In Their Own Words

Criminals on Crime

Fourth Edition

Paul Cromwell
Wichita State University

Roxbury Publishing Company
Los Angeles, California

Library of Congress Cataloging-in-Publication Data

In their own words: criminals on crime / [edited by] Paul Cromwell.—4th ed.
p. cm.
Includes bibliographical references.
ISBN 1-931719-55-1
1. Criminology—Field work. 2. Crime—Research.
3. Criminals—Research. I. Cromwell, Paul F.
HV6030 .I488 2006
364—dc22 2004051097
CIP

IN THEIR OWN WORDS: CRIMINALS ON CRIME (Fourth Edition)

Publisher and Editor: Claude Teweles
Managing Editor: Dawn VanDercreek
Production Editor: Sacha A. Howells
Cover Design: Marnie Kenney
Typography: SDS Design, Info@sds-design.com

Printed on acid-free paper in the United States of America. This paper meets the standards for recycling of the Environmental Protection Agency.

ISBN 1-931719-55-1

Roxbury Publishing Company
P.O. Box 491044
Los Angeles, California 90049-9044
Voice: (310) 473-3312 Fax: (310) 473-4490
Email: roxbury@roxbury.net
Website: www.roxbury.net

Dedication

This volume is dedicated to the generous scholars and researchers whose work appears here.

Contents

Acknowledgments xi

Preface xii

About the Contributors xv

Section I: Introduction to Ethnographic Research in Criminal Justice and Criminology

Introduction 1

1. A Snowball's Chance in Hell: Doing Fieldwork With Active Residential Burglars. 2

Richard T. Wright, Scott H. Decker, Allison K. Redfern, and Dietrich L. Smith

Wright and his associates explain the process and problems associated with designing and conducting a field study of active burglars.

2. Researching Crack Dealers: Dilemmas and Contradictions 9

Bruce A. Jacobs

Jacobs discusses the problems and dangers associated with studying criminals "in the wild."

*3. Why I'll Talk: Offenders' Motives for Participating in Qualitative Research 19

Heith Copes and Andy Hochstetler

Copes and Hochstetler examine the issue of gaining offenders' cooperation in field research on crime.

Section II: Criminal Lifestyles and Decision Making

Introduction 29

4. The Socially Bounded Decision Making of Persistent Property Offenders 30

Neal Shover and David Honaker

Shover and Honaker argue that improved understanding of the decision-making processes of property offenders is gained through exploring how their decisions are shaped by their lifestyles.

*New to the Fourth Edition

Section III: Property Crime

*New to the Fourth Edition

Section IV: Violent Crime

Section V: Occupational Crime

*New to the Fourth Edition

Section VI: Illegal Occupations

Section VII: Gangs and Crime

*New to the Fourth Edition

Section VIII: Drugs and Crime

Section IX: Quitting Crime

*New to the Fourth Edition

Acknowledgments

Like the first three editions, this Fourth Edition of *In Their Own Words* owes its existence first to the researchers and authors whose work is presented here. My task was simply to select the best exemplars of contemporary ethnographic research and to attempt to tie them together in an integrated and effective way. I gratefully acknowledge the scholarly efforts of the authors of the studies presented in this anthology. It is truly their book.

In the process of preparing each new edition I have had the benefit of numerous reviewers who commented on the selections, organization, and integration of materials and on the general worth of the project. Their advice has been invaluable. In most cases I accepted it gratefully. In every case, I benefited from it. To the extent that this book has value for advancing scholarly understanding of crime and criminals and especially as a teaching tool, the credit should be given to them. To the extent that it fails in its purpose, I am to blame. Special appreciation is extended to: Leana Bouffard, North Dakota State University; Shawna Cleary, University of Central Oklahoma; Jo-Ann Della-Giustina, John Jay College; Charles F. Hanna, Duquesne University; Kristi Hoffman, Roanoke College; Jason Jimerson, Franklin College; Louis Kontos, Long Island University; Sarah O'Keefe, University of Massachusetts–Amherst; Peter J. Venturelli, Valparaiso University; John T. Whitehead, East Tennessee University; and Jay R. Williams, Duke University.

Bruce Jacobs and Richard T. Wright at the University of Missouri–St. Louis and Neal Shover at the University of Tennessee also offered valuable insights and advice.

Sacha A. Howells and Scott Carter at Roxbury Publishing Company provided their expertise in all stages of the manuscript preparation. I am particularly appreciative of the efforts and persistence of Claude Teweles, publisher and president at Roxbury Publishing Company. He kept me on track and on schedule.

Special appreciation goes to Christy Circle, my graduate assistant, whose efficient and dedicated work in securing permissions, scanning, and editing articles made my life so much easier while completing this new edition.

My wife, Jimmie, is owed the greatest debt. Her editing skills, attention to detail, and emotional support have always undergirded my efforts. Once again, I express my gratitude to her.

—Paul Cromwell
Wichita, Kansas

Preface

This anthology provides the reader with an opportunity to view the world from the perspective of criminal offenders. *In Their Own Words, Fourth Edition,* is a collection of field studies of crime and criminals derived from a long tradition of field research in criminology (Sutherland 1937; Cressey 1953; Irwin 1970; Shover 1971; Letkemann 1973; Klockars 1974; Inciardi 1977; Campbell 1984). In the Fourth Edition, students will encounter gang members, murderers, burglars, shoplifters, robbers, fences, addicts, pimps, rapists, drug smugglers, bookies, and white-collar offenders—all of whom discuss their motives, perceptions, strategies, and rationalizations of crime. This expanded edition contains 15 new studies, adding accounts of carjackers, drug users and dealers, telemarketing frauds, prostitutes, female gang members, robbers, serial killers, and thieves.

Some changes in organization have occurred. Section I now contains three chapters dealing with the issues and problems associated with conducting ethnographic research. A new chapter in this section by Heith Copes and Andy Hochstetler looks at the issue of how researchers convince offenders to discuss their crimes.

A new section, "Quitting Crime," incorporates research into the controversial issue of desistance—how and why offenders quit criminal activity, reduce the level or intensity of their criminal behavior, or engage in less serious offenses.

Methods of Field Research

Field research is not a single research methodology. Field research, also called *ethnography,* provides a way of looking at the complex contexts in which any research problem exists. Good field research results in what Glassner and Carpenter (1985) call *thick description*—access to the often conflicting and detailed views of the social world held by the subjects being studied.

According to Maxfield and Babbie (1995), field research "encompasses two different methods of obtaining data: direct observation and asking questions." *Asking questions* involves in-depth interviews (also called ethnographic interviews) with research subjects. Field study interviews are much less structured than survey research interviews. At one level, field interviews may be likened to a conversation (Maxfield and Babbie 1995). At a more structured level, researchers ask open-ended questions in which a specific response is elicited, but the respondent is allowed and encouraged to explain more completely and to clarify responses. The question is simply a guide, structuring but not limiting the interviewee's responses. Ressler, Burgess, and Douglas' chapter, "Serial Killers: Antecedent Behaviors and the Act of Murder," Cromwell, Parker, and Mobley's "The Five-Finger Discount: An Analysis of Motivation for Shoplifting," Shover and Honaker's "The Socially Bounded Decision Making of Persistent Property Offenders," and Hochstetler and Copes' "Managing Fear to Commit Felony Theft" are examples of the "asking questions" methodology.

Observation takes several forms in field research. These techniques may be categorized on a continuum according to the role played by the researcher (Gold 1969; Maxfield and Babbie 1995). At one degree of involvement, the researcher observes an activity or individuals without their knowledge. A researcher watching shoplifters through a one-way mirror in a department store is an example of this technique. Gold (1969) labels this method the *complete observer.*

At a more involved level of interaction, the researcher is identified as a researcher and interacts with the participants in the course of their activities but does not actually become a participant (Maxfield and Babbie 1995). Gold (1969) identified this technique as *observer-as-participant.* In "Deciding to Commit a Burglary," Richard Wright and Scott Decker used the technique when observing burglars in their natural habitat ("in the wild") and going with them to houses they had previously burglarized, reconstructing their crimes.

The *participant-as-observer* (Gold 1969) technique involves participating with the group under study while making clear the purpose of conducting research. Wilson Palacios and Melissa Fenwick used a version of this technique in their study of the Ecstasy club scene in South Florida ("'E' Is for Ecstasy: A Participant Observation Study of Ecstasy Use").

The most complete involvement of researcher with subjects is the complete participant. Gold (1969, 33) describes this role:

> The true identity and purpose of the complete participant in field research are not known to those he observes. He interacts with them as naturally as possible in whatever areas of their living interest him and are acceptable to him in situations in which he can play or learn to play requisite day-to-day roles successfully.

A number of ethical, legal, and personal risk considerations are involved in the complete participant role, and the researcher must tread carefully to avoid pitfalls. Because of these problems, complete participation is seldom possible in criminological research. However, some of the material in Patricia Adler's "Dealing Careers" was obtained using this methodology. Adler reports that although most of their subjects (high-level drug dealers) knew that she and her husband were researchers, others did not. They were accepted by these individuals through their friendship and were vouched for by those same subjects. Thus, her study made use of both complete participant and participant-as-observer techniques.

Use of Field Research in Criminal Justice and Criminology

Field studies are particularly well-suited to investigating several important issues in criminology and criminal justice. Only through field research may we observe the everyday activities of offenders: how they interact with others, how they perceive the objects and events in their everyday lives, and how they perceive the sanction threat of the criminal justice system. By understanding the offenders' perspective, decision making, and motivation, field research may inform crime prevention and control strategies. Wright and Decker (1994) point out that criminal justice policymaking is predicated on assumptions about the perceptions of criminals:

> The traditional policy of deterrence rests squarely on the notion that offenders are utilitarian persons who carefully weigh the potential costs and rewards of their illegal actions. . . .

However, the studies in this collection offer strong arguments for other, perhaps as compelling, motivations for many crimes, including so-called economic crimes. Even robbery and burglary, crimes assumed to be driven almost entirely by instrumental (economic) motivations, may have expressive roots as well. Burglars report that excitement, thrills, and a "rush" often accompany the criminal act. Some burglars report having occasionally committed a burglary out of revenge or anger against the victim (see Wright and Decker, "Deciding to Commit a Burglary" and Shover and Honaker, "The Socially Bounded Decision Making of Persistent Property Offenders," both in this volume). On the other hand, gang membership, which traditionally has been thought to be turf-oriented and centered on conflict, is shown to be increasingly about money—drugs and drug sales. Thus, effective crime control strategies must take into account the factors that drive crime. Field research that allows offenders to "speak for themselves" is ideally suited to these issues.

Field studies such as those in this book also have great value in educating students in criminal justice and criminology. The field has sometimes suffered from the "distance" between student and subject of the study. Would anyone argue that it is possible to train a physician without contact with sick people? The essence of medical training is of course the gaining of experience diagnosing and treating the sick. Yet, in 15 years as a criminal justice practitioner and administrator, and 20 years as a criminal justice and criminology educator, I have been troubled by the realization that most graduates never encounter an actual criminal during the course of their education. Some universities provide internships or practicums or arrange field trips to prisons or other correctional facilities. Despite these efforts, however, few students ever experience a "real criminal" during their education. By viewing the criminal event from the perspective of the participants, these studies can make the decision by an individual to engage in crime "up close and personal" and supplement the statistical data from other research.

In Their Own Words enriches the reader's understanding of criminal typologies, criminal decision making, criminological theories, and criminal subcultures and lifestyles. The studies contained in this book vary in terms of the settings, the crimes being studied, and the researcher's involvement and role in the environment. In every case, however, the story is told from the perspective of, and in the words of, the offender. In each case, the researcher places the offender's words in a theoretical context and provides analyses and conclusions.

References

Campbell, A. 1984. *Girls in the Gang.* Oxford, UK: Basil Blackwell.

Cressey, D.R. 1953. *Other People's Money.* Glencoe, IL: Free Press.

Glassner, B. and C. Carpenter. 1985. *The Feasibility of an Ethnographic Study of Property Offenders: A Report Prepared for the National Institute of Justice.* Washington, DC: NIJ Mimeo.

Gold, R. 1969. "Roles in Sociological Field Observation." In *Issues in Participant Observation,* eds. George J. McCall and J.L. Simmons. Reading, MA: Addison-Wesley.

Inciardi, J. 1977. "In Search of Class Cannon: A Field Study of Professional Pickpockets." In *Street Ethnography: Selected Studies of Crime and Drug Use in Natural Settings,* ed. Robert S. Weppner. Beverly Hills: Sage.

Irwin, J. 1970. *The Felon.* Englewood Cliffs, NJ: Prentice-Hall.

Klockars, C. 1974. *The Professional Fence.* New York: Macmillan.

Letkemann, E. 1973. *Crime as Work.* Englewood Cliffs, NJ: Prentice-Hall.

Maxfield, M.G. and E. Babbie. 1995. *Research Methods for Criminal Justice and Criminology.* Belmont, CA: Wadsworth.

Shover, N. 1971. "Burglary as an Occupation." Ph.D. dissertation, University of Illinois.

Sutherland, E.H. 1937. *The Professional Thief.* Chicago: University of Chicago Press.

Wright, R.T. and S.H. Decker. 1994. *Burglars on the Job: Streetlife and Residential Break-Ins.* Boston: Northeastern University Press. ✦

About the Contributors

Patricia A. Adler is a professor of sociology at the University of Colorado–Boulder.

Deborah R. Baskin is a professor and chair in the Department of Criminal Justice at California State University–Los Angeles.

Ann W. Burgess is professor emeritus at the University of Pennsylvania School of Nursing.

Glenn S. Coffey is an assistant professor of sociology, anthropology, and criminal justice at the University of North Florida.

Phyllis Coontz is an associate professor in the Graduate School of Public and International Affairs at the University of Pittsburgh.

Heith Copes is an assistant professor of criminology and criminal justice at the University of Alabama at Birmingham.

Paul Cromwell is a professor of criminal justice and director of the School of Community Affairs at Wichita State University.

Dean Dabney is an associate professor of criminal justice at Georgia State University.

Scott H. Decker is Curator's Professor of criminology and criminal justice at the University of Missouri–St. Louis.

John E. Douglas is a retired FBI agent.

Jeffrey Fagan is a professor of law at Columbia University.

Charles E. Faupel is a professor of sociology at Auburn University.

Melissa E. Fenwick is a doctoral candidate in criminology at the University of South Florida.

Gilbert Geis is professor emeritus at the University of California–Irvine.

John M. Hagedorn is an associate professor of criminal justice at the University of Illinois at Chicago.

Dick Hobbs is a professor of sociology at the University of Durham in the United Kingdom.

Andy Hochstetler is an assistant professor of sociology at Iowa State University.

David Honaker is an independent scholar in Knoxville, Tennessee.

Bruce A. Jacobs is an associate professor of crime and justice studies at the University of Texas–Dallas.

Paul Jesilow is an associate professor of criminology, law, and society in the School of Social Ecology at the University of California–Irvine.

Joseph Marolla is a professor of sociology and anthropology at Virginia Commonwealth University.

Eleanor M. Miller is a professor of sociology and Associate Dean for the Social Sciences at the University of Wisconsin–Milwaukee.

Jody Miller is an associate professor at the University of Missouri–St. Louis.

Shawna Mobley is Director of Correctional Counseling of Kansas in Wichita, Kansas.

Sheigla Murphy is Director of Substance Abuse Studies at the Institute for Scientific Analysis in California.

James N. Olson is a professor of psychology at the University of Texas–Permian Basin.

Wilson R. Palacios is associate professor of criminology at the University of South Florida.

Lee Parker is an attorney and judge in Wichita, Kansas.

Henry M. Pontell is a professor of criminology, law, and society in the School of Social Ecology at the University of California–Irvine.

Allison K. Redfern (now Allison Rooney) is a probation officer for the state of Missouri.

Robert K. Ressler is a retired FBI agent.

Kim Romenesko is Director of the Honors Program at the University of Wisconsin–Milwaukee.

Diana Scully is a professor of sociology at Virginia Commonwealth University.

Neal Shover is a professor of sociology at the University of Tennessee–Knoxville.

Rashi K. Shukla is an assistant professor at the University of Central Oklahoma.

Dietrich L. Smith is Director of Diversity at Chaminade College Prepatory School in St. Louis, Missouri.

Ira Sommers is a professor of criminal justice at California State University–Los Angeles.

Volkan Topalli is an assistant professor of criminal justice at Georgia State University.

Kenneth D. Tunell is a professor of criminal justice and police studies at Eastern Kentucky University.

Dan Waldorf (deceased) was a senior research associate at the Institute for Scientific Analysis in Alameda, California.

Richard T. Wright is a professor in the Department of Criminology and Criminal Justice at the University of Missouri–St. Louis. ✦

Section I

Introduction to Ethnographic Research in Criminal Justice and Criminology

Section I is dedicated to an exploration of the problems, procedures, processes, and dilemmas of ethnographic research. In the first selection, Wright, Decker, Redfern, and Smith ("A Snowball's Chance in Hell: Doing Fieldwork With Active Residential Burglars") present a seminal study of issues relating to locating research subjects in the active criminal population. Wright et al. discuss the value of using active offenders rather than incarcerated individuals as research subjects, and how they recruited subjects for their study of residential burglars. Other issues relating to ethnographic research with active offenders are also presented.

In the next selection, the danger and dilemmas associated with field studies with active criminals are graphically illustrated. Criminologist Bruce A. Jacobs discusses relationships with research subjects, issues of developing trust, concerns about "going native," issues of maintaining social distance from subjects while maintaining trust and confidence, problems in dealing with law enforcement, and the dangerous, changeable, and unpredictable nature of fieldwork with active offenders.

Finally, Copes and Hochstetler discuss the motivations that underlie the willingness of incarcerated inmates to talk freely and honestly about their crimes with researchers.

These selections open the door to the research that follows. They allow the reader to more fully appreciate the methods by which the research was accomplished and the difficulty associated with such studies. ✦

Chapter 1 A Snowball's Chance in Hell

Doing Fieldwork With Active Residential Burglars

Richard T. Wright
Scott H. Decker
Allison K. Redfern
Dietrich L. Smith

Criminologists long have recognized the importance of field studies of active offenders. More than 2 decades ago, for example, Polsky (1969, 116) observed that "we can no longer afford the convenient fiction that in studying criminals in their natural habitat, we would discover nothing really important that could not be discovered from criminals behind bars." Similarly, Sutherland and Cressey (1970) noted that:

> Those who have had intimate contacts with criminals "in the open" know that criminals are not "natural" in police stations, courts, and prisons, and that they must be studied in their everyday life outside of institutions if they are to be understood. By this is meant that the investigator must associate with them as one of them, seeing their lives and conditions as the criminals themselves see them. In this way, he can make observations which can hardly be made in any other way. Also, his observations are of unapprehended criminals, not the criminals selected by the processes of arrest and imprisonment. (68)

And McCall (1978, 27) also cautioned that studies of incarcerated offenders are vulnerable to the charge that they are based on "unsuccessful criminals, on the supposition that successful criminals are not apprehended or at least are able to avoid incarceration." This charge, he asserts, is "the most central bogeyman in the criminologist's demonology" (also see Cromwell, Olson, and Avary 1991; Hagedorn 1990; Watters and Biernacki 1989).

Although generally granting the validity of such critiques, most criminologists have shied away from studying criminals, so to speak, in the wild. Although their reluctance to do so undoubtedly is attributable to a variety of factors (e.g., Wright and Bennett 1990), probably the most important of these is a belief that this type of research is impractical. In particular, how is one to locate active criminals and obtain their cooperation?

The entrenched notion that field-based studies of active offenders are unworkable has been challenged by Chambliss (1975) who asserts that:

> The data on organized crime and professional theft as well as other presumably difficult-to-study events are much more available than we usually think. All we really have to do is to get out of our offices and onto the street. The data are there; the problem is that too often [researchers] are not. (39)

Those who have carried out field research with active criminals would no doubt regard this assertion as overly simplistic, but they probably would concur with Chambliss that it is easier to find and gain the confidence of such offenders than commonly is imagined. As Hagedorn (1990, 251) has stated: "Any good field researcher . . .willing to spend the long hours necessary to develop good informants can solve the problem of access."

We recently completed the fieldwork for a study of residential burglars, exploring, specifically, the factors they take into account when contemplating the commission of an offense. The study is being done on the streets of St. Louis, Missouri, a declining "rust belt" city. As part of this study, we located and interviewed 105 active offenders. We also took 70 of these offenders to the site of a recent burglary and asked them to reconstruct the crime in considerable detail. In the following pages, we will discuss how we found these offenders and obtained their cooperation. Further, we will consider the difficulties involved in maintaining an ongoing field relationship with these offenders, many of whom lead chaotic lives. Lastly, we will outline the characteristics of our sample, suggesting ways in which it differs from one collected through criminal justice channels.

Locating the Subjects

In order to locate the active offenders for our study, we employed a "snowball" or "chain referral" sampling strategy. As described in the literature (e.g., Sudman 1976; Watters and Biernacki 1989), such a strategy begins with the recruitment of an initial subject who then is asked to recommend further participants. This process continues until a suitable sample has been "built."

The most difficult aspect of using a snowball sampling technique is locating an initial contact or two. Various ways of doing so have been suggested. McCall (1978), for instance, recommends using a "chain of referrals":

> If a researcher wants to make contact with, say, a bootlegger, he thinks of the person he knows who is closest in the social structure to bootlegging. Perhaps this person will be a police officer, a judge, a liquor store owner, a crime reporter, or a recently arrived Southern migrant. If he doesn't personally know a judge or a crime reporter, he surely knows someone (his own lawyer or a circulation clerk) who does and who would be willing to introduce him. By means of a very short chain of such referrals, the researcher can obtain an introduction to virtually any type of criminal. (31)

This strategy can be effective and efficient, but can also have pitfalls. In attempting to find active offenders for our study, we avoided seeking referrals from criminal justice officials for both practical and methodological reasons. From a practical standpoint, we elected not to use contacts provided by police or probation officers, fearing that this would arouse the suspicions of offenders that the research was the cover for a "sting" operation. One of the offenders we interviewed, for example, explained that he had not agreed to participate earlier because he was worried about being set up for an arrest: "I thought about it at first because I've seen on T.V. telling how [the police] have sent letters out to people telling 'em they've won new sneakers and then arrested 'em." We also did not use referrals from law enforcement or corrections personnel to locate our subjects owing to a methodological concern that a sample obtained in this way may be highly unrepresentative of the total population of active offenders. It is likely, for instance, that such a sample would include a disproportionate number of unsuccessful criminals, that is, those who have been caught in the past (e.g., Hagedorn 1990). Further, this sample might exclude a number of successful offenders who avoid associating with colleagues known to the police. Rengert and Wasilchick (1989, 6) used a probationer to contact active burglars, observing that the offenders so located "were often very much like the individual who led us to them."

A commonly suggested means of making initial contact with active offenders other than through criminal justice sources involves frequenting locales favored by criminals (see Chambliss 1975; Polsky 1969; West 1980). This strategy, however, requires an extraordinary investment of time as the researcher establishes a street reputation as an "all right square" (Irwin 1972, 123) who can be trusted. Fortunately, we were able to short-cut that process by hiring an ex-offender (who, despite committing hundreds of serious crimes, had few arrests and no felony convictions) with high status among several groups of black street criminals in St. Louis. This person retired from crime after being shot and paralyzed in a gangland-style execution attempt. He then attended a university and earned a bachelor's degree, but continued to live in his old neighborhood, remaining friendly, albeit superficially, with local criminals. We initially met him when he attended a colloquium in our department and disputed the speaker's characterization of street criminals.

Working through an ex-offender with continuing ties to the underworld as a means of locating active criminals has been used successfully by other criminologists (see e.g., Taylor 1985). This approach offers the advantage that such a person already has contacts and trust in the criminal subculture and can vouch for the legitimacy of the research. In order to exploit this advantage fully, however, the ex-offender selected must be someone with a solid street reputation for integrity and must have a strong commitment to accomplishing the goals of the study.

The ex-offender hired to locate subjects for our project began by approaching former criminal associates. Some of these contacts were still "hustling," that is, actively involved in various types of crimes, whereas others either had retired or remained involved only peripherally through, for example, occasional buying and selling of stolen goods. Shortly thereafter, the ex-offender contacted several street-wise law-abiding friends, including a youth worker. He explained the research to the contacts, stressing that it was confidential and that the police were not involved. He also informed them that those who took part would be paid a small sum (typically $25.00).

He then asked the contacts to put him in touch with active residential burglars.

Figure 1 outlines the chain of referrals through which the offenders were located. Perhaps the best way to clarify this process involves selecting a subject, say 064, and identifying the referrals that led us to this person. In this case, the ex-offender working on our project contacted a street-wise, non-criminal acquaintance who put him in touch with the first active burglar in the chain, offender 015. Offender 015 referred 7 colleagues, one of whom—033—put us in touch with 3 more subjects, including 035, who in turn introduced us to 038, who referred 8 more participants. Among these participants was offender 043, a well-connected burglar who provided 12 further contacts, 2 of whom—060 and 061—convinced 064 to participate in the research. This procedure is similar to that described by Watters and Biernacki (1989, 426) in that "the majority of respondents were not referred directly by research staff." As a consequence, our sample was strengthened considerably. After all, we almost certainly would not have been able to find many of these individuals on our own, let alone convince them to cooperate.

Throughout the process of locating subjects, we encountered numerous difficulties and challenges. Contacts that initially appeared to be promising, for example, sometimes proved to be unproductive and had to be dropped. And, of course, even productive contact chains had a tendency to "dry up" eventually. One of the most challenging tasks we confronted involved what Biernacki and Waldorf (1981, 150) have termed the "verification of eligibility," that is, determining whether potential subjects actually met the criteria for inclusion in our research. In order to take part, offenders had to be both "residential burglars" and "currently active." In practice, this meant that they had to have committed a residential burglary within the past 2 weeks. This seems straightforward, but it often was difficult to apply the criteria in the field because offenders were evasive about their activities. In such cases, we frequently had to rely on other members of the sample to verify the eligibility of potential subjects.

We did not pay the contacts for helping us to find subjects and, initially, motivating them to do so proved difficult. Small favors, things like giving them a ride or buying them a pack of cigarettes, produced some cooperation, but yielded only a few introductions. Moreover, the active burglars that we did manage to find often were lackadaisical about referring associates because no financial incentive was offered. Eventually, one of the informants hit on the idea of "pimping" colleagues, that is, arranging an introduction on their behalf in ex-

Figure 1
"Snowball" Referral Chart

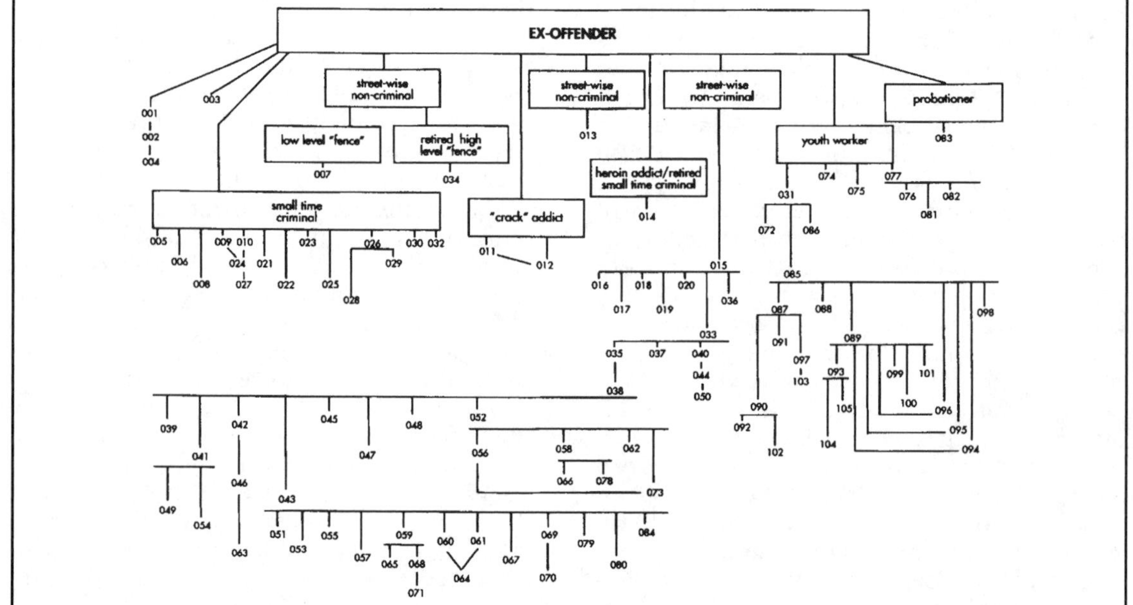

change for a cut of the participation fee (also see Cromwell et al. 1991). This idea was adopted rapidly by other informants and the number of referrals rose accordingly. In effect, these informants became "locators" (Biernacki and Waldorf 1981), helping us to expand referral chains as well as vouching for the legitimacy of the research, and validating potential participants as active residential burglars.

The practice of pimping is consistent with the low-level, underworld economy of street culture, where people are always looking for a way to get in on someone else's deal. One of our contacts put it this way: "If there's money to make out of something, I gotta figure out a way to get me some of it." Over the course of the research, numerous disputes arose between offenders and informants over the payment of referral fees. We resisted becoming involved in these disputes, reckoning that such involvement could only result in the alienation of one or both parties (e.g., Miller 1952). Instead, we made it clear that our funds were intended as interview payments and thus would be given only to interviewees.

Field Relations

The success of our research, of course, hinged on an ability to convince potential subjects to participate. Given that many of the active burglars, especially those located early in the project, were deeply suspicious of our motives, it is reasonable to ask why the offenders were willing to take part in the research. Certainly the fact that we paid them a small sum for their time was an enticement for many, but this is not an adequate explanation. After all, criminal opportunities abound and even the inept "nickel and dime" offenders in the sample could have earned more had they spent the time engaged in illegal activity. Moreover, some of the subjects clearly were not short of cash when they agreed to participate; at the close of one interview, an offender pulled out his wallet to show us that it was stuffed with thousand dollar bills, saying:

> I just wanted to prove that I didn't do this for the money. I don't need the money. I did it to help out [the ex-offender employed on our project]. We know some of the same people and he said you were cool.

Without doubt, many in our sample agreed to participate only because the ex-offender assured them that we were trustworthy. But other factors were at work as well. Letkemann (1973, 44), among others, has observed that the secrecy inherent in criminal work means that offenders have few opportunities to discuss their activities with anyone besides associates which many of them find frustrating. As one of his informants put it: "What's the point of scoring if nobody knows about it?" Under the right conditions, therefore, some offenders may enjoy talking about their work with researchers.

We adopted several additional strategies to maximize the cooperation of the offenders. First, following the recommendations of experienced field researchers (e.g., Irwin 1972; McCall 1978; Walker and Lidz 1977; Wright and Bennett 1990), we made an effort to "fit in" by learning the distinctive terminology and phrasing used by the offenders. Here again, the assistance of the ex-offender proved invaluable. Prior to entering the field, he suggested ways in which questions might be asked so that the subjects would better understand them, and provided us with a working knowledge of popular street terms (e.g, "boy" for heroin, "girl" for cocaine) and pronunciations (e.g., "hair ron" for heroin). What is more, he sat in on the early interviews and critiqued them afterwards, noting areas of difficulty or contention and offering possible solutions.

A second strategy to gain the cooperation of the offenders required us to give as well as take. We expected the subjects to answer our questions frankly and, therefore, often had to reciprocate. Almost all of them had questions about how the information would be used, who would have access to it, and so on. We answered these questions honestly, lest the offenders conclude that we were being evasive. Further, we honored requests from a number of subjects for various forms of assistance. Provided that the help requested was legal and fell within the general set "of norms governing the exchange of money and other kinds of favors" (Berk and Adams 1970, 112) on the street, we offered it. For example, we took subjects to job interviews or work, helped some to enroll in school, and gave others advice on legal matters. We even assisted a juvenile offender who was injured while running away from the police to arrange for emergency surgery when his parents, fearing that they would be charged for the operation, refused to give their consent.

One other way we sought to obtain and keep the offenders' confidence involved demonstrating our trustworthiness by "remaining close-mouthed in regard to potentially harmful information" (Irwin 1972, 125). A number of the offenders tested us by asking what a criminal associate said about a particular matter. We declined to discuss such issues, explaining that the promise of confidentiality extended to all those participating in our research.

Much has been written about the necessity for researchers to be able to withstand official coercion (see Irwin 1972; McCall 1978; Polsky 1969) and we recognized from the start the threat that intrusions from criminal justice officials could pose to our research. The threat of being confronted by police patrols seemed especially great given that we planned to visit the sites of recent successful burglaries with offenders. Therefore, prior to beginning our fieldwork, we negotiated an agreement with police authorities not to interfere in the conduct of the research, and we were not subjected to official coercion.

Although the strategies described above helped to mitigate the dangers inherent in working with active criminals (see e.g., Dunlap et al. 1990), we encountered many potentially dangerous situations over the course of the research. For example, offenders turned up for interviews carrying firearms including, on one occasion, a machine gun; we were challenged on the street by subjects who feared that they were being set up for arrest; we were caught in the middle of a fight over the payment of a $1 debt. Probably the most dangerous situation, however, arose while driving with an offender to the site of his most recent burglary. As we passed a pedestrian, the offender became agitated and demanded that we stop the car: "You want to see me kill someone? Stop the car! I'm gonna kill that motherfucker. Stop the fuckin' car!" We refused to stop and actually sped up to prevent him jumping out of the vehicle; this clearly displeased him, although he eventually calmed down. The development of such situations was largely unpredictable and thus avoiding them was difficult. Often we deferred to the ex-offender's judgment about the safety of a given set of circumstances. The most notable precaution that we took involved money; we made sure that the offenders knew that we carried little more than was necessary to pay them.

Characteristics of the Sample

Unless a sample of active offenders differs significantly from one obtained through criminal justice channels, the difficulties and risks associated with the street-based recruitment of research subjects could not easily be justified. Accordingly, it seems important that we establish whether such a difference exists. In doing so, we will begin by outlining the demographic characteristics of our sample. In terms of race, it nearly parallels the distribution of burglary arrests for the City of St. Louis in 1988, the most recent year for which data [were] available. The St. Louis Metropolitan Police Department's Annual Report (1989) reveals that 64 percent of burglary arrestees in that year were Black, and 36 percent were White. Our sample was 69 percent Black and 31 percent White. There is divergence for the gender variable, however; only 7 percent of all arrestees in the city were female, while 17 percent of our sample fell into this category. This is not surprising. The characteristics of a sample of active criminals, after all, would not be expected to mirror those of one obtained in a criminal justice setting.

Given that our research involved only currently active offenders, it is interesting to note that 21 of the subjects were on probation, parole, or serving a suspended sentence, and that a substantial number of juveniles—27 or 26 percent of the total—were located for the study. The inclusion of such offenders strengthens the research considerably because approximately one-third of arrested burglars are under 18 years of age (Sessions 1989). Juveniles, therefore, need to be taken into account in any comprehensive study of burglars. These offenders, however, seldom are included in studies of burglars located through criminal justice channels because access to them is legally restricted and they often are processed differently than adult criminals and detained in separate facilities.

Prior contact with the criminal justice system is a crucial variable for this research. . . . Of primary interest . . . is the extent to which our snowball sampling technique uncovered a sample of residential burglars unlikely to be encountered in a criminal justice setting, the site of most research on offenders.

More than one-quarter of the offenders (28 percent) claimed never to have been arrested. (We excluded arrests for traffic offenses, "failure to appear" and similar minor transgressions, because such offenses do not adequately distinguish serious criminals from others.) Obviously, these offenders would have been excluded had we based our study on a jail or prison population. Perhaps a more relevant measure in the context of our study, however, is the experience of the offenders with the criminal justice system for the offense of burglary, because most previous studies of burglars not only have been based on incarcerated offenders, but also have used the charge of burglary as a screen to select subjects (e.g., Bennett and Wright 1984; Rengert and Wasilchick 1985). Of the 105 individuals in our sample, 44 (42 percent) had no arrests for burglary, and another 35 (33 percent) had one or more arrests, but no convictions for the offense. Thus 75 percent of our sample would not be included in a study of incarcerated burglars. . . .

Conclusion

By its nature, research involving active criminals is always demanding, often difficult, and occasionally dangerous. However, it is possible and, as the quantitative information reported above suggests, some of the offenders included in such research may differ substantially from those found through criminal justice channels. It is interesting, for example, that those in our sample who had never been arrested for anything, on average, offended more frequently and had committed more lifetime burglaries than their arrested counterparts. These "successful" offenders, obviously, would not have shown up in a study of arrestees, prisoners, or probationers—a fact that calls into question the extent to which a sample obtained through official sources is representative of the total population of criminals.

Beyond this, researching active offenders is important because it provides an opportunity to observe and talk with them outside the institutional context. As Cromwell et al. (1991) have noted, it is difficult to assess the validity of accounts offered by institutionalized criminals. Simply put, a full understanding of criminal behavior requires that criminologists incorporate field studies of active offenders into their research agendas. Without such studies, both the representativeness and the validity of research based on offenders located through criminal justice channels will remain problematic.

Questions for Thought and Discussion

1. The authors suggest that incarcerated offenders may not provide valid information regarding their past crimes. What is the reason for this, and how did they solve the problem?
2. Apart from the money offered to the research subjects, why would a criminal be willing to talk openly about his or her past crimes with researchers?
3. What do the authors means by "snowball sampling?"

References

Bennett, Trevor and Richard Wright. (1984). *Burglars on Burglary: Prevention and the Offender.* Aldershot, England: Gower.

Berk, Richard and Joseph Adams. (1970). Establishing rapport with deviant groups. *Social Problems* 18:102–117.

Biernacki, Patrick and Dan Waldorf. (1981). Snowball sampling: Problems and techniques of chain referral sampling. *Sociological Methods and Research* 10:141–163.

Chambliss, William. (1975). On the paucity of research on organized crime: A reply to Galliher and Cain. *American Sociologist* 10:36–39.

Cromwell, Paul, James Olson, and D'Aunn Avary. (1991). *Breaking and Entering: An Ethnographic Analysis of Burglary.* Newbury Park, CA: Sage.

Dunlap, Eloise, Bruce Johnson, Harry Sanabria, Elbert Holliday, Vicki Lipsey, Maurice Barnett, William Hopkins, Ira Sobel, Doris Randolph, and Ko-Lin Chin. (1990). Studying crack users and their criminal careers: The scientific and artistic aspects of locating hard-to-reach subjects and interviewing them about sensitive topics. *Contemporary Drug Problems* 17:121–144.

Hagedorn, John. (1990). Back in the field again: Gang research in the nineties. Pp. 240–259 in *Gangs in America,* edited by C. Ronald Huff. Newbury Park, CA: Sage.

Irwin, John. (1972). Participant observation of criminals. Pp. 117–137 in *Research on Deviance,* edited by Jack Douglas. New York: Random House.

Letkemann, Peter. (1973). *Crime as Work.* Englewood Cliffs, NJ: Prentice-Hall.

McCall, George. (1978). *Observing the Law.* New York: Free Press.

Miller, S. M. (1952). The participant observer and over-rapport. *American Sociological Review* 17:97–99.

Polsky, Ned. (1969). *Hustlers, Beats, and Others.* Garden City, NJ: Anchor.

Rengert, George and John Wasilchick. (1985). *Suburban Burglary: A Time and a Place for Everything.* Springfield, IL: Charles C. Thomas.

———. (1989). *Space, Time and Crime: Ethnographic Insights into Residential Burglary.* Final report submitted to the National Institute of Justice, Office of Justice Programs, U.S. Department of Justice.

Sessions, William. (1989). *Crime in the United States 1988.* Washington, DC: U.S. Government Printing Office.

St. Louis Metropolitan Police Department. (1989). *Annual Report 1988–1989.* St. Louis, MO: St. Louis Metropolitan Police Department.

Sudman, Seymour. (1976). *Applied Sampling.* New York: Academic Press.

Sutherland, Edwin and Donald Cressey. (1970). *Criminology,* 8th Edition. Philadelphia, PA: Lippincott.

Taylor, Laurie. (1985). *In the Underworld.* London: Unwin.

Walker, Andrew and Charles Lidz. (1977). Methodological notes on the employment of indigenous observers. Pp. 103–123 in *Street Ethnography,* edited by Robert Weppner. Beverly Hills, CA: Sage.

Watters, John and Patrick Biernacki. (1989). Targeted sampling: Options for the study of hidden populations. *Social Problems* 36:416–430.

West, W. Gordon. (1980). Access to adolescent deviants and deviance. Pp. 31–44 in *Fieldwork Experience: Qualitative Approaches to Social Research,* edited by William Shaffir, Robert Stebbins, and Allan Turowitz. New York: St. Martin's.

Wright, Richard and Trevor Bennett. (1990). Exploring the offender's perspective: Observing and interviewing criminals. Pp. 138–151 in *Measurement Issues in Criminology,* edited by Kimberly Kempf. New York: Springer-Verlag.

Chapter 2 Researching Crack Dealers

Dilemmas and Contradictions

Bruce A. Jacobs

"Yo, Bruce, come on down the set [neighborhood]. Meet where we usually do," Luther said, and hung up the phone.[1] A trusted contact for an ongoing study of street-level crack dealers and a crack dealer himself, I had no reason to question him. "Just another interview," I thought. Notebooks and file folders in hand, I went to the bank, withdrew fifty dollars for subject payments, and drove fifteen minutes to the dope set I was coming to know so well.

Luther flagged me down as I turned the corner. The seventeen-year-old high school drop-out opened the door and jumped in. "Swerve over there." He pointed to a parking space behind the dilapidated three-story apartment building he called home. "Stop the car—turn it off." Nothing out of the ordinary; over the previous three months, we often would sit and talk for a while before actually going to an interview. This time, though, there was an urgency in his voice I should have detected but did not. He produced a pistol from under a baggy white T-shirt. "Gimme all your fuckin' money or I'll blow your motherfuckin' head off!"

"What the fuck's your problem?" I said, astonished that someone I trusted had suddenly turned on me. The gun was large, a six-shooter, probably a long-barrel .45. It was ugly and old looking. Most of its chrome had been scratched off. Its black handle was pockmarked from years of abuse. Why was he doing this? How did I get myself into this situation? It was the kind of thing you hear about on the evening news but don't expect to confront, even though I knew studying active offenders risked such a possibility.

I frantically pondered a course of action as Luther's tone became more and more hostile. He was sweating. "Just calm down, Luther, just calm down—everything's cool," I trembled. "Don't shoot—I'll give you what you want." "Gimme all your fuckin' money!" he repeated. "I ain't fuckin' around—I'll waste you right here!" I reached in my left-hand pocket for the fifty dollars and handed it over. As I did so, I cupped my right hand precariously an inch from the muzzle of his gun, which was pointing directly into my abdomen. I can survive a gunshot, I thought to myself, as long as I slow the bullet down.

He snatched the five, crisp ten-dollar bills and made a quick search of the vehicle's storage areas to see if I was holding out. "OK," he said, satisfied there were no more funds. "Now turn your head around." I gazed at him inquisitively. "Turn your motherfuckin' head around!" For all I knew, he was going to shoot and run; his right hand was poised on the door handle, his left on the trigger. "Just take your money, man, I'm not gonna do anything." "Turn the fuck around!" he snapped. "OK," I implored, "I won't look, just lemme put my hand over my eyes." I left small openings between my fingers to see what he was really going to do. If he were truly going to fire, which he appeared to be intent on doing—the gun was being raised from the down-low position in which it had been during the entire encounter to right below head level—I would smack the gun upward, jump out of the car, and run a half block to the relative safety of a commercial street.

As I pondered escape routes, he jammed the gun into his pants as quickly as he had drawn it, flung open the door, and disappeared behind the tenements. I hit the ignition and drove slowly and methodically from the scene, grateful to have escaped injury, but awestruck by his brazen violation of trust. All I could do was look back and wonder why.

If this were the end of the story, things would have normalized, I would have learned a lesson about field research, and I would have gone about my business. But Luther was not through. Over the next six weeks, he called my apartment five to ten times a day, five days a week, harassing, taunting, irritating, baiting me. Perhaps twice over that six-week period, I actually picked up the phone—only to find out it was he and hang up. Luther would call right back and let the phone ring incessantly, knowing I was there and letting the answering machine do the dirty work. On several occasions, it became so bad that I had to disconnect the line and leave the apartment for several hours.

I'd arrive home to see the answering machine lit up with messages. "I can smell the mousse in your hair—huh, huh, huh," his sinister laugh echoing through the apartment. "I know you're there, pick it up." More often than not, I would hear annoying dial tones. One message, however, caught my undivided attention: "897 Longacre—huh, huh, huh," he laughed as I heard him flipping through the phone book pages and identifying my address. "We'll [he and his homeboys] be over tomorrow." I didn't sleep well that night or for the next six weeks.

What was I to do—report the robbery, and go to court and testify to stop what had become tele-stalking? Some researchers contend that when crimes against fieldworkers occur, staff are to "report them to the police to indicate that such violations will have consequences."[2] I did not feel I had this option. Calling the authorities, no matter how much I wanted to, would not only have endangered future research with Luther's set and those connected to it, but would also have risked retaliation—since Luther's homies knew where I lived and worked.

So I called the phone company and got caller ID, call return, and call block. These devices succeeded in providing his phone number and residence name, which I used to trace his actual address, but I could still do nothing to stop him. Changing my number was the last thing I wanted to do, because those who smell fear often attack. As other researchers have noted, concern about "violence may cause ethnographers to appear afraid or react inappropriately to common street situations and dangers. . . . Fearful behavior is easily inferred by violent persons" and may often lead to violence itself.[3] Thus, Berk and Adams stress the importance of maintaining one's cool when threatened: "The investigator will be constantly watched and tested by the very people he is studying. This is especially true [with] delinquents who . . . value poise in the face of danger."[4] Danger, it must be remembered, is "inherent" in fieldwork with active offenders, "if for no other reason than there is always the possibility of dangerous cultural misunderstandings arising between researchers and subjects."[5] This is especially true of research among active streetcorner crack sellers, who routinely use violence or threats of violence to gain complicity.[6]

After enduring six weeks of this post-robbery harassment, and with no end in sight, I had to do something. I called the police and told them the story. An officer came out and listened to messages I had saved. As he listened, the telephone rang, and Luther's number displayed on the caller ID. "Do you want me to talk to him?" the officer asked sternly. "No," I replied, feeling more confident with a cop three feet away. "Lemme see if I can work things out." I picked up the phone and started talking.

"What do you want?"

"Why do you keep hangin' up on me? All I want is to talk."

"What do you expect me to do, *like* you [sardonically, on the verge of losing it]? You fuckin' robbed me and I trusted you and now you call me and leave these fuckin' messages and you want me to *talk* to you [incredulous]?"

"I only did that 'cause you fucked me over. I only ganked [robbed] you 'cause you *fucked me.*"

"What are you talking about?"

He proceeded to explain that without him, none of the forty interviews I obtained would have been possible. True, Luther was the first field contact to believe that I was a researcher, not a cop. He was my first respondent, and he was responsible for starting a snowball of referrals on his word that I was "cool."[7] But after he could no longer provide referrals, I moved on, using his contacts to find new ones and eliminating him from the chain. My newfound independence was inexplicable to him and a slap in the face. He wanted vengeance; the robbery and taunting were exactly that.[8]

Ethnography and Social Distance?

Such are the risks ethnographers take when studying dangerous, unstable offenders. Although "robbery, burglary, and theft from field staff are uncommon, [they] do occur. In fact, many crack distributors are frequent and proficient robbers, burglars, and thieves."[9] Not so ironically, someone I had trusted and considered a "protector"[10] had become someone to be protected from. Such flip-flops are entirely possible in the world of active offenders, who themselves often admit an inability to control or understand their behavior.

All of this merely underscores the changeable, unpredictable nature of fieldwork relations, especially with active offenders. Johnson notes that "[i]t is incumbent on the investigator to assess the influences of these changes."[11] The important point is for researchers to put themselves in a position where they can do this. Unfortunately, the very nature of criminological fieldwork may work against this.

Much of the problem revolves around the dilemma between social distance and immersion in fieldwork, and the difficulty researchers have in resolving it. The notion of "social distance" is thought to be in some ways foreign to the ethnographic enterprise. Wolff, for example, contends that successful fieldwork inevitably requires surrender—psychological, social, and otherwise—to the setting, culture, and respondents one is studying. It requires "total involvement, suspension of received notions, pertinence of everything, identification, and risk of being hurt."[12] Ethnographers are advised to immerse themselves in the native scene,[13] to become a member of what they are studying.[14] They are told to become an actual physical and moral part of the setting.[15] As Berk and Adams put it, "The greater the social distance between the participant observer and the subjects, the greater the difficulty in establishing and maintaining rapport."[16]

Building rapport with active offenders typically becomes more difficult, though, as the "deviantness" of the population one studies increases.[17] With any offender population, trying to become "one of them" too quickly can be downright harmful. Some contend that the most egregious error a fieldworker can make is to assume that the fieldworker can gain the immediate favor of his or her hosts by telling them that he or she wants to " 'become one of them' or by implying, by word or act, that the fact that they tolerate his [or her] presence means that he [or she] is one of them."[18] Similarly, Polsky warns that "you damned well better not pretend to be 'one of them,' because they will test this claim out and one of two things will happen. Either the researcher will get drawn into participating in actions one would otherwise not engage in, or the researcher could be exposed as a result of not doing so, the latter having perhaps even greater negative repercussions."[19] The more attached the researcher gets too early in the process, the more vulnerable she or he may be to exploitation. The researcher is still a researcher, no matter how close the researcher thinks she or he is getting. Subjects know this and may also know there will be few if any serious repercussions if they try to pull something, especially at the beginning of research when the fieldworker tends to be the most desperate for acceptance. Problems are only compounded by the fact that researchers tend to be far more streetwise by the end of fieldwork than they are at the beginning. Perhaps the least important time to be streetwise is at the end; both the number and seriousness of threats tend to decline with time. Where threats are often highest—at the beginning, when the researcher may be labeled a narc, a spy, or simply a suspicious character—the researcher may also be least capable of handling them. This only makes the threats that do materialize more threatening.

Researchers who are victimized at this early stage may often be barred from reporting it; doing so threatens to breach promises of confidentiality and anonymity made to subjects. The practical matter of being labeled a narc who "sold someone out" is a separate issue and potentially more problematic: snitching violates a sacred norm of street etiquette, even if the person being snitched on is in the wrong. At best, snitching will terminate future chains of respondents. At worst, it will label the researcher a "rat" and subject him or her to street justice. Both outcomes are, of course, undesirable and will likely bring an end to one's research.

Being immersed while remaining to some degree objective is the key. Some researchers stress the importance of using "interactional devices and strategies that allow the fieldworker to stay on the edges of unfolding social scenes rather than being drawn into their midst as a central actor."[20] Others recommend engaging in a paradoxical and "peculiar combination of engrossment and distance."[21] Like the Simmelian stranger, researchers are told to be familiar yet not too familiar, involved yet not too involved, all the while making the balance seem natural.[22] Some modicum of social distance is thus critical to the ethnographic enterprise—"as a corrective to bias and overrapport brought on by too strong an identification with those studied."[23]

In some sense, then, social distance between the researcher and the active offenders she or he studies can be beneficial. As Wright and Decker observe, "[T]he secrecy inherent in criminal work means that offenders have few opportunities to discuss their activities with anyone besides associates, a matter which many find frustrating."[24] By definition, criminal respondents will often have "certain knowledge and skills that the researcher does not have."[25] This asymmetry may empower them to open up or to open up sooner than they otherwise would. Offenders may enjoy speaking about their criminal experiences with someone who is "straight." Perhaps it is a satisfaction gained from teaching someone supposedly smarter than they, at least in terms of academic degrees. The fact that respondents may see something in the research that benefits them, or an opportunity to correct faulty impressions of what it is they actually do,[26] only facilitates these dynamics.

All of it may come down to dramaturgy. Yet, the very nature of criminological fieldwork dictates that the researcher either can't or won't "act" in certain ways at certain times. Acting inappropriately can compromise the research itself, the fieldworker's ability to remain in the setting, or the ability to remain there safely. The moral and practical conundrum between social distance, immersion, and "participant" observation in criminological fieldwork may, in many ways, be unresolvable.

My failure to manage the distance, immersion dialectic with Luther appeared to have more to do with a practical shortfall in managing informant relations—a myopia if you will—than with going native. Clearly, I had lost objectivity in the process of "handling" Luther. Whether this was a function of overimmersion is open to question, but it undoubtedly played some role. Whether it was avoidable is also open to question, particularly when one considers the practical and methodological paradoxes involved in fieldwork with active offenders. Although myopic (mis)management led to my exploitation by Luther, without putting myself in such a position, I would never have been able to collect the data I did. In many ways, the "shortfall" was necessary and, at some level, advantageous.

The bottom line is that no matter how deft the fieldworker is at managing relations, he or she ultimately never gains total control. Criminological fieldworkers exist in a dependent relationship with their subjects.[27] This makes one wonder who is indeed the "subject" and what he or she can be "subject to" at any given moment. Some contend that the hierarchical relationship between interviewer and subject in social research is "morally indefensible"[28] and should be thrown out. Perhaps the hierarchy may be jettisoned as a matter of course, by the very nature of the fieldworker–active offender relationship. Luther's actions toward me stand as an exemplary case.[29]

Studying Active Offenders

Studying active drug dealers is problematic precisely because their activity is criminal. Active offenders are generally "hard to locate because they find it necessary to lead clandestine lives. Once located, they are reluctant, for similar reasons, to give accurate and truthful information about themselves."[30] "Outsiders" are often perceived as narcs seeking to obtain damaging evidence for juridical purposes.[31] Indeed, the most common suspicion that subjects have about fieldworkers is that they are spies of some sort. As Sluka notes, "It is difficult to find an [ethnographer] who has done fieldwork who has not encountered this suspicion."[32]

Collecting data from drug dealers, particularly from active ones, is likely to be difficult and dangerous unless one can construct friendships within a dealing community.[33] Because of this difficulty, some researchers target institutional settings.[34] Such settings afford the chance of obtaining data without the risk of physical harm associated with "street" interviews.[35] Unfortunately, collecting valid and reliable data in such settings may not be entirely possible, as criminologists have "long suspected that offenders do not behave naturally" in them.[36] Sutherland and Cressey argue that "[t]hose who have had intimate contacts with criminals 'in the open' know that criminals are not 'natural' in police stations, courts, and prisons and that they must be studied in their everyday life outside of institutions if they are to be understood."[37] Polsky is more emphatic, commenting that "we can no longer afford the convenient fiction that in studying criminals in their natural habitat, we . . . discover nothing really important that [cannot] be discovered from criminals behind bars. What is true for studying the gorilla of zoology is likely to be even truer for studying the gorilla of criminology."[38] There are fundamental qualitative differences between the two types of offenders. Institutionalized drug dealers, for example, may represent those not sophisticated or skilled enough to prevent apprehension, or those who simply do not care about getting caught and who sell to anyone with money. Studies of incarcerated offenders are thus open to the charge of being based on "unsuccessful criminals, on the supposition that successful criminals are not apprehended or are at least able to avoid incarceration." This weakness is "the most central bogeyman in the criminologist's demonology."[39]

Knowing this, I entered the field and began frequenting a district near a major university that is both prestigious and expensive, yet which borders a dilapidated neighborhood with a concentrated African American population and heavy crack sales. A lively commercial district, with restaurants, quaint cafes, bars, theaters, and stores, splits the two. The area is known for racial and ethnic diversity, making it relatively easy for most anyone to blend in. Over a nine-month period, I frequented the area and made myself familiar to the regular crowd of hangers-out in the dividing commercial district. Some of these individuals were marginally homeless and spent entire days in the district smoking, drinking, playing music, and begging. Though not crack dealers themselves, they knew who the dealers were and where they worked. After gaining their trust, I was shown the dealers' congregation spots and quickly took to the area.

At first, I would simply walk by, not explicitly acknowledging that anything was going on. Sometimes I would be escorted by one of the "vagabonds," but most of the time I went alone. My objective was simply to let dealers see me. Over the days and weeks, I walked or drove through slowly to gain recognition, trying to capitalize on what Goffman has called second seeings: "[U]nder some circumstances if he and they see each other seeing each other, they can use this fact as an excuse for an acquaintanceship greeting upon next seeing. . . . "[40] Unfortunately, this did not go as easily as Goffman suggests, as dealers openly yelled "SCAT!"—a term for the police undercover unit—at me.[41] Jump-starting participation was clearly the toughest part of the research because dealers suspected I was the police. Ironically, it was the police who gave me my biggest credibility boost.

Police and Credibility

. . . Ferrell notes that "a researcher's strict conformity to legal codes can be reconceptualized as less a sign of professional success than a possible portent of methodological failure . . . a willingness to break the law," by contrast, "[opens] a variety of methodological possibilities."[42]

Hanging with offenders on street corners, driving them around in my car, and visiting their homes must have been a curious sight. My appearance is somewhat akin to that of a college student. Shorts, T-shirts, cross-trainers, and ball caps with rounded brims, "just like SCAT wear 'em" (as one respondent put it), make up my typical attire. Further, I am white, clean-cut, and affect a middle-class appearance, traits the relatively poor, African American respondents associated with the police. These traits appeared to make them even more leery that I was SCAT, or that I worked for SCAT in some capacity.

To offenders who hadn't gotten to know me well, or to those waiting to pass judgment, I was on a deep-cover assignment designed to unearth their secrets and put them in jail. To cops on the beat, I was just another college boy driving down to crackville with a user in tow to buy for me. Such relations are commonplace in the street-level drug scene and have generalized subcultural currency: users serve as go-betweens and funnel unfamiliar customers to dealers for a finder's fee, usually in drugs and without the customer's consent, but generally with his or her tacit permission. When cops see a relatively nicely dressed, clean-shaven white boy driving a late-model car (with out-of-state plates, I might add) and a black street person in the passenger seat, they lick their chops.

Several police stops of me in a one-month period lent some credibility to this proposition. I had not obtained, as Wright and Decker had, a "prior agreement with the police"[43] whereby the police knew what I was doing and pledged not to interfere. I chose not to; the last thing I wanted was to let police know what I was doing. As Polsky explains, "Most of the danger for the fieldworker comes not from the cannibals and headhunters but from the colonial officials. The criminologist studying uncaught criminals in the open finds sooner or later that law enforcers try to put him on the spot—because, unless he is a complete fool, he uncovers information that law enforcers would like to know. . . . "[44] Because my grant was not a federal one, I could not protect the identity of my respondents with a certificate of confidentiality (which theoretically bars police from obtaining data as it pertains to one's subjects). My work was undercover in a sense and eminently discreditable. However, contrary to admonitions by some to avoid contact with the police while doing research with dangerous populations,[45] my run-ins with police turned out to be the most essential tool for establishing my credibility.

My first run-in came two weeks after making initial contact with offenders. I was driving Luther through a crack-filled neighborhood—a neighborhood which also happened to have the highest murder rate in a city which itself had the fourth-highest murder rate in the nation.[46] We were approaching a group of ten mid-teen youths and were about to stop when a St. Louis city patrol car pulled behind. Should I stop, as I planned on doing, and get out and talk with these youths (some of whom Luther marginally knew), or would that place them in imminent danger of arrest? Or should I continue on as if nothing was really going on, even though I had been driving stop and go, under ten miles an hour, prior to and during the now slow-speed pursuit? I opted for the latter, accelerating slowly in a vain attempt to reassert a "normal appearance."[47]

Sirens went on. I pulled over and reassured Luther there was nothing to worry about since neither of us had contraband (I hoped). As officers approached, I thought about what to tell them. Should I say I was a university professor doing field research on crack dealers (a part I clearly didn't look), lie, or say nothing at all? "Whatcha doin' down here?" one of the officers snapped. "Exit the vehicle, intertwine your fingers behind your heads, and kneel with your ankles crossed," he commanded. The searing June sidewalk was not conducive to clear thinking, but I rattled something off: "We used to work together at _____. I waited tables, he bussed, and we been friends since. I'm a sociology major up at _____ and he said he'd show me around the neighborhood sometime. Here I am." "Yeah right," the cop snapped again while searching for the crack he thought we already had purchased. Three other police cars arrived, as the cop baited Luther and me as to how we really knew each other, what each other's real names were (which neither of us knew at the time), and what we were doing here. Dissatisfied with my answers, a sergeant took over, lecturing me on the evils of crack and how it would destroy a life others in this very neighborhood wished they had. I found no fault with the argument, listened attentively, and said nothing. After a final strip search in the late afternoon sun revealed nothing, they said I was lucky, vowed to take me in if I ever showed my face again, and let us go.

On a second occasion, Luther and his homie Frisco were in my car when we pulled up to a local liquor store. The two became nervous upon seeing two suits in a "tec" (detective) car parked at the phone booth. I told Luther and Frisco to wait, and I went into the store. As I exited, the two men approached and showed their badges. "What you doin' with these guys—do you know 'em?" "Yes," I said, deciding to tell them who I really was and what I was doing. "Mind if we search your car?" one asked. "No problem," I replied. "Go right ahead." As one searched my car (for crack, guns, or whatever else he thought he'd find), his partner cuffed both Luther and Frisco and ran warrants. As I soon learned, both detectives knew the two as repeat violent offenders with long rap sheets. They took Frisco in on an outstanding warrant and let Luther go with me. "I respect what you're doing," the searching officer said as he finished and approached, "but you don't know who you're dealing with. These guys are no good." I told him thanks and promptly left with Luther, feeling remorseful about Frisco being taken in only because he was with me.

On a third occasion, I was sitting on my car making small talk with four or five dealers when a patrol car rolled by. The officers inside gave a stern look and told us to break it up. "All right," I said, not going anywhere. We continued to talk for a few minutes when the officers, clearly agitated, rolled by again and demanded in no uncertain terms, "Break it up and we mean now." I hopped in my car, drove four or five blocks, made a left, and heard sirens. "Here we go again." This time, I was not nearly as nervous as I had been on the other occasions, ready to dispense my professor line, show my consent forms and faculty ID, and see their shocked reaction. "Get out of the car and put your hands on the trunk," the driver predictably ordered as I began my explanation. They searched me anyway, perhaps thinking it was just another mendacious story, but I kept conversing in a relaxed, erudite tone. Cops are known to have perceptual shorthands to render quick and accurate typifications of those with whom they're interacting,[48] and I could tell my conversational style was creating a good impression. I told them that I was doing interviews, that I was paying respondents for their time, and that the research was part of a university grant designed to better understand the everyday lives of urban youth. This was, of course, specious. The study's true purpose was to identify how crack dealers avoid arrest, something I dared not admit, for obvious reasons. "You can do what you want," one of them said, satisfied after a thorough search revealed no contraband, "but if I were you, I'd be real careful. You don't want to mess around with these punks." His words rang all too true several weeks later when Luther pointed the gun at my abdomen.

I did not realize it at the time, but my treatment by police was absolutely essential to my research. Police provided the "vital test"[49] I desperately needed to pass if my study were to be successful. The differential enforcement practices of these police officers (and many others around the country)—in which young, minority males are singled out as "symbolic assailants" and "suspicious characters" deserving of attention[50]—benefitted *me* immensely. Police detained *me* because I was with "them." Driving alone in these same areas at the same time, though suspicious, would not likely have attracted nearly as much attention. I was "guilty by association" and "deserving" of the scrutiny young black males in many urban locales receive consistently. For my research, at least, this differential enforcement was anything but negative.

As Douglas notes, it is often necessary for researchers to convince offenders they are studying that the researchers do not represent the authorities.[51] Sluka adds that subjects "are going to define whose side they think you are on. They will act towards you on the basis of this definition, regardless of your professions."[52] Words may be futile in convincing offenders who or what one really is. Ultimately, "actions speak louder than words. . . . [T]he researcher will have to demonstrate by . . . actions that he is on the side of the deviants, or at least, not on the side of the officials."[53] The police had treated me like just another user, and had done so with offenders present. This treatment provided the "actions" for me, the picture that spoke a thousand words.

Offenders' accounts of my treatment spread rapidly through the grapevine, solidifying my credibility for the remainder of the project and setting up the snowball sampling procedure I would use to recruit additional respondents. Without the actions of *police* I may not have been accepted by *offenders* as readily as I was or, perhaps, never accepted at all. A skillful researcher can use the police—indirectly and without their knowledge or, as in my case, without even the researcher's own intent—to demonstrate to offenders that the researcher is indeed legitimate and not an undercover police officer. Often thought to be a critical barrier to entry, the police may be the key to access. Of course, undercover officers themselves can manipulate this very dynamic to gain credibility with those they target—something savvy law enforcement administrators may exploit by setting up fake arrests in plain view. Such tactics may make a researcher's identity even more precarious; in my case, though, this did not occur.

Why police never attempted to confiscate my notes during these pull-overs I'll never know. Perhaps it was because the notes appeared to be chicken scratch and were indecipherable by anyone but me. Perhaps it was because my notes didn't reveal anything the cops did not already know, or at least thought they knew. Regardless, the law is clearly against ethnographers, who can be held in contempt and sent to jail for protecting sources and withholding information.[54] As Carey points out, "There is no privileged relationship between the . . . researcher and his subject similar to that enjoyed by the lawyer and client or psychiatrist and patient."[55] This, of course, says nothing about issues of guilty knowledge or guilty observation.[56] Being aware of dealing operations and watching transactions take place makes one an accessory to their commission, a felony whether one participates or not. Fieldworkers are co-conspirators by definition, no matter their motive or intent. As Polsky concludes, "If one is effectively to study adult criminals in their natural settings, he must make the moral decision that in some ways he will break the law himself."[57]

Researching Active Crack Sellers: In Perspective

By definition, criminological, fieldworkers regularly intrude into the lives of individuals engaged in felonies—felonies for which these individuals can receive hard time. The more illegal the behavior, the more offenders as research subjects have to lose if found out. Obviously, this makes it tougher—and more risky—for researchers to gain access.

Street-level crack selling is thus a paradox of sorts: there is perhaps no other behavior so openly visible and so negatively sanctioned by law as crack selling. It must be this way for sellers to be available to their customers. This is particularly true in a declining drug market such as St. Louis[58] where demand is finite and dwindling, while the number of sellers has remained constant or increased. To compete in such conditions, sellers will often stand out longer and in more difficult conditions than they previously would, in greater numbers, and in greater numbers together. Individual sellers also may rush to customers to steal sales from competitors, drawing even more attention. This situation creates ideal conditions for police—or researchers—to identify open-air sellers and infiltrate them.

Access notwithstanding, the importance of a strong indigenous tie to the research setting at the beginning of field relations—as a way of vouching for the researcher—cannot be overstated. Access and safe access are two wholly different notions. In my case, this tie was Luther—or at least so I thought. More generally, it is an indigenous offender or ex-offender turned fieldworker who acts as gatekeeper and protector. Yet, in a twist of sorts, field research with active offenders often requires strong ties in order to generate weak ones—that is, to initiate the methodological snowball. Micro-structurally and methodologically, this is unique; multiple weak ties rather than one or two strong ones are thought to be indispensable for social-network creation.[59] Indeed, one or two strong ties may actually cut off an actor from an entire social network.

In field research, developing strong ties with the wrong person or persons can, at a minimum, bias the sample or, worse, generate no sample at all.[60] Researchers may gain entry, but it may be with the wrong person. As my encounter with Luther attests, the outcome can be far more threatening than obtaining a biased sample or no sample. Perhaps the larger point here is that, no matter how strong or safe one's ties, danger is inherent in fieldwork with active offenders. Nowhere is this more true than among streetcorner crack sellers. Although many dangers can be addressed through planning and preparation, more often than not, danger management hinges on a creative process of "trial and blunder"[61] and results from a combination of skill and luck.[62] As Sluka notes, "[G]ood luck can sometimes help overcome a lack of skill, and well-developed skills can go far to help overcome the effects of bad luck. But sometimes no amount of skill will save one from a gross portion of bad luck."[63] Inevitably, criminological fieldwork is unpredictable and less subject to rational planning than we want it to be. How researchers handle this problem ultimately is a personal choice.

Researching active offenders requires one to balance conflicting agendas. Such agendas emanate from specific audiences—whether police or criminals—each with their own biases toward the ethnographic enterprise. Simply taking sides or currying favor with one audience over the other is not the issue, though this may be done at some point. Research strategies must be weighed carefully because their consequences are inevitably dialectical: police can get you "in" with offenders, but offenders can get you "in trouble" with police. Personal security is dependent on offender acceptance, yet security can be compromised by dependency. Police can be researchers' last bastion of hope against volatile offenders, but reliance on authorities may undermine the very purpose for being in the field. Caught among these contradictions stands the researcher, a true one-person "island in the street."[64] In this lonely position, the researcher must decide when to shade the truth and when to be forthright, when to offer and when to omit, when to induce and when to lie back. Such judgments are subjective and context specific, as any ethnographer will tell you. They must be made with the audience in mind, whether that audience is legal or illegal, academic or social. Each choice affects the kinds of data obtained and revealed. And how far an ethnographer is willing to go to get such data intertwines with the results that ethnographer hopes ultimately to obtain—as my encounter with Luther attests.

Questions for Thought and Discussion

1. Unlike the recruitment methods used by Wright and his associates in Chapter 1, how did Jacobs locate and recruit subjects?
2. What do you think about the methods used by Jacobs to conduct this study? Is this type of research too dangerous?
3. Jacobs had several "run-ins" with police during his research. How did these incidents affect his study?

Notes

1. All names are pseudonyms to protect identities.
2. Terry Williams, Eloise Dunlap, Bruce D. Johnson, and Ansley Hamid, "Personal Safety in Dangerous Places," *Journal of Contemporary Ethonography* 21 (1992): 365.
3. Williams et al., "Personal Safety," 350.
4. Richard A. Berk and Joseph M. Adams, "Establishing Rapport with Deviant Groups," *Social Problems* 18 (1970): 110.

5. Jeffrey A. Sluka, "Participant Observation in Violent Social Contexts," *Human Organization* 49 (1990): 114.
6. Williams et al., "Personal Safety," 347.
7. Patrick Biernacki and Dan Waldorf, "Snowball Sampling," *Sociological Methods and Research* 10 (1981): 141–163.
8. See Harold Garfinkel, "Conditions of Successful Degradation Ceremonies," *American Journal of Sociology* 61 (1956): 420–424.
9. Williams et al., "Personal Safety," 364.
10. Williams et al., "Personal Safety," 350.
11. John M. Johnson, "Trust and Personal Involvements in Fieldwork," in *Contemporary Field Research,* ed. Robert M. Emerson (Prospect Heights, IL: Waveland, 1983), 205.
12. Kurt H. Wolff, "Surrender and Community Study: The Study of Loma," in *Reflections on Community Studies,* ed. Arthur J. Vidich, Joseph Bensman, and Maurice R. Stein (New York: Wiley, 1964), 237.
13. Robert H. Lowies, *The History of Ethnological Theory* (New York: Farrar and Rinehart, 1937), 232.
14. Hortense Powdermaker, *Stranger and Friend: The Way of an Anthropologist* (New York: Norton, 1966), 19.
15. E. E. Evans-Pritchard, *Social Anthropology and Other Essays* (New York: Free Press, 1964), 77–79.
16. Berk and Adams, "Establishing Rapport," 103.
17. Berk and Adams, "Establishing Rapport."
18. Rosalie H. Wax, "The Ambiguities of Fieldwork," in *Contemporary Field Research,* ed. Robert M. Emerson (Prospect Heights, IL: Waveland, 1983), 179.
19. Ned Polsky, *Hustlers, Beats, and Others* (Chicago: Aldine, 1967), 124.
20. Robert M. Emerson, ed., *Contemporary Field Research* (Prospect Heights, IL: Waveland, 1983), 179.
21. Ivan Karp and Martha B. Kendall, "Reflexivity in Field Work," in *Explaining Human Behavior: Consciousness, Human Action, and Social Structure,* ed. Paul F. Secord (Beverly Hills, CA: Sage, 1982), 261.
22. Georg Simmel, "The Stranger," in *Georg Simmel,* ed. Donald Levine (Chicago: University of Chicago Press, 1908), 143–149.
23. Emerson, *Contemporary,* 179.
24. Richard T. Wright and Scott H. Decker, *Burglars on the Job: Streetlife and Residential Break-ins* (Boston: Northeastern University Press, 1994), 26.
25. Berk and Adams, "Establishing Rapport," 107.
26. See Polsky, *Hustlers.*
27. Peter K. Manning, "Observing the Police: Deviance, Respectables, and the Law," in *Research on Deviance,* ed. Jack D. Douglas (New York: Random House, 1972), 213–268.
28. Annie Oakley, "Interviewing Women: A Contradiction in Terms," in *Doing Feminist Research,* ed. Helen Roberts (London: Routledge and Kegan Paul, 1981), 41.
29. Luther's stalking came to an end only because police picked him up on two unrelated counts of armed robbery and armed criminal action. He is now serving ten years in a Missouri state penitentiary. With the help of colleagues, I moved. My phone number is now unlisted and unpublished, something I recommend to other ethnographers researching active offenders.
30. John Irwin, "Participant Observation of Criminals," in *Research on Deviance,* ed. Jack D. Douglas (New York: Random House, 1972), 117.
31. See Erich Goode, *The Marijuana Smokers* (New York: Basic, 1970).
32. Sluka, "Participant Observation," 115.
33. See Patricia Adler, *Wheeling and Dealing: An Enthography of an Upper-Level Drug Dealing and Smuggling Community* (New York: Columbia University Press, 1985).
34. Diana Scully, *Understanding Sexual Violence* (Boston: Unwin Inman, 1990).
35. Michael Agar, *Ripping and Running: A Formal Ethnography of Urban Heroin Addicts* (New York: Seminar Press, 1973).
36. Wright and Decker, *Burglars,* 5.
37. Edwin Sutherland and Donald Cressey, *Criminology,* 8th ed. (Philadelphia: Lippincott, 1970), 68.
38. Polsky, *Hustlers,* 123.
39. George McCall, *Observing the Law* (New York: Free Press, 1978), 27.
40. Erving Goffman, *Relations in Public: Micro Studies of the Public Order* (New York: Basic Books, 1971), 323.
41. SCAT is an acronym for "street corner apprehension team." This fifteen-man undercover team is charged with curbing street-level drug sales by apprehending dealers immediately after sales to one of their "buy" officers. Hiding nearby in unmarked cars, personnel "swoop" down on offenders in an attempt to catch them with marked money just given them by buy officers. This money either has traceable dye or serial numbers previously recorded that link dealers to undercover transactions. SCAT units were highly feared because they were reportedly merciless in their arrest procedures (i.e., they conducted strip searches).
42. Jeff Ferrell and Mark S. Hamm, *Ethnography at the Edge: Crime, Deviance and Field Research* (Boston: Northeastern University Press, 1998).

43. Wright and Decker, *Burglars,* 28.
44. Polsky, *Hustlers,* 147.
45. See Sluka, "Participant Observation."
46. Federal Bureau of Investigation, *Crime in the United States* (Washington, DC: Government Printing Office, 1995).
47. See Erving Goffman, *Stigma: Notes on the Management of Spoiled Identity,* (Englewood Cliffs, NJ: Prentice-Hall, 1963).
48. See John Van Maanen, "The Asshole," in *Policing: A View from the Streets,* ed. Peter K. Manning and John Van Maanen (Santa Monica: Goodyear, 1978), 221–238.
49. Erving Goffman, *Frame Analysis: An Essay on the Organization of Experience* (Cambridge, MA: Harvard University Press, 1974).
50. See Jerome Skolnick, "A Sketch of the Policeman's 'Working Personality,'" in *Criminal Justice: Law and Politics,* ed. George F. Cole (North Scituate, MA: Duxbury Press, 1980).
51. Jack D. Douglas, "Observing Deviance," in *Research on Deviance,* ed. Jack D. Douglas (New York: Random House, 1972), 3–34.
52. Sluka, "Participant Observation," 123.
53. Douglas, "Observing Deviance," 12.
54. Irving Soloway and James Walters, "Workin' the Corner: The Ethics and Legality of Fieldwork among Active Heroin Addicts," in *Street Ethnography,* ed. Robert S. Weppner (Beverly Hills, CA: Sage, 1977), 175–176.
55. James T. Carey, "Problems of Access and Risk in Observing Drug Scenes," in *Research on Deviance,* ed. Jack D. Douglas (New York: Random House, 1972), 77.
56. See Adler, *Wheeling,* 24.
57. Polsky, *Hustler,* 133–134.
58. Andrew Gollub, Farrukh Hakeem, and Bruce D. Johnson, "Monitoring the Decline in the Crack Epidemic with Data from the Drug Use Forecasting Program," Unpublished manuscript, 1996.
59. Mark Granovetter, "The Strength of Weak Ties," *American Journal of Sociology* 78 (1973): 1360–1380.
60. Douglas's research on nudist beach goers, for example, was jeopardized because of his early bond with a marginal and generally disliked participant (something Douglas did not know until later)—a participant with whom he was able to bond precisely because of that person's marginality; see Douglas, "Observing Deviance."
61. See Karp and Kendall, "Reflexivity."
62. Robert F. Ellen, *Ethnographic Research: A Guide to General Conduct* (London: Academic Press, 1984), 97.
63. Sluka, "Participant Observation," 124.
64. Marin Sanchez-Jankowski, *Islands in the Street: Gangs in American Urban Society* (Berkeley: University of California Press, 1991).

Chapter 3
Why I'll Talk

Offenders' Motives for Participating in Qualitative Research

Heith Copes
Andy Hochstetler

Criminologists have a long history of interviewing those engaged in illicit behaviors to gain insights into the nature of crime and criminality (see Bennett's 1981 history in *Oral History and Delinquency*). Interviews allow offenders to explain their offenses and lifestyles from their own perspectives. This is important because those engaged in criminal and deviant activities are in the "unique position of being able to describe, in their own words, the motivations and causes of crime, the level and nature of crime calculus, and the perceived effectiveness of crime control activities in deterring crime" (Miethe and McCorkle 2001, 17). When the voices of those engaged in illicit activity are coupled with the researchers' analyses, students and criminal justice professionals can get a more realistic glimpse into the world of offenders, as well as move toward theoretical explanation of their lifestyle (Pogrebin 2004). The researcher's job is to notice and organize patterns in what offenders have to say.

Clearly, posing questions to offenders is vital for a full understanding of crime and criminality. But, if we are to garner the benefits of the offender's perspective it is necessary that researchers both locate these individuals and convince them to talk to us about their misdeeds. To many qualitative investigators this task may seem daunting. Finding people who have direct experience with criminal behavior can be difficult, as they often desire to remain hidden, especially from those outside their social worlds, yet finding them is in no way impossible. Data on "presumably difficult-to-study events are much more available than we usually think. All we really have to do is to get out of our offices and into the streets. The data are there; the problem is that too often sociologists are not" (Chambliss 1975, 39). Thus, for investigators to find those involved in illicit behavior, they must leave the safe environment of the university and enter into uncomfortable and possibly risky environments to talk to people who may be "drunk, high, or in jail" (Shover 1996, 193).

Even if we do leave our offices to find offenders there is still the task of convincing them to share their stories. Finding people to divulge details of their lives requires that researchers put forth extra efforts not required when using less intrusive methods. Ethnographic research requires that we intrude into people's lives and have them reveal personal information that they may not have shared with others before. When the stories they relate involve crime, the details they provide could lead to their arrest or leave them vulnerable to other penalties in the future. And as Wright and Decker (1997, 4) point out, "No matter how much inmates are assured otherwise, many will continue to believe what they say to researchers will get back to the authorities and influence their chances for early release." Still, most offenders of interest have criminal records and related problems known too well by family and friends, and therefore have little to hide when it comes to most subjects.

Despite the inconveniences and potential legal risks of talking to researchers, offenders are often quite willing to discuss their lives and criminal careers in great detail. Many novice interviewers inaccurately assume that research participants, especially those who have something to hide, will not discuss certain topics with them. They mistakenly believe that they will be met with "hostility and a lack of co-operation" from those they wish to interview (Shover 1985, 154). Fortunately, as Berg (2001, 95) notes, "once subjects have been persuaded to participate in an interview, they often tell far more details than the interviewers would ever want to know." Many people engaged in deviant and/or criminal behavior are "willing, able, and often eager to share their thoughts" (Hagan and McCarthy 1997, 244). Girshick (1999, x) found herself "in awe that so many [inmates] were willing to share and reveal." This willingness to talk has been documented by numerous researchers (Jacobs 1996, 1999, 2000; Shover 1985, 1996; Rengert and Wasilchick 2000). Indeed, we too have been astounded by our participants' openness and frankness in their descriptions of their lives and crimes.

What would make someone who has engaged in behavior that society has defined as immoral and illegal disregard the potential risks and inconveniences to sit down and openly discuss their lives and misdeeds? An answer to this question has important implications for qualitative researchers regarding how to recruit participants and the meaningfulness of their finished work. The motives individuals have for participating in research ultimately affect the nature of the stories they relay and the type of information they withhold. It was for these reasons that during a project on street criminals' techniques and motives we posed the question, "Why did you agree to talk to us?" We posed this question to 33 incarcerated individuals (31 males and two females). These individuals were incarcerated in a medium-security prison at the time of the interviews and agreed to talk about their participation in serious violent crimes. The reasons inmates gave for consenting to the interview included the desire to satisfy immediate material needs, to benefit emotionally and psychologically, to give back to others, and, for a few, a misunderstanding about the benefits we were capable of providing.

Immediate Rewards

Many inmates agree to be interviewed for altruistic reasons, such as doing their part to keep the next generation from making similar mistakes or helping out a trusted confederate (Shover 1985). A smaller number of inmates consent to interviews for more self-serving and mundane reasons. Inmates contended that they were willing to tell their stories to us because they could use the money that we offered, they simply desired to have a conversation with someone from the outside, they were eager to get a change of scenery, or they were curious to see what it was like to be interviewed.

Financial Incentives

Researchers who rely on survey and interview methods often provide small monetary incentives to encourage participants to either complete a questionnaire or to consent to an interview. Financial incentives can be powerful motivators, especially among populations that have little means of earning money, such as those confined in institutions. But even those who are interviewed in the streets, who could conceivably make more money through hustling than researchers can offer, are attracted to the prospect of making quick cash (Wright and Decker 1994). For those offenders approached on the street, money is "critical in generating their interest. . . . On the streets, money talks; nobody does anything for nothing" (Jacobs 1999, 14). While there are some ethical dilemmas when deciding how much money to offer, most researchers agree that it is appropriate to compensate study participants for their time and knowledge. We offered the inmates whose words are used here 20 dollars to encourage them to sit down and talk with us.

As others have found, our financial incentive did encourage participation. However, it was uncommon for inmates to state that their primary reason for participating in the research was for the money. Statements such as, "Twenty dollars about the only thing good you know. That's about it. That's about the only thing good [about doing this]," or "I needed [the money], you know what I'm saying. I needed it. It helped," were uncommon. In fact only three inmates claimed that money was the driving force behind their participation. Doubtless, easy money does intrigue offenders and whet other motives for participating.

It was common for inmates to acknowledge that money helped but that other reasons for their cooperation were more important. For these individuals, the "financial reward [was] little more than a pleasant bonus" (Wright and Decker 1997, 24). One offender stated, for example, "I'm gonna be blessed with 20 dollars and hopefully I can help you with your study, your career or whatever you are doing." Here the participant mentions money but underplays its importance, suggesting that altruism was the "real" reason for participating. Regardless of the priority of money as a motivator, it is clear that even small financial gestures can generate compliance.

Conversations With Outsiders

The secrecy inherent in criminal participation means that offenders have few opportunities to relate their exploits to those who are not associates. Offenders often find this inability to share their "war stories" frustrating (Letkemann 1973). This is especially the case when audiences that are familiar with and largely uninterested in such stories other than as diversionary banter surround them. This frustration is possibly even greater among captive populations. Deep reflection on or analysis of one's mistakes is discouraged in most informal contexts of the prison. This is expressed by one offender who stated, "Just to talk to a stranger for thirty minutes, you know what I'm saying, is cool with me cause I'm getting tired of talking to them." Incarcerated individuals have even fewer opportunities to have meaningful conversations with those who are not incarcerated or who are not criminal justice personnel. They have little opportunity to share their stories with people who do not judge them or assume they are being deceptive or hyperbolic. In the words of one participant:

> It's good [talking to you]. It ain't too often that we get to conversate with someone . . . on an intelligent level, you know what I'm saying. [With someone] that's already overcome certain obstacles and is already successful.

Similarly, as one participant explained, "I ain't never got a visit since I been up here. I haven't seen nobody from the streets in seven years. Ain't had a visit, you know. But, you know, it was just cool talking to you." When cut off from the conventional and ordinary world any taste of it can be rewarding, or at least a relief from routine. Offenders welcome the chance to talk to someone who is not in some way connected to the institution (Athens 1997, 103).

Additionally, some offenders are motivated by the desire to teach those with formal educations something about life in the streets. Many ethnographers have fostered the teaching role of respondents to generate cooperation from them (Berk and Adams 1970). As Miller (2001, 30) points out, "providing respondents with the opportunity to act as teachers can afford them with a sense of meaning and importance." Because marginalized individuals seldom have the opportunity to lend their voices to social discourse, the opportunity to do so acts as a lure for their participation. The value of simple conversation with a person whom they need not impress, with whom they have no official or emotional tie, and with whom they can share their expertise cannot be overestimated as a motive for offenders inside and outside of prison walls.

Change of Setting/Pass Time

To effectively manage prison populations it is necessary for prison staff to structure the daily activities of inmates. This creates a predictable, monotonous routine for prisoners, which can make time creep and the days run together. To disrupt this routine inmates often seek out activities in the hopes of making time go a little faster. Many inmates enroll in church services, educational programs, and self-help classes not because of [a] desire to change their ways, but simply to change their setting. As one participant stated, "What are we doing in the dorm? Nothing. This right here, this is passing my time." Undoubtedly, this desire to break the routine of prison life is a motivating factor for many of those who participate in research as it "provides a break from the boredom and monotony of prison life" (Matthews 2002, 10). Inmates often jump at chances to "just get out of the dorm" and have a look at new scenery. As one participant explained:

> Plus, you know, it's a change of scenery, you dig. I didn't know what we was gonna come at or nothing like that there. But, let me tell you something, the dorm, and you can put this in the record, the dorm ain't got no windows in it.

In responding to our question about why they came to talk to us, participants gave statements such as, "I just want a little walk, you know what I'm saying." And, "You stay in the dorm. You be cooped up in there 24 hours a day. Ain't nothing else to do back in the dorm except playing cards or something." Certainly, when people spend most of their time in a confined area any opportunity to travel beyond its borders is welcomed. Doubtless, the motivation increases in bleak settings.

Curiosity

Many of those who are confined in state institutions share an interest in experiencing the unknown. This same trait is what drove several of the participants to consent to the interview (Matthews 2002). One offender exemplifies this curiosity in his response to our question:

> Well, I wanted to see what it was really about. You know, curiosity. Curiosity killed the cat. I just wanted to see what's happening up here, you know. I decided to come down and see.

Several individuals made direct reference to wanting to "come up here and see what it was like." Part of seeing what it is like is to discern whether something is amiss and to exude confidence in the face of what could be a deception. Showing confidence in chaotic or unknown situations is a trait highly valued by many serious street offenders (Katz 1988). Investigators often get the impression when doing research in jails and prisons, as well as on the streets, that some of the first people they interview see themselves as scouts who can speak with authority to others about whether the situation is "cool." If investigators were to press them for names, dates or other sorts of information that could lead to trouble, early participants would caution friends and associates considering the interview.

Psychological Benefits to Self

Many offenders decide to participate in interviews because they have begun to reassess their crimes and related mistakes. Either they are engaged in a new way of life or are exploring the possibility of a new approach. In fact, the interview is often viewed as part of a therapeutic process or as evidence of their recovery. Many believe that talking to professionals, even if they are merely criminologists and not psychiatrists, might "help them come to terms with their personal problems" (Wright and Decker 1997, 25). Thus, sharing their stories acts as a catharsis and is evidence that they are on the right path to recovery.

Catharsis

Talking to others allows offenders to "let it all out" without being perceived as weak or vulnerable. For people who have engaged in illegal behavior the simple act of talking about their misdeeds makes them feel better about what they have done. Several of those we spoke with thanked us for allowing them to talk and acknowledged that they felt better about themselves because of the experience (see Shover 1985). As one participant said:

> It makes me feel better by talking about [my past]. I mean, it's like looking back over all the devious shit that I've done and got away with, I figure, you know, if I can come sit down here and talk to you about half the shit I done did then I can sleep better.

Similarly, another offender stated:

> I'm trying to make a change in my life because I got children out there. I'm trying to go out there and do the right thing, you know. So, it's best to talk about it. It's like having counselors to better myself. So, it doesn't bother me to talk about it.

Interviewing offenders not only benefits social science, but it also allows those directly involved in the behavior to explain away, both to others and to themselves, the guilt caused by criminal participation. For many research participants, the interviews turn "out to be intense, genuine experiences" (Hagedorn 1988, 33).

The Right Track

The interview is a reflective setting. Offenders get the message that they are supposed to be assessing what went wrong for them. Some think that assessments of their prospects for reform should follow the telling of the unfortunate story. After the interview two participants said they were going to go "straight" and do what they could to get back in school (see Wright and Decker 1997, 25). In fact, one of these later contacted us about how to apply for school. We are unaware if he followed through with our advice and actually went "straight." More important for present purposes, such statements of conventional goals and assessments of prospects conclude many interviews, even when they are not requested.

Additionally, participating in research practically requires that the offender adapt or respond to a conventional stance. They explain errors and crimes in a way that might be understood by strangers to the street criminal's world (Maruna and Copes 2004). Offenders, especially those on the slippery path to reform, are likely to portray crime as an aberration and as such, as something interesting and worth exploring. Criminal acts say nothing about who the offenders are deep inside or who they want to be. Loosely structured interviews aid this interpretation and narrative if only by the implicit assumptions that the causes of crime are complex and the choice to offend worthy of reflection.

Offenders experience few settings where an honest recounting of their stories might be interpreted as evidence of noble aims. In the interview, their honesty is more important than the ledger that balances their criminal records and other failures against their accomplishments. Interviews, therefore, fit neatly into offenders' self-improvement projects and help them to refine and construct their stories as honest struggling citizens. Many have only had such conversations with themselves and are eager to voice them in a setting where these stories will not be viewed as overly sentimental, a con game, or whining. Their enthusiasm for relating their stories of change also should be interpreted in light of treatment program designs that emphasize claiming one's mistakes, confessing, and sharing tales of struggle and redemption. Many have participated in such programs and all are aware of them. Being given a chance to tell their story, or testify, represents an opportunity to take a step, however small, in the right direction. For this reason, offenders commonly respond to simple questions about why they chose to participate in a study with answers much more profound and ambitious than researchers, who typically have humble aims, might initially expect. One offender commented, for example, "I don't know it's like even though I consider myself halfway, I am getting my mind right." Another reflects on his motives:

> I'm just trying to get right, you know. I want to go out there and do the right thing and make my mom proud. Settle down, have a little family. I'm tired of coming in here. Selling drugs ain't going to take you nowhere.

Participation in the research process indicates to themselves and to outsiders that they are indeed on the right path to getting their lives in order.

Social Benefits to Others

Many participants choose to take part in research to help others. In some cases this is part of their project to do the right thing and make amends for past misdeeds. Where this is the case, they often want to teach the moral lessons of their stories to an imagined audience of people confronting decisions similar to those that led them astray. In their imaginings, this may occur when someone's life is directly affected, as is hopefully the case when offenders speak to student groups. Most offenders recognize that they are more likely to reach their target audience indirectly. They intend to help a researcher to understand criminal acts in a way that might indirectly benefit those at risk of crime or help others recognize the social problems that might have contributed to their acts.

Helping Abstract Others

Many of those who agree to talk to investigators do so because they recognize that they have acted improperly and wish that their testimonies could help deter young people from making similar bad choices. All who conduct qualitative research hear statements of this type:

> Maybe it might help somebody. Help some young person. Hopefully, they haven't really gotten into [violent crime] yet. Maybe, they might be stealing cars or something like that, you know. Maybe, I might be able to help them or you might be able to help them by hearing what I have to say.

Another informant echoes the sentiment:

> Just knowing that somebody is trying to do something that might help one of them youngsters out there. I hope you will help them because we got a lot of youngsters coming in here now.

These altruistic intentions on the part of the offender have shaped qualitative criminology since its earliest days. The five Martin boys interviewed by Shaw and colleagues claimed that they agreed to give their life histories in the "genuine hope that the documents might be useful in preventing other boys from becoming involved in delinquency and crime" (Shaw, McKay, and McDonald 1938, 143).

In a similar vein, some participants look toward improved community understanding and recognition of some of the external sources of crime as the main reason for participating. As one offender explained:

> I was cool about it because I really want to let people know why people do it. That's the only reason why I participated. You know, just so they can have understanding that it's more than what society would think. Society put a label on them and put them in jail for the rest of their lives. [People should] try to learn something about this person and why he or she did these things. Then, you understand. I mean [understand] why you want to rob, why you want to kill, why you want to jack this or jack that. If you got a good understanding of their background and environment, then you have a better understanding of why people do these things.

Participants with this motivation believe that "their life history would make an entertaining and perhaps useful contribution to understanding crime and those who commit it" (Shover 1996, 190).

Helping the Researcher

These varieties of altruism are common, but participation in a research project can also help others who are more proximate and who are more certain to benefit. Researchers are often impressed at how many participants decide to participate in a project primarily because it will help the researcher. This often comes from a practical recognition that completion of a research project benefits academic careers. While the participants have little understanding of how academic careers advance, they do understand that they are being asked to help and are in a position to aid someone in a conventional pursuit. When asked why he agreed to talk to us one participant responded:

> Oh, you alright. I just heard you was at school. If it can help you out, by me being in here, I mean by me giving you this. . . . I just hope something comes out of this. Maybe, you can get something out of this.

In keeping with the reflective tone of many interviews, the desire to help someone's academic or professional advancement often is accompanied by statements that failure in the workplace and educational advancement is where they went astray. One participant laments, "This is helping you, you know. . . . At least you are doing what you should be doing. I should be in college right now." They also want to help students. As true experts on crime, they desire to give their expertise to those who study it. The fact that students of crime typically are attached to a university gives the offender a way to tap into, if only temporarily and with the loosest connection, this prestigious world and to put experience to good use.

A desire to help us resulted in several participants refusing to take the 20 dollars for the interview, because they believed the money was coming directly from our pockets. Shover (1985) observed a similar reaction from those with whom he spoke. Like Shover, we insisted that these individuals accept the money. After explaining that we had been given a grant and that the university or the state was actually paying for it, all accepted the money.

Favor for Trusted Others

Whether research is conducted in institutions or on the street, word spreads. Soon enough, researchers find that they have gained participants because someone has vouched for them or made a request that the new recruits participate. In institutions, researchers have to be particularly wary of these referrals. When they come from officials they might have a coercive element and when they come from inmates they might have something to do with payment of debts incurred in the illegal inmate economy. Despite these cautions, researchers generally come to understand the value of being referred by a trusted insider. For potential participants it makes what might have been a worrisome decision into a casual and confident choice to participate. The simple request by a respected member of the street or prison community goes a long way for recruiting participants (Athens 1997; Jacobs and Wright 1999; Wright and Decker 1994). Indeed, having those in the participants' social world vouch for investigators is critical to establishing further participation. As Jacobs (1999, 22) noted, "if [contacts] told others it was 'cool' to talk to me and that participants would not be 'burned' as a result, it tended to be believed." One inmate points to a correctional officer as his motive: "Well, I been knowing the Major for awhile. The Major just asked for my cooperation. He just asked me to help you guys out." Another points to an inmate friend, "The guy that I was talking to about it, me and him are cool, you know, and he say, 'Do you want to do the interview?' I said, yeah, that's cool."

Misunderstanding

Ethical guidelines require researchers to disclose the nature and possible dangers of the research to participants. When doing research in a prison setting it is important to inform inmates that their participation is completely voluntary and that their participation will have no effect, either positive or negative, on their status as an inmate. That is, inmates are informed in advance that participation will not affect parole, admittance into work or social programs, or their relations with staff. Despite these acknowledgements, many inmates are motivated to volunteer because they believe they will somehow benefit from cooperation.

Even though we took special care to let inmates know that we neither worked for nor were affiliated with the prison or the Department of Corrections, several inmates believed that we could help them with their criminal justice status. Typically, they believed that the study was one of the many programs that the prison implemented to help ex-cons get back on their feet. For example, one offender acknowledged, "[I agreed because] the prison has a lot of programs that are going on. You don't know what you getting yourself into. It could be something good, you know what I'm saying." Upon further probing it became clear that this individual believed that our research was a part of a program set up by the prison to help inmates. He agreed to talk to us because he thought it was a prerequisite for acceptance into the program. Fortunately, we were able to clarify this misunderstanding and the inmate left with the concluding remark, "Well, if nothing else at least I got out of the dorms."

Another inmate who misinterpreted our solicitation agreed to come and meet with us because, "I didn't know I was coming in here for an interview. I thought I was coming here to sign some papers to go home." Doubtless a few inmates are also under the impression that this is a chance for them to tell stories that may help them with their cases. This is often because they imagine that interviewers are informants or are operating at the behest of criminal justice officials. We believe that inmates participating for this reason are easy to identify by their reluctance to address many questions and their apparent deceptions. By comparing their words with official records, researchers see deception. If we are right, this motivation is exceedingly rare.

Discussion

Offenders have a project when they come to an interview (see Presser 2004). To some extent, their narratives are predetermined and independent of the questions that are asked. Offenders' constructions of their stories may have as much to do with the reasons they consent to the interview as the prompts and probing questions from the researcher. Stories of struggle or reform are, for example, fairly consistent across offenders, and of a limited number of types. They rear their heads in much of what offenders say about a variety of topics. Interviewers become familiar with certain scripts, such as the addiction tales of heroin users, the born again stories of penitents, and the hard-knock stories of early life on the streets of large housing projects. This does not deny that the stories are true or diminish the value of what offenders say for understanding crime. These accounts are part of human and lived experience. Nevertheless, the motivations for sharing and the constructions of accounts by offenders should not escape the attention of qualitative researchers or their readers. One reason is that they introduce an angle into the account that might be missed if researchers do not pay attention to what offenders are attempting to accomplish in interviews. Also, they raise some potential methodological biases.

Participation in almost all research projects and data collection efforts is voluntary. Beyond checking to make sure that those who decline to participate do not differ on potentially important and available variables from those who do, little can be done about selection biases introduced by volunteering. Students of crime must accept that they generally only know the stories of those who choose to tell them as they choose to tell them. Participating offenders are likely to adopt certain postures. At some times and in some settings these may be very different than the identities and images they send off when committing crimes. Offenders may be insightful and careful where they know that such a stance is appropriate and that every word will be analyzed. Conversely, some will choose to play the role of criminal in hope that researchers will not be disappointed with their stories. This act may resemble the inauthentic, over-the-top identities and cool poses that are characteristic of street corners and the decision to offend. In any case, the proportional distribution of accounts is influenced by the decision to participate in a study, the interview setting, the story that is most viable there, and the motives of participants.

Qualitative researchers themselves introduce another source of potential bias. Articulate and interesting respondents are more likely to influence findings at every stage of analysis. These interviews last longer and are drawn from more heavily. To prove this point, one need only recognize how articulate and insightful many participants are whose statements find their way into print. It is the hope of every researcher that an article is interesting, and it is tempting to select colorful statements for inclusion. Participants, especially those whose interviews are heavily relied upon, probably are more reflective, intelligent, and well-spoken than the typical street offender. The bright, self-reflective, and verbose may be more likely to volunteer in the first place because they believe that they have something interesting and worthwhile to say, or suspect that they are capable of saying it well. Their narratives follow a logical plot line and are easy to organize and understand. Despite the selection bias toward articulate volunteers, every qualitative researcher of street crime quickly learns that a good interview that provides insight on more than a few simple points is a rare gem. Readers should not forget that ramblings of intellectually challenged, hopelessly intoxicated, or mentally ill respondents seldom make it to paper, as the data from these interviews are often useless (see Miller 1986, 187). This omission is justifiable but these shortcomings certainly speak to some of the origins and lived experience of crime.

The Value of Talk

For many years, qualitative research was seen as the most appropriate way to gauge criminal motives. Apart from recognition that reasonable offenders would hide a few details and bend the truth on occasion, the offender was viewed as an impartial narrator of events. This is, of course, not the way reconstruction of motives or answers to difficult questions occurs for any of us. Wider academic interest in the formation of accounts and narratives of complex events has turned attention to this fact. For example, those of us who chose to go to college probably cannot really explain accurately the decision-making processes or events that led us to that conclusion, although we do have a story available should anyone ask. Many questions asked of offenders by qualitative researchers require similar narrative construction. Variation in these constructions may be important over and above the facts relayed. In fact, there is great and increasing awareness among criminologists that the way that offenders understand and depict their lives may have significant effects on their prospects for rehabilitation. The story that offenders tell and how they tell it may give indication of their progress toward the end of a criminal career (Maruna 2001).

The decision to participate in a study and the reason given for doing so might be similarly relevant and important. Some offenders see their participation in a study as a reaffirming or generative exercise. This decision and its motivations represent the front board of the stories they will relate. For some, it is a small gesture at restitution. For others, it is an attempt to elicit some understanding from an impartial and attentive outsider. A few see the decision as yet another sign that they are on the right track or as a chance to explore their motives publicly. Some are simply raconteurs or curiosity seekers who want to see what kind of reaction they will get from their stories or what a research effort is about. There is, for many, nothing better to do and nothing to hide. Unfortunately, for researchers who are looking for more, a few use the unusual venue to fictitiously portray themselves as unremorseful hard men or criminal insiders who occupy a strange and exciting world. Like rap artists who posture as pimps, almost none of these are as interesting or exceptional as they think and their insights are familiar, predictable, and fairly easy to tune out. Occasionally, a good qualitative researcher can turn an interview that has this quality or other indications that it is unproductive around. This may well be because offenders' motives shift as the course of an interview proceeds; they can strike on something unexpected and decide to explore it. But, if offenders are really there only for the money or to show off, the good that will come of talking to them is reduced.

Conclusions

Like offenders' words themselves, their motives for participating in a study are of interest for voyeuristic, theoretical, and practical reasons. There are patterns and subtexts in narratives based on the narrator's purpose and understanding of what is appropriate. These form a significant part of the story and how the facts are related. The same is true of participants in qualitative criminological research. Their motives tell something about where the offenders have been, where they are, and where they are going.

It is clear that criminologists have much to gain from interviewing offenders. The accounts of offenders have allowed us to understand the meanings they associate with crime, the criminal decision-making process, and the most effective crime-control strategies. What has been less clear is what these participants have to gain in this research. We have provided a list of many, but certainly not all, of the benefits that offenders associate with talking with interviewers. It is important to point out that we elicited the cooperation of individuals who were incarcerated for violent crimes at the time of the interview. They may have different motives than active offenders for agreeing to be a part of academic research. Those who are living outside prison walls obviously do not participate in research to get a look at new scenery, although they may be looking for a novel activity. Nevertheless, we believe that the reasons these incarcerated individuals gave are similar to the reasons nonincarcerated individuals give.

In addition, one's position in the life-course and social structure may affect interpretation of the research event and motivations for being a part of a study. Those who are approaching the end of their criminal careers surely have different reasons than those just embracing crime, or those in the midst of their careers. Similarly, those who engage in especially egregious criminal acts, like murder and rape, may not have the same motivations as those whose crimes are more mundane. White-collar offenders are likely to devote a great deal of effort in interviews to defending their character. Penitents are rare among them. But once again we contend that differences among types of offenders are merely in the relative frequency of motives for participation, and not in distinct motives. The desire to help others, to get on the right track, or to just share their lives with others are certainly not unique to those in prisons, those considering giving up crime, or those who engage in violent street crimes (see Wright and Decker 1994, 1997).

The current findings and discussion of why offenders consent to interviews also has important implications for how researchers complete Internal Review Board (IRB) reports. The IRB is designed to ensure that researchers treat human participants in a way that is consistent with ethical guidelines. When determining if a certain research project using human subjects is ethical, the researcher must demonstrate that the benefits of the study outweigh potential harm to participants. Those who engage in ethnographic research typically point to the abstract benefits that the research addresses, such as how the study can inform criminal justice personnel on how best to thwart the actions of offenders. Thus, the general public benefits from the words of offenders, but little is said of the actual participants. The current research suggests that the telling of their stories can have direct benefits to participants. An understanding of how the research process can benefit those directly involved in it can go a long way in facilitating the IRB process, making it easier for ethnographic researchers to leave their offices and enter into the world of thieves, hustlers, and heavy drug users.

Questions for Thought and Discussion

1. In this chapter, the authors suggest that many incarcerated offenders are willing to talk about their crimes for altruistic reasons. What do you think?
2. Would the authors of the first two chapters in this book agree that researchers can obtain valid information from incarcerated offenders? Why or why not?
3. What are some of the ethical issues involved in interviewing incarcerated individuals?

References

Athens, Lonnie. 1997. *Violent Criminal Acts and Actors Revisited*. Urbana, IL: University of Illinois Press.

Bennett, James. 1981. *Oral History and Delinquency: The Rhetoric of Criminology.* Chicago: University of Chicago Press.

Berg, Bruce L. 2001. *Qualitative Research Methods for the Social Sciences,* 4th ed. Needham Heights, MA: Allyn and Bacon.

Berk, Richard, and Joseph M. Adams. 1970. "Establishing Rapport with Deviant Groups." *Social Problems* 18:102–117.

Chambliss, William. 1975. "On the Paucity of Original Research on Organized Crime: A Footnote to Galliher and Cain." *The American Sociologist* 10:36–39.

Girshick, Lori. 1999. *No Safe Haven: Stories of Women in Prison.* Boston: Northeastern University Press.

Hagan, John, and Bill McCarthy. 1997. *Mean Streets: Youth Crime and Homelessness.* Cambridge, UK: Cambridge University Press.

Hagedorn, John. 1988. *People and Folks: Gangs, Crime and the Underclass in a Rustbelt City.* Chicago: Lakeview Press.

Jacobs, Bruce A. 1996. "Crack Dealers and Restrictive Deterrence: Identifying Narcs." *Criminology* 34:409–431.

———. 1999. *Dealing Crack: The Social World of Streetcorner Selling.* Boston: Northeastern University Press.

———. 2000. *Robbing Drug Dealers: Violence Beyond the Law.* New York: Aldine de Gruyter.

Jacobs, Bruce A., and Richard Wright. 1999. "Stick-up, Street Culture, and Offender Motivation." *Criminology* 37:149–173.

Katz, Jack. 1988. *Seductions of Crime: The Moral and Sensual Attractions of Doing Evil.* New York: Basic Books.

Letkemann, P. 1973. *Crime as Work.* Englewood Cliffs, NJ: Prentice-Hall.

Maruna, Shadd. 2001. *Making Good: How Ex-convicts Reform and Rebuild Their Lives.* Washington, DC: American Psychological Association.

Maruna, Shadd, and Heith Copes. 2004. "Excuses, Excuses: What Have We Learned From Five Decades of Neutralization Research?" *Crime and Justice: An Annual Review of Research* 32.

Matthews, Roger. 2002. *Armed Robbery.* Portland, OR: Willan.

Miethe, Terance D., and Richard C. McCorkle. 2001. *Crime Profiles: The Anatomy of Danger-*

ous Persons, Places, and Situations. Los Angeles: Roxbury.

Miller, Eleanor M. 1986. *Street Women.* Philadelphia: Temple University Press.

Miller, Jody. 2001. *One of the Guys: Girls, Gangs, and Gender.* Oxford: Oxford University Press.

Pogrebin, Mark (ed.). 2004. *About Criminals: A View of the Offender's World.* Thousand Oaks, CA: Sage.

Presser, Lois. 2004. "Violent Offenders, Moral Selves: Constructing Identities and Accounts in the Research Interview." *Social Problems* 51:82–102.

Rengert, George F., and John Wasilchick. 2000. *Suburban Burglary: A Tale of Two Suburbs,* 2nd ed. Springfield, IL: Charles C Thomas.

Shaw, Clifford R., Henry D. McKay, and James F. McDonald. 1938. *Brothers in Crime.* Chicago: University of Chicago Press.

Shover, Neal. 1985. *Aging Criminals.* Beverly Hills, CA: Sage.

———. 1996. *Great Pretenders: Pursuits and Careers of Persistent Thieves.* Boulder, CO: Westview.

Wright, Richard T., and Scott Decker. 1994. *Burglars on the Job: Streetlife and Residential Break-ins.* Boston: Northeastern University Press.

———. 1997. *Armed Robbers in Action: Stickups and Street Culture.* Boston: Northeastern University Press.

Section II

Criminal Lifestyles and Decision Making

This section explores the lifestyles and decision-making strategies of criminals. We are concerned here with offenders' views and attitudes about both criminal and conventional activities and their perceptions of the risks and benefits associated with a criminal lifestyle. How those perceptions are formed and how they change over time are also examined. Because the nature of the criminal lifestyle is hidden from public view and open only to the initiated, criminologists know little about these important issues. The research studies in this book are a step toward understanding the dynamics of criminal lifestyles and criminal decision making in that context.

In the first selection, Shover and Honaker ("The Socially Bounded Decision Making of Persistent Property Offenders") argue that an adequate understanding of the decision-making processes of property offenders can be gained only through exploring how these offenders' decisions are influenced by their lifestyles. They argue that offenders' risk assessments can best be understood by exploring the personal and social contexts in which decisions are made. They examine how the lifestyles of persistent property offenders affect their assessment of the risks and benefits of crime. The research focuses on the decision to commit a crime, emphasizing how closely that decision fits the rational choice model, in which decisions are based on an "assessment of potential returns from alternative courses of action and the risk of legal sanctions."

In Chapter 5, "The Reasoning Burglar: Motives and Decision-Making Strategies," Cromwell and Olson examine the criminal calculus of residential burglars. They describe the processes by which burglars choose to commit a burglary and select a target.

Baskin and Sommers ("Women, Work, and Crime") analyze how female offenders make a living. They describe the women's progression from early involvement in the legitimate, formal economy to their ultimate embeddedness in the illegal, informal economy. Through a description of their experiences, the women provide us with an understanding of the basis for and types of decisions they make when choosing their "professions."

In the next selection, "Stick-up, Street Culture, and Offender Motivation," Jacobs and Wright draw from a study of active armed robbers in St. Louis an understanding of how robbers arrive at a state of motivation to commit an act of armed robbery. They looked at the immediate concerns of the offenders, the so-called foreground factors, rather than the background characteristics (the factors that led the individuals to consider a criminal lifestyle) that are usually emphasized in the dynamics of criminality. In other words, they examined the factors that led to the commission of the criminal event, rather than those that led to criminality. These motivations are an underexamined area of criminological research. ✦

Chapter 4
The Socially Bounded Decision Making of Persistent Property Offenders

Neal Shover
David Honaker

The past decade has witnessed a renewal of interest in understanding crime based on the degree of rationality attributed to criminals as they contemplate offending. The rational choice model recognizes that individuals choose crime from other possible alternative courses of action. The argument holds that prospective criminals weigh the possible consequences of their actions—potential risks and possible gains—and take advantage of a criminal opportunity only when it is in their self-interest to do so. This model stresses the offender's perceptions of the costs and benefits and the anticipated net utilities of crime, arguing that an objective appraisal of the costs and benefits of any course of action cannot be completely known or acted upon.

In the following selection, Neal Shover and David Honaker argue that the risk assessments of offenders are best understood by exploring the personal and social contexts in which decisions are made. They examine the lifestyles of persistent property offenders as influences on how they assess the risks and benefits of crime. The focus of the research is on the decision to commit a crime with emphasis on how closely that decision fits the rational choice model.

The study population includes a sample of 60 recidivist property offenders incarcerated in Tennessee state prisons who were nearing their release date. Subjects ranged in age from 23 to 70 years of age, with an average age of 34.1 years. Each member of the sample was interviewed approximately one month before his release from prison. Seven to 10 months after release, the authors traced, contacted, and interviewed 46 of the original sample of 60 men. The data used in this study were collected in the postrelease interviews. Semistructured ethnographic interviews were the principal data collection technique.

The interviews produced detailed descriptions of the most recent, easiest recalled crime that each subject had committed prior to the interview. Some of these crimes were committed before their incarceration and some after release. The objective was to gain, through the eyes of the offender, an understanding of the decision to commit a specific criminal act. The subjects were asked to focus their recollection on how the decision was made and to provide a detailed account of the risks and rewards they assessed while doing so.

The 1970s were marked by the eclipse of labeling theory as the dominant individual-level criminological theory and by the reappearance of interest in approaches originally advanced by classical theorists. Economists and cognitive psychologists along with many in the criminological mainstream advanced an interpretation of crime as *choice,* offering models of criminal decision making grounded in the assumption that the decision to commit a criminal act springs from the offender's assessment of its anticipated net utilities (e.g., Becker 1968; Heineke 1978; Carroll 1978; Reynolds 1985). This movement in favor of rational-choice approaches to crime spurred empirical investigation of problems that heretofore were limited primarily to studies of the death penalty and its impact on the homicide rate.

Early investigations of a rational choice interpretation of crime reported a weak but persistent relationship between the certainty of punishment and rates of serious property crimes (Blumstein, Cohen, and Nagin 1978). It was recognized, however, that an understanding of criminal decision making also requires knowledge about individual perceptions and beliefs about legal threats and other constraints on decision making (e.g., Manski 1978). Investigators moved on two main fronts to meet this need. Some used survey methods to explore differential involvement in minor forms of deviance in samples of restricted age ranges, typically high school and college students (e.g., Waldo and Chiricos 1972). Alternatively they examined the link between risk assessments and criminal participation in samples more representative of the general population. . . . Serious shortcomings of these studies are that most either ignore the potential rewards of crime entirely or they fail to examine its emotional and interpersonal utilities. Still other investigators turned attention to serious criminal offenders and began expanding the narrow existing knowledge base (e.g., Claster 1967), chiefly through the use of cross-sectional research designs and survey methods.

For more than a decade now, investigators have studied offenders' attitudes toward legitimate and criminal pursuits, their perceptions of and beliefs about the risks of criminal behavior, and their estimates of the payoffs from conventional and criminal pursuits (e.g., Petersilia et al. 1978; Peterson and Braiker 1980). These studies raise serious questions about the fit between offenders' calculus and a priori assumptions about their utilities and criminal decision making. One investigation of 589 incarcerated property offenders concluded, for example, that the subjects apparently do not utilize "a sensible cost-benefit analysis" when weighing the utilities of crime (Figgie 1988, 25). They substantially underestimate the risk of arrest for most crimes, routinely overestimate the monetary benefit they expect, and seem to have "grossly inaccurate perceptions of the costs and benefits associated with property crime" (Figgie 1988, 81). Unfortunately, both design and conceptual problems undermine confidence in the findings of this and similar studies. Cross-sectional survey methods, for example, are poorly suited for examining dynamic decision-making processes. Most such studies also fail to examine offenders' estimates of the likely payoffs from noncriminal alternatives or their nonmonetary utilities, such as emotional satisfaction (Katz 1998).

As newer, empirically based models of criminal decision making have been developed (e.g., Clarke and Cornish 1985; Cornish and Clarke 1986), a growing number of investigators are using ethnographic methods to examine the offender's criminal calculus, often in real or simulated natural settings (e.g., Carroll 1982; Carroll and Weaver 1986). The research reported here continues this line of ethnographic inquiry by using retrospective interviews to examine criminal decision making by serious and persistent property offenders. The focus of our attention is the decision to commit a crime rather than the target-selection decision that has received substantial attention elsewhere (e.g., Scarr 1973; Repetto 1974; Maguire 1982; Bennett and Wright 1984a; Rengert and Wasilchick 1985; Cromwell, Olson, and Avary 1991). The first objective is to examine how closely the decision to commit crime conforms to a classical rational choice model in which decisions assumedly are based largely on an assessment of potential returns from alternative courses of action and the risk of legal sanctions. A second objective is to examine the influence of the lifestyle pursued by many persistent property offenders on the salience of their utilities and the risks they assess in criminal decision making. . . .

Findings

Analysis reveals the most striking aspect of the subjects' decision making for the crimes they described is that a majority gave little or no thought to the possibility of arrest and confinement. Of 34 subjects who were asked specifically whether they considered the risk of arrest or who spontaneously indicated whether they did so, 21 (62 percent) said they did not. The comments of two subjects are typical:

> Q: Did you think about . . . getting caught?
>
> A: No.
>
> Q: [H]ow did you manage to put that out of your mind?
>
> A: [It] never did come into it.
>
> Q: Never did come into it?
>
> A: Never did, you know. It didn't bother me.
>
> Q: Were you thinking about bad things that might happen to you?
>
> A: None whatsoever.
>
> Q: No?
>
> A: I wasn't worried about getting caught or anything, you know. I was a positive thinker through everything, you know. I didn't have no negative thoughts about it whatsoever.

The 13 remaining subjects (38 percent) acknowledged they gave some thought to the possibility of arrest but most said they managed to dismiss it easily and to carry through with their plans:

Q: Did you worry much about getting caught? On a scale of one to ten, how would you rank your degree of worry that day?

A: [T]he worry was probably a one. You know what I mean? The worry was probably one. I didn't think about the consequences, you know. I know it's stupidity, but it didn't [cross my mind] that I might go to jail, I mean it crossed my mind but it didn't make much difference.

Q: As you thought about doing that [armed robbery], were there things that you were worried about?

A: Well, the only thing that I was worried about was . . . getting arrested didn't even cross my mind just worrying about getting killed is the only thing, you know, getting shot. That's the only thing . . . but, you know, you'd have to really be crazy not to think about that . . . you could possibly get in trouble. It crossed my mind, but I didn't worry about it all that much.

Some members of our sample said they managed deliberately and consciously to put out of mind all thoughts of possible arrest:

When I went out to steal, I didn't think about the negative things. 'Cause if you think negative, negative things are going to happen. And that's the way I looked at it . . . I done it just like it was a job or something. Go out and do it, don't think about getting caught, 'cause that would make you jumpy, edgy, nervous. If you looked like you were doing something wrong, then something wrong is gonna happen to you. . . . You just, you just put [the thought of arrest] out of your mind, you know.

Q: Did you think about [the possibility of getting caught] very much that night?

A: I didn't think about it that much, you know. . . . [I]t comes but, you know, you can wipe it away.

Q: How do you wipe it away?

A: You just blank it out. You blank it out.

Another subject said simply that "I try to put that [thought of arrest] the farthest thing from my mind that I can."

Many subjects attribute their ability to ignore or to dismiss all thought of possible arrest to a state of intoxication or drug altered consciousness:

Q: You didn't think about going to prison?

A: Never did. I guess it was all that alcohol and stuff, and drugs. . . . The day I pulled that robbery? No. I was so high I didn't think about nothing.

Another subject told us that he had been drinking the entire day that he committed the crime and, by the time it occurred, he was in "nightlight city."

While it is clear that the formal risks of crime were not considered carefully by most members of the sample, equally striking is the finding that very few thought about or assessed legitimate alternatives before opting to commit a criminal act. Of 22 subjects who were asked specifically whether they had done so, 16 indicated they gave no thought whatsoever to legitimate alternatives. The six subjects who did either ignored or quickly dismissed them as inapplicable, given their immediate circumstances.

We recognize the methodological shortcomings of the descriptions of criminal decision making and behavior used as data for this study. Since the subjects were questioned in detail only about specific offenses they could remember well, the sample of descriptions may not be representative of the range of crimes they committed. By definition, they are memorable ones. Moreover, the recall period for these crimes ranged from one to 15 years, raising the possibility of errors caused by selective recall. Whether or not this could have produced systematic bias in the data is unknown. We cannot rule out the possibility that past crimes are remembered as being less rational than they actually were at the time of commission. Such a tendency could account in part for our interpretation of the data and our description of their style of decision making. The fact that we limited the sample to recidivists means also that we cannot determine how much their behavior may reflect either innate differences (Gottfredson and Hirschi 1990) or experiential effects, i.e., the effects of past success in committing crime and avoiding arrest (Nagin and Paternoster 1991). It could be argued that the behavior of our subjects, precisely because they had demonstrated a willingness to commit property crimes and had done so in the past, limits the external validity of their reports. Given sample selection criteria and these potential data problems, generalizations beyond the study population must be made with caution.

This said, we believe that the remarkable similarity between our findings and the picture of criminal decision making reported by others who have studied serious property offenders strengthens their credibility significantly. A study of 83 imprisoned burglars revealed that 49 percent did not think about the chances of getting caught for any particular offense during their last period of offending. While 37 percent of them did think about it, most thought there was little or no chance it would happen (Bennett and Wright 1984a, Table A14). Interviews with 113 men convicted of robbery or an offense related to robbery revealed that "over 60 percent . . . said they had not even thought about getting caught." Another 17 percent said that they had thought about the possibility but "did not believe it to be a problem" (Feeney 1986, 59–60). Analysis of prison interviews with 77 robbers and 45 burglars likewise revealed their "general obliviousness toward the consequences [of their crimes] and no thought of being caught" (Walsh 1986, 157). In sum, our findings along with the findings from other studies suggest strongly that many serious property offenders seem to be remarkably casual in weighing the formal risks of criminal participation. As one of our subjects put it, "you think about going to prison about like you think about dying, you know." The impact of alcohol and drug use in diminishing concern with possible penalties also has been reported by many others (e.g., Bennett and Wright 1984b; Cromwell, Olson, and Avary 1991).

If the potential legal consequences of crime do not figure prominently in crime commission decision making by persistent thieves, what do they think about when choosing to commit crime? Walsh (1980; 1986) shows that typically they focus their thoughts on the money that committing a crime may yield and the good times they expect to have with it when the crime is behind them. Carroll's data (1982) likewise indicate that the amount of gain offenders expect to receive is "the most important dimension" in their decision making while the certainty of punishment is the least important of the four dimensions on which his subjects assessed crime opportunities. Our findings are consistent with these reports; our subjects said that they focused on the expected gains from their crimes:

> I didn't think about nothing but what I was going to do when I got that money, how I was going to spend it, what I was going to do with it, you know.

> See, you're not thinking about those things [possibility of being arrested]. You're thinking about that big pay check at the end of thirty to forty-five minutes worth of work.

> [A]t the time [that you commit crime], you throw all your instincts out the window. . . . Because you're just thinking about money, and money only. That's all that's on your mind, because you want that money. And you throw, you block everything off until you get the money.

Although confidence in our findings is bolstered by the number of points on which they are similar to reports by others who have explored crime commission decision making, they do paint a picture of decision making that is different from what is known about the way at least some of them make target selection decisions. Investigators (e.g., Cromwell, Olson, and Avary 1991) have shown that target decisions approximate simple commonsense conceptions of rational behavior (Shover 1991). A resolution of the problem presented by these contradictory findings is suggested by others (Cromwell, Olson, and Avary 1991) and also apparent in our data: Criminal participation often results from a *sequence* of experientially and analytically discrete decisions, all of potentially varying degrees of intentional rationality. Thus, once a *motivational* crime commission decision has been made, offenders may move quickly to selecting, or to exploiting an apparently suitable target. At this stage of the criminal participation process, offenders are preoccupied with the *technical* challenge of avoiding failure at what now is seen as a *practical* task. As one subject put it, "you don't think about getting caught, you think about how in hell you're going to do it *not* to get caught, you know." His comments were echoed by another man: "The only thing you're thinking about is looking and acting and trying *not* to get caught." Last, consider the comments of a third subject: "I wasn't afraid of getting caught, but I was cautious, you know. Like I said, I was thinking only in the way to prevent me from getting caught." Just as bricklayers do not visualize graphically or deliberate over the bodily carnage that could follow from a collapsed scaffold once there is a job to be done, many thieves apparently do not dwell at length on the likelihood of arrest or on the pains of imprisonment when proceeding to search out or exploit suitable criminal opportunities.

The accumulated evidence on crime commission decision making by persistent offenders is substantial and persuasive: the rationality they employ is limited or bounded severely (e.g., Carroll 1982; Cromwell, Olson, and Avary 1991). While unsuccessful persistent offenders may calculate potential benefits and costs before committing criminal acts, they apparently do so differently or weigh utilities differently than as sketched in a priori decision making models. As Walsh (1980, 141) suggests, offenders' "definitions of costs and rewards seem to be at variance with society's estimates of them." This does not mean their decision making is *irrational* but it does point to the difficulties of understanding it and then refining theoretical models of the process. Our objective in the remainder of this [chapter] is an improved understanding of criminal decision making based on analysis of the socially anchored purposes, utilities, and risks of the acts that offenders commit. Put differently, we explore the contextual origins of their bounded rationality.

Lifestyle, Utilities, and Risk

It is instructive to examine the decision making of persistent property offenders in context of the lifestyle that is characteristic of many in their ranks: life as party. The hallmark of *life as party* is the enjoyment of "good times" with minimal concern for obligations and commitments that are external to the person's immediate social setting. It is a lifestyle distinguished in many cases by two repetitively cyclical phases and correspondingly distinctive approaches to crime. When offenders' efforts to maintain the lifestyle (i.e., their party pursuits) are largely successful, crimes are committed in order to sustain circumstances or a pattern of activities they experience as pleasurable. As Walsh (1986, 15) puts it, crimes committed under these circumstances are "part of a continuing satisfactory way of life." By contrast, when offenders are less successful at party pursuits, their crimes are committed in order to forestall or avoid circumstances experienced as threatening, unpleasant or precarious. Corresponding to each of these two phases of party pursuits is a distinctive set of utilities and stance toward legal risk.

Life as Party

Survey and ethnographic studies alike show that persistent property offenders spend much of their criminal gains on alcohol and other drugs (Petersilia et al. 1978; Maguire 1982; Gibbs and Shelley 1982; Figgie 1988; Cromwell, Olson, and Avary 1991). The proceeds of their crimes, as Walsh has noted (1986, 72), "typically [are] used for personal, nonessential consumption (e.g., 'nights out'), rather than, for example, to be given to family or used for basic needs." Thieves spend much of their leisure hours enjoying good times. Our subjects were no different in this regard. For example,

> I smoked an ounce of pot in a day, a day and a half. Every other day I had to go buy a bag of pot, at the least. And sometimes I've went two or three days in a row. . . . And there was never a day went by that I didn't [drink] a case, case and a half of beer. And [I] did a 'script of pills every two days.

While much of their money is consumed by the high cost of drugs, a portion may be used for ostentatious enjoyment and display of luxury items and activities that probably would be unattainable on the returns from blue-collar employment:

> [I]t was all just, it was all just a big money thing to me at the time, you know. Really, what it was was impressing everybody, you know. "Here Floyd is, and he's never had nothing in his life, and now look at him: he's driving new cars, and wearing jewelry," you know.

Life as party is enjoyed in the company of others. Typically it includes shared consumption of alcohol or other drugs in bars and lounges, on street corners, or while cruising in automobiles. In these venues, party pursuers celebrate and affirm values of spontaneity, autonomy, independence, and resourcefulness. Spontaneity means that rationality and long-range planning are eschewed in favor of enjoying the moment and permitting the day's activities and pleasures to develop in an unconstrained fashion. This may mean, for example, getting up late, usually after a night of partying, and then setting out to contact and enjoy the company of friends and associates who are known to be predisposed to partying:

> I got up around about eight-thirty that morning. . . .
>
> Q: Eight-thirty? Was that the usual time that you got up?
>
> A: Yeah, if I didn't have a hangover from the night before. . . .

> Q: What kind of drugs were you doing then?
>
> A: I was doing. . . . Percodans, Dilaudids, taking Valiums, drinking. . . . [A]nyway, I got up that morning about eight-thirty, took me a bath, put on some clothes and . . . decided to walk [over to my mother's home]. [T]his particular day, . . . my nephew was over [there]. . . . We was just sitting in the yard and talking and drinking beer, you know. . . . It was me, him and my sister. We was sitting out there in the yard talking. And this guy that we know, he came up, he pulled up. So my nephew got in the car with him and they left. So, you know, I was sitting there talking to my sister. . . . And then, in the meantime, while we was talking, they come back, about thirty minutes later with a case of beer, some marijuana and everything, and there was another one of my nephews in the car with them. So me, two of my sisters, and two of my nephews, we got in the car with this guy here and we just went riding. So we went to Hadley Park and . . . we stayed out there. There were so many people out there, they were parked on the grass and things, and the vice squad come and run everybody away. So when they done that, we left. . . . So we went back out [toward my mother's home] but instead of going over to my mother's house we went to this little joint [tavern]. Now we're steady drinking and smoking weed all during this day. So when we get there, we park and get out and see a few friends. We [were] talking and getting high, you know, blowing each other a shotgun [sharing marijuana].

Enjoyment of party pursuits in group context is enhanced through the collective emphasis on personal autonomy. Because it is understood by all that participants are free to leave if they no longer enjoy or do not support group activities, the continuing presence of each participant affirms for the remainder the pleasures of the lifestyle. Uncoerced participation thus reinforces the shared assumption that group activities are appropriate and enjoyable. The behavioral result of the emphasis on autonomy is acceptance of or acquiescence in group decisions and activities.

Party pursuits also appeal to offenders because they permit conspicuous display of independence (Persson 1981). This generally means avoidance of the world of routine work and freedom from being "under someone's thumb." It also may include being free to avoid or to escape from restrictive routines:

> I just wanted to be doing something. Instead of being at home, or something like that. I wanted to be running, I wanted to be going to clubs, and picking up women and shooting pool. And I liked to go to [a nearby resort community] and just drive around over there. A lot of things like that. . . . I was drinking two pints or more a day. . . . I was doing Valiums and I was doing Demerol. . . . I didn't want to work.

The proper pursuit and enjoyment of life as party is expensive, due largely to the costs of drugs. As one of our subjects remarked: "We was doing a lot of cocaine, so cash didn't last long, you know. If we made $3,000, two thousand of it almost instantly went for cocaine." Some party pursuers must meet other expenses as well if the lifestyle is to be maintained:

> Believe it or not, I was spending [$700] a day.
>
> Q: On what?
>
> A: Pot, alcohol, women, gas, motel rooms, food.
>
> Q: You were living in hotels, motels?
>
> A: Yeah, a lot of times, I was. I'd take a woman to a motel. I bought a lot of clothes. I used to like to dress pretty nicely, I'd buy suits.

Party pursuits require continuous infusions of money and no single method of generating funds allows enjoyment of it for more than a few days. Consequently, the emphasis on spontaneity, autonomy, and independence is matched by the importance attached to financial resourcefulness. This is evidenced by the ability to sustain the lifestyle over a period of time. Doing so earns for offenders a measure of respect from peers for their demonstrated ability to "get over." It translates into "self-esteem . . . as a folk hero beating the bureaucratic system of routinized dependence" (Walsh 1986, 16). The value of and respect for those who demonstrate resourcefulness means that criminal acts, as a means of sustaining life as party, generally are not condemned by the offender's peers.

The risks of employing criminal solutions to the need for funds are approached blithely but confidently in the same spontaneous and playful manner as are the rewards of life as party. In fact, avoidance of careful and detailed planning is a way of demonstrating possession of valued personal qualities and commitment to the lifestyle. Combined with the twin assumptions that peers have chosen freely and that one should not interfere with their autonomy, avoidance of rational planning finds expression in a reluctance to suggest that peers should weigh carefully the possible consequences of whatever they choose to do. Thus, the interaction that precedes criminal incidents is distinguished by circumspection and the use of linguistic devices that relegate risk and fear to the background of attention. The act of stealing, for example, is referred to obliquely but knowingly as "doing something" or as "making money":

> [After a day of partying,] I [got] to talking about making some money, because I didn't have no money. This guy that we were riding with, he had all the money. . . . So me and him and my nephew, we get together, talking about making some money. This guy tells me, he said, "man, I know where there's a good place at."
>
> Q: Okay, so you suggested you all go somewhere and rob?
>
> A: Yeah, "make some" well, we called it "making money."
>
> Q: Okay. So, then you and this fellow met up in the bar. . . . Tell me about the conversation?
>
> A: Well, there wasn't much of a conversation to it, really. . . . I asked him if he was ready to go, if he wanted to go do something, you know. And he knew what I meant. He wanted to go make some money somehow, any way it took.

To the external observer, inattention to risk at the moment when it would seem most appropriate may seem to border on irrationality. For the offender engaged in party pursuits, however, it is but one aspect of behaviors that are rational in other respects. It opens up opportunities to enjoy life as party and to demonstrate commitment to values shared by peers. Resourcefulness and disdain for conventional rationality affirm individual character and style, both of which are important in the world of party pursuits (Goffman 1967).

Party Pursuits and Eroding Resources

Paradoxically, the pursuit of life as party can be appreciated and enjoyed to the fullest extent only if participants moderate their involvement in it while maintaining identities and routines in the straight world. Doing so maintains its "escape value" but it also requires an uncommon measure of discipline and forbearance. The fact is that extended and enthusiastic enjoyment of life as party threatens constantly to deplete irrevocably the resources needed to sustain enjoyment of its pleasures. Three aspects of the life-as-party lifestyle can contribute to this end.

First, some offenders become ensnared increasingly by the chemical substances and drug using routines that are common there. In doing so, the meaning of drug consumption changes:

> See, I was doing drugs every day. It just wasn't every other day, it was to the point that, after the first few months doing drugs, I would have to do "X amount" of drugs, say, just for instance, just to feel like I do now. Which is normal.

Once the party pursuer's physical or psychological tolerance increases significantly, drugs are consumed not for the high they once produced but instead to maintain a sense of normality by avoiding sickness or withdrawal.

Second, party pursuits erode legitimate fiscal and social capital. They cannot be sustained by legitimate employment and they may in fact undermine both one's ability and inclination to hold a job. Even if offenders are willing to work at the kinds of employment available to them, and evidence suggests that many are not (Cromwell, Olson, and Avary 1991), the time schedules of work and party pursuits conflict. The best times of the day for committing many property crimes are also the times the offender would be at work and it is nearly impossible to do both consistently and well. For those who pursue life as a party, legitimate employment often is foregone or sacrificed (Rengert and Wasilchick 1985). The absence of income from noncriminal sources thus reinforces the need to find other sources of money.

Determined pursuit of life as party also may affect participants' relationships with legitimate significant others. Many offenders manage to enjoy the lifestyle successfully only by exploiting the concern and largesse of family and friends. This may take the form of repeated requests for and receipt of personal loans that go unreturned, occasional thefts, or other forms of exploitation:

> I lived well for awhile. I lived well . . . until I started shooting cocaine real bad, intravenously. . . . [A]nd then everything, you know, went up in smoke, you know. Up my arm. The watches, the rings . . . the car, you know. I used to have a girl, man, and her daddy had two horses. I put them in my arm. You know what I mean? I made her sell them horses. My clothes and all that stuff, a lot of it, they went up in smoke when I started messing with that cocaine.

Eventually, friends and even family members may come to believe that they have been exploited or that continued assistance will only prolong a process that must be terminated. As one subject told us, "Oh, I tried to borrow money, and borrow money and, you know, nobody would loan it to me. Because they knew what I was doing." After first refusing further assistance, acquaintances, friends, and even family members may avoid social contacts with the party pursuer or sever ties altogether. This dialogue occurred between the interviewer and one of our subjects:

> Q: [B]esides doing something wrong, did you think of anything else that you could do to get money? . . . Borrow it?
>
> A: No, I'd done run that in the ground. See, you burn that up. That's burned up, right there, borrowing, you know. . . . Once I borrow, you know, I might get $10 from you today and, see, I'll be expecting to be getting $10 tomorrow, if I could. And then, when I see you [and] you see me coming, you say, "no, I don't have none." [A]s the guys in the penitentiary say, "you absorb all of your remedies," you see. And that's what I did: I burned my remedies up, you know.

Last, when party pursuits are not going well, feelings of shame and self-disgust are not uncommon (Frazier and Meisenhelder 1985). Unsuccessful party pursuers as a result may take steps to reduce these feelings by distancing themselves voluntarily from conventional others:

> Q: You were married to your wife at that time?
>
> A: Yeah, I was married. . . .
>
> Q: Where was she living then?
>
> A: I finally forced her to go home, you know. . . . I made her go home, you know. And it caused an argument, for her to go home to her mother's. I felt like that was the best thing I did for her, you know. She hated me . . . for it at the time, didn't understand none of it. But, really, I intentionally made her go. I really spared her the misery that we were going to have. And it came. It came in bundles.

When party pursuers sustain severe losses of legitimate income and social resources, regardless of how it occurs, they grow increasingly isolated from conventional significant others. The obvious consequence is that this reduces interpersonal constraints on their behavior.

As their pursuit of life as party increasingly assumes qualities of difficulty and struggle, offenders' utilities and risk perceptions also change. Increasingly, crimes are committed not to enhance or sustain the lifestyle so much as to forestall unpleasant circumstances. Those addicted to alcohol or other drugs, for example, must devote increasing time and energy to the quest for monies to purchase their chemicals of choice. Both their drug consumption and the frequency of their criminal acts increase (Ball et al. 1983; Johnson et al. 1985). For them, as for others, inability to draw on legitimate or low-risk resources eventually may precipitate a crisis. One of our respondents retold how, facing a court appearance on a burglary charge, he needed funds to hire an attorney:

> I needed some money bad or if I didn't, if I went to court the following day, I was going to be locked up. The judge was going to lock me up. Because I didn't have no lawyer. And I had went and talked to several lawyers and they told me . . . they wanted a thousand dollars, that if I couldn't come up with no thousand dollars, they couldn't come to court with me. . . . [S]o I went to my sister. I asked my sister, I said, "look here, what about letting me have seven or eight hundred dollars" which I knowed she had the money because she . . . had been in a wreck and she had gotten some money out of a suit. And she said, "well, if I give you the money you won't do the right thing with it." And I was telling her, "no, no, I need a lawyer." But I couldn't convince her to let me have the money. So I left. . . . I said, shit, I'm fixin' to go back to jail. . . . [S]o as I left her house and was walking I was going to catch the bus the [convenience store] and bus stop was right there by

> each other. So, I said I'm going to buy me some gum. . . . [A]nd in the process of me buying the chewing gum, I seen two ladies, they was counting money. So I figured sooner or later one of them was going to come out with the money. . . . I waited on them until . . . one came out with the money, and I got it.

Confronted by crisis and preoccupied increasingly with relieving immediate distress, the offender eventually may experience and define himself as propelled by forces beyond his control. Behavioral options become dichotomized into those that hold out some possibility of relief, however risky, and those that promise little but continued pain. Legitimate options are few and are seen as unlikely solutions. A criminal act may offer some hope of relief, however temporary. The offender may imbue the criminal option with almost magical prospects for ending or reversing the state of discomfort:

> I said, "well, look at it like this"; if I don't do it, then tomorrow morning I've got the same [problems] that I've got right now. I could be hungry. I'm going to want food more. I'm going to want cigarettes more. I'm going to want everything more. But, if I do it, and if I make it, then I've got all I want.

Acts that once were the result of blithe unconcern with risk can over time come to be based on a personal determination to master or reverse what is experienced as desperately unpleasant circumstances. As a result, inattention to risk in the offender's decision making may give way to the perception that he has nothing to lose:

> It . . . gets to the point that you get into such a desperation. You're not working, you can't work. You're drunk as hell, been that way two or three weeks. You're no good to yourself, and you're no good to anybody else. Self-esteem is gone [and you are] spiritually, mentally, physically, financially bankrupt. You ain't got *nothing to lose.*

Desperate to maintain or reestablish a sense of normality, the offender pursues emotional relief with a decision to act decisively, albeit in the face of legal odds recognized as narrowing. By acting boldly and resolutely to make the best of a grim situation, one gains a measure of respect, if not from others, then at least from oneself.

> I think, when you're doing drugs like I was doing, I don't think you tend to rationalize much at all. I think it's just a decision you make. You don't weigh the consequences, the pros and the cons. You just do it.
>
> You know, all kinds of things started running through my mind. If I get caught, then there, there I am with another charge. Then I said, well if I don't do something, I'm going to be in jail. And I just said, "I'm going to do it."

The fact that sustained party pursuits often cause offenders to increase the number of offenses they commit and to exploit criminal opportunities that formerly were seen as risky should not be interpreted as meaning they believe they can continue committing crime with impunity. The opposite is true. Many offenders engaged in crimes intended to halt or reverse eroding fortunes are aware that eventually they will be arrested if they continue doing so:

> Q: How did you manage not to think about, you know, that you could go to prison?
>
> A: Well, you think about it afterwards. You think, "wow, boy, I got away with it again." But you know, sooner or later, the law of averages is gonna catch up with you. You just can't do it [commit crime] forever and ever and ever. And don't think you're not gonna get caught, 'cause you will.

Bennett and Wright (1984a) likewise show that a majority of persistent offenders endorse the statement that they will be caught "eventually." The cyclical transformations of party pursuits from pleasant and enjoyable to desperate and tenuous is one reason they are able to commit crimes despite awareness of inevitable and potentially severe legal penalties.

The threat posed by possible arrest and imprisonment, however, may not seem severe to some desperate offenders. As compared to their marginal and precarious existence, it may be seen as offering a form of relief:

> [When he was straight], I'd think about [getting caught]: I could get this, and that [penalties]. . . . [A]nd then I would think, well, I know this is going to end one day, you know. But, you know, you get so far out there, and get so far off into it that it really don't matter, you know. But you think about that. . . . I knew, eventually, I would get caught, you know. . . . I was off into drugs and I just didn't care if I got caught or not.

> When I [got] caught and they caught me right at the house it's kind of like, you feel good, because you're glad it's over, you know. I mean, a weight being lifted off your head. And you say, well, I don't have to worry about this shit no more, because they've caught me. And it's over, you know.

In sum, due to offenders' eroding access to legitimately secured funds, their diminishing contact with and support from conventional significant others, and their efforts to maintain drug consumption habits, crimes that once were committed for recreational purposes increasingly become desperate attempts to forestall or reverse uncomfortable or frustrating situations. Pursuing the short-term goal of maximizing enjoyment of life, legal threats can appear to the offender either as remote and improbable contingencies when party pursuits fulfill their recreational purposes or as an acceptable risk in the face of continued isolation, penury, and desperation.

We analyzed the descriptions of crime provided by our subjects, and their activities on the day the crime occurred. We focused specifically on: (1) the primary purpose of their crimes, i.e., whether they planned to use the proceeds of crime for pleasure or to cope with unpleasant contingencies, and (2) the extent and subjective meaning of their drug use at the time they decided to commit the crime in question. Based on the analysis, we classified the crimes of 15 subjects as behaviors committed in the enjoyment of life as a party and 13 as behaviors committed in order to enhance or restore enjoyment of this lifestyle. The 12 remaining offenders could not be classified because of insufficient information in the crime descriptions or they [were] isolated criminal acts that do not represent a specific lifestyle. Two subjects, for example, described crimes that were acts of vengeance directed at the property of individuals who had treated them or their relatives improperly. One of the men related how he decided to burglarize a home for reasons of revenge:

> I was mad. . . . When I was in the penitentiary, my wife went to his house for a party and he give her a bunch of cocaine. . . . It happened, I think, about a week before I got out. . . . I just had it in my mind what I wanted to do: I wanted to hurt him like I was hurt. . . . I was pretty drunk, when I went by [his home], and I saw there wasn't no car there. So, I just pulled my car in.

The other subject told how an acquaintance had stolen drugs and other possessions from his automobile. In response the subject "staked out the places where he would be for several days before I caught him, at gunpoint, [and] made him take me to his home, [which] I ransacked, and found some of the narcotics that he had stolen from me." Although neither of these crimes was committed in pursuit of life as party, other crimes committed by both these subjects during their criminal careers did occur as part of that lifestyle. Other investigators have similarly reported that revenge is the dominant motive in a minority of property offenses (e.g., Cromwell, Olson, and Avary 1991, 22).

Implications

We have suggested that daily routines characteristic of the partying lifestyle of persistent and unsuccessful offenders may modify both the salience of their various decision utilities and their perceptions of legal risk in the process of their crime commission decisions. This is not to say that these decisions are irrational, only that they do not conform to decision making as sketched by rational choice theories. Our objective was not to falsify the rational choice approach to criminal decision making, for we know of no way this could be accomplished. Whatever it is, moreover, rationality is not a dichotomous variable. Indeed, offenders' target selection decision making appears more rational in the conventional sense than do crime commission decisions.

The lesson here for theories of criminal decision making is that while utilities and risk assessment may be properties of individuals, they also are shaped by the social and personal contexts in which decisions are made. Whether their pursuit of life as party is interpreted theoretically as the product of structural strain, choice, or even happenstance is of limited importance to an understanding of persistent offenders' discrete criminal forays. What is important is that their lifestyle places them in situations that may facilitate important transformations in the utilities of prospective actions. If nothing else, this means that some situations more than others make it possible to discount or ignore risk. We are not the first to call attention to this phenomenon:

> [The] situational nature of sanction properties has escaped the scales and indicators employed in official record and self-report survey research. In this body of research an arrest and a year in prison are generally assumed to have the same mean-

ing for all persons and across all situations. The situational grounding of sanction properties suggests, [however,] that we look beyond official definitions of sanctions and the attitudinal structure of individuals to the properties of situations. (Ekland-Olson et al. 1984, 174)

Along the same line, a longitudinal survey of adult offenders concludes that decision making "may be conditioned by elements within the immediate situation confronting the individual . . . [such that] perceptions of the opportunity, returns, and support for crime within a given situation may influence . . . perceptions of risks and the extent to which those risks are discounted" (Piliavin et al. 1986, 115). The same interpretation has been suggested by Shover and Thompson (1992) for their failure to find an expected positive relationship between risk estimates and crime desistance among former prison inmates.

In light of the sample and data limitations of this study we cannot and have not argued that the lifestyle we described generates or produces the characteristic decision-making behaviors of persistent property offenders. The evidence does not permit such interpretive liberties. It does seem reasonable to suggest, however, that the focal concerns and shared perspectives of those who pursue life as party may function to sustain offenders' free-wheeling, but purposeful, decision-making style. Without question there is a close correspondence between the two. Our ability to explain and predict decision making requires that we gain a better understanding of how utilities and risk perceptions are constrained by the properties of situations encountered typically by persons in their daily rounds. In other words, we must learn more about the daily worlds that comprise the immediate contexts of criminal decision-making behavior.

Questions for Thought and Discussion

1. What do the authors mean by "socially bounded decision making?"
2. According to the findings in this study, how much weight did offenders give to selecting legal alternatives in their quest for money?
3. How does "life as party" affect the decisions offenders make?
4. What theory or theories of criminal behavior are illustrated in this research?

References

Ball, J. C., Shaffer, J. W. and Nurco, D. N. (1983) The day-to-day criminality of heroin addicts in Baltimore: A study in the continuity of offense rates, *Drug and Alcohol Dependence,* 12, 119–142.

Becker, G. (1968) Crime and punishment: An economic approach, *Journal of Political Economy,* 76, 169–217.

Bennett, T. and Wright, R. (1984a) *Burglars on Burglary,* Hampshire, U.K.: Gower.

———. (1984b) The relationship between alcohol use and burglary, *British Journal of Addiction,* 79, 431–437.

Blumstein, A., Cohen, J. and Nagin, D., editors (1978) *Deterrence and Incapacitation: Estimating the Effects of Criminal Sanctions on Crime Rates,* Washington, D.C.: National Academy of Sciences.

Carroll, J. S. (1978) A psychological approach to deterrence: The evaluation of crime opportunities, *Journal of Personality and Social Psychology,* 36, 1512–1520.

———. (1982) Committing a crime: The offender's decision, in: J. Konecni and E. B. Ebbesen (Eds.), *The Criminal Justice System: A Social-Psychological Analysis,* San Francisco: W. H. Freeman.

Carroll, J. S. and Weaver, F. (1986) Shoplifters' perceptions of crime opportunities: A process-tracing study, in: D. B. Cornish and R. V. Clarke (Eds.), *The Reasoning Criminal: Rational Choice Perspectives on Offending,* New York: Springer-Verlag.

Clarke, R. V. and Cornish, D. B. (1985) Modeling offenders' decisions: A framework for research and policy, in: M. Tonry and N. Morris (Eds.), *Crime and Justice: A Review of Research,* Vol. 4, Chicago: University of Chicago Press.

Claster, D. S. (1967) Comparison of risk perception between delinquents and nondelinquents, *Journal of Criminal Law, Criminology, and Police Science,* 58, 80–86.

Cornish, D. B. and Clarke, R. V., editors (1986) *The Reasoning Criminal: Rational Choice Perspectives on Offending,* New York: Springer-Verlag.

Cromwell, P. F., Olson, J. N. and Avary, D. W. (1991) *Breaking and Entering: An Ethnographic Analysis of Burglary,* Newbury Park, Ca.: Sage.

Ekland-Olson, S., Lieb, J. and Zurcher, L. (1984) The paradoxical impact of criminal sanctions: Some microstructural findings, *Law and Society Review,* 18, 159–178.

Feeney, F. (1986) Robbers as decision-makers, in: D. B. Cornish and R. V. Clarke (Eds.), *The Reasoning Criminal: Rational Choice Perspectives on Offending,* New York: Springer-Verlag.

Figgie International (1988) *The Figgie Report Part VI The Business of Crime: The Criminal Perspective,* Richmond, Va.: Figgie International Inc.

Frazier, C. E. and Meisenhelder, T. (1985) Criminality and emotional ambivalence: Exploratory notes on an overlooked dimension, *Qualitative Sociology,* 8, 266–284.

Gibbs, J. J. and Shelley, P. L. (1982) Life in the fast lane: A retrospective view by commercial thieves, *Journal of Research in Crime and Delinquency,* 19, 299–330.

Goffman, E. (1967) *Interaction Ritual,* Garden City, N.Y.: Anchor.

Gottfredson, M. R. and Hirschi, T. (1990) *A General Theory of Crime,* Stanford, Ca.: Stanford University Press.

Heineke, J. M., editor (1978) *Economic Models of Criminal Behavior,* Amsterdam: North-Holland.

Johnson, B. D., Goldstein, P. J., Preble, E., Schmeidler, J., Lipton, D. D., Spunt, B. and Miller, T. (1985) *Taking Care of Business: The Economics of Crime by Heroin Addicts,* Lexington, Ma.: D.C. Heath.

Katz, J. (1998) *Seductions of Crime,* New York: Basic Books.

Maguire, M. in collaboration with T. Bennett (1982) *Burglary in a Dwelling,* London: Heinemann.

Manski, C. F. (1978) Prospects for inference on deterrence through empirical analysis of individual criminal behavior, in: A. Blumstein, J. Cohen and D. Nagin (Eds.), *Deterrence and Incapacitation: Estimating the Effects of Criminal Sanctions on Crime Rates,* Washington, D.C.: National Academy of Sciences.

Nagin, D. S. and Paternoster, R. (1991) On the relationship of past to future participation in delinquency, *Criminology,* 29, 163–189.

Persson, M. (1981) Time-perspectives amongst criminals, *Acta Sociologica,* 24, 149–165.

Petersilia, J., Greenwood, P. W. and Lavin, M. (1978) *Criminal Careers of Habitual Felons,* Washington, D.C.: U.S. Department of Justice, National Institute of Law Enforcement and Criminal Justice.

Peterson, M. A. and Braiker, H. B. (1980) *Doing Crime: A Survey of California Prison Inmates,* Santa Monica, Ca.: Rand Corporation.

Piliavin, I., Gartner, R. and Matsueda, R. (1986) Crime, deterrence, and rational choice, *American Sociological Review,* 51, 101–119.

Rengert, G. F. and Wasilchick, J. (1985) *Suburban Burglary,* Springfield, Ill.: Charles C. Thomas.

Repetto, T. A. (1974) *Residential Crime,* Cambridge, Ma.: Ballinger.

Reynolds, M. O. (1985) *Crime by Choice: An Economic Analysis,* Dallas, Tx.: Fisher Institute.

Scarr, H. A. (1973) *Patterns of Burglary* (second edition), Washington, D.C.: U.S. Department of Justice, National Institute of Law Enforcement and Criminal Justice.

Shover, N. (1991) Burglary, in: M. Tonry (Ed.), *Crime and Justice: An Annual Review of Research,* Vol. 14, Chicago: University of Chicago Press.

Shover, N. and Thompson, C. Y. (1992) Age, differential expectations, and crime desistance, *Criminology,* 30, 89–104.

Waldo, G. P. and Chiricos, T. G. (1972) Perceived penal sanction and self-reported criminality: A neglected approach to deterrence research, *Social Problems,* 19, 522–540.

Walsh, D. (1980) *Break-Ins: Burglary from Private Houses,* London: Constable.

———. (1986) *Heavy Business,* London: Routledge and Kegan Paul.

Chapter 5
The Reasoning Burglar

Motives and Decision-Making Strategies

Paul Cromwell
James N. Olson

I*f you want to know something about burglary, what better way than to talk with burglars and ask them to recreate their past crimes as you observe and ask questions? This is what the authors of this study did. Using a snowball sampling technique, they selected a group of 30 active burglars and spent many hours with each of them. First they conducted an extensive semistructured interview with the subjects, asking them questions about their decisions to commit burglaries, their drug use, their codefendants, the techniques they used to select targets, methods of breaking into houses, how they searched once inside, and what they did with the stolen items once obtained. Following the interviews, the burglar subjects were asked to ride along with the researchers and to recreate past burglaries (up to the point of actually committing the crime). They were asked to identify the factors that made up their decision to burglarize a particular residence and those factors that deterred them from a burglary. Findings from this study inform crime-prevention policies at both the individual and the community levels. Burglars are found to make decisions based on their perceptions of risk and gain at the site of a prospective target, and on factors that have immediate consequences. Risk variables such as the possibility of future arrest and criminal justice sanctions play a very minor role in their decision-making processes. Thus, criminal justice practices and legislation which establish severe penalties for burglary (and most other property crime) do not usually deter burglars. On-site practices, such as target hardening and increasing visibility and surveillance from the street and neighbors' homes do have a deterrent effect.*

Much of the recent research on property crime (Hochstetler and Copes 2003; Copes 2003; Cromwell and Olson 2004; Cromwell, Olson and Avary 1991; Shover 1996; Wright and Decker 1994; Jacobs 1999; Shachmurove et al. 1997) has focused on the rational processes by which an offender chooses a criminal career, selects targets, and carries out criminal acts. Rational choice theory is predicated on the assumption that individuals *choose* to commit crimes. The theory predicts that individuals evaluate alternative courses of action, weighing the possible rewards against the costs and risks, and choosing the action that maximizes their gain.

The notion of rational choice has its origins in both the classical theories of Cesare Beccaria and Jeremy Bentham in the late eighteenth century and in relatively recent economic theory, specifically in the work of Gary Becker (1968). According to classical theory, criminals are free, rational, and hedonistic. They choose among alternative courses of action according to their perceptions of the risks and gains associated, seeking to maximize gain (or pleasure) and minimize risk (or pain).

Modern classical explanations are derived from economic theory, which views the decision to commit crime as essentially like any other decision—that is, one made on the basis of a calculation of the costs and benefits of the action. The benefits of a criminal action are the net rewards of crime and include not only the gains but also intangible benefits such as emotional pleasure or satisfaction. The individual may receive immense satisfaction from the excitement of crime, from the independent lifestyle afforded by crime, or from outwitting the authorities. The risks or costs of crime are those associated with formal punishment should the individual be discovered, apprehended, and convicted, as well as psychological or social costs, such as pangs of conscience, social disapproval, marital and family discord, or loss of self esteem (Vold and Bernard 1986).

The degree of rationality that can be attributed to offenders in planning and executing their crimes and how rationality is related to crime prevention measures have been central issues of debate (Clarke and Cornish 1985; Cornish and Clarke 1986; Cornish 1993; Cook 1980). Brezina (2002) characterizes the major positions as the "narrow" and the "wide" models of rational choice. The narrow model assumes that offenders consider all possible consequences of their actions and choose the course that maximizes their personal gain and utility. The wide model, in contrast, suggests that offenders do not operate under optimal conditions; that the complete range of possible consequences is always unknown to the actor; and that even if all possible consequences were known, most individuals are not capable of the intricate and complex calculations necessary to choose the course of action to maximize outcomes. In other words, the wide model assumes that information necessary to make good decisions is frequently unavailable and that even if [it] were, most people are not particularly competent decision makers.

The concept of limited rationality proposes that for behavior to be rational, it does not have to be carefully preconceived and planned or require hierarchical, sequential decision making. It is enough that decisions are perceived to be optimal. It does not require deliberate weighing of carefully considered alternatives and consequences. It is sufficient that decision makers choose between alternatives based upon their immediate perception of the risks and gains involved. The decision does not have to be the best possible under the circumstances, nor does it have to be based upon an accurate assessment of the situation. A burglar can never calculate with assurance the value of the property he or she expects to take away in a burglary or know with confidence the extent of the punishment should he or she be apprehended. The concept of limited rationality recognizes the limited capacity and willingness of most persons to acquire and process information from more than one input or source simultaneously.

Cornish and Clarke (1986) concluded that people usually pay attention to only some of the facts or sources at their disposal, employing shortcuts or rules of thumb to speed the decision process. These rules of thumb are analogous to Cook's (1980) concept of "standing decisions," which negate the need to weigh carefully all the alternatives and consequences before making a decision in many cases. A standing decision may simply be a decision made beforehand to take advantage of certain types of criminal opportunities or to avoid others. In effect, these are rational processes that do not require conscious analysis each time they are employed.

In this chapter we consider the rational processes that motivate offenders to commit burglary and the decision strategy they use in committing the crime. When considering the motives that underlie crime, we must first differentiate between *criminality* and *crime*. Crime refers to the criminal event itself. Criminality refers to processes through which individuals originally become involved in crime and which create a "readiness" to offend. . . . Cornish and Clarke (1986, 2) assert that the development of criminality is a process that is usually multistaged and extends over an extended period of time. For example, a person from a broken home might not develop adequate social bonds allowing him or her to perceive of theft as a reasonable means of dealing with an urgent need for cash. Having associates who commit criminal acts might further cement the perception that crime is an appropriate solution to the problem. For purposes of this study, we assume a readiness to commit crimes and we do not delve into the dynamics of the burglar's criminality. Of more immediate concern are those variables which translate the readiness into a criminal event into the criminal event itself.

Motivation for Burglary

The motivation that drives the burglary event is a consistent factor in the literature. Scarr (1973) found that burglars in his study cited four general motives; in order of importance:

(1) need for money to buy drugs and alcohol,

(2) need for money to lead a "fast expensive life,"

(3) social motives (gangs, delinquent subcultures, peer approval, status), and

(4) idiosyncratic motives (kicks, thrills, pathological behavior, rebellion).

Reppetto's (1974) subjects reported satisfaction of their need for money as the primary motivation for their robberies and burglaries. Subsidiary satisfactions such as excitement, revenge, and curiosity were cited by a significant but smaller percentage of the subjects. Excitement as a motive was mentioned most often by the younger burglars and less often by the older. Only 10 percent of Reppetto's subjects stated that they would continue to commit burglary if their need for money, including money for drugs, was satisfied (22).

Rengert and Wasilchick (1985) concluded, "The primary reason stated by burglars we interviewed for deciding to commit a burglary was simply to obtain money. . . . The need for money arose out of psychologically defined needs, not subsistence needs" (54).

Wright and Decker (1994) reported that the decision to commit a burglary was driven primarily by a need for cash. Due to the "then and there" lifestyle of most thieves—living entirely in the present—getting a job and working for the money was not a viable alternative. They explained that much of the offending by the burglars in their study was directed toward obtaining the funds necessary to sustain activities that constituted the essence of "streetlife" (194–195).

Shover (1996) argues that the lives of burglars and other thieves is one of an unending "party." Their crimes are committed to allow them to maintain a lifestyle that is essentially the pursuit of a pattern of activities that they experience as pleasurable (93). They are seeking to "keep the party going." Shover states that those who live this lifestyle share a minimal concern for serious matters in favor of enjoying the moment (93).

> Persistent thieves spend much of their criminal gains on alcohol and other drugs. The proceeds of their crimes "typically" are used for personal, non-essential consumption, rather than, for example, to be given to family or used for basic needs. . . . Thieves and hustlers spend many of their leisure hours enjoying good times, albeit there is a decidedly frenetic and always precarious quality to the way these times are lived. (94)

In an early study of theft and thieves, Jackson (1969) wrote:

> [Burglars] if they had any money . . . [they] wouldn't be out stealing, they'd be partying. It's as simple as that. If they have money they're partying and when they're broke, they start stealing again. (136)

Our subjects lived similar lives and expressed similar motives for their crimes. They stressed the need for money to fulfill expressive needs as the primary motivation for their offending. Only one burglar in our study reported a primary need for money for something other than to purchase drugs or alcohol or for other "partying" activities—and he used the money to support his gambling habit. Although virtually every burglar used some of the money from criminal activity to buy food and clothing and to pay for shelter, transportation, and other licit needs, the greatest percentage of the proceeds from burglary went toward the purchase of drugs and alcohol and to the activity they loosely labeled as partying. Many of the burglars discussed the importance of maintaining a "fast, expensive life." Keeping up appearances was stressed by many as a primary concern. This was especially true for the African-American burglars. One burglar summed up the attitude this way:

> You gotta understand about blacks. It's important to keep up a front, to have money and for people to know you have money. Looking good is important. You can't get women if you don't have some bread.

All 30 of our burglar subjects abused drugs and/or alcohol. Most were addicts. Some were so addicted that they took their stolen items directly to a local drug dealer who was known to trade drugs for quality stolen goods. They did not want to spend the extra time converting their goods to cash before buying drugs. Most, however, converted their loot to money and then went immediately to a drug dealer or to a bar where they ingested or self-administered their way into temporary oblivion. The length of their "party" determined the timespan between burglaries, for when they ran out of drugs and alcohol and had "slept it off," they began again the search for a new burglary target.

We recognize that our sample was not an exact reflection of the nation's population of residential burglars insofar as drug and alcohol abusers may have been overrepresented. However, Shover (1991, 1996) and Wright and Decker (1994) arrived at similar conclusions concerning the lifestyles of burglars and other thieves. Jerry, one of our more articulate burglar subjects, summed it up as follows:

> Once I got into the life, I liked it—a lot. I always liked to party and if you party you can't keep a job for any length of time. I like the ladies too. And the ladies like dudes with lots of folding money. You can't keep it up working for hourly wages. I've had some pretty good jobs before, but it was never enough. Not enough money. Not enough time. Not enough freedom—when you work. Now I work for myself. I'm a self-employed thief. I can party all I want to and when I run out of green, I go get some more.

While drugs, alcohol and "party" were the dominant motives for the burglars in our study, other factors also played a role for some burglars. Excitement and thrills were mentioned by almost every informant; however, only a few would commit a burglary for that purpose only. Like Reppetto (1974), we concluded that the younger, less experienced burglars were more prone to commit crimes for thrills and excitement.

Gerald, a 22-year-old burglar, stated:

> I used to love that adrenaline rush you get when you first go in the window. It's as good as coke. Heart starts thumping and you get shaky and feel super alive. When I was 15–16 years old, I lived for that feeling. I still get scared and get the rush, but now I do it [burglarize] for money.

Another informant, Steve, a 36-year-old, said:

> There's no feeling like it. It's fear and sex and danger and every other exciting feeling you ever had all rolled into one. I'd do crime just for that rush. I do do crime just for that rush. Sometimes.

About 30 percent of the informants reported committing at least one burglary for revenge. They seldom obtained much material reward in revenge burglaries, reporting instead that they "trashed" the victim's house. This tendency was more pronounced among burglars under 25 years of age. One burglar reported:

> I was helping this friend move into a new house and the white lady next door saw that we were black. I heard her tell another neighbor that she was upset about a black man moving in next door. I decided to come back the next day and "do" her house for revenge.

Another said that he had burglarized the house of a former friend after that individual had "snitched" on him. He said:

> I didn't take nothin' except some food. Mainly I just trashed his place. I was really pissed off.

The Decision Strategy and Target Selection

Being motivated to commit a crime is a necessary but not a sufficient condition for the actual commission of the act. Even a highly motivated burglar—one who has immediate need for money—must still locate a vulnerable target and manage to effect entry without detection. These tasks are not as simple as they may appear to be. As Wright and Decker (1994) observe, "In theory, the supply of residential properties seems so vast that finding a target would seem to be a simple matter. In practice, however, potential targets are fairly limited" (62). The potential burglary target must:

- be unoccupied (90 percent of the burglars we interviewed stated that they would not knowingly enter a residence where they knew someone was at home);
- not be easily observed from the street of neighboring homes;
- be in a neighborhood or area where the burglar would not "stand out" or be noticed as a suspicious stranger;
- be accessible—relatively easy to break into; and
- contain items worth stealing.

Gerald, an experienced burglar explained:

> First off, you gotta find a place that's empty, you know, no one's home. Sometimes it's hard to tell. Place look empty but you go check it out and there's somebody there. One time I rang the doorbell to see if anybody was home at this one house and nobody answered, so I go in the back and break in through the sliding door. Next thing I know there's this old lady sleeping in front of the TV. I got the Hell out of there. . . . Sometimes you can check out a whole bunch of places and none look good.

Jerry, an African-American burglar agreed:

> It ain't easy . . . looking for places to hit. Me, I gotta pretty much stay in neighborhoods where I fit in. Some of these rich white neighborhoods are too dangerous. I stand out . . . people watch me and if I hang around too long, somebody be calling the law.

Interestingly, during the initial interview virtually every burglar in our study reported a rational decision-making strategy in selecting burglary targets. The following dialogue is typical of responses during the first interview:

> Q. Before you decide to break into a house, what kinds of things do you think about—I mean what makes you decide whether a house is a good place to burglarize or too risky?
>
> A. First, I gotta case the place. Sometimes I watch the place for two, three days before I go in.

> Q. Really? You take that much time? What are you looking for?
>
> A. Fuckin' A! Can't be too careful. I'm looking for, you know, when they come and go, and how many people live there, when the police come by, have they got good stuff. You know, is it going to be worth it to hit the place?

But, when we went with them to reconstruct their past crimes, we found important variations between what they initially told us (in the semistructured interview) about the process of selecting a target and committing a burglary, and what they actually did when presented with a field simulation. Most of our burglars could design a textbook burglary. However, when subsequently visiting sites of burglaries they had previously committed, the characteristics of the target sites and the techniques used to burglarize those targets were seldom congruent with the completely rational approach they had constructed during the initial interview. The sites, more often than not, were targets of opportunity rather than purposeful selections. There were three common patterns:

(a) the burglar happened by the potential burglary site at an opportune moment when the occupants were clearly absent and the target was perceived as vulnerable (open garage door, windows, etc.);

(b) the site was one that had been previously visited by the burglar for a legitimate purpose (as a guest, delivery person, maintenance worker, or other such activity); or

(c) the site was chosen after "cruising" neighborhoods searching for a criminal opportunity and detecting some overt or subtle cue as to vulnerability or potential for material gain.

One of the purposes of the study was to determine which environmental cue or complexes of cues caused a burglar to perceive of a potential burglary target as vulnerable to burglary. Some researchers (Wright and Decker 1994; Bennett and Wright 1984; Brantingham and Brantingham 1978, 1981; Brown and Altman 1981) have focused on the burglar's use of distinctive environmental stimuli that function as signals or cues to provide salient information about the environment's temporal, spatial, sociocultural, psychological, and legal characteristics. An individual who is motivated to commit a crime uses these discriminative cues to locate and identify target sites. With practice the individual gains experience and learns which discriminative cues and which combination or sequence of cues are associated with "good" targets. These cues then serve as a "template" which is used in victim or target selection. Potential victims or targets are compared to the template and either rejected or accepted, depending on the congruence (Brantingham and Brantingham 1978, 1981, 1991, 1993). In effect, these are standing decisions that do not require conscious analysis each time they are employed. Regardless of whether the individual is consciously aware of the construction and implementation of the template, each time it is successfully employed it is reinforced and becomes relatively automatic. The Brantinghams state:

> The templates are not a simple list of easily identifiable and measurable characteristics, but more a holistic image with a complex interaction of past and relationships seen from varying perspectives. (1993, 12)

As one of our burglary subjects said:

> I just know how I feel about it. I drive around and see a place and think, "This is a good one." It's experience—know what I'm saying? I been doing this a long time and I just know.

Another burglar informant perhaps stated it better. He said:

> I got a criminal mind, you know. Something just tells me a place is hot or cold. It's like intuition.

Finding that most burglars have developed an intuitive mental template of what constitutes a good or a bad burglary target, we set out to determine which discriminative cues or sequence of cues composed the template. Knowing what cues cause a site to be more or less attractive to a burglar should allow development of effective burglary prevention strategies.

We also wished to understand the decision-making processes involved. How does the burglar use cues that represent risk and gain? What factors might cause a burglar to be deterred from burglary? What makes a site more attractive to the burglar? What are the cues that the burglar uses to make the decision to commit the burglary? How does the burglar determine whether a target site is unoccupied? Is there a favored time of day, or day of the week? How does he or she effect entry into a locked residence?

Interviews with our 30 burglar subjects and the recreations of past burglaries by the subjects suggest that a burglar's decision to "hit" a specific target is based primarily on environmental cues that are perceived to have *immediate* consequences. Most burglars seem to attend only to the present; future events or consequences do not appear to weigh heavily in their risk-versus-gain calculation. Drug-using burglars and juveniles are particularly oriented to this immediate-gain and immediate-risk decision process. Non-drug-using experienced burglars are probably less likely to attend only to immediate risks and gains. Our informants, although experienced burglars, were all drug users, and tended to have a "here and now" orientation toward the rewards and costs associated with burglary. As one informant stated:

> I don't think about the future. Today is all that counts with me. You might be dead tomorrow, so live the best you can right now, today. I knew this dude that was always planning what he was gonna do someday—how he was gonna have a big car and a house and be rich and stuff—he got killed by some other dudes in a dope deal. All that planning didn't do no good for him. Wasted all that time, you know. I don't think that way.

Another burglar assessed his life in the following manner:

> Ever[y] day I live past 15–16 years old is just luck. I don't expect to get to 25 or 30. I just ain't goin' to worry about what might happen. I'm just goin' to have a good time while I'm here.

And another stated:

> I don't think about it. I might think about it later, but when I'm doing a crime, I worry about the here and now. The police and the joint aren't part of my thinking, you know what I mean. Can't let those things bother you.

These findings suggest that the rational choice process must be considered as it is perceived through the eyes of the offender. Long-term rewards and future punishment appears to have little effect on most burglars. They are concerned about danger at the crime site and the immediate rewards to be had there.

Assessing Gain

There is considerable research supporting the position that reward or gain is the most important element in the decision to commit a burglary. Shover (1996) found that instead of paying close attention to the potential consequences of their actions and planning carefully to avoid arrest, offenders tend to focus on the money that committing a crime will yield and how they will spend that money. Shover cited one subject, who stated:

> I didn't think about nothing but what I was going to do when I got that money and how I was going to spend it, you know. See, you're not thinking about those things [possibility of being arrested]. You're thinking about that big paycheck at the end of 30 or 40 minutes of work. (1996, 158–59)

The decision strategy employed by our informants began with an appraisal of the circumstances at the potential target site. Most burglars in the study expended minimal energy and time assessing gain cues. They estimated potential gain quickly and intuitively. They tended to make assessments of individual target sites based upon their evaluation of the general affluence of the neighborhood in which the target was located. The assumption is that most residences in a neighborhood contain essentially the same quality and quantity of "stealable" items. As one burglar stated:

> It don't take no Einstein to know [what's in a house]. I can look at a neighborhood and almost tell you what's in every house there. Poor neighborhoods got poor stuff. Rich neighborhoods got rich stuff.

Luis, a heroin addict/burglar, told the interviewer:

> Most houses in this neighborhood have got at least two color TVs, a VCR, some stereo equipment, and some good jewelry. A lot of 'em have got guns, too.

Wright and Decker (1994) found that almost all of the offenders in their study were attracted to residences "which, judging from the outside, appeared to them to contain 'good stuff.' " The most obvious cue was the size of the house. "Other things being equal, a large house was regarded as promising the biggest payoff" (Wright and Decker 1994, 82). Well-maintained property was considered by their burglar informants to contain the most desirable goods. The type of car parked in the driveway was also a gain cue to the subjects in Wright and Decker's study. One of their subjects stated:

> Here's this big old house sittin' up there and in the driveway is two BMWs and a Mercedes. This other house might have a van or something like that. . . . So I visualize that [the intended target] must have more things than that house. (82–83)

Our burglar subjects expressed similar preferences. Donna stated:

> I'm always looking for signs that they got something worthwhile. Big expensive houses, rich cars, stuff like that.

Another subject expressed a preference for houses in a certain part of time where the lots were all over an acre in size and the houses large and expensive. He said:

> These people mostly have gardeners and other people doing their work for them. When I see somebody mowing that ain't the owners and a gardener's truck parked in the street and lots of expensive trees and flowers, I know these people got money. Top of that, if I go on the property, people next door and passing by probably goin' to think I work there.

Inside Information

In some cases, the assessment of gain does not require use of the mental template. The burglar actually knows what is inside the house through the use of informants who have been in the house and have given inside information to the burglar. Experienced burglars often work with "inside men" who have access to potential targets and advise the burglar about things to steal. They may also provide such critical information as times when the owner is away and weaknesses in security. One female informant maintained close contact with several women who worked as maids in affluent sections of the community. She would gain the necessary information from these women and later come back and break into the house, often entering by a door or window left open for her by the accomplice. A more common scenario was for the burglar to learn of the habits and activities of home owners from maids, gardeners, and others who had no intention of knowingly assisting a burglar. Friends who worked in these jobs would alert him to possible burglaries through casual talks about their jobs or their employers, mentioning, for instance, that the family they worked for was leaving for a two-week vacation, or that they had just purchased a new television or VCR. The burglar then used that otherwise innocent information to commit a burglary.

People involved in a variety of service jobs (repair, carpet cleaning, pizza delivery, lawn maintenance, plumbing, carpentry) enter many homes each day and have the opportunity to assess the amount and quality of potential stolen merchandise and security measures taken by the residents. Burglars will often establish contact with employees of these businesses for purposes of obtaining this inside information. One informant said:

> My homie, he works for [a carpet cleaning service] and he in 5–6 different houses every day. He always keeps an eye out for places where they have expensive stuff. I give him somethin' off every job if he clues me in to a place.

One of the burglars in our study worked closely with an employee of a maid service. The maid provided information to the burglar about security, times when the residents were away from home, and a list with specific locations of valuable goods inside the house.

Information about potential targets was frequently gained from fences—persons who purchase stolen property for later resale. Because many fences have legitimate occupations, they may have knowledge of the existence of valuable property from social or business relationships. They can often provide the burglar with information about the owners' schedules and the security arrangements at the target site [see Chapter 19 in this volume, "Fencing: Avenues for the Redistribution of Stolen Property" for a more detailed discussion—Ed.]. Pawnshop employees may also be able to provide burglars with information about potential targets. One professional burglar told the interviewer that an employee at a pawnshop provided him with copies of jewelry appraisals and the addresses of potential targets.

Inside knowledge is also obtained by persons who work regularly in a neighborhood but who never actually enter a potential target residence. Several of our informants worked sporadically as carpenters' helpers or roofers. During the course of residential construction jobs they became aware of the habits of the people living nearby. They used this knowledge later or provided inside information to other burglars for a fee or a split of the take. Larry, a burglar and heroin addict, told us:

> One time I was working on this roofing job in this real nice area. I got to know the schedules of almost everybody on the block. I knew when they left in the morning and came home at night, and who stayed home during the day. About two weeks after the job was done I came back and did [burglarized] almost every house on that block.

Assessing Risk

The risk side of the decision making equation is one of the most difficult to study and one of the most controversial. Do burglars carefully plan their crimes? Do they act spontaneously, taking advantage of opportunity? Do they act without giving thought to short-term or long-term risk? The answer to these questions is central to developing burglary prevention strategies. While it may be difficult for a homeowner to hide or disguise indicators of gain, such as affluence of neighborhood, size of residence or type of automobile driven, controlling risk cues may be more easily accomplished.

As stated earlier, consideration of long-term risk is almost nonexistent in the decision processes of most burglars. Burglars and many other criminals tend to live in the here and now. Not only do they not consider next month or next year, most do not even consider the next day. On the other hand, immediate risks do play a significant role in target selection. Shover (1996) found that "burglars pay close attention to whether or not a residence is occupied and how easily potential entry points can be seen by neighbors and passers-by" (161).

We learned that while most burglars stated a preference for the homes of the affluent as presenting the greatest opportunity for gain, they tended to avoid these houses and neighborhoods due to increased risk. Affluent homes are more likely to have alarm systems and private security patrols, as well as to be occupied during the day by residents and/or servants. Burglars also perceived themselves as more likely to "stand-out"—to be noticed and observed—in such neighborhoods. One of the burglars interviewed for a study by George Rengert (1981), commenting on the possibility of committing a burglary in a very affluent neighborhood near Philadelphia, remarked:

> These houses are too good. Probably have alarms, or servants. And they're rich and probably watch out for each other all the time. (22)

Likewise, an African-American burglar in our study declared:

> Man, I'd stand out in that neighborhood. What's a black man doing over here? That's what they'd be saying. They might think I was working somewhere, but they'd still keep a eye on me all the time I was around. When I'm out doing my thing, I like to be invisible. Man gotta fit in a place, then he be invisible. Can't be invisible in this neighborhood.

The immediate risk cues considered by burglars in the target selection decision fell into three categories: visibility, occupancy, and accessibility.

Visibility

Visibility refers to the extent to which a house is overseen and observable by neighbors or passers-by. Visibility cues include the location of the house on the block and whether or not the windows and doors of the target site can be observed from neighbors' houses, and from the street. The visibility of a potential burglary target was considered by our informants as a primary factor in target selection. These cues provide answers to several questions of primary importance to the burglar. Are there neighbors present? Can the neighbors observe the target house from inside their homes? Can the proposed point of entry into the target site be observed by passers-by? Are there dogs that might bark and arouse neighbors? Are there shrubs, blind doorways, corners, or fences that will hide the burglar during entry? Is there traffic near the house that might see and report the burglar? Are there people in the neighborhood who "watch the street and know who is and who is not at home"?

The location and type of windows both at the target site and at neighbors' houses were considered critical by almost all informants. One burglar in our study stated:

> Notice how that picture window looks out onto the street. The curtains stay open all the time and both the houses across the street can see straight into the living room. I wouldn't do [burglarize] this place.

Another said:

> I'm looking at that upstairs window next door. You can see almost everything that

> goes on at this house from there. I'm worried about that window.

Wright and Decker (1994) also found that burglars considered visibility a major factor in their decision calculus. The burglars in their study preferred to enter from the rear of a house. They stated:

> I never [break in] through the front, unless I go through, like, a porch or something that could hide me. It's too obvious on the front. See, on the back it's not that obvious. The other . . . houses ain't facing the back. You don't find too many [potential onlookers] on the back, you mostly find them on the front.

Although the average burglar fears being seen, many professional burglars do not. Rather, they fear being seen *and reported.* The more experienced burglars stated that it was important to fit into a neighborhood or situation. They attempted to make their presence in a neighborhood seem normal and natural. The most professional of the burglars in our study, Robert, always drove a car that fit the neighborhood's socioeconomic level or a van disguised as a delivery vehicle. He dressed befitting the circumstances: as a plumber, deliveryman, or businessman. He would walk to the door of a potential target residence, open the screen door, and unobtrusively hold it open with his foot while he pretended to be having a conversation with a nonexistent person inside. He would then enter the house if the door was unlocked (he reported that many of his target houses were unlocked). If the door was locked, he pantomimed a conversation that appeared to instruct him to go around to the backyard. He would then walk around the house, sometimes stopping to gaze at some feature of the house or landscape, and take notes on a clipboard. When he got to the backyard, he entered the house from that point. To possible onlookers, he had knocked on the door, talked with the owner, and, following instructions, had gone to the rear of the house on some legitimate errand. Other times he would stop his car near a proposed target residence, open the hood, tinker around under the hood, appear to be angry, kick a tire, and angrily walk over to the potential target house. A neighbor or anyone else who might be watching saw only an angry man with a broken car, walking to a house to ask for assistance. Robert was not concerned about being seen. He expected to be seen, but because of his role-playing he did not expect to be reported (and he seldom was).

Visibility cues also include the extent of natural cover such as trees, shrubbery, and other landscaping. Houses with dense shrubbery near windows and doors were considered very vulnerable by the informants. One of the most important forms of cover was the privacy fence, a six- to eight-foot-high board or masonry fence enclosing a backyard. These fences were common in the area studied, and most informants considered them important in the target-selection process. Some stated that they would not consider burglarizing a house that did not have a privacy fence. Although burglars were at risk while climbing the fence or entering through an unlocked gate, once inside, they were effectively protected from prying eyes by the fence. As one burglar stated:

> Once I'm inside this fence, I can slow down and take my time. The place is mine.

Occupancy

The second category of risk cues are those that indicate *occupancy.* Occupancy cues include the presence of cars in the driveway or garage, visible residents, noise or voices emanating from the house, and other cues that indicate someone is at home. Research both before and after our study confirms the preference for unoccupied targets (Scarr 1973; Reppetto 1974; MacDonald 1980; Bennett and Wright 1984; Wright and Decker 1994). Twenty-eight of the 30 burglars in our study stated that they would never purposely enter an occupied residence. Many reported that their greatest fear was that they would encounter the resident upon entering or that the resident would return home while they were still there.

The typical burglar is much more aware of our use of time than we are. As Rengert and Wasilchick (1985, 52) conclude, "We are all waiting to become victims of a burglar whose intuition about time coincides with our routine." Robert, a professional burglar in our sample revealed that he was not only aware of his victim's use of time, but also that of police and law enforcement:

> You know when is the best time to do a burglary? Three o'clock in the afternoon. Mothers are picking up their kids at school and the police are doing shift change. Even if someone called the cops on me, they'd be in the middle of shift change and it would take longer to get here.

Our research confirmed that burglars work during periods when residences are left unguarded. They concluded that if a home is guarded (occupied) during the day, it is likely to be guarded by women. Rengert and Wasilchick (1985) stated that women who do not work outside the home tend to develop predictable patterns regarding the use of discretionary time for the purpose of shopping, errands, or visiting friends and relatives. Women who work outside the home develop similar patterns of time use on Saturday and Sunday. In either case, the use of discretionary time for the purpose of shopping and running errands is observable and predictable by residential burglars. Whenever the house is left unguarded, it is susceptible to burglary. They wrote, "When we combine the daily activities of many women, we can identify times when the typical house is not likely to be guarded" (Rengert and Wasilchick 1985, 26). They found burglars to be most active between 10:00 and 11:00 a.m. and from 1:00 to 3:00 p.m.

The burglars in our study stated they preferred to work between 9:00 and 11:00 a.m. and in mid-afternoon. Most organized their working hours around school hours, particularly during the times when parents (usually mothers) took children to school and picked them up after school. Several told us that they waited "until the wife left to take the kids to school or go shopping." Most stated that they did not do burglaries on Saturday because people were usually home then. However, Sunday morning during church hours were considered prime time for weekend burglary.

Only a small number (n = 3) of burglars in our study committed residential burglaries at night. Most preferred to commit their crimes during daylight hours when they expected people to be at work and out of the home. Those who did commit nighttime burglary usually knew the victims and their schedules or took advantage of people being away from home in the evening during special events, such as high school football games. Pep squads at the high schools in the area studied decorate the front yards of the football team members with signs that identify the player, position, and uniform number. Burglars told us that they knew these houses would most likely be empty on Friday nights because the families attended the game. One said:

> Man! Wait until football season. I clean up then. When they are at the game, I'm at their house.

Accessibility

Accessibility cues are those factors that indicate how easily the residence can be entered and how well the site is protected. These cues include location and type of doors and windows, as well as the extent of target hardening such as locks, burglar alarms, fences, walls, burglar bars, and dogs. Accessibility also includes neighborhood and street permeability. Houses on corners or on through streets are more accessible than those on dead-end streets, cul-de-sacs and other streets with few intersections. Houses in gated communities are much less susceptible than those open to all. Burglars generally agree (Bennett and Wright 1984; MacDonald 1980; Taylor and Nee 1988; Wright and Decker 1994) that the critical elements in assessing vulnerability to break-in are:

- Larger, more expensive residences are more difficult to break into.
- Houses on cul-de-sacs, streets with few intersections, barricaded streets and those in gated communities are among the least vulnerable to burglary.
- Alarm systems increase the risk.
- Dogs increase the risk.
- Burglar bars and good quality locks increase both the effort and the risk.

Large, Expensive Homes. Although many burglars express a preference for burglarizing homes in the "rich" part of town, all agree that expensive homes are much more risky targets. Not only are burglars less likely to know the neighborhood and more likely to be noticed and identified as outsiders, they also recognize that homes in these areas have more security technology than smaller, less expensive homes. As one of our burglar subjects complained:

> These people got solid wood doors and locks and alarms . . . maybe even laser guns protecting their house. It's just too hard. I don't mess with rich people's houses.

Complex Street Layouts, Barricaded Streets, and Gated Communities. Accessibility also applies to the location of houses and other potential burglary targets. The more difficult the route to the prospective crime site, the less likely it will be targeted by the burglar. There has been a moderate amount of research on the susceptibility of houses on cul-de-sacs or less permeable streets and in gated communities to burglary and other forms of predatory crime. In a study of a residential area of Hartford, Connecticut, R. A. Gardiner (1978) demonstrated that closing off some streets to cars resulted in an overall decrease in crime. A study by James Lasley (1996) found a reduction in drive-by shootings in Los Angeles when some streets were closed to cars. Atlas and LeBlanc (1994) found a significant reduction in burglary in a south Florida community after implementation of street closures and barricades. Others (Bevis and Nutter 1977; Beavon 1984) have shown that the farther a residence is from main thoroughfares and arterial roads, the less likely it is to become a burglary target. The Brantinghams (1975), in a study of residential burglary in Tallahassee, Florida, found that burglary rates decreased sharply towards the core of residential areas.

A recent analysis of burglary in Greenwich, Connecticut, sought to determine the attributes of homes that attract burglars (Shachmurove, Fishman, and Hakin 1997). The researchers obtained self-report data from 3,014 households, of which 339 had experienced burglary incidents. They found that homes closer to major arterial routes (providing escape opportunities for the burglars), corner homes, and those adjacent to wooded areas tended to have a greater probability of being burglarized.

Jesse, one of our experienced burglars, stated:

> I don't like to go too deep [inside a neighborhood]. You get kinda lost once you get in those winding streets and stuff. I like to stay close to the main road so I can find my way out and escape fast.

Roberto, a professional burglar in our sample, adamantly declared:

> [I] don't do cul-de-sacs. Or dead-end streets. Always gotta have an escape route.

Burglar Alarms. Burglar alarms can serve as occupancy proxies. As such, burglars try to avoid them (Wright and Decker 1994). As one burglar told Wright and Decker (96):

> If I see an alarm out, like I say, they usually have them outside the house. I'll leave them alone automatically.

A major study of the effectiveness of burglar alarms was conducted by the Cedar Rapids, Iowa, Police Department. Matched pairs of 100 businesses and schools with previous burglaries were chosen for the experiment. One member of each pair was given a burglar alarm that sounded directly at the police station. The other half served as a control group. There was a reduction of 55 percent in attempted burglaries in sites with alarms compared to a reduction of only 8 percent for the control group (Rubenstein, Murray, Motoyama, and Rouse 1980).

In their study of burglary in Greenwich, Connecticut, Shachmurove et al. (1997) concluded that "if the home is protected by an alarm the probability for a burglary is virtually nil" (11). Our findings confirm these studies. One burglary subject advised:

> Sometimes I pick a house to do and when I get up close I can see the wires taped to the window and I know they got an alarm. I just move on.

Another stated:

> Most houses got a sign, like "This house protected by Westinghouse Security" or one of those other security companies. I just pass them by. People stupid to hit a house with an alarm system. Just go to one without it. That's common sense, you know. . . . Sometimes you see this blue sign that just says something like "This house protected by an electronic alarm system" without no company name on it. That's not real. . . . They just trying to scam you. You can get those signs at Radio Shack. Don't mean nothing.

Wright and Decker (1994) found that, "Most offenders . . . wanted to avoid alarms altogether and, upon encountering such devices, abandoned all thought of attacking the dwelling. Indeed, 56 of 86 subjects we questioned about this issue said that they were not prepared to burglarize an alarmed residence under *any* circumstances" (125). One of their burglar subjects reported:

> When I check the house out and be ready to get in it and I see an alarm, I'm ready to bust a window and I see that, I just back off it. (126)

Although several burglars in our study boasted about disarming alarms, when pressed for details, almost all admitted that they did not know how to accomplish that task. Two informants had disarmed alarm systems and were not particularly deterred by them. They stated that the presence of an alarm system gave them an additional cue as to the affluence of the residents, telling them that there was something worth protecting inside. One informant had purposely taken a job installing alarm systems in order to learn to disarm them. Another informant stated that alarm systems did not deter her because she still had time to complete the burglary and escape before police or private security arrived in response to the alarm. She stated that she never took more than 10 minutes to enter, search, and exit a house. She advised:

> Police take 15 to 20 minutes to respond to an alarm. Security [private security] sometimes gets there a little faster. I'm gone before any of them gets there.

Another professional burglar advised that he did not care whether a house had an alarm or not. He would go ahead and enter and begin to gather the goods he planned to steal. He said that after about five minutes the telephone would ring (the alarm company calling to verify the alarm). After the call, he stated that he had 5 to 15 minutes before someone arrived.

In general, however, burglars agreed that alarms were a definite deterrent to their activities. Other factors being equal, they preferred to locate a target that did not have an alarm rather than to take the additional risk involved in attempting to burglarize a house with an alarm system. Over 90 percent of the informants would not choose a target with an alarm system. Most (about 75 percent) were deterred by a sign or window sticker that stated that the house was protected by an alarm system. As Richard, an experienced burglar, stated:

> Why take a chance? There's lots of places without alarms. Maybe they're bluffing, maybe they ain't.

Locks, Burglar Bars, and Other Target-Hardening Devices. Past research has been inconsistent regarding the importance of locks on windows and doors. Scarr (1973) and Rengert and Wasilchick (1985) found that burglars consider the type of lock installed at a prospective target site. Others (Bennett and Wright 1984; Reppetto 1974; Walsh 1980) did not find locks to be a significant factor in the target selection process.

Early research evaluating "target hardening" techniques in four public housing projects in Seattle (1975) and in Chicago's Cabrini-Green public housing (1979) found that installation of deadbolt locks and other such techniques significantly reduced the burglary rate in those areas. From their review of these programs, Rubenstein et al. (1980) concluded that locks are a factor considered by burglars in target selection. Rengert and Wasilchick (1985) wrote: ". . . most of the burglars we interviewed are easily discouraged by a tough lock. With so many opportunities, many burglars will move on rather than struggle with a deadbolt lock" (90).

Wright and Decker (1994) found that locks and windows and doors were usually not considered during the initial phase of the target selections process because they were not able to be seen from a distance. They wrote, "If locks were considered at all, this usually occurred at a later stage" (98). Once a target was selected, the burglar would deal with the problem of locked doors and windows when the problem was actually encountered:

> Locks play a part [in discouraging burglars], but . . . [if] you got the right tools, you could go up to the front door and open it as quickly and as easy as if you had your own key. . . . (Wright and Decker 120)

The majority of informants in our study initially stated that they were not deterred by locks, just as in the case of alarm systems. However, during burglary reconstructions, we discovered that given two potential target sites, all other factors being equal, burglars prefer not to deal with a deadbolt lock. After the burglar compared a few sites and discovered his or her own preference for doors without deadbolt locks, they were better able to evaluate their own preferences. A typical response to our questions about deadbolt locks was:

> I gotta be in and out in 2–3 minutes. I ain't got time to mess with no tough lock.

Another of our subjects said:

> I never really thought about it. I can bust open a deadbolt if I got time, but going back on it, I usually just find a house without one.

The variation in findings regarding security hardware appears to be related to the degree to which burglars are either rational or opportunistic. To the extent to which burglars are primarily opportunistic, locks appear to have some deterrent value. The opportunistic burglar chooses a target based upon its perceived vulnerability to burglary at a given time. Given a large number of potential targets, the burglar tends to select the most vulnerable of the target pool. A target with a good lock and fitted with other security hardware will usually not be perceived to be as vulnerable as one without those items. The rational, planning burglar chooses targets on the basis of factors other than situational vulnerability and conceives ways in which he or she can overcome impediments to the burglary (such as the target site being fitted with a high quality deadbolt lock). Thus, to the extent that burglars are rational planners, deadbolt locks have limited utility for crime prevention. Our findings, however, support the deterrent value of deadbolt locks; 75 percent of the burglaries reconstructed during our research were opportunistic offenses. Many of those burglaries would have been prevented (or displaced) by the presence of a quality deadbolt lock. It is important to note that nearly one half of the burglary sites in the present study were entered through open or unlocked windows and doors. The findings are very similar to those of Rengert and Wasilchick (1985) who found that burglary through unlocked doors was a "surprisingly frequent occurrence." They wrote:

> Many burglars build their careers on the mistaken belief held by residents that "it can't happen here," or "I'll only be next door for a minute." More than one of the burglars we talked to burglarized open houses while the residents were in the backyard doing yard work.

Dogs. Almost all studies agree that dogs are an effective deterrent to burglary. Wright and Decker (1994, 208) stated that few of the burglars in their study were prepared to tackle a house with a dog. Reppetto (1974) found that only about one-third of burglars under the age of 25 years reported that dogs would not be a deterrent. Although there is some individual variation among burglars, the general rule is to bypass a house with a dog—any dog. Large dogs represent a physical threat to the burglar and small ones are often noisy, attracting attention to the burglar's activities. We found that although many burglars have developed contingency plans to deal with dogs (petting them, feeding them, or even killing them), most burglars prefer to avoid them. When asked what were considered absolute "no go" factors, most burglars responded that dogs were second only to occupancy.

Approximately 30 percent of the informants, however, initially discounted the presence of dogs as a deterrent. Yet, during ride alongs the sight or sound of a dog at a potential target site almost invariably resulted in a "no go" decision. As Richard said:

> I don't mess with no dogs. If they got dogs I go someplace else.

Debbie told us that she was concerned primarily with small dogs:

> Big dogs don't bark much. I talk to them through the fence or door and get them excited. Then I open the gate or the door and when they charge out, I go in and shut the door behind me. They are outside and I'm in. Little dogs yap too much. They [neighbors] look to see what they are so excited about. I don't like little yapping dogs.

Some of the more professional burglars were less concerned with dogs and had developed techniques for dealing with them. In general, however, the presence of a dog was considered an effective deterrent.

Summary

Burglary appears to be a highly instrumental crime, being committed almost exclusively to obtain money. While thrill, excitement and revenge do play a minor role in the etiology of the offense, it is primarily young, inexperienced burglars who report such motives. Once the decision is made to commit a burglary, the burglars must select a likely target. We found that most of them employ a decision-making strategy that has three components. The burglar begins with an assumption that each proposed target site contains at least some minimal potential gain. He or she must then determine whether the target site can be entered without being seen and reported, whether the site might be occupied, and whether the site can be broken into readily. These determinations are made on the basis of evidence obtained from observing environmental cues at or near the target site and employing the mental template constructed through past experience and the recounted experiences of others.

Burglars use three categories of environmental cues to assess these risk factors: (a) cues that indicate the visibility of the proposed target site; (b) cues that indicate whether the target site is occupied; and (c) cues that indicate the degree of difficulty that might be expected in actually breaking into the site. The specific content of these cues has varied widely across prior studies.

We found that burglars are opportunistic and are easily deterred or displaced from one target site to another. Situational factors such as the presence of a dog, an alarm system, security hardware, and alert neighbors may be effective deterrents. However, criminal justice system sanctions appear to have little role in the risk-gain calculus employed by burglars. Their "here and now" orientation tends to negate the role of future consequences in their decision making and thus reduce the impact of most public policy regarding burglary in particular and property crime in general.

Questions for Thought and Discussion

1. This chapter looks at the rational processes used by burglars in selecting targets and committing burglaries. What do the authors mean by "degrees of rationality?" What is the narrow model compared to the wide model of rationality?
2. What are the qualities of a "good" burglary target?
3. According to the authors, what are the three risk cues considered by burglars in their target selection process?
4. What theory or theories of criminal behavior are illustrated in this research?

References

Atlas, Randal, and Will C. LeBlanc. 1994. "The Impact on Crime of Street Closures and Barricades: A Florida Study." *Security Journal,* 5: 140–5.

Beavon, D.J. 1984. *Crime and the Environmental Opportunity Structure: The Influence of Street Networks on the Patterning of Property Offenders.* Unpublished master's thesis. Simon Fraser University, Burnaby, B.C.

Becker, Gary. 1968. "Crime and Punishment: An Economic Approach." *Journal of Political Economy,* 76: 169–217.

Bennett, T., and R. Wright. 1984. *Burglars on Burglary: Prevention and the Offender.* Aldershot, U.K.: Gower.

Bevis, C., and J.B. Nutter. 1977. "Changing Street Layout to Reduce Residential Burglary." Paper presented at American Society of Criminology annual meeting. Atlanta, GA.

Brantingham, Patricia L., and Paul J. Brantingham. 1975. "Residential Burglary and Urban Form." *Urban Studies,* 12: 273–86.

———. 1978. "A Theoretical Model of Crime Site Selection." In *Crime, Law and Sanctions,* eds. M.D. Krohn and R.L. Akers. Beverly Hills, CA: Sage.

———. 1981. *Environmental Criminology.* Beverly Hills, CA: Sage.

———. 1991. *Environmental Criminology.* Prospect Heights, IL.: Waveland Press.

———. 1993. "Nodes, Paths and Edges: Considerations on the Complexity of Crime on the Physical Environment." *Journal of Environmental Psychology,* 13: 3–28.

Brezina, Timothy. 2002. "Assessing the Rationality of Criminal and Delinquent Behavior: A Focus on Actual Utility." In *Rational Choice and Criminal Behavior: Recent Research and Future Challenges,* eds. Alex R. Piquero and Stephen G. Tibbetts, 241–64. New York: Routledge.

Brown, B.B., and I. Altman. 1981. "Territoriality and Residential Crime: A Conceptual Framework." In *Environmental Criminology,* eds. P.J. Brantingham and P.L. Brantingham. Beverly Hills, CA: Sage.

Clarke, R.V., and D.B. Cornish. 1985. "Modeling Offenders' Decisions: A Framework for Policy and Research." In *Crime and Justice: An Annual Review of Research,* 4th ed., eds. M. Tonry and N. Morris. Chicago: University of Chicago Press.

Cook, Philip J. 1980. "Research in Criminal Deterrence: Laying the Groundwork for the Second Decade." In *An Annual Review of Research,* eds. Norval Morris and Michael Tonry, 211–268. Chicago: University of Chicago Press.

Copes, Heith. 2003. "Streetlife and the Rewards of Auto Theft." *Deviant Behavior* 24(4):309–332.

Cornish, D.B. 1993. "Theories of Action in Criminology: Learning Theory and Rational Choice Approaches." In *Advances in Criminological Theory, Vol. 5: Routine Activity and Rational Choice,* eds. Ronald V. Clarke and Marcus Felson, 351–382. New Brunswick, NJ: Transaction.

Cornish, D.B., and R.V. Clarke. 1986. "Situational Prevention, Displacement of Crime and Rational Choice Theory." In *Situational Crime Prevention: From Theory Into Practice,* eds. K. Heal and G. Laycock. London: HMSO.

Cromwell, Paul, and James N. Olson. 2004. *Breaking and Entering: Burglars on Burglars.* Belmont, CA: Wadsworth.

Cromwell, Paul, James Olson, and D. Avary. 1991. *Breaking and Entering: An Ethnographic Analysis of Burglary.* (Newbury Park, CA: Sage).

Gardiner, R.A. 1978. *Design for Safe Neighborhoods.* Washington DC: Law Enforcement Assistance Administration.

Hochstetler, Andy, and Heith Copes. 2003. "Managing Fear to Commit Felony Theft." In *In Their Own Words: Criminals on Crime,* 3rd ed., ed. Paul Cromwell, 87–98. Los Angeles: Roxbury.

Jackson, B. 1969. *Outsdide the Law: A Thief's Primer.* New York: Macmillan.

Jacobs, Bruce A. 1999. *Dealing Crack: The Social World of Streetcorner Selling.* Boston: Northeastern University Press.

Lasley, James R. 1996. *Using Traffic Barriers to "Design Out" Crime: A Program Evaluation of L.A.P.D.'s Operation Cul-de-Sac.* Report to the National Institute of Design. Fullerton: California State University–Fullerton.

MacDonald, John M. 1980. *Burglary and Theft.* Springfield, IL: Charles C. Thomas.

Rengert, G. 1981. "Burglary in Philadelphia: A Critique of an Opportunity Structure Model." In *Environmental Criminology,* eds. Paul J. and Patricia L. Brantingham. Beverly Hills, CA: Sage.

Rengert, G., and J. Wasilchick. 1985. *Suburban Burglary: A Time and a Place for Everything.* Springfield, IL: Charles C. Thomas.

Reppetto, T.G. 1974. *Residential Crime.* Cambridge, MA: Ballinger.

Rubenstein, H., C. Murray, T. Motoyama, and W.V. Rouse. 1980. *The Link Between Crime and the Built Environment: The Current State of the Knowledge* (Vol. 1). Washington, DC: National Institute of Justice.

Scarr, H.A. 1973. *Patterns of Burglary.* Washington, DC: U.S. Government Printing Office.

Shachmurove, Yochanan, Gordon Fishman, and Simon Hakin. 1997. *The Burglar as a Rational Economic Agent.* CARESS Working Paper, 97-7 (mimeo).

Shover, Neal. 1991. "Burglary." In *Crime and Justice: A Review of Research* (Vol. 14), ed. Michael Tonry, 73–114. Chicago: University of Chicago Press.

———. 1996. *The Great Pretenders: Pursuits and Careers of Persistent Thieves.* Boulder, CO: Westview Press.

Taylor, M., and C. Nee. 1988. "The Role of Cues in Residential Burglary." *British Journal of Criminology,* 238:396–401.

Tunnell, Kenneth D. 1992. *Choosing Crime: The Criminal Calculus of Property Offenders.* Chicago: Nelson Hall.

Vold, G., and T.J. Bernard. 1986. *Theoretical Criminology,* 3rd ed. New York: Oxford University Press.

Walsh, D.P. 1980. *Break-ins: Burglary from Private Houses.* London: Constable.

Wright, Richard T., and Scott H. Decker. 1994. *Burglars on the Job: Street Life and Residential Burglary.* Boston: Northeastern University Press.

Paul Cromwell and James N. Olson, "The Reasoning Burglar: Motives and Decision-Making Strategies." Adapted from work originally published in Cromwell and Olson, *Breaking and Entering: Burglars on Burglary.* Belmont, CA: Wadsworth Publishing Company. 2004.

Chapter 6 Women, Work, and Crime

Deborah R. Baskin
Ira Sommers

T*he purpose of this study was to explore the impact of women's life experiences on their involvement in legal and illegal work. The authors consider issues such as how job opportunities, skills, and aspirations affect the work-crime relationship and how illegal activities attract women away from jobs in the licit economy and from involvement in gender stereotypical crimes such as prostitution. The authors describe how a sample of women involved in violent street crime make a living and follows their involvement in the legal and illegal economies.*

The research is based on in-depth life history interviews with 170 women who committed nondomestic violent felony crimes (robbery, assault, homicide) in New York City. The women were recruited from various social settings including (1) those arrested and arraigned for violent crimes (N=49); (2) those in state prison for violent crimes (N=48); and (3) women actively involved in violent criminal offending (N=73).

Interviews were open-ended, in-depth, and, when possible, audiotaped. The open-ended technique created a context in which respondents were able to speak freely and in their own words. Furthermore, it facilitated the pursuit of issues that were raised by the women during the interview but were not recognized beforehand by the researchers. The in-depth interview approach enabled the authors to pursue information about specific events, as well as provide an opportunity for respondents to reflect on those events. As a result, they were able to gain insight into the women's attitudes, feelings, and other subjective orientations to their experiences.

A typical member of the sample was a black woman, 27 years old, a high-school dropout with two children, possessing limited legal work experience. The youngest was 16 years old and the oldest 43. The median age of the respondents was 30 years. Seventy-five percent of the subjects were high-school dropouts, typically leaving school by 11th grade. Although most of the women had worked in a legitimate job (80 percent), the median number of months employed was only 16 and the average was 35.9 months. Most of the women worked in unskilled and semiskilled working-class occupations (e.g., clerical and factory jobs).

The relationship between crime and work has become the focus of much criminological research (Bourgois 1995; Crutchfield 1997; Fagan 1996; Fagan and Freeman 1994; Grogger 1994; Reuter et al. 1990; Sommers et al. 1996; Sullivan 1989; Wilson 1996). This is due, in part, to major shifts over the past two decades in inner-city legal and illegal labor markets as well as to important changes in the social, cultural, and political dynamics within urban communities. Thus far, research in this area has concentrated almost exclusively on males with only passing reference to and/or conjecture regarding women.

Nonetheless, the macro transformations in urban communities that have been identified as affecting males' decisions concerning criminal involvement have also had an impact on women's choices as they relate to work and crime. Therefore, the purpose of the present research is to explore key issues concerning the interaction between legal and illegal work in terms of the impact that the study of women's life experiences had on that relationship. Here, we will explore how such human capital issues as job opportunities, skills and aspirations mediated the work-crime relationship; how illegal work, especially drug distribution and robbery, drew women away from their positions in the licit economy, as well as from their involvement in gender stereotypical crimes such as prostitution; and how an increasing and eventual full-time commitment to street life and drug abuse ended their relationship to careers in both the legal and illegal labor markets altogether.

The Literature on Crime and Work

The sharp rise in violent crime and drug trafficking that characterized many inner cities during the 1980s and early 1990s has often been associated with a precipitous decline in formal employment opportunities. This "disappearance of work" (Wilson 1996) has been seen as altering the basic calculus used by young people to influence their choice of economic activities. By and large, the outcome of such decision-making, in the context of dwindling wages and satisfactory job opportunities in the legal world of work, has been increased participation in illegal income-generating activities (Fagan 1992; Freeman 1983; Hagedorn 1994; Witte and Tauchen 1994).

In recent years, research based on this model of decision-making has flourished. Elements of the economic calculus have been dissected and results supporting the choice of crime *over* legal work have been reported. Increasing unemployment and underemployment have been identified as significantly related to crime participation (Chiricos 1987; Blackburn, Bloom, and Freeman 1990; Corcoran and Parrott 1992; Fagan and Freeman 1994); income from crime, especially from drug dealing, has been found to be higher than income from other, legal sources (Vicusi 1986; Reuter et al. 1990; Fagan 1992, 1994a; Freeman 1992); and the social and psychic payoffs from illegal work seem to outweigh the concern over, if not the risks of legal sanctions (Fagan 1996). Thus, the choice of illegal work is understandable, at least, intellectually.

Once the decision to enter the world of illegal enterprise has been made, another body of research has sought to explain the persistence of illicit income-generation activities. Here, ethnographic studies have documented a renouncement of the secondary labor market by inner-city males. Young males who have turned to the illegal economy now rely on street networks for status (Anderson 1990, 1994; Fagan 1994a, 1994b; Hagedorn 1994; Hagedorn and Macron 1988; Padilla 1992; Taylor 1990; Moore, 1991, 1992). And, they use the discourse of work, like "getting paid," or "going to work" (Sullivan 1989) to describe their criminal careers. Thus, for these young males, money from crime and reputation from criminal success form the bases for commodity consumption and status that would be unavailable to them from the legal workaday world.

The persistence of criminal careers from adolescence to adulthood is also understood in terms of the structural changes in legal employment patterns in urban centers. Where once manufacturing jobs and other semiskilled labor market positions provided egresses from criminal careers as young males moved from adolescence to adulthood, the disappearance of such opportunities has resulted in cross-generational joblessness with attendant cultural, social, and legal disadvantages (Wilson 1996; Tienda 1989; Sullivan 1989). Thus, young males in the transition to adulthood who suffer from social capital deficits (Bourgois 1995), the stigma of legal sanctions (Anderson 1990; Sullivan 1989), and exaggerated tastes and preferences (Anderson 1990; Bourgois 1995) further narrow their options for economic and social success in the world of licit work (Hagan and Pallioni 1990; Bourgois 1995; Anderson 1990; Sampson and Laub 1993).

Over time, the perception that entry into the world of legal work is possible dwindles. At this stage of criminal career development, research points to the rise of a rigid bifurcation between licit and illicit economic activities (Anderson 1990, 1994; Hagedorn 1994; Hagedorn and Macron 1988; Taylor 1990; Moore 1992). Thus, young males eventually choose to *either* abandon their involvement in illegal work and accept the economic and social parameters of the conventional workaday world, or they commit themselves to illegal work and its concomitant social and legal implication. However, once the decision to commit to the illicit economy is made, the option to return to the licit world is narrowed, if not eliminated altogether (Hagan 1993). This bifurcation has become, if not an empirical reality, one that at least characterizes much thinking in this area.

Recent research, however, suggests that participation in the *worlds* of work may not be exclusive. In fact, several studies show a much more dynamic and flexible interaction between legal and illegal work. Some qualitative studies have documented regular career "shifts" from illegal to legal sources of income and even simultaneous participation in both economies over the course of an individual's work history (Shover 1985; Biernacki 1986; Sullivan 1989; Padilla 1992; Adler 1992; Baskin and Sommers 1998).

Despite the talk of "young people," "individuals," and "inner-city residents," much of what we know about the interaction between legal and illegal work is based on information obtained from male respondents. This is unfortunate. Recent research on female offenders has documented dramatic changes in women's participation in income-generating criminal activities. From robbery to drug dealing, women in inner cities have increased their involvement as well as other aspects of their participation in crime, such as roles and statuses. Thus, we find more women acting as principals in criminal events, as crew bosses and owners of drug distribution enterprises, and as recruiters of other women into the illicit world of work (Baskin and Sommers 1998; Fagan 1994b; Inciardi et al. 1993; Mieczkowski 1994; Miller 1998; Taylor 1993). Further, we find more women entering crime apart from domestic partnerships, more within single-sex peer groups, and more ready to employ violence as part of doing business (Baskin and Sommers 1998; Curry, Ball, and Fox 1994). And, we find that for some women, their involvement in other forms of street crime, such as robbery, burglary, and drug dealing, has led to a decrease in their participation in prostitution (Sommers, Baskin, and Fagan 1996).

Nonetheless, these changes do not *erase* the fact that gender does indeed make a difference in daily life experiences and in decision-making patterns (Brown and Gilligan 1992; Pipher 1994), albeit in different ways for different groups of women. Therefore, research needs to focus on women within specific contexts if we are to understand how the dynamics of gender impact on particular criminal career decisions.

The research reported within is a step in that direction. Here, we describe how a sample of women involved in violent street crime tried to make a living. We explore their progression from early involvement in the legal and formal economy, their joint involvement in these two spheres and their ultimate embeddedness in the informal and illicit economy. Through a description of their experiences in these various "work" sectors, the women provide us with an understanding of the bases for and types of decisions they made when choosing their "vocations."

It is clear from their accounts that even from the outset, a tension always existed between their involvement in legal and illegal work and between the asocial world of formal labor and the seemingly social atmosphere promised by criminal involvement. Further, we find that the "economic" calculus so often reported in the literature is only partially the basis for their decision making; and that their maintenance in these criminal activities comes to resemble less the workaday world described in relation to male criminal careers and more the world of drug addicts that the traditional literature on females and crime suggests (Bourgois and Dunlap 1993; Maher and Daly 1996; Hunt 1990).

Participation in the Secondary Labor Market

For the women we interviewed, legal employment was viewed as important, at least initially. By the time they were sixteen, the majority had left school. Therefore, securing a job took on great significance. And, at least at first, they were successful. Unlike their male counterparts, most of whom experienced high rates of joblessness from the start (Wilson 1996), 80 percent of the women we interviewed were able to secure employment in the formal economy. These jobs were exclusively in the secondary labor market.

Research on the effects of labor distribution on criminal involvement has suggested that relegation to the secondary labor market, that is, working at jobs that are low-paying, have few, if any benefits, and offer little in terms of advancement, will result in greater participation in violent crime (Crutchfield 1989).[1] Further, it is hypothesized that the mechanism through which this relationship is fostered is that of social bonding. In other words, the "weaker bonds . . . associated with employment in secondary occupations, will lead to higher crime rates" (Crutchfield 1989). Those who work in the secondary labor market, therefore, are less likely both to develop attachments and commitments to their jobs as well as stakes in conformity as compared to their peers in the primary labor market. Thus, the "qualities" of a job, rather than the presence or absence of employment, seem to affect criminal involvement (Rosenfeld and Messner 1989; Sampson and Laub 1993; Uggen et al. 1992), at least among males.

Of the women in our study who worked, the vast majority were employed in entry level, unskilled positions as office clerks (32 percent), factory laborers (28 percent), and salespeople (25 percent). Fifteen percent of the women were able to obtain "aide" positions in home health care or education. These positions were acquired either through temporary employment agencies or public programs, never through personal networks. They lasted no more than a few months and were characteristically low paying and offered little long term security and no chances for advancement.

The women in our study entered the labor force with an acute awareness that their employment, even in the future, would, in all probability, be sporadic or remain in the lowest echelons of the secondary market. For the few women who hoped for more lucrative futures in the licit job sector, training in cosmetology and having their own "station" at the local beauty salon was their loftiest goal. But, even at the outset, these women did not think that the jobs available to them would bring the "prestige, pride, and self-respect" (Liebow 1967, 60) found in white-collar occupations. Thus, like the men Liebow described in *Tally's Corner* (1967), these women ascribed "no lower value on the job than does the larger society" (57). In other words, these women were keenly aware of the social value of the types of jobs available to them.

The work descriptions offered by the women we interviewed confirmed this perspective. Furthermore, like the men Liebow described and those studied by Bourgois (1995), the women eventually came to view these jobs with an active lack of interest. They were routinely fired due to excessive absenteeism or were absent frequently as a way of quitting. They would often show up for work high on drugs, or coming down from a night of heavy drinking and partying. Often, especially towards the end of their involvement in the formal economy, they used their work environments as settings for their increasingly prevalent criminal activities.

Descriptions of Initial Experiences in the Legal Economy

Herminia told us about her first job:

> I worked for like minimum wage at Duane Read Pharmacy. I enjoyed it cause, you know, I felt, like independent. I was bringing a little money home. But, fast I stopped liking it. I never liked a job that would be just standing like in one place, you know, like doing the same thing over and over. I got tired of it—the monotony, the routine every day, so I stopped showing up. I lasted there about four months. Then, I worked in McDonald's for maybe four weeks. I hated McDonald's. It was boring. I was there for about four weeks. So, I went through a few other jobs. These were the only ones I could get. I had to lie about my age just to get these. I was only 15 and 16 and who was going to hire me?

Herminia's description was typical of the women in this study. For that matter and without exception, regardless of the actual position, and like the men who Liebow spoke with in *Tally's Corner,* the women did not display an "overt interest in job specifics . . . in a large part perhaps because the specifics are not especially relevant" (Liebow 1967, 57). This was due to the fact that the secondary job market was comprised of "a narrow range of nondescript chores calling for nondescript, undifferentiated, unskilled labor" (Liebow 1967, 57).

Danelle, too, described her dissatisfaction with the types of jobs available to her. Furthermore, given her early involvement in violent street crime and drug use, it was especially difficult for her to accept the drudgery and routine of employment in the secondary market. Clearly, these types of jobs did not compete with the excitement she had and enjoyment she received from hanging out and partying with her friends.

> I used to work at—this was when I was 16—I used to work at Wendy's. Yeah, at Roy Rogers too. I worked like, for six months at the first job and two months for the second. I quit because I couldn't function every day, gettin' up and goin' to work and then partyin' the night before. I didn't feel too great about these jobs. Wearing a stupid uniform and flipping burgers. That's lame.
>
> Yeah, I was trying to do something for myself by working these jobs. But it wasn't working. I rather go home and get high and hang out with my people. So, it wasn't workin' and neither was I.

Interestingly, even among those who worked in the human service sector, principally as home attendants, work was viewed similarly as demeaning, boring, and no different from clerical or sales work:

> I started out as a home health aide. It was O.K. for a little while. But then I got sick of it. You know what I'm saying—they like, they were driving me crazy. I felt like a housekeeper. It was nothing special, no different than working burgers or cleaning tables. There's not much else to say about it. (Denise)

Thus, the women in our study came to view their involvement in the licit job world with the same emptiness as the countless ghetto, barrio, and streetcorner males studied by other researchers. The difference for the women in our study, though, was that they were at least initially drawn to the legal economy and remained there for almost three years.

The Intermingling of Licit and Illicit Work

At the beginning of their employment careers, the women attempted to make a living, primarily through legitimate employment. Over time, however, they decided that the low economic and cultural returns from their marginal employment were not satisfactory. They then turned to crime and illegal hustles for supplementation. For many women, the workplace itself came to serve as a setting for these activities. And, it was these activities that provided them with important sources of income, identity, and excitement.

Here Denise, a former home attendant, describes how she combined licit and illicit work to augment her desires for more money, more excitement, and the respect of her peers on the street:

> Yeah, so I hated doing things for these rich people, so after a while me and my friends developed a gimmick. I would go into the house, and I would case it out and get all the necessary information. When they would be out, my friends would come in and like vandalize it. Then we'd all go out and party and celebrate our success. I was really a key connection for them. And, funny thing is, I would go back to work the next day like nothing ever happened and act shocked.
>
> I did that for about six months. But I really couldn't stand cleaning up after these rich people and so I went to work at _____ Hospital in their dietary department. Then I got the key to the supplies and I had my girlfriends come up with a truck and unload the block. This was fun and made us lots of money too. But, I got arrested and had to give them my paycheck. I worked there for about six months too.

Monica, too, used her place of employment for her illegal enterprises. In this case, she dealt drugs from her office.

> I started as a summer youth worker for a City agency. But then they kept me permanently as a floater, which means like I worked diversified duties. I made, like, $9,000 a year. At this point I was already indulging in cocaine and I started selling drugs. So, uh, I started going to work and showing people my material—people that I knew that got high. And they started buying from me. So then they started buying weight which would mean that I would have to get more material—and give it to them. And, uh, it's like I used the messenger companies from the office. I used to call the messenger companies, and they used to pick everything up. And they would come pick it up at the agency and drop it off at someone else not knowing what was really inside. I made like $4000 to $5200 a week. But then I just started using all the money for getting high and I stopped going to the office.

"Doubling up" in crime and work (Fagan 1994a), as these women had done, is not unusual among active offenders, regardless of gender, especially among those involved in drug distribution. Research has indicated that between 25 percent and 57 percent of active offenders report participating in income producing crime, thereby optimizing extant opportunities (Grogger 1994; Hagedorn 1994; Fagan 1992; Reuter et al. 1990). Nonetheless, research in this area, again using predominately male respondents, has explained such behavior solely in economic terms. It has been argued that young males will "double up" for the purpose of optimizing income generation opportunities, plain and simple.What was different for the women in our study was the fact that "doubling up" provided these women with opportunities for optimizing *both* the economic *and* the social facets of their lives; one no less important than the other. Thus, "doubling up" permitted the intermingling of fun, excitement, and adventure with occasions for both legal and illegal income generation—all within the same work setting.

Crime on the Side

For some of the women with whom we spoke, "doubling up" took a different form. These women recounted for us incredible work schedules in which, for the majority of the time that they were employed in the legal sector, they would also hold down "second jobs" during their *off* hours. Many, but not all, of these women had an overarching addiction to drugs that pushed them to secure money by any means possible—legal and otherwise. April was one such woman:

> I was makin' like $7 an hour at this Sears job. That was actually pretty good money, but I was gettin' high. I was stealin', robbin'. I used to forge checks to get more money. I worked there for maybe six months. I guess I was into fast money, a fast life. I needed money to support my habit. So I went out, and, uh, the person that I was buying from, I asked him, you know, how can I get into it.

> So, after I was done with my day at Sears, I was selling on the street. I turned out to be one of the carriers—the person that, uh, pick up the drugs and distribute it to people on the street to sell. I bring in about $2000 to $3000 a week. Sometimes I, I would be up two or three days in a row because the money would be coming so fast that I'd be, I wouldn't want to go to sleep because I knew if I would go to sleep, I would miss money—the Sears money and the other—I wanted both.

For the drug-addicted women, losing sleep, being absent from legal work, partying, and hustling formed their day-to-day experiences.

For other women, crime on the side was a continuation of their long-term involvement in offending. Initially, it counterbalanced the asocial and boring nature of their jobs in the legal sector. It provided these women with the excitement, adventure, and camaraderie absent from jobs in the secondary labor market. Further, and not unimportantly, crime on the side supplemented the meager incomes they received from their marginal jobs.

As L.G. recounts:

> When I was like 15—when I dropped out of school after, you know, a lot of places weren't taking people that didn't have a high school diploma and stuff like that—I went to a temporary agency, you know, which allowed me to work for different companies. I did clerical work for the Department of Probation. I did clerical work for AT&T and Citibank. I worked six or seven months in each of these places. Usually the job itself had ended and I'd go back to the agency and they place me again. But they were all boring—no one to talk to, to hang out with, but I kept going. But even though I was workin' and still doin', you know, the right thing, I always was drawed to doin' the wrong thing somewhere down the line.
>
> When I'd get home from work, I'd go hang out with my friends. We got hooked up with some people who were, uh, transportin' drugs from New York to New Jersey to Washington, and I started doin' that for a while after work, on weekends, or between jobs. I would get paid large sums of money and I, you know, I clung to that for a while. But I was really into [it] for the fun and for things to do with my friends. I did like the real money, though.
>
> I did other stuff during this time, like stealin' in stores and rippin' people off. Me and friends would go to parks and 34th and 42nd streets and stick people up. We got money, real money for clothes, jewelry, and fun. But really soon getting the real money became the important thing.

L.G. was socialized initially into illegal behavior and violence for principally nonpecuniary reasons. The money she received at the early stages of her criminal career was secondary to the excitement and adventure she received from her participation. However, as L.G. and her counterparts entered their late teens and experienced a desire for a more sustained source of income, they applied the criminal "skills" learned earlier to economically motivated activities. But, even within this context, noneconomic motives were still important. For these women, committing crime with friends and enjoying the fruits together were still meaningful.

We should say that at this point in their lives, and unlike their male counterparts, these women were relatively successful in avoiding serious legal sanctions for their already lengthy involvement in criminal activity. On the average, first arrests occurred when these women were in their early (for robberies) to mid-twenties (assault and drugs), later than for males (Fagan 1996; Fagan and Freeman 1994; Grogger 1994; Sampson and Laub 1993; Good et al. 1986). Therefore, commitment to the illegal economy was viewed by these women as a relatively low-risk endeavor and the length of time that they were able to "double up" far exceeded that of their male counterparts.

Furthermore, the deterrent influences of social sanctions, such as family, peer, and community disapproval, also did not seem to affect the decisions of these women in the same way as for men (Fagan 1989). For that matter, by the time these women were in their very early twenties, they were emotionally, if not physically, estranged from their foster families or families of origin. By and large, as the women's commitment to their criminal careers increased, they became increasingly estranged from their families. This estrangement followed several patterns: the women would initially maintain legal residence with their families but come to spend more of their time in and out of apartments with friends, lovers, or other strangers; or these women eventually would be kicked out of their families' households or their own project apartments due to their increasing involvement in criminal and drug careers, most often permanently leaving their children behind with family or friends, or in the custody of child welfare; or, when they experienced a downturn in their criminal careers they would wander the streets, living in abandoned buildings, welfare hotels, or shelters, avoiding contact with their significant others, including children.

There were a few women with children who left their "always nagging and interfering" families when welfare found them and their children an apartment in the projects. And, for those fortunate and very few who were lucky enough to have a steady income from drug dealing, they moved into public housing or low-income apartments. However, the continued involvement of the majority of these women in drug dealing and other street crimes led eventually to eviction and often pushed them into the street.

One thing was clear though, when speaking about families, especially their children, these women considered all such relationships as fetters—fetters, initially on their criminal careers and social lives and later on, in their missions to obtain drugs and stay high. Accounts of children getting in the way abounded. As Wanda told us:

> Yeah, I have a son. I have been away from him for five years while I've been runnin' the streets. I was never with my son. He lives with his grandmother. BCW took him away from me. My mother called them because I was neglectin' him. I was always out leaving him alone in the house. Never thought anything about how my mom and him felt.

Another woman recounted:

> Oh yeah, my kids. I have three of them. But they never stayed with me. They always lived with my mom or my sister. I started dropping them off when I would be out doing stuff. But then I finally stopped bringin' them back to my place. They were always gettin' in the way. What with my hours, I couldn't be there and then, all that cryin'. It used to bother my friends when we'd come back to the apartment to party.

The estrangement of these women from their families reduced the salience of both formal and informal social networks and therefore did not influence their "calculus" on the risks and benefits of participation in the illegal economy. As Danelle explained:

> Who's going to care? My ma gets money from me and doesn't ask where it's from. She just takes care of my kid for me and doesn't complain. Sometimes she tells me to be careful. I got my friends to run with me and we're doin' just fine. No one bothers us, not even the cops. Yeah, my brother's in prison, but he just got stupid. He'll be out and back into it. It's the way things are here. So, I don't get the question. Why should I think about the problems of doing business? They're not my problems. Who cares, anyway?

Here, Danelle expresses a very common theme in the narratives offered by most of the women. Not only did the women not perceive arrest or incarceration as a risk, but when commenting on others' criminal justice involvements, they dismissed them as endurable, temporary, and not the least bit unusual. Furthermore, most perceived their families and communities as highly tolerant or just plain indifferent to their behavior, whether the behavior was "decent" or "street" (Anderson 1994). For some of the women, the fact that their families were receiving "benefits," i.e. money [or] commodities, as a result of their involvement in criminal enterprises, seemed to reduce, further, any perception of familial rejection. Thus, for these women, commitment to the illegal economy did not produce any particularly strong strains between them and their families and communities.

Commitment to the Illegal Economy

Patterns of illegal work varied among the women. As we have heard, some abandoned work after periods of licit employment, others drifted in and out of legal work while firmly committed to the illegal economy. Herminia's account was typical of this latter group of women:

> I had lots of little jobs, but selling cocaine was always how I really made my living. My last job was, I was 18, I was a receptionist at a showroom. I was there maybe one year. It was okay. But I was already into selling cocaine. I started that much earlier when my father went to jail. I felt that as my duty as taking care of my family I started selling coke. My father didn't know anything about it at first. But there came a time when we were doin' it together. We were selling together.
>
> Now, I'd be selling for about seven years. I went up and down. I could make $500. I could make $3000 a week. I never stood on the corner and sold bags or anything like that. It would always be quantity. I had a few customers, four or five customers. I was selling ounces with some Colombians. They became like my suppliers and stuff. I started like with myself,

> when my father came out I started like working with him. Then I stopped working in offices altogether.

Alicia, too, considered her criminal activities as more important and more regular than her sporadic experiences within the legal economy:

> I had two jobs. I used to do factory work. I didn't like . . . it was too much labor, you know. You had to do everything. I did home attendant for a little while. It was okay. But, my main commitment was to doing robberies. After awhile doing both things, the home attendant thing and the robbery thing, I tried to slow down a bit. So, I had to devote myself to one thing. I went full time to robbing people.

Other women from the outset considered the illegal economy as their primary job commitment. They chose *exclusive* "careers" in crime and never participated in the secondary labor market. For these women, given the alternatives of low-wage payoffs from legal work and the expectation of relatively high returns from income-generating criminal activities, they viewed illegal work as a rational choice not unlike choices made among legitimate occupational pursuits and not unlike their male counterparts (Fagan 1994a).

Jocorn and Rose both had a rich history of pre- and early adolescent involvement in violence and crime. For them, by the time they reached their mid-teens, hustling was a way of life. As Rose recalls:

> Like I said, I use to live in a neighborhood full of hustlers. And um, they use to watch me go to school, giving me $5 or $10 to buy clothes off the street for all the kids in the neighborhood. And then just, we started hanging down there by them. Then we started holding drugs for them. And paying us, $100 a day, and we would hold a 100 quarters, now if I would have gotten caught with that, lord knows how much time, but I was too naive and young to know what was going on. The money was good to me. I thought I was rich, you know what I am saying. And I liked to buy. So, by the time I left school, I was already into my job on the streets. I knew how to do the job and I had no problem protecting myself while I was doing it.

Jocorn, too, was deeply entrenched in her "career" by the time she left school. And, she stayed in this one "job," advancing through the ranks until she had her own organization.

> I was about 11 or 12 when I started selling drugs. It was fast money. I guess that's what attracted me to it, the fast money and the fun. I was makin' about $500 a week. Much later on, when I was about 17, I started like putting people to work for me. I was pulling in $10,000 a day.
>
> I sold it all. Crack too. I've been dealing for 19 years. The more I had, you know, the more money I wanted. I had people in Brooklyn, Manhattan, the Bronx, Boston, in upstate. All I was basically doing was gettin' the drugs and receiving the money.

The "career" trajectories of the women in the above accounts reflect the influences of structure and context in shaping their choices and options. With limited access to satisfying legal work, and in segregated neighborhoods with high concentrations of joblessness, alienated views of legal work and diminished expectations for conventional employment became normative. For some of the women, the criminal involvement of family, friends, and neighbors were more likely to integrate them into the criminal world than into referral networks for legal and stable employment. For others, immersion in crime during childhood and early adolescence marginalized them early on from interest in or access to job contacts in the licit workaday world.

But, for those women who had some experience in the secondary labor market, commitment to criminal careers eventually ended their involvement in legal work. Denise, who earlier described her job experiences, told us about her break with marginal labor:

> Well, I still went from job to job pulling new scams. Worked for some lawyers and ran a prostitution thing out of their office. I quit working for the lawyers and with my two babies of my own and I got on welfare. Once I had that system figured out, I took the bus over to another town, and, uh, I got on welfare out there. I used a wig and glasses, somebody else's baby, and I had a birth certificate printed up with my name, and I go on welfare out there too. I tried this from town to town. I was collecting numerous checks. It was good money.
>
> But there was more money to be made. About when I was 20, I started to sell drugs with my father and uncle. I made about $1500 a day! I dealt heroin for about two years. Then I went into business for myself. I sold heroin and coke. I was clearing $4500 to $5500 a week.

For other women, drug use exerted a strong influence on their ultimate commitment to the illegal economy over employment in the secondary labor market. Even at the outset, commitment to licit work was weak. But, with the onset of cocaine smoking, such investments diminished and quickly disappeared. Further, once addicted to harder drugs, i.e., crack cocaine, most of the women in this study experienced the ultimate rupture in ties to the licit workaday world and a decline in the importance of excitement, adventure, and peer participation in criminal activities. Thus, drug addiction and not peers came to organize most of daily life's activities.

Barbara's involvement in legitimate work ended with her abuse of crack:

> I worked for the Board of Education as a teacher's aide from like '84 to '86. When I was working I didn't need to be involved in crime at that time because I had my own income. But I was smoking crack. I was fired from the Board of Ed because of my lateness and absenteeism.
>
> I got so involved in getting high that I was kind of glad that I didn't have to get up in the morning anymore. I didn't care about that job or those people on that job, or even the kids like I was supposed to. That's when I started gettin' into crime.

For some, cocaine smoking intensified the illicit activities in which they already were active. Evelyn recalls:

> What happen was I didn't have any money, I didn't have any way of getting a job, I was already addicted into crack. Like I said, my parents threw me out of the house, there was no way of getting any money from them or anything like that, I had bumped into people who were selling, and I got connected with them Two Spots selling drugs with their bosses. I said [I] can help you out, be your lookout or whatever, and from there I started working and I met the bosses and I started working like that.

From Some Involvement in the Legal Economy to Immersion in the Cocaine Economy and Ultimate Withdrawal From Crime as Work

While the women's stories show that illicit behaviors were continuous over time, their intensification suggests some important transitions. These transitions were structured by economic changes and social opportunities as well as key developments within drug markets. For instance, the development of the cocaine economy created opportunities for drug selling that did not exist in prior, especially heroin, markets. The changing economic structure of inner-city neighborhoods also created the possibility of changes in gender roles that in the past determined options for status and income within street drug networks.

At one time, women were excluded from selling by rigid gender roles and male hegemony in deviant street networks. The expanding cocaine economy and the increasing presence of women in the public domain may have neutralized the social processes that in the past consigned them to secondary roles in street networks. As a result, the women were able to form new organizations for drug selling, or pursue independent careers in drug selling.

For Gayle, making money through drug selling was her career ambition:

> I sold all kinds of drugs. I knew from the start that I wanted to be big in this. From weed I went to selling heroin and to coke. I started dealing weed at 15. I used to steal weed from my father and deal it. Somebody approached me to deal crank [speed]. I was making $200 a week. I sold in this parking lot where kids hung out. I made $800 to $900 a week from speed.
>
> Then I sold heroin. I already had the knowledge of dealing. I went straight to somebody who sold heroin. The idea was strictly to make money. At first I sold it myself. Then I would cut ounces and bag it and let my female friends sell it for me off the street. I was making $2500 a week. I dealt heroin for years and I started dealing coke. At this point I really learned how to make lots of money selling drugs.

Viewing women's involvement in drug markets in economic and career terms suggests an active role in decision-making. Earlier deterministic conceptions of women and drugs described a passive drift into the secondary roles of hustling and prostitution in a street world dominated by men. However, the accounts provided by the women in this [chapter] indicate that within contemporary drug markets, women often made decisions to enter based on a logical evaluation of career options. Here, the women considered both economic (wages) and nonpecuniary (status) returns from work in the secondary labor market. Furthermore, they realistically assessed their chances of obtaining economic and social support from domestic arrangements. Recognizing their constrained options, these women opted for illicit work which to them seemed to represent a rational choice.

Stephanie's account reflects this weighing of options:

> Well, I've been working off and on in different cashiers and stuff like since I'm 15 years old. I always knew that a woman couldn't depend on a man to take care of her. I grew up on Public Assistance. I saw how it affected my mom when we on PA. People always coming to check up on your home.
>
> So, I knew I would have to get a career or something. But work was just menial jobs to me, and they really didn't matter.
>
> But then I saw that dealing drugs was a way to make real money. I started free-lancing. I purchased coke from a guy that I used to cop for myself. So I began to bring people to him. But since I still had a job, in the hair business there's a lot of drugs flowing. So I used to just buy in large quantities and sell to people at work. I sold to people I knew, who I knew were into drugs. When I got off from work, I usually went to a friend's house that I know got high. I sat and got high with them, and I usually sold to whoever was in their home.

For Stephanie and many of the other women, criminal career choices provided them with higher incomes than were reachable by their peers in conventional careers. Furthermore, their involvement and success in these career trajectories placed them in contexts offering status (Williams 1989; Padilla 1992), excitement (Adler 1985; Anderson 1990), and commodities.

Dealing also helped many women avoid or exit from the types of street hustling, including prostitution, that characterized women's illicit income-generating strategies (Goldstein et al. 1992; Ouellet et al. 1993; Ratner 1993). Stephanie's preference for dealing was typical among the women we studied:

> You see, as a prostitute or hooker, you know, I don't know. For me it's like, uh, you would rather sell drugs or even rob somebody than to perform a service. The last thing I wanted to do is lay down for somebody. I'd rather deal or rip people off.

Further, dealing provided new ways to expand their traditionally limited roles, statuses and incomes within the street economy.

For many of the women in our study, however, their involvement in the workaday world of criminal enterprise was shortlived. The same drug—crack—that opened new career opportunities for a lot of them, also brought many of them down. Crack *abuse* resulted in their immersion in a social world where options became narrower and exploitation more likely (Rosenbaum 1981). The narrowing options reflected both the social contexts where crack was used and the effects of the drug itself.

Similar to heroin use in past eras, heavy crack use closed off social exits from drug use or hustling (Fagan 1994b; Rosenbaum 1981). One woman said that the intense pleasure from smoking crack, and the reinforcement when it was repeated, made it impossible "to make any space between [herself] and the world where [she] smoked it."

Reinarman et al. (1989) described the isolation that accompanies obsessive crack use, the suspicions toward friends and family members, the withdrawal from social interactions, the rejection of activities that do not lead to refilling the pipe, and the cashing of limited economic and social assets in pursuit of an elusive but mythically powerful high. Thus, it is not surprising that with an increase in crack use, prostitution returned as an important income source for the women who used crack.

Prolonged crack use eventually led to deeper immersion in the social scenes and behaviors that limited their participation in both the licit and illicit work and social worlds. Although some walked away from crack after experimentation or maintained limits on their use of crack, others immersed themselves in crack use and reconstructed their social and economic lives to accommodate their frequent crack use.

The point of immersion into the world of crack was an important turning point for the women in our study. Their *economic* lives, for instance, became increasingly intertwined with their *social* worlds. They organized their lives around drugs and immersed themselves in those activities and with those people with whom they shared economic and social behaviors. Their roles and identities, as well as their primary sources of status and income, became defined, exclusively, within these street networks. Their options for transition to legal work, marriage, or educational settings were limited. And, their engulfment in street networks reinforced their pathway into an abyss. Any notion of a "calculus" disappeared as "chasing the pipe" became the one and only goal of daily life.

For the majority of women, then, the problem of maintaining an addiction came to take precedence over other interests and participation in both the legal and illegal work worlds. The women also came to define themselves in relationship to their drug problems. They were "junkies," "crackheads," or "cokebitches." Few women came to see themselves as criminals, workers, or in any way other than as addicts. Whatever deviant behaviors they engaged in came to be justified by their "drug compulsion."

The increased salience or primacy of their drug habits led to their "role engulfment." Schur pointed out that one major consequence of the processes through which deviant identity is ascribed is the tendency "of the deviator to become 'caught up in' a deviant role . . . that his behavior is increasingly organized 'around' the role . . . and that cultural expectations attached to the role come to have precedence in the organization of his general way of life" (Schur 1971, 69). As a result, the women progressively became totally immersed in the networks of the drug markets. They became committed to the drug world's norms, values, and lifestyle, and they limited their involvement with nondeviant individuals and groups.

As the circumstances of the women's lives changed, and they became more engulfed in the drug world, it became less and less likely that they actively considered working, even at crime. Thus, for the majority of the women in our study, the short period between adolescence and adulthood took them through various positions vis-à-vis the workaday worlds. For many there was, indeed, an early engagement in the legal economy; all went on to embrace the social and pecuniary benefits of criminal participation; and most disengaged totally from both economies, immersed instead in an all-consuming search for the next hit of crack.

Conclusion

There remains little doubt that women's experiences within the worlds of licit and illicit work remain gendered. This is the case, especially, as one reaches through the upper echelons of both the primary and illegal labor markets. In the primary market, women's gains during the 1970s and 80s were tempered by their placement in lower status specialties, less desirable work settings, lower paying industries and professions, and part-time rather than full-time work (Baca Zinn and Eitzen 1998; Jacobs 1989; Reskin and Roos 1990; Herz and Wooten 1996).

In terms of the upper levels of criminal networks, women continued to confront sex discrimination. In part, the ethnic and family segmentation of drug labor markets made it difficult for women to achieve higher ranks. The retail drug trades, particularly in immigrant communities, reproduced traditional perceptions of women's limited capabilities. Thus, women involved in the drug trade in Hispanic communities were often refused access to upper level roles that required the routine use of violence or involved the handling of large sums of money or drugs (Williams 1989; Waterston 1993).

However, such a pattern seems somewhat moderated in both the legal secondary labor and the lower levels of illicit street markets. In both these venues, the 1980s opened doors for inner-city women. In terms of the secondary labor market, transformations in the economy resulted in poor women having greater success than their male counterparts in claiming service sector and clerical jobs (Baca Zinn and Eitzen 1998; Wilson 1987). At the same time, inner-city women were faced with new opportunities that were brought about by demographic, social, and particularly, drug market changes. These opportunities resulted in increased participation in street crime as well as greater diversification in roles and statuses and types of crimes. For instance, most of the women crack dealers were involved in direct sales either in curbside or indoor locations, a relatively rare role in earlier drug markets (Baskin and Sommers 1998; Johnson et al. 1985).

Nonetheless, the "success" of women in street crimes such as robbery and drug distribution was temporary. And, it is perhaps the transitory nature of their fortuity that is most the result of gendered life experiences. Despite evidence that women enter into street crime for many of the same reasons as their male counterparts (Baskin and Sommers 1998; Miller 1998) and are more successful at avoiding legal sanctions, they are less successful than men at avoiding the pitfalls of addiction. Furthermore, despite the doors opened to these women as a result of changes associated with crack cocaine, it was also this drug that made their downfall so dramatic and their return to gendered crimes, such as prostitution, almost unavoidable.

Again, the role that crack cocaine played in the lives of inner-city women during the 1980s cannot be minimized. It was far reaching and profound. Unlike the underrepresentation of females in street heroin scenes (Rosenbaum 1981), several studies have documented that women accounted for almost 50 percent of crack customers (Bourgois and Dunlap 1993; Deschenes 1988; Greenleaf 1989). Furthermore, whereas males who worked in crack distribution during this time period were less likely to use crack (Ratner 1993), this was not the case for women. In addition, the effects of crack use on females were far more serious than for males (Ouellet et al. 1993) resulting in greater depravation, devastation, and return to prostitution (Bourgois and Dunlap 1993).

In conclusion, the women we interviewed were members of distinct communities that mediated between them and the larger society. It was within these local communities that the women interacted and made decisions regarding school, family, and work. Additionally, it was within these local communities that they devised ways of handling the exigencies that were imposed by the larger economic and political structures. Community levels of family dysfunction, economic and social dislocation, and changing demographics as well as the presence of illegitimate opportunities all contributed to a landscape in which decisions were made concerning key aspects of everyday life, including work.

These landscapes, though, exist within specific time frames. As such, they are dynamic. Therefore, changes both in legal and illegal labor markets as well as in gender socialization should be considered in future research. In this way, we will be able to understand better the complex processes that influence local criminal and drug career decisions. Certainly, it will be interesting to see whether the decline in crack cocaine markets in inner-city neighborhoods have had any impact on women's roles on the street.

Questions for Thought and Discussion

1. According to the authors, what is the relationship between employment opportunities and crime?
2. How does this relationship differ between men and women?
3. How does drug use fit into this pattern?
4. What theory or theories of criminal behavior are illustrated in this research?

Note

1. Similar to the primary labor sector, in the secondary sector there is a white-collar upper level (which includes sales and clerical workers), where working conditions, pay, and benefits are better than in the blue-collar lower level (private household, laborer, and most service jobs). Turnover is high in both levels of this sector because these workers have relatively few marketable skills and are easily replaced (Kelly 1991).

References

Adler, Patricia. 1992. "The Post Phase of Deviant Careers: Reintegrating Drug Traffickers." *Deviant Behavior* 13:103–126.

———. 1985. *Wheeling and Dealing: An Ethnography of an Upper-Level Dealing and Smuggling Community.* New York: Columbia University Press.

Anderson, Elijah. 1994. "The Code of the Streets." *The Atlantic Monthly* May:81–94.

———. 1990. *Streetwise.* Chicago: University of Chicago Press.

Baca Zinn, Maxine and Stanley D. Eitzen. 1998. "Economic Restructuring and Systems of Inequality." In Margaret L. Andersen and Patricia Hill Collins (eds.) *Race, Class and Gender: An Anthology.* Belmont, CA: Wadsworth Publishing Co.

Baskin, Deborah and Ira Sommers. 1998. *Casualties of Community Disorder: Women's Careers in Violent Crime.* Boulder, CO: Westview Press.

Biernacki, P. 1986. *Pathways From Heroin Addiction: Recovery Without Treatment.* Philadelphia: Temple University Press.

Blackburn, M., D. Bloom, and R. Freeman. 1990. "The Declining Economic Position of Less Skilled American Men." In Gary Burtless (ed.) *A Future of Lousy Jobs? The Changing Structure of U.S. Wages.* Washington, DC: The Brookings Institution.

Bourgois, Phillipe. 1995. *In Search of Respect: Selling Crack in El Barrio.* New York: Cambridge University Press.

Bourgois, Phillipe and Eloise Dunlap. 1993. "Exorcising Sex for Crack: An Ethnographic Perspective From Harlem." In Mitchell S. Ratner (ed.) *Crack Pipe as Pimp: An Ethnographic Investigation of Sex-for-Crack Exchanges.* New York: Lexington Books.

Brown, Lyn Mikel and Carol Gilligan. 1992. *Meeting at the Crossroads: Women's Psychology and Girls' Development.* New York: Ballantine Books.

Chiricos, Ted. 1987. "Rates of Crime and Unemployment: An Analysis of Aggregate Research." *Social Problems* 334:187–212.

Corcoran, Mary and Susan Parrott. 1992. "Black Women's Economic Progress." Paper presented at the Research Conference on the Urban Underclass: Perspectives from the Social Sciences. Ann Arbor, MI: June.

Crutchfield, Robert. 1997. "Labor Markets, Employment, and Crime." *National Institute of Justice Research Preview.* Washington, DC: U.S. Department of Justice.

———. 1989. "Labor Stratification and Violent Crime." *Social Forces* 68 (2):513–530.

Curry, David, Richard Ball, and Robert J. Fox. 1994. "Gang Crime and Law Enforcement Record Keeping." *Research in Brief.* Washington, DC: National Institute of Justice.

Deschenes, Elizabeth. 1988. "Cocaine Use and Pregnancy." Drug Abuse Series Paper of the Drug Abuse Information and Monitoring Project, California Department of Alcohol and Drug Programs, Health and Welfare Agency.

Fagan, Jeffrey. 1996. "Legal and Illegal Work: Crime, Work and Unemployment." In Burton Weisbrod and James Worthy (eds.) *Dealing With Urban Crisis: Linking Research to Action.* Evanston, IL: Northwestern University Press.

———. 1994a. "Legal and Illegal Work: Crime, Work and Unemployment." Paper presented at Metropolitan Assembly on Urban Problems: Linking Research to Action. Northwestern University, Center for Urban Affairs and Policy Research.

———. 1994b. "Women and Drugs Revisited: Female Participation in the Cocaine Economy." *Journal of Drug Issues* 24:179–226.

———. 1992. "Drug Selling and Licit Income in Distressed Neighborhoods: The Economic Lives of Drug Users and Drug Sellers." In Adele Harrell and George Peterson (eds.) *Drugs, Crime and Social Isolation: Barriers to Urban Opportunity.* Washington, DC: The Urban Institute Press.

———. 1989. "Cessation of Family Violence: Deterrence and Dissuasion." In Lloyd Ohlin and Michael Tonry (eds.) *Family Violence,* Volume 11 of *Crime and Justice: An Annual Review of Research.* Chicago: University of Chicago Press.

Fagan, Jeffrey and Richard Freeman. 1994. "Crime and Work." Unpublished. Newark, NJ: Rutgers University, School of Criminal Justice.

Freeman, Richard. 1992. "Crime and the Employment of Disadvantaged Youths." In George Peterson and Wayne Vroman (eds.) *Urban Labor Markets and Job Opportunities.* Washington, DC: Urban Institute Press.

———. 1983. "Crime and Unemployment." In James Q. Wilson (ed.) *Crime and Public Policy.* San Francisco: Institute for Contemporary Studies Press.

Goldstein, Paul, Laurence Ouellet, and Michael Fendrich. 1992. "From Bag Brides to Skeezers: An Historical Perspective on Sex-for-Drugs Behavior." *Journal of Psychoactive Drugs* 24:349–361.

Good, David H., Maureen Pirog-Good, and Robin Sickles. 1986. "An Analysis of Youth Crime and Employment Patterns." *Journal of Quantitative Criminology* 2:219–236.

Greenleaf, V. D. 1989. *Women and Cocaine: Personal Stories of Addiction and Recovery.* Los Angeles: Lowell House.

Grogger, Jeffrey. 1994. "Criminal Opportunities, Youth Crime, and Young Men's Labor Supply." Unpublished. Department of Economics, University of California, Santa Barbara.

Hagan, John. 1993. "The Social Embeddedness of Crime and Unemployment." *Criminology* 31:465–492.

Hagan, John and Alberto Pallioni. 1990. "The Social Reproduction of a Criminal Class in Working Class London, Circa 1950–1980." *American Journal of Sociology* 96:265–299.

Hagedorn, John. 1994. "Neighborhoods, Markets and Gang Drug Organization." *Journal of Research in Crime and Delinquency* 31:264–294.

Hagedorn, John and Parry Macron. 1988. *People and Folks: Gangs, Crime and the Underclass in a Rustbelt City.* Chicago: Lake View Press.

Herz, Diane and Barbara Wooten. 1996. "Women in the Workforce: An Overview." In Cynthia Costello and Barbara Kivimae Krimgold (eds.) *The American Woman, 1996–1997.* New York: W. W. Norton.

Hunt, Dana. 1990. "Drugs and Consensual Crimes: Drug Dealing and Prostitution." In Michael Tonry and James Q. Wilson (eds.) *Drugs and Crime. Crime and Justice, Volume 13.* Chicago: University of Chicago Press.

Inciardi, James A., Dorothy Lockwood, and Anne Pottieger. 1993. *Women and Crack Cocaine.* New York: Macmillan.

Jacobs, Jerry. 1989. "Long Term Trends in Occupational Sex Segregation." *American Journal of Sociology* 95:160–173.

Johnson, Bruce, Paul Goldstein, Edward Preble, James Schmeidler, Douglas Lipton, Barry Spunt, and Thomas Miller. 1985. *Taking Care of Business: The Economics of Crime by Heroin Abusers.* Lexington, MA: Lexington Books.

Kelly, Rita Mae. 1991. *The Gendered Economy: Work, Careers, and Success.* Newbury Park, CA: Sage Publications.

Liebow, Elliot. 1967. *Tally's Corner: A Study of Negro Streetcorner Men.* Boston, MA: Little, Brown and Company.

Maher, Lisa and Kathleen Daly. 1996. "Women in the Street-Level Drug Economy: Continuity or Change?" *Criminology* 34:465–492.

Mieczkowski, Thomas. 1994. "The Experiences of Women Who Sell Crack: Some Descriptive Data From the Detroit Crack Ethnography Project." *Journal of Drug Issues* 24:227–248.

Miller, Jody. 1998. "Up It Up: Gender and the Accomplishment of Street Robbery." *Criminology* 36:37–66.

Moore, Joan. 1992. "Institutionalized Youth Gangs: Why White Fence and El Hoyo Maravilla Change So Slowly." In J. Fagan (ed.) *The Ecology of Crime and Drug Use in Inner Cities.* New York: Social Science Research Council.

———. 1991. *Going Down to the Barrio: Homeboys and Homegirls in Change.* Philadelphia: Temple University Press.

Ouellet, Lawrence, W. Wayne Weibel, A. D. Jimenez, and W. A. Johnson. 1993. "Crack Cocaine and the Transformation of Prostitution in Three Chicago Neighborhoods." In Mitchell Ratner (ed.) *Crack Pipe as Pimp An Ethnographic Investigation in Sex-for-Crack Exchanges.* New York: Lexington Books.

Padilla, Felix. 1992. *The Gang as an American Enterprise.* Boston, MA: Northeastern University Press.

Pipher, Mary. 1994. *Reviving Ophelia: Saving the Selves of Adolescent Girls.* New York: Ballantine Books.

Ratner, Mitchell. 1993. "Sex, Drugs and Public Policy: Studying and Understanding the Sex-for-Crack Phenomenon." In Mitchell Ratner (ed.) *Crack Pipe as Pimp: An Ethnographic Investigation of Sex-for-Crack Exchanges.* New York: Lexington Books.

Reinarman, Craig, Dan Waldorf, and Sheila Murphy. 1989. "The Call of the Pipe: Freebasing and Crack Use as Norm-Bound Episodic Compulsion." Paper presented at the Annual Meeting of the American Society of Criminology, Reno, Nevada, November.

Reskin, Barbara and Patricia Roos. 1990. *Job Queues, Gender Cues: Explaining Women's Inroads Into Male Occupations.* Philadelphia, PA: Temple University Press.

Reuter, Peter, Robert MacCoun, and Patrick Murphy. 1990. *Money From Crime.* Report R3894. Santa Monica, CA: The Rand Corporation.

Rosenbaum, Marsha. 1981. *Women and Heroin.* New Brunswick, NJ: Rutgers University Press.

Rosenfeld, Richard, and Steven Messner. 1989. *Crime and the American Dream.* Albany: SUNY Press.

Sampson, Robert J. and John H. Laub. 1993. *Crime in the Making.* Cambridge, MA: Harvard University Press.

Schur, E. 1971. *Labeling Deviant Behavior: Its Sociological Implications.* New York: Harper and Row.

Shover, Neil. 1985. *Aging Criminals.* Newbury Park, CA: Sage.

Sommers, I., D. Baskin, and J. Fagan. 1996. "The Structural Relationship Between Drug Use, Drug Dealing and Other Income Support Activities Among Women Drug Dealers." *Journal of Drug Issues* 26:975–1006.

Sullivan, Mercer. 1989. *Getting Paid.* Ithaca, NY: Cornell University Press.

Taylor, Avril. 1993. *Women Drug Users: An Ethnography of a Female Injecting Community.* Oxford: Clarendon Press.

Taylor, Carl. 1993. *Girls, Gangs, Women and Drugs.* East Lansing: Michigan State University Press.

———. 1990. "Gang Imperialism." In R. Huff (ed.) *Gangs in America.* Newbury Park, CA: Sage Publications.

Tienda, Marta. 1989. "Neighborhood Effects and the Formation of the Underclass." Paper presented at the Annual Meeting of the American Sociological Association, San Francisco, August.

Uggen, Christopher, Irving Piliavin, and Ross Matsueda. 1992. *Job Programs and Criminal Desistance.* Washington, DC: The Urban Institute.

Vicusi, W. Kip. 1986. "The Risks and Rewards of Criminal Activity: A Comprehensive Test of Criminal Deterrence." *Journal of Labor Economics* 4:317–340.

Waterston, Alisse. 1993. *Street Addicts in the Political Economy.* Philadelphia: Temple University Press.

Williams, Terry. 1989. *The Cocaine Kids.* New York: Addison-Wesley.

Wilson, William J. 1996. *When Work Disappears: The World of the New Urban Poor.* New York: Alfred Knopf.

———. 1987. *The Truly Disadvantaged.* Chicago: University of Chicago Press.

Witte, Ann and Helen Tauchen. 1994. "Work and Crime: An Exploration Using Panel Data." Unpublished paper.

Chapter 7
Stick-up, Street Culture, and Offender Motivation

Bruce A. Jacobs
Richard T. Wright

The decision to commit robbery, then, is motivated by a perceived need for cash. Why does this need express itself as robbery? Presumably the offenders have other means of obtaining money. Why do they choose robbery over legal work? Why do they decide to commit robbery rather than borrow money from friends or relatives? Most important, why do they select robbery to the exclusion of other income-generating crimes? Motivation is the central causal variable driving criminal behavior. However, other variables must be considered. While offenders may be motivated to commit a crime, motivation is only a necessary and not a sufficient condition for a crime to occur. Foreground factors such as need for cash, stresses, and pressures of street life are the precipitating factors in the criminal event. In this chapter, the authors explore the decision-making strategies of street predators through interviews with 86 active armed robbers. They found that the decision to commit a robbery is mediated and shaped by active participation in street culture with its constituent conduct norms, representing an essential intervening variable linking criminal motivation to background risk factors and subjective foreground conditions. The conclusion reached is that offenders, when faced with a pressing need for cash, tend to resort to robbery because they know of no other course of action, legal or illegal, that offers as quick and easy a way out of their financial difficulties. Stopping such criminals—in the absence of lengthy incapacitation—is not likely to be successful. Getting offenders to "go straight" is analogous to telling a lawful citizen to "relinquish his history, companions, thoughts, feelings, and fears, and replace them with [something] else" (Fleisher, 1995: 240).

Motivation is the central, yet arguably the most assumed, causal variable in the etiology of criminal behavior. Obviously, persons commit crimes because they are motivated to do so, and virtually no offense can occur in the absence of motivation. Though the concept inheres implicitly or explicitly in every influential theory of crime, this is far from saying that its treatment has been comprehensive, exhaustive, or precise (but see Tittle, 1995). In many ways, motivation is criminology's dirty little secret—manifest yet murky, presupposed but elusive, everywhere and nowhere. If there is a bogey-man lurking in our discipline's theoretical shadows, motivation may well be it.

Much of the reason for this can be located in the time-honored, positivistic tradition of finding the one factor, or set of factors, that accounts for it. Causality has been called criminology's "Holy Grail" (Groves and Lynch, 1990: 360), the quest for which makes other disciplinary pursuits seem tangential, sometimes inconsequential. The search typically revolves around identification of background risk factors (Katz, 1988)—behavioral correlates—that establish nonspurious relationships with criminal behavior (Groves and Lynch, 1990: 358). A panoply of such factors have been implicated over many decades of research—spanning multiple levels, as well as units, of analyses. They include, among other things, anomie, blocked opportunities, deviant self-identity, status frustration, weak social bonds, low self-control, social disorganization, structural oppression, unemployment, age, gender, class, race, deviant peer relations, marital status, body type, IQ, and personality (see e.g., Akers, 1985; Becker, 1963; Chambliss and Seidman, 1971; Cloward and Ohlin, 1960; Cohen, 1955; Cornish and Clarke, 1986; Felson, 1987; Hirschi, 1969; Merton, 1938; Miller, 1958; Quinney, 1970; Sampson and Laub, 1992; Shaw and McKay, 1942; Sutherland, 1947).

Common to all such factors, however, is their independent status from the "foreground" of criminal decision making—the immediate phenomenological context in which decisions to offend are activated (see also Groves and Lynch, 1990; Katz, 1988). Though background factors may predispose persons to crime, they fail to explain why two individuals with identical risk factor profiles do not offend equally (see e.g., Colvin and Pauly, 1983), why persons with particular risk factors go long periods of time without offending, why individuals without the implicated risk factors offend, why persons offend but not in the particular way a theory directs them to, or why persons who are not determined to commit a crime one moment become determined to do so the next (see Katz, 1988: 3–4; see also Tittle, 1995, on "theoretical precision"). Decisions to offend, like all social action, do not take place in a vacuum. Rather, they are bathed in an "ongoing process of human existence" (Bottoms and Wiles, 1992: 19) and mediated by prevailing situational and subcultural conditions.

In this article we attend to these important foreground dynamics, exploring the decision-making processes of active armed robbers in real-life settings and circumstances. Our aim is to understand how and why these offenders move from an unmotivated state to one in which they are determined to commit robbery. We argue that while the decision to commit robbery stems most directly from a perceived need for fast cash, this decision is activated, mediated, and channeled by participation in street culture. Street culture, and its constituent conduct norms, represents an essential intervening variable linking criminal motivation to background risk factors and subjective foreground conditions. . . .

Money, Motivation, and Street Culture

Fast Cash

With few exceptions, the decision to commit a robbery arises in the face of what offenders perceive to be pressing need for fast cash (see also Conklin, 1972; Feeney, 1986; Gabor et al., 1987; Tunnell, 1992). Eighty of 81 offenders who spoke directly to the issue of motivation said that they did robberies simply because they needed money. Many lurched from one financial crisis to the next, the frequency with which they committed robbery being governed largely by the amount of money—or lack of it—in their pockets:

> [The idea of committing a robbery] comes into your mind when your pockets are low; it speaks very loudly when you need things and you are not able to get what you need. It's not a want, it's things that you need, . . . things that if you don't have the money, you have the artillery to go and get it. That's the first thing on my mind; concentrate on how I can get some more money. I don't think there is any one factor that precipitates the commission of a crime, . . . I think it's just the conditions. I think the primary factor is being without. Rent is coming up. A few months ago, the landlord was gonna put us out, rent due, you know. Can't get no money no way else; ask family and friends, you might try a few other ways of getting the money and, as a last resort, I can go get some money [by committing a robbery].

Many offenders appeared to give little thought to the offense until they found themselves unable to meet current expenses.

> [I commit a robbery] about every few months. There's no set pattern, but I guess it's really based on the need. If there is a period of time where there is no need of money . . . then it's not necessary to go out and rob. It's not like I do [robberies] for fun.

The above claims conjure up an image of reluctant criminals doing the best they can to survive in circumstances not of their own making. In one sense, this image is not so far off the mark. Of the 59 offenders who specified a particular use for the proceeds of their crimes, 19 claimed that they needed the cash for basic necessities, such as food or shelter. For them, robbery allegedly was a matter of day-to-day survival. At the same time, the notion that these offenders were driven by conditions entirely beyond their control strains credulity. Reports of "opportunistic" robberies confirm this, that is, offenses motivated by serendipity rather than basic human need:

> If I had $5,000, I wouldn't do [a robbery] like tomorrow. But [i]f I got $5,000 today and I seen you walkin' down the street and you look like you got some money in your pocket, I'm gonna take a chance and see. It's just natural. . . . If you see an opportunity, you take that opportunity. . . . It doesn't matter if I have $5,000 in my pocket, if I see you walkin' and no one else around and it look like you done went in the store and bought somethin' and pulled some money out of your pocket and me or one of my partners has peeped this, we gonna approach you. That's just the way it goes.

Need and opportunity, however, cannot be considered outside the open-ended quest for excitement and sensory stimulation that shaped much of the offenders' daily activities. Perhaps the most central of pursuits in street culture, "life as party" revolves around "the enjoyment of 'good times' with minimal concern for obligations and commitments that are external to the . . . immediate social setting" (Shover and Honaker, 1992: 283).

While the offenders often referred to such activities as partying, there is a danger in accepting their comments at face value. Many gambled, used drugs, and drank alcohol as if there were no tomorrow; they pursued these activities with an intensity and grim determination that suggested something far more serious was at stake. Illicit street action is no party, at least not in the conventional sense of the term. Offenders typically demonstrate little or no inclination to exercise personal restraint. Why should they? Instant gratification and hedonistic sensation seeking are quite functional for those seeking pleasure in what may objectively be viewed as a largely pleasureless world.

The offenders are easily seduced by life as party, at least in part because they view their future prospects as bleak and see little point in long-range planning. As such, there is no mileage to be gained by deferred gratification:

> I really don't dwell on [the future]. One day I might not wake up. I don't even think about what's important to me. What's important to me is getting mine [now].

The offenders' general lack of social stability an absence of conventional sources of support only fueled such a mindset. The majority called the streets home for extended periods of time; a significant number of offenders claimed to seldom sleep at the same address for more than a few nights in a row (see also Fleisher, 1995). Moving from place to place as the mood struck them, these offenders essentially were urban nomads in a perpetual search for good times. The volatile streets and alleyways that crisscrossed St. Louis's crime-ridden central city neighborhoods provided their conduit (see also Stein and McCall, 1994).

Keeping up Appearances

The open-ended pursuit of sensory stimulation was but one way these offenders enacted the imperatives of street culture. No less important was the fetishized consumption of personal, nonessential, status-enhancing items. Shover and Honaker (1992: 283) have argued that the unchecked pursuit of such items—like anomic participation in illicit street action—emerges directly from conduct norms of street culture. The code of the streets (Anderson, 1990) calls for the bold display of the latest status symbol clothing and accessories, a look that loudly proclaims the wearer to be someone who has overcome, if only temporarily, the financial difficulties faced by others on the street corner (see e.g., Katz, 1988). To be seen as "with it," one must flaunt the material trappings of success. The quest is both symbolic and real; such purchases serve as self-enclosed and highly efficient referent systems that assert one's essential character (Shover, 1996) in no uncertain terms.

> You ever notice that some people want to be like other people . . . ? They might want to dress like this person, like dope dealers and stuff like that. They go out there [on the street corner] in diamond jewelry and stuff. "Man, I wish I was like him!" You got to make some kind of money [to look like that], so you want to make a quick hustle.

The functionality of offenders' purchases was tangential, perhaps irrelevant. The overriding goal was to project an image of "cool transcendence" (Katz, 1988), that, in the minds of offenders, knighted them members of a mythic street aristocracy.

Obviously, the relentless pursuit of high living quickly becomes expensive. Offenders seldom had enough cash in their pockets to sustain this lifestyle for long. Even when they did make the occasional "big score," their disdain for long-range planning and desire to live for the moment encouraged spending with reckless abandon. That money earned illegally holds "less intrinsic value" than cash secured through legitimate work only fueled their spendthrift ways (Walters, 1990: 147). The way money is obtained, after all, is a "powerful determinant of how it is defined, husbanded, and spent" (Shover, 1996: 140). Some researchers have gone so far as to suggest that through care-free spending, persistent criminals seek to establish the very conditions that drive them back to crime (Katz, 1988). Whether offenders spend money in a deliberate attempt to create these conditions is open to question; the respondents in our sample gave no indication of doing so. No matter, offenders were under almost constant pressure to generate funds. To the extent that robbery alleviated this stress, it nurtured a tendency for them to view the offense as a reliable method for dealing with similar pressures in the future. A self-enclosed cycle of reinforcing behavior was thereby triggered (see also Lemert, 1953).

Why Robbery?

The decision to commit robbery, then, is motivated by a perceived need for cash. Why does this need express itself as robbery? Presumably the offenders have other means of obtaining money. Why do they choose robbery over legal work? Why do they decide to commit robbery rather than borrow money from friends or relatives? Most important, why do they select robbery to the exclusion of other income-generating crimes?

Legal Work

That the decision to commit robbery typically emerges in the course of illicit street action suggests that legitimate employment is not a realistic solution. Typically, the offenders' need for cash is so pressing and immediate that legal work, as a viable money-making strategy, is untenable: Payment and effort are separated in space and time and these offenders will not, or cannot, wait. Moreover, the jobs realistically available to them—almost all of whom were unskilled and poorly educated—pay wages that fall far short of the funds required to support a cash-intensive lifestyle:

> Education-wise, I fell late on the education. I just think it's too late for that. They say it's never too late, but I'm too far gone for that. . . . I've thought about [getting a job], but I'm too far gone I guess. . . . I done seen more money come out of [doing stick-ups] than I see working.

Legitimate employment also was perceived to be overly restrictive. Working a normal job requires one to take orders, conform to a schedule, minimize informal peer interaction, show up sober and alert, and limit one's freedom of movement for a given period of time.

The "conspicuous display of independence" is a bedrock value on which street-corner culture rests (Shover and Honaker, 1992: 284): To be seen as cool one must do as one pleases. This ethos clearly conflicts with the demands of legitimate employment. Indeed, robbery appealed to a number of offenders precisely because it allowed them to flaunt their independence and escape from the rigors of legal work.

This is not to say that every offender summarily dismissed the prospect of gainful employment. Twenty-five of the 75 unemployed respondents claimed they would stop robbing if someone gave them a "good job"—the emphasis being on good:

> My desire is to be gainfully employed in the right kind of job. . . . If I had a union job making $16 or $17 [an hour], something that I could really take care of my family with, I think that I could become cool with that. Years ago I worked at one of the [local] car factories; I really wanted to be in there. It was the kind of job I'd been looking for. Unfortunately, as soon as I got in there they had a big layoff.

Others alleged that, while a job may not eliminate their offending altogether, it might well slow them down:

> [If a job were to stop me from committing robberies], it would have to be a straight up good-paying job. I ain't talkin' about no $6 an hour. . . . I'm talkin' like $10 to $11 an hour, something like that. But as far as $5 or $6 an hour, no! I would have to get like $10 or $11 an hour, full-time. Now something like that, I would probably quit doing it [robbery]. I would be working, making money, I don't think I would do it [robbery] no more. . . . I don't think I would quit [offending] altogether. It would probably slow down and then eventually I'll stop. I think [my offending] would slow down.

Even if the offenders were able to land a high-paying job, it is doubtful they would keep it for long. The relentless pursuit of street action—especially hard drug use—has a powerful tendency to undermine any commitment to conventional activities (Shover and Honaker, 1992). Life as party ensnares street-culture participants, enticing them to neglect the demands of legitimate employment in favor of enjoying the moment. Though functional in lightening the burdensome present, gambling, drinking, and drugging—for those on the street—become the proverbial "padlock on the exit door" (Davis, 1995) and fertilize the foreground in which the decision to rob becomes rooted.

Borrowing

In theory, the offenders could have borrowed cash from a friend or relative rather than resorting to crime. In practice, this was not feasible. Unemployed, unskilled, and uneducated persons caught in the throes of chronically self-defeating behavior cannot, and often do not, expect to solve their fiscal troubles by borrowing. Borrowing is a short-term solution, and loans granted must be repaid. This in itself could trigger robberies. As one offender explained, "I have people that will loan me money, [but] they will loan me money because of the work [robbery] that I do; they know they gonna get their money [back] one way or another." Asking for money also was perceived by a number of offenders to be emasculating. Given their belief that men should be self-sufficient, the mere prospect of borrowing was repugnant:

> I don't like always asking my girl for nothing because I want to let her keep her own money. . . . I'm gonna go out here and get some money.

The possibility of borrowing may be moot for the vast majority of offenders anyway. Most had long ago exhausted the patience and goodwill of helpful others; not even their closest friends or family members were willing to proffer additional cash:

> I can't borrow the money. Who gonna loan me some money? Ain't nobody gonna loan me no money. Shit, [I use] drugs and they know [that] and I rob and everything else. Ain't nobody gonna loan me no money. If they give you some money, they just give it to you; they know you ain't giving it back.

When confronted with an immediate need for money, then, the offenders perceived themselves as having little hope of securing cash quickly and legally. But this does not explain why the respondents decided to do robbery rather than some other crime. Most of them had committed a wide range of income-generating offenses in the past, and some continued to be quite versatile. Why, then, robbery?

For many, this question was irrelevant; robbery was their "main line" and alternative crimes were not considered when the pressing need for cash arose:

> I have never been able to steal, even when I was little and they would tell me just to be the watch-out man. . . . Shit, I watch out, everybody gets busted. I can't steal, but give me a pistol and I'll go get some money. . . . [Robbery is] just something I just got attached to.

Some of the offenders who favored robbery over other crimes maintained that it was safer than burglary or dope dealing:

> I feel more safer doing a robbery because doing a burglary, I got a fear of breaking into somebody's house not knowing who might be up in there. I got that fear about house burglary. . . . On robbery I can select my victims, I can select my place of business. I can watch and see who all work in there or I can rob a person and pull them around in the alley or push them up in a doorway and rob them. You don't got [that] fear of who . . . in that bedroom or somewhere in another part of the house.

A couple of offenders reported steering clear of dope selling because their strong craving for drugs made it too difficult for them to resist their own merchandise. Being one's own best customer is a sure formula for disaster (Waldorf, 1993), something the following respondent seemed to understand well:

> A dope fiend can't be selling dope because he be his best customer. I couldn't sell dope [nowadays]. I could sell a little weed or something cause I don't smoke too much of it. But selling rock [cocaine] or heroin, I couldn't do that cause I mess around and smoke it myself. [I would] smoke it all up!

Without doubt, some of the offenders were prepared to commit crimes other than robbery; in dire straits one cannot afford to be choosy. More often than not, robbery emerged as the "most proximate and performable" (Lofland, 1969: 61) offense available. The universe of money-making crimes from which these offenders realistically could pick was limited. By and large, they did not hold jobs that would allow them to violate even a low-level position of financial trust. Nor did they possess the technical know-how to commit lucrative commercial break-ins, or the interpersonal skills needed to perpetrate successful frauds. Even street-corner dope dealing was unavailable to many; most lacked the financial wherewithal to purchase baseline inventories—inventories many offenders would undoubtedly have smoked up.

The bottom line is that the offenders, when faced with a pressing need for cash, tend to resort to robbery because they know of no other course of action, legal or illegal, that offers as quick and easy a way out of their financial difficulties. . . .

Discussion

The overall picture that emerges from our research is that of offenders caught up in a cycle of expensive, self-indulgent habits (e.g., gambling, drug use, and heavy drinking) that feed on themselves and constantly call for more of the same (Lemert, 1953). It would be a mistake to conclude that these offenders are being driven to crime by genuine financial hardship; few of them are doing robberies to buy the proverbial loaf of bread to feed their children. Yet, most of their crimes are economically motivated. The offenders perceive themselves as needing money and robbery is a response to that perception.

Though background risk factors, such as pressing financial need, predispose persons to criminality, they fail to provide comprehensive, precise, and deep explanations of the situational pushes, urges, and impulses that energize actual criminal conduct (Tittle, 1995). Nor do such factors identify the "necessary and sufficient" conditions for criminal motivation to eventuate in criminal behavior. Focusing on the foreground attends to these problems. A foreground analytic approach identifies the immediate, situational factors that catalyze criminal motivation and transforms offenders from an indifferent state to one in which they are determined to commit crime. . . .

Although the streets were a prime focus of much early criminological work, the strong influence of street culture on offender motivation has largely been overlooked since (but see Baron and Hartnagel, 1997; Fleisher, 1995; Hagan and McCarthy, 1992, 1997). Below, we attempt a conceptual refocusing by exploring the criminogenic influence of street culture and its constituent conduct norms on offender decision making (see also Hagan and McCarthy, 1997). In doing so, we do not wish to make a Katzian attempt to "outgun positivism" with a sensually deterministic portrait of crime (see Groves and Lynch, 1990: 366). Our goal rather is to highlight the explanatory power and conceptual efficiency of street culture participation as a mediating foreground factor in the etiology of armed robbery.

Street culture subsumes a number of powerful conduct norms, including but not limited to, the hedonistic pursuit of sensory stimulation, disdain for conventional living, lack of future orientation, and persistent eschewal of responsibility (see Fleisher, 1995: 213–214). Street culture puts tremendous emphasis on virtues of spontaneity; it dismisses "rationality and long-range planning . . . in favor of enjoying the moment" (Shover and Honaker, 1992: 283). Offenders typically live life as if there is no tomorrow, confident that tomorrow will somehow take care of itself. On the streets, "every night is a Saturday night" (Hodgson, 1997), and the self-indulgent pursuit of trendy consumerism and open-ended street action becomes a means to this end.

The pursuit of fast living is more than symbolic or dramaturgical, it cuts to the very core of offenders' perceptions of self-identity. To be cool, hip, and "in," one must constantly prove it through conspicuous outlays of cash. The fetishized world of street-corner capitalism dictates that fiscal responsibility be jettisoned and money burned on material objects and illicit action that assert in no uncertain terms one's place in the street hierarchy. Carefree spending creates the "impression of affluence" (Wright and Decker, 1994: 44) by which offenders are judged; it serves to demonstrate that they have indeed "made it"—at least for the time. On the streets, the image one projects is not everything, it is the only thing (see Anderson, 1990). To not buy into such an approach is to abandon a source of recognition offenders can get nowhere else (see Liebow, 1967) or, worse, to stare failure full in the face. It is not hard to fathom why many offenders in our sample regarded a lack of funds as an immediate threat to their social standing.

The problem becomes one of sustenance; the reputational advantages of cash-intensive living can be appreciated and enjoyed to their fullest "only if participants moderate their involvement in it" (Shover and Honaker, 1992: 286). This requires intermittent and disciplined spending, an anomalous and ultimately untenable proposition. Offenders effectively become ensnared by their own self-indulgent habits—habits that feed on themselves and constantly call for more of the same (Lemert, 1953; Shover, 1996). These habits are expensive and create a pressing and pervasive need for cash—a need remedied through robbery but only temporarily, since the proceeds of any given robbery merely "enable" more action (Shover, 1996).[1] The seductive attractions of street life appear to take on a powerful logic of their own (Hagan and McCarthy, 1997); offenders burn money only to create (albeit inadvertently) the conditions that spark their next decision to rob. . . . Predisposing background risk factors also are represented (see Hagan and McCarthy, 1997, for a comprehensive discussion of these factors as they relate to street-culture participation).

As much as these offenders sought liberation through the hedonistic, open-ended pursuit of sensory stimulation, such a quest ultimately is both self-defeating and subordinating. Those hooked on street action may never see it this way, but objective assessments of reality are difficult to render when rationality is as severely bounded (Walsh, 1986) as it is here. Suffice it to say that, for those in our sample, the "choice" to rob occurs in a context in which rationality not only is sharply bounded, it barely exists. If one takes the influence of context seriously, most offenders "decide" to commit robbery in a social and psychological terrain bereft of realistic alternatives (Shover, 1996). Street-culture participation effectively obliterates, or at least severely circumscribes, the range of objectively available options, so much so as to be almost deterministic. Offenders typically are overwhelmed by their own predicament—emotional, financial, pharmacological, and otherwise—and see robbery as the only way out. Chronic isolation from conventional others and lifestyles only reinforces their insularity (Baron and Hartnagel, 1997: 413–414), driving them deeper and deeper into a "downward life trajectory" of ever-increasing criminal embeddedness (see Hagan and McCarthy, 1997; see also Ekland-Olson et al., 1984, on "role engulfment"). . . .

Being a street robber is more than a series of offenses that allow one to meet some arbitrarily specified inclusion criteria: it is a way of behaving, a way of thinking, an approach to life (see e.g., Fleisher, 1995: 253). Stopping such criminals exogenously—in the absence of lengthy incapacitation—is not likely to be successful. Getting offenders to "go straight" is analogous to telling a lawful citizen to "relinquish his history, companions, thoughts, feelings, and fears, and replace them with [something] else" (Fleisher, 1995: 240). Self-directed going-straight talk on the part of offenders more often than not is insincere—akin to young children talking about what they're going to be when they grow up: "Young storytellers and . . . criminals . . . don't care about the [reality]; the pleasure comes in saying the words, the verbal ritual itself brings pleasure" (Fleisher, 1995: 259). Gifting offenders money, in the hopes they will reduce or stop their offending (Farrington, 1993), is similarly misguided. It is but twisted enabling and only likely to set off another round of illicit action that plunges offenders deeper into the abyss of desperation that drives them back to their next crime.

Questions for Thought and Discussion

1. According to the offenders in this study, what is the primary motivation for robbery?
2. Why do robbers say that they choose robbery over legal work?
3. What does the author mean by the "foreground" of criminal decision making?
4. What theory or theories of criminal behavior are illustrated in this research?

Note

1. The idea that these offenders are acting to restore "control balance" (Tittle, 1995) is questionable. They seem rather to be going from deficit to surplus, and back again, without ever pausing to assess their current state of equilibrium.

References

Akers, Ronald L. 1985. *Deviant Behavior: A Social Learning Approach.* 3d ed. Belmont, Calif.: Wadsworth.

Anderson, Elijah. 1990. *Streetwise.* Chicago: University of Chicago Press.

Baron, Stephen and Timothy Hartnagel. 1997. Attributions, affect, and crime: Street youths' reactions to unemployment. *Criminology* 35:409–434.

Becker, Howard S. 1963. *Outsiders.* New York: Free Press.

Bottoms, Anthony and Paul Wiles. 1992. Explanations of crime and place. In David Evans, Nigel Fyfe, and Derek Herbert (eds.), *Policing and Place: Essays in Environmental Criminology.* London: Routledge.

Chambliss, William J. and Robert Seidman. 1971. *Law, Order, and Power.* Reading, Mass.: Addison-Wesley.

Cloward, Richard A. and Lloyd E. Ohlin. 1960. *Delinquency and Opportunity.* New York: Free Press.

Cohen, Albert K. 1955. *Delinquent Boys.* New York: Free Press.

Colvin, Mark and John Pauly. 1983. A critique of criminology: Toward an integrated structural-Marxist theory of delinquent production. *American Journal of Sociology* 89:513–551.

Conklin, John. 1972. *Robbery.* Philadelphia: JB Lippincott.

Cornish, Derek B. and Ronald V. Clarke (eds.). 1986. *The Reasoning Criminal: Rational*

Choice Perspectives on Offending. New York: Springer-Verlag.

Davis, Peter. 1995. Interview, "If You Came This Way." *All Things Considered,* National Public Radio, October 12.

Ekland-Olson, Sheldon, John Lieb, and Louis Zurcher. 1984. The paradoxical impact of criminal sanctions: Some microstructural findings. *Law & Society Review* 18:159–178.

Farrington, David P. 1993. Motivations for conduct disorder and delinquency. *Development and Psychopathology* 5:225–241.

Feeney, Floyd. 1986. Robbers as decision-makers. In Derek B. Cornish and Ronald V. Clarke (eds.), *The Reasoning Criminal: Rational Choice Perspectives on Offending.* New York: Springer-Verlag.

Felson, Marcus. 1987. Routine activities in the developing metropolis. *Criminology* 25:911–931.

Fleisher, Mark S. 1995. *Beggars and Thieves: Lives of Urban Street Criminals.* Madison: University of Wisconsin Press.

Gabor, Thomas, Micheline Baril, Maurice Cusson, Daniel Elie, Marc LeBlanc, and Andre Normandeau. 1987. *Armed Robbery: Cops, Robbers, and Victims.* Springfield, Ill.: Charles C Thomas.

Groves, W. Byron and Michael J. Lynch. 1990. Reconciling structural and subjective approaches to the study of crime. *Journal of Research in Crime and Delinquency* 27:348–375.

Hagan, John and Bill McCarthy. 1992. Streetlife and delinquency. *British Journal of Sociology* 43:533–561.

———. 1997. *Mean Streets: Youth Crime and Homelessness.* Cambridge: Cambridge University Press.

Hirschi, Travis. 1969. *Causes of Delinquency.* Berkeley: University of California Press.

Hodgson, James F. 1997. *Games Pimps Play.* Toronto: Canadian Scholars' Press.

Katz, Jack. 1988. *Seductions of Crime: Moral and Sensual Attractions in Doing Evil.* New York: Basic Books.

Lemert, Edwin. 1953. An isolation and closure theory of naive check forgery. *Journal of Criminal Law, Criminology, and Police Science* 44:296–307.

Liebow, Eliot. 1967. *Tally's Corner.* Boston: Little, Brown.

Lofland, John. 1969. *Deviance and Identity.* Englewood Cliffs, NJ: Prentice-Hall.

Merton, Robert K. 1938. Social structure and anomie. *American Sociological Review* 3:672–682.

Miller, Walter B. 1958. Lower class culture as a generating milieu of gang delinquency. *Journal of Social Issues* 14:5–19.

Quinney, Richard. 1970. *The Social Reality of Crime.* Boston: Little, Brown.

Sampson, Robert J. and John H. Laub. 1992. Crime and deviance in the life course. *Annual Review of Sociology* 24:509–525.

Shaw, Clifford R. and Henry D. McKay. 1942. *Juvenile Delinquency and Urban Areas.* Chicago: University of Chicago Press.

Shover, Neal. 1996. *Great Pretenders: Pursuits and Careers of Persistent Thieves.* Boulder, Colo.: Westview.

Shover, Neal and David Honaker. 1992. The socially-bounded decision making of persistent property offenders. *Howard Journal of Criminal Justice* 31:276–293.

Stein, Michael and George McCall. 1994. Home ranges and daily rounds: Uncovering community among urban nomads. *Research in Community Sociology* 1:77–94.

Sutherland, Edwin. 1947. *Principles of Criminology.* 4th ed. Philadelphia: JB Lippincott.

Tittle, Charles R. 1995. *Control Balance: Toward a General Theory of Deviance.* Boulder, Colo.: Westview.

Tunnell, Kenneth D. 1992. *Choosing Crime: The Criminal Calculus of Property Offenders.* Chicago: Nelson-Hall.

Waldorf, Dan. 1993. Don't be your own best customer: Drug use of San Francisco gang drug sellers. *Crime, Law, and Social Change* 19:1–15.

Walsh, Dermot. 1986. Victim selection procedures among economic criminals: The rational choice perspective. In Derek B. Cornish and Ronald V. Clarke (eds.), *The Reasoning Criminal: Rational Choice Perspectives on Offending.* New York: Springer-Verlag.

Walters, Glenn. 1990. *The Criminal Lifestyle.* Newbury Park, Calif.: Sage.

Wright, Richard T. and Scott H. Decker. 1994. *Burglars on the Job.* Boston: Northeastern University Press.

Section III

Property Crime

Most crime is nonviolent, solely intended to bring financial benefit to the offender. Property crime is usually differentiated from violent crime in its lack of the use of force or serious injury to the victim. Property crimes make up more than 90 percent of all victimizations. In addition to being more frequent than violent crimes, property crimes usually occur without interaction between the victim and the criminal. In contrast, violent offenders and their victims interact with each other and are often known to each other, although stranger-to-stranger violence is becoming more common.

This section includes studies of nonviolent property offenders: burglars, thieves, and buyers and sellers of stolen property. The offenders discuss their perspectives on crime as a way of life and the strategies and decisions involved in their criminal activities.

In the first selection ("Streetlife and the Rewards of Auto Theft"), Copes examines another aspect of criminal behavior that is underresearched, especially using qualitative methods. Copes notes that this is surprising "considering the symbolic importance of automobiles to Americans and the prevalence and cost of auto theft to the public." In this article, Copes examines the decision making, motives, and rationalizations of 45 convicted auto thieves. This selection provides the reader with an in-depth exploration of the relationship between the "life as party" streetlife of the offenders and motor vehicle theft. The crimes of these respondents are primarily committed in order to maintain their indulgent lifestyles.

In the next selection ("Deciding to Commit a Burglary"), Wright and Decker argue that burglars typically decide to commit a burglary in the face of a perceived need, usually the need for money, but occasionally for such subjective needs as self-esteem, identity, or status. Burglary, according to these authors, suggests a mindset of desperation that can weaken the influence of perceived sanctions and neutralize misgivings about the morality of the act.

The article by Hochstetler and Copes ("Managing Fear to Commit Felony Theft") examines fear as an immediate influence on thieves' decision making. The authors conclude that while long-term criminal justice consequences are not factored too heavily into the decision-making processes, the immediate threats of confrontation and injury figure prominently in the criminal calculus.

In the final chapter in this section ("The Five-Finger Discount: An Analysis of Motivations for Shoplifting"), Cromwell, Parker, and Mobley analyze the motivations that underlie shoplifting. They found that although most shoplifters acted to obtain cash or desired merchandise, few individuals used a single, stable criminal calculus.

The studies included in this section and throughout the book illustrate that criminal decision making is neither purely opportunistic nor completely rational. It is frequently directed at solving immediate problems and satisfying immediate needs. Age, lifestyle, and previous criminal experience combine to create a "limited rationality" based on what seems reasonable to the offender. ✦

Chapter 8 Streetlife and the Rewards of Auto Theft

Heith Copes

I*n order to understand offender decision-making processes, we must look to their assessments of the risks and gains associated with their crimes and how their lifestyles mediate those decisions. As Shover and Honaker have argued (see Chapter 4), the lives of most thieves are centered about pursuit of "life as party" to the exclusion of almost all other considerations. Data for this study were drawn from semi-structured interviews with 45 individuals on community supervision in one metropolitan area in Tennessee. All respondents were under probation or parole following convictions for various property crimes and had committed at least one motor vehicle theft. The purpose of the interviews was to determine how participation in streetlife mediated their decisions to engage in auto theft. The author concludes that their crimes provided the economic resources necessary to live their lives of autonomy, excitement, and hedonism, and to maintain an image of having overcome the despair of the streets.*

Understanding the process by which offenders choose crime is critical as it has important implications for both theory and policy. The bulk of research on criminal decision-making is grounded in rational choice theory and assumes that offenders rationally measure the potential penalties of crime against its anticipated rewards (Becker 1968; Cornish and Clarke 1986). Individuals are thought to pursue goals reflecting their self-interest and purposively choose to commit crime if the expected benefits of illegal behavior exceed the benefits of engaging in legitimate activity. Conversely, the decision to forgo criminal behavior may be based on the individual's perception that the benefits have diminished or the risk of detection and subsequent cost is too great. In other words, individuals explore their options and choose the alternative that provides the highest expected gain.

Early rational choice theorists borrowed from economic theories of expected utility and proposed models of criminal decision-making that could be expressed mathematically (e.g., Becker 1968). These theories depicted offenders as "pure" rational calculators; that is, individuals were assumed to choose courses of action that produced optimal rewards from limited effort. Thus, they created an image of offenders as self-maximizing decision-makers who carefully calculated their advantages. Research using this framework typically focused on how offenders weighed the costs of crime, including the certainty and severity of punishment, and how these costs contributed to deterrence (e.g., Grasmick and Bursik 1990; Nagin and Paternoster 1994).

The portrayal of offenders as "pure" economic calculators was criticized on several grounds. The most detrimental criticism was that this self-maximizing model of criminal behavior "does not fit the opportunistic and reckless nature of much crime" (Clarke 1997:9; see Clarke and Felson 1993). Therefore, to better understand the decision-making process of street offenders, investigators began examining the ways offenders evaluate their options and choose crime within a sociocultural context. This line of research eschewed the quantitative methods that characterized earlier rational choice studies for qualitative ones, thereby allowing an understanding of criminal decision-making from the perspective of the offender. These studies examined the components of criminal decisions, including the decision to offend instead of pursuing legitimate alternatives, the target selection process, and individuals' perceptions of various rewards and costs of illegality. This growing empirical emphasis on understanding the decision-making process led to more cautious and subjective theoretical understandings of criminal choice, or what has been termed limited or bounded rationality (Clarke and Cornish 1985; Cornish and Clarke 1986; Opp 1997; Shover and Honaker 1992).

Accumulated evidence persuasively shows that the "rationality they [offenders] employ is limited or bounded severely" (Shover and Honaker 1992:282). This does not imply that their behavior is irrational, but it does suggest that we must look beyond economic models of rationality if we want to better understand the choices offenders make. Bounded models of criminal decision-making take into account the social, physical, and situational context where criminal decisions are made as well as offenders' perceptions of the world around them. Internal calculations are inevitably inadequate because people do not have access to all pertinent information. Everyone does not choose from the same set of universally available options, consequently, crime offers different risks and rewards to those immersed in streetlife than it does to law-abiding citizens. Thus, if we wish to understand the decision-making process of offenders, "it is useful to examine the worlds in which much of their life is spent" (Shover 1996:93; see Jacobs and Wright 1999; Hagan and McCarthy 1997). To do this it is necessary to situate their decisions within the principal lifestyle that frames their choices.

Numerous qualitative studies have elaborated on the indulgent lifestyles that many offenders live (e.g., Fleisher 1995; Hagan and McCarthy 1992, 1997; Jacobs and Wright 1999; Shover 1996). What can be synthesized from this literature is that persistent offenders emphasize the "enjoyment of good times" (Shover 1996:94) at the expense of all else. They live in a social world that emphasizes "partying" and fast living where they are frequently "caught up in a cycle of expensive, self-indulgent habits" (Jacobs and Wright 1999:163). Offenders quickly erode any legitimate resources for obtaining money to support their lifestyle, making criminal behavior appear more rewarding.

Participation in street culture constrains individuals' subjective assessments of the risks and rewards of crime. The paltry financial rewards of most street crimes would not encourage most members of the middle class to pursue this life. Yet, these rewards when coupled with other intrinsic rewards of crime, such as status, autonomy, and action, are enough to turn the heads of many toward street crime. Researchers have explored the role of streetlife on decision-making for a variety of crimes, including burglary, robbery, carjacking, and drug dealing (Jacobs 1999; Jacobs et al. forthcoming; Shover 1996; Wright and Decker 1994, 1997). Absent from this list is an in-depth exploration of the relationship between streetlife and motor vehicle theft.

There has been relatively little research on auto theft (Clarke and Harris 1992a), especially using qualitative methods (notable exceptions include Fleming 2003 and Spencer 1992). This is surprising considering the symbolic importance of automobiles to Americans and the prevalence and cost of auto theft to the public (Freund and Martin 1993). According to current data from the Federal Bureau of Investigation (FBI 2002) approximately 1.2 million cars were illegally taken from their owners in 2001, resulting in a rate of 430.6 per 100,000 inhabitants. With such high numbers of motor vehicle theft it is not surprising that the financial loss from it is enormous. In 2001 alone, the loss due to motor vehicle theft was estimated to be over \$8.2 billion, averaging \$6,646 per vehicle (FBI 2002). This is much larger than the estimated loss from burglary (\$3.3 billion).

Because of the prevalence and high cost of motor vehicle theft and its neglect by researchers, there is a need to understand the criminal decision-making of auto thieves. The current study examines offenders' perceptions of the rewards of auto theft within the sociocultural context of streetlife. It relies on semi-structured interviews with auto thieves to determine how participation in streetlife facilitates offenders' decisions to engage in motor vehicle theft by providing the motivations for their behaviors. The results of this endeavor will increase our understanding of motor vehicle theft and will add to our understanding of criminal decision-making in general. . . .

Streetlife and Motivations for Auto Theft

Previous studies have described the indulgent lifestyles that many offenders live and have shown how this lifestyle impacts offender's decisions to engage in crime (e.g., Fleisher 1995; Hagan and McCarthy 1992, 1997; Jacobs and Wright 1999; Shover 1996; Shover and Honaker 1992; Wright and Decker 1997). These studies suggest that the defining characteristic of streetlife is the quest to lead "a life of desperate partying" (Wright and Decker 1997:35). As Shover (1996) states, "the hallmark of life as party is enjoyment of 'good times' with minimal concerns for obligations and commitments external to the person's immediate social setting" (p. 93). It is a lifestyle that encourages the hedonistic pursuit of sensory stimulation, lack of future orientation, and neglect of responsibility (Fleisher 1995). Continuing the good times takes precedent over all else. This emphasis on partying is illustrated in the writings of a thief (Jackson 1969):

> [the life] is mostly a party. I don't think people understand that it's quite like that, but it is. In other words, you don't work. . . . When you get your money, you usually get it real fast and you have a lot of time to spend it. You can sleep all day if you want to and you can go out and get drunk, get high—you don't have to get up the next morning to go to work. (pp. 146–7)

In this context crime can emerge without warning to continue the good times or to forestall circumstances that are perceived to be unpleasant.

Making Money

This lifestyle of "ostentatious consumption" (Shover 1996:94) entails major expenses. The material excess that is promoted in this lifestyle, especially when it comes to drug use and personal style, dictate that the proceeds from crime be spent quickly. Offenders in the criminal lifestyle spend the spoils of their criminal ventures with seeming abandon, in part because money acquired illegally holds less intrinsic value than income earned through hard work. As one auto thief said, "I don't treasure the money I make. I don't even try to save it. All down in the end I know I won't be able to save it anyway." The income from the minimum-wage jobs that characterize the employment possibilities of people in their social position are woefully inadequate to support this fast lifestyle. Even those with employable skills are left with empty pockets. As one unusually skilled offender explained:

> Well, it's hard to go to work and work 12 hours a day when you got a two hundred dollar drug habit a day. You only make two hundred dollars a day at best, you know. That's at 16 or 17 dollars an hour, when I went to industrial carpentry. You still can't support a drug habit and a family.

Auto theft affords offenders the luxury of living their chosen lifestyle by providing a viable source of income. Seventeen offenders said they stole cars to profit financially from the sale of stolen vehicles. Auto theft can be a profitable business if one has the proper skills and connections. Auto thieves can earn anywhere from $500 to $5,000 per car, depending on their position in the chop shop hierarchy and the type of vehicle stolen. Many are aware that they can potentially make a great deal of money by selling stolen cars. In fact, the perceived ease at making fast money persuaded one offender to quit the "drug game" and begin a career in stealing cars. In his words:

> I was selling drugs and got tired of selling drugs. A friend of mine, he told me I could make more money and it would be easier to take the cars than to sell the drugs. So I gave it a shot because I'm a good mechanic. There ain't nothing I can't do to a car. . . . I come from maybe, I wouldn't say a big-time drug dealer but maybe a second-class drug dealer making maybe two thousand to three thousand dollars a day. It was just so hectic so I stopped selling drugs to steal cars because it was easier. The money come quicker.

While knowledge of chop shops secured higher payoffs, offenders without these connections could still profit from auto theft by stripping cars and selling the parts in a loosely structured network of friends and acquaintances (Fleming 2003). Six offenders stripped stolen cars to sell individual parts. As one offender said:

> Sometimes [we] sold the parts, sometimes [we] just put it on our car. But most time we'll strip the car all the way down to the engine and sell the engine, you know what I'm saying. When we didn't know about going to sell the cars [to chop shops], that's what we were doing. We were selling body parts. . . . We'd sell parts all day.

Even for those who do possess the necessary skills to obtain economically satisfying employment, streetlife makes it nearly impossible to keep the job for any extended amount of time. The resentment of authority and disdain for conventional employment all but prohibits these offenders from maintaining stable employment. Thus, most persistent offenders choose not to work, preferring instead to lead a more autonomous life—a life where they are free from the constraints of the working stiffs' nine-to-five world (Akerstrom 1985, 2003). MacIssac (1968:69), an ex-thief, illustrates this belief, "I was always quite candid in admitting that I was a thief because I enjoyed the stimulation of crime and because I had a marked aversion to the 40-hour week." Auto theft offers offenders the ability to live autonomously and continue their party pursuits by providing the necessary financial resources and by allowing them to travel when the desire arises. When asked if he worked before his arrest one offender replied, "What I need a job for? I make my money with them cars. I got everything I need right here."

Looking Good and Being Seen

Offenders living "life in the fast lane" (Gibbs and Shelly 1982) spend an exorbitant amount of money buying clothes and other items in an attempt to "keep up appearances" (Wright and Decker 1997:40; see also Shover and Honaker 1992; McCall 1994). By spending money conspicuously offenders can "create a look of cool transcendence" and show others that they are "members of the aristocracy of the streets" (Wright and Decker 1997:40). As one offender explained when asked what he did with the money, "Parlay, you know, go buy a new fix [drugs] and shit. Take care of a bill or something like that. Mostly, just to dress with." Another offender replied, "I like lavish clothes. I like to go out to clubs. I had a lot of girlfriends—when you living that lifestyle you going to spend the money, you know." Offenders spend without thinking in order to create an "impression of affluence" (Wright and Decker 1994). On the streets, the image projected is critical and those in "the game" must visually play the role. This includes dressing well and driving the right car.

Offenders often value nice cars and hope to garner the respect of others in their community by "flossing,"[1] and a large proportion of auto thieves steal cars to cruise around in or joyride. Typically, they only keep the car for a short time, usually under three days, but they try to make the most of their time. When asked why he stole cars one young auto thief replied, "I never wanted anything out of the cars, man. I was only interested in the car. I loved riding. Always did, always will. I liked riding." These auto thieves use the stolen vehicle to continue the good times by visiting friends, picking up girls, or just being seen.

For a significant number of offenders who were intent on cruising around in a stolen car, stealing a suitable one was a prerequisite. They searched for vehicles that fit the style and image they wished to project. For instance, one auto thief said:

> I was very choicey. I used to go and look at them. Let me give you an example. If I had a choice between this car and that car. This one here looks more sporty because the windows are dark. I would get that car. [I went for] sportier cars. The girls will go for that one more than the other one because that one there is too plain. This one there is really nice. I had to have something real beautiful sporty because of my taste. I had good taste.

Some avoided stealing cars that were wrecked or too old. Some would not break the windows of the car because they saw no point in cruising in a car that did not look good or that was obviously stolen. As one offender stated, "I would try not to break no window gettin' in. Who wants to ride around in a car with a broken window?"

Auto thieves want to look good by driving the right car but some recognize that trying to sport a stolen car as their own is too risky. To overcome this risk, they use the spoils of auto theft to obtain the car they desired. Offenders can fix up their own cars by purchasing accessories with the proceeds of auto theft, by stripping stolen cars and keeping the desirable parts for themselves, or by stealing the exact vehicle they wanted and keeping it intact. As one offender explains, "I took a car and demolished it to build up my car, you know what I'm saying. I never did steal a car to sell or anything. It was always for my use." Another explained:

> I got a Pontiac and I see you got a Pontiac, and my fenders are bent up. I'll take your car and take the fenders off and put it on my car. Do the paint up real quick and go ditch yours. Nothing might be wrong with yours. Yours might be brand new. Mine is second hand. But I'd jack your car to take the body parts to put on mine. Make my shit look good. And just ditch yours off.

Stereos rank high on the list of sought after accessories. When the beats (stereos) are loud they draw the attention of others, thus, offenders are not only heard they are seen. One car thief stated that his primary motive for the car theft was to take out the stereo. "Sometimes we would jack them just for the music. Sometimes we'd jack a car, take the music out [and] hook our car up with the music." As one joyrider stated, "Every now and then I might take a little radio or some music out of them. Keep a little music or whatever."

Despite the high number of offenders who sold cars to chop shops, it was rare for auto thieves to steal cars to permanently keep for themselves. In fact, only two offenders stated they did so. One offender stole a car for his brother to keep:

> [My brother's] car broke down and couldn't be fixed. It was through. We didn't have no more money. . . . We saw a car that looked just like my brother's. So we waited until everybody went into the store, got in the car and took off. . . . He's still got it. It's legal now.

The other offender stole a motorcycle to keep for himself. He claimed he had always wanted a motorcycle and when the opportunity to steal one presented itself, he took it. In his words, "I took a motorcycle—a little blue Honda motorcycle. It had 'for sale' on it. God knows I didn't have the money to buy no machine like that."

Auto theft provides offenders with the opportunity to cruise in stylish cars. However, if one wants to truly stand out he or she must be "seen" in [his or her] car. One technique for being seen is to develop a distinctive driving style. Evidence that stylistic driving is a means to gain status is illustrated in the following description, "My style of riding in stolen cars I would describe as unique. I wouldn't just sit up and drive, because after I had learned how to drive real well from stealing so many vehicles, I used to like to lean." This style of driving is frequently called a "gangsta lean" by those in the street.

Going Places

> I had went to a club. I was living with [my girl]. I got dropped off at the house and I didn't have the key, or she wasn't there, or she kicked me out or something. I don't remember. But I was stuck way over here. It was like two in the morning. So, I'm drunk and I walk outside and I'm like damn. I didn't know no better. I wasn't even planning on stealing a car. All I knew I was stuck.

The previous quote perhaps best illustrates how some offenders find themselves in situations where they "desperately" need a ride. A hallmark of streetlife is the desire to be up for anything, at any time, especially a party. This desire to party often leaves them stranded far from home with no means of getting back. Fourteen offenders stated they had stolen a car for the purpose of short-term transportation. Several auto thieves wanted to go to a party but had no ride there; others went to a party and were left by their friends. In his words, one auto thief explained:

> I remember one time I was stuck at these apartments. I just came from these girls' house and it was like ten or eleven o'clock and I had no ride to go across town. . . . I jumped into an old Toyota, and I took off with it.

Some just needed a ride after their domestic partners kicked them out of the house or took their car keys. One auto thief explained, "[I stole a car] because my girlfriend took my keys and I wanted to go out. I had to be from one point to another, like a 30-minute drive. And I seen [a car]. It was a spur of the moment thing I guess." One young man went out of town for a drug deal. When the deal went bad he was forced to abandon his car. He later stole a car just to get home:

> I was up there, and they had a dope deal went bad. I was about 16. So, the dope deal went bad, and we had to run. By the time [everything was over], I couldn't find [my car], you know. So, I had some money, but it wasn't enough money, you know what I'm saying. So, I saw a Lincoln on like a store lot. I just went over there. The door was open. . . . So when I popped [the ignition], I turned the music on and I came straight home.

All of these offenders were faced with situational pressures that were the products of the party lifestyle. The desire to maintain or extend the party created a need to get out of town or to another part of town quickly. Thus, in a moment of self-defined desperation, they stole a car to get where they needed to go, so that they could continue their search for good times.

Living for the Moment

While impulsiveness is often portrayed as a psychological shortcoming in the criminology literature (e.g., Gottfredson and Hirschi 1990), a measure of it and other indicators of a "devil may care" attitude are respectable in street offenders' surroundings. Offenders, especially younger ones, are expected by peers to embrace and enjoy adventures ranging from street fights, to heavy drug use binges, to commission of acquisitive felonies. Dozens of studies document the presence of what might be termed the cult of adventure and toughness among males in the lower tiers of the working class (Anderson 1999; Gibbs and Shelly 1982; Jacobs and Wright 1999; MacLeod 1987; Miller 1958). It is spontaneity and action, not reserve, that brings about "good times" for those immersed in this lifestyle. Thus, offenders seek out risky situations (Katz 1988). Many design their crimes with the intent of maximizing the risks so they can boost the level of excitement that crime creates. For instance, one car thief said, "Man, I done stole a fucking car with people right there in their window. I mean a big ole picture window and shit." The added risk was a source of pride and accomplishment for this offender as it was evidence of his ability to "face and overcome dangerous situations" (Jacobs et al. forthcoming).

Offenders can prove their willingness to engage in thrilling and exciting behavior by engaging in auto theft. This is evident by the choice of adjectives used to describe crimes. Words such as "fun," "thrilling," or a "high" are frequently used to explain the overriding emotions that auto theft elicits. One young auto thief said, "Well, a lot of people just do it to make money. I take them for the thrill, the adrenalin rushes." Similarly, another young car thief said, "It was fun because I was doing it so long it was just like I would get a little adrenalin rush off of it. It was just a thrill. Like a thrill." The experience associated with engaging in auto theft is often compared to the physical sensation of drug use. As one offender recalls, "Yeah, I mean it's like just about as good of a rush as snorting a foot-long line of cocaine." The thrill of auto theft is in offenders' abilities to "dance with danger" (Jacobs et al. forthcoming). This can be achieved by putting their physical safety and freedom on the line by driving dangerously, by being chased by police, or by simply doing things that most people do not have the nerve [for] or cannot stomach.

Auto thieves' thirst for excitement is evidenced by their desire to steal cars and drive them recklessly (Fleming 2003). Cars are stolen to race, test drive, tear up, or engage in dangerous car stunts. In other words, to "just raise hell." As one offender stated, "We actually played quite a dangerous game of bumper cars if we got two or more in one night."

Another stated, "When I was younger, [we stole them] for joyrides, demolition derbies. Steal a car and tear it up." Just how much wear some put on these cars is best illustrated by one young car thief:

> There was a Porsche [we stole] that had the front wheel ripped off it completely. In some of the [cars], the radiator would be busted and before we knew it there would be steam coming out and we had to ditch it because the block was about to crack.

Driving chaotically not only threatens offenders' physical safety but it also increases their chances of coming into contact with agents of the law. Few activities can generate the excitement and the ability to prove one's reckless abandon like fleeing from police in a stolen car. Four offenders claimed they stole cars with the deliberate intention of getting chased by police. When asked what motivated him to steal cars, one auto thief stated:

> It wasn't the thrill of stealing the vehicle itself—it was the thrill of being in a stolen vehicle and cops behind you. I don't too much do drugs. It's pretty high. It's pretty awesome. You getting behind a vehicle, behind the wheel of a stolen vehicle, and you run this truck that you have no idea what it's capable of doing. You don't know if you'll be able to escape from them, how fast it can go, how slow it will go, you know. So, you just shaking. [Your] nerves are wrecked.

This same belief was reflected in the words of another offender:

> The fun part about it is.... If the police get after us we going to get in a police chase. That was the excitement you know. . . . That was the fun part.

A major component of the motivation to commit auto theft and part of its inherent thrill is the pleasurable feelings that come with doing the act and being successful, or "getting away with it" (Frazier and Meisenhelder 1985). To many offenders, being successful at crime provides a sense of accomplishment (Gibbens 1958). By getting away with crime they are able to accomplish things most people could not. This is illustrated by the following offenders:

> But, man really though, it was like, it was more of like, a thrilling thing to me. To be able to get away with it. I mean, it would just give me goose pimples. Man I mean, it was like I pulled this off and I made this, you know. How I mean I would manage to keep from getting caught.

For offenders who stole high-end cars equipped with alarms and other security devices, a feeling of accomplishment was especially prevalent. One experienced car thief said:

> I just liked to steal the cars, you know. I used to pride myself on which car I could steal. You know, the harder and more mysterious it was, the more I wanted to get it. So, it's harder to steal the Porsches. All right, I'm going to go get one.... I take the pride in the knowledge of how to beat

the system. It's just like them hackers. Sometimes I just amaze myself.

Getting Even

Justice on the streets seldom involves the criminal justice system. The "code of the street" demands that problems be taken care of informally, thus making street justice a common practice (Anderson 1999). Often offenders steal the property of others as a form of social control; so what may seem as an unprovoked theft is really a response to the perceived misconduct of the victim (Black 1983, 1998; see Jacobs 2000; Jacobs et al. forthcoming). Offenders exact revenge or retribution on those who, in their opinions, deserve it. For example, over one-third of the burglaries in New York resulting in arrest involve grievances between the burglar and victim (Vera Institute 1977). Seven auto thieves said that they had stolen cars because of spite or revenge. For these men, car theft is a way to express their dislike for another person. Auto theft is chosen as a method of revenge because these offenders possess the necessary skills to do so. Those auto thieves motivated by revenge were experienced car thieves, some stealing as many [as] 200 cars in their lifetimes. These skills as car thieves translated into a natural means of exacting revenge or retribution on "deserving" others.

Car thieves who steal for revenge give several reasons for their "moralistic concerns" (Jacobs 2000:33). Being disrespected or unfairly treated by the victim was the primary reason for "punishing" them. But even these insults must be interpreted within the context of streetlife. The "sins" of the victims are often minor transgressions but are interpreted as threats to the offenders' identity as being a legitimate player of the streets. One man described a situation where he was publically humiliated and decided to get back at the instigator. When asked why he stole the particular car in question he responded, "This dude was drinking and kept on putting me down." Another offender was upset with a drug dealer because the dealer refused to provide him with drugs at no cost.

> I always wanted to get some dope from this one dude. All my other little partners he would front them dope and stuff like this. But, we damn near stayed at the same house, but every time I come to get drugs I had to buy it from him. So, I was like fuck him I'm get me something else. I just took his car.

Sometimes car thieves had longstanding feuds with the people whose car[s] they stole. One offender resorted to auto theft in an attempt to get back at the person who shot at him. "The last one, I stole it because the nigger had tried to shoot at me."

Some of the victims highly coveted their cars, often more than any other possession, making it the most obvious way for the offender to exact revenge. One offender believed that his victim "flossed" too much so he took it upon himself to put the braggart in his place.

> [What happened was] one day me and one of my friends—you know we used to be friends back in the day—we got into it. We used to fight about girls and stuff. Well he had a nice car. He used to always come in my neighborhood late at night playing his music loud, loud, loud. Boom, boom, boom! He had like four 18-inch punchers in the back. Nice amps, speakers all over. Bumping. He thought he was bigger than everybody else, you know. Nobody had more sound than him. We used to always fight. I said I'm going to fix him. I'm going to show him. He had nice rims. Nice, nice rims. . . . I showed him a thing or two.

For some offenders retribution is a secondary motive for the auto theft. These offenders were determined to steal a car for any number of reasons. It was when they began searching for a suitable target that they decided to steal from those people whom they saw as deserving. One younger offender wanted to show his friends that he was "man enough" to steal a car. He described why he chose this particular car:

> I stole [this lady's] Lincoln. This lady, she used to come ride around. She was mean. That lady was mean. One time I asked her to go cut her grass, she ain't never looked at me. She never answered me, just rolled her eyes. So, [I thought] I'm going to fix you. I was going to do something to her dogs. Throw them a pill in a burger or something and give it to them. But I never did it. Then one night I wanted to go riding. I was like I wonder if I can [steal a car]. I know I can do it. I bet you I can show them I can [steal a car], you know.

Staying Low

Individuals embedded in street culture engaged in a wide range of illicit behaviors. The desire to avoid being identified when committing other crimes leads them to steal cars to use as getaway vehicles. Since most cannot find people willing to loan a car to them, some offenders turn to auto theft to insure their anonymity. By stealing a car, offenders fulfill the practical need of moving around town while simultaneously concealing their identities. When asked if he ever stole a car to commit another crime one offender stated:

> A few. Maybe like for a drive by, or something like that. We did that a few times, you know. If it was like some situation like that. Don't let the mother fucker know what I got. If its something like that in the 'hood. See, like if I'm in my neighborhood and some mother fucker be done got down bad, and I know he know what I'm driving. [Then] I might go get something from somewhere else and handle up on our business. Because I know if I come by in my shit they know what I'm riding in, so. Like a few times, see like [we stole a] pick-up truck and put a few mother fuckers in the back. They don't know who it is passing through. And we handle our business and we gone, shit. Keep shit down cool like that.

This is perhaps the rarest form of motor vehicle theft (McCaghy et al. 1977). Only four offenders stated they stole cars for the purpose of concealing their identity.

Discussion and Conclusion

Before concluding, a caveat is in order about auto theft typologies. Others have developed motivational typologies of auto theft (e.g., Challinger 1987; Clarke and Harris 1992a; McCaghy et al. 1977). They have even used these typologies to explain the type and frequency of cars stolen (Clarke and Harris 1992b; Tremblay et al. 1994). It is possible to use the data presented to construct a motivational typology; however, doing so may be inappropriate. Typologies imply exclusivity and stability, they are based on the idea that offenders in one group are qualitatively different from the offenders in the other group. Based on the current data, this portrayal does not accurately represent auto thieves because the motivational categories are not mutually exclusive. It is common for car thieves to have multiple motivations over their careers and for a single theft. This progression is illustrated in the words of one offender:

> Just getting somewhere, trying to move, you know. Just being seen mainly. To get different places. You know if you got a car and shit you ride around, you can get with the girls and shit, you know. I mean that's basically what it's about then, you know. It wasn't about no money and shit then, back that early. As time went on and shit, I went to stealing them for like the rims, the tires, or the sound system and shit like that out of them. And me dealing with body shops, I might get it for a different body part that might cost a whole lot, you know. Like one shop I was working with we used to take the cars, say you got a car that is wrecked on the front, we'll go steal another one like it and cut it in half and weld that shit back together. They would make like ten or fifteen G [thousand]—depends on how much damage the insurance company paid for, you know. So I mean, it got to be to a different level as time progressed.

The fluid nature of offender's motivations suggests that typologies may obscure the nature of auto theft more than they illuminate it.

The motivations to engage in auto theft are a product of the hedonistic culture of the street. This is a lifestyle that encourages the enjoyment of good time and the dismissal of all that is restrictive. Those embedded in streetlife paint themselves as autonomous, action-adventurers who cannot be held back by the rigid life of the "working stiff" (Akerstrom 1985). They "relish the independence and autonomy to structure time and daily routines as they wish" (Shover 1996:95). But enjoyment of this life often comes at a major expense, financially and socially, and participants often find themselves "strapped for cash." Faced with eroding legitimate resources, the high cost of the lifestyle makes criminal behavior all the more enticing. Offender's accounts of their crimes reveal that money is typically the primary motive for their crimes (Feeney 1986; Tunnell 1992). This desire for money instigates many auto thefts. The sale of stolen cars goes a long way in filling the pockets of offenders. If auto thieves have the necessary skills and proper connections they can easily bankroll their lifestyle.

Offenders are motivated by other things besides money. Auto theft is uniquely suited to support streetlife in ways other than financially. First, it gives offenders the ability to make their parties mobile. If their current location becomes boring or is uncomfortable they can "hot wire" a car and travel to more thrilling locations. The automobile allows them to move the party off the stoop and travel to places where they imagine real hustlers, party-goers, and girl-getters to be. No other crime affords offenders with this degree of geographic mobility. Second, in the world of the street, appearance is everything. One's style should be reflected in everything they do, including the type of car they drive. Auto theft provides a direct means of acquiring high-end car accessories like stereos and rims. If an offender wants drugs they can rob drug dealers or pharmacies (Jacobs 2000). If they want cash they can engage in armed robbery or check forgery (Lemert 1958; Wright and Decker 1997). If they want to travel in stylish vehicles they can steal cars. Third, auto theft fuels the desire for action more than most other crimes. Interviews with robbers show that they often experience thrills and rushes while they are committing the robbery. But the actual act of robbery lasts a short time, usually under a minute or two. The excitement of auto theft can last for hours and even days, depending on how long offenders want to push their luck and drive in a "hot car."

Finally, and perhaps most importantly, auto theft carries with it symbolic importance. Driving the right car can do more to tell others about themselves than any other activity or personal item. Automobiles project a sense of power, prestige, and status, especially in many urban subcultures (Bright 1998). Displaying material items shows that they are "someone who has overcome—if only temporarily—the financial difficulties faced by others on the streetcorner." (Wright and Decker 1997:40). Thus, the ability to drive around, or "floss," in a car is important for many male youths because it allows them to literally cruise past the poverty and despair of the street.

Recent efforts to understand the criminal calculus using qualitative methods has provided much insight into the process by which offenders weigh the costs and benefits of crime; however, there is still more to learn. If decision-making research is to progress, investigators must explore how gender, age, criminal experience, and other characteristics of offenders shape their assessments of the costs and benefits of crime within their given lifestyle. Doing so would allow for a better understanding of criminal behavior and, consequently, lead to more efficient crime control policies.

Questions for Thought and Discussion

1. How does the concept of rational choice explain the activities of car thieves in this chapter?
2. How does lifestyle influence the decisions of the auto thieves in this chapter?
3. Does "living for the moment" have consequences for deterrence as criminal justice policy? In what way?
4. How might policy be developed through an understanding of the motivations of auto thieves?

Note

1. Flossing is a term meaning "to show off." It is frequently used in the context of driving a nice vehicle.

References

Akerstrom, Malin. 1985. *Crooks and Squares: Lifestyles of Thieves and Addicts in Comparison to Conventional People.* New Brunswick, NJ: Transaction.

———. 2003. "Looking at the Squares: Comparisons with the Square Johns." Pp. 51–9 in *In Their Own Words: Criminals on Crime,* 3rd edition, edited by Paul Cromwell. Los Angeles: Roxbury.

Anderson, Elijah. 1999. *Code of the Street: Decency, Violence and the Moral Life of the Inner City.* New York: W.W. Norton.

Becker, Gary S. 1968. "Crime and Punishment: An Economic Approach." *Journal of Political Economy* 76:169–217.

Black, Donald. 1983. "Crime as Social Control." *American Sociological Review* 48:34–45.

———. 1998. *The Social Structure of Right and Wrong.* San Diego, CA: Academic.

Bright, Brenda. 1998. "Heart Like a Car: Hispano/Chicano Culture in Northern New Mexico." *American Ethologist* 25:583–609.

Challinger, Dennis. 1987. "Car Security Hardware—How Good is it?" In *Car Theft: Putting on the Brakes, Proceedings of Seminar on Car Theft,* May 21. Sydney, Australia: National Road and Motorists' Association and the Australian Institute of Criminology.

Clarke, Ronald. 1997. *Situational Crime Prevention: Successful Case Studies.* Guilderland, NY: Harrow and Heston.

Clarke, Ronald and David Cornish. 1985. "Modeling Offenders' Decisions: A Framework for Research and Policy." Pp. 147–85 in *Crime and Justice: A Review of Research* (Vol. 4), edited by Michael Tonry and N. Morris. Chicago: University of Chicago Press.

Clarke, Ronald and Marcus Felson, eds. 1993. *Routine Activity and Rational Choice: Advances in Criminological Theory,* Vol. 5. New Brunswick, NJ: Transaction.

Clarke, Ronald and Patricia Harris. 1992a. "Auto Theft and its Prevention." Pp. 1–54 in *Crime and Justice: A Review of Research* (Vol. 16), edited by Michael Tonry. Chicago: University of Chicago Press.

———. 1992b. "A Rational Choice Perspective on the Targets of Auto Theft." *Criminal Behavior and Mental Health* 2:25–42.

Cornish, Derek and Ronald Clarke. 1986. *The Reasoning Criminal.* New York: Springer-Verlag.

Federal Bureau of Investigation. 2002. *Uniform Crime Reports: Crime in the United States.* Washington, DC: U.S. Department of Justice.

Feeney, Floyd. 1986. "Robbers as Decision Makers." Pp. 53–71 in *The Reasoning Criminal: Rational Choice Perspectives on Offending,* edited by Derek Cornish and Richard Clarke. New York: Springer-Verlag.

Fleisher, Mark S. 1995. *Beggars and Thieves: Lives of Urban Street Criminals.* Madison, WI: University of Wisconsin Press.

Fleming, Zachary. 2003. "The Thrill of it All: Youthful Offenders and Auto Theft." Pp. 99–107 in *In Their Own Words,* 3rd ed., edited by Paul Cromwell. Los Angeles: Roxbury.

Frazier, Charles and Thomas Meisenhelder. 1985. "Exploratory Notes on Criminality and Emotional Ambivalence." *Qualitative Sociology* 8:266–84.

Freund, Peter and George Martin. 1993. *The Ecology of the Automobile.* Montreal, Canada: Black Rose Books.

Gibbens, Thomas. 1958. "Car Thieves." *British Journal of Delinquency* 8:257–65.

Gibbs, John and Peggy Shelly. 1982. "Life in the Fast-Lane: A Retrospective View by Commercial Thieves." *Journal of Research in Crime and Delinquency* 19:299–330.

Gottfredson, Michael and Travis Hirschi. 1990. *A General Theory of Crime.* Stanford, CA: Stanford University Press.

Grasmick, Harold G. and Robert J. Bursik. 1990. "Conscience, Significant Others, and Rational Choice: Extending the Deterrence Model." *Law and Society Review* 24:837–61.

Hagan, John and Bill McCarthy. 1992. "Street Life and Delinquency." *British Journal of Sociology* 43:533–61.

———. 1997. *Mean Streets: Youth Crime and Homelessness.* Cambridge, MA: Cambridge University Press.

Jackson, Bruce. 1969. *A Thief's Primer.* New York: Macmillan.

Jacobs, Bruce. 1999. *Dealing Crack: The Social World of Streetcorner Selling.* Boston, MA: Northeastern University Press.

———. 2000. *Robbing Drug Dealers: Violence Beyond the Law.* New York: Aldine de Gruyter.

Jacobs, Bruce, Volkan Topalli, and Richard Wright. Forthcoming. "Carjacking, Streetlife, and Offender Motivation." *British Journal of Criminology.*

Jacobs, Bruce and Richard Wright. 1999. "Stick-Up, Street Culture, and Offender Motivation." *Criminology* 37:149–73.

Katz, Jack. 1988. *Seductions of Crime.* New York: Basic.

Lemert, Edwin. 1958. "The Behavior of the Systematic Check Forger." *Social Problems* 6:141–9.

MacIssac, John. 1968. *Half the Fun Was Getting There.* Englewood Cliffs, NJ: Prentice-Hall.

MacLeod, Jay. 1987. *Ain't No Making It: Aspirations and Attainment in a Low-Income Neighborhood.* Boulder, CO: Westview.

McCaghy, Charles, Peggy Giordano, and Trudy Henson. 1977. "Auto Theft: Offender and Offense Characteristics." *Criminology* 15:367–85.

McCall, Nathan. 1994. *Makes Me Wanna Holler: A Young Black Man in America.* New York: Random House.

Miller, Walter. 1958. "Lower-Class Culture as a Generating Milieu of Gang Delinquency." *Journal of Social Issues* 14:5–19.

Nagin, Daniel S. and Raymond Paternoster. 1994. "Personal Capital and Social Control: The Deterrence Implications of a Theory of Individual Differences in Criminal Offending." *Criminology* 32:581–606.

Opp, Karl-Dieter. 1997. "Limited Rationality and Crime." Pp. 47–63 in *Rational Choice and Situational Crime Prevention,* edited by Graeme Newman, Ronald V. Clarke, and S. Giora Shoham. Brookfield, VT: Dartmouth.

Shover, Neal. 1996. *Great Pretenders: Pursuits and Careers of Persistent Thieves.* Boulder, CO: Westview.

Shover, Neal and David Honaker. 1992. "The Socially Bounded Decision Making of Persistent Property Offenders." *Howard Journal of Criminal Justice* 31:276–93.

Spencer, Eileen. 1992. *Car Crime and Young People on a Sunderland Housing Estate.* Crime Prevention Unit Series Paper 40. London: Home Office.

Tremblay, Pierre, Yvan Clermont, and Maurice Cusson. 1994. "Jockeys and Joyriders: Changing Patterns in Car Theft Opportunity Structures." *British Journal of Criminology* 34:307–21.

Tunnell, Kenneth. 1992. *Choosing Crime: The Criminal Calculus of Property Offenders.* Chicago: Nelson Hall.

Vera Institute. 1977. *Felony Arrests: Their Prosecution and Disposition in New York City's Courts.* New York: Vera Institute of Justice.

Wright, Richard and Scott Decker. 1994. *Burglars on the Job: Street Life and Residential Break-Ins.* Boston: Northeastern University Press.

———. 1997. *Armed Robbers in Action.* Boston: Northeastern University Press.

Chapter 9
Deciding to Commit a Burglary

Richard T. Wright
Scott H. Decker

Why burglary? Why do offenders choose burglary over other crimes? Based on their study of residential burglary in St. Louis, Wright and Decker discuss the dynamics underlying the decision to commit a burglary. The authors interviewed 105 active residential burglars, taking them to the scenes of their past crimes and asking them to reconstruct the burglaries in extensive detail. In this chapter they examine the factors which motivated the crime—that is, "why burglary?" The subjects in their study tended to be misfits in a world that values punctuality, schedules, and discipline. Crime appealed to some of the subjects precisely because it allowed them to flaunt their independence from the routine imposed by the world of work (see Chapter 4 in this volume, "The Socially Bounded Decision Making of Persistent Property Offenders"). Their crimes were committed primarily based on their perception of an immediate need for money. Their need for money revolved primarily around maintaining their lifestyle, which the authors described as "high living" and which Shover (1991) termed "life as party," although some committed burglaries for licit activities such as food, clothing, and shelter, and others had committed burglaries for revenge, thrills and other noneconomic reasons.

The demographic characteristics of residential burglars have been well documented. As Shover (1991) has observed, such offenders are, among other things, disproportionately young, male, and poor. These characteristics serve to identify a segment of the population more prone than others to resort to breaking in to dwellings, but they offer little insight into the actual causes of residential burglary. Many poor, young males, after all, never commit any sort of serious offense, let alone a burglary. And even those who carry out such crimes are not offending most of the time. This is not, by and large, a continually motivated group of criminals; the motivation for them to offend is closely tied to their assessment of current circumstances and prospects. The direct cause of residential burglary is a perceptual process through which the offense comes to be seen as a means of meeting an immediate need, that is, through which a motive for the crime is formed.

Walker (1984:viii) has pointed out that, in order to develop a convincing explanation for criminal behavior, we must begin by "distinguishing the states of mind in which offenders commit, or contemplate the commission of, their offenses." Similarly, Katz (1988:4), arguing for increased research into what he calls the foreground of criminality, has noted that all of the demographic information on criminals in the world cannot answer the following question: "Why are people who were not determined to commit a crime one moment determined to do so the next?" This is the question to which the present chapter is addressed. The aim is to explore the extent to which the decision to commit a residential burglary is the result of a process of careful calculation and deliberation.

In the overwhelming majority of cases, the decision to commit a residential burglary arises in the face of what offenders perceive to be a pressing need for cash. Previous research consistently has shown this to be so (Bennett and Wright, 1984; Cromwell et al., 1991) and the results of the present study bear out this point. More than nine out of ten of the offenders in our sample—95 of 102—reported that they broke into dwellings primarily when they needed money.

> Well, it's like, the way it clicks into your head is like, you'll be thinking about something and, you know, it's a problem. Then it, like, all relates. "Hey, I need some money! Then how am I going to get money? Well, how do you know how to get money quick and easy?" Then there it is. Next thing you know, you are watching [a house] or calling to see if [the occupants] are home. (Wild Will—No. 010)

> Usually when I get in my car and drive around I'm thinking, I don't have any money, so what is my means for gettin' money? All of a sudden I'll just take a glance and say, "There it is! There's the

> house." . . . Then I get this feelin', that right moment, I'm movin' then. (Larry William—No. 017)

These offenders were not motivated by a desire for money for its own sake. By and large, they were not accumulating the capital needed to achieve a long-range goal. Rather, they regarded money as providing them with the means to solve an immediate problem. In their view, burglary was a matter of day-to-day survival.

> I didn't have the luxury of laying back in no damn pin-striped [suit]. I'm poor and I'm raggedy and I need some food and I need some shoes. . . . So I got to have some money some kind of way. If it's got to be the wrong way, then so be it. (Mark Smith—No. 030)

> When I first started out, when I was younger, [burglary] was excitement or a high. But now it's to get by, you know, to survive. I don't ask my father for anything. My mother is not able to help. (Larry Harris—No. 035)

Given this view, it is unsurprising that the frequency with which the offenders committed burglaries was governed largely by the amount of money in their pockets. Many of them would not offend so long as they had sufficient cash to meet current expenses.

> Usually what I'll do is a burglary, maybe two or three if I have to, and then this will help me get over the rough spot until I can get my shit straightened out. Once I get it straightened out, I just go with the flow until I hit that rough spot where I need the money again. And then I hit it . . . the only time I would go and commit a burglary is if I needed the money at that point in time. That would be strictly to pay light bill, gas bill, rent. (Dan Whiting—No. 102)

> Long as I got some money, I'm cool. If I ain't got no money and I want to get high, then I go for it. (Janet Wilson—No. 060)

> You know how they say stretch a dollar? I'll stretch it from here to the parking lot. But I can only stretch it so far and then it breaks. Then I say, "Well, I guess I got to go put on my black clothes. Go on out there like a thief in the night." (Ralph Jones—No. 018)

A few of the offenders sometimes committed a burglary even though they had sufficient cash for their immediate needs. These subjects were not purposely saving money, but they were unwilling to pass up opportunities to make more. They attributed their behavior to having become "greedy" or "addicted" to money.

> I have done it out of greed, per se. Just to be doing it and to have more money, you know? Say, for instance, I have two hundred dollars in my pocket now. If I had two more hundreds, then that's four hundred dollars. Go out there and do a burglary. Then I say, "If I have four hundred dollars, then I can have a thousand." Go out there and do a burglary. (No. 018)

> It's like when you smoke a cigarette, you know, you want more and more from the nicotine. Well, from my experience, you can get bigger and better stuff the more times that you do it and you can make more money. I'm addicted to money, I love money. So I just keep doing [burglaries]. (Robert Jones—No. 103)

Typically, the offenders did not save the money that they derived through burglary. Instead, they spent it for one or more of the following purposes: (1) to "keep the party going"; (2) to keep up appearances; or (3) to keep themselves and their families fed, clothed, and sheltered.

Keeping the Party Going

Although the offenders often stated that they committed residential burglaries to "survive," there is a danger in taking this claim at face value. When asked how they spent the proceeds of their burglaries, nearly three-quarters of them—68 of 95—said they used the money for various forms of (for want of a better term) high-living. Most commonly, this involved the use of illicit drugs. Fifty-nine of the 68 offenders who spent the money obtained from burglary on pleasure-seeking pursuits specifically mentioned the purchase of drugs. For many of these respondents, the decision to break into a dwelling often arose as a result of a heavy session of drug use. The objective was to get the money to keep the party going (Shover and Honaker, 1990). The drug most frequently implicated in these situations was "crack" cocaine.

> [Y]ou ever had an urge before? Maybe a cigarette urge or a food urge, where you eat that and you got to have more and more? That's how that crack is. You smoke it and it hits you [in the back of the throat] and you got to have more. I'll smoke that sixteenth up and get through, it's like I never had none. I got to have more. Therefore, I gots to go do another

burglary and gets some more money. (Richard Jackson—No. 009)

> It's usually, say we'll be doing some coke and then you really want more, so we'll go and do [a burglary] and get some money. (Sasha Williams—No. 094)

> I might find somebody with some good crack . . . while I'm high I say, "Damn, I want me some more of this shit!" Go knock a place off, make some more money, go buy some more dope. (Die Leo—No. 079)

Lemert (1953:304) has labelled situations like these "dialectical, self-enclosed systems of behavior" in that they have an internal logic or "false structure" which calls for more of the same. Once locked into such events, he asserts, participants experience considerable pressure to continue, even if this involves breaking the law.

> A man away from home who falls in with a group of persons who have embarked upon a two- or three-day or even a week's period of drinking and carousing . . . tends to have the impetus to continue the pattern which gets mutually reinforced by [the] interaction of the participants, and [the pattern] tends to have an accelerated beginning, a climax and a terminus. If midway through a spree a participant runs out of money, the pressures immediately become critical to take such measures as are necessary to preserve the behavior sequence. A similar behavior sequence is [evident] in that of the alcoholic who reaches a "high point" in his drinking and runs out of money. He might go home and get clothes to pawn or go and borrow money from a friend or even apply for public relief, but these alternatives become irrelevant because of the immediacy of his need for alcohol. (Lemert, 1953:303)

Implicit in this explanation is an image of actors who become involved in offending without significant calculation; having embarked voluntarily on one course of action (e.g., crack smoking), they suddenly find themselves being drawn into an unanticipated activity (e.g., residential burglary) as a means of sustaining that action. Their offending is not the result of a thoughtful, carefully reasoned process. Instead, it emerges as part of the natural flow of events, seemingly coming out of nowhere. In other words, it is not so much that these actors consciously choose to commit crimes as that they elect to get involved in situations that drive them toward lawbreaking (Kennedy and Baron, 1993).

Other subjects, though they claimed that a perceived need for drugs typically triggered their decision to do a burglary, were not under the influence of drugs when the decision was reached. Their aim was to get high rather than to stay high. They regarded themselves as having a drug "habit" which compelled them to crime; the urge for drugs seemed beyond their ability to control and had to be satisfied by whatever means necessary. Although some in this group were addicted to narcotics such as heroin, this was not always the case.

> See, sometimes I wake up and don't have no [marijuana]. I have to go do my [burglary] and get me some money and get me some. (Carl Jackson—No. 022)

Getting and using drugs were major preoccupations for a majority of the offenders, not just a small cadre of addicts. Many of them reported committing burglaries *solely* for the purpose of obtaining money to buy drugs. But even some of those who did burglaries for other reasons ended up spending a portion of the profits on drugs.

> Lot of times when I commit burglary I use some of the money to get drugs, but I don't do the burglaries for that purpose. (Larry Washington—No. 013)

For these offenders, indulgence in drug use represented a crucial aspect of their street identity as "hip"; the street corner culture from which most of them—black and white, male and female—were drawn is oriented largely toward getting high (Anderson, 1990). In the past, this almost exclusively involved the drinking of beer or cheap wine. While drinking remains a feature of street culture—14 offenders, 21 percent of those who spent their money on high-living, mentioned the purchase of alcohol—it is increasingly being accompanied by illicit drug use. The money required to support such use is substantial and this ensured that the offenders were almost perpetually in need of cash (Shover and Honaker, 1992).

Beyond the purchase of illicit drugs and, to a lesser extent, alcohol, 10 of the 68 offenders—15 percent—also used the proceeds from their residential burglaries to pursue sexual conquests. All of these offenders were male. Some liked to flash money about, believing that this was the way to attract women.

I guess I like to flash [money] a lot, impress the girls and stuff. Go out and spend some money, you know? (Wayne Jones—No. 055)

[I commit burglaries to] splurge money with the women, you know, that's they kick, that's what they like to do. (Jon Monroe—No. 011)

[I use the burglary money for] gifts for young ladies—flowers or negligee or somethin'. Some shoes, "Put them shoes on, them pumps." [Then] watch 'em nude. (Jack Daniel—No. 054)

Like getting high, sexual conquest was a much-prized symbol of hipness through which the male subjects in our sample could accrue status among their peers on the street. The greatest prestige was accorded to those who were granted sexual favors solely on the basis of smooth talk and careful impression management. Nevertheless, a few of the offenders took a more direct approach to obtaining sex by paying a streetcorner prostitute (sometimes referred to as a "duck") for it. While this was regarded as less hip than the more subtle approach described above, it had the advantage of being easy and uncomplicated. As such, it appealed to offenders who were wrapped up in partying and therefore reluctant to devote more effort than was necessary to satisfy their immediate sexual desires.

I spend [the money] on something to drink, . . . then get me some [marijuana]. Then I'm gonna find me a duck. (Ricky Davis—No. 105)

It would be misleading to suggest that any of the offenders we spoke to committed burglaries *specifically* to get money for sex, but a number of them often directed a portion of their earnings toward this goal.

In short, among the major purposes for which the offenders used the money derived from burglary was the maintenance of a lifestyle centered on illicit drugs, but frequently incorporating alcohol and sexual conquests as well. This lifestyle reflects the values of the street culture, a culture characterized by an openness to "illicit action" (Katz, 1988:209–15), to which most of our subjects were strongly committed. Viewed from the perspective of the offenders, then, the oft-heard claim that they broke into dwellings to survive does not seem quite so farfetched. The majority of them saw their fate as inextricably linked to an ability to fulfill the imperatives of life on the street.

Keeping up Appearances

Of the 95 offenders who committed residential burglaries primarily for financial reasons, 43 reported that they used the cash to purchase various "status" items. The most popular item was clothing; 39 of the 43 said that they bought clothes with the proceeds of their crimes. At one level, of course, clothing must be regarded as necessary for survival. The responses of most of the offenders, however, left little doubt that they were not buying clothes to protect themselves from the elements, but rather to project a certain image; they were drawn to styles and brand names regarded as chic on the streets.

See, I go steal money and go buy me some clothes. See, I likes to look good. I likes to dress. All I wear is Stacy Adams, that's all I wear. [I own] only one pair of blue jeans cause I likes to dress. (No. 011)

I buy fashionable clothes or whatever, you know, just spend [the money]. (Mike West—No. 049)

[I] buy Stacy Adams clothes, sweaters. When I grew up, I always had the basic shit. [My parents] were wealthy and I always got [cheap] shoes and shit and I was always in competition with other kids and [my parents] never understood that. So I would go out and buy me Nikes. I'd buy three brand new sixty-dollar pairs of shoes and clothes. (Joe Wilson—No. 099)

A lot of times I'll buy clothes or tennis shoes or some jogging outfits, something like that. Some type of jacket or buy a hat. (Maurice Ross—No. 040)

Wearing appropriate clothing is an important aspect of fitting into any social situation. This is no less true for street culture, which has its own "dress code." As Anderson (1990) has observed, dressing in the latest status symbol clothing is virtually mandatory for those who want to be seen as hip on the street. The subjects in our sample were responding to this fact by using the money that they made from burglary to purchase fashionable outfits.

After clothes, cars and car accessories were the next most popular status items bought by the offenders. Seven of the 43 reported spending at least some of the money they got from burglaries on their cars.

I spent [the money] on stuff for my car. Like I said, I put a lot of money into my car. . . . I had a '79 Grand Prix, you know, a nice car. (Matt Detteman—No. 072)

The attributes of a high-status vehicle varied. Not all of these offenders, for example, would have regarded a 1979 Grand Prix as conferring much prestige on its owner. Nevertheless, they were agreed that driving a fancy or customized car, like wearing fashionable clothing, was an effective way of enhancing one's street status.

A sizable portion of the offenders therefore used the profits from their offenses to acquire the material trappings of success. In doing so, they sought to create an impression of affluence and hipness so that they would be admired by their peers on the street and by others. A British burglar interviewed by Bennett and Wright (1984:139) made explicit reference to the desire of offenders to be seen as a "better class of person."

> I don't know if you've ever thought about it, but I think every crook likes the life of thieving and then going and being somebody better. Really, you are deceiving people; letting them think that you are well off. . . . You've got a nice car, you can go about and do this and do that. It takes money to buy that kind of life.

Shover and Honaker (1990:11) have suggested that the concern of offenders with outward appearances, as with their notorious high-living, grows out of what is typically a strong attachment to the values of street culture; values which place great emphasis on the "ostentatious enjoyment and display of luxury items." In a related vein, Katz (1988) has argued that for those who are committed to streetlife, the reckless spending of cash on luxury goods is an end in itself, demonstrating their disdain for the ordinary citizen's pursuit of financial security. Seen through the eyes of the offenders, therefore, money spent on such goods has not been "blown," but rather represents a cost of raising or maintaining one's status on the street.

Keeping Things Together

While most of the offenders spent much of the money they earned through residential burglary on drugs and clothes, a substantial number also used some of it for daily living expenses. Of the 95 who committed burglaries to raise money, 50 claimed that they needed the cash for subsistence.

> I do [burglaries] to keep myself together, keep myself up. (James Brown—No. 025)

Necessities mentioned most frequently were food, shelter, and clothing for the children. Thirty-eight of the 50 offenders (76 percent) reported using money from their burglaries to pay for one or all of these needs. Some of them used the money *solely* for such expenses.

> [I spend the money from my burglaries for] needs, not wants, needs—roof over my head, food in my mouth and things for my kids. (Lynn—No. 095)

The majority, however, paid for their immediate subsistence needs and spent the remaining cash on status-enhancing items and high-living.

> [I use burglary money to buy] food, clothing, drugs—in that order. And a place to stay, that's gon come automatic cause I'm a always find a place to stay. (No. 035)

Quite a few of the offenders—13 of 50—said that they paid bills with the money derived from burglary. Here again, however, there is a danger of being misled by such claims. To be sure, these offenders did use some of their burglary money to take care of bills. Often, though, the bills were badly delinquent because the offenders avoided paying them for as long as possible—even when they had the cash—in favor of buying, most typically, drugs. It was not until the threat of serious repercussions created unbearable pressure for the offenders that they relented and settled their accounts.

> [Sometimes I commit burglaries when] things pressuring me, you know? I got to do somethin' about these bills. Bills. I might let it pass that mornin'. Then I start trippin' on it at night and, next thing you know, it's wakin' me up. Yeah, that's when I got to get out and go do a burglary. I *got* to pay this electric bill off, this gas bill, you know? (No. 009)

Similarly, several of the subjects in our sample reported doing burglaries to pay parking or traffic tickets they had long ignored, having preferred to use their money for high-living.

> I started getting tickets and it was, like, I got four tickets for improper registration plates. Then it was like, "Hey, I need some money, this stuff is calculating up." I [needed] some money and I [didn't] want to run and ask Mom. So I just did [a burglary]. (No. 010)

Spontaneity is a prominent feature of street culture (Shover and Honaker, 1992); it is not surprising that many of the offenders displayed a marked tendency to live for the moment. Often they would give every indication of intending to take care of their obligations, financial or otherwise, only to be distracted by more immediate temptations. For instance, a woman in our sample, after being paid for an interview, asked us to drive her to a place where she could buy a pizza for her children's lunch. On the way to the restaurant, however, she changed her mind and asked to be dropped off at a crack house instead. In another case, we persuaded a male subject to allow three consultants on our research to come along on a visit to the scene of his most recent residential burglary in exchange for a larger than usual participation fee. At the agreed time and place, we arrived to find him sitting with friends in a car in an incoherent state; he had used the promised research payment as a means of obtaining cocaine on credit and was in the process of consuming it despite his scheduled meeting with us!

Katz (1988:216) has suggested that, through irresponsible spending, persistent offenders seek to construct "an environment of pressures that guide[s] them back toward crime." Whether offenders spend money in a conscious attempt to create such pressures is arguable; the subjects in our sample gave no indication of doing so, appearing simply to be financially irresponsible. One offender, for example, told us that he never hesitated to spend money, adding, "Why should I? I can always get some more." However, the inclination of offenders to free-spending leaves them with few alternatives but to continue committing crimes. Their next financial crisis is never far around the corner.

The high-living of the offenders, thus, calls into question the extent to which they are driven to crime by genuine financial hardship. At the same time, though, their spendthrift ways ensure that the crimes they commit will be economically motivated (Katz, 1988). The offenders perceive themselves as needing money, and their offenses typically are a response to this perception. Objectively, however, few are doing burglaries to escape impoverishment.

Why Burglary?

The decision to commit a residential burglary, then, is usually prompted by a perceived need for cash. Burglary, however, is not the only means by which offenders could get some money. Why do they choose burglary over legitimate work? Why do they elect to carry out a burglary rather than borrow the money from a friend or relative? Additionally, why do they select burglary rather than some other crime?

Given the streetcorner context in which most burglary decisions were made, legitimate work did not represent a viable solution for most of the offenders in our sample. These subjects, with few exceptions, wanted money there and then and, in such circumstances, even day labor was irrelevant because it did not respond to the immediacy of their desire for cash (Lemert, 1953). Moreover, the jobs available to most of the offenders were poorly paid and could not sustain their desired lifestyles. It is notable that 17 of the 95 offenders who did burglaries primarily to raise money *were* legitimately employed.

> [I have a job, but] I got tired of waiting on that money. I can get money like that. I got talent, I can do me a burg, man, and get me five or six hundred dollars in less than a hour. Working eight hours a day and waiting for a whole week for a check and it ain't even about shit. (No. 022)

> [E]ven if I had a job, I betcha I couldn't find a job payin' me over minimum wage. Then they probably want to pay me every two weeks, so I would have to supplement that week that I wouldn't get paid with somethin'. (Mike Jackson—No. 046)

Beyond this, a few of the offenders expressed a strong aversion to legitimate employment, saying that a job would impinge upon their way of life.

> I ain't workin' and too lazy to work and just all that. I like it to where I can just run around. I don't got to get up at no certain time, just whenever I wake up. I ain't gotta go to bed a certain time to get up at a certain time. Go to bed around one o'clock or when I want, get up when I want. Ain't got to go to work and work eight hours. Just go in and do a five-minute job, get that money, that's just basically it. (Tony Scott —No.085)

> I done got lazy. . . . I don't even want to work eight hours. I figure I can do maybe only one hour and get paid as much as I would if I worked a full day. (Kip Harris—No. 069)

These subjects closely matched the "high-level thieves" described by Shover (1991:92): "Misfits in a world that values precise schedules, punctuality, and disciplined subordination to authority, high-level thieves value the autonomy to structure life and work as they wish." Indeed, crime appealed to some of the subjects precisely because it allowed them to flaunt their independence from the routine imposed by the world of work (Shover and Honaker, 1992). Not taking orders from anyone—be it a girlfriend, a wife, or an employer—is a bedrock value on which male streetcorner culture rests; to be regarded as hip one must always do as he pleases. Accordingly, those who defined themselves most strongly in terms of their street reputation found the idea of getting a job to be distasteful because legitimate employment would require them to do as they were told by the boss.

> I guess [burglary is] in my blood. I don't too much want to work with a job and listen to no boss. But I can, like, do two or three burglaries and take money home to my kids. (Roger Brown—No. 058)

Nevertheless, a majority of the offenders reported that they wanted lawful employment; 43 of the 78 unemployed subjects who said that they did burglaries mostly for the money claimed they would stop committing offenses if someone gave them a "good" job.

> I'm definitely going to give it up as soon as I get me a good job. I don't mean making fifteen dollars an hour. Give me a job making five-fifty and I'm happy with it. I don't got to burglarize no more. I'm not doing it because I like doing it, I'm doing it because I need some [drugs]. (No. 079)

> Anything like five dollars an hour might slow me down, stop me completely. And the people at the job ain't buggin' me. I'll stay there the rest of my life if the people don't bother me cause I don't take nothing from 'em and therefore I would've went off on one of 'em or either beat 'em up. They don't bother me and I won't bother them and that five dollars is standin' strong. And wouldn't have to steal nothin' cause I'd have my money there. And I might cut down off my drugs—mainly you do drugs cause there's nothing to do. (No. 009)

While such claims may or may not be sincere—some of these subjects had held reasonably high-paying jobs in the past, but lost them owing to dishonesty or drug and alcohol problems—it is unlikely that they will ever be challenged. Decent employment opportunities are limited for inner-city residents (Wilson, 1987) and the offenders, who by and large are poorly educated, unskilled, and heavy illicit drug or alcohol users, are not well placed to compete for the few good jobs available. Most of them realized this and were resigned to being out of work. In their eyes, burglary represented a more realistic means of "earning" some money.

> Look, [there] ain't no job! I been out here lookin' for work, can't find no work. So I do what I do best. (Leroy Robison—No. 045)

Instead of committing burglaries, of course, the offenders perhaps could have borrowed some cash from a friend or relative. But they did not view this as a feasible alternative. Some of them were unwilling to ask for money because they felt that this would damage their status.

> I like to stand on my own two feet as a man, you know what I'm sayin'? I like to pay my way and I don't like to ask nobody for nothin'. Don't want nobody talkin' about me like I won't pay my way. I ain't freeloadin' off nobody. I'm a man, so I take care of myself. (Jeffery Moore—No. 006)

Others had borrowed money in the past, but were reluctant to ask for more.

> I can't keep askin' my wife, my brothers and sister and my mother. They'll tell me the same thing, "You a grown man, go out there and get you a job!" Or [they'll hand me some money and say], "Here, don't come back too soon." You know, you can only do that for so long. (No. 018)

And still others simply found that it was impossible to borrow money.

> After you ask for a few dollars from people—your loved ones or your grandmother—and they tell you what they ain't got, you lay back down and try to go to sleep. You don't have no cigarettes, no beer, no nothing. Yeah, it builds up, animosity builds up inside you. Seems like that old devil just push you on out the door [to do a burglary]. (No. 069)

In any case, borrowing money offers only a short-term solution to financial needs. There usually is an expectation that loans will be repaid and this can provide the impetus for carrying out a burglary. Indeed, Katz (1988: 217) has gone so far as to suggest that this obligation is a major source of the monetary troubles that drive offenders to crime: "Economic pressures toward crime emerge, not as the direct result of particular substantive needs as much as through the pressure of obligations accumulated in social networks. Borrowing and credit relations among offenders form a subtle, elaborate institution." In the course of our interviews we were told of burglaries that had been carried out because the offender owed money or wanted to reclaim a pawned article. We even encountered an offender who recently had broken into the residence of a fellow burglar in order to collect on a bad debt.

When faced with an immediate need for cash, then, the offenders in our sample perceived themselves as having little hope of getting money both quickly *and* legally. Many of the most efficient solutions to financial troubles are against the law (Lofland, 1969). However, this does not explain why the subjects decided specifically on the crime of residential burglary. After all, most of them admitted committing other sorts of offenses in the past, and some still were doing so. Why should they choose burglary?

For some subjects, this question held little relevance because they regarded residential burglary as their "main line" and alternative offenses were seldom considered when the need for money arose.

> I guess the reason why I stick to burglary is because it makes me a lot of money. . . . I guess you could say why I just do [burglary] is because I've been doing it for a while and I'm kind of stuck with it. (Carl Watson—No. 032)

> [I do burglary] because it's easy and because I know it. It's kind of getting a speciality or a career. If you're in one line, or one field, and you know it real well, then you don't have any qualms about doing it. But if you try something new, you could really mess up. . . . At this point, I've gotten away with so much [that] I just don't want to risk it—it's too much to risk at this point. I feel like I have a good pattern, clean; go in the house, come back out, under two minutes every time. (Darlene White—No. 100)

> [Burglary is] easy for me. People have armed robberies and sell crack or whatever; I do burglaries. That's the easiest thing I do. . . . I'm just saying that's what best suits me. (Karl Alverez—No. 081)

> I don't know [why I decided on burglary]. I guess I'm good at it. . . . I just like burglary, that's it. (No. 013)

When these subjects did commit another kind of offense, it typically was triggered by the chance discovery of a vulnerable target. As noted in the first chapter, most of the burglars we interviewed identified themselves as hustlers, people who were always looking to "get over" by making some fast cash; it would have been out of character for them to pass up any kind of presented opportunity to do so.

> If I see another hustle, then I'll do it, but burglary is my pet. (Larry Smith—No. 065)

> Burglars usually just stick to burglary. There's only one time that I was in the process of doing a burglary and I did a robbery. I was gettin' ready to do a burglary and a guy walked up and had a money sack. So I forgot all about the burglary and got the money sack. (No. 055)

The immediacy of their need for money, however, drove most of the offenders to look actively for any illicit opportunity to obtain cash rapidly, and they were open to crimes other than residential burglary. As one put it: "When you need money, you're going to do what you have to." These offenders chose to break into a dwelling when that act represented what they perceived to be the "most proximate and performable" (Lofland, 1969:61) crime available to them. Both their subjective state and the objective characteristics of the situation played a part in shaping this perception. For such offenders, making the decision to commit a residential burglary instead of another type of offense involved more than a cool assessment of the potential costs and benefits associated with the various alternatives; emotion, mood, and intuition also had a powerful influence on this process (Scheff, 1992).

> [S]ometimes you feel better about one thing than you do another and sometimes you know where the money is at. It depends on what's there at the time, whether there is transportation or you are in the area. It's just what looks good at the time. What's more comfortable for you to do, what feels better. (Earl Martin—No. 083)

> [W]hen you high on crack, you want some more crack and you don't want to wait, so you got to do a robbery. Now a burglary, you might be high at three in the morning, now whose house can you go in at

three in the morning and they ain't gonna be there? (Diamond Craig—No. 027)

A few offenders typically did not themselves choose to commit residential burglaries, but went along with offenses suggested by someone else. In need of cash, these subjects were especially receptive to presented criminal opportunities, even if they were not particularly enamored of burglary.

> I got a friend that do burglaries with me. He usually the one that sets them up. If he ain't got one set up, then I might go off into somethin' else. (Larry Brown—No. 052)

Some of these offenders seemed, when on their own, to lack the stomach for any sort of serious wrongdoing. Others had a preference for a different type of crime, but were tempted to do an occasional burglary when asked to lend a hand. One subject told us that he usually stayed away from burglary in favor of drug selling, explaining that he regarded the former as morally worse than the latter because "the victim comes to you in drug selling, [while] in burglary you go to the victim." Nevertheless, he admitted being willing to commit a break-in when presented with a good opportunity by one of his associates.

The range of moneymaking crimes from which the majority of the offenders could choose was fairly limited. By and large, they did not hold jobs that would allow them to violate even a low-level position of financial trust (Cressey, 1953). Similarly, few had the technical expertise required to disarm the sophisticated security systems protecting lucrative commercial targets or the interpersonal skills needed to commit frauds. It is not surprising, therefore, that, besides residential burglary, almost all of them stuck to a limited number of crimes requiring little skill, such as theft (mostly shoplifting), stealing cars, streetcorner drug selling and robbery.

For many of the offenders, the few profitable criminal opportunities objectively available to them were restricted still further by their belief that certain crimes were too risky or were morally unacceptable. A number of them, for instance, had curtailed or severely limited their participation in drug selling because they felt that the risks of apprehension and punishment were too great.

> It's hard right now, man. . . . I can go back to selling drugs which I could lose my ass. A burg, I could get away with four years [imprisonment]. If I get caught on burglary, I know I'm guaranteed four years. I get caught with drugs, I'm a do thirty [years]. So see, I got away from drugs and fell with the number one [offense, burglary]. (Charlie—No. 024)

> See, right now they harder on druggies than a burglar or auto thief. They tryin' to save the younger generation now. They sayin' drugs is the cause of the crimes now. (Joe Outlaw—No. 056)

Likewise, some regarded robbery, especially armed robbery, as carrying too much risk.

> See, if you rob a person, they can identify you cause you lookin' right at 'em, you know? They lookin' right at you and they can identify you. And armed robbery is what? Five to ten [years]? Or ten to fifteen [years]? (No. 006)

> [T]hey givin' too much time for robbin'. After my eight years for robbery, I told myself then I'll never do another robbery because I was locked up with so many guys that was doin' twenty-five to thirty years for robbery and I think that's what made me stick to burglaries, because I had learned that a crime committed with a weapon will get you a lot of time. (No. 013)

One offender decided against committing robberies because he was afraid of being hurt by the victim or witnesses.

> I'm not going to try no strong robberies cause these people could possibly see me out there in the street and I might be full of some alcohol or something and they could get me. They could shoot me or stab me or anything and I wouldn't know. (No. 040)

A couple of the burglars we worked with believed that it was wrong to threaten or to use violence to get money and therefore were reluctant to do robberies. Although the offender quoted below does not say that he avoided robbery for moral reasons, the tone of his voice left no doubt that this was the case.

> I'd never personally rob a human being, like walk up to them and say, "Give me you wallet and give me your purse!" No way. (No. 079)

Even those who were willing to do robberies, however, sometimes were unable to do so because they did not have the "facilitating hardware" (Lofland, 1969:69–72), namely, a firearm.

> Well, lately I haven't did any [robberies]. But when I was doin' it, I robbed every Friday. . . . I ain't got no pistol, that's the only reason [I haven't been doing them], . . . I swear. (No. 011)

Handguns are in great demand on the street. One of the subjects in our sample claimed that he would rather have a pistol than cash because "a gun is money with a trigger." Offenders who are in need of immediate cash often are tempted to sell their weapon instead of resorting to a difficult or risky crime. The result of this is that they do not always have a pistol at their disposal. In such circumstances residential burglary, which typically requires nothing more than readily available objects (e.g., a screwdriver, hammer, or small crowbar) for its commission, becomes correspondingly more attractive.

The Seductions of Residential Burglary

For some offenders, the perceived benefits of residential burglary may transcend the amelioration of financial need. A few of the subjects we interviewed—7 of 102—said that they did not typically commit burglaries as much for the money as for the psychic rewards. These offenders reported breaking into dwellings primarily because they enjoyed doing so. Most of them did not enjoy burglary per se, but rather the risks and challenges inherent in the crime.

> [I]t's really because I like [burglaries]. I know that if I get caught I'm a do more time than the average person, but still, it's the risk. I like doin' them. (No. 013)

> I think [burglary is] fun. It's a challenge. You don't know whether you're getting caught or not and I like challenges. If I can get a challenging [burglary, I] like that. It's more of the risk that you got to take, you know, to see how good you can really be. (No. 103)

These subjects seemingly viewed the successful completion of an offense as "a thrilling demonstration of personal competence" (Katz, 1988:9). Given this, it is not surprising that the catalyst for their crimes often was a mixture of boredom and an acute sense of frustration born of failure at legitimate activities such as work or school.

> [Burglary] just be something to do. I might not be workin' or not going to school—not doing anything. So I just decide to do a burglary. (No. 017)

The offense provided these offenders with more than something exciting to do; it also offered them the chance to "be somebody" by successfully completing a dangerous act. Similarly, Shover and Honaker (1992:288) have noted that, through crime, offenders seek to demonstrate a sense of control or mastery over their lives and thereby to gain "a measure of respect, if not from others, at least from [themselves]."

The purest example of the psychic rewards of residential burglary was provided by a probationer who, because he denied being currently active, was not included in our sample. Nevertheless, we spoke to him at great length. This man described, with obvious glee, breaking into places, rearranging the furniture and leaving, often without taking anything. He portrayed himself as a prankster, explaining that he got a great charge out of picturing the victims trying to make a credible-sounding police report. That his motivations were more sinister, however, was suggested when he commented: "I know that [the victims] are still wondering what I took. And I didn't take a thing!" Though the offenses had occurred months earlier, this individual still appeared to derive satisfaction from having desecrated the living space of his victims; he clearly was pleased by the prospect that his actions continued to unsettle their lives. Katz (1988:69) noted a phenomenon closely akin to this among the offenders he surveyed, concluding that nonacquisitive burglaries were experienced as a "black sacrament," a quasi-religious act of defilement through which criminals attempted "to project something negative into the victim's world."

While only a small number of the subjects in our sample said that they were motivated *primarily* by the psychic rewards of burglary, many of them perceived such rewards as a secondary benefit of the offense. Sixteen of the 95 offenders who did burglaries to raise cash also said that they found the crime to be "exciting" or "thrilling."

> Burglary is excitin'. [I do it] mostly for the money, but a lot of times it arouses my suspicion and curiosity. (No. 046)

> [Beyond money], it's the thrill. If you get out [of the house], you smile and stand on it, breathe out. (No. 045)

> It's just a thrill going in undetected and walking out with all they shit. Man, that shit fucks me up. (No. 022)

Several of those who were motivated predominantly by financial pressures claimed that the offense represented "a challenge" or "an adventure" as well.

> It wasn't just gettin' money . . . it was just the thing of doing it, the thrill out of going in [the house] and doing it. I guess it was a challenge. (No. 055)

> [Burglary] is a challenge . . . like going on a treasure hunt. (Billy Kelly—No. 048)

> [After the money, burglary] is adventure to me. (Rodney Price—No. 057)

And a number of the subjects who reported committing burglaries mostly as a way of making money added that breaking into dwellings was "fun" too.

> [I do burglaries] for the money. Sometimes it is kind of fun. (Ed Alverez—No. 082)

Finally, one of the offenders who did burglaries chiefly for monetary reasons alluded to the fact that the crime also provided him with a valued identity.

> My main reason [for committing burglaries] is because of the money . . . and knowin' that you can hustle, knowin' that you a hustler. (No. 054)

Beyond all of this, quite a few of the offenders who *usually* resorted to burglary out of financial need occasionally committed the offense to get even with someone for a real or imagined wrong. A number of them mentioned doing burglaries from time to time for "revenge." In the case below, for example, a black offender broke into the home of a young white man who had called him "a nigger" during an altercation over a scratched car door.

> I was driving my mother's car and [I pulled into the parking lot of a convenience store]. When I opened my door, I hit this guy's car—a gray Cutlass—and he wanted to fight about it. . . . So we were going to [settle it there], but the police broke it up. So I was thinking about gettin' even . . . I followed him [home]. . . . I just kept him in sight till I seen what house he was staying in. . . . It was Wednesday and, uh, I was plannin' on doing it Friday, but I had to learn their routine first. I watched a little bit the rest of Wednesday and then I came back and watched it a little bit Thursday, but, uh, I had to move quick cause I wanted to get even. . . . That was a grudge there, a payback, so it wasn't too much for the money. I broke up more stuff in there than I stole. . . . Normally when I break in a house, it's so that I can get me a high, cause I be having the urge to smoke a little coke. But this particular day, they just pissed me off. I just wanted to get even. I just wanted to hit 'em where it hurts—in they pocket—and I think I did pretty good. (John Black—No. 008)

Other offenders described break-ins designed to punish an ex-lover, collect on a bad debt, or "pay back" an unscrupulous drug dealer. Black (1983:34) has suggested that crimes such as these are essentially moralistic and involve "the pursuit of justice." Indeed, he has gone so far as to argue that many burglaries are best thought of as a form of self-help or "secret social control" (Black, 1983:37). This may be overstating the matter, but it is clear that, on occasion, some offenders find burglary an appealing means of righting a perceived wrong. For instance, several burglars in our sample who often worked together reported targeting the homes of homosexuals who were buying up and renovating property on the periphery of their own neighborhood. These offenders explained that they did not like gays and broke into their dwellings as a means of forcing them to move out of the area. From their perspective, such crimes were justifiable in the circumstances; they represented an attempt to keep the neighborhood from being overrun by outsiders whose way of life was different and threatening.

Summary

Offenders typically decided to commit a residential burglary in response to a perceived need. In most cases, this need was financial, calling for the immediate acquisition of money. However, it sometimes involved what was interpreted as a need to repel an attack on the status, identity, or self-esteem of the offenders. Whatever its character, the need almost invariably was regarded by the offenders as pressing, that is, as something that had to be dealt with immediately. Lofland (1969:50) has observed that most people, when under pressure, have a tendency to become fixated on removing the perceived cause of that pressure "as quickly as possible." Those in our sample were no exception. In such a state, the offenders were not predisposed to consider unfamiliar, complicated, or long-term solutions (see Lofland, 1969:50) and instead fell back on residential burglary, which they knew well. This often seemed to happen almost automatically, the crime occurring with minimal calculation as part of a more general path of action (e.g., partying). To the extent that the offense ameliorated their distress, it nurtured a tendency for them to view burglary as a reliable means of dealing with similar pressures in the future. In this way, a foundation was laid for the continuation of their present lifestyle which, by and large, revolve around the street culture. The self-indulgent activities supported by this culture, in turn, precipitated new pressures; and thus a vicious cycle developed.

That the offenders, at the time of actually contemplating offenses, typically perceived themselves to be in a situation of immediate need has at least two important implications. First, it suggests a mind-set in which they were seeking less to maximize their gains than to deal with a present crisis. Finally, it indicates an element of desperation which might have weakened the influence of threatened sanctions and neutralized any misgivings about the morality of breaking into dwellings (see Shover and Honaker, 1992). [These and other points will be discussed in chapters throughout the book.—Ed.]

Questions for Thought and Discussion

1. Why do criminals choose burglary over other crimes?
2. Does this study support the findings in Chapters 4 and 6? If so, in what way?
3. What are the elements of street culture that lead to criminal behavior, especially burglary?
4. What theory or theories of criminal behavior are illustrated in this research?

References

Anderson, E. (1990), *Street Wise: Race, Class, and Change in an Urban Community,* Chicago: University of Chicago Press.

Bennett, T., and Wright, R. (1984), "Burglars' Perception of Targets," *Home Office Research Bulletin* 15:18–20, London: Home Office Research and Planning Unit.

Black, D. (1983), "Crime as Social Control," *American Sociological Review* 48:34–45.

Cressey, D. (1953), *Other People's Money,* Glencoe, IL: Free Press.

Cromwell, P., Olson, J., and Avary, D. (1991), *Breaking and Entering: An Ethnographic Analysis of Burglary,* Newbury Park, CA: Sage.

Katz, J. (1988), *Seductions of Crime: Moral and Sensual Attractions in Doing Evil,* New York: Basic Books.

Kennedy, L., and Baron, S. (1993), "Routine Activities and a Subculture of Violence," *Journal of Research in Crime and Delinquency* 30:88–112.

Lemert, E. (1953), "An Isolation and Closure Theory of Naive Check Forgery," *Journal of Criminal Law, Criminology, and Police Science* 44:296–307.

Lofland, J. (1969), *Deviance and Identity,* Englewood Cliffs, NJ: Prentice-Hall.

Scheff, T. (1992), "Rationality and Emotion: Homage To Norbert Elias." In Coleman, J., and Fararo, T., *Rational Choice Theory: Advocacy and Critique,* pp. 101–19, Newbury Park, CA: Sage.

Shover, N. (1991), "Burglary." In Tonry, M., *Crime and Justice: A Review of Research,* vol. 14, pp. 73–113, Chicago: University of Chicago Press.

Shover, N., and Honaker, D. (1990), "The Criminal Calculus of Persistent Property Offenders: A Review of Evidence." Paper presented at the Forty-second Annual Meeting of the American Society of Criminology, Baltimore, November.

———. (1992), "The Socially Bounded Decision Making of Persistent Property Offenders," *Howard Journal of Criminal Justice* 31, no. 4:276–93.

Walker, N. (1984), Foreword. In Bennett, T., and Wright, R., *Burglars on Burglary: Prevention and the Offender,* pp. viii–ix, Aldershot: Gower.

Wilson, W. (1987), *The Truly Disadvantaged: The Inner City, the Underclass, and Public Policy,* Chicago: University of Chicago Press.

Chapter 10 Managing Fear to Commit Felony Theft

Andy Hochstetler
Heith Copes

T*he authors of this study interviewed 92 thieves (motor vehicle thieves, armed robbers, and burglars) on community supervision in a southern state between 1998 and 2000. Interviews lasted from one to two hours and focused on thieves' detailed recollections of specific criminal events. The authors' purpose was to examine immediate influences on thieves' decision making. This paper focuses on techniques and activities that allow those who are considering theft to overcome the central fears associated with the crime. The study found that fears of injury and confrontation figure prominently in thieves' decisions while fears of long-term criminal justice consequences are secondary considerations. Most thieves must face substantial fear before committing crime. Certainly the larger circumstances of offenders' lives makes crime more attractive to them than to people who occupy more deliberative environments and who have much to lose. But, committing felony theft still requires situational mental preparation. Drug use, cognitive tricks, and interpersonal interactions alleviate sufficient fear to make crime possible.*

Increasingly, criminologists look at crime as a choice and draw on what is known about decision making in other fields. Grounded in the tradition of rational choice, the simplest decision-making theories assume that offenders choose to commit crime after rationally calculating the potential rewards of crime as well as the potential costs that might result from being detected and punished. Researchers typically examine the components of criminal decisions, including the decision to offend instead of pursuing legitimate alternatives, the target selection process, and offenders' perceptions of various rewards and costs of illegality. This line of research has provided a wealth of information on both theoretical and practical problems in criminology. It suggests that offenders do weigh the costs and benefits of their crimes, but that decision making is socially bounded and not based on simple economic calculation (Wright and Decker 1994; Shover and Honaker 1992). Persistent street offenders live in a social world that emphasizes "life as party." This lifestyle promotes heavy drug use, spontaneity, and fast living, usually at the expense of conventional responsibilities. Offenders' behavior is not characteristic of economic calculators but of persons who are trying to stay high on drugs and alcohol and make some quick cash (Tunnell 1992; Wright and Decker 1994). Therefore, criminal behavior must be understood in the culturally circumscribed contexts of street life.

As we look to offenders' lifestyles and events prior to their crimes, a picture emerges of life trajectories that have taken recent turns for the worse, albeit many felons never had any degree of stability and security in their family and occupational lives. Criminal decisions are difficult to comprehend without first understanding the effects of extreme drug and alcohol consumption or without reference to the deteriorating life conditions that result from offenders' previous decisions. Continued partying delays confrontation with the consequences and hard facts of street life, but events sometimes force them to realize that their lives are without direction. Unfortunate conditions and recent incidents in their life trajectories, whether divorce, arrest, or banal confrontations with debtors or family members put offenders in a state of mind where devoting themselves more fully to drug consumption and criminal action seems appealing. In this condition, any criminal opportunity is likely to turn their heads (Horney, Osgood, and Marshall 1995). As one thief put it,

> You just don't care, you know. You get that attitude that, hey, whatever happens, happens. I'm not gonna worry about that [consequences] until it happens, and that's . . . the state of mind you are in [when stealing].

Another offender recalls that reckless living makes criminal decisions seem insignificant and logical in light of larger life circumstances.

> Things were crazy anyway. I was worried and paranoid all the time. We sat around the apartment and listened to a police scanner, for Christ-sakes. Our apartment was full of stolen stuff and crank, and we were living off of hot credit cards [purchased from other thieves and hotel bartenders]. If you're like that anyway, why not do a crime so you got something to really worry about?

Undoubtedly, offenders' lifestyles place them in company and situations where they are likely to encounter criminal opportunity and facilitate a mind set where the short-term gains of offending are more salient than the seemingly remote chances of being detected and apprehended.

Despite participation in a lifestyle that predisposes offenders to making careless decisions most must still overcome significant psychological and moral barriers in order to commit a felony. Even highly motivated and persistent offenders experience fear, anxiety, and apprehension about stealing. It is hard to escape completely the discomforting effects on the emotions and the body that accompany risky and dangerous choices. As one offender stated,

> I guess you was nervous but you too stupid to realize you was nervous. The adrenaline gets to pumping. It might seem like you're cool but you not. It's always there, the thought of getting caught. It's always there.

While it may be the longer trajectory of offenders' lives that places them in situations where crime is perceived as attractive, immediate situations, emotional components, and mental devices figure heavily in criminal decisions and are important for understanding criminal choice.

There is much to fear when committing serious property crime. The extreme physical sensations, often described as a "rush" or "butterflies," that occur during offending provide evidence that crime generates fear. Except for the most hardened criminals and those who offend without a second's forethought, crime evokes fears that range from a sense of uncertainty to intense fright. Thieves contend that the things they fear most when committing crime are the possibility that they may be caught and arrested, or worse, that they or their victims may be injured. While some offenders claim that they do not think about being caught by police, a significant number rank encounters with police at the top of their fearful considerations.

> The police, that's what I'm worried about. I can get away [from the owner]. If I can't fight them, I can outrun them. I can get around them. But when you come against the police, I know it ain't good.

The potential for arrest and jail time raises the pulse of thieves, but the majority of the offenders we interviewed contend that the real fear of crime, and the more likely risk, is being caught or confronted by a victim. Thieves are keenly aware that they are imposing on another's rights and property and that if they are detected by the potential victim the situation may turn violent. Getting shot or severely injured during the commission of a crime is a fear that understandably enters the minds of many thieves as they consider a target. It is noteworthy that five offenders we interviewed had suffered serious injuries at the hands of victims: three had been shot and two stabbed. Even the most brazen armed robbers in our sample had a great deal of apprehension about confronting victims who might resist. For them, unquestioned control over their victims at the scene of a robbery is extremely important. Any sudden movements or surprises from victims are seen as dangerous affronts to this control. Of course, most offenders avoid confronting the owners of the property they are stealing. This avoidance is not simply due to the fact that they do not want to be seen and reported to the police, but that they do not want to be killed. A car thief succinctly explains, "The police take ya to jail, but the owner'll kill ya."

When asked whom he feared more, the police or the owner, a young thief who ventured into rural areas to steal responded:

> The owners! Shoot, this is country folk. These people don't believe in calling the cops. You in their yard stealing something; they coming out with shotguns. It might not be nothing but pellet shots in it, but it still going to sting. Like I said, it was dangerous. You don't know who's land you're on. You don't know who or what they are capable of doing. People shoot you around here and bury you in their backyard and no one will ever miss you. Especially if you are in their yard trying to steal something. Don't no one know you're there. Think about, if you in their yard stealing you ain't telling no one you was going to steal this. This ain't orga-

> nized crime where you got a boss. This is small time stuff. So, I was more scared of them coming out finding me.

Another responded:

> I always have fears, you always have worries of people in they windows, if they see you but they just not saying nothing. They loading their guns right now. They waiting and they are going to shoot me, you know all that. Yeah, you have fears. Most times you have fears in everything you do, especially when it's wrongdoing.

It is apparent that fear factors into the decision-making process of many offenders. Few offenders give their crimes and the potential consequences careful consideration, but this is not evidence that dreadful thoughts do not cross their minds at some time. In fact, one reason that criminal penalties do not occupy offenders' attention is that they are more likely to worry about more immediate and dreadful fears, like being shot.

We contend that fear and the excitement it engenders are the overriding emotions during crime commission—and would be even more so if offenders did not take measures to overcome them. Just as offenders must neutralize moral concerns and guilt before proceeding criminally (Sykes and Matza 1957), they must find a way to reduce and manage their fears and anxieties. Offenders engage in social and psychological behaviors that allow them to overcome the immediate deterrent potential of fear associated with crime. In our view, some of the most significant proximal influences on criminal decisions provide a means of overcoming fears associated with the acts. Therefore, criminal decisions are significantly influenced and enabled by events that occur within hours or even minutes of the offense when fear is likely to arise. In what follows, we discuss how offenders more or less intentionally reduce their fears to enable crime.

Drugs, Alcohol, and Courage

> [I] may have a little drink, you know, a little false courage. A little marijuana, you know, false courage. You drinking and smoking marijuana, that brings it on.

As illustrated in the previous quote, an obvious means of fear reduction is alcohol and drug consumption. Drugs and alcohol dull reasoning abilities and reduce fearful reactions caused by risky behavior. And many offenders make criminal decisions through a heavy cognitive fog created by drug use. Over 80 percent of the thieves (76 of 92) that we interviewed were under the influence of drugs or alcohol during their last crime. In many cases, the amounts of drugs and alcohol they had consumed were extreme even by the standards of men who spent much of their time under the influence of one intoxicating substance or another. Crime and drug use were so intertwined in subjects' explanations of their crimes that the causal order of the relationship between drug use and offending usually was difficult to discern. Intoxication inspires and enables thieves; drugs both lure offenders and assist them in fear reduction. Setting the problem of causal order aside, some of our subjects made it clear that the only way that they could still their nerves to commit crime was by getting high.

> Well, I drink my alcohol and start thinking about the money I could get out of the deal. I didn't really . . .when I am drinking I ain't too scared. It kills my nerves. I ain't too scared. That alcohol have me pumped up, you know.

Another offender describes the numbing effects of drugs: "There really wasn't no fear. There is no fear. When I'm on Xanax and stuff like that, there is no fear at all. Nothing." While total alleviation of fear is not the norm, numerous offenders in our study and in other studies make similar statements (Shover 1996; Tunnell 1992).

Nearly 20 percent of the thieves we interviewed suffered from withdrawal from drugs or alcohol when they were arrested. Obviously, avoiding the physical discomfort of drug withdrawal was a goal in most of the crimes committed by the severely addicted. These addicts are among the most motivated offenders and therefore look past fear more easily than others. Drug withdrawal often seems a less appealing prospect than committing a felony. Most addicts must contend with fear of crime, but their desires do not allow them to postpone or waiver on criminal decisions. A heroin addict who routinely vomited from nervousness before he committed burglaries recalls that his desire for the substance allowed him to overcome his unusually strong aversion to criminal danger.

> Believe it or not, I didn't enjoy it. I did it out of necessity. I didn't do it because I enjoyed it period. I can't see any enjoyment. It was pretty miserable really.

In addition to the fear-reducing and addictive qualities of drugs, they provide motivation in other ways. Many offenders are committed to continuing the current party when they offend. Co-offenders who want to extend the current binge often use the promise of drugs and alcohol to "pump up" their potential partners. Sometimes a small taste of the party and substances to come inspires offending. The provision of drugs and alcohol can silence objections to committing a crime and reduce hesitation. A robber explains that when he informed his crime partner that he no longer wanted to participate in a series of robberies, the more enthusiastic of the pair bought more liquor in a successful attempt to "get me drunk . . . to where I didn't give a damn." When drugs are used to influence others criminally the intent is not to manipulate them into doing something they find unacceptable. Instead, drugs are one means of encouragement—a motivational tool. Nevertheless, it is clear that some offenders are much more committed to a criminal trajectory and to the party than others and these persons encourage crime—often as a means of replenishing supplies of intoxicants and expenses accumulated during earlier indulgence.

Incremental Actions

Offenders seldom think out a criminal plan carefully, prepare to carry it out, and then systematically put their plan into action. At first glance, it appears that many criminal decisions are made in an instant. Careful examination reveals that offenders often prepare for a potential criminal decision by taking small steps toward a crime and postponing the final decision to commit an offense until the last moment. By procrastinating on their decision, offenders create an illusion of pure spontaneity for investigators and sometimes for participants in the crime. By approaching crime incrementally, thieves can postpone the realization that they are taking steps toward crime, and maintain the belief that they can easily back out of the situation.

In group crimes, a division of labor and the need to coordinate action between participants in an unstructured environment ensures that criminal decisions are made incrementally. Multiple offenders take successive steps toward crime and then check co-offenders' reactions to make sure that everyone is on the same page. Interaction before a crime is often a series of hints and exploratory actions that allow those who are most committed to crime and those who are still turning over their options to make sense of each other's objectives and form mutual action. The improvisational and incremental nature of many criminal decisions provides opportunity to simultaneously avoid focusing on the dangers of a criminal act and to feel out the development of the act as it progresses. This approach reduces fear and creates the perception of safety because offenders think that in cooperation with partners they can watch for and ferret out signs of danger and abort any crime that looks too risky along the way.

> We would just look at it and kind of walk around and walk up to the house to knock on the door. Sure, lots of times we would change our minds. [If] I have learned one thing over the years its that you don't commit a crime that don't feel right. You go with your gut.

Incremental decision making also allows offenders to concert ignorance of their objective. Even offenders who proceed in a seemingly rational direction toward a crime often assist each other in overcoming fear by avoiding direct discussion of their unrealized objective. The need for money is the primary topic of conversation before a theft, but many offenders engage in small talk, listen to car stereos, or sit in silence as they approach a target. Offenders often think that careful planning would only heighten tensions and be of little benefit. A home invasion robber recalls that the most intriguing element of the conversation that preceded a crime planned by his partners is what was not said.

> We was having a good time on the way down there like usual. Riding around and drinking and smoking marijuana and things like that. I didn't think at first that there was nothing to it other than a night out drinking and partying. They was all just yelling and carrying on like we usually do.

When groups commit crime, concerted ignorance is especially easy to maintain if for no other reason than a single participant cannot be certain of what others will do when faced with a criminal decision. Offenders often note that they did not know exactly what their partners intended to do before the group offended. By speaking ambiguously before crime, thieves maintain their supposed ignorance of the probable outcome. A robber remembers the conversation that set the scene for his crime.

> It is not like you approach him and say "hey, look here, I have this problem." It's more like you are getting high and everything like that. You talkin' about this son of a bitch who did this to you and that son of a bitch who did that to you. And then I said, "I ought to go over there and take my money." One guy goes, "yeah, I ought to! I ought to do this and I ought to do that." And one thing leads to another, and basically I find myself in a situation where like I'm laying on the side of a hill saying, what the hell am I doing this for?

Retrospective claims by offenders that they did not know or were not certain that a crime would occur are common. These claims often come from those who should have known; many of the thieves we interviewed had lengthy criminal records. There was sufficient situational information in the scenes preceding most of their crimes to suggest criminal potential to even the criminally inexperienced. In one interview a young robber was asked, "What did you walk up to the guy for?" His response suggests that everyone involved suspected the interaction could come to no good:

> I was just going to borrow a cigarette. I don't know. I might have kicked him in the ass or something. Might told him to go on and get out of there. I don't know.

This robber maintains that he did not intend to commit a robbery. However, he admits that he had seen similar scenarios develop into robberies and that he recognized the possibility that the confrontation might turn into a serious crime.

Thieves progress toward crime through a series of decisions. Improvisational and incremental decision making allows them to forestall consideration of potential negative consequences. In many cases, they try to ignore the probable outcome of their interaction by leaving noncriminal avenues open. In other cases, offenders recognize criminal potential in a scene, but are able to tell themselves that their personal role and risk in crime is minimal. Interaction in crime groups is structured to allow for both of these techniques of fear management.

Interpersonal Influences

As mentioned in our discussion of drug use, individual offenders' determination to achieve a criminal objective varies. Some leave their homes knowing that they will do something illegal while others have only the faintest notion that the situations they are entering have criminal potential. Most offenders are in the mid-range of this spectrum of intention and some exert considerable effort to see that their role in making plans and carrying out crime is peripheral. In fact, some subjects said that they wanted to gain from the benefits of crime without assuming their share of the risk. By being less quick to act than their partners and keeping some distance from the target and the planning, they hoped to protect themselves physically, minimize their culpability, and to make it seem that their part in crime was incidental and unintentional. Fear is often managed by attempting to let co-offenders shoulder the risk.

> I told them I wasn't going to do it [robbery]. I told them I am going to take no part in it at all. I told them the only way I was going to participate in any of this is that it is my car and I am driving it. And you know as far as the crime goes, I am going to be as much involved in it as you are when it comes down to if anybody gets in any trouble for it, so I am getting my fair share.

Many offenders contend that they would not have participated had their partners been unwilling to take on the most dangerous tasks. Getaway drivers, car thieves who transport co-offenders to their targets, and look-outs often think that they are assuming less risk than other participants. This increases the attractiveness of offending, diminishes fear, and makes refusal of criminal opportunity more difficult. Two burglars explain that they relied on co-offenders to accomplish criminal tasks that seemed excessively dangerous.

> I didn't mind doing it, but I didn't like to go in. I would break the windows with a cinder block or a rock and then they would run in. To me, that was the easy part. They would be in the car . . . I hated the idea of going in there because I knew that somebody would be laying up in there with a shotgun.

A burglar recalls that even without encouragement having co-offenders is reassuring: "safety in numbers I guess. It felt safer in numbers." Several offenders mentioned that they were able to overcome their fears because their co-offenders assured them that they would be warned of any danger. Another set of "eyes and ears" can remove much of the fear of the unknown. As one thief says:

> In the process of doing crime I've learned that it takes two in order for a person to succeed. The pen is full nowadays because the one man wants to sell dope by himself, he wants to go rob this by himself, or he wants to go burglarize this or whatever. He gets caught sooner or later. It takes two in the game. You got to have a backup, somebody you can trust, to be your eyes in whatever you doing and then you will succeed. If not, you ain't going to succeed.

Co-offenders also play an important part in thieves' rapid attempts to weigh the benefits of crime against their fears. Like all decisions, the style of presentation provided for alternatives as well as the objective risk and rewards figure in the choices that actors make. In many cases, immediate pressure from peers to offend easily outweighs the deterrent effect of fear and seemingly remote negative consequences that might arise from crime.

When criminal plans are openly discussed, offenders often build confidence by "talking it up" or "gassing each other up" (Cromwell, Olson, and Avary 1991, 69; Shover 1996; Tunnell 1992). The most outspoken and motivated thieves in a group dominate conversations occurring before crime. These instigators often gloss over information about risks and exaggerate potential rewards. Interestingly, this optimistic conversation characterizes the discussions of thieves whose criminal records show that they probably know that the real rewards of crime are likely to be petty and that the cost of being caught can be severe. Perhaps this indicates that criminal deliberations reflect fear management techniques more than cooperative problem solving. Many of our subjects accompanied partners to crimes where riches were promised only to be disappointed. One young man whose booty consisted of a handful of costume jewelry recalls how his crime came about from a promising proposal:

> She mentioned it, just "my parents are going on vacation and we should go rob them." I said, "well, I don't know." But, that night it sounded a lot better and a lot easier. If someone had said let's go rob a house, I would have been like you're stupid. I mean the only reason I went along was because she said there is a bunch of jewelry and my money is guaranteed.

Several young offenders interpreted the optimistic criminal proposals before them as challenges. It is difficult for many thieves to admit that they do not have the stomach for serving as wheelmen or in other secondary capacities to co-offenders who are ready to assume even greater risks. The desire to avoid being seen as cowardly is an important motivation. When offenders, especially young men who are already partaking in risky activities, are "called out," they feel that they have little choice but to go through with a criminal act. They must act regardless of the fears they may possess, and if they show signs of hesitation, whether in the form of excessive questions or delays, the power of their courageous displays is diminished. Young offenders are especially willing to overlook their fears in order to save face or to gain status in the group. It is the fear that makes what they are doing worthwhile. As one young offender stated:

> You see it was three of us, and they were like "come on." They were the boost I needed to make it. . . . I thought about [backing out], especially the first time. I was like "man what am I doing here," you know. You see really it was like a spur of the moment thing. I was afraid to back out because I didn't want them to think "man he's coward," you know. . . . I was always younger so by my older friend wanting to do it I'm like maybe this is what it's all about, you know. Even though I got butterflies in my stomach, like I'm about to puke or something. Knowing I can't go through with this. I can't even move.

A criminal challenge is often made when bragging by one member attracts attention of his associates or opens their eyes to opportunity. Recalling his youthful days of joyriding in stolen cars, an older offender stated:

> I had a friend named Craig. He used to brag, "Man I can get them [cars] in five minutes, man." But, I could look and tell if [cars] were unlocked. And I would say, "Yea, but you get nervous, I don't. I bet I can get that before you." It was something like . . . we would just be walking around town or around the courthouse, you know. I would say "get it." He was like "check if nobody is looking." I would say "I told you, you was nervous." I'd get in there and start it and take off.

Similarly, a thief describes how a car theft began when he challenged his friend to follow through on his claim of criminal readiness:

> One night me and two of my partners was sitting on the levy smoking weed. For some strange reason my little partner Chip was like, "so and so went on a car lot the other night and you know those little boxes they had the keys in the boxes on the window." I'm like, "they don't have the damn keys in the window. Stop tripping!" [He said] "Man, I'm telling you." So, we end up going to a car dealership. And you know we . . . I am just really being nosy to see if they are lying, to call their bluff. And we break one of the boxes and he was right they had keys in it.

A robber explains how his group prodded their most cautious partner by placing him in an awkward situation that seemed to demand action.

> One of the guys stayed a nervous wreck . . . [mock whines] "I don't want to do it, I don't want to do it, I don't want to do it." The driver just sat there until he done it. He would get mad and everything, just aggravated to death. Finally, [he would] start thinking about it and just get up and do it. We'd sit there for five or ten minutes.

Once offenders begin considering a crime, the influence of the most criminally motivated persons in the group increases. In fearful situations, people are likely to turn to those who seem to be comfortable with unfolding events. In potentially criminal situations, participants who seem to have task-relevant experience are often used to gauge appropriate behavior. Novice criminals rely on older, more experienced offenders for their safety barometers. A young burglar explains his decision to accompany his friend on a spontaneous burglary.

> Whether we wanted to or not, we would, 'cuz we figured he was right. I mean, it was like we knew he had been around more than we had. I mean just getting into things; like just getting high or stealing or whatever. He wasn't scared of nothin'.

In response to the influence granted them based on perceived criminal abilities, persons thought to be in control often instigate and direct an offense. Previous research shows that in most crime groups instigators are easy to identify (Warr 1996). They may assemble guns or other tools to be used in crime, drive the group to a promising target, or begin other preparations. Their confident actions create the sense among others that the group's course is under control. Purposeful action can significantly reduce fears among the novice and hesitant offenders in a group.

By the time an offense is committed, offenders have dropped hints and numerous decisions have been made that set the group's course. To turn back at the last minute is to renege on an implicit obligation. Recall that few offenders are relaxed in the instant before crime. In these tense situations, hesitation draws impatient reactions including scorn and criticisms of cowardice. There is substantial pressure to get on with it. In this regard, a thief does not differ greatly from a soldier who charges out of the foxhole and into combat because of "comrades and fear of their reproaches, and the retaliation if he abandons them in danger; [and] his desire to go where others do without trembling more than they" (Du Picq 1947). A burglar recalls,

> He got the one and put him through the window, I mean what am I gonna do, you know. I didn't want to look like a punk and leave. I wouldn't leave them standing there and me a punk. Then, if they got away from it, then I would be a punk for leaving. That's how I was. I mean I thought I was in a little gang or whatever.

In extreme demonstrations of powerful interpersonal demands to offend, three offenders reported that they had resorted to violence when their partners did not agree with the assessment that certain crimes were too dangerous. Two of the aforementioned reluctant thieves recall their reactions to overenthusiastic co-offenders.

> It was just stupid and I wouldn't go along with it. He got aggravated and [was] wantin' to and I never would. And he got my temper going and I just dragged him out of the car right there and smacked his head against the Coke machine a couple of times and took off walking. I walked a couple of miles I guess before they come and got me.

> He is in front of me and he is itchy and I am noticing how itchy he is. I am standing behind him and I said, "no!" And he says, "yeah man, them's old people." I said "no!" I know where he carries his gun and when I see him go for where he carries his gun, I just pulled out my gun and stuck it in his ribs. I said, "I'll put one through you

> right now." By the time the old lady walked to the door I asked how low is the [hotel] rates and I said, "saw some lower up the road." So, I got in the truck and we rode on.

Although most attempts to abort crime never come to this, these cases demonstrate the difficulty of turning criminal momentum in a group without looking frightened and losing face.

The majority of offenders commit their crimes with others, and interpersonal interactions with others influence many criminal decisions decisively. Drugs and encouraging interpersonal interactions distort risks and reduce fear, but offenders still exercise considerable agency. Ultimately they must overcome their private fears to commit crime. To do this, they rely on mental devices that we term cognitive tricks.

Cognitive Tricks

Offenders are able to define the dangerous situation before them in ways that are more palatable, thereby allowing them to more easily commit crime. They can do this by redefining the act as thrilling, by putting the whole event and its consequences out of their heads, or by relying on the "power of positive thinking" and intuition. When offenders view crime as exciting they are able to confront fear by reinterpreting it as a challenge to their bravery and ability. There are many leisurely displays of fearlessness in our society that set participants apart from the cautious. Theft is an illegal means to the same sense of significance and mastery of fear that these provide. One car thief explains, "It was fun. It was fun because I would get a little adrenalin rush off of it. It was just a thrill. Like a thrill." Another car thief gives a similar response,

> But man really though, it was like, it was more of a thrilling thing to me. To be able to get away with it. I mean it would just give me goose pimples, man. I mean it was like I pulled this off and I made this, you know.

Less adventurous offenders can choose not to think about the theft or its consequences. It is very common for thieves to devote little thought to the possibility of being caught. Offenders are adept at simply puting the consequences of their actions "out of mind" (Tunnell 1992). Many of the offenders we interviewed stated that if the thought of getting caught came up, they pushed it aside. As with many dreadful and fearful activities, participants often focus on completing the task at hand without considering its broader causes or consequences. One of the best strategies for dealing with fear is to simply get the task done. One younger offender stated, "Like I say when I get scared or something, for me, the best way to overcome it is to just do it. Just go ahead and do it." Another stated, "I just blank it out. I never tried to worry about it." Offenders often try to focus their thoughts on rewards and getting the job done.

> Q: How were you still able to do it?
>
> A: I was just like, I got to have money, you know. I wanted money to buy nice clothes and stuff, you dig. I was like, just go and do it. I didn't really think about that at the time. At that time I wasn't really thinking about that, you know. I was just trying to get that money you know.
>
> Q: How would you get past that fear?
>
> A: I just pushed it aside.

By jumping into the act, the offender neutralizes fears that arise through contemplation.

Another cognitive trick that offenders use is positive thinking. Much like the athlete who enters a competitive event with a mind set that they can and will win, offenders enter crime "knowing" that they will be successful. Not only will they not get caught but they will come away richer.

> Yeah, the thought [of being caught] crosses your mind when you are doing it, but I always use this as a rule of thumb when breaking the law, if you think about breaking the law you are going to get busted. If you don't have a conscience about it and just let it go, nothing happens. You just know in your heart and in your mind that what you're doing nobody will ever know about it and you'll never get caught for it. And even if things get hot, you'll get out of it. It's always worked. I guess it's a karma thing.

> I thought about [being caught] a few times but it was the positive thinking thing, you know. If I don't think about it, they won't catch me. If they get behind me, I will get away.

Some superstitiously believe that they have developed the ability to sense trouble, and therefore, if they do not "feel bad" about a crime then they are safe. Signs of impending disaster are thought to be different than normal fears.

> Yeah, you can sense when something is wrong. It's all about going with your first mind. You know you have a sense of something not being right. The way things going like they know something. Sometimes you be paranoid. Look we going to leave this one alone. Another time. We going to go another time. Or we going to go in another area.

Previous investigators note that with experience offenders develop the ability to recognize criminal opportunity and to sense danger in a developing crime (Faupel 1991; Maurer 1951; Sutherland 1937; Wright, Logie, and Decker 1995). Investigators often focus on objective criminal readiness and ability to spot promising targets, but offenders also believe that successful crime requires intangible intuitive skills. For our purposes, whether or not repeat offenders have a heightened ability to sense danger is less important than the fact that many believe they do. Several subjects in this study claimed that they would not have been caught had they paid attention to premonitions that they had during their progress toward crime. This perceived ability to foresee trouble reduces fear when offenders prepare for crime.

Criminal Identity and Crime Continuance

Most of the men in our study were not criminal novices. Other authors have shown that criminal experience provides a perceptual outlook through which criminal opportunities are assessed (Wright, Logie, and Decker 1995). Recent successful crimes often provide offenders with a sense of security that aids them in overcoming their fears in subsequent crimes. For this reason, offenders often strike similar targets in rapid series of crimes. Through routine they hope to remove some of the uncertainty of offending and make crime more predictable and fear more manageable. If they have succeeded before, the same method should work again. With experience, offenders also may build confidence in their partners' abilities. Eventually criminality can become a group identity or a mental device for organizing events and predicting group action. While interaction in experienced groups retains some of its improvisational and incremental character, it brings criminal potential to mind more quickly.

Many offenders developed a criminal identity that set themselves above not only squares but also other criminals. These men believed they possessed special traits, such as technical skills, intuitive skills, and/or intellectual skills that allowed them to escape detection. It is remarkable how many of the car thieves and burglars that we spoke to who implied that they possessed rare skills despite all evidence to the contrary. An identity, or self-perception, as a good thief allowed them to approach crime more confidently. They are not like other thieves; they know what they are doing and think that they can circumvent most of the risks of crime. Experienced offenders often take pride in what they did. As one offender stated, "I had a lot of pride because I would do it so smooth. And I was so classic with it."

Shared criminal experiences are especially salient in ascribing criminal potential in a group. In support of this statement, several subjects who had co-offenders who had never stolen together before, stole every time they got together after that initial offense. Moreover, crime groups tend to be more specialized than individual offenders (Warr 1996). Familiarity with co-offenders and how they will act during a crime goes a long way toward alleviating insecurities and fears. Thieves who exhibit no special criminal skills and who are committing extremely risky crimes can easily come to think that they have discovered a sure means of making money, or that they are good and fortunate criminals who can muster more courage than typical men. A young burglar recalls the discussion after his first crime: "We sat and joked about it how easy it was . . . hey, we can do this every day." A robber who committed multiple convenience store heists recalls his diminishing fear:

> On that first one, my god was I nervous. I stayed up all night pacing the floor and looking out the window. I thought what did I do, I could go to prison. After that it got easier. Eventually [after additional robberies] I thought no one is coming. I just realized ain't no one coming.

Of course, the ability to overcome fear and to stay calm does help in the commission of crime. An extremely experienced crew of burglars reports the security that practice brought to their crimes allowing them to overcome the intrigue and greed that place burglars at increased risk.

> Whenever we went inside, we knew what to do. This one wasn't no different. We knew exactly what would be expected of us. It, you know, was a thing that we had done so much that we knew we had to take control. You have to know that this is someone's home, you're invading their life. They have lived there no telling how long and you're going in invading everything. You know that's scary . . . it's one of those situations where you don't just get caught; you get yourself caught. Just common damn sense, you know, you can't take everything and you can't live in their house. You got to grab and go, get the hell out of there as fast as possible.

Conclusion

At the critical moment when crime occurs, many offenders are faced with fear and apprehension. We have elaborated on a few of the techniques and situational adjustments that allow offenders to engage in dangerous behavior, but many others exist. We should also point out that not all offenders experience great fear; some get only mild butterflies before crime, and others have become so hardened that they feel nothing. Sometimes fears diminish with age and experience. The most experienced of the thieves we interviewed recalled that when they were young they had intense fears but now they no longer do. In their minds, they have become so skilled at what they do that there is no need to be fearful and they have realized that the odds of being caught are long. Some are confident that they know how to design their crimes to avoid worry about being killed or injured. Others state that they have already been to jail and know what it is like, so they no longer fear arrest.

While situational fears are barriers to committing a particular crime they can be easily overcome, especially with support from co-offenders. And when a target evokes too much fear, many offenders simply find a target that is less daunting. While fear certainly affects decision strategies, the thieves we interviewed report that fear served only to turn them away from specific targets. They usually could find a target that evoked a manageable level of fear. As a result, fear had little impact on their criminal careers. After all, many overcame fears of being shot on dark streets in hopes of making only a few dollars. The theme of this article is that offenders' lifestyles not only motivate them but also prepare them for overcoming fear. Just as street culture and interactions with crime-condoning others provide techniques for neutralizing guilt, they also make available sustained and situational techniques for neutralizing fear. For many thieves, overcoming fear is an intrinsic reward and goal of crime.

In a time when criminal justice policy aims to instill fear in the minds of offenders, particularly repeat offenders, we should recognize that this would be difficult if not impossible to do in a humane society. Fearful circumstances and punishments can be created but situational and lasting outlooks held by offenders conditions any deterrent potential of policies and practices that increase the risk and cost of crime. Only when offenders mature to the point of recognizing the lasting damage of a criminal career to their lives and families do they begin to avoid criminal companions and situations altogether. At this point, the threshold of fear necessary to deter them from crime is small by comparison to extreme risks that they once seized.

Questions for Thought and Discussion

1. In this chapter the authors focus on the techniques offenders use to overcome their fears in order to commit crimes. What are some of those fears and how are they overcome?
2. What role does fear of criminal justice sanctions play in the "fears" of criminals?
3. What role do drugs and alcohol play in overcoming fear?
4. What theory or theories of criminal behavior are illustrated in this research?

References

Cromwell, Paul, James Olson, and D'Aunn Wester Avary. 1991. *Breaking and Entering: An Ethnographic Analysis of Burglary.* Newbury Park, CA: Sage.

DuPicq, Charles Ardant. 1947. *Battle Studies: Ancient and Modern Battle.* London: Ams Press.

Faupel, Charles. 1991. *Shooting Dope: Career Patterns of Hard-Core Heroin Users.* Gainesville: University of Florida Press.

Horney, Julie, D. Wayne Osgood, and Ineke Haen Marshall. 1995. "Criminal careers in the short-term: Intra-individual variability in crime and its relation to local life circumstances." *American Sociological Review* 60: 655–673.

Maurer, David. 1951. *Whiz Mob: A Correlation of the Technical Argot of Pickpockets With Their Behavior Patterns.* Gainesville, FL: American Dialect Society.

Shover, Neal. 1996. *Great Pretenders: Pursuits and Careers of Persistent Thieves.* Boulder, CO: Westview.

Shover, Neal, and David Honaker. 1992. "The socially bounded decision making of persistent property offenders." *Howard Journal of Criminal Justice* 31:276–293.

Sutherland, Edwin. 1937. *The Professional Thief.* Chicago: University of Chicago Press.

Sykes, Gresham, and David Matza. 1957. "Techniques of neutralization: A theory of delinquency." *American Sociological Review* 22(6):664–670.

Tunnell, Kenneth. 1992. *Choosing Crime: The Criminal Calculus of Property Offenders.* Chicago: Nelson Hall.

Warr, Mark. 1996. "Organization and instigation in delinquent groups." *Criminology* 34:11–37.

Wright, Richard and Scott Decker. 1994. *Burglars on the Job: Street Life and Residential Break-Ins.* Boston: Northeastern University Press.

Wright, Richard T., Robert H. Logie, and Scott Decker. 1995. "Criminal expertise and offender decision making: An experimental study of the target selection process in residential burglary." *Journal of Research in Crime and Delinquency* 32:39–53.

Chapter 11 The Five-Finger Discount

An Analysis of Motivations for Shoplifting

Paul Cromwell
Lee Parker
Shawna Mobley

The purpose of this study was to analyze the various motives that underlie shoplifting behavior and to suggest prevention strategies based on the types of shoplifters identified and the motives that drive their behavior. The study is based on data obtained over a nine-year period in three states. The initial data were gathered during the course of a field study of burglary in 1988 and 1989 in Texas (Cromwell, Olson, and Avary 1991). Many of the 30 active burglars interviewed for that study were also shoplifters. The data were obtained through extensive interviews with 20 burglars who also shoplifted regularly.

The second wave of shoplifter interviews occurred in Miami, Florida, between 1991 and 1994. The first group of respondents were located with the assistance of a graduate student who was employed part-time in a methadone maintenance clinic in the city. She introduced the first author to a pair of heroin addicts receiving methadone at the clinic. After some initial hesitancy (and assurances from the employee, whom they trusted), they discussed their shoplifting experiences. They related that they supported their considerable heroin habits exclusively through shoplifting. Using a snowball referral technique, 19 additional shoplifter subjects were obtained over the next 12 months. These 22 subjects were extensively interviewed from one to five times each between 1990 and 1991. All were current or former substance abusers, and all were active shoplifters at the time of the study.

Between 1992 and 1994, anonymous surveys were conducted with undergraduate students in sociology classes at a university in Miami. Two hundred and twenty-eight completed surveys were obtained. Of these, 141 (62 percent) admitted to one or more instances of shoplifting and completed an additional survey questionnaire regarding their shoplifting experiences. Thirty-nine agreed to participate in a more extensive interview concerning their shoplifting experiences. These interviews lasted from one to three hours. Several student respondents were interviewed on more than one occasion.

Finally, in 1997, in Wichita, Kansas, the authors obtained access to a court-ordered diversion program for adult "first offenders" charged with theft. Of these, the majority were charged with misdemeanor shoplifting. These individuals were required to attend an eight-hour therapeutic/education program as a condition of having their records expunged. The authors participated in the sessions as observers, recording their stories and experiences and occasionally asking questions. The participants were told that the authors were studying shoplifting and were asked to participate in a more extensive interview after the sessions were concluded. Data were obtained regarding shoplifting experiences from 137 subjects during the eight-hour sessions and the authors subsequently conducted more extensive interviews with 34 of these informants. Although the diversion program was designed for first offenders, many of the participants had lengthy histories of shoplifting and a smaller percentage had been arrested and convicted of shoplifting in the past.

In summary, shoplifting data were gathered from 320 persons who admitted to one or more shoplifting incidents and more extensive interviews were conducted with 115 of those respondents. The respondents ranged from youthful first offenders to professionals who made the bulk of their living from shoplifting.

Although the 115 subjects who were interviewed more extensively provided clarification, detail, and a richer description of their shoplifting, they did not appear to differ significantly in their motivation, extent of shoplifting behavior, or attitude toward shoplifting from those in the group who completed only the survey instrument.

The study found that shoplifting is not simple behavior with a simple causal dynamic. While shoplifters appeared to make conscious decisions to shoplift and did usually attend to considerations of risk and gain in their decision calculus, many reported that they stole for different reasons at different times. There were few individuals who employed a single, stable criminal calculus. While most stole for economic reasons, they also occasionally chose to steal to satisfy some emotional need, and an otherwise rational offender might on occasion steal some item for which he or she had no need or purpose. Although the findings support a rational choice model of offending, some noted cases of shoplifting with apparent nonrational motives.

Shoplifting may be the one crime that most people have committed at one time or another in their lives, and yet it is relatively unstudied. There have been few large-scale studies yielding systematically collected data. Prior research on this subject tends to focus on small convenience or student populations (Katz 1988; Turner and Cashdan 1988; Moore 1983); data gathered from criminal justice or store security records (Cameron 1964; Moore 1984; Robin 1963); special populations, such as the elderly (Feinburg 1984), juveniles (Klemke 1982; Hindelang et al. 1981; Osgood et al. 1989), or psychiatric patients (Arboleda-Florez et al. 1977); or involve a few questions about shoplifting as part of a larger more general survey (Johnston et al. 1984–1995). And, while there have been some large-scale studies (e.g. Griffin 1970, 1971; Fear 1974; Won and Yamamoto 1968), most of these have been conducted with apprehended shoplifters and have concentrated primarily on collecting demographic data on the subjects.

There are several apparent reasons for the lack of interest on the part of scholars and the public. First, most shoplifting is a minor, nonviolent offense. It does not engender public outrage or fear. It is seldom the focus of legislative or media investigations. In fact, most studies place shoplifting near the bottom of the seriousness scale, along with such offenses as painting graffiti and trespassing (Warr 1989). In her classic study, Mary Cameron (1964) wrote:

> Most people have been tempted to steal from stores, and many have been guilty (at least as children) of "snitching" an item or two from counter tops. With merchandise so attractively displayed in department stores and supermarkets, and much of it apparently there for the taking, one may ask why everyone isn't a thief. (xi)

Lloyd Klemke (1992) explains that shoplifting does not result in "eye-catching 'body counts' or astronomical dollar losses generated by individual shoplifters" (5). He argues:

> Without sensational evidence of cataclysmic harm to foster and fuel public concern, most people consider shoplifting to be an interesting but not a very serious type of crime. (6)

Second, shoplifters do not conform to most people's perception of what a criminal is like. Instead, shoplifters tend to be demographically similar to the "average person." In a large-scale study of nondelinquents, Klemke (1982) reported that as many as 63 percent had shoplifted at some point in their lives. Students, housewives, business and professional persons, as well as professional thieves constitute the population of shoplifters. Loss prevention experts routinely counsel retail merchants that there is no "profile" of a potential shoplifter. Klemke (1992) contends, ". . . adult middle-class female shoplifters continue to be a significant segment of the contemporary shoplifting population" (24). Turner and Cashdan (1988) conclude, "While clearly a criminal activity, shoplifting borders on what might be considered a 'folk crime.' "

Another reason for the relative lack of interest in shoplifting is the public's attitude toward the "victim." While most people understand that the costs of shoplifting are passed on to the consumer through higher prices, few people view a large, impersonal department store or other commercial establishment with much sympathy. Shoplifters themselves frequently characterize their crimes as "victimless," or the victim as deserving it.

So, Why Study Shoplifting?

It is for many of these same reasons that shoplifting should be more widely and systematically examined. It is perhaps the most commonly committed crime. It is widely distributed in the population and appears to cross racial, ethnic, gender, and class lines. Studies have shown that one in every 10–15 shoppers shoplifts (Lo 1994; Russell 1973; Turner and Cashdan 1988). The Federal Bureau of Investigation estimates that shoplifting accounts for approximately 15 percent of all larcenies (Freeh 1996). According to the *Monitoring the Future* data, shoplifting is the most prevalent and most frequent crime among high-school seniors over time, with over 30 percent of respondents reporting having taken something from a store without paying on one or more occasions (Johnston et al. 1984–1995). And, a study by Ellen Nimick (1990) identified shoplifting as the most common offense for which youth under the age of 15 are referred to juvenile court. Estimates of losses attributable to shoplifting range from 12 to 30 billion dollars annually (Klemke 1992; Nimick 1990; Griffin 1988).

While shoplifting is considered by most to be a relatively minor offense, it is a violation of the law, and when the stolen items exceed a certain value, it is a felony. Petty offenses, while not as dramatic as more serious ones, raise the same questions of explanation and policy as do more serious offenses.

The very fact that shoplifting is considered to be a "folk crime" enables us to see some things about the origin and motivation for crime that more serious offenses such as burglary and robbery may not. And explaining why people shoplift may help explain why most of us at some time or another engage in deviant behavior and why some persist and some do not.

If shoplifting is as prevalent as studies have shown and the losses attributed to shoplifting as great as estimates indicate, this criminal activity has major economic and social consequences and should be more widely and systematically studied.

Purpose of This Study

The purpose of this study is to analyze the various motives that underlie shoplifting behavior and to suggest prevention policy strategies based on the types of shoplifters identified and the motives which drive their behavior.

Conceptual Framework

Rational Choice Theory

This research focuses on the factors that motivate an offender to commit a crime—in this case, to shoplift. While some studies have attributed shoplifting to psychological maladjustments, to compulsion, or to other forces beyond the conscious control of the offender (Arboleda-Florez et al. 1977; Beck and McEntyre 1977; Solomon and Ray 1984), most research has noted that shoplifters often employ decision strategies involving calculation of the risks and gains associated with committing the offense. This rational choice perspective is predicated on the assumption that individuals choose to commit crimes. It predicts that individuals will evaluate alternative courses of action, weigh the possible rewards against the costs and risks, and choose the action that maximizes their gain. The benefits of a criminal action are the net rewards of crime and include not only the material gains but also intangible benefits such as emotional satisfaction. The individual may receive immense satisfaction from the excitement of crime, from the independent lifestyle afforded by crime, or from outwitting the authorities. The risks or costs of crime are those associated with the formal punishment should the individual be discovered, apprehended, and convicted, as well as psychological or social costs, such as pangs of conscience, social disapproval, marital and family discord, or loss of self-esteem (Vold and Bernard 1986).

Rational choice theory is a theory of crime, not a theory of criminality. It assumes a general "readiness" for crime, that is, someone who has sufficient criminal motivation to act upon a criminal opportunity or to seek out an opportunity to commit a crime (Brantingham and Brantingham 1991). Criminal "readiness" is not constant in any individual. It varies over time and space according to any individual's background, circumstances, and opportunity structure. On one occasion, shoplifting might be a product of the individual's mood and perceptions brought on on by drugs or alcohol, and by the need for money on another (Brantingham and Brantingham 1993).

The degree of rationality that can be attributed to offenders in planning and executing their crimes and how rationality is related to crime prevention measures has been a central issue of debate (Clarke and Cornish 1986; Cook 1989). In the classical version of rational choice, the individual gathers information relevant to risk and gain and combines this information in making a reasoned decision. There is little reason to believe that this "strict" form of rationality is correct. Offenders seldom have all the information regarding risk and gain and have little or no accurate knowledge of the probabilities of reward or punishment associated with the act. However, in order for an act to be rational, it is not necessary that it be carefully preconceived and planned. Behavioral decision making theorists (March 1994; Newell and Simon 1972; Kahneman et al. 1982) have shown that individuals do not behave consistently with normative rationality; rather, they take shortcuts or make simplifications that are reasonable but may not produce maximized outcomes (Carroll and Weaver 1986). This view of rationality does not require deliberate weighing of carefully considered alternatives and consequences. It is sufficient that decision makers choose between alternatives based upon their immediate perception of the risks and gains involved. The decision does not have to be the best possible under the circumstances, nor does it have to be based upon an accurate assessment of the situation. And, as Wilson and Herrnstein (1985) conclude, the value of any reward or punishment associated with a criminal action is always uncertain. It is enough that decisions are perceived to be optimal.

The concept of "limited rationality" recognizes the limited capacity and willingness of most persons to acquire and process information from more than one input or source simultaneously. Clarke and Cornish (1986) concluded that people usually pay attention to only some of the facts or sources at their disposal, employing short cuts or rules of thumb to speed the decision process. These rules of thumb are analogous to Cook's (1989) concept of "standing decisions" which negate the need to carefully weigh all the alternatives and consequences before making a decision in many cases. A standing decision may simply be a decision made beforehand to take advantage of certain types of criminal opportunities or to avoid others. None of this, however, implies irrationality. Rational choice theories need only presume that some minimal degree of planning and foresight occurs (Hirschi 1986).

Many prior studies have noted a rational element in the motivations of shoplifters. Cameron (1964) classified shoplifters into two classes: *boosters,* who "steal merchandise as one way of making a living," and *snitches,* described as "deliberate thieves who manifest intent to steal by preparation beforehand and who carry out their crimes with system and method" (58–59). She noted that they are "not impulsive, erratic individuals who are suddenly 'taken' with an uncontrollable urge for a pretty bauble" (59). She concluded that there may be individuals who act impulsively; however, their numbers are few and their impact on the justice system or on business institutions is minimal.

Moore (1983) also found little evidence that pathology or maladjustment were significant contributing factors in shoplifting. He found no meaningful differences in the MMPI between shoplifters and nonshoplifters. Instead, he found that college students experience psychological satisfaction from acquiring personally attractive goods and saving money for other purposes. Kraut (1976) also argued that the motive for most shoplifting was the acquisition of goods at minimum cost. He claimed that the decision to shoplift is "an inverse function of the perceived risks associated with stealing" (Kraut 1976, 365).

Turner and Cashdan (1988) asked college students to provide information about the reasons their classmates and friends shoplifted. It was assumed that their responses would function as a projective self-report, in effect, revealing information about the respondents' real or potential motives for shoplifting. They found that poverty, "self-indulgence," and some variant of "thrill," "risk," "fun," or "challenge" were the most prevalent motives reported. Those who reported poverty (mentioned by 64 percent of the subjects) as a motive shoplifted to obtain items they needed but could not afford to buy. Self-indulgence (mentioned by 40 percent of the respondents) was defined as stealing items that were desired, but not necessarily needed. Sixty-six percent of the respondents listed "excitement," "thrill," "challenge," or "fun" as a primary motive for their illegal behavior.

Katz (1988), in research with a college student population, concluded that "various property crimes share an appeal to young people, independent of the material gain or esteem from peers" (Katz 1988, 52). He found that such offenses as vandalism, joyriding, and shoplifting are "all sneaky crimes that frequently thrill their practioneers" (53).

Each of these studies—whether attributing shoplifting to the desire to obtain material goods at minimal cost or to attain some psychosocial reward (thrill, excitement, fun, self-indulgence, etc.)—involves a choice by the offender based upon (at least minimally) his or her perceptions of the risks and gains associated with the act.

Results

The subjects were asked to explain the primary motivation for their shoplifting. They were asked, "Why do you shoplift?" They were allowed to list as many reasons as they believed applied to them, but were asked to be specific about the "main reason you shoplift." Many subjects reported more than one motive for their behavior. Table 11.1 illustrates the range of responses reported by the study subjects:

Table 11.1
Reported Motivations for Shoplifting

Primary Motivation	N	Percent
1. Wanted item but did not want to pay for it.	82	25.6
2. Peer pressure.	49	15.3
3. Steal for a living.	46	14.4
4. Wanted the item but could not afford it.	41	12.8
5. I don't know why. It was an impulse thing.	37	11.6
6. I was under the influence of drugs or alcohol.	17	5.3
7. I enjoy the thrill/rush/danger involved.	15	4.7
8. I was under a lot of stress.	13	4.1
9. I can't help myself. It's compulsive.	10	3.1
10. Other.	10	3.1

It was difficult to determine the *primary* motivation driving the shoplifting activity for most of the informants, as they shoplifted for different reasons at different times. Many reported multiple reasons for single shoplifting events. For example, one Wichita subject stated, "I wanted it. It's kind of a rush to take things, and I was mad at my mother at the time." When a subject expressed difficulty listing a primary motivation, the first motivation mentioned was considered primary. In the example above, the primary motive was recorded as "I wanted it." The subject was then asked if he had the money to pay for the item. If he or she said "yes," the motive was classified as "I wanted the item but did not want to pay for it." If he or she said "no," the motive was classified as "I wanted the item but could not afford to pay for it."

A Miami student reported, "My girlfriend dared me to do it. It was real exciting—I was pumped." In this case, the motive was recorded as "peer pressure."

This finding of within-individual variation in motivation may be important, as most of the literature in criminal decision making suggests a single, stable criminal calculus. However, it appears that many of the subjects in this study shoplifted for economic gain on some occasions and to satisfy some psychosocial need on others. Occasionally, the two motives were intertwined in a single offense.

In the following section each of the identified motives for shoplifting and representative statements by study subjects are presented.

'I Wanted the Item(s) but Didn't Want to Pay for It'

Eighty-two subjects listed this motive as primary. These shoplifters admitted to having the money to pay for the items they stole, but preferred to steal them anyway. Over 60 percent (64.6 percent) of males and only 47.5 percent of females reported this motivation as their primary reason for shoplifting. Many of these subjects also reported stealing for the thrill or rush, by impulse, or for some other "noneconomic" reason on occasion. White respondents (42.6 percent) were more likely than black respondents (24.4 percent) or Hispanics (32.9 percent) to report this motivation. Some examples of their responses include:

> I did it because I didn't want to pay for anything. I've got better things to do with my money. (Wichita: 18-year-old white male)

> I have a long shoplifting history. There are a lot of expensive things and I want them. (Miami student: 22-year-old white female)

> I got two kids I gotta raise and I don't get no help from that shit of an ex-husband of mine. They like nice things and it makes me feel good seeing them dressed nice to go to school. It ain't hard to take stuff. I just take what I want, anytime I want it. I've got three televisions and three VCRs in my house. I took 'em all from Wal-Mart. . . . I once went a whole year without washing clothes. Just threw them in the basement when they was dirty and "went shopping" for some more. (Wichita: 29-year-old black female)

> I've got better things to spend my money on. Some things you can't lift—movie tickets, a Big Mac, gas, stuff like that—everything that I can lift, I do. (Miami student: 23-year-old black male)

'It Was Peer Pressure'

Forty-nine (49) subjects reported peer pressure as the primary motivation for their shoplifting. Peer pressure—the second most cited motive in the present study—may be a highly rational motive for behavior as perceived by the offender. Approval from peers is one of the most powerful motivators of youthful behavior. Robert Agnew writes, "This pressure might be direct, with respondents reporting that their friends explicitly encouraged them to commit the delinquent act. This pressure might also be indirect, with respondents stating that they were trying to impress their friends or simply act in conformity with them" (Agnew 1990, 279).

Two-thirds of all the subjects reported shoplifting because of peer influences at one time or another in their life. However, only those subjects who were in the early stages of a shoplifting career or those who had shoplifted only a few times reported peer influence as the primary motivation for their current behavior. White respondents were three to four times more likely to report peer pressure as their main motive. Males were somewhat more likely than females to report peer pressure as a motive for their behavior. Many of the professional thieves reported shoplifting due to peer influence, but they seemed to be referring to their early experiences. Twenty-two Miami students (15 male and 7 female) and 27 Wichita informants (20 male and 7 female) listed peer influence as the primary motivation of their behavior.

> My mom is a shoplifter. Both my sisters do it. I got it from them. My oldest sister said, "Don't be stupid. Take what you want." (Wichita: 20-year-old black female)

> I started out learning from my cousins. They always stole candy from the [neighborhood store]. They let me go with them but at first I just was the lookout—watching if the manager was looking. If he looked at them, I dropped a can or a box on the floor and he looked at me and they knew he was watching. (Wichita: 38-year-old Hispanic male)

> My mother taught me. Ever since I was a baby she used me to hide stuff. She'd push me in my stroller and put things under my blanket. After I got older she would give me stuff to walk out of the store with. Nobody paid any attention to a little kid. (Wichita: 25-year-old white female)

> I never stole anything in my life until I changed schools in the seventh grade. These girls had a sorority and to get in you had to shoplift something. They would tell you what to take. . . . I had to get a pair of earrings from a Woolworth store. Red ones. It was too easy. I still do it sometimes. (Miami student: 22-year-old white female)

In some cases, need or greed supplied the primary motive, but peer pressure facilitated the actual offense. One Wichita subject stated:

> I had been wanting this CD and my friend started egging me on to steal it. I was afraid I'd get caught and stuff, but he just kept bugging me about it and finally I went in the store and put it down my pants and just walked out. It set off the alarm by the door and I just ran out. Now I can't ever go back in there 'cause they know what I look like. (Wichita: 19-year-old female)

'I Steal for a Living'

These subjects shoplifted for resale and much of their income was derived from shoplifting. Most, but not all, were or had been drug addicts with daily habits which ranged from $50 to $500. They engaged in a range of legal and illegal activities to support their habits. Most preferred shoplifting to other criminal activity because of the ease of committing the crime and the minimal sanctions associated with apprehension and conviction. Twenty of the Texas subjects (18 males and 2 females), 22 of the Miami drug clinic informants (21 males and 1 female), and four of the Wichita subjects (1 male and 3 females) were so categorized. In every case, these subjects looked on their shoplifting as "work." One subject in Wichita told the interviewer, "I'm a self-employed thief." Typical responses included:

> I changed from doing houses [burglary] to boosting cause it was getting too hot for me in Odessa. I couldn't go out of the house without being dragged down for some burglary I didn't commit. I've been down to TDC [Texas Department of Corrections] two times already and I could get the "bitch" next time [life imprisonment as a habitual criminal] so I went to boosting. It's a misdemeanor. Oughta have changed years ago. Boosting is easy and safer. [Y]ou steal a TV from a house and maybe you get $50 for it. I got a 19-inch Magnavox at Wal-Mart last week and sold it for half the sticker price. (Texas: 47-year-old Hispanic male)

> I make more than you do [referring to the writer] just stealing from stores. Yesterday I rolled up six silk dresses inside my shirt and walked out of Dillards [an upscale department store in Ft. Lauderdale]. They was worth over $1000 and I sold 'em for $300. That was 30 minutes' work. (Miami drug clinic: 39-year-old white female)

> I'm the Prince of Thieves. Everybody in my family are crooks. My father is a shoplifter. My mother is a shoplifter. My sister is a shoplifter. I'm sure my son will probably be a shoplifter, too. I can't imagine making a living any other way. I'm proud

of what I do and I'm proud that I've only been caught once—after over 20 years. (Wichita: 40-year-old white male)

I don't boost every day. Sometimes not even every week. My girlfriend and I go out whenever we need some money and spend the whole day. We fill up big garbage bags full of stuff—clothes mostly. We make enough to live good for a week, two weeks. (Wichita: 28-year-old black female)

I gotta have $200 every day—day in and day out. I gotta boost a $1000, $1500 worth to get it. I just do what I gotta do. . . . Do I feel bad about what I do? Not really. If I wasn't boosting, I'd be robbing people and maybe somebody would get hurt or killed. (Miami drug addict: 28-year-old white male)

Taking stuff from stores is a lot easier than robbing people or burglary. Nobody ever shoots boosters. Even if I get caught, nothing much gonna happen. Probation—a few days in county. It's like it's my job. (Texas drug addict: 35-year-old black female)

'I Wanted the Item(s) and Could Not Afford It'

Another common response to the motivation question was "I wanted [the item] and didn't have enough money, so I lifted it." This motivation was reported much more often by women (80 percent) than by men. Some of the women who reported this motivation were single parents with few financial resources. However, the majority simply coveted some item they could not then afford to buy and took it. In many cases this was one of the motivations for their first shoplifting experience. Five Miami student respondents (0 males and 5 females) and 36 Wichita subjects (8 males and 28 females) listed this as their primary motive for shoplifting. Typical responses included:

> I want nice things for my family but I can't afford to buy them. My husband and kids have the best wardrobe in town. My husband doesn't know, but I don't know how he doesn't. Where does he think all this stuff comes from? He never asks. Course, he doesn't know how much anything costs. (Wichita: 39-year-old white female)

> My mom wouldn't buy me a pair of $30 jeans . . . so I took 'em. (Wichita: 18-year-old black female)

> I stole a wallet from Sears for my boyfriend. I didn't have the money so I took it. After that I became quite the klepto. If I saw something I wanted, I took it . . . it's hard to raise three children without help and my ex hasn't paid a cent of child support. . . . I was willing to steal to give them things they needed. It's hard to see something you want and can't have it. (Wichita: 33-year-old white female)

> The first time I ever lifted anything, there was this CD I wanted real bad. I didn't have any money and me and my friend decided to steal it. We were scared to death, but it was easy. I've probably stolen $10,000 worth of stuff since. (Miami student: 22-year-old white female)

'I Don't Know Why. It Was Just an Impulse'

A few subjects expressed the belief that their acts were impulsive and done without thought or planning. Nine Miami college students (4 males and 5 females) and 28 Wichita subjects (10 males and 18 females) reported impulse as the primary motive for their shoplifting. Over one-half of all the subjects reported impulse as one of the motives for their first shoplifting experiences. Typical responses included:

> I want to say "spur of the moment." It was a watch and I just wanted that watch then. The amazing thing was that I had the money in my pocket to pay for it. I wish I could say that I had been drinking, but I can't. (Wichita: 33-year-old black male)

> It was sort of an impulse. I didn't plan to do it. I'm really embarrassed by all this. (Wichita: 22-year-old white female)

> I didn't really plan on it. It just kinda happened. I've never stolen anything before. (Wichita student: 19-year-old white male)

> I've been doing it since I was in elementary school. [I] see something in a store and even if I don't need it, I just take it. I don't know why. I'm a klepto. (Miami student: 18-year-old Hispanic female)

> I've done this since I was eight. To me it comes natural. I don't know why I do it. I've done it so many times that I don't think about it. (Wichita: 18-year-old white male)

> I took a shirt at K-Mart. I don't understand why I did it. I have friends who take things, but I never did. I liked this shirt and on the spur of the moment I stuffed it in my purse. (Wichita: 19-year-old white female)

'I Was Under the Influence of Drugs or Alcohol'

Eleven of the subjects in the Wichita diversion sample (7 males and 4 females) and six in the Miami student sample (3 males and 3 females) reported shoplifting only when intoxicated or under the influence of drugs. Many stated that they never stole when sober and blamed the disinhibition of alcohol or drug use for their crimes. In fact, in most cases, they reported taking minor items such as beer, cigarettes, or candy. Subjects reported:

> I picked up a pack of cigarettes and put them into my pocket. I forgot I had them there. I'd been drinking most of the afternoon. (Wichita: 30-year-old white male)

> Drinking causes it. I should stop altogether. Makes me impulsive. That's when I take things. Usually I'm too drunk to be a good thief. (Wichita: 40-year-old black male)

> Sometimes when everybody is drinking or smoking, we go down to the [shopping area] and pick up stuff. It doesn't seem bad then but sometimes I do feel guilty about it the next day. (Miami: 21-year-old white female)

> When I'm drunk or stoned, it's like I'm invisible. No, it's like I'm Superman. I ain't scared of nothing. Nobody can touch me. It seems like that's what always gets me in trouble. I'll just walk in and take something and walk out. (Wichita: 37-year-old white male)

> We were sitting around drinking. My roommate bet me I couldn't go across the street and steal a pack of cigarettes. (Miami: 20-year-old white male)

'I Enjoy the Thrill/ Excitement/Rush/Danger'

Many informants viewed shoplifting as a challenge and a thrill. They enjoyed the risk taking and many discussed the "rush" they received from the act. Many of the subjects reported "excitement" or "rush" as one of the motivations for their illegal behavior; however, only 15 informants, six Miami students (6 males and 0 females) and nine Wichita subjects (7 males and 2 females) considered this motivation as primary.

> I do it for the rush. Adrenaline rush, you know. You get all excited and you feel kinda crazy inside. I can't explain it. It's adrenaline. (Wichita: 25-year-old white male)

> It's like an addiction. I like the feeling I get when I might get caught. Once you get in the car and you got away with it, it's like, wow, I did it. It's a buzz. An adrenaline buzz. I love that feeling—while I'm still in the store, my heart is pumping real loud and fast. It's so loud I know people can hear it. I'm really scared, but once I get away, I'm exhilarated. (Miami student: 21-year-old white female)

> It is really fun. It got to be quite a lark doing it. It was an art and I was good at it. (Wichita: 44-year-old white male)

> It's not hard. Actually, it's fun. It's fun when you get away with it. It's scary in the store. Heart pumping—adrenaline pumping. It's exciting. Addicting. (Wichita: 30-year-old white female)

> It's a thrill—the excitement, danger. Fear. Dude, my heart pounded like a drum. Like it was gonna come out of my chest. It made me feel alive. (Miami: 20-year-old white male)

'I Can't Help Myself. It's Compulsive'

A small number of informants reported that their behavior was beyond their control. This category is differentiated from the "Impulse" category by the subjects' assertions that they could not seem to stop. Many argued that they were addicted to shoplifting. There was significant crossover between those who reported compulsive behavior and those who reported shoplifting for thrill and excitement. Seven Miami students (0 males and 7 females) and six Wichita subjects (2 males and 4 females) reported that they could not easily control their shoplifting behavior. Typical responses include:

> I don't plan on stealing. I tell myself I'm not going to do it again and then I see something I want and I lift it. I already have it in my purse before I think about it. It's like, you know, automatic pilot. I'm addicted—that's all I know. (Miami student: 19-year-old white female)

> I'm a kleptomanic. I steal anything I can get in my purse. The other day I stole a key chain—can you believe it? Took a chance on going to jail with a stupid key chain. (Wichita: 35-year-old white female)

> Shoplifting is an addiction for me. It built up over time. I tried seeing a counselor but it didn't help. Didn't stop me. (Wichita: 44-year-old black male)

'I Was Under a Lot of Stress'

A small number of subjects reported shoplifting as a response to stressful life situations. Five Wichita (2 males and 3 females) and five Miami students (0 males and 5 females) listed stress as the primary factor in their shoplifting behavior. Typical responses included:

> I was worried about my ex-wife back in New York. She was being evicted from her apartment. I also didn't get a promotion I thought I was going to get. (Wichita: 46-year-old black male)

> I was working long hours and not getting along with my wife and we had a lot of bills and some sickness. I don't know what happened to me. Next thing I know I'm stealing things. Books from Barnes and Noble, cigarettes, meat from [grocery store]. (Wichita: 40-year-old white male)

> I used to shoplift before I got married. Then I stopped. . . . The divorce started me up again. It gave me something to think about, I guess. I think maybe I wanted to get caught, but I didn't for a long time. (Wichita: 35-year-old white female)

> I get depressed. Things start to pile up and I start shoplifting. Sometimes it's at finals [final exams] or when I have a fight with my boyfriend. One time when I thought I was pregnant. Who knows why. It's like I take out my feelings on them [the stores]. (Miami student: 24-year-old white female)

Other Responses

Other responses not mentioned often enough to rate a separate category included: "It was so easy" (n=1), "I had a fight with my husband and I wanted to embarrass him" (n=1), "I hate my boss. When he gives me shit about something, I give myself a little reward" (n=1), "I needed some condoms and was too embarrassed to take them to the check-out" (n=2), and "the check-out line was too long and I didn't want to wait" (n=5). Six Wichita respondents (3 males and 3 females) and four Miami students (2 males and 2 females) listed these motives.

Conclusions and Discussion

It is obvious, now, that to speak of shoplifting as having a simple causal dynamic is to misunderstand the diversity and complexity of the behavior. When asked "Why do you shoplift?" the 320 shoplifters in this study revealed motivations that ranged from purely economic to apparent manifestations of emotional maladjustment. Most of the subjects reported that they shoplifted for some economic benefit. These subjects chose to steal as a means of satisfying their material needs and desires. Others satisfied some emotional need by their shoplifting activity. Still others sought to avoid some unpleasant or painful encounter or activity. These behaviors—satisfying economic or emotional needs—may be seen as highly utilitarian and rational. Motivations in these categories included (1) wanting the item but not being able to afford it, (2) wanting the item but not wanting to pay for it, (3) pressure from peers, (4) stealing for a living, and (5) feelings of thrill, rush, or danger. A small number of subjects reported that they stole to avoid embarrassment of paying for condoms, to avoid long lines at the check-out station, to embarrass a spouse or parent, or to exact revenge on an employer or store where they perceived they had been mistreated.

Of critical importance, however, was the finding that people who shoplift steal for different reasons at different times. In the 115 cases more extensively interviewed, there were few individuals who reported a single, stable criminal calculus. An otherwise "rational" shoplifter might occasionally act impulsively, stealing some item for which he or she had no need or purpose. The informants often expressed bewilderment over their motives in such cases. Of course, it is recognized that subjects may not have good insight into their own behavior or motives. Subjects may have reported their motive as "impulse" or "compulsive" because they could not articulate the dynamics of their behavior. Others may have reported stealing because of the disinhibition brought on by drugs or alcohol as a rationalization for behavior which they could not otherwise justify.

This points out the situational nature of offending. The motivation to shoplift is closely tied to the offenders' current circumstances. In most instances offenders perceive the act as a means of satisfying some need. The "need" may be for cash, for some item(s) they wish to obtain for their personal use, or to satisfy some psychosocial need, such as revenge, self-esteem, peer approval, or for thrill and excitement. However, the same individuals might also commit offenses without a clear motive. Several informants reported that they simply went along with friends who decided to shoplift during an otherwise legitimate shopping excursion.

They joined in for no reason other than, as one informant said, "It seemed like a good idea at the time." Crozier and Friedberg (1977) argued that people seldom have clear objectives. They do not know exactly where they are going or what they want. Maurice Cusson (1983) notes that to imagine that people carry out only projects that are conceived in advance and act in terms that are clearly foreseen is "sheer idealism" (p. 19). A shoplifter may drift into crime on one day, following the lead of a friend or acquaintance, while on another occasion he or she may utilize a more thoughtful planning strategy before committing a crime. Wright and Decker (1994) argued that this type of offending is not the result of a thoughtful decision strategy, but rather "emerges out of the natural flow of events, seemingly coming out of nowhere" (40). They conclude:

> [i]t is not so much that these actors consciously choose to commit crime, as they elect to get involved in situations that drive them toward lawbreaking. (40)

Some "otherwise rational" shoplifters reported that they occasionally took an item, not out of need or because they wanted it, but because they could do so without being observed. In these cases, the relative lack of risk appeared to be the major factor in the offenders' calculus. They were individuals with a "readiness" to commit offenses if the circumstances were favorable, and they did so even when they had no specific need for the items taken. Like the proverbial mountain that was climbed "because it was there," these shoplifters stole because they could.

Approximately 20 percent (n=60) of the informants reported occasionally committing offenses for what appeared to be nonrational motives. These included shoplifting as a response to stress, as a result of compulsion, or an impulse. Women were more than twice as likely to report a nonrational motive than men. Of the 60 individuals who reported a nonrational motive for their shoplifting, 42 were women. Such shoplifters often asserted that they did not know why they committed their acts or that they did not understand their own behavior. The behavior was seldom obviously goal-oriented and it frequently did not have a significant acquisitive element. Many of these shoplifters took small, inexpensive items such as candy, cigarettes, and nonsensical items like keychains or small toys for which they had no use. However, upon closer examination, we found that all of these individuals recognized that they had a tendency to "compulsively" or "impulsively" shoplift, and yet they consciously entered places of business for that very purpose. Others appeared to attribute their shoplifting to forces over which they had no control as a means of maintaining their sense of self-worth or to impress the interviewer with their "basic goodness." One informant summed it up stating, "I'm basically a good person. Sometimes I lift things and when it's over, I can't even tell you why. It's not like me at all."

These findings are important because they call attention to a wider range of behaviors and motives associated with shoplifting than have previous studies, which depended upon limited samples or on data developed through criminal justice sources. They also suggest the need for further systematic research with both apprehended and nonapprehended shoplifter populations.

Implications for Prevention Strategies

The study suggests that shoplifting is not simple behavior with simple motives. Shoplifting is more complex than previously thought and the motives of shoplifters, while not stable, are more rational than those noted in some previous research. These findings, if borne out by further research, have policy implications both for law enforcement and for businesses.

If a substantial proportion of shoplifters are compulsive and nonrational, policies based on deterrence have little impact. They do not calculate the risks and gains, but rather steal without "reason." However, if shoplifting is perceived as rational behavior, then deterrence-based policies may be effective. The existence of a strong deterrent effect does not require that the individual be fully informed or fully rational in their decisions. The deterrence argument holds that an increase in the probability or severity of punishment for a particular crime will reduce the rate at which that crime is committed, other things being equal (Cook 1989, 51). This suggests that arrest and prosecution for shoplifting might reduce its incidence. However, during the course of this study we discussed store policy regarding shoplifting with store mangers and loss-control personnel. A substantial number of these individuals reported that they prosecuted few shoplifters because of fear of lawsuits by those arrested or belief that penalties for the offense were so minor compared to the time and effort required for the store to carry out the prosecution as to render prosecution not worthwhile. Others reported that their loss-control technology or manpower was too limited to provide the evidence needed to prosecute suspected shoplifters. In many of these stores, suspected shoplifters were detained briefly, the stolen items recovered, and the thieves warned not to return to the store under threat of prosecution.

Interviews revealed that shoplifters are easily deterred if the threat of apprehension is obvious. Their perceptions of the risks involved at a particular store were gained from their own experiences and those of friends and acquaintances. They said that when a store had a reputation for arresting and prosecuting shoplifters, they tended to give it a wide berth. They also reported that once in a store, if they were being overtly watched by clerks or loss-prevention staff, they left the store immediately. These findings have several implications for loss control.

First, effective shoplifting control requires visible and obvious threat communication. Stores should post signs stating their policies regarding shoplifting. Clarke (1992) has shown that "rule setting" has a significant effect on behavior. Where the rules are clearly and openly established and stated, people tend to adhere to them. Where the rules are ambiguous or unclear, there is less adherence.

Second, shoplifting can be effectively reduced by strategic siting of store clerks' work stations and proper layout of display counters, check-out areas, and dressing rooms. Stores which pile merchandise high, crowd aisles, and do not maintain adequate sight line between aisles and check-out stations may expect higher rates of shoplifting. Unattended dressing rooms and inattentive clerks also facilitate theft. Some small but expensive items, such as cigarettes, batteries, and razor blades should be placed in locked display cabinets or immediately under the watchful eyes of clerks. Clerks should be trained in shoplifting prevention and incentives should be established to encourage attentiveness. Closed-circuit television, strategically placed mirrors, and merchandise tagging, bar-coding, and "electronic point of sales" systems also play a major role in theft reduction.

Third, if store personnel openly and overtly observed suspected shoplifters, following them about the store, most of them would leave without committing an offense. However, there is little glory or credit given to employees who "scare off" potential thieves. Most store security personnel prefer to apprehend suspected shoplifters and will thus observe them covertly, waiting for a theft to occur before revealing themselves. This course of action results in lost time spent processing the shoplifter in the store, taking statements, calling the police, if warranted by the evidence and store policy, and subsequently testifying in court if necessary.

Fourth, if store policy demands that the shoplifter be apprehended, then the store should be committed to carrying out the prosecution to the end. If word gets out in the shoplifter population (and it will) that a store releases apprehended shoplifters with a warning, or does not follow up with charges and court appearances by its staff, shoplifters will not weigh risk too heavily in their risk-gain calculus. That store will become a favorite for shoplifters.

Finally, police, prosecutors, and courts must agree to aggressively prosecute shoplifting. If shoplifters find that they are rarely arrested, unlikely to be convicted if arrested, and unlikely to receive a substantial punishment if convicted, then they may justifiably begin to believe that they are free to commit their offenses at will.

Policies, once established and communicated to the public, should be carried out faithfully. If the policy is to prosecute "to the fullest extent of the law," as the anti-shoplifting signs often threaten, then stores should follow through on the promise. These actions reverberate throughout the shoplifter population and should quickly pay dividends in reduced levels of theft.

These conclusions suggest that most shoplifters can be deterred. Their behavior, while not rational in the Benthamite sense, has a rational component in most cases.

Questions for Thought and Discussion

1. On the surface, shoplifting appears to be a relatively minor offense committed by low-level offenders for small rewards. If this is true, what is the value of studying this offense and these offenders?
2. How widespread is shoplifting in society?
3. What are the major motivations for shoplifting and how might this knowl-

edge be used in developing prevention strategies?

4. What theory or theories of criminal behavior are illustrated in this research?

References

Agnew, Robert (1990) The Origins of Delinquent Events: An Examination of Offender Accounts. *Journal of Research in Crime and Delinquency* 27(3): 267–294.

Arboleda-Florez, J., Helen Durie, and John Costello (1977) Shoplifting—An Ordinary Crime. *Journal of Offender Therapy and Comparative Criminology* 21(3): 201–207.

Beck, E. A. and S. C. McEntyre (1977) MMPI Patterns of Shoplifters within a College Population. *Psychological Reports* 41: 1035–1040.

Brantingham, Paul J. and Patricia L. Brantingham (1991) *Environmental Criminology* (Prospect Heights, IL: Waveland Press).

Brantingham, Patricia L. and Paul J. Brantingham (1993) Environment, Routine, and Situation: Toward a Pattern Theory of Crime. In Ronald V. Clarke and Marcus Felson (Eds.) *Routine Activity and Rational Choice* (New Brunswick, NJ: Transaction Publishers).

Cameron, Mary (1964) *The Booster and the Snitch* (New York: The Free Press).

Carroll, John and Frances Weaver (1986) Shoplifters' Perceptions of Crime Opportunities: A Process Tracing Study. In Derek B. Cornish and Ronald V. Clarke (Eds.) *The Reasoning Criminal: Rational Choice Perspectives on Offending* (New York: Springer-Verlag).

Clarke, Ronald V. (Ed.) (1992) *Situational Crime Prevention: Successful Case Studies* (New York: Harrow and Heston).

Clarke, Ronald V. and Derek Cornish (1986) *The Reasoning Criminal: Rational Choice Perspectives on Offending* (New York: Springer-Verlag).

Cook, Philip J. (1989) The Economics of Criminal Sanctions, pp. 50–78, in M. L. Friedland (Ed.) *Sanctions and Rewards in the Legal System: A Multidisciplinary Approach* (Toronto: University of Toronto Press).

Cromwell, Paul, James N. Olson, and D. W. Avary (1991) *Breaking and Entering: An Ethnographic Analysis of Burglary.* (Beverly Hills, CA: Sage).

Crozier, M. and E. Friedberg (1977) *L'Acteur et le systeme* (Paris: Le Seuil). Cited in Cusson (1983).

Cusson, Maurice (1983) *Why Delinquency?* (Toronto: University of Toronto Press).

Fear, R. W. G. (1974) An Analysis of Shoplifting. *Security Gazette* (July): 262–263.

Feinburg, Gary (1984) Profile of the Elderly Offender. In Evelyn Newman, Donald J. Newman, and Mindy Gerwitz (Eds.) *Elderly Criminals* (Cambridge, MA: Oelgeshlager, Gunn and Hain).

Freeh, Louis (1996) *Crime in the United States—1995* (Washington, DC: U.S. Department of Justice).

Griffin, R. K. (1970) Shoplifting: A Statistical Survey. *Security World* 7, Part 10: 21–25.

——— (1971) Behavioral Patterns in Shoplifting. *Security World* 10, Part 2: 21–25.

Griffin, Roger (1988) *Annual Report: Shoplifting in Supermarkets* (Van Nuys, CA: Commercial Service Systems).

Hindelang, Michael, Travis Hirschi, and Joseph Weis (1981) *Measuring Delinquency* (Beverly Hills, CA: Sage).

Hirschi, Travis (1986) On the Compatibility of Rational Choice and Social Control Theories. In Derek R. Cornish and Ronald V. Clarke (Eds.) *The Reasoning Criminal: Rational Choice Perspectives on Offending* (New York: Springer-Verlag).

Johnston, Lloyd D., Jerald G. O'Malley, and Patrick M. O'Malley (1984–1995) *Monitoring the Future* (Ann Arbor, MI: Institute for Social Research, University of Michigan). Data adapted by and cited from Bureau of Justice Statistics (1997). *Sourcebook of Criminal Justice Statistics—1996* (Washington, D.C.: United States Department of Justice).

Kahneman, D., P. Slovic, and A. Tversky (Eds.) (1982) *Judgement Under Uncertainty: Heuristics and Biases* (New York: Cambridge University Press).

Katz, Jack (1988) *The Seductions of Crime* (New York: Basic Books).

Klemke, Lloyd W. (1982) Exploring Juvenile Shoplifting. *Sociology and Social Research* 67: 59–75.

——— (1992) *The Sociology of Shoplifting: Boosters and Snitches Today* (Westport, CT: Praeger).

Kraut, Robert (1976) Deterrent and Definitional Influences on Shoplifting. *Social Problems* 25 (February): 358–368.

Lo, Lucia (1994) Exploring Teenage Shoplifting Behavior. *Environment and Behavior* 26(5): 613–639.

March, James G. (1994) *A Primer on Decision Making: How Decisions Happen* (New York: Free Press).

Moore, Richard (1983) College Shoplifters: Rebuttal of Beck and McIntyre. *Psychological Reports* 53: 1111–1116.

———(1984) Shoplifting in Middle America: Patterns and Motivational Correlates. *International Journal of Offender Therapy and Comparative Criminology* 28(1): 53–64.

Newell, A. and H. A. Simon (1972) *Human Problem Solving* (Englewood Cliff, NJ: Prentice-Hall).

Nimick, Ellen (November, 1990) Juvenile Court Property Cases. *OJJDP Update on Statistics.* (Washington, D.C.: United States Department of Justice) 1–5.

Osgood, Wayne D., Patrick M. O'Malley, Gerald G. Bachman, and Lloyd D. Johnston (1989) Time Trends and Age Trends in Arrests and Self-Reported Behavior. *Criminology* 27(3): 389–415.

Robin, Gerald D. (1963). Patterns of Department Store Shoplifting. *Crime and Delinquency* 9 (April): 163–172.

Russell, D. H. (1973) Emotional Aspects of Shoplifting. *Psychiatric Annals* 3: 77–79.

Solomon, G. S. and J. B. Ray (1984) Irrational Beliefs of Shoplifters. *Journal of Clinical Psychology,* 40(4).

Turner, C. T. and S. Cashdan (1988) Perceptions of College Students Motivations for Shoplifting. *Psychological Reports* 62: 855–862.

Vold, George and Thomas Bernard (1986) *Theoretical Criminology* (New York: Oxford University Press).

Warr, Mark (1989) What Is the Perceived Seriousness of Crimes? *Criminology* 27(4): 801.

Wilson, James Q. and Richard J. Herrnstein (1985) *Crime and Human Nature* (New York: Simon and Schuster).

Won, G. and G. Yamamoto (1968) Social Structure and Deviant Behavior: A Study of Shoplifting. *Sociology and Social Research* 53, Part 1: 45–55.

Wright, Richard T., and Scott Decker. 1994. *Burglars on the Job: Streetlife and Residential Break-ins.* Boston: Northeastern University Press.

Section IV

Violent Crime

Violent crime refers to any criminal act committed through the threat of harm or actual physical harm to the victim. Violent crimes such as robbery, rape, and murder have profoundly affected the way we live and have clearly altered our lifestyles. While the per capita crime rates for violent crime decreased slightly in the 1990s, because of increased population, the overall incidence of violent crime has increased significantly in the past two decades.

In a new selection in this volume, "Dubs and Dees, Beats and Rims: Carjackers and Urban Violence," Topalli and Wright examine the highly violent crime of carjacking. Little is known about the thought and behaviors of those who commit this "hybrid" form of crime that bridges property and violent crime. Topalli and Wright interviewed 28 active offenders to illustrate how they plan and commit the crime of carjacking. Like the findings of many other studies in this volume, the offenders chose to commit their crime out of peer pressure, boredom, or for a need for cash or drugs. Most of the subjects engaged in what Topalli and Wright referred to as "soft opportunism, taking advantage of opportunities which presented themselves during their normal daily activities."

Ressler, Burgess, and Douglas' "Serial Killers: Antecedent Behaviors and the Act of Murder" is another new selection. These experts on sexual homicide and serial killers (Ressler and Douglas are both former profilers with the Behavioral Sciences Unit of the FBI) present the results of a long-term study of 36 convicted and incarcerated sexual murderers and serial killers. Often using the killer's own words, the authors convey the murderer's thoughts, feelings, and actions as he contemplates, commits, and reacts to his crimes.

Scully and Marolla ("Convicted Rapists' Vocabulary of Motive: Excuses and Justifications") analyze the excuses and justifications used by convicted rapists to explain their behavior. The authors view rape as learned behavior. The learning also includes the excuses and justifications used to diminish responsibility. In this sense, the rapist responds more like the occupational criminal than other violent offenders do. The occupational criminal has difficulty perceiving him- or herself as a criminal and thus attempts to negotiate a nondeviant identity. The rapist has committed one of the most socially repugnant crimes, repudiated by criminals and noncriminals alike. His excuses and justifications are thus designed to place the act in a more appropriate context. In much the same way, the occupational criminal attempts to recast his or her criminal behavior as "necessary" for the survival of the business, or as merely sharp business practice.

Violent crime is often considered to be less rationally conceived than property crime. Violent behavior is often expressed in the "heat of passion"—during periods of great emotional turmoil. The violent act is thought to be more expressive than instrumental, having no real functional purpose or acceptable rationale.

However, recent studies have shown that violence can be highly instrumental. Wright and Decker ("Creating the Illusion of Impending Death: Armed Robbers in Action") reported that violence can play an important role in the commission of armed robberies by overcoming the resistance of the victims. Violence is thus rationally employed to accomplish the goal of the robbery.

In these selections we see violent crime as having both expressive and instrumental roots. The motives for their behavior, strategies used by the offenders to accomplish their crimes, and rationalizations used to avoid responsibility for their acts are graphically illustrated in this anthology. ✦

Chapter 12
Dubs and Dees, Beats and Rims

Carjackers and Urban Violence

Volkan Topalli
Richard T. Wright

Carjacking—stealing a car by force or threat of force—has captured headlines across the country. The crime has increased dramatically over the past decade. An average of 49,000 completed and attempted carjackings takes place each year in the United States compared to approximately 35,000 annually in the late 1980s and early '90s. Most of the participants were opportunists who simply took advantage of circumstances, either for economic reasons or in order to develop and enhance their reputations among their peers. Many cars so taken are used initially for transportation, but eventually are converted to cash through selling to third parties or chop shops, or are stripped of valuable accessories and abandoned. The authors use Shover's (1996) term "alert opportunism" to refer to offenders who take advantage of situationally vulnerable targets while not actively seeking a car to hijack. They use the term "motivated opportunism" to describe the motivation state of those who actively seek out targets. Like various studies reproduced in this volume (Wright and Decker, Copes, Jacobs and Wright,) the subjects in this study lived "life as party," utilizing the money received from the cars they stole for drugs, alcohol, sex, and other accouterments of the "streetlife" culture.

With the exception of homicide, probably no offense is more symbolic of contemporary urban violence than carjacking. Carjacking, the taking of a motor vehicle by force or threat of force, has attained almost mythical status in the annals of urban violence and has played an undeniable role in fueling the fear of crime that keeps urban residents off of their own streets. What is more, carjacking has increased dramatically in recent years. According to a recent study (BJS, 1999), an average of 49,000 carjackings were attempted each year between 1992–96, with about half of those attempts being successful. This is up from an average of 35,000 attempted and completed carjackings between 1987–92—a 40 percent increase.

Although carjacking has been practiced for decades, the offense first made national headlines in 1992 when a badly botched carjacking in suburban Washington, D.C., ended in homicide. Pamela Basu was dropping her 22 month old daughter at preschool when two men commandeered her BMW at a stop sign. In full view of neighborhood residents, municipal workers, and a school bus driver, the two men tossed her daughter (still strapped to her car seat) from the vehicle and attempted to drive off with Basu's arm tangled in the car seat belt. She was dragged over a mile to her death. This incident focused a nationwide spotlight on carjacking and legislative action soon followed with the passing of the Anti Car Theft Act of 1992. Carjacking was made a federal crime punishable by up to a 25-year term in prison or—if the victim is killed—by death.

Like other forms of robbery, carjacking bridges property and violent crimes. Although a manifestly violent activity, it appears often to retain elements of planning and calculation typically associated with instrumental property crimes such as burglary. Unlike most robberies, however, carjacking apparently is directed at an object rather than a subject. Most of the research on carjackings is based on official police reports or large pre-existing data sets such as the National Crime Victimization Survey. From this research, we know that carjackings are highly concentrated in space and time, occurring in limited areas and at particular hours (Friday and Wellford, 1994). These studies also indicate that carjackers tend to target individuals comparable to themselves across demographic characteristics such as race, gender, and age (Friday and Wellford, 1994; Armstrong, 1994). We know that weapons are used in 66–78 percent of carjackings, and that weapon usage increases the chance that an offense will be successful (BJS, 1999; Donahue, McLaughlin, and Datum, 1994; Fisher, 1995; Rand, 1994). Finally, these studies suggest that carjacking is often a violent offense; approximately 24–38 percent of victims are injured during carjacking (BJS, 1999; Fisher, 1995; Rand, 1994).

Despite these studies, much about carjacking remains poorly understood. By their very large-scale nature, such studies are incapable of providing insight into the interaction between motivational and situational characteristics that govern carjacking at the individual level. What is more, they overrepresent incidents in which the offenders and victims are strangers. Recent literature on the nature of acquaintance robbery (e.g., Felson, Baumer, and Messner, in press) and drug robbery (see Jacobs, Topalli, and Wright, 2000; Topalli, Wright, and Fornango, 2002) suggests that this limitation may represent a crucial gap in our understanding of the social and perceptual dynamics associated with carjacking. If, for example, offenders target victims who they know or "know of," the chance of serious injury or death may increase because within-offense resistance and post-offense retaliation both are more likely.

We conducted a field-based study of active carjackers, focusing on the situational and interactional factors (opportunities, risks, rewards) that carjackers take into account when contemplating and carrying out their crimes. Drawing on a tried and tested research strategy (Jacobs, Topalli, and Wright, 2000; Jacobs, 1999; Wright and Decker, 1994, 1997), we recruited 28 active offenders (with three asked back to participate in follow-ups) from the streets of St. Louis, Missouri, and interviewed them at length about their day-to-day activities, focusing on the motivations, planning, execution, and aftermath of carjackings. This methodological strategy allowed us to examine the perceptual links between offenders' lifestyles and the immediate situational context in which decisions to offend emerge, illuminating the contextual uses that mediate the carjacking decision. Interviews focused on two broad issues: (1) motivation to carjack and vehicle/victim target selection, and (2) aftermath of carjacking offenses (including vehicle disposal, formal and informal sanction risk management, use of cash, etc.). The issue of how carjacking occurs (i.e., offense enactment) is covered across the discussion of these two broader themes, because enactment represents a behavioral bridge that unites them. Thus, the procedural characteristics of carjacking naturally emanated from discourse regarding motivation, target selection, and aftermath.

Motivation and Target Selection

In the area of motivation, our interviews focused on the situational and interactional factors that underlie the decision to commit a carjacking, and the transition from unmotivated states to those in which offenses are being contemplated. On its face carjacking seems risky. Why risk a personal confrontation with the vehicle owner when one could steal a parked car off the street? Respondents felt that car theft was more dangerous because they never knew if the vehicle's owner or law enforcement might surprise them. Low-Down explains:

> **Low-Down:** I done did that a couple of times too, but that ain't nothing I really want to do 'cause I might get in a car [parked on] the street and the motherfucker [the owner of the vehicle] might be sitting there and then it [might not] be running [any] ways. I done got caught like that before, got locked up, so I don't do that no more. I can't risk no motherfucking life just to get into a car and then the car don't start. That's a waste of time. I would rather catch somebody at a light [or] a restaurant drive-thru or something like that.

Throughout the interviews, two global factors emerged as governing motivation, planning, and target selection: the nature of a given carjacking *opportunity* (that is, its potential risks and rewards) and the level of *situational inducements* (such as peer pressure, need for cash or drugs, or revenge). When these factors, in some combination, reached a critical minimal level, the decision to carjack became certain.

Internal and External Pressures: Situational Inducements and Carjacking

Many of the offenders we spoke to indicated that their carjackings were guided by the power of immediate situational inducements. Such inducements could be internal (e.g., money, drugs, the avoidance of drug withdrawal, need to display a certain status level, desire for revenge, jealousy) or external (objective or subjective strains, such as pressure from family members to put food on the table, the need to have a vehicle for use in a subsequent crime). Situational inducements could be intensely compelling, pressing offenders to engage in carjacking even under unfavorable circumstances, where the risk of arrest, injury, or death was high or the potential reward was low. Here, the individuals' increased desperation caused them to target a vehicle or victim they would not otherwise consider (such as a substandard car, or one occupied by several passengers), initiate an offense at a time or location that was inherently more hazardous (e.g., day-time, at a busy intersection), or attempt a carjacking with no planning whatsoever.

Internal situational inducements usually were linked to the immediate need for cash. Most street offenders (including carjackers) are notoriously poor planners. They lead cash-intensive lifestyles in which money is spent as quickly as it is obtained (due to routine drug use, street gambling, acquisition of the latest fashions, heavy partying; see e.g., Jacobs, 1999; Wright and Decker, 1994, 1997; Shover, 1996). As a result, they rapidly run out of money, creating pressing fiscal crises, which then produce other internal situational inducements such as the need to feed oneself or to avoid drug withdrawal.

The sale of stolen vehicles and parts can be a lucrative endeavor. Experienced carjackers sometimes stripped the vehicles themselves (in an abandoned alley or remote lot) and sold the items on the street corner or delivered them to a chop shop owner with whom they had a working relationship. Of particular value were "portable" after-market items, such as gold or silver plated rims, hub caps, and expensive stereo components. Across our 28 respondents, profits from carjacking per offense ranged anywhere from $200 to $5,000, with the average running at $1,750. The cash obtained from carjacking served to alleviate ever emergent financial needs.

Little Rag, a diminutive teen-aged gang-banger, indicated that without cash the prospect of heroin withdrawl loomed ahead.

> **INT:** So, why did you do that? Why did you jack that car?
>
> **Little Rag:** For real? 'Cause it's the high, it's the way I live. I was broke. I was fiending [needed drugs]. I had to get off my scene real quick [wanted to get back on my feet]. I sold crack but I'd fallen off [ran out of money] and I had to go and get another lick [tempting crime target] or something to get back on the top. I blow it on weed, clothes, shoes, shit like that. Yeah, I truly fuck money up.

The need for drugs was a frequent topic in our discussions with carjackers. Even the youngest offenders had built up such tolerances to drugs like heroin and crack that they required fixes on a daily basis. Many were involved in drug dealing and had fallen into a well known trap; using their own supply. Whether they sold for themselves or in the service of someone else, the need for cash to replenish the supply or feed the habit was a powerful internal motivator. L-Dawg, a young drug dealer from the north side of St. Louis also had developed a strong addiction to heroin. Only two days before his interview with us, he had taken a car from a man leaving a local night club.

> **L-Dawg:** I didn't have no money and I was sick and due some heroin so I knew I had to do something. I was at my auntie's house [and] my stomach started cramping. I just had to kill this sickness, 'cause I can't stay sick. If I'd stayed sick I would [have to] do something worse. The worse I get sick, to me, the worse I'm going to do. That's how I feel. If I've got to wait on it a long time, the worse the crime may be. If it hadn't been him then I probably would have done a robbery. One way or another I was going to get me some money to take me off this sickness. I just seen him and I got it.

External situational inducements could be just as compelling. Pressures from friends, family, other criminal acquaintances, or even the threat of injury or death were capable of pushing offenders to carjacking. For example, C-Low described an incident that occurred while he was with a friend in New Orleans. The two were waiting in the reception room of a neighborhood dentist when a group of men hostile to C-Low's friend walked into the office.

> **C-Low:** They knew him. I didn't know them. It was something about some fake dope. I think it was some heroin. He got caught. We weren't strapped [armed] at the time. We booked out. We left. We just left 'cause he know this person's gonna be strapped, and I didn't know this. So my partner was like, "Man, just burn out man, just leave." So we was leaving and they was coming up behind us [and started] popping [shooting] at us just like that, popping at my partner, just started shooting at him, so my partner he was wounded. We had no car or nothing so we were running through and the guy was popping at us. So, there was a lady getting out of her car, and he stole it. We had to take her car because we had no ride. She worked at the [dentist's]. She like a nurse or something. It was a nice little brand

new car. Brand new, not the kind you sort of sport off in like. She saw I was running. She heard the gun shots. I know she heard them, but she didn't see the guy that was shooting at us though. She had the keys in her hand. She was getting out her car, locking her door, yeah. She had her purse and everything. [My partner] just came on her blind side, just grabbed her, hit her. She just looked like she was shocked, like she was in a state of shock. She was really scared. And [we] took her car and we left. We could've got her purse and everything, but we were just trying to get away from the scene 'cause we had no strap and they were all shooting at us. We just burnt on out of there. Got away. But then [later that day] he got caught though . . . somebody snitched on him and they told them [the police] that he had the car. He gave me the car but he got caught for it, they couldn't find the car 'cause I'd taken it to the chop shop. I sold the car for like twenty-seven hundred bucks and about 2 ounces of weed.

Similarly, Nicole, a seasoned car thief and sometime carjacker, described a harrowing spur-of-the-moment episode. She and a friend had been following a young couple from the drive-in, casually discussing the prospect of robbing them, when her partner suddenly stopped their vehicle, jumped out and initiated a carjacking without warning. Nicole was instantly drawn into abetting her partner in the commission of the offense.

Nicole: My partner just jumped out of the car. He jumped out of the car and right then when I seen him with the gun I [realized] what was happening. I had to move. Once he got the guy out of the car he told me, "Come get the car." The girl was already out of the car screaming, "Please don't kill me, please don't kill me!" She was afraid because [she could see] I was high. You do things [when] you high. She's running so I'm in the car waiting on him. He's saying, "Run bitch and don't look back." She just started running . . . across the parking lot. [At] the same time he made the guy get up and run, "Nigger you do something, you look back, I'm gonna kill your motherfucking ass." As he got up and ran he shot him anyways.

Risks and Rewards: How Opportunity Drives Carjacking

Need was not the only factor implicated in carjacking. Some carjackers indicated that they were influenced by the appeal of targets that represented effortless or unique opportunities (e.g., isolated or weak victims, vehicles with exceptionally desirable options). Here, risks were so low or potential rewards so great that, even the absence of substantive internal or external situational inducements, they decided to commit a carjacking. Such opportunities were simply too good to pass up.

Po-Po (short for "Piss Off the Police") described just such an opportunity-driven incident. She and her brother had spent the day successfully pickpocketing individuals at Union Station, a St. Louis mall complex. On their way out, she noticed an easy target, an isolated woman in the parking lot, preoccupied with the lock on her car door.

Po-Po: It was a fancy little car. I don't know too much about names of cars, I just know what I like. A little sporty little car like a Mercedes Benz–like car. It was black and it was shiny and it looked good. I just had to joy ride it. She was a white lady. It looked like she worked for [a news station] or somebody. We just already pick pocket[ed] people down at Union Station, but fuck. So we just walked down stairs and [I] said, "You want to steal a car? Come on dude, let me get this car." I didn't have a gun on me. I just made her think I had a gun. I had a stick and I just ran up there to her and told her, "Don't move, don't breathe, don't do nothing. Give me the keys and ease your ass away from the car." I said, "You make one sound I'm going to blow your motherfucker head off and I'm not playing with you!" I said, "Just go on around the car, just scoot on around the car." Threw the keys to my little brother and told him go on and open the door. And she stood around there at the building like she waiting on the bus until we zoomed off. We got away real slow and easy.

Likewise, Kow, an older carjacker and sometimes street robber, was on his way to a friend's house to complete a potentially lucrative drug deal when he happened on an easy situation—a man sitting in a parked car, talking to someone on a pay phone at 2 A.M.

INT: What drew you to this guy? What were you doing? Why did you decide to do this guy?

Kow: Man, it ain't be no, "What you be doing?," [it's] just the thought that cross your mind be like, you need whatever it is you see, so you get it, you just get it. I was going to do something totally different [a drug deal] but along the way something

> totally different popped up so I just take it as it comes. I was like, "Whew! Get that!" I don't know man, your mind is a hell of thing. On our way to this other thing. It just something that just hit you, you know what I'm saying? Plus, [he looked like] a bitch. I don't know, it's just something, he look like a bitch, just like we could whip him, like a bitch, you know what I'm saying? Easy.

Not all irresistible opportunities were driven solely by the prospect of monetary gain. In a city the size of St. Louis, offenders run into one another all the time, at restaurants, malls, movie theaters and night-clubs. As a result, individuals with shared histories often encounter unique chances for retaliation or personal satisfaction. Goldie emphasized how such opportunities could pop up at a moment's notice. While cruising the north side of St. Louis, he spotted an individual who had sexually assaulted one of his girlfriends.

> **Goldie:** I did it on the humbug [spontaneously]. I peeped this dude, [saw that] he [was] pulling up at the liquor store. I'm tripping [excited] you know what I'm saying, [as I'm] walking there [towards the target]. You know, peep him out, you dig? He [was] reaching in the door to open the door. His handle outside must have been broke cause he had to reach in [the window] to open the door. And I just came around you know what I'm saying. [I] put it [the gun] to his head, "You want to give me them keys, brother?" He's like, "No, I'm not givin' you these keys." I'm like, "You gonna give me them keys, brother. It's as simple as that!" Man, he's like, "Take these, motherfucker, fuck you and this car. Fuck you." I'm like, "Man, just go on and get your ass home." [Then I] kicked him in his ass, you know what I'm saying, and I was like, "Fuck that, as a matter of fact get on your knees. Get on your knees, motherfucker. . . ." Then I seen this old lady right, that I know from around this neighborhood. I was like "Fuck!," jumped on in the car [and] rolled by. I wanted to hit him but she was just standing there, just looking. That's the only thing what made me don't shoot him, know what I'm saying? 'Cause he's fucking with one of my little gals. 'Cause he fucked one of my little gals. Well, she was saying that he didn't really fuck her, you know, he took the pussy, you know what I'm saying? He got killed the next week so I didn't have to worry about him. Motherfuckers said they found him dead in the basement in a vacant house.

Alert and Motivated Opportunism

Offenses motivated purely by either irresistible opportunities or overwhelming situational inducements are relatively rare. Most carjackings occur between these extremes, where situational inducements merge with potential opportunities to create circumstances ripe for offending. What follows are descriptions of offenses spurred by the combination of internal or external situational inducements and acceptable (or near acceptable) levels of risk and reward. The degree to which a given situation was comprised of rewards and risk on the one hand and internal and external pressures on the other varied, but when the combination reached a certain critical level, a carjacking resulted.

Offenders often described situation in which inducements were present, but *not* pressing, where they had *some* money or *some* drugs on them, but realized that the supply of either or both was limited and would soon run out. In such cases, the carjackers engaged in a state of what Bennett and Wright (1984; see also, Feeney, 1986) refer to as *alert opportunism*. In other words, offenders are not desperate, but they anticipate need in the near term and become increasingly open to opportunities that may present themselves during the course of their day-to-day activities. Here, would-be carjackers prowled neighborhoods, monitoring their surroundings for good opportunities, allowing potential victims to present themselves.

Corleone, a 16-year-old with over a dozen carjackings under his belt, had been committing such offenses with his cousin since the age of 13. The two were walking the streets of St. Louis one afternoon looking for opportunities for quick cash when they saw a man walking out of a barbershop toward his parked car, keys in hand. Motivated by the obliviousness of their prey and the lightness of their wallets, they decided to take his car.

> **Corleone:** It was down in the city on St. Louis Avenue. We was just walking around, you know. We just look for things to happen you see just to get money. We just walk around and just see something that's gonna make us money. We just happened to be going to the Chinaman [a restaurant] to get something to eat. [We had] about five or six dollars in our pocket which ain't nothing. It was this man driving a blue Cutlass. It has some chrome wheels on there. He just drove up and we was going to the Chinaman and . . . my

cousin was like, "Look at that car, man, that's tough [nice]. I'm getting that. I want that." [I was] like, "Straight up, you want to do it?" He was like, "Yeah." He was all G[ood] for it. Then he [the victim] came out the barbershop. It was kind of crowded and we just did what we had to do. There was this little spot where [my cousin] stash[es] his money, drugs and all that type of stuff and then he got the gun [from the stash]. He got around the corner. He say, "Hey, hey." I asked him for a cigarette so he went to the passenger's side [of the vehicle to get one]. I ran on the driver's side with a gun. Put it to his head and told him to get out the car.

INT: Did you know that you were going to do carjacking or. . . ?

Corleone: No. Not necessarily. But since that was what came up, that's what we did.

No matter how alert one is, however, good opportunities do not always present themselves. Over the course of time, situational inducements mount (that is, supplies of money and drugs inevitably dry up), and the option of waiting for ideal opportunities correspondingly diminishes. Such conditions cause offenders to move from a "passive" state of alert opportunism to an "active" state of what could be referred to as *motivated opportunism* (creating opportunities where none previously existed or modifying existing non-optimal opportunities to make them less hazardous or more rewarding). Here, attention and openness to possibilities expands to allow offenders to tolerate more risk. Situations that previously seemed unsuitable start to look better.

Binge, a 45-year-old veteran offender who had engaged in burglary, robbery, and carjacking for over 20 years, discussed his most recent decision to get a car on a wintry January day. He had been carrying a weapon (a 9mm Glock) since that morning, looking to commit a home invasion. After prowling the streets for hours and encountering few reasonable prospects, he happened on an easy opportunity—a man sitting parked in a car, its engine running, at a Metrolink (trolley) station.

Binge: Well, I was out hustling, trying to get me a little money and I was walking around. I was cold. I was frustrated. I couldn't get in [any] house[s] or nothing, so I say [to myself], "Well I'll try and get me a little car, and you know, just jam off the heat and shit that he [the vehicle's owner] got," you know? I was strapped [carrying a firearm] and all that, you know and I was worried about the police catching me, trying to pull my pistol off, and I see this guy. Well, he was at the Metrolink you know, nodding [falling asleep] in his car. So, I went up to the window. I just think that I just peeped it on [happened on the situation]. I was at the Metrolink you know, I was standing at the bus station trying to keep warm and so I just walked around with no houses to rob, and I seen this dude you know sitting in his car, you know, with the car running. And I said "Ah man, if I can get a wag at this [take advantage of this opportunity]," you know. It wasn't just an idea to keep warm or nothing like that. I was cold and worried, and it just crossed my mind and I thought I can get away with it, and I just did it. I'd do anything man, I'd do anything. If I want something and I see I can get away with it I'm gonna do it. That's what I'm saying. That night I saw an opportunity and I took it, you know. It just occurred to me.

Just as compelling were instances where third parties placed demands on offenders. A number of our respondents indicated that they engaged in carjacking to fulfill specific orders or requests from chop shop owners or other individuals interested in a particular make and model of car or certain valuable car parts. The desire to fulfill such orders quickly created conditions ripe for motivated opportunism.

Goldie, for instance, was experiencing strong internal situational pressures (the need for cash) and external pressures (the demand for a particular vehicle by some of his criminal associates) combined with a moderately favorable opportunity (inside information on the driver of the wanted vehicle and its location):

Goldie: He's from my neighborhood. He's called Mucho. He's from the same neighborhood but like two streets over. Them two streets don't come over on our street. You know, we not allowed to go over on they street. It was a nice car. The paint, the sound system in it, and the rims. [It] had some beats, rims. Rims cost about $3,000, some chrome Daytons. Hundred-spokes platinums.

INT: OK. That's a lot of money to be putting on a car. What does he do for a living?

Goldie: I don't know. I don't ask. What they told me was they wanted this car and they are going to give me a certain amount of money.

INT: You say they told you they wanted this car. You mean they told you they wanted his car or they wanted a car like that?

Goldie: His car. His car. They want [Mucho's] car. They said, "I need one of these, can you get it for me?" And they knew this guy. So now, I need that car. That car.

Low-Down also specialized in taking orders from chop shops,

Low-Down: What I do, I basically have me a customer before I even go do it. I ask a few guys that I know that fix up cars, you know what I'm saying. I ask them what they need then I take the car. But see, I basically really got a customer. I'm talking about this guy over in East St. Louis. Me and Bob, we real cool. He buy 'em 'cause he break 'em down, the whole car down and he got an autobody shop. He sell parts. He'll take the car and strip it down to the nitty gritty and sell the parts. He get more money out of selling it part by part than selling the car. And, before I get it I already set the price.

He also had a drug habit:

Low-Down: The main reason basically why I did it was I be messing with heroin, you know what I'm saying. I be using buttons [heroin housed in pill-form]. I be snorting some, but I be snorting too much, you know? I got a habit for snorting cause I be snorting too much at a time, that's how I call it a habit. I probably drop about five or six [buttons] down first [thing in the morning]. [So] I was basically really sick and my daughter needed shoes and shit like that and my girlfriend was pressuring me about getting her some shoes. She had been pressing me about two or three days. Baby food and stuff like that. But the money I had, I had been trying to satisfy my habit with it. Basically, I just thought it was a good thing to do. It was a good opportunity.

Aftermath

The second portion of our interviews with carjackers dealt with the aftermath of carjackings. Here, we were concerned with basic questions: What did they do with the vehicles? What did they do with their money? Given the propensity of many carjackers to target other offenders, how did they manage the threat of retaliation? The majority of our respondents immediately disposed of the vehicle, liquidating it for cash. As Corleone put it, "there's a possibility they report[ed] the car stolen and while I'm driving around the police [could] pull me over. I ain't got time to hop out [of the vehicle] and run with no gun. I just want to get the money that I wanted."

Although most of our respondents immediately delivered the vehicle to a chop shop or dismantled it themselves, a fair number of them chose to drive the vehicle around first, showing it off or "flossing" to other neighborhood residents and associates. Despite the possibility that the vehicle's owner or the police might catch up with them, they chose to floss.

INT: What do you like to do after a carjacking?

Binge: Well, what I like to do is just like to, see my friends. They don't give a damn either, I just go pick them up and ride around, smoke a little bit [of] weed, and get some gals, and to partying or something like that you know. I know it's taking a chance but, you know like I say, they don't give a damn.

INT: Is that what you did with the car that you took off the guy at the Metrolink?

Binge: Yeah. I was just riding around listening to the music, picked up a couple of friends of mine. We rode around. I told them it was a stolen car. It was a nice little car too. Black with a kind of rag top with the three windows on the side. The front and back ones had a little mirror and another window right in the roof. Oh yeah, oh yeah—[it had] nice sounds. I was chilling man, I was chilling, you know? I was driving along with the music playing up loud. Ha ha.You know I wasn't even worried. I was just feeling good. 'Cause I'm not used to driving that much you know 'cause I don't have a car you know. That's why when I do a carjacking I just play it off to the tee, run all the gas off, keep the sounds up as loud as I can, keep the heat on, you know just abuse the car you know. That's all about carjacking like that.

C-Low described his desire to floss as having to do with the ability to gain status in his neighborhood.

C-Low: Put it this way, you got people you know that's driving around. We just wanna know how it feels. We're young and we ain't doing shit else. So they [people from the neighborhood] see you driving the car, they gonna say, "Hey, there's C-Low!" and such and such. That makes us feel good 'cause we're riding, and then when we're done riding we wreck the car or give it to somebody else and let him ride. We took the car and drove around the hood, flossing everything. And then we wrecked it on purpose. We ran it into a ditch. I don't know, we were flicked up high, we were high man, just wild! Wrecked the thing.

But even for offenders like these, the prospect of getting caught and losing profits eventually began to outweigh the benefits of showing off.

INT: So how long did you drive around in the [Chevrolet] Suburban before you stripped it?

Loco: Oh, we was rolling that. We drove for a good thirty minutes, then I said that I want[ed] to get up out of it because they might report it stolen. We was [still driving] right there [near] the scene [of the crime] and they [the police] would have probably tried to flag me [pull me over]. And if they tried to flag me, I would [have to] have taken them through a high-speed chase. Fuck that.

Sleezee-E informed us (as did other respondents) that disposing of the vehicle quickly was the key to getting away with a carjacking. Indeed, almost all respondents were aware of the police department's "hot sheet" for stolen vehicles (although their estimations of how long it took for a vehicle to show up on the hot-sheet varied greatly, from as soon as the vehicle was reported stolen to 24 hours or even longer afterwards).

Sleezee-E: [People think that] the cops will wait 24 hours just to see what you are going to do with the car. Because some idiots, when they jack a car, they just drive it around and then they leave it someplace. I don't do that. That's how you get caught. Driving it around. You take that car right to the chop shop and let them cut that sucker up.

Once the vehicle was stripped, most carjackers disposed of the vehicle by destroying it somehow.

Little Rag: 'Cause it was hot man! It was too hot. All I [wanted] was to take the rims, take the beats, the equalizer, the detachable face. Got all that off, then I just pour gas on it and burnt that motherfucker up. I had fingerprints [on it]. I didn't have no gloves on. I had my own hands on the steering wheel. I left my fingerprints.

Nicole and a boyfriend chose a less conventional method of getting rid of their stolen vehicle.

Nicole: We got rid of the car first. We drove the car two blocks and went back down a ways to the park. We drove the car up there, we parked right there and sat for about ten minutes, made sure how many cars come down this street before we can push it over there. It's a pond, like it's a lake out there with ducks and geeses in it.

Cash for Cars: Life as Party

While a few respondents reported that they used the proceeds from carjacking to pay for necessities or bills, the overwhelming majority indicated that they blew their cash indiscriminately on drugs, women, and gambling.

We had interviewed Tone on a number of previous occasions for his involvement in strong-arm drug robbery. Although robbery was his preferred crime, he engaged in carjacking occasionally (about once every two months) when easy opportunities presented themselves. During his most recent offense, he and three of his associates took a Cadillac from a neighborhood drug dealer and made $6000. When we asked what he did with his portion, he indicated that he, ". . . spent that shit in like, two days."

INT: You can go through $1500 in two days?

Tone: Shit, it probably wasn't even two days, it probably was a day, shit.

INT: What did you spend 1500 on?

Tone: It ain't shit that you really want. Just got the money to blow so fuck it, blow it. Whatever, it don't even matter. Whatever you see you get, fuck it. Spend that shit. It wasn't yours from the gettyup, you know what I'm saying? You didn't have it from the jump so. . . . Can't act like you careful with it, it wasn't yours to care for. Easy come, easy go. The easy it came, it go even easier. Fuck that, fuck all that. I ain't trying to think about keeping nothing. You can get it again.

INT: So what does money mean to you?

Tone: What money mean? Shit, money just some shit everybody need, that's all. I mean, it ain't jack shit.

INT: Ok, so it's not really important to you?

Tone: Fuck no. 'Cause I told you, easy come, easy go.

Mo had taken a Monte Carlo from two men residing in another neighborhood. He had planned the offense over the course of a month and finally, posing as a street window cleaner, carjacked them as they exited a local restaurant. The vehicle's after-market items netted $5,000 in cash.

INT: I'm just kind of curious how you spend like $5,000!

Mo: Just get high, get high. I just blow money. Money is not something that is going to achieve for nobody, you know what I'm saying? So everyday, there's not a promise that there'll be another [day] so I just spend it, you know what I'm saying? It ain't mine, you know what I'm saying, I just got it, it's just in my possession. This is mine now, so I'm gonna do what I've got to do. It's a lot of fun. At a job you've got to work a lot for it, you know what I'm saying? You got to punch the clock, do what somebody else tells you. I ain't got time for that. Oh yeah, there ain't nothing like gettin' high on $5000!

Binge and others confirmed that the proceeds from their illegal activities went to support this form of conspicuous consumption.

Binge: I just blowed it man. With the money me and my girlfriend went and did a bit of shopping, stuff for Christmas. But, the money I got from his wallet? I just blowed that, drinking and smoking marijuana.

For Corleone, the motivation to carjack was directly related to his desire to manage the impressions of others in his social milieu. His remarks served as a poignant comment on sociocultural and peer pressures experienced by many inner city youths. The purpose of carjacking was to obtain the money he needed to purchase clothing and items that would improve his stature in the neighborhood.

Corleone: [$1500 is] a lot. [I bought] shoes, shoes, everything you need. Guys be styling around our neighborhood. The brand you wear, shoes cost $150 in my size. Air Jordans, everybody want those. Everybody have them. I see everybody wearing those in the neighborhood. I mean come on, let's go get a car. I'm getting those, too.

INT: How many pairs of sneakers have you got?

Corleone: Millions. I got, I got, I got a lot of shoes. Clothes, gotta get jackets.

INT: Well, why do you have to look good, what's so big about looking good?

Corleone: It's for the projects, man. You can't be dressing like no bum. I mean you can't, you can't go ask for no job looking like anything.

INT: So you're saying like if you don't look good, you can't get girls, if you don't have the nicest shoes?

Corleone: You can't. Not nowadays, not where I'm from. You try to walk up to a girl, boy, you got on some raggedy tore up, cut up shoes they're gonna spit on you or something. Look at you like you crazy. Let's say you walking with me. I got on creased up pants, nice shoes, nice shirt and you looking like a bum. Got on old jeans. And that dude, that dude, he clean as a motherfucker and you look like a bum.

INT: So you're competing with each other, too?

Corleone: Something like that. Something like a popularity contest.

INT: Well, you know, you can look nice and clean and not have to spend $150 bucks on shoes, you know.

Corleone: It's just this thing, it's a black thing. You ain't going [to] understand, you don't come from the projects.

The Hazards of Carjacking: Retaliation and the Spread of Violence

Interestingly, a sizeable proportion of our respondents purposely targeted people who themselves were involved in crime. Such individuals make excellent targets. Their participation in street culture encourages the acquisition of vehicles most prized by carjackers (those with valuable, if often gaudy, after-market items). And, because they are involved in a number of illegal activities (such as drug selling), they cannot go to the police. As Mr. Dee put it;

Mr. Dee: You can't go to no police when you selling drugs to buy that car with your drug money. So, I wasn't really worried about that. If he would have went to the police he would have went to jail automatically 'cause they would have been like, "Where'd you get this thousand dollar car from?" He put about $4,000 into the car. So, he ain't got no job, he ain't doin it like that bro. He'd be goin' to the police station lookin' like a fool tellin' his story. I [could] see if he's workin' or something . . . and slinging. It'd be different 'cause he could show them his check stub from work.

However, there is a considerable danger associated with targeting such individuals because, unable to report the robbery of illegal goods to the police, they have a strong incentive to engage in retaliation—those who fail to do so risk being perceived as soft or easy (see e.g., Topalli, Wright, and Fornango, 2002). This introduces the possibility that incidents of carjacking likely are substantially higher than officially reported.

When asked about the possibility of retaliation many of the carjackers, displaying typical street offender bravado, indicated that they had no fear. The need to see oneself as capable and tough was essential to respondents. Such self-beliefs served to create a sense of invulnerability that allowed carjackers to continue to engage in a crime considered by many to be hazardous. As Playboy put it, "It [can't be] a fear thing. If you're gonna be scared then you shouldn't even go through with stuff like that [carjacking people]."

Likewise, Big-Mix expressed an almost complete disregard for the consequences of his actions. His comments confirm the short-term thinking characteristic of many street offenders, "I don't give a damn. I don't care what happens really. I don't care. That's how it always is. Whether they kill us or whether we kill them, same damn shit. Whatever. I don't fucking care." Pacman, a younger carjacker who worked exclusively with his brother-in-law, indicated that thinking about the possible negative consequences was detrimental to one's ability to execute an offense. When asked if he was worried about retaliation, he was dismissive.

Pacman: Yeah, you be pretty pissed. But like I say, I'm not looking over my back, you know what I'm saying? Because, I wouldn't be here for sure. I couldn't [keep carjacking]. I definitely wouldn't last man. I wouldn't have lasted as long as I lasted. Because it would be too many motherfuckers [that I've victimized], you know what I'm saying, [for me to look] over my shoulder all the time. When I look what the fuck could I do anyhow? I could get a few of them, but it would take a lot of motherfucking looking over my shoulder. I try to avoid that altogether. I'm going to avoid all that.

Other carjackers relied on hypervigilance (obsessive attention to one's surroundings and to the behavior of others), or anonymity maintenance (e.g., targeting strangers, not talking about the crime, using of disguises, carjacking in areas away from one's home ground; see Jacobs, Topalli, and Wright, 2000; Jacobs, 1999) to minimize the possibility of pay-back. Sexy-Diva, a female carjacker who worked with Sleezee-E, often spent hours with potential victims at night clubs before taking their cars, "I just disguises myself. I change my hair . . . my clothes. I change whatever location I was at. And then I don't even go to that area no more. They can't find me. No way, no how."

Nukie sacrificed a great deal of his day-to-day freedom by engaging in behaviors designed to anticipate and neutralize the threat of retaliation.

Nukie: That's why I don't go out. If I go somewhere to get me a beer, if I'm gonna get me some bud [marijuana] or something, I stay in the hood. I don't go to the clubs. There's too many people going there at night, you know what I'm saying? I don't need to be spotted like that. That's why I keep on the DL [down-low, out of sight]. You see, I stay in the hood. [If] I be riding [in a car], while I'm riding I might have my cats [friends] with me. You know, no motherfucker's gonna try to fuck with us like that. Yeah, I be with some motherfucker most of the time. If we're [going] to do something, go get blowed [high]—see, we get blowed every day—I be with people, shit.

Pookie choose[s] to employ similar preemptive tactics, but also emphasized the need to be proactive when dealing with the threat of retaliation, predicated on the philosophy that, "the best defense is a good offense."

Pookie: Well, you know the best thing [to deal] with retaliation like this here, you know, in order for you to get some action you got to bring some action. If I see you coming at me and you don't look right, then this is another story here. If you doing it like you're reaching for something, I'm gonna tear the top of your head off real quick, you know. I'm gonna be near you, where you're at because they ain't nothing but some punk-ass tires and rims that I took from you, that's all it is.

What you gotta understand is that you worked hard for it, and I just came along and just took them, you know. You go back and get yourself another set son, 'cause if I like them then I'm gonna take them again.

In the end, there were no guarantees. No matter how many steps a carjacker took to prevent retaliation, the possibility of payback remained. As self-confidence bred the perception of security, so too did it breed over-confidence. This was true in the case of Goldie, whose motivation to carjack a known drug dealer named Mucho was described above. His attempt did not go as planned.

Goldie: He was going to put up a fight trying to spin off with [the car], I jumped in and threw it in Park so now I'm tussling with him, "Give me this motherfucker!" He's trying to speed off. He got like in the middle of the intersection. I dropped my gun on the seat and he grabbed me like around here [the neck], trying to hold me down in the car, and throw it back in Drive, with me in the car, you dig? You know, I'm like no, I ain't going for that shit. I had my feet up on the gear [shift], you know what I'm saying? He ain't tripping off the gun. He trying to hold me, "Nigger motherfucker, you ain't going to get this car! Punk-ass nigger! What the fuck wrong with you? What the fuck do you want my car for?" [I said], "Look boy, I don't want that punk ass shit dude! I'm getting this car. This is mine. Fuck you!" The gun flew on the passenger's seat. So I grabbed the gun and put it to his throat, "So what you gonna to do? Is you gonna die or give up this car?" [He replied], "Motherfucker, you're going to have to do what you are going to have to do." He don't want to give up his car, right? So I cocked it one time, you know, just to let him know I wasn't playing, you dig? But I ain't shoot him on his head, put it on his thigh. Boom! Shot him on his leg. He got to screaming and shit hollering, you know what I'm saying, "You shot me! You shot me! You shot me!" like a motherfucker gonna hear him or something. Cars just steady drive past and shit, you know what I'm saying. By this time I opened up the door, "Fuck you!" Forced his ass on up out of there. He laying on the ground talking about, "This motherfucker shot me! Help, help!" Hollering for help and shit. But before I drove off I backed up, ran over him I think on the ankles like. While he was laying on the street, after I shot him. Ran over his bottom of his feet or whatever, you know what I'm saying. Oh, yeah. I felt that. Yeah. Boom, boom. "Aaaah!" scream. I hear bones break, like all this down here was just crushed. I didn't give a fuck though. Sped off. Went and flossed for a minute.

INT: I don't know—two streets over and he sounds like he's pretty scandalous. You're not worried about him coming up on you for this?

Goldie: No. I pretty much left him not walking. And he don't know who I am. [Later on] I heard about that. [People were saying], "Motherfucker Mucho, he got knocked [attacked], motherfucker tried to knock him, took his car, you know what I'm saying, on the block." I'm like, "Yeah, I heard about that." You know what I'm saying. "I wonder who did this shit." You know what I'm saying?

Three months later, we spoke to Goldie from his hospital bed. Mucho had tracked him down and shot him in the back and stomach as he crossed the street to buy some marijuana.

Goldie: I call them a bad day. . . . I got shot. I saw him [Mucho] drive by but I didn't think he seen me. He caught up to me later. [I got shot] in the abdomen (pointing at his stomach) . . . here's where they sewed me up. I had twenty staples.

INT: How did it go down?

Goldie: I wanted [to] stop on the North-[side] and get me a bag of grass, grab me a bag of weed or something. So, [we were] going around to the set [the dealer's home turf] and I'm getting out, I see [Mucho's] car parked this time. He wasn't in it. I'm thinking in my mind like you know, "That's that puss ass." So I'm like, "Damn I'm having bad vibes already." So I instantly just turned around like, "Fuck it. I'll go somewhere else to get some grass." I'm walking [back] to [my] car and hear a gunshot. Jump in the car. You know . . . you [don't] feel it for a minute. [Then,] my side just start hurting, hurting bad you know what I'm saying? I'm like damn. Looked down, I'm in a puddle of blood, you know. She freaking out and screaming, "You shot! You shot!" and shit. [She] jumped out the car like she almost should be done with me, you know what I'm saying? So I had to immediately take myself to the hospital. [They] stuffed this tube all the way down my dick all the way to my stomach . . . fucking with my side, pushing all of it aside. [I was there] about a good week. I done lost about 15 or 20

> pounds. That probably wouldn't have happened if I wouldn't have to go do that. Wanted some more grass. At the wrong spot at the wrong time.

Goldie made it clear during the interview that he felt the need to counter-retaliate to protect himself from future attack by maintaining a tough reputation, a valuable mechanism of deterrence.

> **INT:** You don't feel like you all are even now? You shot him—he shot you. Why go after him?
>
> **Goldie:** It's [about] retaliation. When I feel good is when he taken care of . . . and I don't have to worry about him no more. I mean my little BG's [Baby Gangsters, younger criminal protégées] look up to me. Me getting shot and not going and do [something about, it they would say], "Ah [Goldie's] a bitch. Aw, he's a fag." Now down there [in the neighborhood], when they hit you, you hit them back. You know, if someone shoot you, you gotta shoot them back. That's how it is down there or you'll be a bitch. Everybody will shoot you up, whoop your ass. Know what I'm saying? Treat you like a punk. It's just I got to do what I have to do, you know what I'm saying.

Many carjackers echoed such sentiments, indicating a common belief in the importance of following unwritten rules of conduct and behavior related to street offending, especially when they refer to matters of honor or reputation (see Anderson, 1999; Katz, 1988).

Conclusion

This chapter has demonstrated that the decision to commit a carjacking is governed by two things: perceived situational inducements and perceived opportunity (see Hepburn, 1984; Lofland, 1969). Situational inducements involve immediate pressures on the would-be offender to act. They can be internal (e.g., the need for money or desire for revenge) or external (e.g., the peer pressure of co-offenders). Opportunities refer to risks and rewards ties to a particular crime target in its particular environmental setting. . . .

Carjackings occur when perceived situational inducements and a perceived opportunity, alone or in combination, reach a critical level, thereby triggering that criminogenic moment when an individual commits to the offense. It is important to reiterate that either a perceived opportunity or perceived situational inducement on its own may be sufficient to entice an individual to commit a carjacking (see Hepburn, 1984). Numerous examples of this have been detailed throughout the first part of the chapter. It is also important to note that background and foreground factors (such as membership in a criminogenic street culture) can increase the chance that a carjacker will go after a vehicle by lowering his/her capacity to resist the temptation to offend.

More often, carjackings were motivated through the combined influence of opportunity and inducement. The carjackers' responses indicate that offenses triggered by *pure* opportunity or *pure* need are relatively rare. Most carjackings occur between the extremes, where opportunities and situational inducements overlap.

Owing to their precarious day-to-day existence—conditioned by risk factors such as persistent poverty, and exacerbated by "boom and bust" cycles of free-spending when money *is* available—carjackers are always under some degree of pressure and thus are encouraged to maintain a general openness to offending. During a "boom" period, carjackers anticipate future needs, but are not desperate to offend. This encourages Bennett and Wright's (1984) previously described notion of alert opportunism—a general willingness to offend if a particularly good opportunity presents itself.

But as time passes and no acceptable opportunities emerge, situational pressures to offend begin to mount in the face of diminishing resources. Approaching "bust" periods increasingly promote an active willingness to offend, driven by heightened situational inducements. Dormant or anticipated needs become pressing ones, moving carjackers from a state of alert opportunism to a state of motivated opportunism. As they continue to become more situationally desperate, their openness to offending expands to include opportunities perceived to have greater risk or lower reward (see Lofland, 1969). Targets that previously seemed unsuitable become increasingly attractive and permissible. The logical outcome is a carjacking triggered almost exclusively by pressing needs.

It is also possible for carjackers to move from a state of motivated opportunism to the lower state of alert opportunism, especially where the decision to commit such an offense is a driven desire for revenge. Retaliatory urges tend to be high initially, and then to dissipate over time. This is not to say, however, that an offended party has necessarily forgiven the offending party. They may simply be getting on with their lives, even as they keep their eyes open for the object of their wrath.

Although infrequent when compared to strong-arm robbery or drug robbery, carjacking's proportional impact on the spread of violence is probably more significant than has been suspected. When offenders themselves are targeted [for] carjacking, like other forms of violent crime, [it] can produce retaliatory behavior patterns that serve to perpetuate and proliferate cycles of violence on the streets. In addition, their sensationalist nature increases the public's general fear of crime when law-abiding citizens are victimized. In either case, the preceding evidence and discussion indicate that carjacking is a unique and dynamic form of crime that probably deserves its own categorization (separate from robbery or auto theft) or, at the very least, further study and attention by those interested in criminal decision-making.

Questions for Thought and Discussion

1. What are the major motivations (goals) of carjacking?
2. How does carjacking differ from ordinary auto theft?
3. What are dubs, dees, beats, and rims? Why are they desirable items to steal?
4. What theory or theories of criminal behavior are illustrated in this research?

References

Anderson, Elijah. (1999). *Code of the streets: Decency, violence, and the moral life of the inner city.* New York: W. W. Norton.

Armstrong, L. (1994). *Carjacking, District of Columbia.* Washington, D.C.: Bureau of Justice Statistics.

Bennett, Trevor & Richard Wright. (1984). *Burglars on burglary: Prevention and the offender.* Brookfield,VT: Gower.

Bureau of Justice Statistics. (1999). *Carjacking: National crime victimization survey.* Washington, D.C.: U.S. Department of Justice, Bureau of Justice Statistics.

Donahue, M., C. McLaughlin & L. Datum. (1994). *Accounting for carjackings: An analysis of police records in a Southeastern city.* Washington, D.C.: U.S. Department of Justice, Bureau of Justice Statistics.

Feeney, Floyd. (1986). Robbers as decision-makers. In D. B. Cornish & R. V. Clarke (Eds.), *The reasoning criminal: Rational choice perspectives on offending.* New York: Springer-Verlag.

Felson, Richard, Eric Baumer & Steven Messner. (in press). Acquaintance robbery. *Justice Quarterly.*

Fisher, R. (1995). *Carjackers: A study of forcible motor vehicle thieves among new commitments.* Washington, D.C.: Bureau of Justice Statistics.

Friday, S. & C. Wellford. (1994). *Carjacking: A descriptive analysis of carjacking in four states, preliminary report.* Washington, D.C.: U.S. Department of Justice, Bureau of Justice Statistics.

Hepburn, John. (1984). Occasional property crime. In R. Meier (Ed.), *Major forms of crime* (pp. 73–94). Newbury Park, Calif.: Sage.

Jacobs, Bruce A. (1999). *Dealing crack: The social world of streetcorner selling.* Boston: Northeastern University Press.

Jacobs, Bruce A.,Volkan Topalli & Richard Wright. (2000). Managing retaliation: The case of drug robbery. *Criminology* 38, 171–198.

Katz, Jack. (1988). *Seductions of crime: The sensual attractions of doing evil.* New York: Basic Books.

Lofland, John. (1969). *Deviance and identity.* Englewood Cliffs, NJ.: Prentice-Hall.

Rand, Michael R. (1994). *Carjacking.* Washington, D.C.: U.S. Department of Justice, Bureau of Justice Statistics.

Shover, Neal. (1996). *Great pretenders: Pursuits and careers of persistent thieves.* Boulder, Colo.: Westview.

Topalli, Volkan, Richard Wright & Robert Fornango. (2002). Drug dealers, robbery and retaliation: Vulnerability, deterrence, and the contagion of violence. *British Journal of Criminology* 42 (in press).

Wright, Richard & Scott H. Decker. (1994). *Burglars on the job: Streetlife and residential break-ins.* Boston: Northeastern University Press.

———. (1997). *Armed robbers in action: Stickups and street culture.* Boston: Northeastern University Press.

Chapter 13
Serial Killers

Antecedent Behaviors and the Act of Murder

Robert K. Ressler
Ann W. Burgess
John E. Douglas

This chapter differs somewhat from the others in the book. The research was conducted by the Behavioral Science Unit of the Federal Bureau of Investigation. Specially trained agents extensively interviewed 36 incarcerated sexual murderers over a period of several years. These subjects included many of the most notorious and best known serial killers. Two of those agents, Robert Ressler and John Douglas, are joined by Dr. Ann W. Burgess, an expert on the psychology of violence, to provide this insightful and unique look at sexual homicide. Based on extensive interviews, this chapter examines the first two phases of murder, the killer's antecedent behavior that forms the backdrop against which the crime occurs and the actual act of murder.

Putting thoughts and plans of murder into action presents the murderer with various behavioral options. The manner in which he chooses to act reveals much about the man behind the crime; thus, it often forms the basis for law enforcement investigation of crime scene patterns. We view the act of murder as being divided into four distinct phases: (1) antecedent behavior and planning, (2) the act of murder, (3) disposing of the body, and (4) postcrime behavior. At each of these phases, the murderer's thinking patterns . . . influence his choice of how he will act. Although these phases are discussed as separate components, they are overlapping segments of one event: murder. In this chapter, we describe phases one and two and the range of behavioral choices exhibited by the thirty-six murderers in our study.

Phase One: Antecedent Behavior and Planning

The first phase of murder, the killer's antecedent behavior, forms the backdrop against which the crime occurs. Precrime stress factors, frame of mind, and planning combine to influence the murderer's actions during this stage.

Precrime Stress Factors

The killer's mental and emotional state, his frame of mind, and hence his behavior before he murders are influenced to varying degrees by what is happening around him. Murderers often cite certain precipitating stresses as the causes for their behavior. They are not necessarily aware of the basic issues behind these stress factors, issues that play a powerful role in motivation. Yet in the mind of the murderer, stress factors (such as a disagreement with parents) are more than sufficient to justify aggression toward others, even toward strangers. Stress factors described by the men in our study as being present immediately prior to murder include conflict with females, parental conflict, financial stress, marital problems, conflict with males, birth of a child, physical injury, legal problems, employment problems, and stress from a death.

Conflict With Females. The men were able to state in forty-eight (59 percent) of eighty-one murder cases with data that their perceptions of what set the stage for murder involved a conflict with a woman. In one instance, a murderer described meeting a woman in a bar and having some drinks with her. She began ridiculing him. He later picked up another woman and took her to his apartment where he brutally murdered her.

However, some murderers revealed that although stress initially appeared to be caused by conflicts with women, other factors were underlying. One murderer described this additional stress.

> I had broken up with my girlfriend three days before, and I was feeling a lot of anxiety and pressure. Then the day after this [the murder] happened, she called to say she was sorry and she wanted to see me. Knowing what I'd done and everything, I didn't want to see her. So I stayed away from her for about two weeks. . . . I didn't [commit the murder] just because I was mad at my girlfriend. . . . There was peer pressure; there was outside pressure from school. I had been slacking off in my

> studies because my girl and I started to have trouble a month or so before this all happened. I felt a combination of things as far as [causing] what actually took place. It was pressure from home to bring up my grades, to get a job, etc.

Parental Conflict. Another major stress factor for the murderers immediately prior to murder is conflict with parents. For forty-six (53 percent) of eighty-six murder cases, murderers described parental problems. In one case, the killer had numerous fights with his stepfather and tried to kill him with a .45-caliber gun. In another case, a young man who had been adopted at an early age contacted his natural mother after obtaining her name and address. He went to visit her, fully prepared to be accepted into her home. However, he was rejected by her and then learned that he had a sister whom their natural mother had raised. His unconscious rage over his sister's acceptance and his rejection was transferred to victims the age and general appearance of his sister.

Financial Problems. In 48 percent of eighty-six murder cases, the murderers stated that financial difficulties were present at the time of their crimes. Again, this stress factor may be closely related to another, as is revealed in the following example:

> I had some financial difficulties, [although] my wife and I were getting along pretty good. I was arguing with my parents because I was always drunk. I had some conflicts with my mother-in-law, my father-in-law, and my brother-in-law. We'd usually end up in an argument [over] something.

The man's high level of aggression was linked with financial, alcohol, and family member problems, the factors contributing to his emotional state.

Employment Problems. Difficulties with employment were given as precipitating stress factors in 39 percent of ninety murders and were suspected in an additional 26 percent. Employment problems involved situations in which the murderer was unemployed or was having difficulty at work. The employer of one of the murderers made the following report:

> [The offender] did not take orders or advice. He did not get along with other employees. He would usually get into arguments with other employees over nothing. The employees were afraid to say much to him or cross him in any way. He had bad body odor, and I could not get him to do anything about it. [Although] he did my delivery work well and I had few complaints from the customers, my trouble with him was his trouble with other employees.

Marital Problems. Because only a minority of murderers were married, marriage was less frequently an identified cause of stress. However, in 21 percent of eighty-nine murders it was identified as a problem. For example, one murderer admitted he was seeing other women, and he had learned that his wife was also involved in an affair. During this time, his fantasies of rape and murder intensified.

Additional Stress Factors. Other precipitating stressful events identified by the murderers included legal problems (28 percent of eighty-nine cases), conflict with a male (11 percent of eighty-one cases), physical injury (11 percent of eighty-three), death of a significant person (8 percent of seventy-eight), and birth of a child (8 percent of eighty-nine cases). The following excerpt from a prison record is an example of this latter event as a precipitant for murder.

> Shortly after learning of his wife's pregnancy, [the murderer] purchased a pistol he [later] kept at home, claiming he was afraid his wife might be assaulted or his home burglarized while he was at work. After the birth of this first child, there was a marked change in [the offender]. He became more preoccupied, complained of physical pain, his sleep was restless, and his relationships with others deteriorated. He had little interest in sexual relations with his wife. . . . Three murders were in specific reference to this birth. The first murder was committed six weeks after the birth of the child, the second murder occurred when his wife was pregnant with their second child, and the third murder occurred on the day after the first birthday of the first child and coincided with the child's birthday party.

One final example of a precipitating stress factor illustrates the complexity of these factors.

> The murderer, a drug user, reported a long-standing problem with depression, which was evidenced by his frequent need for psychiatric hospitalization. The man had aspirations to become an actor, and he expressed great disappointment in his failure to gain employment as such. Hospital records from several weeks before the crime was committed revealed the

man was depressed, suffered from insomnia and diarrhea, and talked of suicide. The day after he was discussing discharge from the hospital with staff, he committed murder.

Frame of Mind

Frame of mind is a general descriptive term for a dominant emotional state that acts as a primary filter and interpreting mechanism regarding external events. The frame of mind of offenders just before the crime revealed highly negative emotional states such as frustration (50 percent), hostility and anger (46 percent), agitation (43 percent), and excitement (41 percent). Of equal interest are those symptoms and mood states associated with internalized distress—that is, nervousness (17 percent), depression (14.6 percent), fear (10 percent), calm (8.8 percent), or confusion (7 percent). These findings suggest that there is little emotion experienced by the killer that reflects any sense of vulnerability, thereby permitting the killer to interpret the behavior of the victim in the most negative manner. The frame of mind and mood states illustrate how the killer supports his negative cognitions and justification for the crime. There is no emotional reservoir to relate to the vulnerability, pain, and fear of the victim.

Precrime Planning

In relationship to precrime planning or premeditation, 50 percent of the murderers rated their act as intentional in planning who, when, and where they were going to murder. Another 34 percent recognized that they had a congruent mood state to murder and were open to opportunities. This figure suggests an aura of impulsiveness for the act; however, in the structure and organization of thinking, it fits in with the style of these killers. They know of places and strategies by which to obtain victims; when the right combination exists, they commit the crime and label it opportunistic. The remaining 16 percent of the offenders viewed their murderous acts as purely spontaneous and unplanned. These men were without self-appraisal or awareness of any thoughts or emotions building up to a murderous expression. Nevertheless, it appears that sexual murderers may preplan and be more intentional in their crime than has been previously reported in the literature.

Motivations for murder may include a conscious fantasy, plan, directive, or reason to kill. Murderers operating on a conscious motivational level usually remember their thoughts prior to the murder. One of the murderers we interviewed described his preoccupation with murder immediately prior to killing someone: "I had a compulsion during the day and hoped it would settle down—hoped I could wipe it out drinking."

These men have conscious, detailed plans for murder. Often the plans are improved upon with each successive killing; each new experience gives the offender insight into his next murder. Although the man who killed after breaking up with his girlfriend had no conscious plan for his first murder, he carefully planned subsequent murders to avoid being apprehended. With each new murder, the killer improved on his fantasy planning.

Other murderers may be motivated to kill by triggering environmental factors. Although their murderous actions are cued by external occurrences (which we address in our discussion of phase two) their plan for murder is not spontaneous. Some people, such as Samenow, question whether there is any such thing as a spontaneous homicide (Samenow 1984).

In one apparently spontaneous murder, the murderer met the victim in an apartment building hallway; as he passed her, he hit her and dragged her to a landing near the roof. However, crime scene evidence indicated that the killer had previously fantasized about such a murder. The victim's body was placed in a ritualized position, the victim had been tied up after death, and the crime scene displayed a certain symmetry, all of which pointed to a planned crime.

Precrime Actions

The precrime actions of the murderers in the days and hours before they killed provide clues to their mental states at the time of the murders.

In the days before they murdered, several offenders were involved in criminal or violent activities. At least two men committed fetish burglaries, breaking into homes to steal items that, for them, had sexual connotations. An offender who later killed three women assaulted and threatened his wife, forcing her to write a suicide note; another offender killed neighborhood dogs shortly before committing murder. One murderer, who killed five people within one week, set several fires and shot off his gun inside his apartment and from his car in the days preceding the murders. On the day of the first murder, homeowners in the area reported break-ins and thefts.

During the hours immediately before the murders, some murderers go looking for victims. Several described cruising the single bars, parking lots, gay bars, or the gay districts to locate victims. In other cases, they cruise the highways to pick up hitchhikers for victims. The men's actions sometimes involved alcohol and/or drug use. One murderer stabbed to death and eviscerated one woman and attempted to eviscerate another after spending the evening drinking beer and smoking marijuana with them.

The murderer's precrime behavior moves him toward the actual act of murder. In this phase, the murderer's selection of a victim and the onset of certain triggering factors culminate in the murder itself.

Victim Selection

For the murderer with a conscious plan or fantasy, selecting a victim begins the acting-out level of behavior. The plan or fantasy constructed earlier may call for a victim who meets certain criteria, and many murderers have been known to seek out a victim who is exactly right for the fantasy. The history and circumstances of the victim are often important. The victim may be symbolic of someone in the murderer's past, as in the case of the man who killed older women, close to his mother in age. Before his invalid mother died, the man exhumed female bodies from a graveyard and used the corpses in bizarre sexual activities. The man had been caring for his mother, and after her death he murdered the first of his two victims. In another case, the murderer had deep-seated conflicts with his mother, who often ridiculed his inability to form a relationship with a certain type of woman. The man sought and killed attractive, wealthy, female college students—the women his mother claimed were unattainable for him.

Other murderers may look for certain actions in their victims. One man who chose his victims from hitchhikers said, "She was playing up the role, the big beautiful smile and getting in the car, which was kind of tragic, but she had advertised to get blown away." Another murderer sought women to model hosiery and shoes for photographs; after forcing them to pose nude in high-heeled shoes, he killed them.

For the killer without a conscious plan or fantasy, a person may become a victim by eliciting certain responses. For example, someone may remind him of his belief in an unjust world. He may feel unfairly treated, and this sets into motion the justification to kill. One killer felt that his continued rejection by women was an injustice. In response to his frustration over this feeling, he shot and killed women who either were accompanied by men or were attractive enough to be sought by men. Other murderers respond to victims with rage and anger.

Triggering Factors

When discussing their first murders, the men we interviewed generally indicated that something happened to move them either to act out their fantasies of killing or to murder to preserve other fantasies. These occurrences, which we call triggering factors, are often closely connected with how the murderer selects his victim. The murderer with a well-rehearsed fantasy of murder kills to preserve the fantasy, as does the fetish burglar who kills when someone intrudes on his ritual. The murderer with a history of violent fantasies directed against women acts out these fantasies, often claiming that alcohol or the woman herself triggered the murder.

A variety of triggering factors can activate the violence, and the murderer's emotional state may leave him especially open to such factors. Many triggering factors center around some aspect of control. Often the killer's feeling of control and dominance is interrupted by the behavior of the victim. The victim's natural attempt to run away may enrage or upset the murderer because it indicates he may lose control. To another murderer, the victim's offer to comply with his demands may be inflammatory, as it indicates that the victim, rather than the attacker, has made a decision about how the assault will proceed.

The triggering factor in one case was that a victim's behavior did not match the rapist's fantasy of an exceptionally good sexual experience. This man kept giving orders to the woman, thus indicating his fantasy for how he intended the sexual assault to proceed. Her lack of "cooperation" shattered his fantasy. He became enraged and killed her. Another murderer recalled the triggering factor of the victim's trying to escape, although he did not recall the murder itself. His fantasy had centered around control and dominance; the victim's resisting behavior made him murder to preserve his fantasy.

> We were upstairs and I was taking my clothes off. That's when she started back

> downstairs. As a matter of fact, that's the only time I hit her. I caught her at the stairs. . . . She wanted to know why I hit her. I just told her to be quiet. She was complaining about what time she would get home and she said her parents would worry. She consented to sex . . . then I remember nothing else except waking up and her dead in the bed.

Some murderers kill to fulfill a specific fantasy. Several men mentioned going "hunting" every night for a victim. Because they had a specific type of victim in mind, they would wait until an appropriate one appeared. The victim's meeting the killer's criteria would, in fact, trigger the murder. The murderer may be looking for a woman with a male companion in a parked car or a woman alone driving a specific type of car. When such a victim appears, the murderous action is triggered.

Other killers become compelled by their fantasy of murder prior to committing the crime. One murderer, who killed seemingly at random, said he was ordered to murder by flying saucers. To these men, the identity of the victim is irrelevant; the act itself has primary importance.

> I'm all up to kill somebody. It's cold and it's cut and dried. I told the police the first [person] that got into the car . . . it didn't matter if it was male or female, I was going to blow somebody away.

In this case, just the accessibility of someone triggered the murder.

Although some of the murderers in our study did not report fantasies in a conscious way, their description of murders they committed reveal hidden fantasies of violence, often against women. Several of the men described the factors that triggered the killing as their not feeling well, depression, alcohol, or drugs. Out of 118 victim cases, half (49 percent) of the murderers said they had been drinking prior to the crime. The murderers were asked if their use of alcohol at the time of the offense differed significantly from typical drinking. Thirty percent said yes. Drug use at the time of the offense was 35 percent; however, only 12.5 percent said that drug use differed significantly from their typical drug habits. The following example illustrates the statement of a killer who had been drinking.

> It was the same as with the other one. I had been drinking at the bar. I don't even remember leaving. I don't know what made me kill her. I don't even know why I raped her. I had a good-looking wife at home. I saw her get into her car and I walked up and got in the car with her, yelled at her, took her down there where I raped her. I kept telling her I didn't want to hurt her, but I just started choking her.

We suspect that these murderers are preoccupied with a kind of internal dialogue that sustains anger, discontent, irritability, or depression. Use of alcohol or drugs is an attempt to moderate such internal stress, but the fantasy continues. Such an offender is often unaware of the extent of this internal dialogue. For example, when chastised by a teacher or boss, he may talk to himself: "If I ever got that son of a bitch, I'd rip him apart; I'd smash him up." One murderer, after performing poorly in the service and being intimidated by his sergeant, went AWOL on a drinking binge. While out on the street, he beat a drunk to death after the man grabbed him. The murderer felt justified in his actions and was unaware of the intensity of his rage or the impact of his blows. He then beat to death a second man. Finally, he abducted a female acquaintance. When he awoke the next morning, her dead body was beside him with a broomstick thrust into her vagina with such force that it had penetrated her lungs. Although he believes he killed her, he claims no recollection of the incident.

To the men with unconscious plans, violent thoughts are not acknowledged as serious contributors to their behavior. Rather, they believe external circumstances trigger the murderous behavior. One murderer described incarcerated men as "good guys." However, he alluded to a fantasy of dominance when he noted the sense of power bestowed by alcohol.

> If it hadn't been for beer and whiskey, I wouldn't be here [in prison] today. I've seen a lot of men come in and out since I've been here. They go out and they come in. The only reason they do is that they get hold of a bottle. Ninety percent of the guys that are in here are pretty good people, but when they get hold of that bottle, it makes them feel like they are superman.

Phase Two: The Act of Murder

The Actual Murder

Killing the victim moves the murderer to the reality of murder. The victim may not die as in the fantasy or in the way the offender planned. He may have to use more violence, he may feel more frightened than he anticipated, or he may be startled by the fact that he feels excited. Some murderers are exhilarated—they broke the rules, they killed. This feeling will induce some to kill again, while others will, in horror over what they have done, turn themselves in to the police.

For some men the actual murder goes beyond their fantasies of killing. There is confirmation and reinforcement of the fantasy, and pleasure or triumph in the power of the act. One murderer described his heightened excitement when driving his car with the dead bodies of two victims inside.

> I drive up to my apartment with two murdered girls in my car. The trunk is a mess, with one body stabbed to death. The other [body] is on the back seat. The landlord is [at my apartment] with two friends. I [drove] right up and they kept on talking and I thought, wow, would they freak out if I just got out and opened my trunk and back seat and just threw bodies out in front of them. . . . I took the heads up to my room. I could sit there looking at the heads on an overstuffed chair, tripping on them on my bed, looking at them [when] one of them somehow becomes unsettled, comes rolling down the chair, very grisly. Tumbling down the chair, rolls across the cushion and hits the rug, bonk. The neighbor downstairs hates my guts. I'm always making noise late at night. He gets a broom and whacks on the ceiling. "Buddy," I say "I'm sorry for that, dropped my head, sorry." That helped bring me out of the depressions. I would trip on that.

Other murderers feel a surprising sense of horror over the act they committed. The following case illustrates how one murderer reacted to the second of his three murders.

> A thirty-year-old woman was strangled, stabbed, and shot. She had also been cleaned up and positioned in bed after death. Fingerprints were left at the crime scene, along with a message written in lipstick on the wall: "For heaven's sake, catch me before I kill more. I cannot control myself." Six months later the murderer kidnapped and killed a six-year-old girl; a ransom note left at the scene matched the handwriting of the earlier message.

The Sexual Element of Homicide

Although all the murders in our study contained a sexual element, it is apparent that the execution of this element and its meaning to the offender vary. Some victims were raped and then murdered; others were sexually mutilated only after death. In one case, there were no obvious signs of sexual assault; however, the disembowelment of the victim was later found to have a sexual meaning for the killer. Rapists who murder, according to Rada (1978), rarely report any sexual satisfaction from the murder nor do they perform postmortem sexual acts. In contrast, the sadistic murderer (Brittain 1970), sometimes called the lust murderer (Hazelwood and Douglas 1980), kills as part of a ritualized sadistic fantasy.

Rape Murder. In our study, 56 percent of 108 cases with data had victims who were raped prior to death. One murderer recalled how he sexually assaulted the woman in one location and then transported her elsewhere to kill her:

> We got to my apartment. Inside my apartment I tied her up. I wanted to have intercourse. . . . Afterwards we went out to my car, and I took her to a deserted area where I killed her.

The rape murder may be prompted by an emotional frame of mind, as in the following case in which the rage was evident in the stabbing of one of his victims.

> We were walking along, through the culverts, underneath the highway. That's when I pulled out the knife and without even saying [anything] I stabbed her. I had the gun in this hand and the knife came from my back pocket, and I just came around like this and hit her like this. She fell right there, and she screamed as she was falling. I kept stabbing. She fell down and landed on the ground. I kept on stabbing—maybe fifty to one hundred times.

Mutilation Murder. The killer may rape a victim both before and after the victim dies, and these acts may often be sadistic and include mutilation and torture of the victim. For example, in one case the offender raped the victim and then slowly strangled her manually with a garrote. After death he also raped her.

A sexual act was committed only after the victim's death in 42 percent of ninety-two cases with data we studied. In one case, the murderer ejaculated into a knife wound he made into the victim. In another, the killer sexually assaulted both of his victims after he shot them.

Components of torture, mutilation, and overkill, or the infliction of more injury than is necessary to kill a person, are evident in many of these murders. Unusual or bizarre imagery or acts may be necessary to elicit feelings of sexual excitement in the killer. The level of complexity and bizarreness that is needed to obtain and sustain emotional arousal suggests that the ultimate expression of the murderer's perversion may be his mutilation of the victim.

FBI criminal profiling experience finds a frequent component of sexual murder to be the insertion of foreign objects into the vaginal and anal cavities of victims. This act is often combined with other acts of mutilation, such as slashing of the body, cutting of the breasts and buttocks, and biting of various parts of the body. It is noted that these acts, particularly in the case of the disorganized offender, do not coincide with completed acts of sexual penetration. Thus, evidence of sexual fluids are not present in the cavities of the victims. When sexual fluids do appear, they are more often found on or around the body and have been produced by masturbation rather than sexual contact with the victim. This indicates the homicide and assault have triggered a sexual fantasy that excited the killer. Since his sexual history is that of solo sex, and he finds interpersonal relationships difficult, if not impossible, he reverts to masturbatory acts even when a real partner (his victim) is available. Masturbation generally occurs after death, when the fantasy is strongest.

It is theorized by FBI research that the act of placing foreign objects into the victims by the disorganized offender may be a form of regressive necrophilia. This act, therefore, is a substitute for actual sexual intercourse. The insertion becomes the sexual act through fantasy, leaving no sexual evidence for the homicide investigator. It is for this reason that the sexual element of the crime is often missed by police investigators, psychologists, or psychiatrists who evaluate the case. Mental health professionals rarely have access to or examine crime scene photographs in their evaluations and rely solely on narrative descriptions of the murderous acts. Therefore, insertion of a foreign object in the vaginal cavity is often erroneously viewed as an act of mutilation rather than that of sexual substitution. The understanding of the sexual substitution concept provides a criminal profiler with a clearer and more accurate mental picture of the killer. . . .

One-third of the ninety-two victims with data showed evidence of torture. One killer picked up female hitchhikers and, after driving them to remote areas, first raped the women and then beat them on the head with a hammer. Victims of one murderer were also forced to perform fellatio on the offender while he forcefully inserted a hammer handle into their vaginas.

Mutilations often occur when the victim is already dead, a time when the killer has ultimate control over the victim. One victim was found with genitals mutilated and breasts amputated; the murderer had returned to the crime scene 14 hours after killing her and had cut off her breasts.

Another victim was found with stab wounds in the vagina and groin and with her throat slashed. Her nipples had been removed and her face severely beaten, and her cut-off hair was found hanging from a nearby tree branch.

Some murderers volunteered information on the intention of the mutilations. One murderer said that the mutilation after death was a way of disposing of the body, implying that he had a pragmatic reason. However, in addition to cutting up the body, he pulled out the victim's fingernails. The man later claimed not to remember this.

Depersonalization is one form of mutilation that was evident in several of the cases we studied. The term *depersonalization* is used to describe actions taken by the murderer to obscure the personal identity of the victim. These actions may occur before the victim is murdered, as in the case of the offender who mutilated nearly beyond recognition the faces of the young boys he sexually assaulted and killed. Another offender covered his elderly victims' faces with such items as blankets, pillows, towels, and bedspreads. However, not all depersonalization is as overt as these examples imply. The act of rolling a victim over onto his or her stomach so the face is not visible may be a subtle form of depersonalization.

The acting on the murderous thoughts and fantasies sets into motion the early phases of murder. Important to this action in the first phase are precrime stress factors, frame of mind, precrime planning and actions, victim selection, and triggering factors. The behaviors of the murderer confront him with the reality of his act and constitute the second phase of murder.

Questions for Thought and Discussion

1. Why do you think that serial killers, a very small percentage of murders, attract so much attention and have such a fascination to the public?
2. According to the authors, what are some of the precrime stress factors that led to the murders committed by the subjects in this research?
3. What were the major triggering factors that moved the offenders to act out their fantasies of killing?
4. What theory or theories of criminal behavior are illustrated in this research?

References

Brittain, R.P. The sadistic murderer. *Medical Science and the Law,* 1970, 10:98–207.

Hazelwood, R.R., and Douglas, J.E. The lust murderer. *FBI Law Enforcement Bulletin,* April 1980, 18–22.

Rada, R.T. *Clinical Aspects of the Rapist,* New York: Grune and Stratton, Inc., 1978.

Samenow, S.E. *Inside the Criminal Mind,* New York Times Books, 1984.

Chapter 14 Convicted Rapists' Vocabulary of Motive

Excuses and Justifications

Diana Scully
Joseph Marolla

In this chapter, Diana Scully and Joseph Marolla analyze the excuses and justifications that a group of convicted rapists used to explain themselves and their crimes. The researchers conducted extensive interviews with 114 male convicted rapists incarcerated in seven maximum- or medium-security prisons in Virginia. For the purpose of determining the validity of the information obtained, the offenders' accounts were cross-checked with information contained in presentence investigation reports on file at the prison. These reports contained, among other things, police and victims' versions of the crimes for which the rapists had been convicted. Scully and Marolla classified the participants as admitters or deniers. Admitters told essentially the same account of their crimes as police and victims did. Interview accounts by deniers differed significantly from police and victims' versions.

The rapists utilized excuses and justifications that allowed a majority of them to view themselves as nonrapists or "ex-rapists." Many of the rapists, through this form of self-delusion, saw their behavior as appropriate to the situation or as a reasonable adaptation or rational response to the situation they found themselves in.

The following selection, excerpted from the research, is divided into two sections. In the first, the authors discuss the accounts the rapists used to justify their behavior. In the second, they discuss the accounts the rapists used to excuse the rape. The authors' analysis and conclusions follow.

Justifying Rape

. . . Deniers attempted to justify their behavior by presenting the victim in a light that made her appear culpable, regardless of their own actions. Five themes run through attempts to justify their rapes: (1) women as seductresses; (2) women mean "yes" when they say "no"; (3) most women eventually relax and enjoy it; (4) nice girls don't get raped; and (5) guilty of a minor wrongdoing.

1. Women as Seductresses

Men who rape need not search far for cultural language which supports the premise that women provoke or are responsible for rape. In addition to common cultural stereotypes, the fields of psychiatry and criminology (particularly the subfield of victimology) have traditionally provided justifications for rape, often by portraying raped women as the victims of their own seduction (Albin 1977; Marolla and Scully 1979). For example, Hollander (1924, 130) argues:

> Considering the amount of illicit intercourse, rape of women is very rare indeed. Flirtation and provocative conduct, i.e. tacit (if not actual) consent is generally the prelude to intercourse.

Since women are supposed to be coy about their sexual availability, refusal to comply with a man's sexual demands lacks meaning and rape appears normal. The fact that violence and, often, a weapon are used to accomplish the rape is not considered. As an example, Abrahamsen (1960, 61) writes:

> The conscious or unconscious biological or psychological attraction between man and woman does not exist only on the part of the offender toward the woman but, also, on her part toward him, which in many instances may, to some extent, be the impetus for his sexual attack. Often a women [sic] unconsciously wishes to be taken by force—consider the theft of the bride in Peer Gynt.

Like Peer Gynt, the deniers we interviewed tried to demonstrate that their victims were willing and, in some cases, enthusiastic participants. In these accounts, the rape became more dependent upon the victims' behavior than upon their own actions.

Thirty-one percent . . . of the deniers presented an extreme view of the victim. Not only willing, she was the aggressor, a seductress who lured them, unsuspecting, into sexual action. Typical was a denier convicted of his first rape and accompanying crimes of burglary, sodomy, and abduction. According to the pre-sentence reports, he had broken into the victim's house and raped her at knifepoint. While he admitted to the breaking and entry, which he claimed was for altruistic purposes ("to pay for the prenatal care of a friend's girlfriend"), he also argued that when the victim discovered him, he had tried to leave but she had asked him to stay. Telling him that she cheated on her husband, she had voluntarily removed her clothes and seduced him. She was, according to him, an exemplary sex partner who "enjoyed it very much and asked for oral sex. Can I have it now?" he reported her as saying. He claimed they had spent hours in bed, after which the victim had told him he was good looking and asked to see him again. "Who would believe I'd meet a fellow like this?" he reported her as saying.

In addition to this extreme group, 25 percent . . . of the deniers said the victim was willing and had made some sexual advances. An additional 9 percent . . . said the victim was willing to have sex for money or drugs. In two of these three cases, the victim had been either an acquaintance or picked up, which the rapists said led them to expect sex.

2. Women Mean 'Yes' When They Say 'No'

Thirty-four percent . . . of the deniers described their victim as unwilling, at least initially, indicating either that she had resisted or that she had said no. Despite this, and even though according to pre-sentence reports a weapon had been present in 64 percent . . . of these 11 cases, the rapists justified their behavior by arguing that either the victim had not resisted enough or that her "no" had really meant "yes." For example, one denier who was serving time for a previous rape was subsequently convicted of attempting to rape a prison hospital nurse. He insisted he had actually completed the second rape, and said of his victim: "She semi-struggled but deep down inside I think she felt it was a fantasy come true." The nurse, according to him, had asked a question about his conviction for rape, which he interpreted as teasing. "It was like she was saying, 'rape me.'" Further, he stated that she had helped him along with oral sex and "from her actions, she was enjoying it." In another case, a 34-year-old man convicted of abducting and raping a 15-year-old teenager at knife point as she walked on the beach, claimed it was a pickup. This rapist said women like to be overpowered before sex, but to dominate after it begins.

> A man's body is like a Coke bottle, shake it up, put your thumb over the opening and feel the tension. When you take a woman out, woo her, then she says "no, I'm a nice girl," you have to use force. All men do this. She said "no" but it was a societal no, she wanted to be coaxed. All women say "no" when they mean "yes" but it's a societal no, so they won't have to feel responsible later.

Claims that the victim didn't resist or, if she did, didn't resist enough, were also used by 24 percent . . . of admitters to explain why, during the incident, they believed the victim was willing and that they were not raping. These rapists didn't redefine their acts until some time after the crime. For example, an admitter who used a bayonet to threaten his victim, an employee of the store he had been robbing, stated:

> At the time I didn't think it was rape. I just asked her nicely and she didn't resist. I never considered prison. I just felt like I had met a friend. It took about five years of reading and going to school to change my mind about whether it was rape. I became familiar with the subtlety of violence. But at the time, I believed that as long as I didn't hurt anyone it wasn't wrong. At the time, I didn't think I would go to prison, I thought I would beat it.

Another typical case involved a gang rape in which the victim was abducted at knife point as she walked home about midnight. According to two of the rapists, both of whom were interviewed, at the time they had thought the victim had willingly accepted a ride from the third rapist (who was not interviewed). They claimed the victim didn't resist and one reported her as saying she would do anything if they would take her home. In this rapist's view, "She acted like she enjoyed it, but maybe she was just acting. She wasn't crying, she was engaging in it." He reported that she had been friendly to the rapist who abducted her and, claiming not to have a home phone, she gave him her office number, a tactic eventually used to catch the three. In retrospect, this young man had decided, "She was scared and just relaxed and enjoyed it to avoid getting hurt." Note, however, that while he had redefined the act as rape, he continued to believe she enjoyed it.

Men who claimed to have been unaware that they were raping viewed sexual aggression as a man's prerogative at the time of the rape. Thus they regarded their act as little more than a minor wrongdoing even though most possessed or used a weapon. As long as the victim survived without major physical injury, from their perspective, a rape had not taken place. Indeed, even U.S. courts have often taken the position that physical injury is a necessary ingredient for a rape conviction.

3. Most Women Eventually Relax and Enjoy It

Many of the rapists expected us to accept the image, drawn from cultural stereotype, that once the rape began, the victim relaxed and enjoyed it. Indeed, 69 percent . . . of deniers justified their behavior by claiming not only that the victim was willing, but also that she enjoyed herself, in some cases to an immense degree. Several men suggested that they had fulfilled their victims' dreams. Additionally, while most admitters used adjectives such as "dirty," "humiliated," and "disgusted," to describe how they thought rape made women feel, 20 percent . . . believed that their victim enjoyed herself. For example, one denier had posed as a salesman to gain entry to his victim's house. But he claimed he had a previous sexual relationship with the victim, that she agreed to have sex for drugs, and that the opportunity to have sex with him produced "a glow, because she was really into oral stuff and fascinated by the idea of sex with a black man. She felt satisfied, fulfilled, wanted me to stay, but I didn't want her." In another case, a denier who had broken into his victim's house but who insisted the victim was his lover and let him in voluntarily, declared "She felt good, kept kissing me and wanted me to stay the night. She felt proud after sex with me." And another denier, who had hid in his victim's closet and later attacked her while she slept, argued that while she was scared at first, "once we got into it, she was ok." He continued to believe he hadn't committed rape because "she enjoyed it and it was like she consented."

4. Nice Girls Don't Get Raped

The belief that "nice girls don't get raped" affects perception of fault. The victim's reputation, as well as characteristics or behavior which violate normative sex role expectations, are perceived as contributing to the commission of the crime. For example, Nelson and Amir (1975) defined hitchhike rape as a victim-precipitated offense.

In our study, 69 percent . . . of deniers and 22 percent . . . of admitters referred to their victims' sexual reputation, thereby evoking the stereotype that "nice girls don't get raped." They claimed that the victim was known to have been a prostitute, or a "loose" woman, or to have had a lot of affairs, or to have given birth to a child out of wedlock. For example, a denier who claimed he had picked up his victim while she was hitchhiking stated, "To be honest, we [his family] knew she was a damn whore and whether she screwed one or 50 guys didn't matter." According to pre-sentence reports this victim didn't know her attacker and he abducted her at knife point from the street. In another case, a denier who claimed to have known his victim by reputation stated:

> If you wanted drugs or a quick piece of ass, she would do it. In court she said she was a virgin, but I could tell during sex [rape] that she was very experienced.

When other types of discrediting biographical information were added to these sexual slurs, a total of 78 percent . . . of the deniers used the victim's reputation to substantiate their accounts. Most frequently, they referred to the victim's emotional state or drug use. For example, one denier claimed his victim had been known to be loose and, additionally, had turned state's evidence against her husband to put him in prison and save herself from a burglary conviction. Further, he asserted that she had met her current boyfriend, who was himself in and out of prison, in a drug rehabilitation center where they were both clients.

Evoking the stereotype that women provoke rape by the way they dress, a description of the victim as seductively attired appeared in the accounts of 22 percent . . . of deniers and 17 percent . . . of admitters. Typically, these descriptions were used to substantiate their claims about the victim's reputation. Some men went to extremes to paint a tarnished picture of the victim, describing her as dressed in tight black clothes and without a bra; in one case, the victim was portrayed as sexually provocative in dress and carriage. Not only did she wear short skirts, but she was observed to "spread her legs while getting out of cars." Not all of the men attempted to assassinate their victim's reputation with equal vengeance. Numerous times they made subtle and offhand remarks like, "She was a waitress and you know how they are."

The intent of these discrediting statements is clear. Deniers argued that the woman was a "legitimate" victim who got what she deserved. For example, one denier stated that all of his victims had been prostitutes; pre-sentence reports indicated they were not. Several times during his interview, he referred to them as "dirty sluts," and argued "anything I did to them was justified." Deniers also claimed their victim had wrongly accused them and was the type of woman who would perjure herself in court.

5. Only a Minor Wrongdoing

The majority of deniers did not claim to be completely innocent and they also accepted some accountability for their actions. Only 16 percent . . . of deniers argued that they were totally free of blame. Instead, the majority of deniers pleaded guilty to a lesser charge. That is, they obfuscated the rape by pleading guilty to a less serious, more acceptable charge. They accepted being over-sexed, accused of poor judgement or trickery, even some violence, or guilty of adultery or contributing to the delinquency of a minor, charges that are hardly the equivalent of rape.

Typical of this reasoning is a denier who met his victim in a bar when the bartender asked him if he would try to repair her stalled car. After attempting unsuccessfully, he claimed the victim drank with him and later accepted a ride. Out riding, he pulled into a deserted area "to see how my luck would go." When the victim resisted his advances, he beat her and he stated:

> I did something stupid. I pulled a knife on her and I hit her as hard as I would hit a man. But I shouldn't be in prison for what I did. I shouldn't have all this time [sentence] for going to bed with a broad.

This rapist continued to believe that while the knife was wrong, his sexual behavior was justified.

In another case, the denier claimed he picked up his under-age victim at a party and that she voluntarily went with him to a motel. According to pre-sentence reports, the victim had been abducted at knife point from a party. He explained:

> After I paid for a motel, she would have to have sex but I wouldn't use a weapon. I would have explained. I spent money and, if she still said no, I would have forced her. If it had happened that way, it would have been rape to some people but not to my way of thinking. I've done that kind of thing before. I'm guilty of sex and contributing to the delinquency of a minor, but not rape.

In sum, deniers argued that, while their behavior may not have been completely proper, it should not have been considered rape. To accomplish this, they attempted to discredit and blame the victim while presenting their own actions as justified in the context. Not surprisingly, none of the deniers thought of himself as a rapist. A minority of the admitters attempted to lessen the impact of their crime by claiming the victim enjoyed being raped. But despite this similarity, the nature and tone of admitters' and deniers' accounts were essentially different.

Excusing Rape

In stark contrast to deniers, admitters regarded their behavior as morally wrong and beyond justification. They blamed themselves rather than the victim, although some continued to cling to the belief that the victim had contributed to the crime somewhat, for example, by not resisting enough.

Several of the admitters expressed the view that rape was an act of such moral outrage that it was unforgivable. Several admitters broke into tears at intervals during their interviews. A typical sentiment was,

> I equate rape with someone throwing you up against a wall and tearing your liver and guts out of you. . . . Rape is worse than murder . . . and I'm disgusting.

Another young admitter frequently referred to himself as repulsive and confided:

> I'm in here for rape and in my own mind, it's the most disgusting crime, sickening. When people see me and know, I get sick.

Admitters tried to explain their crime in a way that allowed them to retain a semblance of moral integrity. Thus, in contrast to deniers' justifications, admitters used excuses to explain how they were compelled to rape. These excuses appealed to the existence of forces outside of the rapists' control. Through the use of excuses, they attempted to demonstrate that either intent was absent or responsibility was diminished. This allowed them to admit rape while reducing the threat to their identity as a moral person. Excuses also permitted them to view their behavior as idiosyncratic rather than typical and, thus, to believe they were not "really" rapists. Three themes run through these accounts: (1) the use of alcohol and drugs; (2) emotional problems; and (3) [a] nice guy image.

1. The Use of Alcohol and Drugs

A number of studies have noted a high incidence of alcohol and drug consumption by convicted rapists prior to their crime (Groth 1979; Queen's Bench Foundation 1976). However, more recent research has tentatively concluded that the connection between substance use and crime is not as direct as previously thought (Ladouceur 1983). Another facet of alcohol and drug use mentioned in the literature is its utility in disavowing deviance. McCaghy (1968) found that child molesters used alcohol as a technique for neutralizing their deviant identity. Marolla and Scully (1979), in a review of psychiatric literature, demonstrated how alcohol consumption is applied differently as a vocabulary of motive. Rapists can use alcohol both as an excuse for their behavior and to discredit the victim and make her more responsible. We found the former common among admitters and the latter common among deniers.

Alcohol and/or drugs were mentioned in the accounts of 77 percent . . . of admitters and 84 percent . . . of deniers and both groups were equally likely to have acknowledged consuming a substance (admitters, 77 percent . . . ; deniers, 72 percent). . . . However, admitters said they had been affected by the substance; if not the cause of their behavior, it was at least a contributing factor. For example, an admitter who estimated his consumption to have been eight beers and four "hits of acid" reported:

> Straight, I don't have the guts to rape. I could fight a man but not that. To say, "I'm going to do it to a woman," knowing it will scare and hurt her, takes guts or you have to be sick.

Another admitter believed that his alcohol and drug use,

> . . . brought out what was already there but in such intensity it was uncontrollable. Feelings of being dominant, powerful, using someone for my own gratification, all rose to the surface.

In contrast, deniers' justifications required that they not be substantially impaired. To say that they had been drunk or high would cast doubt on their ability to control themsel[ves] or to remember events as they actually happened. Consistent with this, when we asked if the alcohol and/or drugs had an effect on their behavior, 69 percent . . . of admitters, but only 40 percent . . . of deniers said they had been affected.

Even more interesting were references to the victim's alcohol and/or drug use. Since admitters had already relieved themselves of responsibility through claims of being drunk or high, they had nothing to gain from the assertion that the victim had used or been affected by alcohol and/or drugs. On the other hand, it was very much in the interest of deniers to declare that their victim had been intoxicated or high: that fact lessened her credibility and made her more responsible for the act. Reflecting these observations, 72 percent . . . of deniers and 26 percent . . . of admitters maintained that alcohol or drugs had been consumed by the victim. Further, while 56 percent . . . of deniers declared she had been affected by this use, only 15 percent . . . of admitters made a similar claim. Typically, deniers argued that the alcohol and drugs had sexually aroused their victim or rendered her out of control. For example, one denier insisted that his victim had become hysterical from drugs, not from being raped, and it was because of the drugs that she had reported him to the police. In addition, 40 percent . . . of deniers argued that while the victim had been drunk or high, they themselves either hadn't ingested or weren't affected by alcohol and/or drugs. None of the admitters made this claim. In fact, in all of the 15 percent . . . of cases where an admitter said the victim was drunk or high, he also admitted to being similarly affected.

These data strongly suggest that whatever role alcohol and drugs play in sexual and other types of violent crime, rapists have learned the advantage to be gained from using alcohol and drugs as an account. Our sample were aware that their victim would be discredited and their own behavior excused or justified by referring to alcohol and/or drugs.

2. Emotional Problems

Admitters frequently attributed their acts to emotional problems. Forty percent . . . of admitters said they believed an emotional problem had been at the root of their rape behavior, and 33 percent . . . specifically related the problem to an unhappy, unstable childhood or a marital-domestic situation. Still others claimed to have been in a general state of unease. For example, one admitter said that at the time of the rape he had been depressed, feeling he couldn't do anything right, and that something had been missing from his life. But he also added, "being a rapist is not part of my personality." Even admitters who could locate no source for an emotional problem evoked the popular image of rapists as the product of disordered personalities to argue they also must have problems:

> The fact that I'm a rapist makes me different. Rapists aren't all there. They have problems. It was wrong so there must be a reason why I did it. I must have a problem.

Our data do indicate that a precipitating event, involving an upsetting problem of everyday living, appeared in the accounts of 80 percent . . . of admitters and 25 percent . . . of deniers. Of those experiencing a precipitating event, including deniers, 76 percent . . . involved a wife or girlfriend. Over and over, these men described themselves as having been in a rage because of an incident involving a woman with whom they believed they were in love.

Frequently, the upsetting event was related to a rigid and unrealistic double standard for sexual conduct and virtue which they applied to "their" woman but which they didn't expect from men, didn't apply to themselves, and, obviously, didn't honor in other women. To discover that the "pedestal" didn't apply to their wife or girlfriend sent them into a fury. One especially articulate and typical admitter described his feeling as follows. After serving a short prison term for auto theft, he married his "childhood sweetheart" and secured a well-paying job. Between his job and the volunteer work he was doing with an ex-offender group, he was spending long hours away from home, a situation that had bothered his wife. In response to her request, he gave up his volunteer work, though it was clearly meaningful to him. Then, one day, he discovered his wife with her former boyfriend "and my life fell apart." During the next several days, he said his anger had made him withdraw into himself and, after three days of drinking in a motel room, he abducted and raped a stranger. He stated:

> My parents have been married for many years and I had high expectations about marriage. I put my wife on a pedestal. When I walked in on her, I felt like my life had been destroyed, it was such a shock. I was bitter and angry about the fact that I hadn't done anything to my wife for cheating. I didn't want to hurt her [the victim], only to scare and degrade her.

It is clear that many admitters, and a minority of deniers, were under stress at the time of their rapes. However, their problems were ordinary—the types of upsetting events that everyone experiences at some point in life. The overwhelming majority of the men were not clinically defined as mentally ill in court-ordered psychiatric examinations prior to their trials. Indeed, our sample is consistent with Abel et al. (1980) who found fewer than 5 percent of rapists were psychotic at the time of their offense.

As with alcohol and drug intoxication, a claim of emotional problems works differently depending upon whether the behavior in question is being justified or excused. It would have been counter-productive for deniers to have claimed to have had emotional problems at the time of the rape. Admitters used psychological explanations to portray themselves as having been temporarily "sick" at the time of the rape. Sick people are usually blamed for neither the cause of their illness nor for acts committed while in that state of diminished capacity. Thus, adopting the sick role removed responsibility by excusing the behavior as having been beyond the ability of the individual to control. Since the rapists were not "themselves," the rape was idiosyncratic rather than typical behavior. Admitters asserted a nondeviant identity despite their self-proclaimed disgust with what they had done. Although admitters were willing to assume the sick role, they did not view their problem as a chronic condition, nor did they believe themselves to be insane or permanently impaired. Said one admitter, who believed that he needed psychological counseling: "I have a mental disorder, but I'm not crazy." Instead, admitters viewed their "problem" as mild, transient, and curable. Indeed, part of the appeal of this excuse was that not only did it relieve responsibility, but, as with alcohol and drug addiction, it allowed the rapist to "recover." Thus, at the time of their interviews, only 31 . . . percent of admitters indicated that "being a rapist" was part of their self-concept. Twenty-eight percent . . . of admitters stated they had never thought of themselves as a rapist, 8 percent . . . said they were unsure, and 33 percent . . . asserted they had been a rapist at one time but now were recovered. A multiple "ex-rapist," who believed his "problem" was due to "something buried in my subconscious" that was triggered when his girlfriend broke up with him, expressed a typical opinion:

> I was a rapist, but not now. I've grown up, had to live with it. I've hit the bottom of the well and it can't get worse. I feel born again to deal with my problems.

3. Nice Guy Image

Admitters attempted to further neutralize their crime and negotiate a nonrapist identity by painting an image of themselves as a "nice guy." Admitters projected the image of someone who had made a serious mistake but, in every other respect, was a decent person. Fifty-seven percent . . . expressed regret and sorrow for their victim indicating that they wished there were a way to apologize for or amend their behavior. For example, a participant in a rape-murder, who insisted his partner did the murder, confided, "I wish there was something I could do besides saying 'I'm sorry, I'm sorry.' I live with it 24 hours a day and, sometimes, I wake up crying in the middle of the night because of it."

Schlenker and Darby (1981) explain the significance of apologies beyond the obvious expression of regret. An apology allows a person to admit guilt while at the same time seeking a pardon by signalling that the event should not be considered a fair representation of what the person is really like. An apology separates the bad self from the good self, and promises more acceptable behavior in the future. When apologizing, an individual is attempting to say: "I have repented and should be forgiven," thus making it appear that no further rehabilitation is required.

The "nice guy" statements of the admitters reflected an attempt to communicate a message consistent with Schlenker's and Darby's analysis of apologies. It was an attempt to convey that rape was not a representation of their "true" self. For example,

> It's different from anything else I've ever done. I feel more guilt about this. It's not consistent with me. When I talk about it, it's like being assaulted myself. I don't know why I did it, but once I started, I got into it. Armed robbery was a way of life for me, but not rape. I feel like I wasn't being myself.

Admitters also used "nice guy" statements to register their moral opposition to violence and harming women, even though, in some cases, they had seriously injured their victims. Such was the case of an admitter convicted of a gang rape:

> I'm against hurting women. She should have resisted. None of us were the type of person that would use force on a woman. I never positioned myself on a woman unless she showed an interest in me. They would play to me, not me to them. My weakness is to follow. I never would have stopped, let alone pick her up without the others. I never would have let anyone beat her. I never bothered women who didn't want sex; never had a problem with sex or getting it. I loved her—like all women.

Finally, a number of admitters attempted to improve their self-image by demonstrating that, while they had raped, it could have been worse if they had not been a "nice guy." For example, one admitter professed to being especially gentle with his victim after she told him she had just had a baby. Others claimed to have given the victim money to get home or make a phone call, or to have made sure the victim's children were not in the room. A multiple rapist, whose pattern was to break in and attack sleeping victims in their homes, stated:

> I never beat any of my victims and I told them I wouldn't hurt them if they cooperated. I'm a professional thief. But I never robbed the women I raped because I felt so bad about what I had already done to them.

Even a young man, who raped his five victims at gun point and then stabbed them to death, attempted to improve his image by stating:

> Physically they enjoyed the sex [rape]. Once they got involved, it would be difficult to resist. I was always gentle and kind until I started to kill them. And the killing was always sudden, so they wouldn't know it was coming.

Summary and Conclusions

Convicted rapists' accounts of their crimes include both excuses and justifications. Those who deny what they did was rape justify their actions; those who admit it was rape attempt to excuse it or themselves. This study does not address why some men admit while others deny, but future research might address this question. This paper does provide insight on how men who are sexually aggressive or violent construct reality, describing the different strategies of admitters and deniers.

Admitters expressed the belief that rape was morally reprehensible. But they explained themselves and their acts by appealing to forces beyond their control, forces which reduced their capacity to act rationally and thus compelled to rape. Two types of excuses predominated: alcohol/drug intoxication and emotional problems. Admitters used these excuses to negotiate a moral identity for themselves by viewing rape as idiosyncratic rather than typical behavior. This allowed them to reconceptualize themselves as recovered or "ex-rapists," someone who had made a serious mistake which did not represent their "true" self.

In contrast, deniers' accounts indicate that these men raped because their value system provided no compelling reason not to do so. When sex is viewed as a male entitlement, rape is no longer seen as criminal. However, the deniers had been convicted of rape, and like the admitters, they attempted to negotiate an identity. Through justifications, they constructed a "controversial" rape and attempted to demonstrate how their behavior, even if not quite right, was appropriate in the situation. Their denials, drawn from common cultural rape stereotypes, took two forms, both of which ultimately denied the existence of a victim.

The first form of denial was buttressed by the cultural view of men as sexually masterful and women as coy but seductive. Injury was denied by portraying the victim as willing, even enthusiastic, or as politely resistant at first but eventually yielding to "relax and enjoy it." In these accounts, force appeared merely as a seductive technique. Rape was disclaimed: rather than harm the woman, the rapist had fulfilled her dreams. In the second form of denial, the victim was portrayed as the type of woman who "got what she deserved." Through attacks on the victim's sexual reputation and, to a lesser degree, her emotional state, deniers attempted to demonstrate that since the victim wasn't a "nice girl," they were not rapists. Consistent with both forms of denial was the self-interested use of alcohol and drugs as a justification. Thus, in contrast to admitters, who accentuated their own use as an excuse, deniers emphasized the victim's consumption in an effort to both discredit her and make her appear more responsible for the rape. It is important to remember that deniers did not invent these justifications. Rather, they reflect a belief system which has historically victimized women by promulgating the myth that women both enjoy and are responsible for their own rape.

While admitters and deniers present an essentially contrasting view of men who rape, there were some shared characteristics. Justifications particularly, but also excuses, are buttressed by the cultural view of women as sexual commodities, dehumanized and devoid of autonomy and dignity. In this sense, the sexual objectification of women must be understood as an important factor contributing to an environment that trivializes, neutralizes, and, perhaps, facilitates rape.

Finally, we must comment on the consequences of allowing one perspective to dominate thought on a social problem. Rape, like any complex continuum of behavior, has multiple causes and is influenced by a number of social factors. Yet, dominated by psychiatry and the medical model, the underlying assumption that rapists are "sick" has pervaded research. Although methodologically unsound, conclusions have been based almost exclusively on small clinical populations of rapists—that extreme group of rapists who seek counseling in prison and are the most likely to exhibit psychopathology. From this small, atypical group of men, psychiatric findings have been generalized to all men who rape. Our research, however, based on volunteers from the entire prison population, indicates that some rapists, like deniers, viewed and understood their behavior from a popular cultural perspective. This strongly suggests that cultural perspectives, and not an idiosyncratic illness, motivated their behavior. Indeed, we can argue that the psychiatric perspective has contributed to the vocabulary of motive that rapists use to excuse and justify their behavior (Scully and Marolla 1984).

Efforts to arrive at a general explanation for rape have been retarded by the narrow focus of the medical model and the preoccupation with clinical populations. The continued reduction of such complex behavior to a singular cause hinders, rather than enhances, our understanding of rape.

Questions for Thought and Discussion

1. Why do you think that serial killers, a very small percentage of murderers, attract so much attention and have such a fascination to the public?

2. According to the authors, what are some of the precrime stress factors that led to the murders committed by the subjects in this research?
3. What were the major triggering factors that moved the offenders to act out their fantasies of killing?
4. What theory or theories of criminal behavior are illustrated in this research?

References

Abel, Gene, Judith Becker, and Linda Skinner (1980) "Aggressive behavior and sex." *Psychiatric Clinics of North America* 3(2):133–151.

Abrahamsen, David (1960) *The Psychology of Crime.* New York: John Wiley.

Albin, Rochelle (1977) "Psychological studies of rape." *Signs* 3(2):423–435.

——— (1979) "Rape: Sexual disruption and recovery." *American Journal of Orthopsychiatry* 49(4):648–657.

Groth, Nicholas A. (1979) *Men Who Rape.* New York: Plenum Press.

Hollander, Bernard (1924) *The Psychology of Misconduct, Vice, and Crime.* New York: Macmillan.

Ladouceur, Patricia (1983) "The relative impact of drugs and alcohol on serious felons." Paper presented at the annual meetings of the American Society of Criminology, Denver, November 9–12.

Marolla, Joseph, and Diana Scully (1979) "Rape and psychiatric vocabularies of motive." Pp. 301–318 in Edith S. Gomberg and Violet Franks (eds.), *Gender and Disordered Behavior: Sex Differences in Psychopathology.* New York: Brunner/Mazel.

McCaghy, Charles (1968) "Drinking and deviance disavowal: The case of child molesters." *Social Problems* 16(1):43–49.

Nelson, Steve, and Menachem Amir (1975) "The hitchhike victim of rape: A research report." Pp. 47–65 in Israel Drapkin and Emilio Viano (eds.), *Victimology: A New Focus.* Lexington, KY: Lexington Books.

Queen's Bench Foundation (1976) *Rape: Prevention and Resistance.* San Francisco: Queen's Bench Foundation.

Schlenker, Barry R., and Bruce W. Darby (1981) "The use of apologies in social predicaments." *Social Psychology Quarterly* 44(3):271–278.

Scully, Diana, and Joseph Marolla (1984) "Rape and psychiatric vocabularies of motive: Alternative perspectives." In Ann Wolbert Burgess (ed.), *Handbook on Rape and Sexual Assault.* New York: Garland Publishing.

Chapter 15
Creating the Illusion of Impending Death

Armed Robbers in Action

Richard T. Wright
Scott H. Decker

This selection is derived from a larger study by Wright and Decker in which they interviewed 86 active armed robbers in St. Louis. The interviews were semistructured and conducted in a casual manner. The researchers focused on the robbers' thoughts and actions before, during, and after their crimes. In this selection they report on the strategies used by the robbers to compel their victims' compliance.

As such, violence is seen as instrumental to the commission of the crime. Wright and Decker's subjects reported that they created an illusion of impending death to scare victims into a state of compliance. The robbers attempted to maintain the illusion without having to actually make good on the threat. When, however, the victims did not comply as expected, the offenders usually responded with severe violence to bring victims back to compliance. The robbers reported that seldom did they want to kill their victims, although some were prepared to do so if necessary.

Unlike most sorts of street crime, successful armed robberies are never secret or ambiguous. By definition, they require offenders to confront intended victims directly. As David Luckenbill (1981, 25) has observed, there is a strong interactional component to armed robbery; offenders and victims must develop "a common definition of the situation" and co-orient their actions to meet the demands of the offense. This does not happen automatically. After all, why should stick-up victims willingly participate in their own fleecing?

It is important to develop a clear understanding of the strategies used by armed robbers to compel the cooperation of would-be victims. Such information could offer citizens some guidance about how best to act and react should they be confronted by a robber. It also could provide policy makers and criminal justice officials with a better appreciation of offenders' aims and intentions during robberies, thereby enabling them to make more informed crime prevention and sentencing decisions.

In an attempt to learn more about the tactics employed by offenders to commit stick-ups, we located and interviewed 86 currently active armed robbers in St. Louis, Missouri. Armed robbery is a serious problem in St. Louis. In 1994, the year our research began, the city had 6,025 stick-ups reported to the police and ranked second in the nation in robberies per capita. The armed robbers for our study were recruited through the efforts of two field-based informants—an ex-offender, and a small-time heroin dealer and street criminal. Working through chains of street referrals, the field recruiters contacted active armed robbers, convinced them to take part in our project, and assisted us in conducting interviews that lasted up to two hours. In the pages that follow, we report just a small portion of what the offenders said during those interviews, focusing on how they actually commit their offenses.

Approaching the Victim

To be successful, armed robbers must take control of the offense from the start. They immediately have to impose on the interaction a definition favorable to their ends, allowing intended victims no room for negotiation. This typically is accomplished by creating an illusion of impending death.

> Robbery itself is an illusion. That's what it's about. . . . Here is a person that you stick a gun in his face, they've never died, they don't know how it feels, but the illusion of death causes them to do what you want them to do. (aka Robert Jones)

A large part of creating such an illusion involves catching potential victims off guard; the element of surprise denies them the opportunity to adopt an oppositional stance.

> Sometimes people be alert; they be watchin' so you got to be careful of what

you do. You got to be alert. . . . Pretty soon [the intended victim] falls asleep, and then [h]e ain't even trippin'. He over there lookin' at some girl. . . . [H]e probably just take his eyes off what he's doin', watchin' out, [which is] what he's supposed to be doin', and just turn his head on some girls. And [the stick-up] be on. (aka Andrew)

The offenders in our sample employ two different methods to approach would-be victims without arousing their suspicion. The first method involves using stealth or speed to sneak up on unwitting prey.

[Whoever I am going to rob. I] just come up on you. You could be going to your car. If you are facing this way, I want to be on your blind side. If you are going this way, I want to be on that side where I can get up on you [without you noticing me] and grab you: "This is a robbery, motherfucker, don't make it no murder!" I kind of like shake you. That's my approach. (aka Richard L. Brown)

The second method involves "managing a normal appearance" (Luckenbill 1981, 29). The offenders' aim is to fit into the social setting such that victims see their presence as normal and nonthreatening, thereby allowing them to get close enough for a surprise attack.

Well, if I'm walking, say you got something that I want, I might come up there [and say], "Do you have the time?" or "Can I get a light from you?" something like that. "Yeah, it's three o'clock." By then I'm up on you, getting what I want. (aka Loco)

The method chosen to approach potential victims typically is dictated more by situational factors than by the idiosyncratic preferences of individual offenders. Depending on the situation, most of the armed robbers are prepared to use either speed and stealth or the presentation of a nonthreatening self to move within striking range of their victims. The offender quoted below, for example, reported that he and his partners usually initiate their commercial stick-ups simply by charging through the front door of the establishment, ski masks pulled down and guns drawn.

When I approach the door [of a would-be commercial target] generally we got ski masks that rolls up into a skull cap; it's a skull cap right now and as we get to the door, right prior to walking in the door, we pull our masks down. Once we come in, we got these masks down [so] we got to come in pulling our weapons, might even have them out prior to going in, just concealed. As soon as we pull those masks down, we are committed [because our intention is obvious]. (aka Robert Gibson)

He added, however, that circumstances occasionally require them to enter intended targets posing as customers. Doing so helps them to avoid tipping their hand too early, which is crucial in situations where the victim is likely to be armed.

Say for instance [the target is] a tavern and the guy behind the bar . . . might be the kind of guy that got a pistol. Most bartenders and most people that's cashing checks, they got pistols on them. Believe me, they got pistols. . . . So in that particular situation, you got to . . . get in the door before you go into motion because you got to know where they are at. You've got to make sure that you've got a real chance to . . . get up on them and make it not worth their risk to try to reach the pistol [before you betray your intentions]. (aka Robert Gibson)

Regardless of the manner in which the offenders make their approach, the aim almost invariably is the same: to "establish co-presence" with the victim without betraying their intentions (Luckenbill 1981, 29). This gives would-be victims little opportunity to recognize the danger and to take steps to repel the attack. Not only is this far safer for the offenders, it also puts them in a strong position when it comes to compelling the victim's immediate cooperation.

Announcing the Crime

By announcing a stick-up, armed robbers commit themselves irrevocably to the offense. Any semblance of normality has been shattered; from this point onward, the victim will act and react in the knowledge that a robbery is being committed. The offenders we interviewed saw this as the "make or break" moment. The challenge for them was "to dramatize with unarguable clarity that the situation ha[d] suddenly and irreversibly been transformed into a crime" (Katz 1988, 176). In effecting this transformation, they seek to establish dominance over their intended prey, thereby placing themselves in a position to dictate the terms of the unfolding interaction.

When I first come up on [my victims], I might scare them, but then I calm them down. It's a control thing. If you can get a person to listen to you, you can get them

> to do just about anything. . . . That's the way the world is made. (aka Tony Wright)

Most of the offenders said that they typically open their armed robberies with a demand that the would-be victim stop and listen to them.

> I say [to the victim], "Look here, hey, just hold up right where you at! Don't move! Don't say nothing!" (aka James Minor)

They often couple this demand with an unambiguous declaration of their predatory intentions.

> [I tell my victims], "It's a robbery! Don't nobody move!" (aka John Lee)

That declaration, in turn, usually is backed by a warning about the dire consequences of failing to do as they instruct.

> [I say to the victim], "This is a robbery, don't make it a murder! It's a robbery, don't make it a murder!" (aka Wallie Cleaver)

All of the above pronouncements are intended to "soften up" victims; to inform them that they're about to be robbed and to convince them that they are not in a position to resist. Having seized initial control of the interaction, offenders then must let victims know what is expected of them. As one armed robber reminded us: "You have to talk to victims to get them to cooperate. . . . They don't know what to do, whether to lay down, jump over the counter, dance, or whatever." This information typically is communicated to victims in the form of short, sharp orders laced with profanity and, often, racial epithets.

> [I say to victims], "Hey motherfucker, give me your shit! Move slow and take everything out of your pockets!" (aka James Love)

> [I grab my victims and say], "Take it off girl! Nigger, come up off of it!" (aka Libbie Jones)

The "expressive economy" with which the offenders issue instructions can in part be accounted for by a desire to keep victims off balance by demonstrating an ominous insensitivity to their precarious emotional state (see Katz 1988, 177). Clearly, the swearing and racial putdowns help to reinforce this impression.

Almost all of the offenders typically used a gun to announce their stick-ups. They recognized that displaying a firearm usually obviated the need to do much talking. One put it this way: "A gun kinda speaks for itself." Most of them believed that "big, ugly guns" such as 9MMs or 45s were the best weapons for inducing cooperation.

> [The 9MM] got that look about it like it gonna kill you. It talk for itself. "I'm gonna kill you." Looking at a 9 pointed at you, that's what goes through your head: "He gonna kill me if I don't give him this money." (aka Prauch)

In practice, however, many of the armed robbers actually carried somewhat smaller firearms because they were more easily concealed and simpler to handle.

> I like the 32 because it's like a 38, small, easy and accessible. And it will knock [the victim] down if you have to use it. (aka Bob Jones)

A few offenders maintained that very small caliber pistols (e.g., 22s, 25s) made poor robbery weapons because many potential victims were not afraid of them.

> [With] 22s or 25s people gonna be like, "Man, he using this little gun. I ain't worried." A 22 is real little, they gonna be, "Man, that ain't gonna do nothing but hurt me. Give me a little sting." (aka Syco)

That said, the majority of respondents felt that even the smallest handguns were big enough to intimidate most people. As one observed: "A person's gonna fear any kind of gun you put in their face. So it don't matter [what you use]. If it's a gun, it's gonna put fear in you."

The dilemma faced by offenders in relying on a gun to induce fear is that the strategy might work too well. Jack Katz (1988) has noted that the display of a firearm can easily be misinterpreted by victims as the precursor to an offense far more serious than robbery (e.g., rape, kidnapping, murder). Offenders are keen to avoid such misinterpretations because they can stun victims into a state of incomprehension or convince them that determined resistance represents their only chance of survival. When armed offenders warn victims—"This is a robbery, don't make it a murder!"—they are doing more than issuing a credible death threat. Paradoxically, they also are seeking to reassure the victims that submission will not put their lives in jeopardy.

Transferring the Goods

No doubt the most difficult aspect of pulling off an armed robbery involves managing the transfer of goods. The difficulty inheres in the fact that offenders must keep victims under strict control while, at the same time, attempting to make sure that they have gotten everything worth taking. What is more, all of this must be accomplished as quickly as possible. The longer the stick-up lasts, the more risk offenders run of being discovered by police or passersby.

The armed robbers we talked to used two different strategies to manage the transfer of goods. The first involved simply ordering victims to hand over their possessions.

> I tell [my victims], "Man, if you don't want to die, give me your money! If you want to survive, give me your money! I'm not bullshitting!" So he will either go in his back pocket and give me the wallet or the woman will give me her purse. (aka Tony Brown)

By making victims responsible for the transfer of goods, the offenders are able to devote their undivided attention to watching for signs of danger.

> I rather for [victims] to give [their valuables] to me because I have to be alert. If they reach for something, I'll have to shoot them. (aka K-Money)

There is, however, one serious drawback to giving victims responsibility for the transfer; it is difficult to know whether they really have turned over all of their valuables. Recognizing this, many of the offenders employed tough talk and a fierce demeanor to discourage victims from attempting to shortchange them.

> You say, "Is that everything?" You can kinda tell if they lyin' sometimes: "That's all I got, man, that's all!" You'll say, "You're lyin', man, you lyin'!" and just make them think that you're getting pissed because he's lying to you. So basically you got this gun [pointed] at they head, so sometimes it be like, "Okay, I got some more." (aka Damon Jones)

A few of them went so far as to rough up their victims, especially those who appeared confused or hesitant, to reinforce the message that holding something back would be a risky proposition.

> Well, if [the victim] hesitates like that, undecided, you get a little aggressive and you push 'em. Let them know you mean business. I might take [the] pistol and crack their head with it. "Come on with that money and quit bullcrapping or else you gonna get into some real trouble!" Normally when they see you mean that kind of business they . . . come on out with it. (aka Burle)

But most of the offenders who allowed victims to hand over their own possessions simply accepted what was offered and made good their escape. As one explained: "You just got to be like, 'Well, it's cool right here what I got.' When you get too greedy, that's when [bad] stuff starts to happen."

The second strategy used by the armed robbers to accomplish the transfer of goods involved taking the victims' possessions from them without waiting for what was offered.

> I get [the victim's money] because everybody not gonna give you all they got. They gonna find some kind of way to keep from giving it all. (aka Richard L. Brown)

A number of the offenders who preferred this strategy were reluctant to let victims empty their own pockets for fear that they were carrying a concealed weapon.

> I don't let nobody give me nothing. Cause if you let somebody go in they pockets, they could pull out a gun, they could pull out anything. You make sure they are where you can see their hands at all times. (aka Cooper)

To outsiders, these offenders may appear to be greatly overestimating the risk of encountering an armed victim. Such a perspective, however, betrays a respectable, middle-class upbringing. In the desperate inner-city neighborhoods in which almost all of the armed robbers reside, and in which many of them ply their trade, weapons are a ubiquitous feature of everyday life.

As already noted, all of the crime commission strategies adopted by the offenders are intended, at least in part, to minimize the possibility of victim resistance. Generally speaking, these strategies work very well. Nevertheless, almost all of the armed robbers we talked to said that they occasionally encountered victims who steadfastly refused to comply with their demands.

> [O]n the parking lot, if you grab somebody and say, "This is a robbery, don't make it a murder!" I've had it happen that [the victim just says], "Well, you got to kill me then." (aka Richard L. Brown)

Faced with a recalcitrant victim, most of the offenders responded with severe, but nonlethal, violence in the hope of convincing the person to cooperate. Often this violence involved smacking or beating the victim about the head with a pistol.

> It's happened [that some of my victims initially refuse to hand over their money, but] you would be surprised how cooperative a person will be once he been smashed across the face with a 357 Magnum. (aka Tony Wright)

Occasionally, however, a robbery involved shooting the victim in the leg or some other spot unlikely to prove fatal.

> [If the person refuses to do what I say] most of the time I just grab my pistol, take the clip out and just slap 'em. If I see [the victim] trying to get tough, then sometimes I just straight out have to shoot somebody, just shoot 'em. I ain't never shot nobody in the head or nothing, nowhere that I know would kill 'em, just shoot them in they leg. Just to let them know that I'm for real [and that they should] just come up off the stuff. (aka Cooper)

While a majority of the armed robbers preferred to use nonlethal violence to subdue resistant victims, several of them admitted to having been involved in fatal encounters in the past. One of the female offenders, for instance, described how she had watched from the car while one of her male companions shot and killed an uncooperative robbery victim.

> We was in the car and, I didn't get out this time, one of the dudes got out. The [victim], he wasn't gonna let nobody rob him: "Nigger, you got to kill me! You got to kill me!" And that's what happened to him. Just shot him in the head. It was like, God!, I had never seen that. When [my accomplice] shot him, it wasn't like he was rushing to get away. He shot him, walked back to the car, put the gun back up under the seat and just, you know, we watched [the victim] when he fell, blood was coming out of his mouth, he was shaking or something. (aka Ne-Ne)

Such incidents are rare; few of the offenders entered into armed robberies intending to kill or seriously injure their prey. Indeed, some admitted that they probably would abandon an intended offense rather than use deadly force to subdue an uncooperative victim.

> I really ain't gonna shoot nobody. I think a lot of people are like that. I wouldn't shoot nobody myself, if they gave me too much of a problem, I might just take off. (aka Mike J.)

That said, it must be noted that armed robbers typically are acting under intense emotional pressure to generate some fast cash by any means necessary in an interactional environment shot through with uncertainty and danger. Is it any wonder that the slightest hint of victim resistance may provoke some of them to respond with potentially deadly force? As one observed: "When you're doing stuff like this, you just real edgy; you'll pull the trigger at anything, at the first thing that go wrong."

Making an Escape

Once offenders have accomplished the transfer of goods, it only remains for them to make their getaway. Doing that, however, is more difficult than it might appear. Up to this point, the offenders have managed to keep victims in check by creating a convincing illusion of impending death. But the maintenance of that illusion becomes increasingly more difficult as the time comes for offenders to make good their escape. How can they continue to control victims who are becoming physically more distant from them?

In broad terms, the offenders can effect a getaway in one of two ways; they can leave the scene themselves or they can stay put and force the victim to flee. Other things being equal, most of them preferred to be the ones to depart. Before doing so, however, they had to make sure that the victim would not attempt to follow them or to raise the alarm. A majority of the offenders responded to this need by using verbal threats designed to extend the illusion of impending death just long enough for them to escape unobserved.

> I done left people in gangways and alleys and I've told them, "If you come out of this alley, I'm gonna hurt you. Just give me 5 or 10 minutes to get away. If you come out of this alley in 3 or 4 minutes, I'm gonna shoot the shit out of you!" (aka Bennie Simmons)

A few offenders, however, attempted to prolong this illusion indefinitely by threatening to kill their victims if they *ever* mentioned the stick-up to anyone.

> I done actually took [the victim's] ID and told them, "If you call the police, I got your address and everything. I know where you stay at and, if you call the police, I'm gonna come back and kill you!" (aka Melvin Walker)

Some of the armed robbers were uncomfortable relying on verbal threats to dissuade their prey from pursuing them. Instead, they took steps to make it difficult or impossible for victims to leave the crime scene by tying them up or incapacitating them through injury.

> [I hit my victims before I escape so as to] give them less time to call for the police. Especially if it's somebody else's neighborhood [and] we don't know how to get out. You hit them with a bat just to slow his pace. If you hit him in the leg with a bat, he can't walk for a minute; he gonna be limping, gonna try to limp to a payphone. By then it be 15 or 20 minutes, we be hitting the highway and on our way back to the southside where our neighborhood is. (aka Antwon Wright)

While most of the offenders wanted to be the first to leave the crime scene, a number of them preferred to order the victim to flee instead. This allowed the offenders to depart in a calm, leisurely manner, thereby reducing the chances of drawing attention to themselves.

> I try not to have to run away. A very important thing that I have learned is that when you run away, too many things can happen running away. Police could just be cruising by and see you running down the street. I just prefer to be able to walk away, which is one of the reasons why I tend, rather than to make an exit, I tell the victim to walk and don't look back: "Walk away, and walk fast!" When they walk, I can make my exit walking. (aka Stick Going)

What is more, forcing the victim to leave first permitted the offenders to escape without worrying about being attacked from behind—a crucial consideration for those unwilling or unable to incapacitate their prey prior to departure.

> [Afterward,] I will tell [the victim] to run. You wouldn't just get the stuff and run because he may have a gun and shoot you while you are turning around running or something like that. (aka Damon Jones)

Beyond such instrumental concerns, several of the armed robbers indicated that they forced the victim to flee for expressive reasons as well; it demonstrated their continuing ability to dominate and control the situation. The clearest example of this involved an offender who routinely taunted his victims by ordering them to leave the scene in humiliating circumstances: "I like laughing at what I do, like, I told . . . one dude to take off his clothes. I just do a whole bunch of stuff. Sometimes I'll make a dude crawl away. I'll tell him to crawl all the way up the street. And I'll sit there in the alley watching him crawl and crack up laughing."

Conclusion

In short, the active armed robbers we interviewed typically compel the cooperation of intended victims through the creation of a convincing illusion of impending death. They create this illusion by catching would-be victims off guard, and then using tough talk, a fierce demeanor, and the display of a deadly weapon to scare them into a state of unquestioning compliance. The goal is to maintain the illusion for as long as possible without having to make good on the threat. This is easier said than done. Armed robbery is an interactive event and, for any number of reasons, victims may fail to behave in the expected fashion. When this happens, the offenders usually respond with severe, but nonlethal, violence, relying on brute force to bring victims' behavior back into line with their expectations. Very few of them want to kill their victims, although some clearly are prepared to resort to deadly force if need be.

Questions for Thought and Discussion

1. What did the robbers in Wright and Decker's study do to compel their victims to compliance?
2. How could knowledge gained from this research be used to provide citizens with some guidance should they become a victim of robbery?
3. In making their escape, it is necessary for robbers to continue to control their victims while becoming increasingly distant from them. How is this accomplished?
4. What theory or theories of criminal behavior are illustrated in this research?

References

Katz, Jack. 1988. *Seductions of Crime.* New York: Basic Books.

Luckenbill, David. 1981. "Generating Compliance: The Case of Robbery." *Urban Life* 10:25–46.

Section V

Occupational Crime

The term *occupational crime* refers to crimes committed through opportunities created in the course of a legal occupation. In the past, the label *white-collar crime* almost always connoted crimes committed by the rich and powerful. Today, most criminologists have broadened the term to refer to crimes committed by persons in a wide range of situations. The focus today is on the nature of the crime and not on the person committing it—thus the term *occupational crime*.

Much of the research reported in this book tends to support the idea that most offenders accept responsibility for their crimes. However, the most consistent theme in the following articles, which deal with occupational crime, is that these offenders concoct elaborate justifications, excuses, and rationalizations to avoid accepting responsibility for their criminal behavior. Perhaps that is because, for most, their primary identity is noncriminal. They are health-care workers, lawyers, bankers, stockbrokers, and so on. To conceive of themselves as criminals is difficult, if not impossible.

In this section Shover, Coffey, and Hobbs ("Crime on the Line: Telemarketing and the Changing Nature of Professional Crime") explore the world of telemarketing fraud. Shover and his associates interviewed 47 criminal telemarketers drawn from federal prison and parolee populations. Unlike their fellow thieves, telemarketing criminals are disproportionately drawn from the middle class. They are drawn to the business of telemarketing crime because they find the work attractive and rewarding. They are also drawn to the lifestyle and the income it provides. The authors found that their subjects, like those who engage in "street crimes," pursue a hedonistic lifestyle featuring alcohol, drugs, and conspicuous consumption.

In the next selection, Jesilow and his associates ("How Doctors Defraud Medicaid: Doctors Tell Their Stories") focus on occupational criminals' use of "techniques of neutralization" to cast their actions in a more favorable light.

Dabney ("Neutralization and Deviance in the Workplace: Theft of Supplies and Medicines by Hospital Nurses") discovers that most of the nurses in a study in three hospitals who admitted stealing supplies and medicines also concocted rationalizations and neutralizations regarding their behavior.

These studies are somewhat unusual in that ethnographic research of crime "in the suites" is much more difficult to accomplish than studies of crime "in the streets." Potential subjects are less likely to talk with researchers, and are not as easily approached. Patricia Adler (1995) correctly noted that it is easier to "study down than to study up." Thus, the pool of field studies of so-called "white-collar" crime is small; however, the papers included here are excellent examples of what can be accomplished with a difficult population.

Reference

Adler, Patricia. 1995. Personal communication. ✦

Chapter 16
Crime on the Line

Telemarketing and the Changing Nature of Professional Crime

Neal Shover
Glenn S. Coffey
Dick Hobbs

C*riminals have been quick to exploit the opportunities presented by telemarketing. Today, virtually everyone has experienced calls from telemarketers attempting to sell some product or service based on untrue or illegal claims. In many cases, the sales pitch is fraudulent, the goods or services are not delivered, or they are not as represented by the caller. The extent of this practice has led the federal government to pass legislation limiting telemarketing activities. The criminological consequences of this development are poorly charted. In this chapter, the authors examine offenders who have stepped forward to exploit one category of the new opportunities. Drawing from interviews with 47 criminal telemarketers, the authors present a picture and interpretation of them, their pursuits, and their lifestyles. As vocational predators, they share several important characteristics with the professional thieves sketched by earlier generations of investigators. Like the latter, they pursue a hedonistic lifestyle featuring illicit drugs and conspicuous consumption, and they acquire and employ an ideology of legitimation and defence that insulates them from moral rejection. Unlike professional thieves, however, telemarketing criminals disproportionately are drawn from middle-class, entrepreneurial backgrounds. They are markedly individualistic in their dealings with one another and with law enforcement. Finally, their work organizations are more permanent and conventional in outward appearance than the criminal organizations created by blue-collar offenders, which were grounded in the culture of the industrial proletariat. The findings show how the backgrounds and pursuits of vocational predators reflect the qualities and challenges of contemporary lucrative criminal opportunities. Like the markets that they seek to manipulate and plunder, the enacted environments of professional criminals embrace infinite variations, and are largely indistinguishable from the arenas that capacitate legitimate entrepreneurial pursuits.*

Writing at the dawn of the twentieth century, E. A. Ross (1907: 3) was one of the first sociologists to call attention to the fact that crime 'changes its quality as society develops.' Ross focused specifically on growing social and economic interdependence and the variety of ways this permits both exploitation of trust and the commission of crime at a distance from victims. The transformative social and economic changes he noted only gained speed as the century progressed. In the United States and other Western nations, the middle decades of the century saw the emergence or the expansion of state policies and corporate practices with enormous criminological significance. These include a fundamental shift in the state's public welfare functions, which had the effect of expanding programmes and subsidies for citizens across the income spectrum. One measure of this is the fact that by 1992, 51.7 per cent of American families received some form of federal payments, ranging from social security, Medicare and military retirement benefits to agricultural subsidies (Samuelson 1995: 158).

In addition, the years following World War II witnessed a rapid growth of the domestic economy, which made available goods that either were unknown or were unattainable by most citizens just a decade earlier. Houses, automobiles, refrigerators, television sets and a host of other commodities now were within the reach of a growing segment of the population. The disposable income available to the new owners of these commodities allowed them also to purchase the new comprehensive insurance policies offered by insurance underwriters. Increasingly, the middle-class family now was insured against not only major hazards to life, home and business but also loss of or damage to household items (Clarke 1990).

As the century drew to a close, there were fundamental changes also in the structure and dynamics of economic relationships and in communications technology (Adler 1992; Lash and Urry 1994). Most important, widespread use of telecommunications (Batty and

Barr 1994; Turkle 1995), electronic financial transactions and consumer credit (Tickell 1996) presage a depersonalized, cashless economy. Electronic financial transfers among banks and businesses, automatic teller machines (Hirschhorn 1985) and home banking increasingly are used across the globe (Silverstone 1991). In the new world of personal computers and virtual identities, individuals and organizations conduct business with remote others whose credentials and intentions cannot be easily determined.

The net result of these political and economic developments is a cornucopia of new criminal opportunities (Grabosky et al. 2001; Taylor 1999). Federally funded health care programmes, for example, have given physicians and hospitals access to new pools of tax revenue for which oversight is so weak that it has been called a 'licence to steal' (Sparrow 1996). The growth of health insurance fraud, therefore, can be seen as 'emblematic of the emerging forms of . . . crime that reflect the changing economy of the late twentieth century' (Tillman 1998: 197). The new criminal opportunities extend far beyond health care, however.

The changing landscape of criminal opportunities is strikingly apparent in crimes of fraud. Fraud is committed when misrepresentation or deception is used to secure unfair or unlawful gain, typically by perpetrators who create and exploit the appearance of a routine transaction. Fraud violates trust, it is non-confrontational, and it can be carried out over long distance. In organizational complexity and reach, it ranges from itinerant vinyl siding scamsters to international banking crimes that can destabilize national economies. The number of Americans victimized by it is large and substantially exceeds the number victimized by serious street crime (Rebovich et al. 2000; Titus 2001). A 1991 survey of US households found that compared to crimes of burglary, robbery, assault and theft, fraud 'appears to be very common' (Titus et al. 1995: 65). Although a number of methodological shortcomings limit confidence in the findings of previous studies of fraud victimization, there seems little doubt that it is an increasingly commonplace crime.

Telemarketing and Fraud

The rapid growth of telemarketing is one of several consequential changes in the nature of economic relationships in recent decades. In 2000, telemarketing sales accounted for $611.7bn in revenue in the United States, an increase of 167 per cent over comparable sales for 1995. Total annual sales from telephone marketing are expected to reach $939.5bn by the year 2005 (Direct Marketing Association 2001). The reasons for the growth of telemarketing are understood easily in context of the 'general acceleration of everyday life, characterized by increasingly complicated personal and domestic timetables' (Taylor 1999: 45). The daily schedule no longer permits either the pace or the style of shopping that were commonplace a few decades ago, and the need to coordinate personal schedules and to economize on time now drives many household activities. In the search for convenience, telemarketing sales have gained in popularity.

But while it has become an important part of the legitimate economy, criminals also have been quick to exploit the opportunities presented by telemarketing. Although it was nearly unheard of until recent decades, few adults today are unfamiliar with telemarketing fraud. There are countless variations on the basic scheme, but typically a consumer receives a phone call from a high-pressure salesperson who solicits funds or sells products based on untrue assertions or enticing claims. Callers offer an enormous variety of products and services, and often they use names that sound similar to bona fide charities or reputable organizations (US Senate 1993). Goods or services either are not delivered at all, or they are substantially inferior to what was promised. Telemarketing fraud touches the lives of many citizens. A 1992 poll of a national sample of Americans showed that 2 per cent of respondents had been victimized in the preceding six months (Harris et al. 1992). . . .

Findings

Of all who begin employment in criminal telemarketing, some quickly discover it is not their cup of tea; they dislike it or they do not perform well. Others find the work attractive and rewarding but see it only as a means to other life and career goals. Most, therefore, pursue it only temporarily. Others, however, discover they are good at fraudulent telephone sales, and they are drawn to the income and the lifestyle it can provide. On average, the members of our interview sample were employed in these endeavours for 8.25 years. Their ages when interviewed range from 26 to 69, with a mean of 42.4

years. Their ranks include 38 white males, three African American males, and six white females. Nearly all have been married at least once, and most have children.

Organization and Routine

Like its legitimate forms, criminal telemarketing is a productive enterprise that requires the coordinated efforts of two or more individuals. To work in it, therefore, is to work in an organizational setting (Francis 1988; Schulte 1995; Stevenson 2000). The size of criminal telemarketing organizations can vary substantially. Some are very small, consisting of only two or three persons, but others are considerably larger (e.g. Atlanta Journal-Constitution 2000). Their permanence and mobility vary also, ranging from those that operate and remain in one locale for a year or more to others that may set up and operate for only a few weeks before moving on. These 'rip and tear' operators count on the fact that up to six months' time may pass before law-enforcement agencies become aware of and target them. 'Boiler rooms', operations featuring extensive telephone banks and large numbers of sales agents, have become less common in the United States in recent years, largely because of the law-enforcement interest they attract. There is reason to believe, however, that criminal telemarketers increasingly are locating them in countries with weak laws and oversight and operating across international borders (e.g. Australian Broadcasting Corporation 2001).

Larger telemarketing operations commonly take on the characteristics and dynamics of formal organizations; they are hierarchical, with a division of labour, graduated pay and advancement opportunities. Established by individuals with previous experience in fraudulent sales, they generally employ commissioned sales agents to call potential customers, to make the initial pitch, and to weed out the cautious and the steadfastly [un]interested. We took steps to insure that our offender interview sample included persons who formerly held a variety of positions in criminal telemarketing firms. It includes 22 owners, eight managers, and 17 sales agents.

Experienced telemarketers generally do not call individuals randomly but work instead from 'lead lists' (also known as 'mooch lists'). These are purchased from any of dozens of businesses that compile and sell information on consumer behaviour and expressed preferences. Individuals whose names appear on lead lists typically are distinguished by past demonstrated interest or participation in promotions of one kind or another. When a person is contacted by telephone, the sales agent generally works from a script. Scripts are written materials that lay out both successful sales approaches and responses to whatever reception sales agents meet with from those they reach by phone. Promising contacts are turned over to a 'closer', a more experienced and better paid sales agent. 'Reloaders' are the most effective closers; much like account executives in legitimate businesses, they maintain contacts with individuals who previously sent money to the company (i.e. 'purchased' from it) in hopes of persuading them to send more. As one subject told us:

> I had it so perfected that I could get these customers to buy again. . . . I made sure they were happy so I could sell them again. It didn't do me—I didn't want the one time, I didn't want the two-timer. I wanted to sell these people ten times.[1]

The organization of larger telemarketing firms and the routine employees follow when handling promising calls explains why those who 'buy' from them typically report contact with multiple 'salespersons' (American Association of Retired Persons 1996).

The products and services offered by criminal telemarketers span a wide gamut. In one scam, subjects identified and located unaware owners of vacant property, led them to believe that buyers for the property could be found easily, and then charged high fees to advertise it. Other schemes we encountered included collection for charities, drug education programmes, and sale of 'private' stocks. One subject sold inexpensive gemstones with fraudulent certificates of grossly inflated value and authenticity. The stones were sealed in display cases such that purchasers would have difficulty getting them appraised, particularly since they were told that if they broke the seal, the value of the stones would decrease and the certificate of authenticity would become invalid. 'Private stocks', by definition, are not listed or traded on a stock exchange, but telemarketers are able to entice investors with smooth talk and promising prospectives. Dependent upon their salesmen for market reports, those who purchase soon discover that the non-existent stocks take a nose-dive, and they lose their investments. A high proportion of the companies represented by our interview subjects promised that those who purchased products from them were odds-on winners of a prize soon to be awarded once other matters were settled. Typically this required the customers to pay fees of one kind or another. Some of our subjects solicited money for nonexistent charities or legitimate organizations they did not represent. In the products they sell, criminal telemarketers clearly are limited only by the human imagination.

Backgrounds and Careers

A substantial body of research into the lives and careers of street criminals has shown that many are products of disadvantaged and disorderly parental homes. We were interested in determining if the homes in which our subjects were reared reveal similar or functionally equivalent criminogenic characteristics. They do not. Overwhelmingly, the members of our sample describe their parents as conventional and hard working and family financial circumstances as secure if not comfortable. Their parental families were traditional in nature, with the father providing the main source of income. Nevertheless, one-half of the mothers also were employed outside the home. Although the fathers' reported occupations ranged from machinist to owner of a chain of retail stores, 32 were business owners or held managerial positions. A substantial proportion of our subjects were exposed to and acquired entrepreneurial perspectives and skills while young. Business ownership appealed to many of them:

> You're always pursuing more money, most of us are. We're raised that way, we are in this country. And that's the way I was raised. But I also wanted to do my own thing. I wanted to be in business for myself, I wanted the freedom that came with that.

Clearly, telemarketing criminals are not drawn from the demographic pools or locales that stock and replenish the ranks of street criminals. Although we questioned them at length about their early and adolescent years, their responses reveal little that distinguishes them from others of similar age and class background. Certainly, the disadvantages and pathologies commonplace in the early lives of most street criminals are in scant evidence here.

If our subjects' early years reveal few clues to their later criminality, there also are few signs that they distinguished themselves in conventional ways. Their educational careers, for example, are unremarkable; eight dropped out of high school, although most graduated. Twenty-one attended college, but on average they invested only two years in the quest for a degree. Five claimed a baccalaureate degree. When invited to reflect upon how they differ from their siblings or peers, many reported they were aware of an interest in money from an early age. One subject told us:

> I had certain goals when I was a teenager, you know. And I had a picture of a Mercedes convertible on my bedroom mirror for years.

Another subject said:

> You know, I do have a major addiction, and I don't think I'll ever lose it. And I don't think there's any classes [treatment] for it. And it's money, it's Ben Franklin.

He and others like him were aware also that there are ways of earning a good income that do not require hard work and subordination to others. Another subject said:

> You know, I was, I've never been a firm believer [that] you got to work for a company for 30 years and get a retirement. Like my dad thinks. I'm all about going out [and] making that million and doing it, doing it very easily. And there's a lot of ways to do it.

Typically, they began working for pay while young and maintained employment throughout their adolescent years.

None of our subjects said that as children they aspired to a career in telemarketing, either legitimate or criminal. Some had previous sales experience before beginning the work, but most did not. Their introduction to it was both fortuitous and fateful; while still in high school or, more common, while in college, they either responded to attractive ads in the newspaper or were recruited by friends or acquaintances who boasted about the amount of money they were making.

> [A former acquaintance] . . . looked me up, found me and said 'you gotta come out here. . . . We're gonna make a ton of money.' I went out for three weeks—left my wife back home. And I got on the phones, and I was making a thousand dollars a week. I'm like, 'oh, my God, Jenni, pack the stuff, we're going to Arizona.' . . . He was like, 'man, you're, you're a pro at this shit.' And I just, I don't know what it

> was. I was number one. . . . I don't know, I loved it.

The influence of others is remarkably similar to what is known about the criminal careers of street criminals, particularly those who go on to pursue crime with a high degree of skill and success (Hobbs 1995: ch. 2; Winlow 2001: 66–86).

For our subjects, many of whom were foundering on conventional paths, criminal telemarketing was a godsend; it came along at a time when they needed to show that they could make something of themselves. In the words of one of them, it was 'a salvation to me as a means of income. And being able to actually accomplish something without an education'. Criminal telemarketing was the reason some reported for dropping out of college:

> [It] was just something I picked up as a part time job, when I was sixteen. . . . When I was in college, my second year in college, [fellow students] were talking about finishing their four years of college and making $28,000 or $30,000 a year. And I was making $1,000 a week part time, you know. . . . And I just couldn't see doing it. I mean, I wound up, after the end of my second year of college, I never went back. I was making too much money. It just seemed so easy.

New recruits generally start as sales agents, although most of our subjects later worked also as closers and reloaders. Employment mobility is common; individuals move from one firm to another, with some eventually taking managerial positions (Doocy et al. 2001).

After gaining experience, former managers told us they were confident they knew enough about the business to strike out on their own. They did so expecting to increase their income substantially. As one put it:

> [I]n my mind I believed I was smarter than the owners of these other companies that were making millions of dollars. And I just said, 'I can do this on my own.'

Typically, defectors lure productive personnel from their current employer with promises of more money, and on the way out they are not above plundering the business's files and lead lists:

> I downloaded every lead in his file. I took it all. I opened up . . . my own office, took all those people and said 'now, watch me.'

Based in part on the widely shared assumption that the market is never saturated, they generally open a company based on similar products and sales approaches.

What about the criminal histories of fraudulent telemarketers? Information elicited in the interviews and a review of information contained in pre-sentence investigation reports shows that 13 of our subjects had previous criminal records, seven for minor offences (e.g. petty theft and possession of marijuana) and six for felonies. Of the latter, three were convicted previously of telemarketing offences. Clearly, many of our subjects are not one-time or accidental violators; they have histories of multiple arrests and convictions. Others have reported similar findings. Thirty per cent of 162 sales agents employed by a California-based fraudulent telemarketing firm, for example, had records of at least one criminal offence, and another 16.4 per cent had records of alcohol or drug offences (Doocy et al. 2001). For members of our sample who have previous arrests, the age of onset for criminal activity is considerably higher than for street criminals. Our data do show persuasively, however, that many appear to have recurrent trouble with the law and, like street criminals, they are persistent users of alcohol and other drugs. This picture is confirmed also by information contained in their pre-sentence reports.

Attractions and Lifestyles

Overwhelmingly, our subjects told us they got into and persisted at telemarketing for 'the money'. How well does it pay? Only one subject reported earning less than $1,000 weekly, and most said their annual earnings were in the range of $100,000 to $250,000. Five told us their annual earnings exceeded $1m. The fact that they can make money quickly and do so without incurring restrictive responsibilities adds to the attractiveness of the work. They find appealing both the flexible hours and the fact that it requires neither extensive training nor advanced education. Few employers impose rigid rules or strictures; generally there are neither dress codes nor uniforms. The work can be done in shorts and a tee shirt (Doocy et al. 2001).

As important as the income it yields and the casual approach to employment it permits, criminal telemarketing appeals to many who persist at it for reasons of career and identity. Despite class and parental expectations, most of our subjects had not previously settled upon promising or rewarding occupations. Asked what he 'liked about telemarketing', one subject's reply was typical: 'Well, obviously, it was the money.' Immediately, however, he added that 'it gave me a career, [and] to me it was my salvation.' As with him, criminal telemarketing enables others to own their own business despite their unimpressive educational background, their limited credentials and the absence of venture capital. As president of their own corporation, telemarketing provides both outward respectability and an income sufficient to maintain the good life.

Other aspects of the work are attractive as well. Its interpersonal and psychological challenge, for example,

> has strong appeal to many salespersons. The ability to impose one's will upon another person—and to achieve a measurable financial reward for doing so—is highlighted in many of the reports of illegal telemarketing practices. . . . Enforcement officials told us that sellers often have mirrors in the cubicles in which they work. They are told to look into the mirror and see the face of a hot shot salesperson. Sometimes there will be a motto on the wall, such as: 'Each No gets me closer to the Yes I want.' Boiler room owners and managers . . . may put large bills on a bulletin board and say that the next sale or the highest total for the day will qualify for this extra reward. Often the sales people have to stand up when they consummate a transaction, so that the boss can note them and they can take pleasure in the achievement. (Doocy et al. 2001: 17)

Characteristically, our subjects believe they are outstanding salespersons; they are supremely confident of their ability to sell over the telephone despite resistance from those they contact. Doing so successfully is a high. One subject told us:

> You could be selling a $10,000 ticket, you could be selling a $49.95 ticket. And it's the same principle, it's the same rules. It's the same game. I like to win. I like to win in all the games I play, you know. And the money is a reason to be there, and a reason to have that job. But winning is what I want to do. I want to beat everybody else in the office. I want to beat that person I am talking to on the phone.

His remarks were echoed by others:

> [I] sold the first person I ever talked to on the phone. And it was just like that first shot of heroin, you know. I'm not a heroin addict . . . I've only done heroin a couple of times. But it was amazing. It was like, 'I can't believe I just did this!' It was incredible. It was never about the money after that. . . . Yeah, it was about the money initially, but when I realized that I could do this every day, it was no longer about the money. It was about the competition, you know. I wanted to be the best salesman, and I want to make the most money that day. And then it became just the sale. It wasn't the money. I didn't even add the figures in my head anymore. It was just whether or not I can turn this person around, you know, walk him down that mutual path of agreement, you know. That was exciting to me. It was power, you know; I can make people do what I wanted them to do. And they would do it.

> It was the money, but it was [also] the ability to control people, to be able to say over the phone, 'John, go pick up your pen and write this down.' And you write it down! You do exactly like a robot—they would do exactly what they were told to do. And they would do it pleasingly, they would do it without hesitation, because, again, they had enough confidence and faith in you to believe that you were gonna do the right thing about it.

Another subject said simply that the work 'gives you power. It gives you power'. The importance of this dimension of the payoff from fraud has been commented on by others as well (e.g. Duffield and Grabosky 2001).

Criminal telemarketers generally distinguish between working hard and 'working smart'. When asked, therefore, how he viewed those who work hard for modest wages, one replied, 'I guess somebody's gotta do it.' By contrast, work weeks of 20–30 hours are common for them, and even for owners and managers, the need for close oversight of operations decreases substantially once things are up and running. The short work week and their ample income provides considerable latitude in the use of leisure time and in consumption patterns.

The lifestyles of telemarketing participants vary by age and the aspects of the work that employees find most appealing, but ostentatious consumption is common to all. The young, and those attracted to the work and leisure it permits, live life as party (Shover 1996) . Use of cocaine and other illicit drugs is common among this segment of the criminal telemarketing workforce.

> The hours were good. You'd work, sometimes, from about 9 to 2, 9 to 3, sometimes from 12 to 4. Basically, we set our own hours. It was freedom. The money was fantastic. . . . You got the best of the girls. For me, it wasn't really about the job, it was a way of life. . . . I had an alcohol problem at a young age, and to be able to support the alcohol and drug habit with the kind of money that we were making seems to go hand in hand. And then you've got the fast lifestyle, . . . up all night, sleep all day, you know. So, everything kinda coincided with that fast lifestyle, that addictive lifestyle.

Asked how he spent the money he made, another subject responded saying:

> Houses, girls, just going out to nightclubs. And a lot of blow [cocaine]. . . . Lots and lots of blow, enormous amounts. And other than that, you know, I look back, I get sick when I think about how much we spent, where the hell I put it all. I'm making all this money [but] I don't have a whole hell of a lot to show for it, you know. That lifestyle didn't allow you to save.

Heavy gambling is commonplace. One subject said that they 'would go out to the casinos and blow two, three, four, five thousand dollars a night. That was nothing—to go spend five grand, you know, every weekend. And wake up broke!' Commenting on one of his employees, a subject who owned a telemarketing firm when he was arrested said that the man had a Porsche Speedster after he sold his Porsche 911. He had a Dodge Viper, he had a Ferrari 348, he had a Lexus LS400, he had a BMW 850i, he had a Jeep Grand Cherokee. He liked his cars. Now, he didn't have all these at one time, but he ran through them, you know. He traded the Dodge Viper . . . in for the Ferrari. He always had a Porsche.

What we learned about the lifestyles and spending habits of criminal telemarketers differs little from what is known about street criminals and other vocational predators. It also confirms what has been learned about the relationship between easy, unearned income and profligacy: 'The way money is acquired is a powerful determinant of how it is defined, husbanded, and spent' (Shover 1996: 104).

The lifestyles of telemarketers change somewhat as they get older and take on more conventional responsibilities:

> I started to realize that, as I was getting older in the industry, it was affecting my children and my relationship with my wife. To the point that it wasn't what I wanted. I wanted more of a home-type of family, where I got home at six o'clock and have dinner and spend time with my wife and children. And with that industry, it doesn't really do that. My lifestyle? Play golf, go to the lake, you know. I had a family, but . . . I was also, you know, making good money. And I wanted to party and that kind of thing. So, I did that a lot. We got together and partied a lot and went here and there and went to, you know—nightlife go out to clubs occasionally, but, when you're married and have kids, it's limited. It changes. It changed a lot over those years.

For older and more experienced telemarketers, the lifestyle centres around home and family and impressing others with signs of their apparent success:

> I played some golf. [In the summer] water skiing, fishing. I'm real heavy into bass fishing, me and my dad and my brothers. Hunting. Doing things with my wife and kids. I spent a lot of time with them. Evenings, maybe just walking the golf course, or whatever. Watching the sunset.

Another subject told us that after he moved up in the telemarketing ranks: 'My partner and I played, we played a lot of golf. The office was right down from the golf course. We'd go to the golf course and play two or three times a week.' Save for the unrestrained hedonism of their lives when young and neophytes at criminal telemarketing, the broad outlines of their occupational careers, particularly for those who went on to form their own businesses, resemble the work careers of more conventional citizens.

Legitimation and Defence

Doocy et at. (2001: 18) remark that the telemarketing offender they interviewed 'conveyed the assured appearance of a most respectable entrepreneur' and 'conveyed no hint that what he was doing might not be altogether legitimate'. Our subjects are no different. Notwithstanding the fact that all were convicted felons, most reject the labels *criminal* and *crime* as fitting descriptions of them and their activities. They instead employ a range of mitigating explanations and excuses for their offences, although claims of ignorance figure in most (Scott and Stanford 1968; Sykes and Matza 1957). Some former business owners told us, for example, that they set out to maintain a legitimate operation, emulated the operations of their previous employers and assumed, therefore, that their activities violated no laws. Others said they are guilty only of expanding their business so rapidly that they could not properly oversee day-to-day operations. Some said that indulgence in alcohol and illicit drugs caused them to become neglectful of or indifferent toward their businesses. Most claimed that the allure of money caused them to 'look the other way'. Those who owned or managed firms are prone also to blame rogue sales agents for any fraudulent or deceptive activities. As one put it: 'The owners are trying to do the right thing. They're just attracting the wrong people. It's the salesmen'. Another subject likewise suggested: 'I guess I let the business get too big and couldn't watch over all of the agents to prevent what they were doing.' For their part, sales agents charge that their owners and managers kept them in the dark about the business and its criminal nature.

Fraud offenders typically derive moral justification for their activities from the fact that their crimes cannot succeed without acquiescence or cooperation from their victims; unlike victims of burglary and robbery, those who fall prey to fraud usually are willing, if halting or confused, participants in their own victimization (Goffman 1952). Chief among the legitimating and defensive tenets of telemarketing criminals is belief that 'the mooch is going to send his money to someone, so it might as well be me' (Sanger 1999: 9). In other words, 'customers' are thought to be so greedy, ignorant, or incapable that it is only a matter of time before they throw away their money on something impossible. The tendency of fraud offenders to see their victims as deserving of what befalls them was noted by Maurer (1940) more than six decades ago, and it remains true of contemporary telemarketing criminals. One of our subjects told us, 'They know what they're doing. They're bargaining for something, and when they lose, they realize that they were at fault.' There is neither concern nor sympathy for them. Another subject said:

> If these people can't read, so be it. Screw them, you know. It [doesn't say] everybody's gonna get the diamond and sapphire tennis bracelet. They're dumb enough not to read, dumb enough to send me the money, I really don't care, you know. I'm doing what I have to do to stay out of jail. They're doing what they have to do to fix their fix. They're promo junkies, and we're gonna find them and get them, and we're gonna keep getting them. And they're gonna keep buying. And, you know what I used to say, 'they're gonna blow their money in Vegas, they're gonna spend it somewhere. I want to be the one to get it'.

Telemarketing criminals selectively seize upon aspects of their victims' behaviour and point to these as justification or excuse for their crimes. They maintain that they were not victimizing their customers but engaging in a routine sales transaction, no different than a retail establishment selling a shirt that is marked up 1,000 per cent. Telemarketing fraud is therefore construed by its practitioners as perfectly in tune with mainstream commercial interactions: a 'subculture of business' (Ditton 1977: 173).

Ensconced in their outwardly respectable and self-indulgent lifestyles, our subjects professed belief that, so far as the law was concerned, they were risking nothing more severe than a fine, an adverse civil judgment or a requirement they make restitution. They claim the entire problem more appropriately was a 'civil matter' and 'should not be in criminal court.' As one put it: 'if you have people that are not satisfied, we would be happy to give their money back'.

Interpretation

Our description of telemarketing crime and criminals is noteworthy for several reasons, but principally for what it reveals about the relationship between social change and the changing character of lucrative professional theft (Taylor 1999). Defined by cultural criteria rather than legal yardsticks (cf. Sykes 1978: 109), the concept of professional crime has become infused with contradiction and ambiguity by the evolution of this new kind of 'respectable' predator.

Sociological debate over the descriptive validity of professional theft has been carried out largely as a dialogue with the tradition of Sutherland (1937), who located a behaviour system of criminal specialists featuring technical skill, consensus via a shared ideology, differential association, status and, most importantly, informal organization grounded in a shared cultural identity. Subsequently, scholars presented alternative perspectives regarding crimes other than theft (Lemert 1958; Einstadter 1969). However, Shover (1973) perhaps came closest to Sutherland's original conception by locating the social organization of burglary based upon highly instrumental, and constantly evolving networks of dependency as the key variable. In his view, these networks continue to evolve due to innovative strategies in policing, security and technology, and telemarketing fraudsters resemble Shover's professional burglar, in their adaptive pragmatic organization.

Telemarketers also share many core characteristics with 'hustlers' (President's Commission 1966; Shover 1996), or 'rounders' (Letkemann 1973), offenders whose lack of commonality or consensus contradicts the notion of a cohesive tightly knit behaviour system (see also Holzman 1983; Polsky 1964; Roebuck and Johnson 1962). Yet Letkemann suggests that explicit commitment to criminal activity as a means of making a living is the best criterion for differentiating between professional and non-professional criminals, which also echoes Sutherland's classic work, and offers some support for the notion of an occupational group defined by their commitment to illegal economic activities (Becker 1960).

While the investigation of professional thieves and their pursuits has a long history in criminology, the canon is replete with portraits of offenders who have passed from the scene. However, for contemporary observers, 'fraud masters' (Jackson 1994) deservedly command more attention than 'cut purses' (Tobias 1967), 'cannons' (Maurer 1955) and 'good burglars' (Shover 1973). Economic and social change inevitably transform the worlds in which offenders entertain options and organize for pursuit of criminal income (Hobbs 1997; McIntosh 1975; Shover 1983). The classic criminal subcultures of shared practices and beliefs as the basis of criminal community have met the same fate as blue-collar communities based upon traditional industries (Soja 1989). The new entrepreneurial milieu is an enabling environment for a great range and variety of money making schemes (Ruggiero and South 1997), and the perceptual templates of contemporary professional criminals feature cues that are geared to success in a sphere emptied out of anachronistic practice (Wright and Decker 1994).

Automobile theft and 'chop shops' were not found in [nineteenth] century society, for the obvious reason there were no automobiles to steal or sell. The shift to a post-industrial order inevitably changed selectively the human qualities and social capital requisite for successful exploitation of criminal opportunities. Traditional professional thieves hailed from locations in the class and social structure where the young generally do not acquire the human capital requisite to success in the world of well paid and respectable work. The blue-collar skills of an industrial society, however, are not equal to the challenge of exploiting contemporary, increasingly white-collar, criminal opportunities. The post-industrial service-oriented economy instead places a premium on entrepreneurial, interpersonal, communicative and organizational skills, and it is the children of the middle-class who are most likely to be exposed to and acquire these.

The knowledge and skills needed to exploit criminal opportunities vocationally and successfully do not differ greatly from those required for success in the legitimate world. Like the professional thief, the new and increasingly white-collar vocational predators commit planned violations of the law for profit (van Duyne 1996), but they do so in the style of the middle class. They take on and publicly espouse a belief system that defends against moral condemnation from outsiders, and they are dismissive of both the world of hourly employment and the lives of those confined to it. But while the professional thieves of an earlier era publicly endorsed and were expected to adhere to norms of loyalty and integrity in dealings with one another (Maurer 1955; Shover 1973; Irwin 1970; Irwin and Cressey 1962; Cohen and Taylor 1972; McVicar 1982; Mason 1994; Taylor 1984), criminal telemarketers by contrast are extremely individualistic and self-centred in their contacts with criminal justice officials and agencies. Whether this is because of their privileged backgrounds or because the nature of criminal relationships has been 'transformed by the advent of a market culture', their illicit pursuits manifest qualities not only of entrepreneurial creativity but also independence and 'possessive individualism' (Taylor 1999).

Professional thieves of earlier eras found a measure of success in crime despite their humble beginnings, and much about what they made of themselves is understandable in the light of their blue-collar roots. The lives they constructed emphasized freedom to live 'life as party' (Shover and Honaker 1991) by 'earning and burning money' (Katz 1988: 215), to roam without restraint and to celebrate these achievements with others of similar perspective. The class origins of contemporary garden-variety white-collar criminals are more advantaged, but they live their lives in substantially similar fashion. Unlike the 'foot pads' of Elizabethan England, they generally do not gravitate to a criminal netherworld or a self-contained criminal fraternity. Nor do they confine their leisure pursuits to others of similar work. The proletarian underworld was an essential network for exchanging, controlling and disseminating information (McIntosh 1971; Hobbs 1995: 21–3), but the telemarketing fraudster depends on networks of information that are largely indistinguishable from those that underpin the non-criminal sector.

What Benney (1936: 263) called 'the fabulous underworld of bourgeois invention' ironically has been decimated by the embourgeoisement of crime. Criminals now emerge from the economic mainstream and engage both socially and pragmatically with derivations of normative economic activity. The acquisitive entrepreneurial ethic that underpins both legal and illegal performances within the post-industrial market place thrives upon 'new technical, social, psychological and existential skills' (Bauman 1992: 98), which in turn are bordered by new configurations of cultural and technological capital.

While the old underworld was safely ensconced in the locales, occupational practices, leisure cultures and oppositional strategies of the industrial proletariat (Hobbs 1997; Samuel 1981), it is the bourgeois who have emerged with the education and ideological flexibility to engage with lucrative contemporary professional crime, which is located not within a proletarian outpost of traditional transgression, but within rhetorics that legitimate and enable the entire 'spectrum of legitimacy' (Albanese 1989: 101).

Telemarketing fraudsters should be seen as 'fluid sets of mobile marauders in the urban landscape, alert to institutional weakness in both legitimate and illegitimate spheres' (Block 1983: 245). These spheres are pliant and not territorially embedded (Chaney 1994: 149). Detached from an 'underworld' (Haller 1990: 228–9), contemporary professional crime has mutated from an overworld in which the bourgeoisie rather than blue-collar culture is sovereign. This helps explain why telemarketing fraudsters, unlike the professional thieves of previous generations, are likely to spend their weekends on the lake, playing golf, or having friends over for a barbeque. Still, they blow their earnings on drugs, gambling, fast living and conspicuous consumption. They earn a reasonably good return from crime, but like 'box men' of yore, few spend appreciable time in jails and prisons.

Questions for Thought and Discussion

1. Illegal telemarketing is a relatively new crime. How prevalent has it become? In what ways do criminal telemarketers share characteristics with other professional thieves?
2. What social and economic factors led to the growth of telemarketing crime?
3. Compare Shover's subjects in this study and those from his study in Chapter 4. How are they different and how are they alike?
4. What theory or theories of criminal behavior are illustrated in this research?

Note

1. Criminal telemarketers unstintingly employ the rhetoric of legitimate business when describing their operations and activities. Their accounts are filled with references to 'customers', 'purchases', 'account executives', 'premiums' and such. Consequently, when this subject talks of customers who 'bought' from his establishment in the past, he is referring to victims who sent him money and who he hopes can be induced to make additional 'purchases' despite receiving little of value in return for earlier ones.

References

ADLER, P. S. (1992), *Technology and the Future of Work.* New York: Oxford University Press.

ALBANESE, J. (1989), *Organised Crime in America.* Cincinnati: Anderson.

AMERICAN ASSOCIATION OF RETIRED PERSONS (1996), *Telemarketing Fraud and Older Americans: An AARP Survey.* New York: American Association of Retired Persons.

ATLANTA JOURNAL-CONSTITUTION (2000), 'Alleged Scam on Elderly by Telemarketers is Revealed', 6 September: B3.

AUSTRALIAN BROADCASTING CORPORATION (2001), 'Beyond the Boiler Room', 24 September, www.abc.net.au/4corners/.

BATTY, M. and BARR, B. (1994), 'The Electronic Frontier: Exploring and Mapping Cyberspace', *Futures,* 26/7: 699–712.

BAUMAN, Z. (1992), *Intimations of Modernity.* London: Routledge.

BECKER, H. (1960), 'Notes on the Concept of Commitment', *American Journal of Sociology,* 66: 32–40.

BENNEY, M. (1936/1981), *Low Company.* Sussex: Caliban Books.

BLOCK, A. (1983), *East Side-West Side: Organizing Crime in New York, 1930–1950.* Newark, NJ: Transaction.

CHANEY, D. (1994), *The Cultural Turn.* London: Routledge.

CLARKE, M. (1990), 'Control of Insurance Fraud: A Comparative View', *British Journal of Criminology,* 30: 1–23.

COHEN, S. and TAYLOR, L. (1972), *Psychological Survival.* Harmondsworth: Penguin.

DIRECT MARKETING ASSOCIATION (2001), www.the-dma.org.

DITTON, J. (1977), *Part Time Crime.* London: Macmillan.

DOOCY, J., SHICHOR, D. SECHREST, D., and GEIS, G. (2001), 'Telemarketing Fraud: Who Are the Tricksters and What Makes Them Trick?', *Securities Journal,* 14: 7–26.

DUFFIELD, G. and GRABOSKY, P. (2001), 'The Psychology of Fraud', Paper 199. Australian Institute of Criminology.

EINSTADTER, W. J. (1969), 'The Social Organization of Armed Robbery', *Social Problems,* 17: 54–83.

FRANCIS, D. (1988), *Contrepreneurs.* Toronto: Macmillan.

GOFFMAN, E. (1952), 'On Cooling the Mark Out: Some Aspects of Adaptation to Failure', *Psychiatry,* 15: 451–63.

GRABOSKY, P. N., SMITH, R. G. and DEMPSEY, G. (2001), *Electronic Theft: Unlawful Acquisition in Cyberspace.* New York: Cambridge University Press.

HALLER, M. (1990), 'Illegal Enterprise: A Theoretical and Historical Interpretation', *Criminology,* 28/2: 207–35.

HARRIS, L. et al. (1992), 'Telemarketing Fraud', University of North Carolina, Institute for Research in Social Science.

HIRSCHHORN, L. (1985), 'Information Technology and the New Services Game', in M. Castells, ed., *High Technology, Space and Society,* 172–90. Beverly Hills, CA: Sage.

HOBBS, R. (1995), *Bad Business: Professional Crime in Contemporary Britain.* Oxford: Oxford University Press.

——— (1997), 'Professional Crime: Change, Continuity and the Enduring Myth of the Underworld', *Sociology,* 31: 57–72.

HOLZMAN, H. (1983), 'The Serious Habitual Property Offender as Moonlighter: An Empirical Study of Labour Force Participation among Robbers and Burglars', *Journal of Criminal Law and Criminology,* 73: 1774–92.

IRWIN, J. (1970), *The Felon.* Englewood Cliffs, NJ: Prentice-Hall.

IRWIN, J. and CRESSEY, D. (1962), 'Thieves, Convicts and the Inmate Culture', *Social Problems,* 10: 142-55.

JACKSON, J. (1994), 'Fraud Masters: Professional Credit Card Offenders and Crime', *Criminal Justice Review,* 19: 24–55.

KATZ, J. (1988), *Seductions of Crime.* New York: Basic Books.

LASH, S. and URRY, J. (1994), *Economies of Signs and Space.* London: Sage.

LEMERT, E. (1958), 'The Behaviour of the Systematic Check Forger', *Social Problems,* 6: 141–9.

LETKEMANN, P. (1973), *Crime as Work.* Englewood Cliffs, NJ: Prentice-Hall.

MASON, E. (1994), *Inside Story.* London: Pan.

MAURER, D. W. (1940), *The Big Con.* Indianapolis: Bobbs-Merrill.

——— (1955/1964), *Whiz Mob.* New Haven, CT: College and University Press.

MCINTOSH, M. (1971), 'Changes in the Organisation of Thieving', in S. Cohen, ed., *Images of Deviance.* Harmondsworth: Penguin.

——— (1975), The Organization of Crime. New York: Macmillan.

MCVICAR, J. (1982), 'Violence in Prisons', in P. Marsh and A. Campbell, eds., *Aggression and Violence.* Oxford: Blackwell.

POLSKY, N. (1964), 'The Hustler', *Social Problems,* 12: 3–15.

PRESIDENT'S COMMISSION ON LAW ENFORCEMENT AND ADMINISTRATION OF JUSTICE (1966), 'Professional Crime', Task Force Report, ch. 7. Washington DC: US Government Printing Office.

REBOVICH, D. and LAYNE, J. JIANDANI, J. and HALE, S. (2000), *The National Public Survey on White Collar Crime.* National White Collar Crime Center.

ROEBUCK, J. and JOHNSON, R. (1962), 'The Jack of All Trades Offender', *Crime and Delinquency,* 8: 172–81.

ROSS, E. A. (1907), *Sin and Society: An Analysis of Latter-Day Iniquity.* Boston: Houghton Mifflin.

RUGGIERO, V. and SOUTH, N. (1997), 'The Late Modern City as a Bazaar', *British Journal of Sociology,* 48: 54–70.

SAMUEL, R. (1981), *East End Underworld: The Life and Times of Arthur Harding.* London: Routledge and Kegan Paul.

SAMUELSON, R. J. (1995), *The Good Life and Its Discontents.* New York: Random House.

SANGER, D. (1999), 'Confessions of a Phone-Scam Artist', *Saturday Night,* 114: 86–98.

SCHULTE, F. (1995), *Fleeced! Telemarketing Rip-offs and How to Avoid Them.* Amherst, NY: Prometheus Books.

SCOTT, M. B. and STANFORD, M. L. (1968), 'Accounts', *American Sociological Review,* 33: 46–62.

SHOVER, N. (1973), 'The Social Organization of Burglary', *Social Problems,* 20: 499–514.

——— (1983), 'Professional Crime: Major Offender', in Sanford H. Kadish, ed., *Encyclopedia of Crime and Justice,* 1263–71. New York: Macmillan.

——— (1996), *Great Pretenders: Pursuits and Careers of Persistent Thieves.* Boulder, CO: Westview.

SHOVER, N. and HONAKER, D. (1991), 'The Socially Bounded Decision Making of Persistent Property Offenders', *The Howard Journal,* 31: 276–93.

SILVERSTONE, R. (1991), *Beneath the Bottom Line: Households and Information and Communication Technologies in the Age of the Consumer.* London: Brunel University Centre for Research on Innovation, Culture, and Technology.

SOJA, E. (1989), *Postmodern Geographies.* London: Verso.

SPARROW, M. K. (1996), *License to Steal: Why Fraud Plagues America's Health Care System.* Boulder, CO: Westview.

STEVENSON, R. J. (2000), *The Boiler Room and Other Telephone Sales Scams.* Urbana, IL: University of Illinois Press.

SUTHERLAND, E. H. (1937), *The Professional Thief.* Chicago, IL: University of Chicago Press.

SYKES, G. (1978), *Criminology.* New York: Harcourt Brace Jovanovitch.

SYKES, G. and MATZA, D. (1957), 'Techniques of Neutralization: A Theory of Delinquency', *American Sociological Review,* 22: 667–70.

TAYLOR, I. (1999), *Crime in Context: A Critical Criminology of Market Societies.* Boulder, CO: Westview.

TAYLOR, L. (1984), *In the Underworld.* Oxford: Blackwell.

TICKELL, A. (1996), 'Taking the Initiative: Leeds' Financial Centre', in G. Haughton and C. Williams, eds., *Corporate City? Partnerships Participation in Urban Development in Leeds.* Aldershot: Avebury.

TILLMAN, R. (1998), *Broken Promises: Fraud by Small Business Health Insurers.* Boston: Northeastern University Press.

TITUS, R. (2001), 'Personal Fraud and Its Victims', in N. Shover and J. P. Wright, eds., *Crimes of Privilege: Readings in White-Collar Crime,* 57–67. New York: Oxford University Press.

TITUS, R. M., HEINZELMANN, F. and BOYLE, J. M. (1995), 'Victimization of Persons by Fraud', *Crime and Delinquency,* 41: 54–72.

TOBIAS, J. J. (1967), *Crime and Industrial Society in the 19th Century.* London: Batsford.

TURKLE, S. (1995), *Life on the Screen: Identity in the Age of the Internet.* New York: Simon and Schuster.

US SENATE, CONGRESS (1993), Hearing before the Subcommittee on Consumer of the Committee on Commerce, Science, and Transportation, *Telemarketing Fraud and S. 568, The Telemarketing and Consumer Fraud and Abuse Protection Act.* 103d Congress, 1st Session. Washington, DC: US Government Printing Office.

VAN DUYNE, P. (1996), 'The Phantom and Threat of Organized Crime', *Crime, Law and Social Change,* 21: 241–77.

WINLOW, S. (2001), *Badfellas.* Oxford: Berg.

WRIGHT, R. and DECKER, S. (1994), *Burglars on the Job: Streetlife and Residential Break-ins.* Boston: Northeastern University Press.

Chapter 17 How Doctors Defraud Medicaid

Doctors Tell Their Stories

Paul Jesilow
Henry M. Pontell
Gilbert Geis

For this selection, an excerpt from their book, Prescription for Profit: How Doctors Defraud Medicaid, *Jesilow, Pontell, and Geis interviewed 42 physicians who had been sanctioned for Medicaid violations in California and New York. All of the sanctioned doctors had been suspended from practice and two-thirds of them had been convicted of crimes associated with Medicaid fraud. The researchers compared the responses of the sanctioned physicians with a control group of nonsanctioned physicians.*

The authors found that while the physicians admitted the basic facts of their cases, they explained away the criminality of the acts through the use of rationalization and justification. Scully and Marolla ("Convicted Rapists' Vocabulary of Motive," Chapter 14 in this volume) reported similar uses of rationalization and excuse with a study population of convicted rapists.

In the course of our research we interviewed forty-two physicians apprehended for Medicaid scams. To hear them tell it, they were innocent sacrificial lambs led to the slaughter because of perfidy, stupid laws, bureaucratic nonsense, and incompetent bookkeepers. At worst, they had been a bit careless in their record keeping; but mostly they had been more interested in the welfare of their patients than in deciphering the arcane requirements of benefit programs. Certainly, the Medicaid laws are complex and, by many reasonable standards, unreasonable. But we were surprised by the number of rationalizations that these doctors offered, by the intensity of their defenses of their misconduct, and by their consummate skill in identifying the villains who, out of malevolence or ineptitude, had caused their downfall. In these doctors' system of moral accounting, their humanitarian deeds far outweighed their petty trespasses against Medicaid. . . .

Rationales and Rationalizations

The sanctioned doctors generally appeared open and candid, at ease and involved with the subject. Most were perfectly accurate in response to our opening question—which asked them to provide the factual details of their cases—though these recitals were interladen with a plethora of self-excusatory observations. Throughout the interview, we gave the respondents a great deal of leeway in responding, and we sought to avoid putting words in their mouths or guiding them in any particular direction. They could be rude or polite to us (most were very polite), satisfied or disgusted with the government, and optimistic or pessimistic about the futures of their careers. At times, some doctors told us more than they realized. It is difficult in a long, sometimes emotional interview to camouflage strongly held convictions.

All the doctors in the sanctioned group had been suspended from billing the Medicaid program, and about two-thirds had been convicted of a criminal offense. Nonetheless, a doctor often would ask us, "What did I do that was so bad?" Clearly, their interpretations of the ethical and legal character of their actions were quite unlike those made by the law enforcement authorities.

One way to explain this dissonance is by reference to the classic sociological work of Gresham Sykes and David Matza on juvenile delinquents. According to Sykes and Matza, these young criminals "neutralize" the negative definitions that they know "respectable" people apply to their delinquent behaviors. By learning these neutralization techniques in delinquent subcultures, juveniles can render social controls inoperative and be free to engage in delinquency without serious harm to their self-images. Thus, the delinquent can remain committed to law-abiding norms but can also "qualify" them in order to make violations excusable, if not altogether "right." Sykes and Matza observe that "much delinquency is based on what is essentially an unrecognized extension of defenses to crimes, in the form of justifications for deviance that are seen as valid by the delinquent but not by the legal system or society at large." From a study of embezzlers incarcerated in federal prisons, Donald Cressey concluded that these wrongdoers used "vocabularies of adjustment" to justify their behaviors to themselves. They told themselves that they were merely "borrowing" the money, which they would replace just as soon as they resolved a momentary problem. This self-deception enabled the embezzlers to see themselves as basically decent although they were altering records and stealing money.

Because we carried out our interviews several years after the offenses had taken place, we could not determine whether the doctors had fashioned their explanations before or after they committed the abuses—an analytical issue that has bedeviled all researchers attempting to verify the importance of neutralization techniques in lawbreaking. Most likely, we heard explanations of both types. Our data do tend to support the hypothesis that neutralization often constitutes an important element of what has been called the "drift" into illegal behavior, a period during which the perpetrator's episodic lawbreaking often goes unattended and thus begins to lose whatever unsavory moral flavor it might have possessed.

Denial of Responsibility

Few physicians took full personal blame for their violations in the sense of describing them as volitional, deliberate acts of wrongdoing. They were apt to call their activities "mistakes," and some blamed themselves for not having been more careful. This neutralization practice corresponds to what Sykes and Matza call denial of responsibility: "Denial of responsibility . . . extends much further than the claim that deviant acts are an 'accident' or some similar negation of personal accountability. . . . By learning to view himself as more acted upon than acting, the delinquent prepares the way for deviance from the normative system without the necessity of a frontal assault on the norms themselves."

The wrongdoing physicians did engage in a frontal assault on Medicaid norms, but they typically laid the blame on a wide variety of persons other than themselves. Several blamed patients' demands, portraying their own behavior as altruistic. One insisted she was doing no more than trying to see to the essential health of needy people: "Some of the kids didn't have any Medicaid, and you get a mother saying, 'Look, my child is sick. I don't have any Medicaid. Could you put it on the other kid's Medicaid?' It probably wasn't their child to begin with. It was like a sister's child." The physician admitted that she complied with the mother's request, and her "goodheartedness" got her into trouble with the government. She says that during the investigation, "the mother who brought in her sister's child forgot that this kid was treated because it was like a year ago." The mother's lapse of memory or fabrication, the doctor suspected, occurred because the mother hoped to avoid implicating herself in the fraud.

The same physician also insisted she had been victimized by thieves who stole Medicaid cards from beneficiaries and then presented themselves for treatment. Her practice was in "a bad area," and such thefts were common, she pointed out. When the itemization of treatment services came to the legitimate cardholders, they would complain to the authorities. Even if this was true, however, her explanation sidestepped the issue of her responsibility to match the Medicaid card with the person presenting it. . . .

Another physician got into trouble for accepting kickbacks from a laboratory. (Physicians can bill Medicaid for laboratory tests if they own the testing facility; otherwise the laboratory bills Medicaid.) This physician told us he had decided to do his own lab work in order to increase his income. A former employee, whom the physician held responsible for his misfortune, offered the doctor a deal:

> My lab technician quit to start his own laboratory. He said: "Why don't you give me all the lab work." I said: "Fine, you bill Medicaid, and I'll bill my private patients."
>
> They were doing the tests for so much, and I charged them the going rate, and he was giving me a good deal, and that was a private deal. The Medi-Cal, he was doing it all and billing it himself.
>
> Then I told him: "I'm going to get a technician so I can have the benefits of the laboratory, of Medi-Cal too." [But] eventually he says: "I'll give you some benefits on your private patients. For instance, your bill is $300. I'll cut it down to $200 or something so we'll make it up somehow." I said: "All right."

Another physician who took kickbacks portrayed himself as an unwary, passive participant, motivated only by amiability and generosity, in a plan hatched by a hospital. The initiative came from the hospital, and the direct beneficiaries were his employees, so, as far as he was concerned, he had done nothing wrong in allowing the hospital to underwrite his payroll:

> [The] [h]ospital, privately owned, was in the habit of giving kickbacks to physicians using the hospital. I had arranged for three of the girls that worked for me to receive part-time pay to the tune of about $250 each, per month.
>
> This lasted about two years before it was stopped, and the amount of work that they did for the money they received was negligible. So they were able to show in court that this was an indirect type of kickback. Even though the money was not paid to me, by the girls receiving this money, it obviously made them happier or better employees or whatever you want to call it.
>
> I felt that if I didn't accept it, that if I let the girls take it, and then made sure that they got their full salaries and their Christmas bonuses, that I wasn't actually getting any benefit out of it. I thought that therefore I was immune.
>
> And I really wasn't getting any benefit out of it. I had three employees—two of them were getting divorces, and one of them had a third child. The hospital wanted to give kickbacks, let them have it, you know.

An obstetrician, perhaps truthfully, cast responsibility on the welfare department, which had told him how to circumvent an inconvenient regulation:

> Even the [welfare] department told me to change dates . . . to be within the letter of the law. For example, some girl delivers the baby, she decides to have her tubes tied. Now, according to the state, there has to be an application thirty days ahead of tubular ligation, and it has to be submitted, approved, and thirty days given for the patient to make up her mind, to decide.
>
> If she hadn't given us any indication to the ligation, and she has to have one, what do we do now? I can't say, "You have to go home and come back in thirty days." And so they [the welfare caseworkers] told me, as well as the other doctors for Medicaid, they'd just say: "Backdate the request thirty days."

Commonly, denials of responsibility were blended with other self-justifications. A psychiatrist who illegally submitted bills under his name (and took a cut) for work done by psychologists not qualified for payment under Medicaid blamed the therapists but also added that he did it for the benefit of his patients:

> There were times I wanted to quit, but the therapist would say that these people are in need of therapy, and it is going well. It seemed to make sense at the time. They were qualified people. I couldn't do it myself; I wasn't there all the time. It was partly a moral thing. I was persuaded to keep doing it, and a good percentage of patients were getting something out of it. I should have been more responsible, but it also had to do with my trust in people, and that trust was misplaced.

This physician, perhaps as a reflexive bow to a major postulate of his vocation, commented, "I don't want to think of myself as a victim, so I want to take responsibility for what I did." Yet he found irresistible the idea that it was his essential goodness—his trust in people and his sympathy for patients—that had led him astray.

Denial of Injury

Justifying lawbreaking by citing the superordinate benefits of the act—such as the psychiatrist's comment on the value of the therapy for his patients—is called denial of injury in the roster of Sykes and Matza's techniques of neutralization. As they point out, "wrongfulness may turn on the question of whether or not anyone has clearly been hurt by [the] deviance, and this matter is open to a variety of interpretations." Physicians often depicted Medicaid regulations, which assuredly can be both onerous and mercilessly nitpicking, as bureaucratic obstacles, erected by laypeople, that threatened patient care. By breaking or bending the Medicaid rules, the sanctioned physicians argued, they were responding to their higher calling and helping—not hurting—patients.

Taking this tack, a physician who treated obesity by performing surgery emphasized that he was motivated only by "medical reasons" and "didn't give a goddamn what Medi-Cal said":

> Consider patients on welfare. There's a huge group of people who are on welfare because they cannot work. Nobody will give them a job. Their obesity serves as an excuse for remaining in the welfare system. To themselves they just say: "Well, I'm fat; I cannot get a job; therefore, I have to be on welfare." And they're satisfied with it. To alter that situation is haz-

ardous, both from the emotional standpoint, but particularly in terms of physical aspects of it because if they eat enough, no matter how you loused up their gut, they're going to manage to remain obese. Earlier on, fifteen years ago, I did a few welfare patients, and I soon recognized the problem that particular group has especially. The bottom line is that there is a subconscious need for obesity.

Well, I came up with the idea many years ago of saying: "OK, if you want this done, I've got no handle on what your subconscious state is, how much you need your obesity; there's no test for it. But the pocketbook is pretty close to the subconscious mind. If you are willing to pay for something, chances are you want it." Doesn't work that great; but at least it's a way. So what I started doing was charging them in advance: You want surgery, you come up with the money. Your insurance company happens to pay it back, you know, pay the full fee; well, I'll give it right back to them.

I must admit that I did some Medi-Cal patients before I came up with this gimmick. And one or two of them worked very well. They became employable and very successful. But on the other hand, for every successful one, I would find two or three that became a disaster and had to be taken down and reoperated, all kinds of problems.

So, anyway, I started this business. So I go: "OK, you want this surgery; you pay half of it." Now, at that particular point in time, I didn't give a goddamn what Medi-Cal said. I mean, if the patient wants this done, whether it's legal or illegal. I said I'm doing this for my reasons—medical reasons. What they'd have to come up with was maybe $100 or $500, whatever. The fee that Medi-Cal was paying at that time, plus the $500, was still less than what it would be for a private patient. Medi-Cal was paying maybe $500 or $600.

I didn't give a damn about the money. It wasn't as if I got a patient in the emergency room and Medi-Cal only paid me $150, but my fee was $600, and so I tried to collect the balance. That wasn't my intent at all. Welfare patients do not expect to pay you. But this was a volitional thing. They knew about it in advance. It was not an emergency. It was purely elective, cosmetic. I knew I couldn't bill. That's the only part of the regulations I knew and recognized.

It wasn't as though there was fraud involved. I wasn't defrauding anybody. If you want this surgery, you pay me before surgery, not afterwards. If I were billing them afterwards, I recognize that was bad. But this isn't the same thing. I still don't think so.

I really thought I had some really nice results on a few of them. I did have some disasters. That is why I started this. If I had just had the disasters and said "the hell with it, there's no answer to this, get out," I would have avoided it, because I didn't need it. It didn't amount to that much money. I could have been doing a private patient and come out way ahead.

Of course, the physician could have employed tactics other than reaching into a beneficiary's wallet to determine the patient's motivation—for example, adherence to a diet and exercise regimen prior to the operation. That the preoperative payment was intended to preclude reneging on the fee, rather than to measure motivation, is implicit in the physician's subsequent statement:

> Now, plastic surgeons, for example, have done this for years. If you want to have your nose fixed, you pay them right up front. And for the same reason. Because they know that if you have to try to collect afterwards, the patient's going to find five hundred reasons why their nose isn't the way they thought it was going to be. If you've already paid for it, they'll be happy and satisfied.

Such comparisons with other specialties were common among doctors seeking to explain away their violations of the law. The Medicaid rules were capricious, and their own interpretation of fairness was far more sensible than that of the bureaucrats. Consider this psychiatrist's self-righteous indignation:

> My wife is an eminently qualified psychiatric nurse. She had a medical teaching appointment on a medical school staff, supervisor of their inpatients, very qualified individual. So, anyhow, the basic problem was, she worked for me. They accused me—I don't know what the hell they accused me of—charging [Medicaid] for her services.
>
> She was my nurse employee, just like I've had nurse employees everywhere I've been. I have always billed, like when the nurse gave a shot, you didn't bill it through her name. I don't even under-

stand this concept, you know. I still don't understand what basis they can say arbitrarily that she is any different than a nurse that works for an obstetrician.

The way people are supervised in psychiatry is different than for general medicine. They never understood the difference, and still don't, and don't want to know. You can't talk with other physicians about it because they don't know anything about psychiatry, and don't want to know. You are in an esoteric field, that you have to be in to understand.

In a similar vein, another psychiatrist found the regulations senseless and the work he was doing eminently valuable for his patients. Besides, he had been able to bill in another setting for therapy provided by nonphysicians, so he could not comprehend why such an action was not permitted under Medi-Cal:

> I worked as a convalescent lead psychiatrist at one time. Now that means working in one of these county clinics where you are seeing patients and the social worker is seeing patients. These people are being charged the full rate, and it is only the psychiatrist who has a Medi-Cal number. If it is all right in the agency, why isn't it all right in private practice?
>
> I was aware of putting down my name and not any other therapist, you know, who wouldn't be honored. But nevertheless, they were still my patients, and everything that went on was under my signature and my supervision. Some social workers are better than some psychiatrists in the analysis of a problem. Some psychiatrists are not that good in understanding human behavior.
>
> I will stand by unequivocally that the patients that were seen by me, in conjunction with others, were getting far more for their dollar, whether it is paid for by them, their company, or by Medi-Cal. They were getting far more from my clinic than they would get anywhere from one practitioner, and it was because there were certain areas in my training and intuition, my skills, where someone else could do better, and vice versa. As far as I am concerned, they are quality people—something I insisted upon.
>
> My idea was with Medi-Cal, or with whatever I was doing, do what was right for the patients and for the patients' good. I consider four eyes better than two eyes, four arms better than two arms, and four ears better than two ears, and these patients were getting more in their hourly fee. . . .

Denial of a Victim

A third neutralization technique, denial of a victim, occurs when an offender grants that his or her behavior caused injury but insists "the injury is not wrong in light of the circumstances." In our interviews, the sanctioned physicians claimed that although the law had been broken, the excess reimbursement they had received represented only what they deserved for their work. They saw overcharging for services and ordering excessive tests as ways to "make back" what they *should* have been paid.

One physician, for example, granted that his excessive billings were wrong, especially because Medicaid participation was voluntary; but he maintained that the regulations and payment schedules encouraged—even necessitated—cheating, so that doctors in the program could earn fees equivalent to those paid by private insurance:

> If you voluntarily choose to accept Medicaid patients, you have to put up with their baloney, and if you're not willing to put up with their baloney, then maybe you shouldn't take Medicaid patients. So in that sense, it's difficult to say something is not fair and you shouldn't do it. . . .
>
> But the system has got many flaws in it and loopholes and irregularities which necessitate abuses to take place. Otherwise, you can't see patients because of the reimbursement attitude.
>
> Let's take an example. A patient comes in for the first time and is examined. For that it would be, let's say, $60. Now, if the patient goes to a general practitioner for the first time with a cold, he [the doctor] will get that amount. If the patient goes to an internist, who has to evaluate the patient for a complicated situation, such as diabetes, heart disease, god knows what, and spends a lot of time with that patient, he will get compensated the same amount. So it's all the same because it is a new patient visit.
>
> Now for that reason, it is virtually impossible to [receive treatment] at this time in this area. There are virtually no internists in this area that I know who accept Medicaid, because if a patient comes to an internist, they expect a thorough going-over, which they devote anywhere from half an hour to forty-five minutes, and yet the reimbursement rate is exactly the same as if the patient went to a gen-

eral practitioner with a cold and spent five minutes with him.

> Now the system, of course, does ask, when you bill for this visit, whether you spent a lot of time with the patient or a little time. You are supposed to voluntarily say that it was a brief visit and, if you state that, they will pay you a less amount. However, very few people I know do that. They will always bill the maximum amount because that maximum amount is actually less than we charge our private patients. This is one door of abuse that virtually everyone I know who takes Medicaid is using. If they billed the patient with a cold for a very brief visit, then they get paid as little as $12. There's no one I know who can function in this area, with an office and a staff and insurance and all these things, and accept a patient for $12. I would say that form of abuse exists in 90 to 100 percent of doctors that I know who take Medicaid. They're all using the maximum [reimbursement] levels.

This physician's conviction that virtually all his colleagues engaged in billing scams provided fuel for self-justification. As Sykes and Matza note, such a belief allows the perpetrator to transform the violation from a "gesture of complete opposition" to one that represents no more than "an extension of common practice."

An anesthesiologist, caught billing the government for excess time, argued that he was reasonably charging for the patients' recovery time—a charge he knew was against Medicaid regulations:

> We saw no reason why we should do abortions on the garbage of the ghettos and barrios and be responsible for their recovery time and not be paid for it. I really think that it was gray, not black. I'm not defending it. In the context of the time, it wasn't really that bad. But it was stupid to try and do it considering how little money was involved and the horrible consequences. I should have known better. If you are going to steal from the system, it was a very stupid act. I don't think it was really a basically crooked act. I guess you could say it was, but it depends on how you look at it.
>
> When I did it, it was being done by at least 50 percent or 70 percent of the anesthesiologists in Southern California—at least 50 percent. People were fudging time, particularly on Medicaid.

Another physician also blamed the government for creating intolerable conditions that pressed practitioners toward fraud in order to meet patients' needs.

The doctor illustrated what he saw as his dilemma by telling of a fourteen-year-old girl who was having her third abortion in less than six months. He had given the girl birth control pills, but she obviously hadn't taken them. When she came back for the third abortion, he coaxed her into allowing him to insert an IUD: "It's very simple, very easy. We'll put it in right now, immediately after the abortion." The doctor then billed Medicaid for the IUD and its insertion, but the program would not pay because the insertion was done at the same time as the abortion for a fee the agency decreed reasonably covered both procedures. The doctor was irritated:

> So they don't give a damn. It has to be a separate visit. So, then there's the question of getting this patient back. She's already got a local anesthetic in for the abortion. She says, "OK, do it. I won't feel it." You try to convince that same girl a week later or two weeks later? "Oh, no, I don't want those shots again" or "No, it's going to hurt. I don't want an IUD. I'll take the pill." It's another way of driving up costs. It drives up costs because they're going to have the girl pregnant again, and they're going to be perfectly willing to pay for more abortions rather than violate their rule. I paid $7, $8, $9 for an IUD. If I've been foolish enough to insert it immediately after an abortion—I can just forget getting paid. That's too bad. That's my problem. I should have made her come back in two weeks.
>
> Now that's a medical decision that they have no business getting involved in. One of the ways I can handle this problem with this fourteen-year-old, if I've decided that the most important thing is her welfare, is I'm going to put in the goddamn IUD and put on the chart that I put it in tomorrow. Right? Because your health really should come before some bureaucrat, and there's no reason why I should be asked to throw away my money. . . .

Various complaints about the nature of Medicaid recipients were offered by physicians in support of their view that Medicaid practice was more demanding than "normal" medicine and, by implication, should pay more rather than less. One doctor flaunted his disgust to us: "The Medicaid patients are filthy. They keep the place in turmoil. They are the toughest type to treat. The Medicaid patient is more demanding as a rule, and is not as cooperative in their treatment programs. I found this to be very troublesome at times."

Even if one were to accept the doctors' premise that the regulations were too inflexible given the difficulties of working with Medicaid patients, one has to wonder about the structural conflict between the physicians' interest in their patients' well-being and their own financial self-interest. For example, the physician who inserted IUDs after performing abortions argued that he was offering important care to patients. Yet he was unwilling to assume the small cost of the IUD and the minimal extra time to insert it; instead, he chose to cheat Medicaid and reap illegitimate profits. Before the advent of Medicaid, of course, many physicians performed services for indigent patients without charge. They spread the cost of care for the indigent among their fee-paying and insured patients. Government benefit programs now offer—if one is willing to cheat—the opportunity both to proclaim a humanitarian interest in the welfare of poor patients and to get paid at or above the going rate for that interest.

One physician we spoke with harkened to the theme of pro bono service, but quickly added that he was always ready to circumvent the law in order to obtain his fee from Medicaid:

> I would say personally I am disappointed with my colleagues in medicine. All of them are interested in their business. They are not concerned about the health of their patients. They want to make money. And, of course, they will make money. But the primary objective should be the care of patients. In medicine, the fee you get is a side effect.
>
> I was satisfied with the Medicaid reimbursement because I always knew that if somebody didn't pay me, my conscience would make me treat them anyway. I figured it was better to get Medicaid than to treat them free. Some of the regulations are annoying, but you could always get around them. I would first treat the patient, then deal with Medicaid.

This blend of decency, self-righteousness, and a thoroughly high-handed attitude about "annoying" regulations that "you could always get around" nicely satisfied this doctor's conscience and cash flow.

Getting around the rules, playing the Medicaid game, working the system for maximum profit—many of the doctors we spoke with defined their illegal activities in such terms. . . .

Condemning the Condemners

Sykes and Matza describe condemning the condemners as a fourth neutralization technique: "The delinquent shifts the focus of attention from his own deviant acts to the motives and behavior of those who disapprove of his violations." This shift enables violators to minimize responsibility for their behavior by construing it as trivial compared to the misdeeds of the rule makers or as rational compared to the irrational expectations of the rule makers.

In a typical condemnation of the Medicaid program, one of our respondents insisted that Medicaid not only invited but demanded cheating:

> It's not related to reality, you know. It's done by people who are not medical people, who know nothing about the services being provided. One of the peculiarities that they do is that they make arbitrary decisions about things totally unrelated to the services you provide. They're constantly irritating and aggravating the doctors and their staff.
>
> They say, "What we used to do, we're not going to do anymore." And you're already three months into your new billing system. I could keep you here the rest of the day giving you examples of their kind of idiocy, that they somehow manage to make sense out of in their little peculiar world that's unrelated to ours. They've built in systems that either ask for somebody to cheat, you know, or to cheat the patient on the type of care that's provided. You put somebody in the position where lying is the most reasonable course, and they will lie. The patients will lie; the doctor may even lie on what they say about what happened.

This physician illustrated his point by citing the often criticized Medicaid rule that three months must elapse between compensable abortions. Suppose, he argued, a young woman had undergone an abortion in his office one week short of three months ago. According to the rules, he should tell her to come back the following week. But suppose she insists that she has to visit her sick mother in another state. This puts "everybody in a position because somebody has made some rule that doesn't make sense." A "naive" doctor would do the young woman "a favor" and postdate the reimbursement form. But, he concluded, "I don't know whether there's any naive doctors around anymore; they've been so hassled and harassed by this system."

That the Medicaid regulations might represent an attempt, however flawed, to control abuse, rather than an effort to harass or second-guess doctors, did not enter into the thinking of doctors who condemned the system as arbitrary, capricious, and unreasonable. One doctor could only fall back on the word "ridiculous":

> I think they are ridiculous. We ask permission; we send them proof, we send them everything. One of them even asked me for a picture of the patient. I told him: "Who do you think I am, a crook or what? I am telling you this big long hernia there is hanging out of the testicles." I said: "Well, what do I send a picture of? Oh man, you are crazy." And that's what I do; I sent a picture, but it was absolutely ridiculous.
>
> They are spending so much money. So many secretaries they have. They check all the cases in the hospitals, the Medicaid cases that go in, all the welfare cases they check. . . .

Although the sanctioned physicians focused their scorn on particular aspects of the program that related to their own misconduct, they had fewer complaints about reimbursement levels and "unnecessary" regulation than our comparison group of nonsanctioned physicians. Slightly more than half (57 percent) of the sanctioned physicians felt reimbursement was too low, an opinion shared by 73 percent of the nonsanctioned doctors. And almost two-thirds of the sanctioned physicians (62 percent), compared to only 23 percent of the nonsanctioned, said they had no complaints about unnecessary Medicaid regulations. This pattern of self-serving selective disapproval resembles a phenomenon observed in prison culture, where "common criminals" are notably hostile to child molesters and traitors.

Appeal to Higher Loyalties

The fifth and final neutralization technique discussed by Sykes and Matza is the appeal to higher loyalties. Delinquents engage in law-breaking, they say, to benefit smaller and more intimate groups to which they belong, such as their gangs or their friendship networks. Laws are broken "because other norms, held to be more pressing or involving a higher loyalty, are accorded precedence." For the sanctioned physicians, such higher loyalties included service to patients and adherence to professional standards. In an unusual case, one physician insisted that being diagnosed with cancer prompted his cheating. He was worried about whether his infant son would have an adequate inheritance. In addition, he said he was despondent, angry, and bitter and wanted to get caught because of a wish to destroy himself or "to get back at the world" for his illness.

A Subculture of Delinquency?

Every sanctioned doctor we interviewed relied on one or more neutralization techniques to explain what had happened, and only rarely did we hear even the most elemental acknowledgment of self-serving motives. The structure of Medicaid, as we have noted, offers more than ample opportunities to harvest rationalizations that locate blame on factors other than the offender's lack of restraint. At times, doctors agreed that they might have been more careful and diligent about supervising others or challenging unusual goings-on, but such admissions were most often accompanied by claims to have been concerned with more important, socially valuable matters. On occasion, we heard physicians suggest that their own stupidity led to their apprehension—but it was the method of cheating, not the cheating itself, that they regretted.

The tenor of the interviews indicated that the cavalier attitudes these doctors had adopted toward the government benefit programs had been at least partially absorbed from others in the profession, and that professional values may effectively neutralize conflicts of conscience. Here we took our cue from Matza's discussion of a "subculture of juvenile delinquency—a setting in which the commission of delinquency is common knowledge among a group" and which provides norms and beliefs that "function as the extenuating conditions under which delinquency is permissible." A subculture of medical delinquency, we concluded, arises, thrives, and grows in large part because of the tension between bureaucratic regulation and professional norms of autonomy.

Physicians who cheated government programs were not committed to a life of crime and undoubtedly did not cheat on all their billings. Nor did they always steal from Medicaid or from private insurance programs; they probably were honest in much of their work. But when these doctors did defy Medicaid's legal requirements, they typically offered professional justifications in lieu of defining their activities as deviant, illegal, or criminal. . . .

Conclusion

The establishment of the Medicaid program provided new opportunities for doctors and other medical practitioners and organizations to commit criminal acts and to violate administrative regulations. Our research did not yield a composite portrait of physicians who typically get into trouble with Medicaid, though there are some recurring traits in the roster of physicians dealt with by the authorities. The stereotypical image of the violator as an inner-city doctor associated with a Medicaid mill is misleading: Offenders include some of the most respectable members of the profession and physicians of all ages, specialties, and attitudes toward patients and government medical benefit programs.

Questions for Thought and Discussion

1. Unlike many other criminals in this book, some doctors who have been sanctioned for defrauding Medicaid justify their behavior as contributing to the public good. What is the basis of their argument?
2. What are some examples of excuses and justifications used by doctors when asked about their crimes?
3. Should physicians who commit fraud in their billing practices be treated like other criminals and punished accordingly? Why or why not?
4. What theory or theories of criminal behavior are illustrated in this research?

References

Cressey, D. 1953. *Other People's Money.* Glencoe, IL: Free Press.

Sykes, G. and D. Matza. 1957. "Techniques of Neutralization: A Theory of Delinquency." *American Sociological Review* 22:667–70.

Chapter 18 Neutralization and Deviance in the Workplace

Theft of Supplies and Medicines by Hospital Nurses

Dean Dabney

T*his article focuses on the phenomenon of on-the-job deviance among nurses. Deviant behaviors such as supply theft, drug theft, drug use, and procedural shortcuts are addressed from a theoretical perspective that incorporates components of differential association, social learning, and techniques of neutralization theories. The author interviewed 25 registered nurses in critical care units in three hospitals. A snowball sample technique was used, beginning with three nurses who served as interview participants and as the core of the snowball. Each interview lasted 60 to 90 minutes. The data illustrate how nurses readily neutralize their deviant behaviors by using established rationalization schemes. The data suggest that the nature and limits of these rationalizations are created, perpetuated, and disseminated by the nursing work group. Moreover, evidence is presented that suggests that these rationalizations function as* a priori *discriminate stimuli, not simply as* post hoc *justifications for deviant behaviors.*

The nursing profession is not without its share of employee deviance. This deviance takes many forms. Some of the most prevalent and potentially destructive examples of nursing deviance are the theft of drugs or supplies. A nationwide study of drug theft in hospitals (McCormick et al. 1986) found that nurses were implicated in 70 percent of the drug losses (more than 112,000 dosage units over a 1-year period). Moreover, a large-scale survey of nurses' on-the-job substance abuse behaviors conducted by the American Nurses Association (1984) estimated that 8–10 percent of the nation's 1.7 million nurses are dependent on drugs or alcohol. A similar large scale study conducted by the Michigan Nurses Association (1986) estimated that nurses are five times more likely to abuse substances than are members of the general public. The Michigan study went on to estimate that one in seven nurses will abuse substances during their careers. With these figures in mind, the research reported here attempts to provide contextuality to nurses' involvements in organizational deviance, using existing criminological theory. Specifically, this analysis draws on components of differential association, social learning theory, and techniques of neutralization to explain the aforementioned forms of nursing deviance. The goal is to identify both the positive and the negative normative definitions associated with nurses' deviant behavior and to illustrate how the nursing work group supplies its members with a series of neutralizing rationalizations that are then used to modify these definitions.

Theoretical Orientation

The learning process that leads to deviant behavior has long fascinated criminologists. Sutherland's (Sutherland 1949; Sutherland and Cressey 1970) differential association theory was the first to suggest that the learning process behind criminal behavior is the same as that behind noncriminal behavior. At the center of Sutherland's theory is the concept of "definitions." According to Sutherland, these definitions serve as the normative attitudes and beliefs toward behavior. When an individual has the knowledge of how to commit an act and the opportunity presents itself, that individual's behavior will hinge on his or her normative perception of the act. An excess of definitions favorable to an act increases the likelihood of its occurrence, and an excess of negative definitions decreases the likelihood of its occurrence.

Social learning theory (Akers 1985) expands on Sutherland's (Sutherland 1949; Sutherland and Cressey 1970) concept of definitions. According to social learning theory, normative definitions are the result not only of association, but of imitation and differential reinforcement. More important, social learning theory asserts that definitions favorable to deviant acts can take on one of two forms: They can simply define the act as morally correct or they can redefine a morally incorrect act in a favorable light. In the latter case, a set of excuses, justifications, or rationalizations serves as vocal or internal discriminative stimuli for the deviant act. These discriminant stimuli then serve to redefine the act in one of two ways: as not really deviant or as a justifiable act.

Social learning theory incorporates the notion of neutralization from Sykes and Matza's (1957) "techniques of neutralization" theory. Sykes and Matza formulated five distinct typologies of justifications or rationalizations: *denial of responsibility, denial of injury, denial of victim, condemnation of condemner,* and the *appeal to higher loyalties.* These authors posit that each of the above-mentioned neutralization typologies serves as a cognitive mechanism used by individuals to redefine normatively unfavorable behaviors as acceptable. The exact form of this rationalization mechanism, as well as its subsequent verbal manifestation (i.e., the excuses offered by the individual), will differ depending on which of the seven typologies is being used.

Building on the concept of normative definitions, I attempt in this analysis to identify neutralizing definitions that manifest themselves within the nursing work group and thus facilitate various forms of organizational deviance. Interview data are used to demonstrate that the nursing work group creates and maintains its own system of work group norms. For the most part, these definitions correspond with the accepted norms of the hospital and even those of the larger society. However, in some cases, the established organizational norms of the hospital conflict with work group norms. In this case, the work group either provides the individual nurses with a set of rationalizations for violating the hospital's organizational and legal rules or institutes procedural shortcuts or innovative adaptations to circumvent existing hospital policy.

I argue that incoming nurses are aware of the formal organizational definitions against taking supplies and medicines for personal or unauthorized use. Nevertheless, observations in hospitals reveal that nurses readily engage in taking such properties. The contention here is that such behaviors are facilitated by nurses learning a series of justifications and rationalizations that portray theft as not really deviant when committed under certain conditions. Consistent with social learning theory, I argue that these rationalizations are the direct result of reinforcement from other nurses. As nurses are socialized into a particular work group, they tend to change their general normative definition to conform to that held by the work group. These norms do not compel, or require deviations from the hospital or legal regulations. Nor do they portray such deviations as something a "good" nurse should do. Rather, they simply excuse the acts as not really wrong when committed under some circumstances.

Social learning theory and techniques of neutralization theory alike have been challenged on the grounds that they do not adequately address the causal ordering issue required of etiological theories (Hamlin 1988). In short, critics have suggested that there has been little if any conclusive evidence that demonstrates that neutralizing definitions are present before the conception of deviant behaviors. As such, theories such as techniques of neutralization (and, indirectly, social learning theory) are often labeled as little more than ex post facto explanations of deviant behavior.

In this analysis, I propose an etiological explanation of deviant behavior that borrows the issue of neutralizing normative definitions directly from social learning theory and techniques of neutralization paradigms. Thus, the causal ordering issue must be addressed. I use verbatim interview data to illustrate a number of different rationalization techniques used by the nurses, and I use retroactive neutralizations to demonstrate how individuals engage in after-the-fact rationalization that allows them to reconstruct the reality of the situation in question in such a way that it coincides with their predetermined notions of acceptable behavior. Also, evidence that nurses routinize the use of retroactive rationalizations is offered as testimony that they use these neutralization mechanisms as discriminant stimuli that serve to shape future behaviors of the same type. In short, the causal argument is as follows: Nurses are offered certain rationalizations from the nursing work group that excuse or condone certain forms of deviant behavior. In turn, the habitual use of these rationalizations increases the probability that individual nurses will internalize such redefined definitions of acceptable behavior for future reference.

I give evidence of the proactive application of the neutralization concept by presenting accounts in which nurses apply neutralizing definitions to deviant behavior committed in the past and then imply or directly assert that they will continue to engage in these behaviors in the future. Situations like this suggest that nurses have internalized the neutralizing definitions and are using them as discriminant stimuli that shape subsequent behaviors.

Deviance and Neutralizations in the Workplace

Several past research efforts have approached the issue of employee deviance from a similar theoretical perspective. For example, in studying what he called "blue-collar theft" among workers at an electronics factory, Horning (1970) found evidence that employees constructed their own definitions of what did and did not constitute "real" theft within the organization. These definitions depend on the property involved. The respondents classified property into three categories: company property, personal property, and property of uncertain origin. The misappropriation of personal property or company property was seen as theft. However, a similar definition was not applied to property of uncertain origin. In this case, the workers felt justified in taking the property. The origins of these definitions were traced back to the work group. The worker was taught what was acceptable behavior and what was not. These behaviors often directly contradicted company policies, but the workers adhered to the group norms, not company policy.

Other researchers who have applied the neutralization concept to organizational deviance include Cressey (1953), Geis (1967), Benson (1985), Hollinger (1991), Tathum (1974), Sieh (1987), Dalton (1959), Gouldner (1954), Ditton (1977), and Mars (1982). Although each of these studies took on a different theoretical twist and focused on a different work setting, each illustrates how the normative definitions of the work group enable employees to redefine deviant acts that they commit while at work.

In this research, I applied the neutralization concept to a sample of nurses. Specifically, I hypothesized that certain types of hospital property, such as supplies and some forms of medicines, would be afforded uncertain ownership status. At the same time, "harder" drugs such as narcotics should clearly be defined as hospital property and should not be taken. Thus, one would expect that, in addition to offering individual nurses the motives and techniques needed to steal drugs and supplies from the hospital, the nursing work group will also offer the individual an arsenal of justifications that can be used to make these behaviors acceptable in the light of societal or administrative norms.

Results

Theft of General Supplies

All of the nurses claimed to have seen other nurses stealing supplies from hospital stock, and 23 admitted to personal involvements in these activities. In fact, most of the nurses laughed when asked if they had ever seen nurses stealing supplies. When discussing the topic of supply theft, it was customary for the nurses to offer a long and diverse list of popular theft items.

All of the nurses implied that supply theft was accepted behavior among the nursing work group. This is evidenced by the fact that most nurses estimated that 100 percent of the nursing staff reported involvements in supply theft. Only 4 nurses estimated that fewer than 50 percent of the nursing staff were involved in supply theft.

The nurses often made statements that clearly illustrated the group acceptance of supply theft. This can be seen in the following exchange that took place between the interviewer and a 37-year-old intensive care unit nurse:

> "Do they try to hide it [supply theft] from colleagues?"
>
> "No, not at all."
>
> "So it is accepted behavior?"
>
> "Yes, it kind of bothers me, but. . . ."

Despite this group acceptance of supply theft, the nurses were very cognizant of the fact that their behaviors were against the law as well as the norms established by hospital policy. For example, one 28-year-old nurse offered the following normative definition of supply theft: "Probably if you get deep down to it, it is probably morally wrong because it is not yours. But it doesn't bother me in the least. Not in the least! Isn't that awful?" Another nurse, this one a 26-year-old ICU nurse had this to say about the normative definition of supply theft:

> I steal scrubs. I have a million pairs at home. I cut them off and make shorts. I realize it is a debt but you don't think about it. You think that they won't miss it

but you know they do. I mean the scrub loss is $11,000 a month. They take a beating.

Faced with a conflict between the negative societal-administrative definition and a positive work group definition, nurses chose to neutralize the negative definition and enhance the favorable work group definition through the use of work group rationalizations. The most common rationalization justified supply theft as a fringe benefit that goes along with the job. For example, a 47-year-old ICU step-down (an intermediate care unit) nurse claimed that her supply theft was "a way of supplementing one's income." In full, 88 percent of the nurses justified their own, and their observed, theft of general supplies in this manner. This trend is obvious in the statement made by another 28-year-old ICU nurse. When asked if she saw supply theft as a fringe benefit, she said, "Yeah, it's kind of a compensation. . . . I really don't think about it. You just take it. It is no big deal."

It is interesting to note that the scope of this neutralization of supply theft was tempered by work group limitations. Not all forms of supply theft were positively defined by the work group. Only theft in moderation was rationalized. This is obvious in the quote offered by a 33-year-old ICU step-down unit nurse. She said, "If they were taking garbage bags full, people would be upset, but everyone takes something once in a while. It is a kind of fringe benefit for us."

Theft of Over-the-Counter Medicines

A similar trend emerged regarding the theft of over-the-counter medicines. Twenty-one of the nurses admitted that they had themselves stolen certain medicines, usually Tylenol, from hospital stock. Once again, the theft appeared to be quite extensive. For example, when asked to clarify her claim that someone steals Tylenol every day on her unit, a 26-year-old ICU nurse said, "Yeah, if you have a headache, you go take one [Tylenol] out of the drawer."

It was also not uncommon for nurses to say that they had engaged in over-the-counter drug theft on a regular basis. For instance, when asked how many times he had engaged in such thefts, a 48-year-old ICU nurse replied, "I don't know. I have been a nurse for 22 years and this job has given me a lot of headaches. So I guess I couldn't even give you a number." As was the case with supply theft, the theft of over-the-counter drugs was rationalized by work group definitions. This point is illustrated in the following exchange, which occurred with a 25-year-old ICU step-down nurse:

"Is drug theft looked down on by nurses?"

"Probably drugs but not stuff like Tylenol."

"Have you ever taken over-the-counter meds?"

"Oh yeah, things like Tylenol or Motrin."

"How did you get them?"

"I just walk up to the drawer and take them."

"So people see you and they don't say anything?"

"That's right."

Once again, nurses had to justify the theft of over-the-counter drugs as it was known to be against hospital regulations. These rationalizations were also usually based on the fringe benefit rationalization and were tempered by the amount taken and the frequency with which it occurred.

Theft of Nonnarcotic Medicines

A slightly different pattern arose, however, concerning the theft of medicines other than simple pain and headache remedies. In this case, nonnarcotic drugs such as Darvoset N100, a mild analgesic, or tranquilizers such as Xanax or Ativan were frequently mentioned. Although these drugs do require a doctor's prescription, they are dispensed in the same way as other nonnarcotic medicines, through the unit dose system. Under this system, each patient is given his or her daily allotment of these medicines, and they are kept in each patient's room. A nurse must chart the administration of these medicines, but a key is not required to gain access to them. The majority of the nurses explained that there is often an excess of these types of medicines left on the unit. This is sometimes due to over-prescribing by physicians or because the intended patient dies or is transferred before the medication is dispensed. In the latter case, what results is a lag period between when the hospital pharmacy workers realize that the patient is no longer receiving the medicines and when they quit sending them. During this time lag, these excess medicines are stockpiled, without supervision, at the nursing station.

In all, 15 nurses described eyewitness accounts in which nurses took advantage of these stockpiled nonnarcotic drugs by taking them. For example, a 26-year-old clinical coordinator of an ICU stated, "Today one of the nurses had a sore leg so she took some Darvoset out of her patient's drawer."

The misappropriation of these stockpiled nonnarcotic drugs appeared to be accepted behavior among the nurses. For example, one 23-year-old ICU step-down nurse said, "At 6:00 anything that is left in the drawers is free game because it should have been given throughout the day."

Evidence of nurses comparing the theft of these mild analgesics to over-the-counter drugs was offered by a 25-year-old nurse working in an ICU step-down unit. When asked if she had ever seen another nurse take medicines from the hospital, she replied "Yes, stuff like Valium, Tylenol, Motrin, or even Xanax." Further questioning of this nurse showed that she made no distinction between the severity of these thefts. She brushed off the Valium and Xanax as if they were Tylenol or Motrin. Another nurse, this one a 22-year-old ICU nurse, had this to say:

> "What do you think of nurses who take meds?"
>
> "I don't think it is right to take narcs."
>
> "Are you saying that you compare nonnarcs to taking supplies?"
>
> "Yeah."
>
> "Even stuff like the Ativan?"
>
> "I don't see anything wrong with taking Ativan as long as it isn't abused."

This attitude was echoed by other nurses. For example, one 47-year-old recovery room nurse said, "I don't consider a nonscheduled drug much worse than Band-Aids."

The general acceptance of nonnarcotic drug theft is underscored by the finding that, although 22 nurses reported having witnessed theft and or use of controlled substances, none reported these situations to superiors. It is relevant to note that 10 of these respondents indicated their estimates of theft incidents were likely conservative. Few of the nurses who had seen other nurses take drugs could offer what they felt were completely accurate estimates of how many different times they had seen such behavior. For instance, one female, 28-year-old step-down unit nurse explained,

> "Yes, nurses do it for their own use but they only take the stuff that isn't locked up. If it isn't locked up it is fair game. I don't know how many times I have seen it happen."

This inability to estimate the prevalence of theft of these mild analgesics and tranquilizers was also illustrated by a 26-year-old clinical coordinator of an ICU. When asked how many times she had seen these drugs taken, she said, "too many times to count."

All of the nurses explained that pharmacy policy disapproved of stockpiling nonnarcotic medicines. These nurses also understood that hospital regulations did not allow them to misappropriate or ingest these drugs. Still, they rationalized doing so. These rationalizations usually resembled Horning's (1970) notion of property of uncertain ownership. He found that over time, the factory workers in his study had come to collectively redefine some forms of company property as having an uncertain ownership status and thus normatively accepted the removal of these materials for personal use. The idea was that the materials were no longer "really" the property of the company. In the present case of the stockpiled drugs, the nurses engaged in a similar process. In short, because there were no direct controls on these accumulated drugs, the work group saw them as fair game.

Theft of Narcotic Medicines

Each of the 25 nurses made a clear distinction between the theft of unit dose drugs, which are all controlled substances, and the narcotic drugs that are kept under constant lock and key. Although nurses routinely used terminology such as "no big deal" to describe the use or theft of medicines such as Darvoset N100, no such definition was afforded to the locked-down narcotics. Here, the work group norms were clearly in line with the societal and administrative definitions. When asked about narcotic drug theft, one 33-year-old ICU step-down nurse replied,

> I think it is terrible. Narcotics you mean? Yeah, I think it is terrible. They are highly addictive and it ends up being a problem. It turns into a vicious circle and something bad happens.

When asked how narcotic drug theft was viewed among nurses, a 34-year-old ICU nurse said, "I don't know of anyone who would approve of it." This trend was seen throughout the interviews. For example, a 26-year-old operating room nurse said that the theft of narcotics is viewed poorly.

> It is very bad. For instance, one day I was doing the count and came up short on the p.o. [prescribed orally] Tylenol 3's or something. I was really nervous that someone was gonna accuse me of stealing. I looked for them for like an hour.

A negative work group definition of narcotic drug theft translated into minimal reported incidents of theft. Only one nurse admitted to stealing narcotics, and this was an isolated case that had occurred many years earlier. Furthermore, there were only four eyewitness reports of narcotics theft. Although these nurses brushed off the other forms of theft discussed earlier, they claimed that they would report nurses who stole narcotics. This once again illustrates the strong work group controls placed on employee theft among nurses. For example, one 27-year-old oncology nurse said, "it depends on what they are taking. If it is something minor then okay, but if it is something like a narc, I would report them."

A 48-year-old ICU nurse amplified this point about the theft of narcotics. He said, "I don't put up with that. If I saw it, I would have no problem busting them and turning them in."

Procedural Shortcuts

As one can see, there is a clear distinction that can be made between the work group definitions that apply to the theft of narcotics as opposed to other forms of nursing theft (i.e., other forms of medication and supplies). The nurses claim that the former is not tolerated, whereas the latter appears to be condoned if done in moderation. However, these nurses use several procedural activities that increase the opportunity for nurses to steal narcotics. These shortcut procedures in the dispensing and monitoring systems are themselves violations of the rules of governing narcotic medicines. Federal regulations, namely the Controlled Substance Act of 1970, mandate strict regulations on drugs that are categorized as narcotics. For example, all of these drugs must be kept in a secure room or cart. The keys to these facilities are to be kept in the possession of designated charge nurses. When a patient requires a narcotic, the administering nurse must have the charge nurse open the cart for him or her. Also, each dosage unit must be signed out by the administering nurse before it can be given to the patient. Finally, all narcotics in a unit must be counted by two separate nurses at the end of each 8- or 12-hr. shift to verify that all of the narcotics are accounted for. If there is a discrepancy in the count, a lengthy set of administrative forms must be filled out and delivered immediately to the pharmacy. In this event, an official investigation involving security and pharmacy officials must take place.

All of these mandated procedures translate into added time and energy that the nurses must expend. Nurses view these procedures as laborious and distrusting of nurses. As a result, they have modified these procedures, using a number of shortcuts. The nurses rationalize deviant short-cutting strategies as serving to increase the quality of patient care. Work group norms accept the shortcuts, and they appeared to be routine. No nurse claimed to have a charge nurse (the nurse who monitors access to narcotics) who limited the access to narcotic keys. Instead, the keys to the narcotic cart were routinely left on or in the cart itself, a clear violation of the rules. A 26-year-old ICU nurse described this procedural shortcut as follows:

> There is a med cart that is supposed to be locked but the keys are on top. . . . The only time these are locked is when JCAH [Joint Commission on the Accreditation of Healthcare Organizations] comes once a year.

Similarly, a 28-year-old ICU nurse said:

> With the narc box, it is locked but the keys are usually hanging in the lock so anyone that walks by can turn that key and open it. . . . That is unless JCAH is coming. Then, we have to lock everything up and carry the keys but that is only for 1 or 2 days a year.

The nurses have also adapted a modified set of procedures that govern how drug counts are conducted. For example, they do not always adhere to the requirement that states that two nurses must conduct drug counts. Instead, one nurse often conducts the count, and a colleague simply signs the form. In these cases, it is assumed that the initial nurse conducted an accurate count. All 25 nurses described this type of modification in the interviews. A 27-year-old oncology nurse said, "Sometimes one nurse will count and the other will sign, or sometimes two do it together."

These nurses have also adapted a work group strategy for dealing with drug count discrepancies. Nurses are aware of the labor involved in filing drug discrepancy forms. They are also aware of the fact that filing these forms brings them and the work group under suspicion. As an alternative to the mandated paperwork, nurses described a more relaxed way of accounting for missing drugs that has evolved. In this accommodation, a patient who was prescribed the missing medication is simply charged with the missing dose. In all, 21 nurses either admitted to taking part in this mischarting of medicines or claimed to have seen it done by other nurses. For example, one 22-year-old ICU nurse described this mischarting as follows: "Usually you just find someone [a patient] that is using a lot and sign it out to them."

Another nurse, this one a 34-year-old ICU nurse, offered the following description of how mischarting takes place:

> Well a lot of the times, people forget [to sign out a drug] so we kind of go back and make it up as we go [laughing]. There have been times where you have been short and you say . . . I am sure that they used it on this person.

These accounts of nurses' mischarting were widespread and varied in their scope and complexity. For example, a 26-year-old clinical coordinator of one of the medical ICUs described the following incident where the narcotic counts for her unit were not done for an entire weekend:

> This is a good one. I went to work yesterday morning after the weekend and they had not counted the narcs since Saturday. Here I am trying to count on Monday. There were like five things missing for every day . . . I was losing it. I was so pissed off at them. There were five Phentonols, five Ativans, the morphine were missing, the Versed [a type of drug; spelling phonetic] were bad. And then they had four codes over the weekend where all four patients died so there was no way for me to track who got what. So, I just signed them out to who I thought used them.

The systematic dismissal of drug theft as the result of nurses' mischarting of drug errors was rationaized by nurses in several ways. Usually, the nurses insisted that they did not suspect drug theft among their present group of colleagues. This rationalization seemed to rest firmly on the integrity of the nursing profession. Several nurses suggested that they were certain they would know if a fellow nurse was using drugs and mischarting to acquire them. Most assumed that they were sufficiently adept to identify drug users among coworkers. For example, one 48-year-old ICU nurse said, "I think I could tell if someone was doing that [using drugs at work]."

In each case in which a nurse described the mischarting procedure, probes were used to see what the nurses thought of this behavior. None of the nurses originally thought that the missing drugs had been stolen. When I presented this possibility to the respondents, they unequivocally ruled it out.

For example, one 47-year-old female recovery room nurse had this to say when asked if mischarting might serve as a coverup for drug theft:

> I never thought of it that way. We deal in so many units that, when you are short one dosage unit, you just assume that someone forgot to chart it.

After the interview, this nurse suggested that this type of trusting attitude is customary in the nursing profession. She thought that it might be my criminological background that led me to think so suspiciously of what she called "an obviously honest mistake." In his case, an "honest mistake" serves to justify both the missing drug and the mischarting.

Discussion

There are clearly two types of normative definitions functioning in the nurses' work environment: formally stated hospital policies and informal work group mores. Both of these forces serve as guides for nurses' behavior. However, these two sets of definitions are sometimes at odds with one another. For example, in the case of supply theft, over-the-counter medicine theft, or nonnarcotic drug theft, nurses are presented with two very different definitions of acceptable behavior. The administrative policies establish these behaviors as theft that is not permitted. At the same time, the work group socializes its members to tolerate and even condone such behavior as nontheft. Faced with this predicament, nurses appear more inclined to choose the latter alternative. It appears that the strength and persistence of these work group norms increase the probability that nurses will engage in these forms of behavior. This is evidenced by the fact that, for each of the above-mentioned forms of deviance (i.e., supply theft, over-the-counter drug theft, and nonnarcotic drug theft), nurses reported substantial knowledge of and involvement in these activities.

Nurses neutralize the administrative definitions and redefine the theft in a way that lessens inhibitions against the behaviors. These definitions favorable to theft take many forms. They are often determined by the nature and extent of the improprieties. The one commonality shared by all of these neutralizations is the fact that they originate from within the work group and are disseminated to the nurses through an informal socialization process. As a consequence, violations are widespread. This process is directly in line with the theoretical propositions of differential association and social learning theory.

These data illustrate situations in which administrative policies are in agreement with work group norms. The most obvious example revolves around narcotic drug theft. Here, the work group as well as the administrative policies present unfavorable definitions of such behavior. Not only does the work group not condone narcotic drug theft, but it was suggested that they will not tolerate it. If a nurse is thought to be stealing narcotics, he or she is not afforded the same protection as a nonnarcotics diverter would be. Similarly, the work group does not present the nurses with any viable rationalization or justification for narcotic drug theft. This situation appears to have a substantial effect on the prevalence of narcotic drug theft in this sample. Far fewer nurses offered eyewitness accounts or admitted to personal involvement in narcotic drug theft than they did with the other forms of employee theft. Violations of this type were uncommon.

The findings presented in this article lend support to the facilitating role that neutralizing definitions play in differential association and social learning theory. The accounts given by the nurses in this study portray on-the-job deviance as being closely linked to definitions favorable to the deviance. As expected theoretically, normative definitions appear to originate from various sources and are often in conflict with one another. Those definitions that receive strong work group support were more apt to prevail. When these informal work group norms allow nurses to justify theft on the job, it is likely to occur. These justifications may originally have developed following the commission of various forms of employee theft to change the normative perception of the behavior in question. However, once they become part of the work subculture, they seem to be incorporated into the occupational socialization process. Thus, new nurses appear to learn them before committing theft. This temporal ordering issue is also evidenced by the fact that nurses indicated that they will continue engaging in these various forms of employee deviance. This suggests that these normative definitions are being used as discriminant stimuli that serve to shape future behaviors.

The sources of the normative conflict between the nursing work group's and the hospital administration's definitions of proper behavior may well be traced to the overarching way in which nurses conceive of their work objective. As Hollinger and Clark (1983) observed in a study of hospital employees, nurses tend to see themselves as caregivers whose job is to help their patients at any cost. Within this self-conception, nurses are able to justify certain behaviors such as taking supplies as the patient is not harmed. Instead, it is the hospital, who they claim does not appreciate them, that incurs the loss. Similarly, when nurses condone over-the-counter or nonnarcotic drug theft, it is done under the premise that taking the drugs is done to improve the nurse's disposition. The thinking is that this allows them to better treat the patients (e.g., How can I treat a patient if I am stressed out or have a headache?). From this perspective, nurses' impairment actually enhances patient care. At the same time, taking narcotics does not fit into this paradigm as these drugs are thought to have an adverse effect on patient care. This pattern of nurses' behavior leads one to agree with Hollinger and Clark's notion that although many hospital employees enjoy their jobs from a care-giving perspective, they dislike the hospitals in which they must deliver this care. As such, the neutralizations used to justify and even condone nurses' deviance against the hosptial would seem to make a great deal of sense as they are done to benefit the patients.

This research has some obvious methodological limitations. At every step of the research process, one can see problems that could affect the generalizability of these conclusions. For example, the use of such a small, nonrandom sample immediately raises questions. Moreover, one must keep in mind that these interviews involved a small number of respondents in a limited number of settings. As such, it is conceivable that these nurses' behaviors and attitudes differ substantially from those of other nurses in different settings. Similarly, the nature of the interview instrument as well as the use of content analysis raises several questions about researcher objectivity and respondent reactivity.

However, these conclusions serve as a starting point from which one may begin to explain the nature and extent of nursing deviance. One possible explanation for nursing deviance lies within a social learning perspective. By drawing on the concept of normative definitions, as is presented in social learning theory, this research attempted to shed some light on the phenomenon of nursing deviance. Of course, this is only one approach, and the reader may readily devise plausible alternatives.

Questions for Thought and Discussion

1. Of all the crimes and workplace deviance illustrated in this study, which do you think is the most serious? Why?
2. How did the nurses justify or excuse their deviant and illegal activities?
3. Aside from the illegality, what are the dangers involved in mischarting?
4. What theory or theories of criminal behavior are illustrated in this research?

References

Akers, Ronald L. 1985. *Deviant Behavior: A Social Learning Approach.* Belmont, CA: Wadsworth.

American Nurses Association. 1984. *ANA Cabinet on Nursing Practice: Statement on Scope for Addiction Nursing Practice.* Kansas City, MO: Author.

Benson, Michael L. 1985. "Denying the Guilty Mind: Accounting for Involvement in a White Collar Crime." *Criminology* 23:583–607.

Cressey, Donald R. 1953. *Other People's Money.* Glencoe, IL: Free Press.

Dalton, Melville. 1959. *Men Who Manage.* New York: Wiley.

Ditton, Jason. 1977. *Part-Time Crime: An Ethnography of Fiddling and Pilferage.* New York: Macmillan Press.

Geis, Gilbert. 1967. "The Heavy Electrical Equipment Antitrust Cases of 1961." Pp. 139–151 in *Criminal Behavior Systems: A Typology,* edited by M. B. Clinard and R. Quinney. New York: Holt, Rinehart and Winston.

Gouldner, Alvin. 1954. *Patterns of Industrial Bureaucracy.* New York: Free Press.

Hamlin, John E. 1988. "The Misplaced Role of Rational Choice in Neutralization Theory." *Criminology* 26:425–38.

Hollinger, Richard C. 1991. "Neutralizing in the Workplace: An Empirical Analysis of Property Theft and Production Deviance." *Deviant Behavior* 12:169–202.

Hollinger, Richard C., and John P. Clark. 1983. *Theft by Employees.* Lexington, MA: Lexington Books.

Horning, Donald. 1970. "Blue Collar Theft: Conceptions of Property, Attitudes Toward Pilfering, and Work Group Norms in a Modern Industrial Plant." Pp. 46–64 in *Crimes Against Bureaucracy,* edited by E. O. Smigel and H. L. Ross. New York: Van Nostrand Reinhold.

Mars, Gerald. 1982. *Cheats at Work: An Anthropology of Workplace Crime.* London: Allen and Unwin.

McCormick, William C., Ronald C. Hoover, and Joseph B. Murphy. 1986. "Drug Diversion From Hospitals Analyzed." *Security Management* 30:41–48.

Michigan Nurses Association. 1986. *Fact Sheet: Chemical Dependency of Nurses.* East Lansing, MI: Author.

Sieh, Edward W. 1987. "Garment Workers: Perceptions of Inequity and Employee Theft." *British Journal of Criminology* 27:174–190.

Sutherland, Edwin H. 1949. *White Collar Crime.* New York: Dryden.

Sutherland, Edwin H., and Donald R. Cressey. 1970. *Criminology,* 8th Edition. Philadelphia: J. B. Lippincott.

Sykes, Gresham M., and David Matza. 1957. "Techniques of Neutralization: A Theory of Delinquency." *American Sociological Review* 22:664–670.

Tathum, Ronald L. 1974. "Employee Views of Theft in Retailing." *Journal of Retailing* 50:49–55.

Section VI

Illegal Occupations

In the previous section we examined crimes committed by persons in the course of their legal occupations. Here we consider offenders whose occupations violate formal norms. The central activities of such work are illegal, yet they share many commonalities with legal occupations. Most of those who engage in illegal occupations have regular customers, suppliers, and a formal set of roles and activities that do not substantially differ from those of people who perform legal work. Drug dealing, operating an illegal gambling operation, fencing, prostitution, and engaging in confidence games all fall under the rubric of illegal work.

In the first selection in this section, Cromwell and Olson ("Fencing: Avenues for the Redistribution of Stolen Property") report on a study of the relationships between burglars and fences—receivers of stolen property. They found that while professional fences in the tradition of Klockars (1974) and Steffensmeier (1986) remain a significant outlet for the stolen goods of many thieves, there are also many other categories of receiver. These "nonprofessional" fences provide a wide and diverse market for stolen property, especially for thieves who do not have access to professional fences, such as juveniles, drug addicts (whom professional fences often do not trust) and others without a network of criminal associates. Many thieves resort to selling their "booty" to ordinary citizens on the street, in shopping-center parking lots, bars, and other places where people gather. They argue that markets for stolen goods provide the catalyst and continuing motivation for property and that more attention and further research should be focused on this relatively unstudied crime.

In the next selection ("The Second Step in Double Jeopardy: Appropriating the Labor of Female Street Hustlers"), Romenesko and Miller report on women who make their living from street-level prostitution. They draw parallels between the patriarchal structure of the world of prostitution and that which exists in the noncriminal world. The authors report the existence of a street institution known as a pseudo-family, comprised of the pimp and the women who work for him. Within this structure, women street hustlers attempt to obtain status, but working for men in a secondary role serves to further oppress women socially and economically, making it more difficult for them to give up a life of drugs and crime. The pseudo-family is explicitly organized to exploit the female members, who relinquish control of their resources for the affection and recognition of their "man" and the material goods necessary for survival.

Patricia Adler provides a rare glimpse into a community of high-level drug dealers in "Dealing Careers." In this classic study, Adler examines recruitment into drug smuggling and dealing, learning the trade, upward mobility, aging in the career, career shifts, and ultimately phasing out (retirement). This chapter, perhaps more than others, draws a parallel between the "occupation" of drug smuggler/dealer and legitimate occupations.

Gambling is one of the most ubiquitous of illegal occupations. In "Managing the Action: Sports Bookmakers as Entrepreneurs," Coontz focuses on the social, organizational, and occupational features of bookmaking. Her analysis is based on interviews with 47 sports bookmakers in the Rust Belt region of middle America. Coontz argues that despite the "myth" of organized crime involvement in bookmaking, her study found bookmakers to be mostly independent entrepreneurs without ties to larger crime organizations (at least in Pittsburgh).

These studies illustrate that while the participants are involved in illegal activities, they tend to see themselves as "businessmen" with a product or a service for sale to the public. They have similar goals and are faced with many of the same problems and goals prevalent in legitimate enterprises.

References

Steffensmeier, D. 1986. *The Fence: In the Shadow of Two Worlds*. Totowa, NJ.: Rowman and Littlefield.

Klockars, C. B. 1974. *The Professional Fence*. New York: Macmillan. ✦

Chapter 19
Fencing

Avenues for the Redistribution of Stolen Property

Paul Cromwell
James N. Olson

This chapter is based on a study of active burglars in Texas. The authors interviewed 30 active burglars over an 18-month period. The subjects were interviewed on at least three occasions regarding their motivations to commit burglary, their target selection processes and the strategies they utilized to convert their stolen good to cash. In this chapter, the authors explore the fencing of stolen property from the perspectives of the thieves and those who purchase their goods—the fences. They found that markets for stolen goods provide the catalyst and continuing motivation for property. Some young burglars find that they cannot sell their stolen goods successfully and consequently soon give up stealing. However, burglars who are able to convert their goods to cash at the first attempt may continue to repeat this rewarding behavior. They also noted that receivers of stolen property vary widely in the extent of their fencing activities and the level of professionalism involved. A typology of fences is developed.

Our study of burglary led us to consider the important role of the fence—the market for the burglar's stolen goods. If burglary is the supply side of stolen property, then fencing is the demand side. Without a reliable outlet for stolen goods, burglary would have no point. Felson (1998, 38) states that the significance of the fence for producing more crime cannot be overstated. Without the opportunity to sell stolen goods, the thief is limited to stealing money only, or to very inefficient ways of selling on their own. We sought, therefore, to ascertain the dynamics of the thief–fence relationship; to determine the strategies employed by receivers of stolen property; and, how these strategies are implemented and understood by the participants in this activity.

The role of the fence in initiating and sustaining property crime has been recognized for centuries. F. L. Attenborough (1922), in *The Laws of the Earliest English Kings,* refers to a law from 690 A.D., which prohibited "harboring stolen cattle." However, as Steffensmeier (1986) reports, until 1691, under common law, receiving stolen goods was only a misdemeanor. He stated, "While there was no strict law against receiving stolen property prior to the seventeenth century, it was recognized that the activity went on and that it was as bad as theft, which it may actually cause" (63). Finally, in 1691 a statute (Act 3 and 4, William and Mary, c.9.s.4) made the fence an accessory after the fact and liable for severe corporal punishment or transportation. However, prosecution of the receiver was not possible unless the thief was first apprehended and convicted. In 1827, an act of Parliament made provision for an independent trial for the fence whether or not the thief was arrested (Act 7 and 8, Geo. IV c.29).

Perhaps the most notorious fence in criminal justice history was an Englishman, Jonathon Wild. McDonald (1980) described Wild as a notorious leader of a London criminal band of pickpockets, burglars, and other thieves. He set himself up as a "recoverer of stolen property," advertising in newspapers and pamphlets offering rewards for the return of stolen property with no questions asked. He bought the stolen goods and then conveyed them back to their original owners for a percent of their value. Thieves flocked to his "lost property office" with their stolen goods. Those items that were not claimed by their rightful owners, he altered so that they could not be identified and then sold them. Wild was so successful in this fencing venture that he even bought a ship to carry his plunder to Holland and other European ports. Thieves who did not cooperate with Wild were frequently turned in for the reward. It is estimated that he "captured" over 100 thieves during his 15-year career. In fact, as a well-known "thief taker" he was consulted by the Privy Council on occasion for his advice on crime control. However, becoming a public figure is something that no criminal should aspire to, for his high profile eventually brought him down. A notorious criminal who had been captured by Wild escaped from prison and publicly testified to Wild's activities. Soon other witnesses began to appear and Wild's activities resulted in his arrest and conviction. He was hanged in 1725 (McDonald 1980).

State of Knowledge About Fences and Fencing

Despite the fence's acknowledged contribution to crime, there has been a paucity of systematic study of this important category of offender. Due to the clandestine nature of the fence's activities, it is not surprising that so little research has been done. The professional fence has attracted the attention of some researchers, policy makers, and law enforcers (Blakely and Goldsmith 1976; Klockars 1974; . . . Steffensmeier 1986; Walsh 1977; Maguire 1982). Taken as a whole, although these studies provide a good overview of the activities of the professional fence, they ignore almost completely other categories of receivers. However, the nonprofessional receiver has not been overlooked completely. Hall (1952) included part-time receivers in his typology of fences. He identified the "lay receiver," who buys for personal consumption, and the "occasional receiver," who purchases for resale, but only infrequently. Stuart Henry (1978), who studied property crimes committed by ordinary people in legitimate jobs, concluded that receiving stolen property is not exclusively the province of professional criminals, but is an "everyday feature of ordinary people's lives." He states:

> The artificial distinction between "honest" and "dishonest" masks the fact that the hidden economy is the on-the-side, illegal activity of "honest" people who have legitimate jobs and who would never admit to being dishonest. (12)

Henry found that many otherwise legitimate businessmen purchased stolen property when such purchases could be passed on to their customers at a profit.

Cromwell and McElrath (1994) surveyed 739 randomly selected adults in a southwestern city. Respondents were asked if they had ever been offered stolen property for sale, if they had bought stolen property, and if they had friends or neighbors who had bought stolen goods. Thirty-six percent reported having been offered stolen goods. Thirteen percent had knowingly bought stolen goods and 39 percent reported that friends had bought stolen items. They reported that opportunity to purchase stolen goods and the motivation to buy them is related to a person's age, gender, ethnicity, and income. They stated:

> Routine activities theory predicts that buyers and sellers of stolen property must converge in time and space before an illegal transaction can occur. This convergence is facilitated when the lifestyles of buyers and sellers bring them together. . . . Younger persons and males were much more likely than older persons and females to be offered stolen goods for sale. These groups are also more likely to engage in "high risk" activities which might bring them into physical proximity with sellers of stolen goods. (306)

A recent British study, The British Crime Survey (BCS), revealed that a large number of persons are offered stolen property by thieves. Eleven percent of respondents said that they had been offered stolen property in the previous year. A further 11 percent admitted that they had bought stolen goods in the past five years, while 70 percent thought that at least some of their friends and neighbors had purchased stolen goods for use in their home (Sutton, 1998). Further, the Youth Lifestyle Survey, also conducted in England, found that 49 percent of youths aged 14 to 25 years who admitted offending in the last year, admitted that they had bought or sold stolen property in that period (Graham and Bowling 1995).

There is little reliable and valid information regarding the extent of the fencing activities among nonprofessional receivers of stolen property, or the degree to which these amateur fences contribute to the initiation and continuing support of property crime. Some earlier studies concluded that thieves are unable to deal directly with the consuming public and must therefore operate through middlemen who have the financial resources to purchase stolen goods and the contacts to help in their redistribution (Blakely and Goldsmith 1976, 1515). Indeed, this is true in large-scale theft where a thief must dispose of a truckload of television sets or a collection of fine jewelry. Most property crime, however, involves smaller quantities of stolen goods, of lesser value. Televisions, computers, CD players, car radios, most jewelry, handguns, VCRs, microwave ovens—the items that constitute the loot of the average burglar or shoplifter—may be redistributed without the assistance of a professional fence. The thief may sell many of these items directly to the ultimate consumer, to individuals who know or suspect that the items they buy are stolen property.

Some items may be traded for drugs, or sold to part-time receivers—those whose primary business activity is something other than buying and selling stolen property. Other stolen merchandise may be sold in pawn shops, flea markets, and garage sales to consumers who do not know or suspect that it was stolen.

We found that many burglars sought alternative outlets for their stolen goods. They reported selling their stolen items to ordinary citizens in bars, stores, parking lots, and even door-to-door. Others had regular customers for certain types of goods, and still others sold to otherwise legitimate businesses (bars, truck stops, etc.) who were known to be open to an opportunity to buy stolen items.

In order to understand how burglars and other thieves converted stolen property to cash, we interviewed both thieves and those who bought from them. We analyzed the thief's perspective by observations and interviews with active burglars and shoplifters, and through analysis of statements given to the police by arrested burglars and shoplifters. We obtained the receiver's outlook through interviews with professional and nonprofessional fences. We believe that amateur receivers who purchase stolen property do so primarily for personal consumption.

Interviews With Burglars

Burglar subjects were asked to describe (1) the process of locating and selecting a buyer for property they stole; (2) how items obtained in burglaries are sold or bartered; (3) the extent to which the fence determines the goods to be stolen; (4) the extent to which receivers provide aid and strategy to thieves in selecting targets; (5) the decision-making processes that determine what items are offered to which receivers; (6) the prices expected and paid for certain items; and (7) the extent, if any, to which fences specialize in one type or class of merchandise.

Interviews With Fences and Other Receivers

During the course of this study our burglar informants introduced us to many of their regular receivers. Because we had been vouched for by burglars whom they knew and trusted, we had little trouble in obtaining their consent to be interviewed. We approached eight fences in this manner and six of them agreed to be interviewed. Four of them were interviewed extensively over several days or weeks. Interviews with two others were concluded in a session lasting an hour or two. One, a professional fence, allowed us to observe his activities from the back room of a small liquor store, which was a front for his fencing activities.

We also interviewed 19 persons who had purchased stolen property directly from a thief. These subjects were students in our classes, friends and acquaintances, or friends of friends who heard about the study and agreed to talk to us about their experiences. Some of these individuals were one-time purchasers only. Others, however, were regular customers of a thief or thieves.

These interviews—with thieves, fences, and others who knowingly bought stolen property—were subjected to qualitative analysis wherein we derived patterns and constructed typologies from the extensive descriptions.

Interviews With Professional Burglars and Fences

Professional burglars must have reliable outlets for their stolen merchandise. Most sell their goods to one or more professional fences. Dealing directly with the consumer is too irregular and an uncertain way of doing business. Other burglars, however, have limited access to the professional fence. Novice burglars, juveniles, and drug addicts often find it hard to establish regular business relationships with fences. Novices and juvenile burglars do not often steal "quality" merchandise and have not been "tested" regarding their trustworthiness. Drug addicts have a similar handicap in marketing their goods. They are considered unreliable and untrustworthy because of their drug habits. While several addict-burglars reported that they occasionally sold their stolen merchandise to a professional fence, most had to seek less rewarding and more risky alternative channels for their goods. Many resorted regularly to direct sales to the consuming public. One young burglar, who regularly sold his stolen goods directly to consumers, said:

> I hear about somebody who want a TV or a VCR. I ask 'em how much they want to pay, and then I go get them one. If I already got some stuff, I ask around if anybody want to buy it.

A heroin addict burglar reported:

> I sell my stuff to [a local fence, name deleted] when I can. Sometimes he buys stuff from me. Most of the time he don't. He don't trust addicts.

Another informant told the interviewer that he had regular customers for his merchandise. He described his "self-fencing" in the following manner:

> There is this lady who buys big dresses—like bigger than size 16. She pays good too. Another lady will buy jewelry and stuff if I have it. I know about 10 people who buy meat. Whatever is on the price tag, they give me half-price. There is even a policeman—he used to be a policeman—he buys guns if I get one.

Most of the burglars interviewed would have preferred to sell their goods to a fence. They believed the fence to be a more reliable and less risky market. However, of the 30 informants in the study, only seven (23 percent) reported that they could absolutely depend on the professional fences in the community to take their goods. Others reported only occasional business dealings with professional fences. The following statement was typical:

> If I get guns. Not junk—like Saturday-night specials—stuff like Smith and Wessons—I can sell to the fences. I sold some big diamond rings and a Rolex to [local fence, name deleted] last year. They don't buy TVs and VCRs though.

Professional fences reported a strong aversion to doing business with drug addicts and juveniles. However, one fence, while expressing his contempt for drug addicts, bought stolen items from several obvious drug users while we were observing. He explained that, "So many thieves these days are addicts that you got to do a little business with them or you go broke." Another fence, more adamant in his refusal to do business with drug addicts, posted a sign over his cash register. It stated, "NO ADDICTS."

The fences reported that amateurs, drug users, "kids," and other "flakes" could not be trusted. They "snitch" and turn in their buyers when arrested. Professional thieves do not so readily "give up" their meal tickets—their market for stolen goods. Several reported that they would give up their co-offenders before their fence. One expressed his attitude as follows:

> Shit! Thieves are easy to find. I can get somebody to help me do a crime anywhere. Fences—they harder to replace. You turn in [local fences] and nobody gonna do no business with you after that.

Interviews With Nonprofessional Receivers

We also interviewed 19 nonprofessional receivers. These were persons who had bought stolen items for personal consumption and/or resale, but who did not depend upon fencing for all or most of their livelihood. Some had bought stolen property only once or twice. Others were regular consumers of stolen goods. One of these fence/consumers, a college professor who had been buying clothing for himself and his family from a group of burglars and shoplifters for over 20 years, described his activities as follows:

> I go to [department store] and pick out what I want, and tell [thief]. He brings it around in a few days. I pay one-third of the price tag. . . . I know this guy. He's a pot head. He gets speakers and CD players, and all kind of stuff like that. I've bought stuff from him a lot.

A homemaker in a low-income neighborhood explained how she became a customer of a shoplifter:

> My friend said she bought meat from this drug addict. She said she could get me some meat at half-price. First, I bought some steaks for half-price. Now he comes by my house every payday and we get all our meat from him. Other stuff too, sometimes.

More than one-half (n = 11) of the nonprofessional receivers we interviewed own or are employed by legitimate businesses, and occasionally buy stolen property at their place of business, primarily for resale. But, unlike the professional fence, they do not rely on buying and selling stolen property as their principal means of livelihood. To them, fencing is a part-time enterprise, secondary to, but usually associated with, their primary business activity. One of these part-time receivers justified his regular purchases from a thief, saying:

> It's not like you have anything to do with the guy stealing the stuff. He has already stole it. If I didn't buy it someone else would. I just take advantage of a good deal when I can. It's good business.

Another explained, saying:

> I don't even know for sure the stuff is hot. All I know is I can buy brand new tires for

> 20 bucks apiece. The last ones I got from him were Michelins . . . I'm going to turn that down?

A dry-cleaner whose sideline was buying and selling stolen men's suits from shoplifters reported:

> I can put them in a bag and run them in with my regular cleaning. I don't make a big profit. Some weeks I don't buy anything. Mostly I sell to some friends and family. It helps out when business is slow.

Analysis of Arrest Reports

We analyzed 190 statements (confessions) given to police by arrested burglars in the study jurisdiction for one year, in which the burglars told police where and how they had disposed of the stolen property. The alleged receiver(s) of the stolen property were noted and classified as either a professional fence, drug-dealer, part-time receiver, ordinary citizen, etc., through information derived as follows: that contained in the police report; with the help of knowledgeable police detectives; with the assistance of thief "informants"; or, in some cases, through our own knowledge of the criminal community. Other information in the police report which related to the receiver (the thief's reason for choosing a particular receiver or class of receiver, the amount paid for the items, etc.) was also analyzed.The analysis revealed that only 21 percent of the stolen property was sold to professional fences. More than half (56.4 percent) was sold to nonprofessional receivers, including drug dealers. Only 12.1 percent was sold to pawn shops. The remaining 10.5 percent was reported to have been kept by the thief for personal consumption, thrown away, given away, or recovered by police before redistribution. The following statements are representative:

> We took the microwave to [address deleted] and we sold it to an elderly Mexican lady for $30.

> I traded this stuff [cartons of cigarettes] to a man named Mario on the south side for heroin.

> The place where we took the guns was a house on [street name deleted] in [town]. A man named [name deleted] lives there. He is in a motorcycle gang named the Outlaws. They buy guns.

> Then I went back to the 7-Eleven and sold the VCR to [a customer in the parking lot].

> I went in [local tavern] and asked if anyone wanted to buy some cigarettes. Three or four people asked me how much. All I had was Salems and they wanted Marlboros. The bartender said he'd take 'em and sell them to some guy he knows smokes Salems.

> I sold the disc player and the VCR to [name deleted] at [name deleted] liquor store.

> About two weeks ago I met a man named [name deleted]. I met him through the wife of a friend of mine. She told me that [name deleted] might be willing to buy some stolen TVs I had from a burglary a few days before. I took the TVs over there and we plugged them in to see if they worked, and they did and he gave me $50 each for them.

Why Buy Stolen Property?

Buying stolen property involves many different motives. It represents a means of livelihood for some people—individuals who earn all or a significant proportion of their income from fencing. For others, as Steffensmeier (1986) suggests, "fencing they do more or less helps keep them afloat, get over the hump in their legitimate business, or gives them a little extra pocket money" (118). For many others, buying (and occasionally selling) stolen property is a means of economic adaptation. Henry (1978) and Smith (1987) refer to this activity as constituting an "informal economy" or "hidden economy." Participation means more than stretching the dollar. It may, as Gaughan and Ferman (1987) suggest, be a means of economic survival. They write:

> A number of case studies have shown that low-income communities rely on informal economic resources. The importance of hustling in the black ghetto, the persistence of tight kinship networks in working-class urban communities, and the increasing visibility of street peddlers and entertainers testify to this. (23)

Several informants told us that they could not survive [economically] without "hustling." One reported:

> I buy my baby's clothes from this booster [shoplifter]. He sells lots of stuff—even deodorant, aspirin, and medicine. I get cigarettes from another thief. My mother gets all her meat from a booster.

A housewife/informant reported that she occasionally bought from a burglar of her acquaintance and then resold some of the various items. She stated that the income from this source allowed her to stay at home with her children rather than having to seek outside employment.

While for some, buying and/or selling stolen property was a purely economic activity, we were unable to differentiate subjective motivations from economic motivations in many transactions. Psychosocial dynamics were often inextricably bound with economic motives. Some informants reported that they simply could not resist a bargain. Both thieves and receivers reported that "getting a good deal" was an important motivation for the buyer of stolen goods. Some reported buying items for which they had no immediate use, because the "price was right" or that they liked "beating the system." For still others, the occasional purchase of stolen property provided excitement in an otherwise pedestrian existence. One lawyer, for instance, asserted that he bought stolen property not just because he wanted certain items or for the money he might make reselling the items, but also for the "insider feeling" he got through these associations (also see Shover 1971, 153). Another "amateur" receiver reported that she was a member of a group of office workers who bought clothing from several shoplifters who "made the rounds" in various offices and businesses in the area. The women frequently placed orders for items of clothing and paid a prearranged price for the items when the shoplifter returned with the goods. Our informant revealed that the items they purchased were often bought as gifts for friends and relatives. She described a sort of "party atmosphere" around the office on the day the shoplifter was due to arrive with the goods they had ordered days before. As described by our informant, the transaction appeared to be as much social as economic in nature.

One theme that appeared to characterize nonprofessional receivers was the tendency to neutralize or rationalize their involvement in the purchase of stolen property. Almost all of those interviewed disassociated themselves from the theft, and by extension, the victim(s). Many rationalized that "It was already stolen. If I didn't buy it, someone would." They appeared to view the purchase of stolen property as victimless crime, if crime at all. Many neutralized their purchases as "Simply getting a bargain," or that the victim was an insurance company or a big business that "expects to lose a certain amount of merchandise," and makes up for the loss by increasing prices. Many reported that they did not know for sure that the items were stolen. One informant justified her purchase of a new VCR for $50, stating:

> Okay, it's maybe too good a deal to be completely honest. I asked him if it was stolen and he said, "No," and I took his word for it. That's all I can do. I don't want to know either.

Burglars and other thieves appeared to intuitively understand the psychology of selling stolen property directly to the consumer. Most reported that the items must not be explicitly represented as stolen, yet the buyer must believe them to be illegally obtained, and therefore a "good deal." One burglar/informant occasionally purchased cheap costume jewelry from a discount store and sold it as genuine on street corners to passersby. While he did not specifically represent the jewelry as stolen, he implied that it was. He reported that he usually made a good profit from this scam. He concluded:

> People are basically dishonest. They just don't like to admit it to themselves.

Shover's (1971) informant described the same phenomenon, stating: "It's the excitement of buying a piece of stolen goods. If you told them . . . that it was legitimate, they wouldn't buy it" (153).

Several burglars reported that they devised elaborate stories about the source of their stolen items. They explained that buyers like a good story, even if they don't really believe it. The cover story serves to relieve the buyer's anxiety over buying stolen property. An articulate burglar, a college graduate who turned to burglary after becoming addicted to heroin, analyzed the citizen-receivers he did business with, saying:

> People need to feel good about themselves. Most folks can't accept that they are as crooked as us [burglars]. You gotta help 'em out a little. Give 'em a story about the stuff. They know you're lying. Doesn't matter. They need it to keep you and them separated in their minds. You're the thief and they're the good guys.

A Typology of Receivers

It is impossible to characterize those who buy stolen property as a homogeneous category. Rather, they are a diverse group ranging from professional criminals with ties to organized crime (Klockars 1974; Steffensmeier

1986) to respected citizens such as schoolteachers, businesspersons and office workers who buy stolen goods for personal consumption (Henry 1978; Cromwell and McElrath 1994). They may be differentiated by: (1) the frequency with which they purchase stolen property; (2) the scale or volume of purchases of stolen property; (3) the purpose of purchase (for personal consumption or for resale); and (4) the level of commitment to purchasing stolen property. On the basis of these criteria, we distinguished six categories of receivers or fences:

1. Professional fences
2. Part-time fences
3. Professionals who trade services for stolen property
4. Neighborhood hustlers
5. Drug dealers who barter drugs for stolen property
6. Amateurs

Professional Fences

The professional fence is one whose principal enterprise is the purchase and redistribution of stolen property (Blakely and Goldsmith 1976; Chappell and Walsh 1974; Klockars 1974; Steffensmeier 1986). Professional receivers may transact for any stolen property for which there is a resale potential, or may specialize in stolen property that they can commingle with their legitimate stock or legitimate business (e.g., jewelry, dry cleaning, appliance sales or service). The professional receiver generally makes purchases directly from the thief and almost exclusively for resale. These receivers operate proactively, establishing a reliable and persistent flow of merchandise and buying regularly and on a large scale. As a result of this commitment, the professional receiver acquires "a reputation among law breakers, law enforcers and others in the criminal community" (Klockars 1974, 172). Although professional fences frequently operate legitimate businesses as fronts for their fencing activities, fencing is their primary occupation.

Part-Time Fences

The part-time fence functions in a somewhat nebulous domain between the true professional fence and other categories of receivers. The part-time fence is differentiated from the "professional" fence by frequency of purchase, volume of business, and degree of commitment to the fencing enterprise. Usually they do not buy as regularly as do professional fences, nor do they buy in volume. Further, part-time fences do not depend on fencing as their principal means of livelihood. We identified two general subtypes of part-time fences: (a) the passive receiver—who purchases stolen goods either for personal use, or for resale to an undifferentiated secondary consumer; and (b) the proactive receiver—who buys for resale only, and who may take an active role in the theft by placing orders for specific merchandise and providing offenders with information about potentially lucrative targets for burglary in the same way as professional fences.

Passive buyers are known (by thieves) to be buyers of stolen goods. They are "passive" because they do not actively solicit thieves as suppliers, nor do they contract to buy certain items from thieves. Their commitment as receivers is only at the level of being occasionally available to buy certain items of stolen property when offered by a thief. We identified several passive buyers during the study, including a truck stop operator who bought stolen tires and tools, the manager of a video rental business who bought stolen VCRs and videotapes, and a jewelry store proprietor who bought gold jewelry and silverware. Like all part-time receivers, the passive receiver does not buy in volume, and does not depend on fencing as a principal means of livelihood. They may integrate the stolen items into their regular stock, or may personally use the stolen goods—as with the case of an automobile mechanic who buys stolen tools. Like all part-time fences, they are not considered reliable outlets by thieves. They buy only when they have funds available, and/or when they need the particular item(s) offered by the thief. They usually do not have in mind a specific customer to whom they might resell the merchandise.

Proactive receivers mimic professional fences in many respects; however, they do not rely on buying and selling stolen goods for the major part of their livelihood. Their fencing activity is an on-the-side activity, part-time crime. The proactive buyer may contract with a thief for certain items for which he or she has a market. They may actually "take orders" from customers for certain items and arrange to purchase those items from a thief or thieves. Several burglar/shoplifter informants reported that they occasionally stole certain items "on order" from both professional fences and from part-time receivers.

The part-time receiver might even have greater access than the professional fence to strategic information regarding potential victims. Because they are otherwise legitimate citizens and businesspersons, they may be trusted by their colleagues and friends with information regarding their possessions, schedules, and security precautions.

We identified three proactive part-time fences. They were each otherwise legitimate businesspersons. One owned a jewelry store and the majority of his income was from the legitimate profits of the store. However, he occasionally contracted to buy certain specific items of jewelry from a professional thief. In many cases the jeweler had originally sold the items to the victim—only to steal them back. Another proactive part-time receiver, a gunsmith, gained extensive knowledge about a customer's gun collection through his profession, and used that information to provide inside information to a thief about security arrangements and particular items to be stolen. In another case, a pawnbroker provided a thief with descriptions of a customer's jewelry and the details of the customer's vacation plans, which the customer had revealed to him during a conversation.

Professionals Who Trade Services for Stolen Property

These fences are persons whose legitimate occupations place them in close association and interaction with thieves, as in the case of police officers, criminal defense attorneys, or bail bond agents. These receivers may operate from a different economic motivation than other receivers in that they stand to lose financially by refusing to participate in the redistribution of stolen property. This is particularly true for bail bond agents and criminal defense attorneys, who may provide legitimate professional services to property offenders who cannot pay for these services with anything but stolen property (or the proceeds from their illegal activities). Thieves constitute a significant market for the services that these receivers provide legitimately. To refuse such trade would eliminate these "customers" and would severely curtail earnings. For some, it is but a small step from accepting stolen property in return for professional services to placing orders for items to be stolen. During the study, a bail bond agent showed the interviewer a matched pair of stainless steel .357 magnum revolvers that had been stolen for him "on order" by a client for whom he had posted bond. He freely acknowledged accepting stolen property occasionally in exchange for his services, justifying his actions by saying, "When they are in a bind and don't have any money, I try to help out." Another individual, a criminal defense lawyer, was completely candid about his occasional purchases of stolen property from clients, enthusiastically describing items he had received in exchange for his legal services. He described how he had agreed to represent a burglar in a criminal case, telling him that he wanted a gold Rolex in exchange for his services. He proudly displayed the $12,000 watch to the interviewer and stated, "This is a special order."

Neighborhood Hustlers

The neighborhood hustler buys and sells stolen property as one of many hustles—small-time crime and confidence games—which provide a (usually) marginal living outside the conventional economic system. The neighborhood hustler may be a small-time fence, or he or she may be a middleman who brings thieves and customers together, earning a percentage of the sale for service rendered. The neighborhood hustler may also be a burglar who, on occasion, tries a hand at marketing stolen items for others. By definition, he or she is a small-time operator (Blakely and Goldsmith 1976). Most do not have a place of business, as such. Instead, they work out of the trunk of a car, or from their home. One such entrepreneur described himself as follows: "I'm a hustler. I can get you what you want. You got something you want to sell? Tell me. I know where to go and who to see. Ain't nothing happens over here in the Flats [the area of town where he lived] that I don't know about." According to others who knew him, although he was grossly exaggerating his abilities, he was an almost stereotypical neighborhood hustler. Few experienced thieves would trust him to buy directly or to sell their merchandise for them. Several informants described him as a snitch whose hustles included "giving up" the thieves with whom he did business. He was therefore limited to buying from juveniles, drug addicts, and novice thieves who could not market their goods in a more reliable manner.

For some, hustling involves both buying stolen goods for personal consumption and dealing in stolen merchandise. One such neighborhood hustler among our informants bought cigarettes, food, and clothing for personal use, and bought other items for resale. At the time of our interview, she had recently bought 20 rolls of roofing tar paper and 100 gallons of house paint from a thief and resold the items to a building contractor for a $75 profit. Her hustles also included some low-level street drug dealing, which occasionally involved bartering drugs for stolen goods, which she then resold.

Drug Dealers Who Barter Drugs for Stolen Property

Although not every drug dealer will barter for drugs, our interviews with thieves and fences suggest that many street-level dealers consider fencing and drug sales to be logically compatible enterprises. There are two apparent economic motivations for their willingness to barter: (1) bartering increases their drug sales, opening their market to those with stolen property but without cash; and (2) they can increase their profits by marketing the stolen property at a price well above that given in trade to the addict/thief. One such fence, in discussing the advantages of the arrangement, said: "Lot of people come to me 'cause I'll take trades. Won't take no junk or TVs or shit like that. If they got guns, jewelry—then we can do business."

Several of the burglar/drug users we interviewed regularly bartered stolen property for drugs. Rather than searching for an outlet for the goods, they went directly to the drug dealer and obtained drugs in exchange. Although they reported that they did not receive the best possible price for their merchandise from the drug dealer, the speed and efficiency of the operation made the arrangement attractive. One subject said, "This is like one-stop shopping."

Wright and Decker (1974) also found that some burglars in their study sold their stolen goods to drug dealers or traded them for drugs.

> Many of the tough inner-city neighborhoods of St. Louis have an informal economy that operates in part on the sale of stolen property. Local drug dealers often play a prominent role in this economy, both as buyers and sellers, because they have access to ready cash and good illicit connections to potential customers. (181)

One of their informants explained: "Most of the time I want to buy drugs, so I take them stuff to the drug man. Instead of giving me money—he don't want to give out money 'cause he's making money—so he'll trade you his merchandise for your merchandise" (182).

Amateurs

With the exception of the professional thieves in the sample (n = 5), all had sold their goods directly to consumers on one or more occasions. The least experienced, the juvenile and drug-using thieves, were most likely to sell directly to the consumer on a regular basis. We distinguished two general categories of amateur receivers: (1) strangers approached in public places; and (2) persons with whom the thief has developed a relationship and who buys more or less regularly, for personal consumption.

Approaching strangers in public places is risky behavior with a relatively low success rate. It is looked upon with contempt by almost all thieves, and practiced regularly only by those with no other outlets available for their merchandise. Juveniles and drug addicts are most likely to use this technique for disposing of their merchandise. While many thieves in our study expressed their disdain for selling stolen items in this manner, the analysis of confessions given to police by burglars and other thieves revealed that much of the stolen items of these thieves was sold in this manner. Furthermore, many of the nonprofessional receivers we interviewed reported that they had previously bought stolen items from thieves who approached them in a public place. This suggests that the practice may be more widespread than was indicated in the interviews with burglars.

Wright and Decker (1974) also found that a percentage of their burglar subjects approached strangers in public places offering their stolen goods for sale. Twelve of 90 offenders in their sample said they usually sold, at least in part, to strangers. One of their subjects reported: "Man, just like if I see you on the street I walk up and say, 'Hey, you want to buy a brand new 19-inch color TV?' You say, 'Yeah,' and give me $75. I'll plug it up for you" (189).

Our burglar informants expressed similar sentiments:

> I hang at the parking lot at [local chain food store] when I got something to sell. I go up to people that looks like they might buy something. Ask them if they wanna buy whatever I got.

> Don't go up to no rich-looking people or old people. Mostly young white dudes is interested. Course, ya gotta be careful cause cops is mostly like that too—young, white dudes.

A second category of amateur receivers includes those who have developed relationships with one or more thieves and buy stolen property with some regularity. Most buy primarily for personal consumption. Others occasionally resell the stolen property they buy. Several reported reselling their "hot" merchandise at garage sales or through flea markets. Two of the "amateurs" resold the merchandise to friends and coworkers. One amateur fence, a public schoolteacher, began her criminal career when she was approached by a student who offered her a "really good deal" on a microwave oven. She stated that she originally bought the oven to help the student, whose family was suffering financial problems. Afterward, the student began to offer her "bargains" regularly, and she became a frequent customer. Eventually she began to offer her colleagues the opportunity to "get in on a good deal," and even posted the following note in the teachers' lounge:

> **NEED A TV, VCR, MICROWAVE, ETC. ?????**
> **SEE ME BEFORE YOU BUY.**
> **1/2 OFF RETAIL.**

Usually the teacher did not profit financially in this exchange. Instead, she garnered the goodwill and appreciation of those to whom she afforded merchandise at well below wholesale prices. Although she admitted to the interviewer that she "probably knew, deep down inside" that the items were stolen, she had never previously admitted it to herself. In explaining her motivation for purchasing goods in such an unconventional manner, she ironically described them as "a real steal."

Some individuals begin as amateur fences and become more deeply involved as a result of the irresistible gains and the virtual absence of sanctions entailed in purchasing stolen property. The overwhelming increase in profits and the thrill of "beating the system" (or at least making a good deal) tempt them into increasing their participation in the distribution of stolen property. One such amateur turned part-time fence—a social worker—began her fencing activities when her husband purchased a household appliance from a thief he met in the course of his business as a plumber. At first their purchases were for their own consumption. Later, they bought Christmas presents for family members. Eventually they established a thriving family business buying stolen property from thieves and selling it in garage sales and flea markets, as well as to amateur receivers cultivated by the husband through his business colleagues and customers. The informant told the interviewer that she and her husband had put their son through college with the proceeds.

Summary and Discussion

The extent to which fences contribute to the incidence of property theft has been a central issue of debate. In the late 18th century, English magistrate Patrick Colquhoun (1969 [1797]) called for vigorous action against fences in London, stating, "Nothing can be more just than the old observation, 'that if there were no Receivers there would be no Thieves' " (298). Colquhoun's observation continues to have currency. Many believe that if fences could be put out of business, property crime rates would be dramatically reduced (Blakely and Goldsmith 1976; Walsh 1977). The fence is portrayed as not only providing a market for stolen goods, but also serving as an instigator and initiator of property theft.

This perspective has been criticized by other observers who argue that the "conception of the fence's role in property theft is bigger and more important than it ought to be, and that the involvement of other participants in an illegal trade is overlooked" (Steffensmeier 1986, 285). Stuart Henry argues that viewing the fence as the prime mover of property theft rests on pretending that real crimes are committed by "real" criminals, not by ordinary people, and certainly not by oneself (cited in Steffensmeier 1986, 286).

The extent to which ordinary people participate in the hidden economy (buying and selling stolen goods) is yet undetermined. However, our findings suggest that this part-time crime is ubiquitous (see also Henry 1978; Cromwell and McElrath 1994; Sutton 1998). Unlike the professional fence, these individuals do not perceive themselves as criminal, or as part of the impetus for property crime. Yet, they provide a ready market for stolen property, particularly for the young, inexperienced, and drug-addicted thieves who lack connections with professional fences.

Markets for stolen goods provide the catalyst and continuing motivation for property. Some young burglars find that they cannot sell their stolen goods successfully and consequently soon give up stealing. However, burglars who are able to convert their goods to cash at the first attempt may continue to repeat this rewarding behavior. Mitigating the market for stolen goods might have a positive effect on halting some criminal careers before they begin (Sutton et al. 2001).

These relatively unstudied channels of redistribution of stolen property may have important implications for crime control. Research that identifies these channels and determines the extent to which stolen property is purchased directly by the consuming public or by "otherwise honest" businesspeople and citizens will assist in the development of strategies to inhibit and disrupt the distribution process.

Questions for Thought and Discussion

1. How do "otherwise honest persons" justify or excuse their purchases of stolen property?
2. Why do juvenile thieves have trouble selling their goods to professional fences?
3. The authors state that crime-control policies that focus on arresting and prosecuting receivers of stolen property might be more effective than simply prosecuting thieves. On what do they base this argument? What do you think?
4. What theory or theories of criminal behavior are illustrated in this reseach?

References

Attenborough, F. L., ed. and trans. 1922. *The Laws of the Earliest English Kings*. Cambridge: The University Press.

Blakely, R., and M. Goldsmith. 1976. "Criminal Redistribution of Stolen Property: The Need for Law Reform." *Michigan Law Review,* 74: 1511–4613.

Chappell, R., and M. Walsh. 1974. "Receiving Stolen Property: The Need for Systematic Inquiry Into the Fencing Process. *Criminology,* 11.

Colquhoun, Patrick. 1969 (1797). *A Treatise on the Commerce and Police on the River Thames*. Montclair, NJ: Patterson Smith.

Cromwell, Paul, and Karen McElrath. 1994. "Buying Stolen Property: An Opportunity Perspective." *Journal of Research in Crime and Delinquency,* 31: 295–310.

Felson, Marcus. 1998. *Crime and Everyday Life,* 2nd ed. Thousand Oaks, CA: Pine Forge.

Gaughan, J. P., and L. A. Ferman. 1987. "Issues and Prospects for the Study of Informal Economics: Research Strategies and Policy." *Annals of the American Academy of Political and Social Science,* 493: 154–72.

Graham, J., and B. Bowling. 1995. "Young People and Crime Survey 1992–93." London: Home Office.

Hall, J. 1952. *Theft, Law and Society.* Indianapolis, IN: Bobbs-Merrill.

Henry, S. 1978. *The Hidden Economy.* London: Martin Robertson.

Klockars, C. B. 1974. *The Professional Fence.* New York: Macmillan.

Maguire, Mike. 1982. *Burglary in a Dwelling.* London: Heinemann.

McDonald, John M. 1980. *Burglary and Theft.* Springfield, IL: Charles C. Thomas.

Shover, N. 1971. *Burglary as an Occupation.* Doctoral dissertation, at the University of Illinois. Ann Arbor, MI: University Microfilms.

Smith, J. D. 1987. "Measuring the Informal Economy." *Annals of the American Academy of Political and Social Science,* 493: 83–99.

Steffensmeier, D. 1986. *The Fence: In the Shadow of Two Worlds.* Totowa, NJ: Rowman and Littlefield.

Sutton, M. 1998. "Handling Stolen Goods and Theft: A Market Reduction Approach." *Home Office Research Study, No. 178.* London: Home Office.

Sutton, Mike, Jacqueline Schneider, and Sarah Hetherington. 2001. "Tackling Stolen Goods With the Market Reduction Approach." *Briefing Note. Paper 8.* London: Home Office.

Walsh, M. 1977. *The Fence: A New Look at the World of Property Theft.* Westport, CT: Greenwood Press.

Wright, Richard T., and Scott H. Decker. 1974. *Burglars on the Job: Street Life and Residential Burglary.* Boston: Northeastern University Press.

Paul Cromwell and James N. Olson, "Fencing: Avenues for the Redistribution of Stolen Property." Adapted from work originally published in Cromwell and Olson, *Breaking and Entering: Burglars on Burglary.* Belmont, CA: Wadsworth Publishing Company. 2004.

Chapter 20
The Second Step in Double Jeopardy

Appropriating the Labor of Female Street Hustlers

Kim Romenesko
Eleanor M. Miller

"*Topical" life histories were obtained from 14 Milwaukee female street hustlers, aged 18 to 35, 11 of whom were members (or former members) of a "street" institution termed the "pseudo-family" (made up of a "man" and the women who work for him). The majority of the women interviewed were institutionalized at the time either at the Milwaukee House of Correction or at a residential drug treatment facility in Milwaukee. A putative and potential refuge for women responding to a dearth of licit employment opportunities and to the glitter and economic potential of the street, the pseudo-family actually emerges as a heteropatriarchal mechanism whose character, organization, and context serve to depress further, rather than enhance, the life chances of its female members. Once a woman is "turned out" by the "man" and enlisted in the pseudo-family, she is enmeshed in a tangled skein of conflicting emotions and motives; "wives-in-law" vie for the coveted position of "bottom woman" and for the attentions and regard of their "man," and the "man" schemes (in concert with other "men") to maintain his dominance and, above all, the profitability of the union. As female hustlers age and as their criminal records lengthen, they become marginal even to this world of last resort. Traded as chattel, often stripped entirely of property in the process of exchanging "men," and finally disowned when competition from other more naïve, more attractive, and more obedient women becomes too strong, street women find themselves doubly jeopardized by capitalistic-patriarchal structures that are pervasive in "straight" society and profound upon the street.*

This article is about Milwaukee women who make their living from street hustling. We attempt to document the operation of a patriarchal structure within the world of women's illicit work that parallels that which exists in the licit world of women's work and, ironically, further marginalizes females who hustle the streets of American cities primarily because of preexisting economic marginalization. The socioeconomic status of these women is, as a result of their experiences in this alternative labor market, even further reduced with respect to the licit market because of the criminal involvement, frequent drug and alcohol dependency, psychological and physical abuse, and ill-health connected with the work of street hustling. A particularly tragic element of this process resides in the fact that for many, the world of the streets appears an attractive array of alternative work opportunities when compared to their experience of "straight" work. The impoverishment, dependency, and, ultimately, redundancy of women, particularly women of color, who work in "women's jobs" in the licit world of work *and* the impoverishment, dependency, and redundancy they experience in the illicit work world, we argue, constitute a situation of "double jeopardy."

That there are few viable opportunities for poorly educated, unskilled women like themselves in the licit job market is very clear to women who eventually become female street hustlers. That a parallel situation exists in the illicit job market, however, escapes the view of new female recruits to street hustling because that view is clouded by the appeal of *feeling,* many for the first time, personally desirable, agentive, and productive as *women* workers. Furthermore, we will attempt to demonstrate that the central mechanism by which female street hustlers are made dependent, and financially, socially, and physically insecure, the mechanism by which they, themselves, are commodified is the "pseudo-family"—a patriarchal unit made up of a "man" and the women who work for him.

Since nearly all of the literature written about street-level prostitutes (which we prefer to call female street hustlers because of the clear diversity in their everyday work that includes a broad array of street hustles), indicates that a major reason women enter street life is because of the perceived financial rewards available to them (Miller, 1986; Brown, 1979; James and Meyerding, 1976; Laner, 1974), we became interested in learning how participation in street life in general, and the pseudo-family in particular, actually affects women's financial situation and, more broadly, their life chances. It is the embeddedness of women's hustling work in the social network that is the "pseudo-family," then, that is the focus of this article. . . .

Background

Given the inaccessibility of lucrative legal work to most women in our society and the failure of our welfare system to maintain women and their children at a livable standard (Sidel, 1986), participation in the illegal activities of street life is a route that a certain proportion of women see as an occupational alternative. As James and Meyerding (1976, p. 178) say:

> Money-making options are still quite limited for women in this society, especially for unskilled or low-skilled women. Recognition of this basic sex inequality in the economic structure helps us see prostitution as a viable occupational choice, rather than as a symptom of the immorality or "deviance" of individual women.

One of our respondents, Elsie, described how and why she became involved in street life.

> I got married when I was eighteen. My husband, okay, when I got married, that was my biggest mistake 'cuz he never was around. I had all these little babies. When I was eighteen I had two [babies], when I was nineteen I had three. He wouldn't work, he wouldn't help support them, and there I'd sit in this little apartment with nothin'—no TV, nothin'—no milk for your babies and, you know, they gotta have milk and stuff. You know, I was so tired of runnin' to my people askin' 'em for, you know, favors: "Would you go buy the babies some milk?" You know, I was embarrassed doin' that. So then that's when I learned to take a check that wasn't mine and go cash it. You know that's what really drove me into it. For their sake, not to benefit myself—not at first it wasn't.

The women of this study, we argue, look to street life to obtain the status and economic stability that is largely unachievable for the children of the poor and near poor, be they male or female. The commodification of female sexuality offers them entree to the streets, often initially as prostitutes. As this analysis will show, however, street women are doubly jeopardized: Involvement in illicit street life is not a viable avenue to financial stability for women because of the institutionalized obstacles that exist in the underworld—obstacles as difficult to circumvent as those in "straight" society.

Work History

Most of the fourteen female street hustlers included in this analysis worked at straight jobs at some point in their lives. (The few that did not, became participants in street hustling in their early teens.) Straight work usually took place before the women's entrance into street life; however, in a few cases, women tried straight jobs in an attempt to leave street life. While some have not given up on the idea that there is some kind of straight work that they could do as the basis of a career, most admitted that they could not go back to boring, low-paying work with inflexible hours. They believe that "the life" (short for street life, also called "the fast life") will pay off sometime in the near future. They think that things will improve, money will be saved, and they will retire from "the life" in comfort. If our analysis is correct, they are probably mistaken.

The types of straight jobs our respondents performed were low-status, low-paying, often part-time jobs that are heavily dominated by females. Examples of the types of jobs the women worked at are fast food attendant or cook, box checker at a department store, house-keeper, dietary aide, beautician, bakery shop clerk, assembly line worker for a manufacturing company, child care aide, hot dog stand attendant, cashier, waitress, hostess, receptionist, go-go dancer, and secretary.

Some women who tried to make it in straight society have been frustrated by their experience and have, essentially, given up. Brandy, a young black woman who participated in the study, had her first straight job when she was 18 years old. She performed clerical duties in Chicago but was eventually laid off. She said:

> I got laid off 'cuz the plant closed down and opened up in Oak Park and I didn't have a way out to Oak Park from the South Side of Chicago. After that, believe it or not, I was working at [a] hotel on Michigan Avenue in Chicago, Illinois, as a maid. After I took two tests, they gave me

a promotion—I was supervisor of housecleaning. . . . That's why it's weird for me to be goin' through the things I'm goin' through now [Brandy was incarcerated at the Milwaukee House of Correction at the time of the interview]. I'm not a bad person at all.

How long were you supervisor of housecleaning?

Brandy: About two and a half years [until she was 21 years old].

What did you do then?

Brandy: Stayed at home and collect unemployment . . . and was lookin' for another job, but I never found one.

Other women, although they had no problem finding jobs, were not satisfied with the pay. Once women get a taste for making "fast money" on the street, it is difficult to go back. Tina describes this attraction to the street in the following comments:

What [type of work] were you doing?

Tina: Oh, I did a lot of things. . . . I was workin' at Marc's Bigboy as a waitress. I've been a waiter, I've been a host, I've been a private secretary, I've been a cashier. I've got a lot of job skills, also.

You've had all these straight jobs and you've got lots of skills. What's the attraction to the streets?

Tina: The money, the fast money. That sums it up.

Elsie, in the passage below, relates not only how difficult it is to live on the wages paid by many employers, but also how sexism worked (and works) to keep women marginal to the job market. She is describing the first straight job that she had as a dietary aide and why she became disaffected.

Elsie: I got the job 'cuz I really needed it. In fact, I had just turned 18 so they was payin' me $1.30 an hour. This was like in '67. Yea, '67 cuz my son was about a year old. They was payin' me $1.30 an hour. . . . See, I was stayin' at home. My mother, she was keepin' my baby. I'd get my check, I'd give her half and I'd keep half. Then, the shop was in walkin' distance, you know, from her house where we was stayin' and we'd get our lunch and stuff free cuz I was workin' in the kitchen. But still, that wasn't enough money for that hard work.

How long did you work there?

Elsie: I worked there nine months. . . . I would have stayed there but I was pregnant again. I was tryin' to keep it from them 'cuz back then you could only work 'til you was five or six months pregnant. And so I tried to keep it from 'em. I worked until I was nine months 'cuz, you know, I never got real big. So I was tellin' 'em I was like four months and I was really eight—so I could keep my job.

Finally, a few women reported simply being intolerant of supervised nine-to-five work and ending up getting fired from their jobs or quitting. It is interesting to note that the women who fall into this category tended to have the least skills.

What did you do then?

Rita: Worked in a hospital in the laundry department and hated it because it was hot, it was hard work, and I hated my boss.

How much did it pay?

Rita: Minimum wage.

How long did you work there?

Rita: Three months.

Why did you leave?

Rita: I've always gotten fired. But, okay, you could say that I've always gotten fired, but before they could fire me, I know when they're going to fire me, [so] I always quit. Before that "You're fired" comes out, I always quit.

What other kinds of straight jobs have you had?

Rita: Okay, my first job was in the hospital. Nurse's aide was my last—I got fired there. A security guard for the telephone company.

What was the reason behind quitting most of them?

Rita: I just am not a nine-to-five person. . . . Most of my jobs were during the day. I had to be there in the morning. I didn't have a car; transportation by bus, I didn't like that. So, it was like, I don't like to take buses. I like being my own boss. Work when I want to work, make good money.

For the uneducated and largely unskilled women of this study—whose experience with straight work was unfulfilling or whose jobs were unstable due to a volatile and sexist market place—participation in street life, with its promise of money, excitement, and independence, seemed the answer to their problems.

Street Life

According to the women of this study, a prerequisite to working as a street hustler is that a woman must have a male sponsor, a "man," to act as a "keep-away" from other "men" who vie for a living on the street. She must turn her earnings over to this "man" in order to be considered "his woman" and to enjoy the "man's" protection. The "man," besides providing protection from other "men," gives his women material necessities and gifts and, most important, sex and love (Merry, 1980).

The following, from an interview with a respondent whom we have named "Chris," illustrates why street women need "men" to work. When asked why she worked and turned her earnings over to a "man" instead of working for herself and keeping her money, she said:

> **Chris:** You can't really work the streets for yourself unless you got a man—not for a long length of time . . . 'cuz the other pimps are not going to like it because you don't have anybody to represent you. They'll rob you, they'll hit you in the head if you don't have nobody to take up for you. Yea, it happens. They give you a hassle. . . . [The men] will say, "Hey baby, what's your name? Where your man at? You got a man?"
>
> So you can't hustle on your own?
>
> **Chris:** Not really, no. You can, you know, but not for long.

Women who do hustle on their own are called "outlaw" women, a term that clearly indicates that their solo activities are proscribed. Women who work as outlaws lose any protection that they had formerly been granted under the "law" of the street and are open targets for "men" who wish to harass them, take their money, or exploit them sexually.

Street life is male dominated and so structured that "men" reap the profits of women's labor. A "man" demands from his women not only money, but respect as well. Showing respect for "men" means total obedience and complete dedication to them. Mary reports that in the company of "men" she had to "talk mainly to the women—try not to look at the men if possible at all—try not to have conversation with them." Rita, when asked about the rules of the street, said, "Just basic, obey. Do what he wants to do. Don't disrespect him. . . . I could not disrespect him in any verbal or physical way. I never attempted to hit him back. Never." And, in the same vein, Tina said that when her "man" had others over to socialize, the women of the family were relegated to the role of servant. "We couldn't speak to them when we wasn't spoken to, and we could not foul up on their orders. And you cannot disrespect them."

Clearly, "men" are the rulers of the underworld. Hartmann's (1984, p. 177) definition of patriarchy is particularly apropos of "street-level" male domination.

> We can usefully define patriarchy as a set of social relations between men, which have a material base, and which, though hierarchical, establish or create interdependence and solidarity among men that enable them to dominate women. Though patriarchy is hierarchical and men of different classes, races, or ethnic groups have different places in the patriarchy, they also are united in their shared relationship of dominance over their women; they are dependent on each other to maintain that domination. . . . In the hierarchy of patriarchy, all men, whatever their rank in the patriarchy, are bought off by being able to control at least some women.

"Men," as the quotations below illustrate, and as Milner and Milner (1972) have written with regard to pimps, maintain a strong coalition among themselves allowing them to dominate women. As the number of women a "man" has working for him increases, the time he can spend supervising each female's activities decreases. It becomes very important that "men" be in contact with one another to assure the social and economic control of street women. With watchful "men" keeping tabs on their own and other "men's" women, women know that they must always work hard and follow the rules.

Rose gives an example, below, of one of the many ways in which "men" protect one another. Rose's sister, who is also involved in street life, was badly beaten by her "man" and decided to press charges against him. She decided to drop the charges because:

> **Rose:** She got scared 'cuz he kept threatening her. . . . His friends [were] callin' her and tellin' her if she didn't drop the charges they was gonna do somethin' to her. So she dropped the charges.

It is interesting to note that when working women are caught talking with "men" who are not their own, it is considered to be at the women's initiative and they are reprimanded. In other words, "men" can speak with whom they please, when they please, but women are not allowed to speak, or even look, at other "men." Ann gives another example of this element of the cohesiveness of "men":

> If another pimp see you "out of pocket" [breaking a rule] or bent over talkin' to another pimp or somethin' in their car, they will tell your man, "Yea, she was talkin' to some dude in a Cadillac—he try and 'knock your bitch.' " That the word they use.
>
> What does it mean?
>
> **Ann:** He tryin' to come up with her. He tryin' to have her for himself. That what they mean. That what they be sayin' all the time: "He tryin' to 'knock your bitch,' man. You better put her 'in check.' " In other words, you better, how should I say it? "In check" mean, tell her what's happenin', keep her under control.
>
> Or, if you be walkin' around on the stroll and stuff and somebody might see you sittin' down on the bench and they say, "Man, your ho [whore] is lazy! All the cars were passin' by—that girl didn't even catch none of 'em." 'Cuz they [the "men"] know you and stuff.

The mechanisms that keep women oppressed at the street level are parallel to those of the broader culture. The wage structure in the United States is such that many women cannot financially endure without men. On the street, women also need men to survive, because they are not allowed to earn money in their absence. In addition, women of the street must give all of the money they earn to their "man." A "man," in turn, uses the money to take care of his needs and the needs of his women—although, as we shall see, money is usually not distributed unconditionally but, rather, is based upon a system of rewards and punishments that are dependent upon the behavior of women.

The Pseudo-Family

The pseudo-family is a familylike institution made up of a "man" and the women who work for him. Its female members refer to each other as "wives-in-law" and to the man for whom they work as "my man." By focusing on the pseudo-family, we try to isolate and expose a street-level mechanism for female oppression, and to explain why the "wife-in-law" is unlikely to revolt or leave her oppressive situation. Specifically, we attempt to describe how the pseudo-family, while seeming to offer love, money, and stability to the women who participate in it, is structured so that women, in fact, gain little. Our thesis, in other words, is that the security of the pseudo-family for the female street hustler is largely illusory.

The structure of the family is hierarchical and the "man" holds the top position. He collects all of the money that women earn and makes decisions about how it is spent. He is also the disciplinarian of the family: When a rule is broken, he is the person who decides upon and metes out the punishment. The "man" also has the final say about who is recruited into his family. Despite the fact that his women may oppose the idea of additional "wives-in-law," there is typically little they can do about it. If women refuse to accept their "wives-in-law" or try to make life difficult for them, they are likely to be thought "disrespectful" and, as such, will be punished. Next in the hierarchy of the pseudo-family is the position of "bottom woman." When a "man" and woman start out working only as an entrepreneurial couple who, at some later date, recruit another woman into the family to become the first woman's "wife-in-law," the most senior woman is accorded the privileged position of "bottom woman." "Bottom women" help to make sure that household is in good working order. "Bottom women" are also expected to keep tabs on their "wives-in-law" and to smooth out any differences that may occur between them.

The "man" of the family places a special trust in the woman that occupies the position of "bottom woman." It is, therefore, an enviable position and one to which "wives-in-law" aspire. To safeguard the position, then, and to control the jealousy that her "wives-in-law" may feel toward her because of her higher status, the "bottom woman" must convince her "wives-in-law"—each individually—that they, in fact, are the "man's" favorite.

Dee, a 26-year-old, self-described Puerto Rican/white woman, has been involved in street life since she was 15. She has an extensive background as "bottom woman" and described how she kept her families (of up to six "wives-in-law") together.

Were you always bottom woman?

Dee: Any man I had, yea. Because it was the mind, the mental thing. If you can avoid jealousy and all that and keep a family together, and me being from keepin' families together, it was an easy thing—right up my alley. [You'd have to] make them feel they were number one and you were just a peon. [It] kept them around, kept them bringin' in $400.00 and $500.00 dollars a night.

Did you get along with your wives-in-law?

Dee: I would force myself to get along with them. . . . I would be protection for them so, consequently, they wouldn't really fight with me, per se, but with each other. So that I would say that I'm . . . [your] . . . friend and her friend and be the mediator between the two. I never really had any problems unless one of them violated some type of code.

To gain the trust of the "bottom woman" and to prove that she is held in high esteem, the "man" often passes on privileged information to the "bottom woman" about her "wives-in-law." Having this information increases the "bottom woman's" feelings of power and prestige and instills confidence in her and her position, motivating the "bottom woman" to do a better job for the "man." Although the information she receives could be used to flaunt the fact that she is her "man's" favorite, the "bottom woman" must remain discreet if she is to retain her position and keep the family together.

A female street hustler can also become a "bottom woman" by working her way up through the ranks of the family. Depending upon the situation, becoming a "bottom woman" in this way can take anywhere from a week to a number of years. Generally, young white women have the best chance of promotion because they make the most money (due to the racism of customers and to the fact that they can work in more and "better" locations than black women without attracting attention from the police), are without lengthy criminal records when first recruited to the streets, and tend to be more obedient. At least one of our respondents said:

Rose: ["Men"] go for young womens and for the white womens. . . . They figure the young womens will get out there and maybe catch a case occasionally until she catch on [but] she won't go to jail . . . and then they think that white women can work anywhere, make more money . . . without catching no heat from the police.

Although there is limited advancement for women, they can never rise to a status equal to the "man." The rules of "the game" explicitly state that "men" are to dominate women, and women, as subservient creatures, are to respect and appreciate that fact (Milner and Milner, 1972). As there are opportunities for promotions within the family, and into safer and more prestigious hustles outside of the family, women cling to the false hope that "their day will come." In addition, the competition among women for these positions, and for their "man's" affection, creates such divisiveness that it is unlikely that women will conspire to fight for significant changes in the street or pseudo-family structure. Thus "men" are assured that the status quo is maintained.

Male Control

The maintenance of male dominance at the street level is dependent upon "men's" ability to control women. The control of women by "men" is made possible, first of all, by the very fact that women are not allowed involvement in the life without "men" as their sponsors. As "men" are well aware, however, women will not accept them and their rule as against the rule and control of another "man" unless given adequate enticements. These take the form of love, money, and the accompanying sense of security. Once a woman has become attached to the "man," he is then in a position to control her more effectively. Lastly, when all else fails, "men" will resort to physical violence in order to maintain control.

Getting women into positions where they can be dominated begins during the "turning out" process—the process whereby a "man" teaches a woman how to become a street hustler. The "turning out" process, as Miller (1978, p. 142) notes:

> [I]nvolves a variety of subtle techniques of social control and persuasion on the part of the pimp. . . . [It] involves several steps in which the pimp initially attracts the woman through his sexual and economic appeal and later changes her mind about the propriety of prostitution and the proper relationship between men and women. . . . The critical factor in the beginning of the relationship is the establishment of control over the relationship by the pimp.

Elsie, whom we heard from earlier, is a 38-year-old black woman. She first met her "man" when she was 28 years old; he was 35. Since about the age of 19, Elsie had been intermittently involved in forgery and other petty street crimes. She was still on the fringe of the life, however, and therefore had never worked with a "man." Elsie described for us how, and under what circumstances, she was turned out by her "man."

> Okay, I had met this guy . . . I knew about stuff like that but I had never indulged in it [prostitution]. I'd done, you know, check forgin' and stealin' but that's it. Me and him was talking—he was dressed up all nice and nice lookin' and he had a big nice Continental outside. So I'm lookin,' you know? So I asked him, I said, "What kind of work do you do?" He said, "I sell insurance. . . ." He said, "You married?" I said, "No, I'm separated but livin' by myself." He said, "Well, could I call you or come by your house, could you give me your number?" I said, "Yea." So I gave him the number. He called me a couple of times and I said, "Well, come back to my house!" I was all excited—I had the house all spic and span and he came over. Right about that time I was having a few problems 'cuz I owed some back bills and stuff—my phone was gettin' ready to be cut off and stuff. I didn't have no stereo or nothin'. So he come by there that night, looked around. I still didn't really know what was happening, you know. I told him I was in financial trouble, they were gettin' ready to cut my phone off—I need a TV and stereo and stuff. He said, "Well, I'm goin' to pay your phone bill and everything for you." And he did! He paid the phone bill the next day, he brought me a stereo, he did all that. He bought me a new outfit.
>
> One of my girlfriends . . . she said, "Elsie, you're too naive." She said, "You don't know what he's supposed to be?" I said, "No." She said, "I think he calls himself a pimp." I said, "He's nice, look what he did." She said, "You know, that's the way they do. He trying to set you up." I said, "Girl, go away. I know what I'm doin." I was older than she was, you know, and she's trying to tell me. And sure enough, that's what it was.
>
> How did you find out?
>
> **Elsie:** He told me about it, okay. When I found out, I found out on the telephone. I said, "Yea, I heard you was, you know." He said, "No, who told you that?" I said, "I just heard it 'cuz a pimp is noticed on the streets." And he used the name Peachy, that was his street name. So I said, "If that's what you is, stay away from me, 'cuz I don't even want to get involved with nobody like that." He said, "No, it ain't like that with me and you, we can just be friends." I said, "Well, I don't even want nothin' to do with you if it's like that. I got four kids, I ain't got time for nothin' like you." He said, "Elsie, it ain't like that. If you don't wanna do nothin' like that." He said, "I admit, I do do that. I got some ladies that, you know, give me money and stuff, but you ain't gonna have to be like that." He said we could just be friends, that we could have a relationship different from that, you know.
>
> Did you believe him?
>
> **Elsie:** Yea, I did! 'Cuz I liked him! So I fell for it. And then the next thing I knew, he came by and said, "Elsie, I got somethin' set up for you."

After Elsie had serviced her first trick, her "man" came to pick her up. She said:

> I got in the car and I was sittin' up, lookin' all quiet and stuff. He said, "Did you get the money?" I said, "Yea." He said, "Where is it?" I said, "I got it." He said, "Give it here." I said, "All of it?" He said, "Yea, and then if you want some I'll give it to you." That's the part that hurted. I gave it to him. [I thought], "I'll never do that no more." But then, after that, I got smart, not really smart but I got a little wiser. Okay, when I would do somethin' like that, I would stash me some money.

Rita, a 26-year-old white woman, first met her "man" when she was 18. However, as she describes it, "I was 18 when I met my man, but I was 19 when I first put money in his hand." Rita said that for some months she had had a girlfriend/boyfriend relationship with her "man." He had a 30-year-old white woman working for him but, according to Rita:

> He wanted a white girl he could turn out himself. Apparently, she [his first woman] had been turned out by somebody else. But I was his turn out completely.

Her "man," like Elsie's, made sure that there was a strong emotional attachment before any money changed hands. Rita said:

> He made me fall in love with him before I put any type of money in his hand. I was working three months and still dating him and not paying him. But he knew that he was getting me.

So he was turning you out but you weren't giving him any money?

Rita: No I was not. He knew I was falling in love with him, okay? Finally, that day came where we sat in the car. We had just gone out. I was sitting in the car with him, he had brought me home from going out—we'd gone out drinking. I was sittin' in the car with him and he turns to me and says, "Well, you know, we've been going out . . . and you know what I'm about and my lady's gettin' kind of mad that ain't nothin' happening and you are working. It's either, you gotta start giving me some money or I can't see you no more." And I did not want that, I fell in love with the man. So it was like, okay, here you go buddy, am I yours now?

Rita also said that her "man" would not bail her out of jail during that initial period when she was not giving him any money. She said that the reason he wouldn't bail her out was that

He was just tryin' to show me, "Look, if you go to jail, I'm there and I'm yours and you're mine, I'll get you out. But you're alone and I can't get you out. That's going against what this is all about."

As these excerpts illustrate, the establishment of an emotional tie between the "man" and the woman is an extremely important element of the "turning out" process. Even though a woman discovers relatively early that a "man's" affection is conditional (depending upon her payment, respect, and obedience to him), she believes the payoff—being "taken care of" financially, socially, and emotionally—to be worth it. When "wives-in-law" enter the picture, however, and the woman finds that she must "share" her "man" with others, jealousy and conflict arise, creating instability within the family.

Getting Disentangled From the Pseudo-Family

Changes in the composition of the pseudo-family are frequent and occur for various reasons. The intervention of the criminal justice system, the inability of "men" to control adequately the jealously of their women, the heavy drug use of street women and their men, and the decreased marketability of women as they age are all factors that affect family stability.

Criminal Justice System

Because of the highly visible hustles in which street women engage, frequent contact with criminal justice authorities is inevitable. When a woman is arrested and incarcerated, a new woman is often recruited into the pseudo-family to replace the lost earnings of the incarcerated woman. When the incarcerated woman is released and returns to her family, the family must adapt to the new amalgam of personalities. Often, however, the adaptation is unsuccessful and the result is that one of the women may leave the family in search of a better situation. The woman who leaves is replaced by another, creating new stresses within the pseudo-family, and the whole process is repeated.

Also, while incarcerated, women may be recruited into new families. One of the women interviewed—a veteran of the game—chose her new "man" by telephone from the House of Correction. She was recruited by one of his women who was also serving time. Another woman reported that she was considering leaving her "man" of nine years for a new "man" whom she met and corresponded with in the House of Correction via smuggled letters. Women who are unhappy with their current family situation, then, or women who are "between" men, have opportunities while incarcerated to join new families.

Drug Use

Excessive drug use by street hustlers and their "men" also erodes family stability. "Men" have a responsibility to their women to take care of business—to pay bills and post bond, dispense clothing and pocket money, and generally behave as a responsive (if not caring) family member—and women, in return, must provide "men" with money and respect. As Joan says, a real pimp "gonna take care of her 'cuz she's takin' care of him." In other words, there are mutual obligations between "men" and women. When "men" use hard drugs excessively, they are unable to hold up their end of the bargain adequately. Similarly, women who are heavy users are unable to maintain good work habits. Both addicted "men" and women drain the financial resources of the family. In addition, "men" become dependent on their women to support their habits and thereby lose the respect of other "men" and women of the street.

> **Dee:** They ["men" in Milwaukee] would take and allow a woman to hold the fact that they're givin' 'em money over their heads. Where, in Chicago or New York, they would get rid of the woman—'cuz women come too easy. The women here are the pimps. And if they're payin' the man they're payin' 'em not because of some strategic level he's at, it's because they want someone to protect them. But he's shootin' so much dope nine times out of ten, that the woman runs it [the family]. She says she's not going to work—he might get down on his hands and knees and beg her 'cuz he's such a punk he needs to go pop from the dopeman. . . . They're shootin' too much dope, they're doin' too much dope. Dope has become a big problem as far as the players and the females. That's taken a lot of good men who have taken the money that women have made 'em, put it in businesses, and smoked up the business. So the drugs alone has killed a lot of the men. It's a vicious circle—it all goes back to the dopeman.

Aging Out

As women age, their value as street hustlers declines and they are often discarded by "men" who favor younger, naive women who have yet to establish criminal records. As a woman becomes both increasingly cynical and less attractive (compared to her younger competitors), she is less assimilable into the pseudo-family. Jody, for example, said that she and her "man" permitted a "wife-in-law" of two years to remain in jail (pending $500.00 bail) because, "we wanted to leave the state and she was old and I had learned everything from her so she was no longer needed." When Rita, another respondent, entered a family, her "wife-in-law" left because, as Rita reported, "she knew that I was prettier than her, younger. She was 30 years old. I [was] 19 and freshly turned out."

In addition, older women are more inclined to consider their own needs rather than the needs of their man. Toni, a 29-year-old, after working as a street hustler for eleven years, seeks a secure life with a "good" man. As she says:

> You become more and more experienced and you have to do serious time and you have so much time to think about what you want. If you're going to stay in this life, [you begin to think] about what you want out of it instead of what he wants out of it. It becomes more of a priority. Now, I want someone who does not mess around with drugs. . . . Who has enough money of his own, has enough things going for himself, to where he doesn't need me. That's what I want now.

Since older women hustlers are less financially successful than younger women, and often are chary of exploitative "men," they are frequently spurned by "men."

Instability

Though women are not allowed control over their earnings, they often receive costly gifts from their "men." The process of leaving "men," however, is such that women frequently lose the material wealth that they have acquired during the relationship. Since the decision to leave a "man" is usually made in anger—after a beating, or after being left to "sit" in jail, or in a fit of jealousy—women commonly leave their families without their treasured material possessions. As Toni says, "I've had to leave without my stuff a few times. Then you gotta start all over each time. But there's been times when I've got to keep my stuff, too." In addition, women who have accomplished some occupational mobility while with a "man" must start at the bottom of the occupational hierarchy when they choose a new one.

The more frequently women change men, then, the less likely their chance of accumulating any material wealth for themselves.

Summary and Conclusions

The pseudo-family, in addition to addressing the emotional and sexual needs of its members, is explicitly organized to realize and exploit the "profitability" that inheres in its female members—that is, their sexuality. But if female street hustlers are both labor and capital "rolled into one," it is difficult to imagine how the "man" can interject himself into the lives of women who, logically, are self-sufficient—in a purely entrepreneurial sense. In fact, the women who join pseudo-families "barter" their way through their family lives, endlessly exchanging their resources as women for, variously, the affections (and recognition) of the "man" and the material goods necessary to survival. There is a twofold answer to the question, therefore, of why women relinquish control of their natural assets in the sexual market of the street. One is that they bring to the street emotional and financial vulnerabilities and so fall prey to "men" prepared to exploit them; the second is that the "sexual" street scene represents a deeply entrenched, patriarchal structure that quickly and effectively punishes independent female hustlers.

Questions for Thought and Discussion

1. What does the author mean by "pseudo-family," and how does this street institution provide support for the prostitute?
2. What drew these women to prostitution? Why do they stay in the life?
3. Explain the "turning out" process.
4. What theory or theories of criminal behavior are illustrated in this research?

References

Brown, M. 1979. "Teenage Prostitution." *Adolescence* 14:665–680.

Hartmann, H. I. 1984. "The Unhappy Marriage of Marxism and Feminism: Towards a More Progressive Union." Pp. 172–189 in *Feminist Frameworks,* edited by A. M. Jaggar and P. S. Rothenberg. New York: McGraw-Hill.

James, J. and J. Meyerding. 1976. "Motivations for Entrance into Prostitution." Pp. 177–205 in *The Female Offender,* edited by L. Cites. Washington, DC: Heath.

Laner, M. R. 1974. "Prostitution as an Illegal Vocation: A Sociological Overview." Pp. 406–418 in *Deviant Behavior: Occupational and Organizational Bases,* edited by C. Bryant. Chicago: Rand McNally.

Merry, S. 1980. "Manipulating Anonymity: Streetwalkers, Strategies for Safety in the City." *Ethnos* 45:157–175.

Miller, E. M. 1986. *Street Woman.* Philadelphia: Temple University Press.

Miller, G. 1978. *The World of Deviant Work.* Englewood Cliffs, NJ: Prentice-Hall.

Milner, C. and R. Milner. 1972. *Black Players: The Secret World of Black Pimps.* Boston: Little, Brown.

Sidel, R. 1986. *Women and Children Last.* New York: Penguin.

Chapter 21 Dealing Careers

Patricia A. Adler

In the early 1970s Patricia Adler and her husband Peter moved to Southwest County (pseudonym) to begin their graduate studies in sociology. There they made friends with "Dave," a neighbor whom they later learned was involved in high-level drug smuggling and dealing. As their friendship with Dave developed, they were introduced to a group of Dave's friends and associates, all involved in illegal drug dealing. As friendship and trust continued to develop between the Adlers and Dave and his associates, the two were slowly granted access to the world of smuggling, dealing, and drug use. For the next six years, with the knowledge and active assistance of Dave and his friends, the Adlers studied this drug-dealing and smuggling community, conducting interviews and observing their activities.

In this selection taken from her book, Wheeling and Dealing: An Ethnography of an Upper-Level Drug Dealing and Smuggling Community, *Patricia Adler explains how thrill seeking, spontaneity, emotionality, and other expressive concerns characterize the lifestyle of these upper-level drug dealers. She follows their careers, first by examining the process of becoming a drug trafficker, then considering the various routes to upward mobility, and finally the experience of aging in the career. Clearly noted are themes of the "glamour and excitement," the hedonism and fast life that attract some to the criminal lifestyle. Like Shover's persistent property offenders, Adler's drug dealers experienced "burnout" in the later stages of their careers. They reported disillusionment with the glamour and increased concern with the risks associated with a criminal life.*

Becoming a Drug Trafficker

Becoming a drug trafficker was a gradual process, where individuals progressively shifted perspective as they became increasingly involved in the social networks of dealers and smugglers (Lieb and Olson 1976). As Ray (1961) has noted for the careers of heroin addicts, joining these social networks required a commitment to the drug world's norms, values, and lifestyle, and limited the degree of involvement individuals subsequently had with nondeviant groups.

Recruitment

I observed three entry routes to this deviant career. These routes were different for dealing and smuggling, and varied according to the level of trafficking where individuals entered the field.

Dealing. Individuals began dealing drugs through their own initiative, entering the occupation via *self-propulsion.* They fell into two groups, marked by different levels of entry and characterized by significantly varied experiences.

People who began dealing with a low-level entry followed the classic path portrayed in the literature (see Anonymous 1969; Blum et al. 1968; Carey 1972; Goode 1970; Johnson 1973). These initiates came from among the ranks of regular drug users, since, in practice, using drugs heavily and dealing for "stash" (one's personal supply) were nearly inseparable. Out of this multitude of low-level dealers, however, most abandoned the practice after they encountered their first legal or financial bust, lasting in the business for a fairly short period (see Anonymous 1969; Carey 1972; Lieb and Olson 1976). Those who sought bigger profits gradually drifted into a full-time career in drug trafficking. Their careers as dealers were therefore entwined with their careers as drug users, which usually began by late adolescence (between the ages of 15 and 22). Because of this early recruitment into dealing, low-level entrants generally developed few, if any, occupational skills other than dealing. Although it was difficult to attain the upper level of the drug trade from these humble beginnings, a small but significant percentage of the dealers I observed in Southwest County got their start in this fashion.

A larger percentage of Southwest County dealers made a middle-level entry. Future big dealers usually jumped into transacting in substantial quantities from the outset, buying 50 kilos of commercial marijuana or one to two ounces of cocaine. One dealer explained this phenomenon:

> Someone who thinks of himself as an executive or an entrepreneur is not going to get into the dope business on a small level. The average executive just jumps

> right into the middle. Or else he's not going to jump.

This was the route taken by Southwest County residents who had little or no previous involvement in drug trafficking. For them, entry into dealing was precipitated by their social relations with local dealers and smugglers (naturally, this implies a self-selecting sample of outsiders who became accepted and trusted by these upper-level traffickers, based on mutual interests, orientation, and values). Through their friendships with dealers, these individuals were introduced to other members of the dealing scene and to their fast life. Individuals who found this lifestyle attractive became increasingly drawn to the subculture, building networks of social associations within it. Eventually, some of these people decided to participate more actively. This step was usually motivated by their attraction to the money and the lifestyle. Dave recounted how he fell in with the drug world set:

> I used to be in real estate making good money. Through my property management and investment services I started meeting some rich people. I was the only person at my firm renting to longhairs and dealing with their money. They all paid me in cash from a giant wad of bills. They never asked for a receipt and always had cash, 24 hours a day. I slowly started getting friendly with them, although I didn't realize how heavy they were. I knew ways of buying real estate and putting it under fictitious names, laundering money so that it went in as hot cash and came out as spendable income. I invested their money in gems, metals, cars. But the whole time I never asked any questions. I just took my commission and was happy. Then one guy asked me to clear some checks for him through my bank account—said he was hiding the money from his ex-wife and the Treasury people. This was the beginning. I slowly got more and more involved with him until I was neglecting my real estate business and just partying with him all the time. My spending went up, but my income went down, and suddenly I had to look around for another way to make money fast. I took the money I was cashing for him, bought some bricks from another dealer friend of his and sold them out of state before I gave him back the cash. Eventually I started to deal with him too, on a front basis. Within six months I was turning 100 bricks at a time.

Once individuals decided to try dealing, they rarely abandoned it after one transaction. Earning money was intoxicatingly alluring, stimulating their greed for more, while losing money usually necessitated becoming involved in another deal to recoup what they lost.

People who entered drug dealing at these middle levels were usually between the ages of 25 and 35, and had worked in some other occupation before dealing seriously. Many drifted into the lifestyle from jobs already concentrated in the night hours, such as bartending, waiting tables, and nightclub door bouncing. Still others came from fields where the working hours were irregular and adaptable to their special schedules, such as acting, real estate, inventing, graduate school, construction, and creative "entrepreneurship" (more aptly called hand-to-mouth survival, for many). The smallest group was tempted into the drug world from structured occupations and the professions.

Smuggling. Smuggling, in contrast, was rarely entered in this self-directed manner. Only a small minority of upper-level dealers were able to make the leap into importation on their own. The rest became involved in smuggling through a form of *solicitation.* The complex task of importing illegal drugs required more knowledge, experience, equipment, and connections than most people possessed. Those who got into drug smuggling usually did so at the invitation of an established smuggler. About half of the people smugglers recruited had not dealt before, but came directly into importation from the drug world's social scene. This implies, like middle-level entry into dealing, that recruits were attracted to the drug crowd and its lifestyle, and that they had prior acquaintance with dealers and smugglers. The other half of the recruits were solicited from among the ranks of middle-level Southwest County dealers.

Recruits who were solicited were likely to have some skill or asset which the experienced smuggler needed to put his operation together. This included piloting or navigating ability, equipment, money, or simply the willingness to handle drugs while they were being transported. One smuggler described the criteria he used to screen potential recruits for his smuggling crew:

> Pilots are really at a premium. They burn out so fast that I have to replace them every six months to a year. But I'm also

> looking for people who are cool: people who will carry out their jobs according to the plan, who won't panic if the load arrives late or something goes wrong, 'cause this happens a lot . . . and I try not to get people who've been to prison before, because if they haven't they'll be more likely to take foolish risks, the kind that I don't want to have to.

Learning the Trade

Once people experienced some initial success in dealing, their attitude shifted from hesitancy to enthusiasm. Despite the amount of time and effort they invested, most people felt as if they had earned a lot of money for very little work. This was because dealing time and work differed structurally from legitimate work: the latter usually took place within a well-defined physical and temporal framework (the 9-to-5 hours at the office), while dealing was accomplished during discretionary, or recreational, hours and settings.

As business began to go well, the danger translated into excitement, making it seem like fun. Novice drug traffickers felt as if they were earning "gravy" money while simultaneously enjoying themselves. This definition of the situation helped them overcome any remaining reluctance and plunge themselves more deeply into the occupation. They then became eager to learn more about concrete strategies of conducting business safely and successfully.

Learning the trade involved acquiring specific knowledge of potential business connections, ways of organizing transactions profitably, ways of avoiding legal detection and arrest, ways of transporting illegal goods, ways of coordinating participants, types of equipment, and myriad other details. This knowledge was acquired through either *on-the-job training* (Miller and Ritzer 1977, 89) or *sponsorship.*

Dealers underwent on-the-job training, refining their knowledge and skills by getting experience and learning from their mistakes. Their early experiences often included getting burned with inferior merchandise, getting "short counted" with low volume, and getting ripped off through carelessness in selecting their dealing associates. While some people abandoned dealing because of these early errors, many returned, better educated, to try again.

Socialization into the technical aspects of smuggling was not as isolated as it was for dealing. Most future smugglers were recruited and trained by a sponsor with whom they had an apprentice/mentor relationship. Those who had been dealers previously knew the rudiments of drug transactions. What they learned from the smuggler was how to fill a particular role in his crew. From there they became familiar with many other roles, learned the scope of the whole operation, and began to meet suppliers and customers. This mentor relationship often led apprentices to form an enduring loyalty to their sponsor. . . .

Identity Shift

Developing a dealing or smuggling self-conception involved more than simply committing illegal acts. A transition in the locus of self was required. Some people assumed the dealing identity immediately and eagerly, having made a conscious decision to pursue dealing as an occupation. Others displayed a more subtle identity shift, as they gradually drifted into membership in the drug world (Matza 1964). Many individuals, then, became drug dealers by their actions well before they consciously admitted this to themselves. One dealer described his transformation:

> I had a job, school, and I was doing volunteer work, but I was also deviant and the deviant part was the part I secretly got off on. I was like a Dr. Jekyll with a Mr. Hyde side. When I got into my dealing bag people would pay homage to me; I'd get respect and recognition. . . . Eventually the two worlds intermingled and the facade [dealing side] became the reality.

Becker and Carper (1956) have asserted that individuals' identities are based on their degree of commitment to an occupation. Thus, those people who maintained their ties to other occupations took longer to form a dealing identity. They did not become fully committed to dealing until some external event (i.e., an arrest, or the conflicting demands of their legitimate and illegitimate businesses) forced them to make a conscious choice. One dealer related how he faced this decision:

> I had been putting off thinking about it for all those months but the time squeeze finally became such a thing that I couldn't ignore it any more. I was working at the office all day and staying up dealing and doing drugs all night. My wife was complaining because I'd fall asleep at odd hours and I never had any time for the kids. I knew I had to choose between my

> two lives—the straight and the dealing. I hated to give up my job because it had always been my security, and besides, it was a good business cover, but I finally decided I was more attracted to dealing. I was making better money there in fewer hours and this way, I'd have more time to be with my kids during the day.

Upward Mobility

Once they had gotten in and learned the trade, most dealers and smugglers strove for upward mobility. This advancement took different forms, varying between dealing and smuggling.

Dealers experienced two types of upward mobility: *rising through the ranks* and *stage-jumping*. The gradual rise exemplifies the way upward mobility has historically been portrayed in the sociological literature on dealing (Anonymous 1969; Carey 1972; Redlinger 1975). Individuals from the lowest levels expanded their range of contacts, realized that they could earn greater profits by buying in greater quantities, and began to move up the hierarchy of dealing levels. Rick described his early stage of involvement with dealing:

> I had dealt a limited amount of lids and psychedelics in my early college days without hardly taking it seriously. But after a while something changed in me and I decided to try to work my way up. I probably was a classic case—started out buying a kilo for $150 and selling two pounds for $100 each. I did that twice, then I took the money and bought two bricks, then three, then five, then seven.

This type of upward mobility, though characteristic of low-level dealers, was fairly atypical of the upper-level drug crowd. Two factors combined to make it less likely for low-level entrants to rise through the ranks to the top. The first was psychological. People who started small thought small; most had neither the motivation nor the vision to deal large quantities of drugs. The second and more critical factor was social. People who started at the bottom and tried to work their way up the ladder often had a hard time finding connections at the upper levels. The few people who did rise through the ranks generally began dealing in another part of the country, moving to Southwest County only after they had already progressed to the middle levels. These people were lured to the region by its reputation within drug circles as an importation and wholesale trafficking market.

More commonly, dealers and smugglers stage-jumped to the higher levels of drug trafficking. Beginning at a middle level, and progressing so rapidly that they could hardly acclimate to their increasing involvement and volume, these people moved quickly to the top. Jean described her mode of escalation:

> When I started to deal I was mostly looking for a quick buck here or there, something to pay some pressing bill. I was middling 50 or 100 bricks at a time. But then I met a guy who said he would front me half a pound of coke, and if I turned it fast, I could have more, and on a regular basis. Pretty soon I was turning 6, 7, 8, 9, 10 pounds a week—they were passing through real fast. I was clearing at least 10 grand a month. It was too much money too fast. I didn't know what to do with it. It got ridiculous, I wasn't relating to anyone anymore. I was never home, always gone. . . . The biggest ego trip came when all of a sudden I turned around and I was selling to the people I had been buying from. I skipped their level of doing business entirely and stage-jumped straight past them.

Southwest County's social milieu, with its concentration of upper-level dealers and smugglers, thus facilitated forming connections and doing business at the upper levels of the drug world.

Within smuggling, upward mobility took the form of individuals *branching out on their own* (Redlinger 1975). By working for a smuggler, some crew members developed the expertise and connections to run their own operation. There were several requirements for such a move. They could fairly easily acquire the technical knowledge of equipment, air routes, stopovers, and how to coordinate personnel after working in a smuggling area for six months to a year. It was difficult to put together their own crew, though, because skilled employees, especially pilots, were hard to find. Most new smugglers borrowed people from other crews until they were established enough to recruit and train their own personnel. Finally, they needed connections for buying and selling drugs. Customers were plentiful, but it often required special breaks or networks to serve a foreign supplier.

Another way for employees to head their own smuggling operations was to take over when their boss retired. This had the advantage of keeping the crew and style of operation intact. Various financial arrangements were worked out for such a transfer of authority, from straight cash purchases to deals involving residual payments. One marijuana smuggler described how he acquired his operation:

> I had been Jake's main pilot for about a year and next after him I knew the most about how his operation was run. We were really tight, and he had taken me all up and down the coast with him, meeting his customers. Naturally I knew the Mexican end of the operation and his supplier, Cesar, since I used to make the runs, flying down the money and picking up the dope. So when he told me he wanted to get out of the business, we made a deal. I took over the set-up and gave him a residual for every run I made. I kept all the drivers, all the dealers, all the connections—everything the guy had—but I found myself a new pilot.

In sum, most dealers and smugglers reached the upper levels of doing business not so much as a result of their individual entrepreneurial initiative but through the social networks they formed in the drug subculture. Their ability to remain in these strata was largely tied to the way they treated these drug world relationships.

Aging in the Career

Up to this point I have discussed dealers and smugglers separately because they displayed distinctive career patterns. However, once individuals rose to the highest levels, they faced a common set of problems and experiences. I will therefore discuss them together below.

Once they entered the drug world and established themselves at its upper levels, dealers and smugglers were capable of wheeling and dealing on a major scale. Yet this period brought with it a growth of malaise. As they aged in the career, the dark side of their occupation began to surface.

The first part of their disillusionment lay in the fading of glamour and excitement. While participation in the drug world brought thrills and status to novices, the occupation's allure faded over time. Their initial feelings of exhilaration began to dull as they became increasingly jaded by their exorbitant drug consumption. Already inclined toward regular use, upper-level dealers and smugglers set no limits on their drug intake once they began trafficking and could afford all the cocaine they desired. One smuggler described how he eventually came to feel:

> It was fun, those three or four years. I never worried about money or anything. But after a while it got real boring, there was no feeling or emotion or anything about it. I wasn't even hardly relating to my old lady anymore. Everything was just one big rush.

After a year or more of serious drug trafficking, dealers and smugglers became increasingly sensitized to the extreme risks they faced. Cases of friends and associates who were arrested, imprisoned, or killed (because of natural hazards) began to mount. The probability that they were known to the police increased. They gradually realized that the potential legal consequences they faced were less remote than they had earlier imagined. Many individuals became convinced that continued drug trafficking would inevitably lead to arrest ("It's only a matter of time before you get caught").

Dealers and smugglers generally repressed their awareness of danger, treating it as a taken-for-granted part of their daily existence. Periodic crises shattered their casual attitudes, however, evoking strong underlying feelings of fears. One dealer talked about his feelings of paranoia:

> You're always on the line. You don't lead a normal life. You're always looking over your shoulder, wondering who's at the door, having to hide everything. You learn to look behind you so well you could probably bend over and look up your ass. That's paranoia. It's a really scary, hard feeling. That's what makes you get out.

These feelings caused dealers and smugglers to assume greater security precautions. After especially close brushes with danger, they intensified their precautions temporarily, retreating into near isolation until they felt that the heat was off. They also gradually incorporated more precautions into their everyday routines, abandoning their earlier casualness for greater inflexibility and adherence to their rational rules of operating (see Lieb and Olson 1976). This went against their natural preference, and they found it unspontaneous and cumbersome.

Drug world members also grew progressively weary of their exclusion from the legitimate world and the series of deceptions they had to manage to sustain that separation.

Initially, the separation had been surrounded by an alluring mystique. As they aged in the career, however, the mystique was replaced by the hassle of everyday boundary maintenance and their feelings of being expatriated from conventional society. One smuggler described the effects of this separation:

> I'm so sick of looking over my shoulder, having to sit in my house and worry about one of my nondrug world friends stopping in when I'm doing business. Do you know how awful that is? It's like leading a double life. That's what makes it not worth it.

Thus, while the drug world was somewhat restricted, it was not an encapsulated community. As Reuter (1983, 174) has noted, criminals maintain an involvement with the legitimate world:

> Criminals do not inhabit a social and physical world that is different from the rest of society. They walk the same streets, dine in the same restaurants, and send their children to the same schools.

This constant contact with the straight world reminded them of the comforts and social ease they had left behind, and tempted them to go straight.

For upper-level dealers and smugglers, then, the process of aging in the career was one of progressive *burnout*. With the novelty worn off, most dealers and smugglers felt that the occupation no longer resembled their earlier impressions of it. Once they had reached the upper levels, their experience began to change and they changed with it. No longer were they the carefree people who lived from day to day without a thought for the future. No longer were they so intoxicated with their glamour that their only care in the world was the search for new heights of pleasure. Elements of this lifestyle remained, but they were tempered with the harsher side of the reality. In between episodes of intensive partying, veteran dealers and smugglers were struck by anxiety. They began to structure their work to encompass greater planning, caution, secrecy, and insulation. They isolated themselves from the straight world for days or weeks at a time, imprisoned and haunted by their own suspicions. They never renounced their hedonism or materialism, but the price they paid increased. Eventually, the rewards of trafficking no longer seemed to justify the strain. It was at this point that the straight world's formerly dull ambience became transformed (at least in theory) into a potential haven.

Shifts and Oscillations

Despite the gratifications dealers and smugglers derived from the easy money, material comfort, freedom, prestige, and power associated with their careers, most of them decided, at some point, to quit the business. This stemmed, in part, from their initial perceptions of the career as temporary ("Hell, nobody wants to be a drug dealer all their life"). Supplementing these early intentions was the process of rapid aging in the career, where dealers and smugglers became increasingly aware of the sacrifices their occupations required and got tired of living the fugitive life. As the dealing life began to look more troubling than rewarding, drug traffickers focused their energies on returning to the straight life. They thought about, talked about, and in many cases, took steps toward getting out of the drug business. But like entering the field, disengaging from drug trafficking was rarely an abrupt act (Lieb and Olson 1976, 364). Instead, it more often resembled a series of transitions, or oscillations out of and back into the business. For once out of the drug world, dealers and smugglers were rarely successful at making it in the legitimate world because they failed to cut down on their extravagant lifestyle or drug consumption. Many thus abandoned their efforts to reform and returned to deviance, sometimes picking up where they left off and other times shifting to a new mode of operating. For example, some shifted from trafficking in cocaine to trafficking in marijuana, some dropped to a lower level of dealing, and others shifted their role within the same group of traffickers. This series of phase-outs and reentries, combined with career shifts, endured for years, dominating the pattern of their remaining involvement with the business. It also represented the method by which many eventually broke away from drug trafficking, for each phase-out had the potential to be an individual's final departure.

Phasing Out

Making the decision to quit a deviant occupation is difficult. Several factors served to hold dealers and smugglers to the drug world. First, the hedonistic and materialistic satisfactions were primary. Once individuals became accustomed to earning large amounts of easy money, they found it exceedingly difficult to go back to the income scale of the straight world. They were also reluctant to abandon the pleasures of the fast life and its accompanying drugs, sex, and power. Second, dealers and smugglers formed an identification with and commitment to the occupation of drug trafficking. Their self-images were tied to that role and could not be easily disengaged. Their years invested learning the trade, forming connections, building reputations served as "side-bets" (Becker 1960), strengthening their involvement with both the deviant occupation and the drug community. And since their relationships were social as well as business-oriented, members' friendship ties bound them to dealing. As one dealer, in the midst of struggling to phase out, explained:

> The biggest threat to me is to get caught up sitting around the house with friends that are into dealing. I'm trying to stay away from them, change my habits.

Third, dealers and smugglers hesitated to voluntarily quit the field because they knew it would be difficult to find another way of earning a living. They feared that they would be unable to account to prospective employers for their years spent in illicit activities. This narrowed their occupational choices considerably, leaving self-employment as one of the few remaining avenues open.

Once dealers and smugglers made the decision to phase out, they generally pursued one of several routes out of dealing. The most frequent pattern involved resolving to quit after they executed one last big deal. While the intention was sincerely uttered, individuals who chose this route rarely succeeded; the big deal too often remained elusive. One marijuana smuggler offered a variation on this theme:

> My plan is to make a quarter of a million dollars in four months during the prime smuggling season and get the hell out of the business.

A second pattern involved individuals who planned to get out immediately, but never did. They announced that they were quitting, yet their outward actions never varied. Bruce, with his problems of overconsumption and debt escalation, described his involvement with this syndrome:

> When I wake up I'll say, "Hey, I'm going to quit this cycle and just run my other business." But when you're dealing you constantly have people dropping by ounces and asking, "Can you move this?" What's your first response? Always, "Sure, for a toot."

In the third pattern of phasing-out, individuals actually suspended their dealing or smuggling activities, but did not replace them with an alternative source of income. Such withdrawals were usually spontaneous and prompted by exhaustion, the influence of a person from outside the drug world, or problems with the police or other associates. As one dealer's case illustrated, these phase-outs usually lasted only until their money ran out:

> I got into heavy legal trouble with the FBI a while back and I was forced to quit dealing. Everybody just cut me off completely, and I saw the danger in continuing myself. But my high class tastes never dwindled. I borrowed money here and there. Before I knew it I was in hock over $30,000. Even though I was hot, I was forced to get back into dealing to relieve some of my debts.

In the fourth pattern of phasing-out, traffickers attempted a move into another line of work. Alternative occupations they tried included: occupations they had pursued before dealing or smuggling; front businesses maintained on the side while they were trafficking in drugs; and new occupations altogether. While some people successfully accomplished this transition, there were problems in all three alternatives.

Most people who tried to resume their former occupations found that these had changed too much while they were away from the field. In addition, they themselves had changed: they enjoyed the self-directed freedom and spontaneity associated with dealing and smuggling, and were unwilling to relinquish it.

Those who turned to their legitimate front business often found that these businesses were unable to support them. Designed to launder rather than earn money, most of these ventures had become accustomed to operating under a continuous subsidy from illegal funds. Once their drug funding was cut off, they could not survive for long.

Many dealers and smugglers utilized the business skills and connections they had developed in drug trafficking to create a new occupation. For some, the decision to prepare a legitimate career for retirement followed an unsuccessful attempt to phase out into a front business. One husband-and-wife dealing team explained how these legitimate side businesses differed from front businesses:

> We always had a little legitimate scam going, like mail-order shirts, wallets, jewelry, and the kids were always involved in that. We made a little bit of money on them. Their main purpose was for a cover and a legitimate business both. But [this business] was different; right from the start this was going to be a legal thing to push us out of the drug business.

Dealers and smugglers often formed these legitimate side occupations by exchanging their illegal commodity for a legal one, going into import/export, manufacturing, wholesaling, or retailing other merchandise. One former dealer described his current business and how he got into it:

> A friend of mine knew one of the major wholesalers in Tijuana for buying Mexican blankets, ponchos, and sweatshirts. After I helped him out with a favor when he was down, he turned me on to his connections. Now, I've cornered the market on wholesaling them to surf shops and swap meet sellers by undercutting everybody else.

The most future-oriented dealers and smugglers thus began gradually tapering off their drug world involvement, transferring their time and money into a selected legitimate endeavor. They did not try to quit drug trafficking altogether until they felt confident that their legitimate business could support them. But like spontaneous phase-outs, many of these planned withdrawals into legitimate businesses failed to generate enough money to keep individuals from being lured back into the drug world.

In addition to the voluntary phase-outs dealers and smugglers attempted after they became sufficiently burned out, many of them experienced an involuntary "bustout" at some point in their careers. Forced withdrawals from dealing or smuggling were usually sudden and necessitated by external factors, either financial, legal, or reputational. Financial bustouts generally occurred when dealers or smugglers were either burned or ripped off by others, leaving them in too much debt to rebuild their operation. Legal bustouts occurred when individuals got so hot from arrest or incarceration that few of their former associates would deal with them. Reputational bustouts occurred when individuals burned or ripped off others (regardless of whether they intended to do so) and were banned from business by their former associates. One smuggler gave his opinion on the pervasive nature of forced phase-outs:

> Some people are smart enough to get out of it because they realize, physically, they have to. Others realize, monetarily, that they want to get out of this world before this world gets them. Those are the lucky ones. Then there are the ones who have to get out because they're hot or someone else so close to them is hot that they'd better get out. But in the end when you get out of it, nobody gets out of it out of free choice; you do it because you have to.

Death, of course, was the ultimate bustout. Some pilots met this fate because of the dangerous routes they navigated (hugging mountains, treetops, other aircraft) and because of the sometimes ill-maintained and overloaded planes they flew. However, despite much talk of violence, few Southwest County drug traffickers died at the hands of fellow dealers.

Reentry

Phasing out of the drug world was usually only temporary. For many, it represented merely another stage in their dealing careers (although this may not have been their original intention), to be followed by a period of reinvolvement. Depending on the situation, reentry into the drug world represented either a *comeback* (from a forced withdrawal) or a *relapse* (from a voluntary withdrawal).

Most people forced out of drug trafficking were anxious to return. They had never decided to withdraw, and their desire to get back was based on many of the same reasons which drew them into the field originally. While it was possible to come back from financial, legal, and reputational bustouts, it was difficult and not always successfully accomplished. Dealers and smugglers had to reestablish their contacts, rebuild their organization and fronting arrangements, and raise any necessary operating capital. More important, they had to overcome the circumstances surrounding their departure; once they resumed operating they often found their former colleagues suspicious of them. They were therefore informally subjected to a trial period in which they had to re-prove their reliability before they could once again move easily through the drug world.

Dealers and smugglers usually found that reentering the drug world after they had voluntarily withdrawn from it involved a more difficult decision-making process, but was easier to implement. As I noted earlier, experienced dealers and smugglers often grappled with conflicting reasons for wanting to quit and wanting to stay with the occupation. When the forces propelling them out of the drug world were strongest, they left. But once out, these forces weakened. Their images of and hopes for the straight world often failed to materialize. Many could not make the shift to the norms, values, and lifestyle of the straight society and could not earn a living within it. Yet the factors enticing individuals to resume drug trafficking were not the same as those which motivated their original entry. They were no longer awestruck by the glamorous lifestyle or the thrill of danger. Instead, they got back in to make money both to pay off the debts they had accumulated while "retired" and to build up and save so that their next phase-out would be more successful. Dealers and smugglers made the decision to reenter the drug world, then, for some very basic reasons: the material perquisites; the drugs; the social ties; and the fact that they had nowhere else to go.

Once this decision was made, the actual process of reentry was relatively simple. One dealer described how the door back into dealing remained open for those "who left voluntarily":

> I still see my dealer friends, I can still buy grams from them when I want to. It's the respect they have for me because I stepped out of it without being busted or burning someone. I'm coming out with a good reputation, and even though the scene is a whirlwind—people moving up, moving down, in, out—if I didn't see anybody for a year I could call them up and get right back in that day.

People who relapsed thus had few problems obtaining fronts, reestablishing their reputations, or readjusting to the scene. Yet once back in, they generally were again unsuccessful in accumulating enough of a nest egg to ensure the success of their subsequent phase-outs. Each time they relapsed into drug trafficking they became caught up once again in the drug world's lifestyle of hedonism and consumption. They thus spent the money they were earning almost as fast as they earned it (or in some cases, faster). The fast life, with its irrationality and present orientation, held a grip on them partly because of the drugs they were consuming, but most especially because of the pervasive dominance of the drug subculture. They thus started the treadmill spinning again so that they never got enough ahead; they never amassed the stockpile that they had reentered the drug world to achieve.

Career Shifts

Dealers and smugglers who reentered the drug world, whether from a voluntary or forced phase-out, did not always return to the same activity, level, or commodity which characterized their previous style of operation. Upon returning after a hiatus, many individuals underwent a "career shift" (Luckenbill and Best 1981) and became involved in some new segment of the drug world. The shifts were sometimes lateral, as when a member of a smuggling crew took on a new specialization, switching from piloting to operating a stash house, for example. One dealer described how he used friendship networks upon his reentry to shift from cocaine to marijuana trafficking:

> Before, when I was dealing cocaine, I was too caught up in using the drug, and people around me were starting to go under from getting into base. That's why I got out. But now I think I've got myself together and even though I'm dealing again I'm staying away from coke. I've switched over to dealing grass. It's a whole different circle of people. I got into it through a close friend I used to know before, but I never did business with him because he did grass and I did coke.

Vertical shifts moved operators to different levels. For example, one former smuggler returned and took up dealing; another wholesale marijuana dealer came back to find that the smugglers he knew had disappeared and he was forced to buy from other dealers.

A third type of shift relocated drug traffickers in different styles of operation. One dealer described how, after being arrested, he tightened his security measures:

> I just had to cut back after I went through those changes. Hell, I'm not getting any younger and the idea of going to prison bothers me a lot more than it did ten years ago. The risks are no longer worth it when I can have a comfortable income with less risk. So I only sell to four people now. I don't care if they buy a pound or a gram.

A former smuggler who sold his operation and lost all his money during his phase-out returned as a consultant to the industry, selling his expertise to individuals with new money and fresh manpower:

> What I've been doing lately is setting up deals for people. I've got foolproof plans for smuggling cocaine up here from Colombia. I tell them how to modify their airplanes to add on extra fuel tanks and to fit in more weed, coke, or whatever they bring up. Then I set them up with refueling points all up and down Central America, telling them how to bring it up here, what points to come in at, and what kind of receiving unit to use. Then they do it all, and I get 10 percent of what they make.

Reentry did not always imply a shift to a new niche, however. Some returned to the same circle of associates, trafficking activity, and commodity they worked with before their departure. Thus, drug traffickers' careers often peaked early and then displayed a variety of shifts from lateral mobility, to decline, to holding fairly steady.

A final alternative involved neither completely leaving nor remaining in this deviant occupation. Many individuals straddled the deviant and respectable worlds forever by continuing to dabble in drug trafficking. As a result of their experiences in the drug world they had developed a deviant self-identity and a deviant *modus operandi.* They did not want to bear the social and legal burden of full-time deviant work, but neither were they willing to assume the drudgery of the straight world. They therefore moved into the entrepreneurial realm, where their daily activities involved some sort of hustling in an assortment of legitimate, quasi-legitimate, and deviant ventures, and where they were their own boss. In this way they were able to retain certain elements of the deviant lifestyle and to socialize on the fringes of the drug community. For these individuals, drug dealing shifted from a primary occupation to a sideline, but they never abandoned it altogether.

Leaving Drug Trafficking

This pattern of oscillation into and out of active drug trafficking makes it somewhat problematic to speak of leaving deviance in the sense of a final retirement. Clearly, some people succeeded in voluntarily retiring. Of these, a few managed to prepare a post-deviant career for themselves by transferring their drug money into a legitimate enterprise. A larger group was forced out of dealing and either did not or could not return; their bustouts were sufficiently damaging that either they never attempted reentry or they abandoned their efforts after a series of unsuccessful comeback attempts. But there was no way of determining in advance whether an exit from the business would be temporary or permanent. Here, dealers' and smugglers' vacillating intentions were compounded by the complexity of operating successfully in the drug world. For many, then, no phase-out could ever be definitively assessed as permanent. As long as individuals had the skills, knowledge, and connections to deal, they could potentially reenter the occupation at any time. Leaving drug trafficking was thus a relative phenomenon, characterized by a trailing-off process where spurts of involvement occurred with decreasing frequency and intensity. This disengagement was characterized by a progressive reorientation to the legitimate world, where former drug traffickers once again shifted their social networks and changed their self-conceptions (Lieb and Olson 1976).

Summary

Dealing and smuggling careers were temporary, fraught with multiple attempts at retirement. Veteran drug traffickers quit their occupation because of the ambivalent feelings they developed toward their deviant life. As they aged in the career their experience changed, shifting from a work life that was exhilarating and free to one that became increasingly dangerous and confining. Just as their deviant careers were temporary, so too were their retirements. Potential recruits, therefore, were lured into the business by materialism, hedonism, glamour, and excitement. Established dealers were lured away from the deviant life and back into the mainstream by the attractions of security and social ease. But once out, retired dealers and smugglers were lured back in by their expertise, by their ability to make money quickly and easily. People who were exposed to the upper levels of drug trafficking found it extremely difficult to quit permanently. This stemmed, in part, from their difficulty in moving from the illegitimate to the legitimate business sector. Even more significant was the affinity they formed for their deviant values and lifestyle. Thus few of the people I observed were successful in leaving deviance entirely. What dealers and smugglers intended, at the time, to be a permanent withdrawal from drug trafficking can be seen in retrospect as a pervasive occupational pattern of shifts and oscillations.

Questions for Thought and Discussion

1. What are the three routes into the world of drug dealing identified by the author?
2. How did the author gain entry into the drug-dealing world? What do you think about this method? Is it ethical?
3. How did the eventual "burnout" of the dealers as they aged compare with the same phenomenon discussed by Shover and Honaker (Chapter 4) and Sommers, Baskin, and Fagan (Chapter 30)?
4. What theory or theories of criminal behavior are illustrated in this research?

References

Anonymous. 1969. "On selling marijuana." In Erich Goode, ed., *Marijuana*, pp. 92–202. New York: Atherton.

Becker, Howard. 1960. "Notes on the concept of commitment." *American Journal of Sociology* LXVI: 32–44.

Becker, Howard, and James Carper. 1956. "The development of identification with an occupation." *American Journal of Sociology* 66:32–42.

Blum, Richard, et al. 1968. *The Dream Sellers*. San Francisco: Jossey-Bass.

Carey, James T. 1972. *The College Drug Scene*. Englewood Cliffs, NJ: Prentice-Hall.

Goode, Erich. 1970. *The Marijuana Smokers*. New York: Basic.

Johnson, Bruce D. 1973. *Marijuana Users and Drug Subcultures*. New York: Wiley.

Lieb, John, and Sheldon Olson. 1976. "Prestige, paranoia and profit: On becoming a dealer of illicit drugs on a university community." *Journal of Drug Issues* 6:356–369.

Luckenbill, David F., and Joel Best. 1981. "Careers in deviance and respectability: The analogy's limitations." *Social Problems* 29:197–206.

Matza, David. 1964. *Delinquency and Drift*. New York: Wiley.

Miller, Gale, and George Ritzer. 1977. "Informal socialization: Deviant occupations." In George Ritzer, *Working*, 2nd ed., 83–94. Englewood Cliffs, NJ: Prentice-Hall.

Ray, Marsh. 1961. "The cycle of abstinence and relapse among heroin addicts." *Social Problems* 9:132–140.

Redlinger, Lawrence J. 1975. "Marketing and distributing heroin." *Journal of Psychedelic Drugs* 7:331–353.

Reuter, Peter. 1983. *Disorganized Crime: The Economics of the Visible Hand*. Cambridge: MIT Press.

Chapter 22 Managing the Action

Sports Bookmakers as Entrepreneurs

Phyllis Coontz

M*ore and more states have moved to legalize various forms of gambling as a viable way to raise substantial revenues. And while some have considered adding sports betting to their menu of games, Nevada continues to be the only state where placing a bet on sports events is legal. Despite the lack of concrete knowledge about illegal sports betting, two justifications for keeping it illegal have dominated the public debate. The first has to do with whether legal sports betting could successfully compete with illegal operations were it to be legalized, and the second has to do with a purported link between gambling on sports and organized crime.*

This paper focuses on the second line of argument and examines the social, organizational, and occupational features of bookmaking. If bookmakers are conduits for organized crime, as is claimed, there should be evidence of this in the day-to-day activities of bookmaking and in the career trajectories of bookmakers. The analysis is based upon interviews with 47 sports bookmakers working in the Rust Belt region. Drawing upon what sports bookies themselves have to say about their experiences in the business and their career trajectories, there appears to be little merit to the organized crime link argument. The analysis suggests that unlike other types of deviance, the social organization of bookmaking insulates bookies from the more typical consequences associated with frequent and prolonged deviant activity, for example, getting arrested, being prosecuted, serving time in prison, and forced association with other criminals. In fact, the findings suggest that bookies are more like entrepreneurs than criminals. While a single study cannot resolve the normative question about whether sports bookmaking should be criminalized, the findings do show that the social construction of bookmaking and bookmakers found in the public debate and popular culture does not reflect the reality of sports bookmaking.

As a cultural phenomenon, gambling in the United States has been an enduring contradiction—while it is widespread it is also heavily regulated. Despite the growth of commercialized gambling since the 1960s, some forms of gambling remain off limits. One of these is sports betting. Betting on sports events is illegal in every state except Nevada. This is somewhat puzzling given the popularity of both gambling and sports.

One of the ironies of this is that while Nevada is the only state that allows sports betting, one of the accoutrements for gambling on sports, i.e., the "line" or "point spread," can be found everywhere. It appears daily in the sports section of most major newspapers; it is a link on numerous sports news websites; it is central to sports commentary about winners, losers, and outcomes on network and cable television; it is packaged as advice that can be purchased through various sports services through 900 telephone numbers; and it is woven into conversations that take place at work, in restaurants, classrooms, dorms, country clubs, bars, and parties every day around the country. It is even available through one of the more than 700 gambling casinos operating on the Internet.

Some have suggested that sports betting might be the number one form of gambling (legal or illegal) in the United States (Scarne 1974; Reuter 1983; Congressional Hearings 1995). Industry analysts (e.g., *Moody's* and *Standard and Poor*) report that sports betting is one of the biggest growth areas in commercialized gambling (*Moody's Industry Review* 1995, 1–46). For example, by the end of fiscal year 1996, bookmakers in Las Vegas handled $2.5 billion in wagers (O'Brien 1998). And according to the Gaming Control Board of Nevada, the amount wagered on sports events has been increasing every year and more sports events are being added to the menu. For example, sports books in Las Vegas added last year's Women's World Cup soccer final to their array of events. Focusing on only a single event, the Super Bowl, the amount wagered almost doubled from $40 million in 1991 to $70 million in 1997 (personal communication, Research Division, June 1998). While illicit wagers are far more difficult to track, it is estimated that in 1997 alone, over $100 billion was wagered illegally on sports (McGraw 1997).

Given the magnitude of legal or illegal sports betting and the popularity of sports, it is difficult to understand why it continues to be outlawed. Of course, sociologists have long recognized that a behavior's legal status has little to do with its popularity, intrinsic harm, or even desirability. Far more important in determining legal status is the way the behavior is socially constructed. In the case of sports betting, we see that one of the dominant social constructions involves bookmakers as unsavory characters with ties to the underworld. For example, supporters of the Professional and Amateur Sports Protection Act of 1992 argued that

> [I]nstead of standing for healthy competition through team work and honest preparation, professional sport contests would come to represent the fast buck, the quick fix, and the desire to get something for nothing. Betting would undermine the integrity of team sports and public confidence in them. . . . Fans could not help but wonder if a missed free throw, a dropped fly ball, or a missed extra point was part of a player's scheme to fix the game (S-474, pg S-7302 Temp. Record).

Other advocates of criminalization allege a link between bookmaking and organized crime and argue that it is a major source of its total gambling revenue (Cressey 1969; The President's Commission on Law Enforcement and the Administration of Justice 1967; Clark 1971). The criminal construction is also common in our popular culture, particularly in films such as *Wiseguy* (1986), *Goodfellas* (1990), and *Casino* (1995) and novels such Gay Talese's *Honor Thy Father* (1971), Mario Puzo's *The Godfather* (1969), and most recently Bill Bonanno's *Bound by Honor* (1999).

How closely do the social constructions presented in the public debate and the popular cultural mirror reality? The research on bookmaking shows that what is known about sports bookies, their methods of operation, career trajectories, life styles, and relationships with each other is limited, fragmented, and largely inferred. Some research on bookmaking generally suggests that instead of being members of a larger criminal syndicate, bookmakers are more likely to operate as a loose confederation of independents that may at times cooperate with one another (Chambliss 1978; Anderson 1979; Reuter and Rubinstein 1982; Reuter 1983; Rosencrance 1987; Sasuly 1982). Despite the lack of empirical evidence about the nature of sports bookmaking, the image of the sports bookie as criminal is pervasive.

This study set out to learn about sports bookmaking from those who do it. The assumption was that if sports bookies are a part of an organized crime syndicate, then there should be some evidence of it in the day-to-day operations of bookmaking. The study examines the social organization of bookmaking and the occupational features of being a sports bookie. This approach is useful because it allows us to move beyond the criminal aspects of sports bookmaking and consider what is actually involved in operating a sports book. That is, what sorts of skills, knowledge, processes, and contexts are needed to get into and manage a sports book.

The analysis draws upon face-to-face interviews with 47 different bookmakers operating in Western Pennsylvania. This researcher examines how one becomes a sports bookmaker; how sports bookmakers manage and grow their business; their relationships with bettors, other sports bookmakers, law enforcement officials, and family; and finally, how they exit the business. If sports bookmaking is indeed a part of a larger criminal organization then it is reasonable to expect that entry into and departure from the business would be determined by the larger organization; that the day-to-day operations would follow norms and practices dictated and monitored by an outside organization; and that the conditions under which bookmakers transact business with bettors would involve criminal elements such as coercion, dishonesty, and bribery.

Background for the Study

Although I have been interested in deviant behavior for more than 20 years, I became interested in sports betting only recently through a friend. It happened during dinner with this friend about six years ago when she excused herself so that she could call her bookie to place a bet on a football game. I didn't know she gambled on sports, and she certainly did not fit my image of someone who would know a bookie. She was a professional and civic minded and did not resemble my image of someone who associated with bookies. This contradiction between my friend and my beliefs piqued my curiosity and is what led to this research.

When I thought about the source of my beliefs, I realized they came mostly from the literature on organized crime and popular culture. I did a thorough literature review and discovered that there was little empirical knowledge about sports bookmaking. In order to learn what sports bookmaking was all about I would need to do some field work and find bookies who were willing to talk about bookmaking. Like most field work on illicit activities, one needs a contact to gain access. I explained my growing interest to my friend and asked whether she would vouch for me with her bookie. My plan was to place bets with her bookie, develop a relationship with him, and then explore whether he would talk to me about the business. For the next several months I placed bets on different football games for an entire season. Eventually, I shared my research interest with my bookie and he agreed to be interviewed. The first interview took place in my home. Simultaneously, I began talking more openly and frequently with friends, acquaintances, and colleagues about betting on sports events and discovered that many of the people I came into contact with—both socially and professionally—bet on sporting events. These interactions led to contacts with other bookies, many of whom agreed to be interviewed. Over the course of a two-year period I interviewed a total of 47 bookies at least once and had follow-up interviews with 11 of them. All of the interviews were tape recorded, transcribed, and analyzed using NUD*IST (a computer based text analysis program). The findings presented here reflect major aspects of the organizational and occupations dimensions of the bookmaking business.

With the exception of the interviews with my bookie, all other interviews took place in locations selected by the bookmakers. Typically we met in restaurants, private clubs, and bars. The interview format focused on the process by which sports bookmakers got involved in the business; their strategies for building and maintaining their business; the duration of their involvement in the business; their relationships with other bookmakers; experiences with outside pressure (from law enforcement, other bookmakers, or professional criminals); the size of their business; the volume of the action; their families and friends; and their perceptions of the business, themselves, and its legal status. I begin the analysis with a general profile of the bookies that participated in this study.

Demographic and General Information About Sports Bookies

All bookmakers were male and ranged in age from 22–72 years old. The mean age for this group was 46. When asked about female bookmakers, I was told that none operated in this region, although some had heard about female sports bookies working elsewhere. All of my informants were originally from the region. All but two of my informants were currently married or living with someone, and all but five had children. Five had gotten divorced as a result of their bookmaking activities, and four remarried. Ninety-one percent (n = 43) were currently employed or self-employed in a legitimate job and five reported relying solely on earnings from bookmaking at different times. Four of my informants did not finish high school, 34 completed high school, and 7 completed college. Of those who completed college, one had a graduate degree and another was studying for an MBA.

On average these men had been involved in bookmaking for 17 years, ranging from a low of 2 years to a high of 45 years. None would reveal the amount of income earned from their bookmaking activities explaining their actual income was contingent on a number of factors such as the amount of a bet, the kind of bet made, the number of winners and losers, and whether losers paid their losses. However, all of the bookies in this study reported making money from bookmaking. Most experienced occasional "off" periods meaning they paid out more than they brought in. And one informant revealed he lost $96,000 the first year he went into business.

Like other illegal markets, sports betting is a cash business. Payouts were usually made midweek (typically Wednesdays) while collections were made the first part of the week (typically Mondays) and took place at designated locations, which were typically public. If a customer was unable to pay their losses in full, terms were established without an interest penalty. Although there are numerous kinds of wagers that can be made, the four most common were: straight bets, over and under bets, teasers, and parlays. The amount wagered varied by customer, but the average wager was $50.00 per game. All of these bookies established a minimum and maximum amount they would accept with the majority not willing to accept wagers over $5,000. Five, however, accepted bets for $10,000 and occasionally more. The majority accepted wagers only on the day of the game (and usually approximately 30 minutes before the start of a game), but some would accept bets when the line first came out.

The Mechanics of Sports Bookmaking

The "line" which is the basis for taking bets serves two general purposes: (1) to encourage the gambling public to gamble on both opponents playing a game, and (2) to balance the amount of money wagered equally between both teams so that amount is equally divided between both teams. According to the "Boxy" Roxborough, the guru of the Las Vegas Line, "the fundamental concept of bookmaking is to force people to gamble . . . at odds favorable to the house. The line is used to encourage gambling by equalizing the contest" (Cook 1992). Sports bookies do not care who wins or loses a game; they are interested in the final score and whether they have more losers than winners for any given game. The point spread then is the bookie's management tool for balancing the betting action on individual games.

The following illustrates how the point spread works. The Super Bowl is the final championship game between the two Conferences in the National Football League (NFL). Although each Conference has a champion, one is usually perceived to be stronger than the other (this is based on a combination of record, performance, and hype). In Super Bowl XXX (for the 1995–96 season) the Dallas Cowboys (the National Football Conference champions) and the Pittsburgh Steelers (the American Football Conference champions) played for the championship. At the time, the NFC and Dallas Cowboys were perceived to be superior to the AFC and Pittsburgh Steelers. Based on this alone, the outcome of the game was seen as a foregone conclusion—Dallas would win.

If you know the outcome of a game before it starts, it will not be very interesting. Because so many matchups are between unequal teams, the line equalizes the contest by giving the underdog an advantage. When the line came out for Super Bowl XXX it was set at 14 points, favoring Dallas. Translated, a 14-point spread meant that the Cowboys would need to win by more than two touchdowns. The question raised by such a high point spread for the bettor, and the question the bookie hopes the bettor will ask, is whether the Cowboys can beat the Steelers by more than 14 points. The line alters what is otherwise a foregone conclusion and entices bettors to put money on the underdog.

Getting Into the Business

As argued earlier, if sports bookmaking is controlled by outside interests then getting into the business should be determined by those associated with these interests. At a minimum, if the external control allegation has merit, there should be accounts of being recruited, coerced, pressured, or getting permission to get started from bookies. None of the bookies reported external pressure—all entered the business voluntarily and most viewed their entry as an opportunity to make money. The oldest bookie in the study, Artie, started out as a numbers runner for another bookmaker when he was only 8 years old. He stated that during his early years (which he characterized as "hard times") he was the sole support for his family (including his parents and siblings). Artie was the only bookie I interviewed who progressed from numbers to sports bookmaking. He worked in the numbers business for over 30 years and then moved into sports bookmaking when he was in his early 40s.

> I ran numbers and made a pretty nice income for a kid. If you hustled $400–$500 worth, you could make a nice piece of change. I took care of my family—I literally paid the bills. I learned from one of the smartest guys in the area. He's dead now, but he was smart, very wise—he was a cousin of my mother's. He liked me, and he took me under his wing. I used to hang around him and one day he asked me if I wanted to do something for him. He sent me out to pick up the day's business—in a paper bag. I brought it back and he put me to work. He trusted me even though I was just a kid, he had confidence in me. You can't imagine how good I felt cause I looked up to him, he had something and everybody, they admired him too. He trusted me—this skinny kid. My mother didn't like it, but at the time, I was the only one working and bringing any money in. I made enough to pay the rent, food, and utilities. Times were hard back then.

Before setting up their own bookmaking operations, betting on sports had been an integral part of every bookie's everyday experiences. Joe, who is in his 50s and operated a legitimate sports book in the Caribbean, grew up around bookies and bettors. He entered the business as a young man while working in the steel mills and began his involvement as a favor to a coworker.

> I was helping a guy I worked with out. A lotta guys bet with him and he couldn't handle it one weekend cause he was sick. We were buddies, he trusted me and asked me to help him out. I took all the action that weekend even though I didn't know what I was doin'. After spending that weekend on the phone I told my buddy I wanted to work with him and I did. The rest is history as they say. After a while I went on my own, I worked every day which is tough when you're workin too, especially during basketball and baseball season. You're takin' action all day and all night long. You gotta time everything. You're on the phone all day and sometimes all night. How many games are played in a day during March Madness? You could have a couple dozen games in one day. My first wife really hated it cause I couldn't leave, we didn't go out—I worked all week and I was on the phone all weekend till the games were over. And if I had a bad day, if I got upset—I was an animal. One time I got so upset, I threw a chair through the TV. That was a long time ago, I'm still embarrassed by it. My kids hated it, too. Like now, they'd never get involved with it cause they saw what it did to me—my wife left me 'cause of it—it's your whole life. Things are different now though. The business in the islands, it's legitimate, it's totally different. I have time to enjoy all my hard work—I'm making so much money down there it'd make you crazy. I'm paying taxes, everything's legitimate. My second wife and I can travel, we can go wherever we want and do whatever we want. I could never make this kind of money at anything else. And the way I look at it, I've earned it cause I worked hard for over 30 years.

Steve, a student studying for his MBA at an area university at the time I interviewed him, said he was motivated by what he saw was a way to make money. Steve explains:

> There was a guy in the dorm and everyone bet with him. I started watching him and saw the potential for making money and thought to myself, "hey I can do that." So, one Saturday I started, just like that, with just a few guys I knew. At first I used the local line in the newspaper and I'd talk to other guys to see what they were gettin'. I only deal with students around here, so it's not too complicated. I mean, at first I kept track of everything in my head, but as I took on more customers I had to write things down—I couldn't keep them straight. I was doin' pretty well and after a couple of months I had over 70 regulars. Then I got a couple of friends of mine involved, 'cause I needed the help—I give 'em a few bucks to help me out. You know, I'm not doin' this forever, but for right now it pays the bills—I'm paying for school. I really don't want to have any debt when I graduate.

With all the respondents in the study, there was no indication of coercion, pressure, or an apprenticeship to get into the business. The two main routes through which bookies got into the business were through their personal relationships and perceived economic opportunities. In all cases, entry was voluntary and situational.

Managing and Building the Business

Since bookies can never be certain of the number of bets that will be made on a given game or the amount wagered, being successful involves more than simply taking the action. While several factors affect success, five appear to be common among all bookies: knowledge of sports, building a credible customer base, volatility in the market, productivity of the bookmaker, and avoiding arrest. Roger, a young former bookie who now operates a legitimate sports betting advice service, explains how knowledge of sports plays an integral role in bookmaking and succeeding in the business.

> I read everything that's printed about the games and players. I did that when I was in the business and I'm doing it right now. Every morning I'm on the Internet reading what the sports writers have to say, looking at statistics, checkin' the weather conditions, going over last year's statistics, everything. I study; study so I can handicap each game. Half my day is spent digesting information. We offer 1 or 2 picks each week—and my track record is pretty good on this, mostly winners. I miss it now and then, but when you put all the facts and figures together with what the sports experts are saying, then you're more likely to come up with winners. Even though I'm on the other side of the

business now, the same rules apply. Rule number one is that you've got to pay attention to the details.

When I was takin' bets, the only way you could make money was if your people picked losers. They're always looking at the Internet, the paper, and checkin' with friends. So if you're gonna make money, you gotta have a solid line—one that's based on the facts and figures of the game. I handicapped all my games, see some guys get their lines from the books in Vegas, but not me, I did it myself. I always prided myself on offering a precise line especially on close games—you know, ½-point difference or maybe a 1-point difference on a close game can make a huge difference. And ½ point is appealing to a lot of bettors. You gotta be firm about your line too. Once you set it, it's the same for everybody. I like to think of myself as an expert on these games—you know, Jimmy the Greek. I've studied them all my life—ask me anything and I can tell you. Bettors are emotional, so they don't think about that ½-point difference—they're gonna go with their hearts. If the bookie's gonna make money, you gotta get 'em to go with their favorites and you do that by a solid line. You don't have to be perfect all the time, 50 percent of the time will do.

The illegal status of bookmaking limits what bookmakers can do to attract customers. They cannot advertise or make cold calls from the phonebook or random digit dialing, yet a successful bookmaking business requires a customer base. How do bookies build a customer base? Jimmy, a 22-year veteran, claims that the customers are just there waiting for bookies because of the popularity of sports.

Who doesn't like sports? Everybody loves sports—and betting on them is part of the entertainment. Ever been to a Steelers game? Look around right before a game. You see all these guys on the horn talking to guys like me. Betting makes a game interesting. Every guy I ever knew from my neighborhood and school bet on games. My Dad even bet—on boxing matches. My brother bet. Since I got into the business, I never had any trouble findin' customers. Listen, they're just there waiting to give you their business. Some of my customers I've known since school, some of 'em I work with, some I've met here or there. I've even had guys give me customers. You know my brother brought customers to me. My sister's husband bets with me. My biggest problem is keeping it manageable and making sure I got good people. I don't want too many customers, you know I work and that complicates things a little. Fifty, sixty's about all I can handle at a time. It seems like if I lose one, then I pick up another one or two.

In addition to building a customer base, bookmakers assume the financial risks in their business. Like any for-profit business, the focus is on the bottom line, which means bookies must be attuned to the market, especially patterns and changes in betting action. Volatility of the market affects success and while the line enables the bookie to balance the action between opposing teams, it is insufficient by itself for ensuring a profit. Knowing this, bookies take other steps to minimize potential risks from dramatic swings in the action. According to Carl, who has been in the business for 18 years, limiting your customer base and setting a maximum limit on wagers are two such steps.

If you're gonna hold everything yourself, you've got to have a minimum of 40 players. Right now I got about 100 people. You've gotta have a strong limit, say $500 and not take any more on a game from any one person because if you get 20 of those people giving you a $500 bet, you've got $10,000 you could lose.

An instrumental factor that affects success is knowing how closely specific customers fit the average customer profile. For example, bookies know that bettors tend to wager on multiple games. Multiple game bettors always work to the bookie's advantage and Tony, who has been in the business for 25 years, explains why:

As you research this, you'll find out that the more games people play, the more chance the bookie has to make money. They gotta pick about 66 percent to break even. They don't realize it 'cause everybody thinks if they pick 50 percent they're even, but they're not, they're losing money cause you gotta pay the juice. For the customer to come out ahead, they gotta pick about 66 percent of the time. There's only one way to make money betting and that's to bet one game. Of course, most people bet a lot of games and they bet their hearts—which is good for the bookie.

Like many small businesses, bookmaking requires a high degree of commitment from the bookie. I frequently heard this level of commitment described in terms of bookmaking being a bookie's life. Bookmaking has a higher priority than other activities. To sustain a business for any length of time, bookies must set aside their other interests and be on call for their customers. Depending on the sports season this could range from every day to every weekend of that season. The bookie must learn to manage his time and balance his bookmaking responsibilities against other responsibilities. Sam describes the various ways that bookmaking consumes the bookie's life.

> You can work year round or you can work a couple seasons. See there's a sport for every season. I work year round. Football's not so bad, but basketball, baseball, and hockey'll kill you—every single day, six and seven days a week. If you're gonna work year round, you basically have no life outside of this. It's not over just cause the phones stop ringin' either. You gotta keep track of everything and I don't know many guys who can just turn out the light after the phones stop. I have my set times see, so half hour before a game starts I'm taking action. I get all my 7:00 and 8:00 games startin at 6:30. Now Sunday football, I've got my 1:00 games and I start around 12:40, my 4:00 games I start around 3:40, and my 9:00 game I start at 8:45. You've gotta little free time in between, but then you're watchin the game to see whether you're makin money. Some games don't end till after midnight. Then I gotta get up and go to work. My wife complains, less now than she used to. I guess she's used to it now. I think the extra money helps. She likes to go out, so I get someone to take over for a day or night. I got a couple of guys who'll do that, you know, answer the phone for me. We always go away in the summer, but I don't relax, 'cause I'm worrying about things. I'm checking every day when I'm away. It's just part of you, it's there all the time.

With the exception of online sports books (who accept credit cards), bookmaking is strictly a cash business. Thus, having customers who are willing to pay their losses is essential for profitability. In lieu of a credit report, the bookie depends on informal means of scrutinizing customers. Typically customers are acquired in two ways: either by referral from other customers (which happened in my case) or directly by knowing the customer. What happens when a customer refuses to pay the bookie? Although proponents of criminalization argue that bookies resort to corruption and extortion to collect gambling debts, none of the bookies I talked to engaged in these practices. Instead, they avoid potential losses by screening their customer. Ray, who has been in the business for 35 years, describes how this process works:

> You see, it's not illegal to place a bet, but you can't take bets—that's why you always gotta watch yourself; most guys know that. You gotta know who you're dealing with. I don't take on anybody I don't know. I check, check, check. Say some guy calls me and wants me to take his action. If I don't know him, I won't do it 'cause I don't need the aggravation. I had to learn this though. There was a guy—oh this was about 15 years ago—who bet with a bunch of different guys. Back then what I thought was important was the numbers. I didn't know the guy so well, but I took his bets anyway. He ran up quite a number with me—he owed me about $10,000. I'd call him and he'd tell me he'd have something for me next week. Well, he never gave me a thing—this happened over and over again. Then one night I see the guy out, and he's buying drinks for everybody, playing the big shot. The guy owes me $10,000 and he's buying people drinks. I was mad. I went up to him and said, "hey where's my money?" The guy was a jerk; he stammered around and told me that if I didn't leave him alone he'd call the feds. He owes me and he's gonna call the feds. I don't want the feds bothering me, I'm not interested in goin' to prison and I don't want anybody checking up on what I'm doing. I knew right then I'd never see any of it and that the guy was a jerk. So what I did was put the word out that he wasn't paying up, that he wasn't good for his bets. You gotta understand, this is a disease for someone like this guy—he just has to bet and there's nothin worse you can do to somebody who likes to bet than to cut him off. When the word is out, nobody will take their action. The only way someone would take his action is if he put money up first.

As discussed earlier, the line is used to balance the action between two teams. There are times however when the betting public is not enticed by fluctuations in the line. When there is more money wagered on one team than another, the bookie could end up having to pay out more than he takes in—a situation he wants to avoid. A degree of bettor psychology is relevant in such cases. Bookies know that sentimentality motivates many bettors. Sentimentality is the tendency to bet on the hometown team—or as one bookie described it, to "bet with your heart." For example, in the recent NBA championship game between the Indiana Pacers and the Los Angeles Lakers, the majority of bettors in the L.A. area bet on the Lakers while the majority of bettors from the Midwest bet on the Pacers. Sentimentality also can explain regional variations in betting patterns, and bookies must always be aware of potential regional differences in betting patterns, and adjust accordingly. When it is impossible to balance the action, bookies can hedge their losses by selling their action to other bookmakers. This practice is called "laying off." Every bookmaker in this study had connections with a layoff bookmaker. Sam, a 17-year veteran, discusses the way sentimentality works:

> What you wanna do is get equal amounts of money on both sides. This is a Steeler town so when the line first came out at 14 then 13 and ½ for the Super Bowl [1995], all the money was on Pittsburgh. I lowered it to 12, but still everyone was takin' Pittsburgh. Even at 12—nobody was taking Dallas. Even though I thought Dallas would win, I was worried. You know, Super Bowl is big, big, big. I was holding a lotta money. I checked around to see what was happening and after thinkin' about it, I figured I'd better get rid of it, that's called a layoff, and if I hadn't gotten rid of it, I'd a been ruined.

Layoff bookmakers charge a fee for taking unwanted action. This can be thought of in terms of Juice. The existence of layoff operations is essential because of the sentimentality factor. If movement in the line does not affect the direction of incoming wagers on a Pittsburgh/Dallas game, then the Pittsburgh layoff bookie could layoff with a Dallas bookie. Six of the bookies in this study took layoff action from other bookies and would sometimes layoff their layoff action with larger operators. It is important to distinguish the relationships bookies have with layoff bookies from organized crime associations. Bookies choose whether to layoff their action and they have choices of who to lay it off with. Instead of reflecting organized crime connections, these relationships more closely resemble what Reuter (1983, 42) calls networks. Occasionally, bookies in these networks combined their bookmaking business with social activities, but this appears to be infrequent.

Although the typical bettor is the bookie's bread and butter, there are always exceptions to typicality and in bookmaking the exception is the wiseguy. The wiseguy almost always beats the bookie. Since bookies lose money to wiseguys they must know who the wiseguy bettors are and limit the action they will accept from them. Eddy, a 52-year old who has been in the business since high school, differentiates the wiseguy from the typical bettor.

> The wiseguy is someone who follows the games—they really do. They know who they wanta bet before the line comes out of Las Vegas—oh, that's the outlaw line that comes out on Sunday night. They'll bet the game with you Sunday night. They know who they want to bet. They take a chance on the line going up or down. They're sharp, but remember this is their livelihood, that's what they do, they don't do anything else. The way it works is that when the game plays, the line might be at 16 and they're locked in at 10. Being locked in they have an option, they can keep the bet at 10 or take the 16 backup with somebody else and hope it falls in between, take the game, and make twice the money. They always bet with a couple of people and they study the games. I did that myself one Saturday a couple of weeks ago, it was the playoff games. I took 17 basketball games. I bet a couple of hundred per game. I was trying to catch it in the middle. I made $17,000 that afternoon. A lot of bookies have quit basketball because you can get destroyed with basketball. If you get a wiseguy who's hot, he'll beat you to death. Those guys just don't bet $100, they want to bet your limit—whatever it is, $500, $1,000, $5,000 whatever, and if they're hot, they'll win 9 out of 10 games.

In addition to developing a reliable client base and learning how to avoid losses, sports bookies can affect their profits by the number of hours they work and the sports they will accept. If they choose to, bookies can work year round or limit their business to particular seasons. Harry, who operated one of the larger businesses, took action on all sports events and explains the relation of this to being successful.

> I got into this for the money; I figured that the more I worked, the more money I'd make. And I'm good at this. But I've had to put in hundreds of thousands of hours at this thing and that's year round. I mean I take every kind of game there is. I take horses, baseball, boxing, football, the

> baskets, hockey, jai lai, you name it. If there's some esoteric thing going on, I'll take it too. You should see my house, I got TVs everywhere. I got one of those dishes so I can watch what's going on all over the world and I got a computer to keep up with the scores and see what other people are doin'. If you wanta make money you've got to put the hours in and you have to know what's going on. See it's not the bookie that puts the fix in, but gamblers. You see they're lookin' for the big win. But like anything else, if you wanna make money you gotta have a work ethic and you gotta know what's going on. I'll buy whatever I need that gives me an edge.

One of the biggest risks from any form of illicit activity is arrest, but unlike other forms of deviant behavior bookies are not afraid of getting arrested. In fact, none of the bookies in this study had been arrested for their bookmaking activities. Tony explains why:

> The cops don't care about guys like me. I don't cause any trouble. I don't drink or do drugs and I don't know of any guys who do, cause for one thing you gotta be alert in this business and drinking and drugs will mess up your thought processes. So what kind of a danger am I? What I'm doing is providing a service, that's all, like any other service type of business. That doesn't mean I'm out there advertising what I'm doin', no way. I just don't do anything that's gonna draw attention to me. My customer's are happy. So I'm clean, my people are happy, and everything's okay. The idea that we go out and break people's legs is something you see on TV. What sense does that make? I mean, if I broke some guy's legs, I'd get arrested. Just doin this, nobody's gonna arrest me.

Retiring From Bookmaking

Like getting into the business, retirement is a personal and voluntary decision. While not all of the bookies talked about retirement, those who did identified three factors that influenced their decision to leave the business: the desire to spend more time with family, having achieved their economic goals, and retirement from their legitimate job. Pete, who has been in the business approximately 15 years, plans to retire within the next year because he wants to spend more time with his family. Pete discusses how the business interferes with spending time with his family and the preparation involved in leaving the business.

> I don't need to do this any more. Financially, things are different now, my wife is working a little and I'm working a lot of hours, I've got seniority. I'm thinking in about a year this thing will come to an end. I mean I don't have the time anymore. I'm coaching my kids, spending a lotta time with them. With the money I've made, I've put it into my house. We couldn't afford the house we're in without this. When I look back on the years, they've been good to me. I made some money where I could buy some things—my house, I got Debbie a new car, and for my kids I've been putting money away for their tuition for school. You know I don't want them going to public school. With my kids, when I'm doing this, they're with me. And to be honest with you, I don't want them growing up with this thing all the time. Everyone in my family, even my wife's family, knows what I do. The way things are now, when there's a family thing, I'm tied up with this—I can't go cause I'm answering the phone all the time. I've talked about leaving with George, he doesn't have the responsibilities I have with my family and all, so he can just step right in 'cause the business is running smoothly. He wants to take it over, it's a good deal for him—I've got good customers, I know them, there's no trouble, and things are real good now.

Unlike Pete, Joe's retirement plan does not involve a successor; instead he shifted his business to the Caribbean where he owns a legitimate sports book. Joe views the earnings from his legitimate enterprise as his retirement cushion. In the following excerpt, Joe discusses how his legitimate operation will provide a comfortable lifestyle without the worry that accompanies an illegal operation.

> The island operation is easy. You can advertise. We do, we have a full page advertisement in Las Vegas, in fact, even in some of the local papers we've got ads with a sports book number. You can call, set up an account. You can use a credit card, wire money, or send us a certified check. Somebody puts money into their account, we give them 10 percent interest on their money, sometimes 15 percent depending on the amount they have and the type of bets they make. If somebody puts a considerable amount of money in there, we give 'em 15 percent right off the bat. If the person is a bettor, you have the money in an account, you know you're

> getting paid, and that's a big part of the business, getting paid. So we give 'em those extra bucks back to use. It works, it works great. Your regular bettors, guys that have the money and want to bet have no problem puttin' the money up front. It's a beautiful way to do business. So, I'm looking at this as my retirement plan. 'Cause, I'm out of everything here and I don't work any work. I've got eight people employed around the clock there and the action comes in 24 hours a day and a woman who manages the operation for me. She's real good. The business grows each week. Even though I worked all my life, I'm not depending on social security to live on—I never trusted the government. I gotta look out for myself. So by the time I'm 65, I'll have enough money saved up from this business to continue to enjoy my life. Like I told you before, me and my wife like to travel, so this way, we can do whatever we want. You know, I'm not a flamboyant guy, I drive a modest car and we live in a nice house, but nothing outrageous. People know me, I belong to the club here, me and my wife come up here a couple times a week, have dinner, watch a game here and there. I'm just beginning to enjoy all that time I've put into this thing 'cause I'll tell you I've worked hard in this business, all those hours. For years, I couldn't leave the house 'cause I was on the phone all day and all night. But now, I can relax now.

Frank, who is 60, is planning to retire from his legitimate job and quit bookmaking at the same time within a year.

> I plan to retire in a year and I've been savin' the money I've made so I can enjoy myself. I got this house in Florida, so as soon as I retire I'm gone. I don't have anybody to worry about, my wife left me 30 years ago, no kids, so it's just me. I saved up a little nest egg so I can go here or there. If I wanta go to Atlantic City or out to Vegas every now and then for a week or so, I'll go. You know, I like to play blackjack. Right now, I'm only working with about 45 people anyway, so when I leave they can find somebody else. Some of my people already work with a couple of bookies, so I'm not worrying, they're set up.

Although Pete, Joe, and Frank give different reasons for leaving the business, their accounts show that retirement is their choice. Pete wants to spend more time with his family and has designated a successor; Joe has worked hard and wants to enjoy his life more fully and is depending on the income from his Caribbean operation; and Frank is planning to retire from bookmaking when he retires from his legitimate job and expects his customers to find another bookie. In all three cases, the decision to retire was voluntary. The different paths to retirement further indicate that not only is the decision to retire voluntary, but also the way that one retires is a choice.

Ties to Organized Crime

I asked about the alleged link to organized crime and found no support in bookies' accounts. Joe offers an interesting counterperspective suggesting that the allegation is a government ploy to control competition from bookies.

> The idea that the Mafia is pullin' the strings on guys like me is a myth. We keep sports honest, believe me. If you're looking for the crooked angle, then government's the real criminal cause they really don't want competition from independents like me. So they keep betting illegal. The truth is that the independents do a better job than the government. Look, our payout is higher, we don't use gimmicks—think about all the gimmicks for the lottery—we don't have the overhead, and we don't cheat. Remember that Nick Perry incident? Bookies have integrity. You gotta have integrity, 'cause if I cheated I'd be outta business. And remember this, we're not on every corner or in every retail store either, pushing people to gamble. But the government can't do it right cause they're greedy and most people know that. Just look at the OTB [Off Track Betting]. How could you lose money with horses? Think about it. When the government's involved there are too many hands in the till. Guys like me make the government look bad 'cause we know what we're doin' and they don't want us out there. So they gotta make it seem like we're a bunch of thugs fixin' games and workin' players. The only games I ever heard about being fixed are the ones you read about in the paper. I'm not saying that it never happens, but when it does, bookies aren't doing the fixin'. It's usually gamblers.

According to Sasuly (1982), all of the major sporting associations (i.e., the NCAA, NBA, NFL, and Thoroughbred Tracks of America) maintain contact with illegal bookmakers as a way of monitoring irregularities. Bookies can be thought of as barometers of irregularities for the world of sports.

Since there have been numerous reports of athletes shaving points, I asked whether bookies had firsthand knowledge of professional athletes betting on games. None of the bookies I talked to knew of any instances where athletes placed bets on or against teams they played for. However, bookies did acknowledge having customers who were professional athletes and who wagered on sports events. Roger describes his experiences with a professional athlete who bets with him.

> I knew players who gambled. I took bets from _____. He didn't call me every week, but once in a while he'd bet on this game or that game. Sometimes he'd win and sometimes he'd lose. If you're askin' whether he'd bet his own game, the answer is no. In fact, he wouldn't bet on any games while he was playing. You know, he had to keep it low key because he could be kicked out of the pros if anyone ever found out. So we kept it quiet. We'd meet at _____, you know a lot of guys worked out there, you could be sorta invisible there, and you know no one noticed, so we'd square up in the locker room. Players gamble. Believe me, all the players know what the line is on their own game and every other game. But me, personally, I've never known a player who bet his own game. I have known guys who are no longer in the pros who bet on their team. The way I look at it is, it's just part of sports.

When unusual or irregular betting patterns emerge, bookies stop taking bets on the game. This practice is referred to as "taking it off the board." It would not be in the bookie's best interests to try to rig or fix games since it is the bookie that stands to lose. Moreover, rigged games would disrupt the logic of bookmaking and the inherent parity in sports betting.

Discussion and Conclusions

Contrary to the image found in the public debate and popular culture, namely that bookies are slick operators looking for the "fast buck, the quick fix, or the desire to get something for nothing" and have ties to organized crime, this analysis shows that bookmakers work hard, are dedicated, possess skill and specialized knowledge, and operate with integrity. Bookies put in long hours and make many sacrifices in other parts of their life in order build a successful business.

Despite the maxim that "you can't beat the bookie," bookies need paying customers and since they cannot recruit or solicit their customers openly, they must devise ways that weed out the poor risks. Bookies must also be attuned to betting patterns and know when to raise or lower the line in order to balance the action. When it is not possible to balance the action, bookies need to know when to layoff with another bookmaker to avoid heavy losses. Finally, successful bookies operate with honesty and integrity. The relationship between the bookie and his customer is based on trust, and bookies know that if they cheat their customers they will lose them.

While the findings show that bookies are fully aware that what they are doing is illegal (Ray captures this by saying "You see, it's not illegal to place a bet, but you can't take bets—that's why you always gotta watch yourself"), they do not define themselves or other bookies as deviant or criminal. Instead they perceive themselves as providing a service to a niche market. What accounts for this non-deviant identity? One possible explanation has to do with the way bookmaking is socially organized. To the lay observer deviance appears to lack order, but sociologists know that like the social world of which it is a part, deviance is highly organized. The social organization of all forms of deviance is a microcosm of society—there are distinct roles, norms of interaction, relationships, and distinct settings and contexts for its occurrence. Best and Luckenbill (1994) argue that the social organization of deviance is an endless source of knowledge because it is where the relationship between the individual and the larger society is mediated (5).

Like many service transactions, the product in the transaction (i.e., the bet), is nonmaterial—it consists of a verbal agreement about the outcome of a sports event. But unlike most illegal service transactions, the bet does not require face-to-face interaction. This fact sets bookmaking apart from other types of deviant transactions. Bookies and customers communicate by phone which means that the transaction can take place anywhere—at work, at home, in a car, in a restaurant, or even while walking down the street. This distances the bookie and the bettor from typical deviant or subcultural settings such as back alleys, street corners, or designated areas like red light districts. The deviant transaction is integrated into the rhythms of everyday actions within the context of normal everyday settings.

In addition to occurring outside a criminal milieu, the structure of the transaction is unlike other illegal transactions because it is nonhierarchical. No middlemen are involved. While it is true that most bookies get their line from oddsmakers (usually working out of Las Vegas), the line nevertheless is in the public domain; you can find it anywhere. Consequently, nothing in the transaction requires the involvement of suppliers, venders, or front men. Because the transaction is between the bookie and the bettor, bookies have autonomy, discretion, control, and independence over their business.

There are three major phases of the bookmaking process: establishing the terms for betting, taking bets, and settling accounts. Within each of these processes, the bookies maintain independence, autonomy, discretion, and control. The conditions and terms for the transaction are determined by the bookie. This involves making decisions about what the line will be, the maximum and minimum amount to be accepted, the types of bets that will be accepted (a straight bet, over/under bet, parlay, etc.), and whether to extend credit to customers. Bookies know that if their terms are not competitive with other bookies, they could lose customers. Taking the bet consummates the transaction. Bettors tell the bookie who they want to wager on, the amount of the bet, and the type of bet they want to make. Bookies repeat this information back to the customer so that there is no misunderstanding about the wager and both wait for the outcome. Settling accounts involves the transfer of money either from losing bettors to bookies or from bookies to winning bettors and is the only phase that involves face-to-face interaction. Since bookmaking is illegal, bookies have no legal right to collect monies owed them nor can bettors demand monies owed to them. Instead of being coercive, settling accounts is based on trust between the bookie and bettor. In every aspect of the bookmaking process we see that bookies are the innovators, decision makers, and risk-takers. They initiate their involvement in bookmaking and see it as an opportunity to provide a service to a growing market; they hone their skills, gather the resources, and manage the process of building their own business.

There is further evidence that bookies differ from other types of deviants when we examine their career trajectories. On average, the bookies in this study were involved in bookmaking for 17 years, which can only be thought of in terms of a lengthy career. Throughout this period, the majority held full-time legitimate jobs, were committed to their families, planned for the future of their families, set economic goals, were involved in community activities, and generally were committed to conventional values. It also is worth noting that only one of the bookies in this study had ever been arrested. Yet in the literature on deviant careers, it is argued that prolonged deviant involvement requires rejecting conventional values (Stebbins 1971, 63).

Best and Luckenbill (1994, 235–237) argue that the social organization of deviance affects the duration of deviant careers in at least four ways. First, most deviant careers are dependent on the support of other deviants, the more contacts they have with other deviants: the longer the career. Second, career deviants have connections to other deviant organizations because of the resources such organizations offer. Third, since illegal activities are characterized by unregulated competition, career deviants must minimize competition, and this is usually done through negotiating with other deviants and by sharing or dividing the territory or resources. The final way career length is affected is through contacts with social control agents—the more contacts, the higher the risk and the shorter the career. The analysis shows that bookmakers' careers are distinct from other deviant careers in the following ways. First, while bookies may associate with other bookies, this occurs only occasionally. Most importantly, their bookmaking business does not depend on these associations or on other deviants. In short, bookies are independent of other deviants. Second, since bookies assume all of the risks (financial and otherwise) involved in the bookmaking enterprise, they do not need to divide or share their customers nor do they have ties to other deviant organizations. Third, the most effective device against competition is the bookie's honesty and integrity. Finally, bookies are buffered from contact with social control agents because the enterprise has such low criminal visibility. Gambling on sports is integrated into the rhythms of everyday life, particularly male culture, and the bookie is a feature of that culture.

This leads to the question of whether it is time that the organized crime, corruption, and sports betting link be put to rest. The findings presented here provide a compelling ar gument for doing so. Although there is evidence showing organized crime's involvement in bookmaking, the findings presented here show bookies to be small entrepreneurs who operate independently. They see themselves as providing a service that is in great demand. It could be argued that major media that promote sports events increase the demand for this service. The line is readily available to the public and is very much a part of the hype that accompanies sports events. The line increases public interest in sporting events and betting on events ensures that millions of fans will watch them. Given the ubiquity of these accoutrements of gambling on sports, it is not surprising that sports betting is widespread and that our anti-gambling policies against it have little impact.

Although the sample for this study is small, confined to a single geographical area, and was selected by word of mouth, the accounts show remarkable consistency. It is possible that the bookies I interviewed represent an unusual group of bookies. Since there is no way of knowing just how large the population of bookies is, it is difficult to assess the representativeness of this study's sample. More research is needed, particularly research done in other gegraphical areas. Nevertheless, the findings presented here show that while bookmaking is illegal, sports betting is widespread, and that bookmakers are more like small business entrepreneurs than petty criminals.

Questions for Thought and Discussion

1. Compare the entry into bookmaking with the entry into drug dealing (Chapter 21). How is it alike? Different?
2. According to the author, does bookmaking have links to organized crime?
3. Bookmakers "retire." Burglars "desist." How are they alike? Different?
4. What theory or theories of criminal behavior are illustrated in this research?

References

Anderson, Annelies. 1979. *The Business of Organized Crime.* Stanford, CA: Hoover Institute.

Best, Joel and David Luckenbill. 1994. *Organizing Deviance.* Englewood Cliffs, NJ: Prentice Hall.

Bonanno, Bill. 1999. *Bound by Honour.* New York: St. Martin's Press.

Chambliss, William. 1978. *On the Take.* Bloomington, IN: University of Indiana Press.

Clark, Ramsey. 1971. *Crime in America.* New York: Simon and Schuster.

Congressional Hearings for H. R. 497, National Gambling Impact and Policy Commission Act, September, 1995.

Cook, James. "If Roxborough Says the Spread Is 7 It's 7." *Forbes,* September 14, 1992, pp. 350–363.

Cressey, Donald. 1969. *Theft of the Nation.* New York: Harper & Row.

DeFina, B., Pustin, B., and Winkler, I. (Producers) & Scorsese, M. (Director). (1990). *Goodfellas* [Film]. (Available from Warner Bros).

DeFina, B., Reidy, J. P. (Producers) & Scorsese, M. (Director). (1995). *Casino* [Film]. (Available from Universal Pictures).

Holcomb, R. & Marshall, P. D. (Directors). (1987). *Wiseguy* [Film]. (Available from Cannell Films).

McGraw, Dan. "The National Bet." *U.S. News & World Report,* April 7, 1997, pp. 50–55.

Moody's Industry Review. "Gaming." April 6, 1995.

National Amateur and Professional Sports Protection Act, S. 474, 1992.

Nevada Gaming Commission and State Gaming Control Board, personal communication with Research Division, June 1998.

O'Brien, Timothy. 1998. *Bad Bet.* New York: Times Business.

President's Commission on Law Enforcement and the Administration of Justice. 1967. *Task Force Report: Organized Crime.* Washington, DC: US Government Printing Office.

Puzo, Mario. 1969. *The Godfather.* New York: Putnum.

Reuter, Peter. 1983. *Disorganized Crime: Illegal Markets and the Mafia.* Cambridge, MA: MIT Press.

Reuter, Peter and Jonathan Rubinstein. 1982. *Illegal Gambling in New York.* Washington, DC: National Institute of Justice.

Rosencrance, John. 1987. "Bookmaking: A Case Where Honesty Is the Best Policy." *Sociology and Social Research* 72(1):7–11.

Sasuly, Richard. 1982. *Bookies and Bettors: Two Hundred Years of Gambling.* New York: Holt Rinehart & Winston.

Scarne, John. 1974. *Scarne's New Complete Guide to Gambling.* New York: Simon & Schuster.

Stebbins, Robert. 1971. *Commitment to Deviance.* Westport, CT: Greenwood.

Talese, Gay. 1971. *Honour Thy Father.* New York: World Publishing.

Section VII

Gangs and Crime

The past 15 years have witnessed a renewed interest in gangs by the criminal justice system and academic researchers. Street youth gangs are increasing sharply in numbers and in violence. Unlike the turf-oriented gangs of the 1950s and 1960s, the youth gangs of today are heavily involved in a variety of criminal activities, including drug trafficking.

In one of the "new" classics of gang scholarship, gang researcher John M. Hagedorn ("Homeboys, Dope Fiends, Legits, and New Jacks") identifies four categories of gang members based on commitment to gang life and drug dealing. He addresses a number of issues critical to understanding the phenomenon of gang life: What happens to gang members as they age? How are drug sales and gang activity related? How might these findings be translated into effective social policy?

Violence characterizes much of gang activity. In the next selection ("Collective and Normative Features of Gang Violence"), Decker explores another aspect of gang life, the culture of gang violence. He explores the normative and behavioral aspects of gang street crime and how these factors shape and routinize the violence of its members. Decker views the violence as having a role in creating and maintaining gang solidarity while also serving as a catalyst for further violence through threat and retaliation. In cases where sustained violence escalates beyond the tolerance of some of its members, the gang may be fractured and split into new, smaller groups, and some members may leave the gang altogether.

In recent years, female gang activity has increased considerably. Where women once served primarily in adjunct roles, mixed-gender gangs have become more common. In an analysis of gender and victimization in gangs, Miller ("Gender and Victimization Risk Among Young Women in Gangs") found that females experience a high risk of victimization at the hands of the gang peers and from assaultive victimization from other gangs.

In each selection, the offenders—both male and female members of street gangs—provide an unfiltered glimpse into their lives and activities. ✦

Chapter 23 Homeboys, Dope Fiends, Legits, and New Jacks

John M. Hagedorn

Based on field research with Milwaukee gangs, gang researcher John Hagedorn delineates four categories of gang members based on their orientation to conventional values and social institutions. Focusing on core members of drug-dealing gangs, Hagedorn argues that gang members may be classified along a "continuum of conventionality," ranging from former gang members now living a legitimate life to those who regard drug-dealing as a career. The study addresses several issues important to both social science and public policy. First, what happens to gang members as they age? Do most gang members graduate from gangbanging to drug sales, as popular stereotypes might suggest? Is drug dealing so lucrative that adult gang members eschew work and become committed to the drug economy? Have changes in economic conditions produced underclass gangs so detached from the labor market that the only effective policies are more police and more prisons? Second, and related to these questions, are adult gang members basically similar kinds of people, or are gangs made up of different types? Might some gang members be more conventional and others less so? What are the implications of this "continuum of conventionality" within drug-dealing gangs for public policy?

The following selection includes interviews with present and former gang members Hagedorn classified as homeboys, dope fiends, legits, and new jacks. They discuss their attitudes toward drug-dealing and conventional lifestyles, attitudes toward themselves, values, future plans, and their life chances. Gang members were largely classified according to their level of commitment to crime as a lifestyle and particularly to drug dealing.

In the conclusion, Hagedorn discusses criminal justice policy relating to gangs, drugs, and the "underclass" in society.

A Typology of Male Adult Gang Members

We developed four ideal types on a continuum of conventional behaviors and values: (1) those few who had gone *legit,* or had matured out of the gang; (2) *homeboys,* a majority of both African American and Latino adult gang members, who alternately worked conventional jobs and took various roles in drug sales; (3) *dope fiends,* who were addicted to cocaine and participated in the dope business as a way to maintain access to the drug; and (4) *new jacks,* who regarded the dope game as a career.

Some gang members, we found, moved over time between categories, some had characteristics of more than one category, and others straddled the boundaries (see Hannerz 1969, 57). Thus a few homeboys were in the process of becoming legit, many moved into and out of cocaine addiction, and others gave up and adopted a new jack orientation. Some new jacks returned to conventional life; others received long prison terms or became addicted to dope. Our categories are not discrete, but our typology seemed to fit the population of gang members we were researching. Our "member checks" (Lincoln and Guba 1985, 314–316) of the constructs with gang members validated these categories for male gang members.

Legits

Legits were those young men who had walked away from the gang. They were working or may have gone on to school. Legits had not been involved in the dope game at all, or not for at least five years. They did not use cocaine heavily, though some may have done so in the past. Some had moved out of the old neighborhood; others, like our project staff, stayed to help out or "give back" to the community. These are prime examples of Whyte's "college boys" (1943) or Cloward and Ohlin's Type I (1960), oriented to economic gain and class mobility. The following quote is an example of a young African American man who "went legit" and is now working and going to college.

> Q: Looking back over the past five years, what major changes took place in your life—things that happened that really made things different for you?
>
> R#105: I had got into a relationship with my girl, that's one thing. I just knew I

couldn't be out on the streets trying to hustle all the time. That's what changed me, I just got a sense of responsibility.

Today's underclass gangs appear to be fundamentally different from those in Thrasher's or Cloward and Ohlin's time, when most gang members "matured out" of the gang. Of the 236 Milwaukee male founders, only 12 (5.1 percent) could be categorized as having matured out: that is, they were working full time and had not sold cocaine in the past five years. When these data are disaggregated by race, the reality of the situation becomes even clearer. We could verify only two of 117 African-American and one of 87 Latino male gang founders who were currently working and had not sold dope in the past five years. One-third of the white members fell into this category.

Few African-American and Latino gang founders, however, were resigned to a life of crime, jail, and violence. After a period of rebellion and living the fast life, the majority of gang founders, or "homeboys," wanted to settle down and go legit, but the path proved to be very difficult.

Homeboys

Homeboys were the majority of all adult gang members. They were not firmly committed to the drug economy, especially after the early thrill of fast money and "easy women" wore off. They had reached an age, the mid-twenties, when criminal offenses normally decline (Gottfredson and Hirschi 1990). Most of these men were unskilled, lacked education, and had largely negative experiences in the secondary labor market. Some homeboys were committed more strongly to the streets, others to a more conventional life. Most had used cocaine, some heavily at times, but their use was largely in conjunction with selling from a house or corner with their gang "homies." Most homeboys either were married or had a "steady" lady. They also had strong feelings of loyalty to their fellow gang members.

Here, two different homeboys explain how they had changed, and how hard that change was:

Q: Looking back over the past five years, what major changes took place in your life—things that happened that really made things different for you?

R#211: The things that we went through wasn't worth it, and I had a family, you know, and kids, and I had to think about them first, and the thing with the drug game was, that money was quick, easy, and fast, and it went like that, the more money you make the more popular you was. You know, as I see it now it wasn't worth it because the time that I done in penitentiaries I lost my sanity. To me it feels like I lost a part of my kids, because, you know, I know they still care, and they know I'm daddy, but I just lost out. Somebody else won and I lost.

Q: Is she with somebody else now?

R#211: Yeah. She hung in there about four or five months after I went to jail.

Q: It must have been tough for her to be alone with all those kids.

R#211: Yeah.

Q: What kind of person are you?

R#217: Mad. I'm a mad young man. I'm a poor young man. I'm a good person to my kids and stuff, and given the opportunity to have something nice and stop working for this petty-ass money I would try to change a lot of things. . . . I feel I'm the type of person that given the opportunity to try to have something legit, I will take it, but I'm not going to go by the slow way, taking no four, five years working at no chicken job and trying to get up to a manager just to start making six, seven dollars. And then get fired when I come in high or drunk or something. Or miss a day or something because I got high smoking weed, drinking beer, and the next day come in and get fired; then I'm back in where I started from. So I'm just a cool person, and if I'm given the opportunity and if I can get a job making nine, ten dollars an hour, I'd let everything go; I'd just sit back and work my job and go home. That kind of money I can live with. But I'm not going to settle for no three, four dollars an hour, know what I'm saying?

Homeboys present a more confused theoretical picture than legits. Cloward and Ohlin's Type III delinquents were rebels, who had a "sense of injustice" or felt "unjust deprivation" at a failed system (1960, 117). Their gang delinquency is a collective solution to the failure of institutional arrangements. They reject traditional societal norms; other, success-oriented illegitimate norms replace conventionality.

Others have questioned whether gang members' basic outlook actually rejects conventionality. Matza (1964) viewed delinquents' rationalizations of their conduct as evidence of techniques meant to "neutralize" deeply held conventional beliefs. Cohen (1955, 129–137) regarded delinquency as a nonutilitarian "reaction formation" to middle-class standards, though middle-class morality lingers, repressed and unacknowledged. What appears to be gang "pathological" behavior, Cohen points out, is the result of the delinquent's striving to attain core values of "the American way of life." Short and Strodtbeck (1965), testing various gang theories, found that white and African American gang members, and lower- and middle-class youths, had similar conventional values.

Our homeboys are older versions of Cohen's and Matza's delinquents, and are even more similar to Short and Strodtbeck's study subjects. Milwaukee homeboys shared three basic characteristics: (1) They worked regularly at legitimate jobs, although they ventured into the drug economy when they believed it was necessary for survival. (2) They had very conventional aspirations; their core values centered on finding a secure place in the American way of life. (3) They had some surprisingly conventional ethical beliefs about the immorality of drug dealing. To a man, they justified their own involvement in drug sales by very Matza-like techniques of "neutralization."

Homeboys are defined by their in-and-out involvement in the legal and illegal economies. Recall that about half of our male respondents had sold drugs no more than 12 of the past 36 months. More than one-third never served any time in jail. Nearly 60 percent had worked legitimate jobs at least 12 months of the last 36, with a mean of 14.5 months. Homeboys' work patterns thus differed both from those of legits, who worked solely legal jobs, and new jacks, who considered dope dealing a career.

To which goal did homeboys aspire, being big-time dope dealers or holding a legitimate job? Rather than having any expectations of staying in the dope game, homeboys aspired to settling down, getting married, and living at least a watered-down version of the American dream. Like Padilla's (1992, 157) Diamonds, they strongly desired to "go legit." Although they may have enjoyed the fast life for a while, it soon went stale. Listen to this homeboy, the one who lost his lady when he went to jail:

> Q: Five years from now, what would you want to be doing?
>
> R#211: Five years from now? I want to have a steady job, I want to have been working that job for about five years, and just with a family somewhere.
>
> Q: Do you think that's gonna come true?
>
> R#211: Yeah, that's basically what I'm working on. I mean, this bullshit is over now, I'm twenty-five, I've played games long enough, it don't benefit nobody. If you fuck yourself away, all you gonna be is fucked, I see it now.

Others had more hopeful or wilder dreams, but a more sobering outlook on the future. The other homeboy, who said he wouldn't settle for three or four dollars an hour, speaks as follows:

> Q: Five years from now, what would you want to be doing?
>
> R#217: Owning my own business. And rich. A billionaire.
>
> Q: What do you realistically expect you'll be doing in five years?
>
> R#217: Probably working at McDonald's. That's the truth.

Homeboys' aspirations were divided between finding a steady full-time job and setting up their own business. Their strivings pertained less to being for or against "middle-class status" than to finding a practical, legitimate occupation that could support them (see Short and Strodtbeck 1965). Many homeboys believed that using skills learned in selling drugs to set up a small business would give them a better chance at a decent life than trying to succeed as an employee.

Most important, homeboys "grew up" and were taking a realistic look at their life chances. This homeboy spoke for most:

> Q: Looking back over the past five years, what major changes have taken place in your life—things that made a difference about where you are now?
>
> R#220: I don't know, maybe maturity. . . . Just seeing life in a different perspective . . . realizing that from sixteen to twenty-three, man, just shot past. And just realizing that it did, shucks, you just realizing how quick it zoomed past me. And it really just passed me up without really having any enjoyment of a teenager. And hell, before I know it I'm going to hit thirty or forty, and I ain't going to have nothing to stand on. I don't want that shit. Because I see a lot of brothers out here now, that's forty-three, forty-four and ain't got shit. They's still standing out

on the corner trying to make a hustle. Doing this, no family, no stable home and nothing. I don't want that shit. . . . I don't give a fuck about getting rich or nothing, but I want a comfortable life, a decent woman, a family to come home to. I mean, everybody needs somebody to care for. This ain't where it's at.

Finally, homeboys were characterized by their ethical views about selling dope. As a group, they believed dope selling was "unmoral"—wrong, but necessary for survival. Homeboys' values were conventional, but in keeping with Matza's findings, they justified their conduct by neutralizing their violation of norms. Homeboys believed that economic necessity was the overriding reason why they could not live up to their values (see Liebow 1967, 214). They were the epitome of ambivalence, ardently believing that dope selling was both wrong and absolutely necessary. One longtime dealer expressed this contradiction:

Q: Do you consider it wrong or immoral to sell dope?

R#129: Um-hum, very wrong.

Q: Why?

R#129: Why, because it's killing people.

Q: Well how come you do it?

R#129: It's also a money maker.

Q: Well how do you balance those things out? I mean, here you're doing something that you think is wrong, making money. How does that make you feel when you're doing it, or don't you think about it when you're doing it?

R#129: Once you get a [dollar] bill, once you look at, I say this a lot, once you look at those dead white men [presidents' pictures on currency], you care about nothing else, you don't care about nothing else. Once you see those famous dead white men. That's it.

Q: Do you ever feel bad about selling drugs, doing something that was wrong?

R#129: How do I feel? Well a lady will come in and sell all the food stamps, all of them. When they're sold, what are the kids gonna eat? They can't eat the dope cause she's gonna go smoke that up, or do whatever with it. And then you feel like "wrong." But then, in the back of your mind, man, you just got a hundred dollars worth of food stamps for thirty dollars worth of dope, and you can sell them at the store for seven dollars on ten, so you got seventy coming. So you get seventy dollars for thirty dollars. It is not wrong to do this. It is not wrong to do this!

Homeboys also refused to sell to pregnant women or to juveniles. Contrary to Jankowski's (1991, 102) assertion that in gangs "there is no ethical code that regulates business ventures," Milwaukee homeboys had some strong moral feelings about how they carried out their business:

R#109: I won't sell to no little kids. And, ah, if he gonna get it, he gonna get it from someone else besides me. I won't sell to no pregnant woman. If she gonna kill her baby, I want to sleep not knowing that I had anything to do with it. Ah, for anybody else, hey, it's their life, you choose your life how you want.

Q: But how come—I want to challenge you. You know if kids are coming or a pregnant woman's coming, you know they're going to get it somewhere else, right? Someone else will make their money on it; why not you?

R#109: 'Cause the difference is I'll be able to sleep without a guilty conscience.

Homeboys were young adults living on the edge. On the one hand, like most Americans, they had relatively conservative views on social issues and wanted to settle down with a job, a wife, and children. On the other hand, they were afraid they would never succeed, and that long stays in prison would close doors and lock them out of a conventional life. They did not want to continue to live on the streets, but they feared that hustling might be the only way to survive.

Dope Fiends

Dope fiends are gang members who are addicted to cocaine. Thirty-eight percent of all African-American founders were using cocaine at the time of our interview, as were 55 percent of Latinos and 53 percent of whites. African Americans used cocaine at lower rates than white gang members but went to jail twice as often. The main focus in a dope fiend's life is getting the drug. Asked what they regretted most about their life, dope fiends invariably said "drug use," whereas most homeboys said "dropping out of school."

Most Milwaukee gang dope fiends, or daily users of cocaine, smoked it as "rocks." More casual users, or reformed dope fiends, if they used cocaine at all, snorted it or sprinkled it on marijuana (called a "primo") to enhance the high. Injection was rare among African-Americans but more common among Latinos. About one-quarter of those we interviewed, however, abstained totally from use of cocaine. A majority of the gang members on our rosters had used cocaine since its use escalated in Milwaukee in the late 1980s.

Of 110 gang founders who were reported to be currently using cocaine, 37 percent were reported to be using "heavily" (every day, in our data), 44 percent "moderately" (several times per week), and 19 percent "lightly" (sporadically). More than 70 percent of all founders on our rosters who were not locked up were currently using cocaine to some extent. More than one-third of our male respondents considered themselves, at some time in their lives, to be "heavy" cocaine users.

More than one-quarter of our respondents had used cocaine for seven years or more, roughly the total amount of time cocaine has dominated the illegal drug market in Milwaukee. Latinos had used cocaine slightly longer than African Americans, for a mean of 75 months compared with 65. Cocaine use followed a steady pattern in our respondents' lives; most homeboys had used cocaine as part of their day-to-day life, especially while in the dope business.

Dope fiends were quite unlike Cloward and Ohlin's "double failures," gang members who used drugs as part of a "retreatist subculture." Milwaukee dope fiends participated regularly in conventional labor markets. Of the 110 founders who were reported as currently using cocaine, slightly more were working legitimate jobs than were not working. Most dope fiends worked at some time in their homies' dope houses or were fronted an ounce or an "eightball" (3.5 grams) of cocaine to sell. Unlike Anderson's "wineheads," gang dope fiends were not predominantly "has-beens" and did not "lack the ability and motivation to hustle" (Anderson 1978, 96–97). Milwaukee cocaine users, like heroin users (Johnson et al. 1985; Moore 1978; Preble and Casey 1969), played an active role in the drug-selling business.

Rather than spending their income from drug dealing on family, clothes, or women, dope fiends smoked up their profits. Eventually many stole dope belonging to the boss or "dopeman" and got into trouble. At times their dope use made them so erratic that they were no longer trusted and were forced to leave the neighborhood. Often, however, the gang members who were selling took them back and fronted them cocaine to sell to put them back on their feet. Many had experienced problems in violating the cardinal rule, "Don't get high on your own supply," as in this typical story:

> R#131: . . . if you ain't the type that's a user, yeah, you'll make fabulous money but if you was the type that sells it and uses it and do it at the same time, you know, you get restless. Sometimes you get used to taking your own drugs. . . . I'll just use the profits and just do it . . . and then the next day if I get something again, I'd just take the money to pay up and keep the profits. . . . You sell a couple of hundred and you do a hundred. That's how I was doing it.

Cocaine use was a regular part of the lives of most Milwaukee gang members engaged in the drug economy. More than half of our respondents had never attended a treatment program; more than half of those who had been in treatment went through court-ordered programs. Few of our respondents stopped use by going to a treatment program. Even heavy cocaine use was an "on-again, off-again" situation in which most gang members alternately quit by themselves and started use again (Waldorf et al. 1991).

Alcohol use among dope fiends and homeboys (particularly 40-ounce bottles of Olde English 800 ale) appears to be even more of a problem than cocaine use. Like homeboys, however, most dope fiends aspired to have a family, to hold a steady job, and to find some peace. The wild life of the dope game had played itself out; the main problem was how to quit using.

New Jacks

Whereas homeboys had a tentative relationship with conventional labor markets and held some strong moral beliefs, new jacks had chosen the dope game as a career. They were often loners, strong individualists like Jankowski's (1991) gang members, who cared little about group norms. Frequently they posed as the embodiment of media stereotypes. About one-quarter of our interview respondents could be described as new jacks: they had done nothing in the last 36 months except hustle or spend time in jail.

In some ways, new jacks mirror the criminal subculture described by Cloward and Ohlin. If a criminal subculture is to develop, Cloward and Ohlin argued, opportunities to learn a criminal career must be present, and close ties to conventional markets or customers must exist. This situation distinguishes the criminal from the violent and the retreatist subcultures. The emergence of the cocaine economy and a large market for illegal drugs provided precisely such an opportunity structure for this generation of gang members. New jacks are those who took advantage of the opportunities, and who, at least for the present, have committed themselves to a career in the dope game.

> Q: Do you consider it wrong or immoral to sell dope?
>
> R#203: I think it's right because can't no motherfucker live your life but you.
>
> Q: Why?
>
> R#203: Why? I'll put it this way . . . I love selling dope. I know there's other niggers out here love the money just like I do. And ain't no motherfucker gonna stop a nigger from selling dope. . . . I'd sell to my own mother if she had the money.

New jacks, like other gang cocaine dealers, lived up to media stereotypes of the "drug dealer" role and often were emulated by impressionable youths. Some new jacks were homeboys from Milwaukee's original neighborhood gangs, who had given up their conventional dreams; others were members of gangs that were formed solely for drug dealing (see Klein and Maxson 1993). A founder of one new jack gang described the scene as his gang set up shop in Milwaukee. Note the strong mimicking of media stereotypes:

> R#126: . . . it was crime and drug problems before we even came into the scene. It was just controlled by somebody else. We just came on with a whole new attitude, outlook, at the whole situation. It's like, have you ever seen the movie *New Jack City,* about the kid in New York? You see, they was already there. We just came out with a better idea, you know what I'm saying?

New jacks rejected the homeboys' moral outlook. Many were raised by families with long traditions of hustling or a generation of gang affiliations, and had few hopes of a conventional future. They are the voice of the desperate ghetto dweller, those who live in Carl Taylor's (1990, 36) "third culture" made up of "underclass and urban gang members who exhibit signs of moral erosion and anarchy" or propagators of Bourgois's (1990, 631) "culture of terror." New jacks fit the media stereotype of all gang members, even though they represent fewer than 25 percent of Milwaukee's adult gang members.

Discussion: Gangs, the Underclass, and Public Policy

Our study was conducted in one aging postindustrial city, with a population of 600,000. How much can be generalized from our findings can be determined only by researchers in other cities, looking at our categories and determining whether they are useful. Cloward and Ohlin's opportunity theory is a workable general theoretical framework, but more case studies are needed in order to recast their theory to reflect three decades of economic and social changes. We present our typology to encourage others to observe variation within and between gangs, and to assist in the creation of new taxonomies and new theory.

Our paper raises several empirical questions for researchers: Are the behavior patterns of the founding gang members in our sample representative of adult gang members in other cities? In larger cities, are most gang members now new jacks who have long given up the hope of a conventional life, or are most still homeboys? Are there "homeboy" gangs and "new jack" gangs, following the "street gang/drug gang" notion of Klein and Maxson (1993)? If so, what distinguishes one from the other? Does gang members' orientation to conventionality vary by ethnicity or by region? How does it change over time? Can this typology help account for variation in rates of violence between gang members? Can female gang members be typed in the same way as males?

Our data also support the life course perspective of Sampson and Laub (1993, 255), who ask whether present criminal justice policies "are producing unintended criminogenic effects." Milwaukee gang members are like the persistent, serious offenders in the Gluecks' data (Glueck and Glueck 1950). The key to their future lies in building social capital that comes from steady employment and a supportive relationship, without the constant threat of incarceration (Sampson and Laub 1993, 162–168). Homeboys largely had a wife or a steady lady, were unhappily enduring "the silent, subtle humiliations" of the secondary labor market (Bourgois 1990, 629), and lived in dread of prison. Incarceration for drug charges undercut their efforts to find steady work and led them almost inevitably back to the drug economy.

Long and mandatory prison terms for use and intent to sell cocaine lump those who are committed to the drug economy with those who are using or are selling in order to survive. Our prisons are filled disproportionately with minority drug offenders (Blumstein 1993) like our homeboys, who in essence are being punished for the "crime" of not accepting poverty or of being addicted to cocaine. Our data suggest that jobs, more accessible drug treatment, alternative sentences, or even decriminalization of nonviolent drug offenses would be better approaches than the iron fist of the war on drugs (see Hagedorn 1991; Reinarman and Levine 1990; Spergel and Curry 1990).

Finally, our typology raises ethical questions for researchers. Wilson (1987, 8) called the underclass "collectively different" from the poor of the past, and many studies focus on underclass deviance. Our study found that some underclass gang members had embraced the drug economy and had forsaken conventionality, but we also found that the majority of adult gang members are still struggling to hold onto a conventional orientation to life.

Hannerz (1969, 36) commented more than two decades ago that dichotomizing community residents into "respectables" and "disrespectables" "seems often to emerge from social science writing about poor black people or the lower classes in general." Social science that emphasizes differences within poor communities, without noting commonalities, is one-sided and often distorts and demonizes underclass life.

Our data emphasize that there is no Great Wall separating the underclass from the rest of the central-city poor and working class. Social research should not build one either. Researchers who describe violent and criminal gang actions without also addressing gang members' orientation to conventionality do a disservice to the public, to policy makers, and to social science.

Questions for Thought and Discussion

1. What happens to gang members as they age? Are their experiences different or similar to those of the thieves, burglars, and other offenders discussed in previous chapters?
2. How have economic conditions affected the growth of gangs?
3. Do most gang members graduate from "gangbanging" to drug dealing as much research suggests?
4. What theory or theories of criminal behavior are illustrated in this research?

References

Anderson, Elijah (1978) *A Place on the Corner.* Chicago: University of Chicago Press.

Blumstein, Alfred (1993) Making rationality relevant. *Criminology* 31:1–16.

Bourgois, Phillippe (1990) In search of Horatio Alger: Culture and ideology in the crack economy. *Contemporary Drug Problems* 16:619–649.

Cloward, Richard and Lloyd Ohlin (1960) *Delinquency and Opportunity.* Glencoe, Ill.: Free Press.

Cohen, Albert (1955) *Delinquent Boys.* Glencoe, Ill.: Free Press.

Glueck, Sheldon and Eleanor Glueck (1950) *Unraveling Juvenile Delinquency.* New York: Commonwealth Fund.

Gottfredson, Michael and Travis Hirschi (1990) *A General Theory of Crime.* Stanford: Stanford University Press.

Hagedorn, John M. (1991) Gangs, neighborhoods, and public policy. *Social Problems* 38:529–542.

Hannerz, Ulf (1969) *Soulside: Inquiries into Ghetto Culture and Community.* New York: Columbia University Press.

Jankowski, Martin Sanchez (1991) *Islands in the Street: Gangs and American Urban Society.* Berkeley: University of California Press.

Johnson, Bruce D., Paul J. Goldstein, Edward Preble, James Schmeidler, Douglas S. Lipton, Barry Spunt, and Thomas Miller (1985) *Taking Care of Business: The Economics of Crime by Heroin Abusers.* Lexington, Mass.: Heath.

Klein, Malcolm W. and Cheryl L. Maxson (1993) Gangs and cocaine trafficking. In Craig Uchida and Doris Mackenzie (eds.), *Drugs and the Criminal Justice System.* Newbury Park: Sage.

Liebow, Elliot (1967) *Tally's Corner.* Boston: Little, Brown.

Lincoln, Yvonna S. and Egon G. Guba (1985) *Naturalistic Inquiry.* Beverly Hills: Sage.

Matza, David (1964) *Delinquency and Drift.* New York: Wiley.

Moore, Joan W. (1978) *Homeboys: Gangs, Drugs, and Prison in the Barrios of Los Angeles.* Philadelphia: Temple University Press.

Padilla, Felix (1992) *The Gang as an American Enterprise.* New Brunswick: Rutgers University Press.

Preble, Edward and John H. Casey (1969) Taking care of business: The heroin user's life on the street. *International Journal of the Addictions* 4:1–24.

Reinarman, Craig and Harry G. Levine (1990) Crack in context: Politics and media in the making of a drug scare. *Contemporary Drug Problems* 16:535–577.

Sampson, Robert J. and John H. Laub (1993) *Crime in the Making: Pathways and Turning Points through Life.* Cambridge: Harvard University Press.

Short, James F. and Fred L. Strodtbeck (1965) *Group Process and Gang Delinquency.* Chicago: University of Chicago Press.

Spergel, Irving A. and G. David Curry (1990) Strategies and perceived agency effectiveness in dealing with the youth gang problem. In C. Ronald Huff (ed.), *Gangs in America.* Beverly Hills: Sage.

Taylor, Carl (1990) *Dangerous Society.* East Lansing: Michigan State University Press.

Thrasher, Frederick (1927) *The Gang.* 1963. Chicago: University of Chicago Press.

Waldorf, Dan, Craig Reinarman, and Sheigla Murphy (1991) *Cocaine Changes: The Experience of Using and Quitting.* Philadelphia: Temple University Press.

Whyte, William Foote (1943) *Street Corner Society.* Chicago: University of Chicago Press.

Wilson, William Julius (1987) *The Truly Disadvantaged.* Chicago: University of Chicago.

Chapter 24 Collective and Normative Features of Gang Violence

Scott H. Decker

G*ang violence has become a serious problem in many large American cities. Based on his study of street gangs in St. Louis, Scott Decker examines the processes and mechanisms which help to shape, escalate, and spread gang violence. With the assistance of a "street ethnographer," himself a former gang member, Decker and his associates conducted extensive interviews with 99 active gang members. The interviews revealed that violence serves many purposes within the gang subculture. First, it produces even more violence through the process of threat and contagion. Second, it serves to solidify the cohesiveness of the gang members by increasing their dependence on each other. Finally, as Decker notes, when violence reaches a certain intolerable level, it may result in breaking up of the gang into new subgroups or in members leaving the gang altogether.*

In 1927, Frederic Thrasher observed that gangs shared many of the properties of mobs, crowds, and other collectives, and engaged in many forms of collective behavior. Despite the prominent role of his work in gang research, few attempts have been made to link the behavior of gangs to theories of collective behavior. This omission is noteworthy because, despite disagreements about most other criteria—turf, symbols, organizational structure, permanence, criminality—all gang researchers include "group" as a part of their definition of gangs. Gang members are individuals with diverse motives, behaviors, and socialization experiences. Their *group* membership, behavior, and values, however, make them interesting to criminologists who study gangs.

In this paper we explore the mechanisms and processes that result in the spread and escalation of gang violence. In particular, we focus on contagion as an aspect of collective behavior that produces expressive gang violence. Collective behavior explanations provide insights into gang processes, particularly the escalation of violence, the spread of gangs from one community to another, and increases in gang membership in specific communities.

Gang Violence

Violence is integral to life in the gang, as Klein and Maxson (1989) observed, and gang members engage in more violence than other youths. Thrasher (1927) noted that gangs developed through strife and flourish on conflict. According to Klein (1971: 85), violence is a "predominant 'myth system'" among gang members and is constantly present.

Our analysis of gang violence focuses on the role of *threat,* actual or perceived, in explaining the functions and consequences of gang violence. We define threat as the potential for transgressions against or physical harm to the gang, represented by the acts or presence of a rival group. Threats of violence are important because they have consequences for future violence. Threat plays a role in the origin and growth of gangs, their daily activities, and their belief systems. In a sense, it helps to define them to rival gangs, to the community, and to social institutions.

Katz (1988) argues that gangs are set apart from other groups by their ability to create "dread," a direct consequence of involvement in and willingness to use violence. Dread elevates these individuals to street elites through community members' perceptions of gang members as violent. In many neighborhoods, groups form for protection against the threat of outside groups (Suttles, 1972). Sometimes these groups are established along ethnic lines, though territorial concerns often guide their formation. Both Suttles (1972: 98) and Sullivan (1989) underscored the natural progression from a neighborhood group to a gang, particularly in the face of "adversarial relations" with outside groups. The emergence of many splinter gangs can be traced to the escalation of violence within larger gangs, and to the corresponding threat that the larger gang comes to represent to certain territorial or age-graded subgroups.

Threat also may contribute to the growth of gangs. This mechanism works in two ways: through building cohesiveness and through contagion. Threats of physical violence increase the solidarity or cohesiveness of gangs within neighborhoods as well as across neighborhoods. Klein (1971) identified the source of cohesion in gangs as primarily external—the results of intergang conflict; Hagedorn (1988) also made this observation. According to Klein, cohesion within the gang grows in proportion to the perceived threat represented by rival gangs. Padilla (1992) reported a similar finding, noting that threat maintains gang boundaries by strengthening the ties among gang members and increasing their commitment to each other, thus enabling them to overcome any initial reluctance about staying in the gang and ultimately engaging in violence. Thus the threat of a gang in a geographically proximate neighborhood increases the solidarity of the gang, motivates more young men to join their neighborhood gang (see Vigil, 1988), and enables them to engage in acts of violence that they might not have committed otherwise.

The growth of gangs and gang violence contains elements of what Loftin (1984) calls "contagion." In this context, contagion refers to subsequent acts of violence caused by an initial act; such acts typically take the form of retaliation. Violence—or its threat—is the mechanism that spreads gang from one neighborhood to another, as well as contributing to their growth.

The threat of attack by a group of organized youths from another neighborhood is part of the gang "myth" or belief system, and helps to create the need for protection as well as to generate unity in a previously unorganized group of neighborhood youths. The origin and spread of such beliefs explain, among other things, the viability of the gang. Threat performs an additional function: it enhances the mythic nature of violence in the gang by increasing the talk about violence and preparedness for violent engagements.

The threat of violence also "enables" gang members to engage in violent acts (especially retaliatory violence) that they might not have chosen under other circumstances. The need to respond effectively to rival gang violence escalates weaponry and increases the "tension" that often precedes violent encounters between gangs.

Threat has an additional function, however. As gangs and gang members engage in acts of violence and create "dread" (Katz, 1988: 135), they are viewed as threatening by other (gang and non-gang) groups and individuals. Also, over time, the threats that gang members face and pose isolate them from legitimate social institutions such as schools, families, and the labor market. This isolation, in turn, prevents them from engaging in the very activities and relationships that might reintegrate them into legitimate roles and reduce their criminal involvement. It weakens their ties to the socialization power and the controlling norms of such mainstream institutions, and frees them to commit acts of violence.

Collective Behavior

Collective behavior and social organizations such as gangs share many common elements, including group behavior, collective processes, and group structure. Thus it is productive to view collective behavior on a continuum with social organizations rather than regarding them as separate topics of study. Thrasher (1927) observed that collective behavior processes operated within the gang, and could be used to account for the emergence of collective violence. Such processes included games, fights, meetings, and defining common enemies. His theoretical formulation, and the supporting distinctions between gangs and other forms of social organizations (e.g., groups, mobs, crowds, publics) make clear the role that he perceived for collective behavior explanations of gang activity.

We adopt our definition of collective behavior from McPhail (1991), who identified three elements of collective behavior: (1) group, (2) behavior, and (3) common actions that vary on one or more dimensions such as purpose, organization, or duration. McPhail observed that gang violence is a form of collective behavior because it emerges from a group process involving common actions that have a defined purpose.

Collective Violence Processes Within the Gang

Gang violence includes a number of acts and is most likely to involve assaults and the use of weapons. Although the motives for these acts are diverse, much gang violence (as discussed above) is retaliatory. This quality is evident in the disproportionate number of assaults and shootings committed in response to the acts of other gangs. This finding is similar to those of other gang researchers including Hagedorn (1988), Klein and Maxson (1989), Maxson, Gordon, and Klein (1985), Moore (1978), Sanders (1993), and Vigil (1988). Initial interviews made clear that a number of violent acts were committed by gang members outside the gang. It would be inappropriate to classify these acts as gang-related, even though they were committed by gang members. Our classification of gang violence included only those acts committed by gang members which were organized by gang members and motivated by gang concerns, especially revenge, retaliation, reputation, and representation of membership. This classification corresponds to the more restrictive of the two definitions applied by Maxson and Klein (1990).

The centrality of violence to gang life was illustrated by counts of the times a topic was mentioned during an interview. Except for drugs (which were mentioned more than 2,000 times), our subjects mentioned violence more often than any other topic. They referred to violence 1,681 times, including hundreds of references to specific acts such as killing or murder (246), assault (148), and robbery (71). As further evidence of the importance of violence, nine of our ninety-nine subjects have been killed since the study began in 1990; several showed us bullet wounds during the interview. As stated earlier, this group had extensive arrest histories: 80 percent had been arrested at least once, the mean number of arrests per subject was eight, and one-third reported that their most recent arrest was for assault or weapons violations.

Other incidents also illustrate the salience of violence in the lives of gang members. One day three gang members were sitting on their front porch, waiting for the field ethnographer to pick up one of them for an interview. As he drove up their street, he heard shots and saw the three subjects being shot in a drive-by. Their wounds were superficial, but this incident underscored the daily potential for violence as well as our ability to observe it firsthand. During the course of our research, several gang members offered to demonstrate their ability to use violence, typically by inviting us to accompany them on a drive-by shooting or to drop them off in rival territory and watch them shoot a rival gang member. We declined all such invitations, but they are not uncommon in field research (Wright and Decker, 1994). On a few occasions during interviews, gang members displayed a firearm when asked whether they possessed a gun. Most subjects reported beginning their life in the gang with a violent encounter; usually they were "beaten in" by members of the gang they were joining. The process of leaving the gang was also described in violent terms: by being "beaten out," leaving through fear of violence, suffering serious injury, or death.

The research reported here attempts to provide a framework for understanding the peaks and valleys of gang violence. As Short and Strodtbeck (1974) observed, efforts to understand gang violence must focus both on process variables (such as interactions) and on situational characteristics (such as neighborhood structure, age, race, and sex). For these reasons we concentrate on stages in the gang process that illustrate important aspects of gang violence, and we examine such violence in the context of five spheres of gang activity: (1) the role of violence in defining life in the gang, (2) the role of violence in the process of joining the gang, (3) the use of violence by the gang, (4) staging grounds for violence, and (5) gang members' recommendations for ending their gang.

The Role of Violence in Defining Life in the Gang

A fundamental way to demonstrate the centrality of violence to life in the gang is to examine how gang members defined a gang. Most answers to this question included some mention of violence. Our subjects were able to distinguish between violence within the gang and that which was unrelated to the gang.

INT: What is a gang to you?

007: A gang is, I don't know, just a gang where people hang out together and get into fights. A lot of members of your group will help you fight.

INT: So if you just got into a fight with another girl because you didn't like her?

007: Then it would be a one-on-one fight, but then like if somebody else jump in, then somebody would come from my side.

INT: Why do you call the group you belong to a gang?

047: Violence, I guess. There is more violence than a family. With a gang it's like fighting all the time, killing, shooting.

INT: What kind of things do members of your organization do together?

085: We have drive-bys, shootings, go to parties, we even go to the mall. Most of the things we do together is dealing with fighting.

Most often the violence was protective, reflecting the belief that belonging to a gang at least would reduce the chance of being attacked.

INT: Are you claiming a gang now?

046: I'm cool with a gang, real cool.

INT: What does that mean to be cool?

046: You don't got to worry about nobody jumping you. You don't got to worry about getting beat up.

Other subjects found the violence in their gang an attractive feature of membership. These individuals were attracted not so much by protection as by the opportunity to engage in violence.

INT: Why did you start to call that group a gang?

009: It's good to be in a gang cause there's a lot of violence and stuff.

INT: So the reason you call it a gang is basically why?

101: Because I beat up on folks and shoot them. The last person I shot I was in jail for five years.

INT: What's good about being in a gang?

101: You can get to fight whoever you want and shoot whoever you want. To me, it's kind of fun. Then again, it's not . . . because you have to go to jail for that shit. But other than that, being down for who you want to be with, it's fun.

INT: What's the most important reason to be in the gang?

057: Beating Crabs. If it wasn't for beating Crabs, I don't think I would be in a gang right now.

Whether for protection or for the opportunity to engage in violence, the members of our sample attached considerable importance to the role of violence in their definition of a gang. Many of the comments evoke what Klein (1971) termed "mythic violence"—discussions of violent activities between gangs that reinforce the ties of membership and maintain boundaries between neighborhood gangs and those in "rival" neighborhoods. In this sense, violence is a central feature of the normative system of the gang; it is the defining feature and the central value of gang life.

Violence in Joining the Gang

Most gangs require an initiation process that includes participation in violent activities. This ritual fulfills a number of important functions. First, it determines whether a prospective member is tough enough to endure the level of violence he or she will face as a gang member. Equally important, the gang must learn how tough a potential member is because they may have to count on this individual for support in fights or shootings. The initiation serves other purposes as well. Most important, it increases solidarity among gang members by engaging them in a collective ritual. The initiation reminds active members of their earlier status, and gives the new member something in common with other gang members. In addition, a violent initiation provides a rehearsal for a prospective member for life in the gang. In short, it demonstrates the centrality of violence to gang life.

Three-quarters of our subjects were initiated into their gangs through the process known as "beating in." This ritual took many forms; in its most common version a prospective gang member walked between lines of gang members or stood inside a circle of gang members who beat the initiate with their fists.

020: I had to stand in a circle and there was about ten of them. Out of these ten there was just me standing in the circle. I had to take six to the chest by all ten of them. Or I can try to go to the weakest one and get out. If you don't get out, they are going to keep beating you. I said "I will take the circle."

One leader, who reported that he had been in charge of several initiations, described the typical form:

001: They had to get jumped on.

INT: How many guys jump on em?

001: Ten.

INT: And then how long do they go?

001: Until I tell em to stop.

INT: When do you tell em to stop?

> **001:** I just let em beat em for bout two or three minutes to see if they can take a punishment.

Other gang members reported that they had the choice of either being beaten in or "going on a mission." On a mission, a prospective member had to engage in an act of violence, usually against a rival gang member on rival turf. Initiates often were required to confront a rival gang member face-to-face.

> **041:** You have to fly your colors through enemy territory. Some step to you; you have to take care of them by yourself; you don't get no help.

> **084:** To be a Crip, you have to put your blue rag on your head and wear all blue and go in a Blood neighborhood—that is the hardest of all of them—and walk through the Blood neighborhood and fight Bloods. If you come out without getting killed, that's the way you get initiated.

Every gang member we interviewed reported that his or her initiation involved participating in some form of violence. This violence was rarely directed against members of other gangs; most often it took place within the gang. Then in each successive initiation, recently initiated members participated in "beating in" new members. Such violence always has a group context and a normative purpose: to reinforce the ties between members while reminding them that violence lies at the core of life in the gang.

The Use of Gang Violence

To understand gang violence more clearly, it is critical to know when such violence is used. In the four following situations, gang members did not regard themselves as initiating violence; rather, because its purpose was to respond to the violent activities of a rival gang. Retaliatory violence corresponds to the concept of contagion (Loftin, 1984) as well as to the principle of crime as social control (Black, 1983). According to this view, gang violence is an attempt to enact private justice for wrongs committed against the gang, one of its members, or a symbol of the gang. These wrongs may be actual or perceived; often the perceived threat of impending violence is as powerful motivator as violence itself.

This view of gang violence helps to explain the rapid escalation of intergang hostilities that lead to assaults, drive-by shootings, or murders between gangs. Such actions reflect the collective behavior processes at work, in which acts of violence against the gang serve as the catalyst that brings together subgroups within the gang and unites them against a common enemy. Such violent events are rare, but are important in gang culture. Collective violence is one of the few activities involving the majority of gang members, including fringe members. The precipitation of such activities pulls fringe members into the gang and increases cohesion.

When Violence Comes to the Gang. We asked gang members when they used violence. Typically they claimed that violence was seldom initiated by the gang itself, but was a response to "trouble" that was "brought" to them. In these instances, the object of violence was loosely defined and was rarely identified; it represented a symbolic enemy against whom violence would be used. These statements, however, indicate an attempt to provide justifications for gang violence.

> **INT:** How often do gang members use violence?

> **005:** When trouble comes to them.

> **INT:** When do you guys use violence?

> **018:** When people start bringing violence to us. They bring it to us and set it up. We take it from there.

> **INT:** When do members of the gang use violence?

> **037:** When somebody approaches us. We don't go out looking for trouble. We let trouble come to us.

> **INT:** When do you guys use violence?

> **042:** Only when it's called for. We don't start trouble. That's the secret of our success.

The view of gang members passively sitting back and waiting for violence to come to them is inconsistent with much of what we know about gang life. After all, many gang members reported that they joined the gang expressly for the opportunity to engage in violence; many lived in neighborhoods where acts of violence occurred several times each day; and most had engaged in violence before joining the gang. Even so, unprovoked violence against another gang is difficult to justify; retaliatory actions against parties that wronged them can be justified more easily. Also, such actions are consistent with the view of the gang as a legitimate social organization serving the legitimate purpose of protecting its members—a central value in the gang's normative structure.

Retaliation. A number of gang members told us that they used violence to even the score with a specific group or individual. Unlike the subjects above, who reported generalized responses, these individuals identified a specific target for their violence: someone who had committed a violent act against them or their gang in the past.

> **002:** I had on a blue rag and he say what's up cuz, what's up blood, and I say uh, what's up cuz, just like that, and then me and him got to arguin' and everything, and teachers would stop it, and then me and him met up one day when nobody was round. We got to fightin. Naw, cause I told Ron, my cousin, my cousin and em came up to the school and beat em up. And the next day when he seen me, he gonna ask me where my cousin and em at. I say I don't need my cousin and em for you. They just came up there cause they heard you was a Blood. And they whooped em. Then me and him had a fight the next day, yeah. And then I had to fight some other dudes that was his friends and I beat em up. Then he brought some boys up to the school and they, uh, pulled out a gun on me and I ran up in the school. And then I brought my boys up the next day and we beat on em.

Specific examples of retaliation against rival gangs were mentioned less frequently than was general gang violence. This point underscores the important symbolic function of gang violence, a value that members must be ready to support. The idea that rival gangs will "bring violence" to the gang is an important part of the gang belief system; it is pivotal in increasing cohesion among members of otherwise loosely confederated organizations.

Graffiti. A third type of gang violence occurred in response to defacing gang graffiti. Organizational symbols are important to all groups, and perhaps more so to those whose members are adolescents. The significance of graffiti to gangs has been documented by a number of observers in a variety of circumstances (Block and Block, 1993; Hagedorn, 1988; Moore, 1978; Vigil, 1988). In particular, graffiti identify gang territory, and maintaining territory is an important feature of gang activity in St. Louis and other cities. As Block and Block observed in Chicago, battles over turf often originated in attempts by rival gangs to "strike out" graffiti. Several gang members told us that attempts to paint over their graffiti by rival gangs were met with a violent response, but no gang members could recall a specific instance. Claiming to use violence in response to such insults again reflects the mythic character of gang violence; it emphasizes the symbolic importance of violence for group processes such as cohesion, boundary maintenance, and identity. Further, such responses underscore the threat represented by rivals who would encroach on gang territory to strike out gang graffiti.

> **INT:** What does the removal of graffiti mean?
>
> **043:** That's a person that we have to go kill. We put our enemies up on the wall. If there is a certain person, we "X" that out and know who to kill.
>
> **INT:** What if somebody comes and paints a pitchfork or paints over your graffiti? What does that mean to your gang?
>
> **046:** First time we just paint it back up there, no sweat. Next time they come do it, we go find out who did it and go paint over theirs. If they come back a third time, it's like three times you out. Obviously that means something if they keep painting over us. They telling us they ready to fight.

Territory. Most gang members continued to live in the neighborhood where their gang started. Even for those who had moved away, it retained a symbolic value. Protecting gang turf is viewed as an important responsibility, which extends well beyond its symbolic importance as the site where the gang began. Our subjects' allegiance to the neighborhood was deeply embedded in the history of neighborhood friendship groups that evolved into gangs. Thus, turf protection was an important value.

When we asked gang members about defending their turf, we received some generalized responses about their willingness to use violence to do so.

> **INT:** If someone from another gang comes to your turf, what does your gang do?
>
> **019:** First try to tell him to leave.
>
> **INT:** If he don't leave?
>
> **019:** He'll leave one way or the other—carry him out in a Hefty bag.

In other instances, however, the responses identified an individual or an incident in which the gang used violence to protect its turf.

> **INT:** What kind of things does the gang have to do to defend its turf?
>
> **013:** Kill. That's all it is, kill.
>
> **INT:** Tell me about your most recent turf defense. What happened, a guy came in?
>
> **013:** A guy came in, he had the wrong colors on, he got to move out. He got his head split open with a sledgehammer, he got two ribs broken, he got his face torn up.
>
> **INT:** Did he die from that?
>
> **013:** I don't know. We dropped him off on the other side of town. If he did die, it was on the other side of town.

Staging Grounds for Violence

Gang members expect that when they go to certain locations they will be the targets of violence from other gangs or will be expected by members of their own gang to engage in violence. In some cases, large-scale violence will occur. Other encounters result only in "face-offs." These encounters highlight the role of situational characteristics in gang violence. Most often the staging grounds are public places such as a restaurant.

> **INT:** Do they ever bring weapons to school?
>
> **011:** No, cause we really don't have no trouble. We mainly fight up at the White Castle. That's where our trouble starts, at the White Castle.

The expectation of violence at certain locations was so strong that some members avoided going to those places.

> **INT:** Do you go to dances or parties?
>
> **047:** I don't. I stay away from house parties. Too many fights come out of there.

According to another gang member, violence at house parties had reached such a level that many hosts searched their guests for weapons.

> **074:** Sometimes people wait until they get out of the party and start shooting. Now at these parties they have people at the door searching people, even at house parties.

In general, gang members reported that they "hung out" in small cliques or subgroups and that it was rare for the entire gang to be together. This reflects the general character of social organization in the gangs we studied. An external threat—usually from another gang—was needed to strengthen cohesion among gang members and to bring the larger gang together. Many members of our sample reported that they did not go skating, to the mall, or to dances alone or in small groups because they knew that gang violence was likely to erupt at such locations. Thus the gang went *en masse* to these locations, prepared to start or respond to violence. These expectations contributed to the eventual use of violence. In this way, the gang's belief system contributed to the likelihood of violent encounters.

Ending Gangs

When we asked for gang members' perspectives on the best way to end gangs, we expected to find a variety of recommendations targeted at fundamental causes (racism, unemployment, education) as well as more proximate solutions (detached workers, recreation centers, job training). Instead the modal response reflected the centrality of violence in the gang. Twenty-five of our 99 subjects told us that the only way to get rid of their gang would be to use violence to get rid of the members. This response was confirmed by gang members in their conversations with the field ethnographer. For many gang members, life in the gang had become synonymous with violence; for one respondent, even job offers were not sufficient to end the gang.

> **INT:** What would be the best way to get rid of your gang, the Rolling Sixties?
>
> **033:** Smoke us all.
>
> **INT:** Kill you all?
>
> **033:** Yeah.
>
> **INT:** We couldn't give you guys jobs?
>
> **033:** No, just smoke us.

Others recommended using extreme violence to get rid of their gang.

> **INT:** What would it take to get rid of your gang?
>
> **035:** Whole lot of machine guns. Kill us all. We just going to multiply anyway cause the Pee Wees gonna take over.
>
> **INT:** What would be the best way to get rid of the Sixties?

035: Kill us all at once. Put them in one place and blow them up.

Violence is so central a part of gang culture that even the members' recommendations about ending gangs include elements of violence.

The Process of Gang Violence

The analysis above suggests a model that accounts for the escalation of gang violence and is consistent with the nature of gang process and normative structure: it reflects the lack of strong leadership, structure, and group goals. The key element is the collective identification of threat, a process that unites the gang and overcomes the general lack of unity by increasing cohesion. This occurred in response to threats against the gang, either real or perceived, by rival gangs. The role of mythic violence is particularly important in this context; it is the agent through which talk about violence most frequently unites gang members.

We suggest that a seven-step process accounts for the peaks and valleys of gang violence. The key to understanding violence is the nature of organization within gangs. Most gangs originate as neighborhood groups and are characterized by loose ties between their members and the larger gang. These groups generally lack effective leadership; cohesion in small cliques is stronger than the ties to the larger gang. Against this backdrop, symbolic enemies are identified when subgroups interact with other gangs near them. Threats from those groups—whether real or perceived—expand the number of participants, and may increase cohesion among members and heighten their willingness to use violence. Violence between gangs is most often the result of a mobilizing event that pushes a ready and willing group beyond the constraints against violence. Such events may include the deployment of gang members to protect or attack certain locations, to engage in actions in cars, or simply to act "loco." Violent encounters typically are short-lived and de-escalate rapidly. This de-escalation, however, may be only a respite before the next retaliation. The process moves through the following seven steps:

1. Loose bonds to the gang;
2. Collective identification of threat from a rival gang (through rumors, symbolic shows of force, cruising, and mythic violence), reinforcing the centrality of violence that expands the number of participants and increases cohesion;
3. A mobilizing event possibly, but not necessarily, violence;
4. Escalation of activity;
5. Violent event;
6. Rapid de-escalation;
7. Retaliation.

Conclusion

Gang violence, like other gang activities, reflects the gang's organizational and normative structure. Such violence, especially retaliatory violence, is an outgrowth of a collective process that reflects the loose organizational structure of gangs with diffuse goals, little allegiance among members, and few leaders.

If gangs are composed of diffuse subgroups, how is violence organized? Our answer to this question is "Not very well and not very often," because most gang violence serves important symbolic purposes within the gang. In addition, most gang violence is retaliatory, a response to violence—real or perceived—against the gang.

Gang violence serves many functions in the life of the gang. First, and most important, it produces more violence through the processes of threat and contagion. These mechanisms strongly reflect elements of collective behavior. Second, it temporarily increases the solidarity of gang members, uniting them against a common enemy by heightening their dependence on each other. When gang violence exceeds tolerable limits, a third function may be evident: the splintering of gangs into subgroups and the decision by some individuals to leave the gang.

Questions for Thought and Discussion

1. What are the various roles of violence in the gang?
2. What are the major factors that bring about violence by gangs?
3. What roles do gangs play in the lives of their members?
4. What theory or theories of criminal behavior are illustrated in this research?

References

Black, D. 1983. "Crime as Social Control." *American Sociological Review* 43:34–45.

Block, C.R. and R. Block. 1993. "Street Gang Crime in Chicago." *Research in Brief* {December}. Washington, DC: National Institute of Justice.

Hagedorn, J. 1988. *People and Folks.* Chicago: Lakeview Press.

Katz, J. 1988. *The Seductions of Crime.* New York: Basic Books.

Klein, M. 1971. *Street Gangs and Street Workers.* Englewood Cliffs, NJ: Prentice Hall.

Klein, M. and C. Maxson. 1989. "Street Gang Violence." Pp. 198–234 in *Violent Crimes, Violent Criminals,* edited by N. Weiner. Beverly Hills: Sage.

Loftin, C. 1984. "Assaultive Violence as Contagious Process." *Bulletin of the New York Academy of Medicine* 62:550–55.

Maxson, C., M. Gordon, and M. Klein. 1985. "Differences between Gang and Nongang Homicides." *Criminology* 21:209–22.

Maxson, C. and M. Klein. 1990. "Street Gang Violence: Twice as Great or Half as Great?" Pp. 71–102 in *Gangs in America,* edited by R. Huff. Newbury Park, CA: Sage.

McPhail, C. 1991. *The Myth of the Madding Crowd.* New York: Aldine.

Moore, J. 1978. *Homeboys.* Philadelphia: Temple University Press.

Padilla, F. 1992. *The Gang as an American Enterprise.* New Brunswick, NJ: Rutgers University Press.

Sanders, W. 1993. *Drive-Bys and Gang Bangs: Gangs and Grounded Culture.* Chicago: Aldine.

Short, J. and F. Strodtbeck. 1974. *Group Process and Gang Delinquency.* Chicago: University of Chicago Press.

Sullivan, M. 1989. *Getting Paid: Youth Crime and Work in the Inner City.* Ithaca: Cornell University Press.

Suttles, G. 1972. *The Social Construction of Communities.* Chicago: University of Chicago Press.

Thrasher, F. 1927. *The Gang.* Chicago: University of Chicago Press.

Vigil, D. 1988. *Barrio Gangs.* Austin: University of Texas Press.

Wright, R.T., and S.H. Decker. 1994. *Burglars on the Job: Streetlife Culture & Residential Burglary.* Boston: Northeastern University Press.

Chapter 25
Gender and Victimization Risk Among Young Women in Gangs

Jody Miller

This selection examines how gendered situational dynamics shape gang violence, including participation in violent offending and experiences of violent victimization. Although there are numerous studies of gangs and gang involved individuals, few have explored the concept of victimization of gang members. The author found that young women, even regular offenders, highlight the significance of gender in shaping and limiting their involvement in serious violence. Based on interviews with 20 female gang members in Columbus, Ohio, Miller found that being a member increases one's risk of assaults and other physical victimization and that these risks are greater for females than for males. She suggests that the act of joining a gang often involves submission to victimization at the hands of other members of the gang and that gang activities thereafter place them at risk for further victimization.

Girls, Gangs, and Crime

Until recently . . . little attention was paid to young women's participation in serious and violent gang-related crime. Most traditional gang research emphasized the auxiliary and peripheral nature of girls' gang involvement and often resulted in an almost exclusive emphasis on girls' sexuality and sexual activities with male gang members, downplaying their participation in delinquency (for critiques of gender bias in gender research, see Campbell 1984, 1990). . . .

However, recent estimates of female gang involvement have caused researchers to pay greater attention to gang girls' activities. This evidence suggests that young women approximate anywhere from 10 to 38 percent of gang members (Campbell 1984; Chesney-Lind 1993; Esbensen 1996; . . . Moore 1991), that female gang participation may be increasing (. . . Spergel and Curry 1993; . . .), and that in some urban areas, upward of one-fifth of girls report gang affiliations (Bjerregaard and Smith 1993; Winfree et al. 1992). As female gang members have become recognized as a group worthy of criminologists' attention, we have garnered new information regarding their involvement in delinquency in general, and violence in particular.

Few would dispute that when it comes to serious delinquency, male gang members are involved more frequently than their female counterparts. However, this evidence does suggest that young women in gangs are more involved in serious criminal activities than was previously believed and also tend to be more involved than nongang youths—male or female. As such, they likely are exposed to greater victimization risk than nongang youths as well.

In addition, given the social contexts described above, it is reasonable to assume that young women's victimization risk within gangs is also shaped by gender. Gang activities (such as fighting for status and retaliation) create a particular set of factors that increase gang members' victimization risk and repeat victimization risk. Constructions of gender identity may shape these risks in particular ways for girls. For instance, young women's adoption of masculine attributes may provide a means of participating and gaining status within gangs but may also lead to increased risk of victimization as a result of deeper immersion in delinquent activities. On the other hand, experiences of victimization may contribute to girls' denigration and thus increase their risk for repeat victimization through gendered responses and labeling—for example, when sexual victimization leads to perceptions of sexual availability or when victimization leads an individual to be viewed as weak. In addition, femaleness is an individual attribute that has the capacity to mark young women as "safe" crime victims (e.g., easy targets) or, conversely, to deem them "off limits." My goal here is to examine the gendered nature of violence within gangs, with a specific focus on how gender shapes young women's victimization risk.

Methodology

Data presented in this article come from survey and semistructured in-depth interviews with 20 female members of mixed-gender gangs in Columbus, Ohio. The interviewees ranged in age from 12 to 17; just over three-quarters were African American or multiracial (16 of 20), and the rest (4 of 20) were white.

Girls who admitted gang involvement during the survey participated in a follow-up interview to talk in more depth about their gangs and gang activities. The goal of the in-depth interview was to gain a greater understanding of the nature and meanings of gang life from the point of view of its female members.

The in-depth interviews were open-ended and all but one were audiotaped. They were structured around several groupings of questions. We began by discussing girls' entry into their gangs—when and how they became involved, and what other things were going on in their lives at the time. Then we discussed the structure of the gang—its history, size, leadership, and organization, and their place in the group. The next series of questions concerned gender within the gang; for example, how girls get involved, what activities they engage in and whether these are the same as the young men's activities, and what kind of males and females have the most influence in the gang and why. The next series of questions explored gang involvement more generally—what being in the gang means, what kinds of things they do together, and so on. Then, I asked how safe or dangerous they feel gang membership is and how they deal with risk. I concluded by asking them to speculate about why people their age join gangs, what things they like, what they dislike and have learned by being in the gang, and what they like best about themselves. This basic guideline was followed for each interview subject, although when additional topics arose in the context of the interview we often deviated from the interview guide to pursue them. Throughout the interviews, issues related to violence emerged; these issues form the core of the discussion that follows.

Setting

The young women I interviewed described their gangs in ways that are very much in keeping with these findings. All 20 are members of Folks, Crips, or Bloods sets. All but 3 described gangs with fewer than 30 members, and most reported relatively narrow age ranges between members. Half were in gangs with members who were 21 or over, but almost without exception, their gangs were made up primarily of teenagers, with either one adult who was considered the OG ("Original Gangster," leader) or just a handful of young adults. The majority (14 of 20) reported that their gangs did not include members under the age of 13.

Although the gangs these young women were members of were composed of both female and male members, they varied in their gender composition, with the vast majority being predominantly male. Six girls reported that girls were one-fifth or fewer of the members of their gang; 8 were in gangs in which girls were between a quarter and a third of the overall membership; 4 said girls were between 44 and 50 percent of the members; and 1 girl reported that her gang was two-thirds female and one-third male. Overall, girls were typically a minority within these groups numerically, with 11 girls reporting that there were 5 or fewer girls in their set.

This structure—male-dominated, integrated mixed-gender gangs—likely shapes gender dynamics in particular ways. Much past gang research has assumed that female members of gangs are in auxiliary subgroups of male gangs, but there is increasing evidence—including from the young women I spoke with—that many gangs can be characterized as integrated, mixed-gender groups.

Gender, Gangs, and Violence

Gangs as Protection and Risk

An irony of gang involvement is that although many members suggest one thing they get out of the gang is a sense of protection (see also Decker 1996; Joe and Chesney-Lind 1995; Lauderback et al. 1992), gang membership itself means exposure to victimization risk and even a willingness to be victimized. These contradictions are apparent when girls talk about what they get out of the gang, and what being in the gang means in terms of other members' expectations of their behavior. In general, a number of girls suggested that being a gang member is a source of protection around the neighborhood. Erica, a 17-year-old African American, explained, "It's like people look at us and that's exactly what they think, there's a gang, and they respect us for that. They won't bother us. . . . It's like you put that intimidation in somebody." Likewise, Lisa, a 14-year-old white girl, described being in the gang as empowering: "You just feel like, oh my God, you know, they got my back. I don't need to worry about it." Given the violence endemic in many inner-city communities, these beliefs are understandable, and to a certain extent, accurate.

In addition, some young women articulated a specifically gendered sense of protection that they felt as a result of being a member of a group that was predominantly male. Gangs operate within larger social milieus that are characterized by gender inequality and sexual exploitation. Being in a gang with young men means at least the semblance of protection from, and retaliation against, predatory men in the social environment. Heather, a 15-year-old white girl, noted, "You feel more secure when, you know, a guy's around protectin' you, you know, than you would a girl." She explained that as a gang member, because "you get protected by guys . . . not as many people mess with you." Other young women concurred and also described that male gang members could retaliate against specific acts of violence against girls in the gang. Nikkie, a 13-year-old African American girl, had a friend who was raped by a rival gang member, and she said, "It was a Crab [Crip] that raped my girl in Miller Ales, and um, they was ready to kill him." Keisha, an African American 14-year-old, explained, "if I got beat up by a guy, all I gotta do is go tell one of the niggers, you know what I'm sayin'? Or one of the guys, they'd take care of it."

At the same time, members recognized that they may be targets of rival gang members and were expected to "be down" for their gang at those times even when it meant being physically hurt. In addition, initiation rites and internal rules were structured in ways that required individuals to submit to, and be exposed to, violence. For example, young women's descriptions of the qualities they valued in members revealed the extent to which exposure to violence was an expected element of gang involvement. Potential members, they explained, should be tough, able to fight and to engage in criminal activities, and also should be loyal to the group and willing to put themselves at risk for it. Erica explained that they didn't want "punks" in her gang: "When you join something like that, you might as well expect that there's gonna be fights. . . . And, if you're a punk, or if you're scared of stuff like that, then don't join." Likewise, the following dialogue with Cathy, a white 16-year-old, reveals similar themes. I asked her what her gang expected out of members and she responded, "to be true to our gang and to have our backs." When I asked her to elaborate, she explained,

> **Cathy:** Like, uh, if you say you're a Blood, you be a Blood. You wear your rag even when you're by yourself. You know, don't let anybody intimidate you and be like, "Take that rag off." You know, "you better get with our set." Or something like that.
>
> **JM:** Ok. Anything else that being true to the set means?
>
> **Cathy:** Um. Yeah, I mean, just, just, you know, I mean it's, you got a whole bunch of people comin', up in your face and if you're by yourself they ask you what's your claimin', you tell 'em. Don't say "nothin."
>
> **JM:** Even if it means getting beat up or something?
>
> **Cathy:** Mmhmm.

One measure of these qualities came through the initiation process, which involved the individual submitting to victimization at the hands of the gang's members. Typically this entailed either taking a fixed number of "blows" to the head and/or chest or being "beaten in" by members for a given duration (e.g., 60 seconds). Heather described the initiation as an important event for determining whether someone would make a good member:

> When you get beat in if you don't fight back and if you just like stop and you start cryin' or somethin' or beggin' 'em to stop and stuff like that, then, they ain't gonna, they'll just stop and they'll say that you're not gang material because you gotta be hard, gotta be able to fight, take punches.

In addition to the initiation, and threats from rival gangs, members were expected to adhere to the gang's internal rules (which included such things as not fighting with one another, being "true" to the gang, respecting the leader, not spreading gang business outside the gang, and not dating members of rival gangs). Breaking the rules was grounds for physical punishment, either in the form of a spontaneous assault or a formal "violation," which involved taking a specified number of blows to the head. For example, Keisha reported that she talked back to the leader of her set and "got slapped pretty hard" for doing so. Likewise, Veronica, an African American 15-year-old, described her leader as "crazy, but we gotta listen to 'im. He's just the type that if you don't listen to 'im, he gonna blow your head off. He's just crazy."

It is clear that regardless of members' perceptions of the gang as a form of "protection," being a gang member also involves a willingness to open oneself up to the possibility of victimization. Gang victimization is governed by rules and expectations, however, and thus does not involve the random vulnerability that being out on the streets without a gang might entail in high-crime neighborhoods. Because of its structured nature, this victimization risk may be perceived as more palatable by gang members. For young women in particular, the gendered nature of the streets may make the empowerment available through gang involvement an appealing alternative to the individualized vulnerability they otherwise would face. However, as the next sections highlight, girls' victimization risks continue to be shaped by gender, even within their gangs, because these groups are structured around gender hierarchies as well.

Gender and Status, Crime and Victimization

Status hierarchies within Columbus gangs, like elsewhere, were male dominated (Bowker et al. 1980; Campbell 1990). Again, it is important to highlight that the structure of the gangs these young women belonged to—that is, male-dominated, integrated mixed-gender gangs—likely shaped the particular ways in which gender dynamics played themselves out. Autonomous female gangs, as well as gangs in which girls are in auxiliary subgroups, may be shaped by different gender relations, as well as differences in orientations toward status, and criminal involvement.

All the young women reported having established leaders in their gang, and this leadership was almost exclusively male. While LaShawna, a 17-year-old African American, reported being the leader of her set (which had a membership that is two-thirds girls, many of whom resided in the same residential facility as her), all the other girls in mixed-gender gangs reported that their OG was male. In fact, a number of young women stated explicitly that only male gang members could be leaders. Leadership qualities, and qualities attributed to high-status members of the gangs—being tough, able to fight, and willing to "do dirt" (e.g., commit crime, engage in violence) for the gang—were perceived as characteristically masculine. Keisha noted, "The guys, they just harder." She explained, "Guys is more rougher. We have our G's back but, it ain't gonna be like the guys, they just don't give a fuck. They gonna shoot you in a minute."

For the most part, status in the gang was related to traits such as the willingness to use serious violence and commit dangerous crimes and, though not exclusively, these traits were viewed primarily as qualities more likely and more intensely located among male gang members.

Because these respected traits were characterized specifically as masculine, young women actually may have had greater flexibility in their gang involvement than young men. Young women had fewer expectations placed on them—by both their male and female peers—in regard to involvement in criminal activities such as fighting, using weapons, and committing other crimes. This tended to decrease girls' exposure to victimization risk compared to male members, because they were able to avoid activities likely to place them in danger. Girls could gain status in the gang by being particularly hard and true to the set. Heather, for example, described the most influential girl in her set as "the hardest girl, the one that don't take no crap, will stand up to anybody." Likewise, Diane, a white 15-year-old, described a highly respected female member in her set as follows:

> People look up to Janeen just 'cause she's so crazy. People just look up to her 'cause she don't care about nothin'. She don't even care about makin' money. Her, her thing is, "Oh, you're a Slob [Blood]? You're a Slob? You talkin' to me? You talkin' shit to me?" Pow, pow! And that's it. That's it.

However, young women also had a second route to status that was less available to young men. This came via their connections—as sisters, girlfriends, cousins—to influential, high-status young men. In Veronica's set, for example, the girl with the most power was the OG's "sister or his cousin, one of 'em." His girlfriend also had status, although Veronica noted that "most of us just look up to our OG." Monica, a 16-year-old African American, and Tamika, a 15-year-old

African American, both had older brothers in their gangs, and both reported getting respect, recognition, and protection because of this connection. This route to status and the masculinization of high-status traits functioned to maintain gender inequality within gangs, but they also could put young women at less risk of victimization than young men. This was both because young women were perceived as less threatening and thus were less likely to be targeted by rivals, and because they were not expected to prove themselves in the ways that young men were, thus decreasing their participation in those delinquent activities likely to increase exposure to violence. Thus, gender inequality could have a protective edge for young women.

Young men's perceptions of girls as lesser members typically functioned to keep girls from being targets of serious violence at the hands of rival young men, who instead left routine confrontations with rival female gang members to the girls in their own gang. Diane said that young men in her gang "don't wanna waste their time hittin' on some little girls. They're gonna go get their little cats [females] to go get 'em." Lisa remarked, "girls don't face as much violence as [guys]. They see a girl, they say, 'we'll just smack her and send her on.' They see a guy—'cause guys are like a lot more into it than girls are, I've noticed that—and they like, 'well, we'll shoot him.' In addition, the girls I interviewed suggested that, in comparison with young men, young women were less likely to resort to serious violence, such as that involving a weapon, when confronting rivals. Thus, when girls' routine confrontations were more likely to be female on female than male on female, girls' risk of serious victimization was lessened further.

Also, because participation in serious and violent crime was defined primarily as a masculine endeavor, young women could use gender as a means of avoiding participation in those aspects of gang life they found risky, threatening, or morally troubling. Of the young women I interviewed, about one-fifth were involved in serious gang violence: A few had been involved [in] aggravated assaults on rival gang members, and one admitted to having killed a rival gang member, but they were by far the exception. Most girls tended not to be involved in serious gang crime, and some reported that they chose to exclude themselves because they felt ambivalent about this aspect of gang life. Angie, an African American 15-year-old, explained,

> I don't get involved like that, be out there goin' and just beat up people like that or go stealin', things like that. That's not me. The boys, mostly the boys do all that, the girls we just sit back and chill, you know.

Likewise, Diane noted,

> For maybe a drive-by they might wanna have a bunch of dudes. They might not put the females in that. Maybe the females might be weak inside, not strong enough to do something like that, just on the insides. . . . If a female wants to go forward and doin' that, and she wants to risk her whole life for doin' that, then she can. But the majority of the time, that job is given to a man.

Diane was not just alluding to the idea that young men were stronger than young women. She also inferred that young women were able to get out of committing serious crime, more so than young men, because a girl shouldn't have to "risk her whole life" for the gang. In accepting that young men were more central members of the gang, young women could more easily participate in gangs without putting themselves in jeopardy—they could engage in the more routine, everyday activities of the gang, like hanging out, listening to music, and smoking bud (marijuana). These male-dominated mixed-gender gangs thus appeared to provide young women with flexibility in their involvement in gang activities. As a result, it is likely that their risk of victimization at the hands of rivals was less than that of young men in gangs who were engaged in greater amounts of crime.

Girls' Devaluation and Victimization

In addition to girls choosing not to participate in serious gang crimes, they also faced exclusion at the hands of young men or the gang as a whole (see also Bowker et al. 1980). In particular, the two types of crime mentioned most frequently as "off-limits" for girls were drug sales and drive-by shootings. LaShawna explained, "We don't really let our females [sell drugs] unless they really wanna and they know how to do it and not to get caught and everything." Veronica described a drive-by that her gang participated in and said, "They wouldn't let us [females] go. But we wanted to go, but they wouldn't let us." Often, the exclusion was couched in terms of protection. When I asked Veronica why the girls couldn't go, she said, "so we won't go to jail if they was to get caught. Or if one of 'em was to get shot, they wouldn't want it to happen to us." Likewise, Sonita, a 13-year-old African American, noted, "If they gonna do somethin' bad and they think one of the females gonna get hurt they don't let 'em do it with them. . . . Like if they involved with shooting or whatever, [girls] can't go."

Although girls' exclusion from some gang crime may be framed as protective (and may reduce their victimization risk vis-à-vis rival gangs), it also served to perpetuate the devaluation of female members as less significant to the gang—not as tough, true, or "down" for the gang as male members. When LaShawna said her gang blocked girls' involvement in serious crime, I pointed out that she was actively involved herself. She explained, "Yeah, I do a lot of stuff 'cause I'm tough. I likes, I likes messin' with boys. I fight boys. Girls ain't nothin' to me." Similarly, Tamika said, "girls, they little peons."

Some young women found the perception of them as weak a frustrating one. Brandi, an African American 13-year-old, explained, "Sometimes I dislike that the boys, sometimes, always gotta take charge and they think sometimes, that the girls don't know how to take charge 'cause we're like girls, we're females, and like that." And Chantell, an African American 14-year-old, noted that rival gang members "think that you're more of a punk." Beliefs that girls were weaker than boys meant that young women had a harder time proving that they were serious about their commitment to the gang. Diane explained,

> A female has to show that she's tough. A guy can just, you can just look at him. But a female, she's gotta show. She's gotta go out and do some dirt. She's gotta go whip some girl's ass, shoot somebody, rob somebody or something. To show that she is tough.

In terms of gender-specific victimization risk, the devaluation of young women suggests several things. It could lead to the mistreatment and victimization of girls by members of their own gang when they didn't have specific male protection (i.e., a brother, boyfriend) in the gang or when they weren't able to stand up for themselves to male members. This was exacerbated by activities that led young women to be viewed as sexually available. In addition, because young women typically were not seen as a threat by young men, when they did pose one, they could be punished even more harshly than young men, not only for having challenged a rival gang or gang member but also for having overstepped "appropriate" gender boundaries.

Monica had status and respect in her gang, both because she had proven herself through fights and criminal activities, and because her older brothers were members of her set. She contrasted her own treatment with that of other young women in the gang:

> They just be puttin' the other girls off. Like Andrea, man. Oh my God, they dog Andrea so bad. They like, "Bitch, go to the store." She like, "All right, I be right back." She will go to the store and go and get them whatever they want and come back with it. If she don't get it right, they be like, "Why you do that bitch?" I mean, and one dude even smacked ha. And, I mean, and, I don't, I told my brother once. I was like, "Man, it ain't even like that. If you ever see someone tryin' to disrespect me like that or hit me, if you do not hit them or at least say somethin' to them. . . ." So my brothers, they kinda watch out for me.

However, Monica put the responsibility for Andrea's treatment squarely on the young woman: "I put that on her. They ain't gotta do her like that, but she don't gotta let them do her like that either." Andrea was seen as "weak" because she did not stand up to the male members in the gang; thus, her mistreatment was framed as partially deserved because she did not exhibit the valued traits of toughness and willingness to fight that would allow her to defend herself.

An additional but related problem was when the devaluation of young women within gangs was sexual in nature. Girls, but not boys, could be initiated into the gang by being "sexed in"—having sexual relations with multiple male members of the gang. Other members viewed the young women initiated in this way as sexually available and promiscuous, thus increasing their subsequent mistreatment. In addition, the stigma could extend to female members in general, creating a sexual devaluation that all girls had to contend with. The dynamics of "sexing in" as a form of gang initiation placed young women in a position that increased their risk of ongoing mistreatment at the hands of their gang peers. According to Keisha, "If you get sexed in, you have no respect. That means you gotta go ho'in' for 'em; when they say you give 'em the pussy, you gotta give it to 'em. If you don't, you gonna get your ass beat. I ain't down for that." One girl in her set was sexed in and Keisha said the girl "just do everything they tell her to do, like a dummy." Nikkie reported that two girls who were sexed into her set eventually quit hanging around with the gang because they were harassed so much. In fact, Veronica said the young men in her set purposely tricked girls into believing they were being sexed into the gang and targeted girls they did not like:

> If some girls wanted to get in, if they don't like the girl they have sex with 'em. They run trains on 'em or either have the girl suck their thang. And then they used to, the girls used to think they was in. So, then the girls used to just come try to hang around us and all this little bull, just 'cause, 'cause they thinkin' they in.

Young women who were sexed into the gang were viewed as sexually promiscuous, weak, and not "true" members. They were subject to revictimization and mistreatment, and were viewed as deserving of abuse by other members, both male and female. Veronica continued, "They [girls who are sexed in] gotta do whatever, whatever the boys tell 'em to do when they want 'em to do it, right then and there, in front of whoever. And, I think, that's just sick. That's nasty, that's dumb." Keisha concurred, "She brought that on herself, by bein' the fact, bein' sexed in." There was evidence, however, that girls could overcome the stigma of having been sexed in through their subsequent behavior, by challenging members that disrespect them and being willing to fight. Tamika described a girl in her set who was sexed in, and stigmatized as a result, but successfully fought to rebuild her reputation:

> Some people, at first, they call her "little ho" and all that. But then, now she startin' to get bold. . . . Like, like, they be like, "Ooh, look at the little ho. She fucked me and my boy." She be like, "Man, forget y'all. Man, what? What?" She be ready to squat [fight] with 'em. I be like, "Ah, look at her!" Uh huh. . . . At first we looked at her like, "Ooh, man, she a ho, man." But now we look at her like she just our kickin' it partner. You know, however she got in that's her business.

The fact that there was such an option as "sexing in" served to keep girls disempowered, because they always faced the question of how they got in and of whether they were "true" members. In addition, it contributed to a milieu in which young women's sexuality was seen as exploitable. This may help explain why young women were so harshly judgmental of those girls who were sexed in. Young women who were privy to male gang members' conversations reported that male members routinely disrespect girls in the gang by disparaging them sexually. Monica explained,

> I mean the guys, they have their little comments about 'em [girls in the gang] because, I hear more because my brothers are all up there with the guys and everything and I hear more just sittin' around, just listenin'. And they'll have their little jokes about "Well, ha I had her," and then and everybody else will jump in and say, "Well, I had her, too." And then they'll laugh about it.

In general, because gender constructions defined young women as weaker than young men, young women were often seen as lesser members of the gang. In addition to the mistreatment these perceptions entailed, young women also faced particularly harsh sanctions for crossing gender boundaries—causing harm to rival male members when they had been viewed as nonthreatening. One young woman participated in the assault of a rival female gang member, who had set up a member of the girl's gang. She explained, "The female was supposingly goin' out with one of ours, went back and told a bunch of [rivals] what was goin' on and got the [rivals] to jump my boy. And he ended up in the hospital." The story she told was unique but nonetheless significant for what it indicates about the gendered nature of gang violence and victimization. Several young men in her set saw the girl walking down the street, kidnapped her, then brought her to a member's house. The young woman I interviewed, along with several other girls in her set, viciously beat the girl, then to their surprise the young men took over the beating, ripped off the girl's clothes, brutally gang-raped her, then dumped her in a park. The interviewee noted, "I don't know what happened to her. Maybe she died. Maybe, maybe someone came and helped her. I mean, I don't know." The experience scared the young woman who told me about it. She explained,

> I don't never want anythin' like that to happen to me. And I pray to God that it doesn't. 'Cause God said that whatever you sow you're gonna reap. And like, you know, beatin' a girl up and then sittin' there watchin' somethin' like that happen, well, Jesus that could come back on

> me. I mean, I felt, I really did feel sorry for her even though my boy was in the hospital and was really hurt. I mean, we coulda just shot her. You know, and it coulda been just over. We coulda just taken her life. But they went farther than that.

This young woman described the gang rape she witnessed as "the most brutal thing I've ever seen in my life." While the gang rape itself was an unusual event, it remained a specifically gendered act that could take place precisely because young women were not perceived as equals. Had the victim been an "equal," the attack would have remained a physical one. As the interviewee herself noted, "we coulda just shot her." Instead, the young men who gang-raped the girl were not just enacting revenge on a rival but on a young woman who had dared to treat a young man in this way. The issue is not the question of which is worse—to be shot and killed, or gang-raped and left for dead. Rather, this particular act sheds light on how gender may function to structure victimization risk within gangs.

Discussion

Gender dynamics in mixed-gender gangs are complex and thus may have multiple and contradictory effects on young women's risk of victimization and repeat victimization. My findings suggest that participation in the delinquent lifestyles associated with gangs clearly places young women at risk for victimization. The act of joining a gang involves the initiate's submission to victimization at the hands of her gang peers. In addition, the rules governing gang members' activities place them in situations in which they are vulnerable to assaults that are specifically gang related. Many acts of violence that girls described would not have occurred had they not been in gangs.

It seems, though, that young women in gangs believed they have traded unknown risks for known ones—that victimization at the hands of friends, or at least under specified conditions, was an alternative preferable to the potential of random, unknown victimization by strangers. Moreover, the gang offered both a semblance of protection from others on the streets, especially young men, and a means of achieving retaliation when victimization did occur.

Lauritsen and Quinet (1995) suggest that both individual-specific heterogeneity (unchanging attributes of individuals that contribute to a propensity for victimization, such as physical size or temperament) and state-dependent factors (factors that can alter individuals' victimization risks over time, such as labeling or behavior changes that are a consequence of victimization) are related to youths' victimization and repeat victimization risk. My findings here suggest that, within gangs, gender can function in both capacities to shape girls' risks of victimization.

Girls' gender, as an individual attribute, can function to lessen their exposure to victimization risk by defining them as inappropriate targets of rival male gang members' assaults. The young women I interviewed repeatedly commented that young men were typically not as violent in their routine confrontations with rival young women as with rival young men. On the other hand, when young women are targets of serious assault, they may face brutality that is particularly harsh and sexual in nature because they are female—thus, particular types of assault, such as rape, are deemed more appropriate when young women are the victims.

Gender can also function as a state-dependent factor, because constructions of gender and the enactment of gender identities are fluid. On the one hand, young women can call upon gender as a means of avoiding exposure to activities they find risky, threatening, or morally troubling. Doing so does not expose them to the sanctions likely faced by male gang members who attempt to avoid participation in violence. Although these choices may insulate young women from the risk of assault at the hands of rival gang members, perceptions of female gang members—and of women in general—as weak may contribute to more routinized victimization at the hands of the male members of their gangs. Moreover, sexual exploitation in the form of "sexing in" as an initiation ritual may define young women as sexually available, contributing to a likelihood of repeat victimization unless the young woman can stand up for herself and fight to gain other members' respect.

Finally, given constructions of gender that define young women as nonthreatening, when young women do pose a threat to male gang members, the sanctions they face may be particularly harsh because they not only have caused harm to rival gang members but also have crossed appropriate gender boundaries in doing so. In sum, my findings suggest that gender may function to insulate young women from some types of physical assault and lessen their exposure to risks from rival gang members, but also to make them vulnerable to particular types of violence, including routine victimization by their male peers, sexual exploitation, and sexual assault.

Questions for Thought and Discussion

1. How do the roles of males and females differ in gangs? Compare the gang members' lifestyle in the previous chapter to those of the women in this chapter.
2. The author states that female gang members are generally not allowed to participate in gang wars or drug dealing. Why?
3. What are the purposes of initiation rituals?
4. What theory or theories of criminal behavior are illustrated by this research?

References

Bjerregaard, Beth and Carolyn Smith. 1993. "Gender Differences in Gang Participation, Delinquency, and Substance Use." *Journal of Quantitative Criminology* 4:329–355.

Bowker, Lee H., Helen Shimota Gross, and Malcolm W. Klein. 1980. "Female Participation in Delinquent Gang Activities." *Adolescence* 15(59): 509–519.

Campbell, Anne. 1984. *The Girls in the Gang.* New York: Basil Blackwell.

———. 1990. "Female Participation in Gangs." Pp. 163–182 in *Gangs in America,* edited by C. Ronald Huff. Beverly Hills, CA: Sage.

Chesney-Lind, Meda. 1993. "Girls, Gangs and Violence: Anatomy of a Backlash." *Humanity & Society* 17(3):321–344.

Decker, Scott H. 1996. "Collective and Normative Features of Gang Violence." *Justice Quarterly* 13 (2):243–264.

Esbensen, Finn-Aage. 1996. Comments presented at the National Institute of Justice/Office of Juvenile Justice and Deliquency Prevention Cluster Meetings, June, Dallas, TX.

Joe, Karen A. and Meda Chesney-Lind. 1995. "Just Every Mother's Angel: An Analysis of Gender and Ethnic Variations in Youth Gang Membership." *Gender & Society* 9(4):408–430.

Lauderback David, Joy Hansen, and Dan Waldorf. 1992. " 'Sisters Are Doin' It for Themselves': A Black Female Gang in San Francisco." *The Gang Journal* 1(1):57–70.

Lauritsen, Janet L. and Kenna F. Davis Quinet. 1995. "Repeat Victimization Among Adolescents and Young Adults." *Journal of Quantitative Criminology* 1(2):143–166.

Moore, Joan. 1991. *Going Down to the Barrio: Homeboys and Homegirls in Change.* Philadelphia: Temple University Press.

Spergel, Irving A. and G. David Curry. 1993. "The National Youth Gang Survey: A Research and Development Process." Pp. 359–400 in *The Gang Intervention Handbook,* edited by Arnold P. Goldstein and C. Ronald Huff. Champaign, IL: Research Press.

Winfree, L. Thomas, Jr., Kathy Fuller, Teresa Vigil, and G. Larry Mays. 1992. "The Definition and Measurement of 'Gang Status': Policy Implications for Juvenile Justice." *Juvenile and Family Court Journal* 43:29–37

Section VIII

Drugs and Crime

One of the most enduring controversies in criminology is that surrounding the relationship between drugs and crime. While no one disputes the correlation—that drugs and crime seem to be interrelated in some manner—the issue of causation is controversial. Do drugs cause crime, or are they related in some other manner?

Recent U.S. Department of Justice data show clearly that a majority of arrestees tend to test positive for drugs. During one period, 78 percent of arrestees in Philadelphia tested positive for at least one illegal drug. Drug use for female arrestees ranged from less than 50 percent in San Antonio to over 85 percent in Manhattan.

In the first selection, " 'E' Is for Ecstasy: A Participant Observation Study of Ecstasy Use," Palacios and Fenwick present a unique inside perspective on drug use in the club culture of south Florida. The authors are particularly concerned with how and when Ecstasy is obtained and used by participants, and the steps they take to avoid detection and arrest.

In the next selection, "The Drugs-Crime Connection Among Stable Addicts," Faupel considers the role that criminal activity plays in facilitating drug use. Using ethnographic interviews with a population of stable addicts (seasoned, mature heroin users), Faupel argues that the drugs-crime connection is much more complex than the "drugs cause crime" hypothesis of popular currency. Instead, he reports that increased heroin consumption is preceded by increased criminal activity. He further debunks the myth of "crazed drug fiends" by examining the rational processes involved in maintaining a drug habit through criminal activity.

In the third chapter in this section, "Inside the Drug Trade: Trafficking From the Dealer's Perspective," Tunnell examines the dealer's perspective on the relationship between dealing and drug use, the nature of making connections with buyers and sellers, and the impact of severe penalties imposed on those caught up in the war on drugs.

In the final selection in this section, "Perceived Risks and Criminal Justice Pressures on Middle-Class Cocaine Dealers," Waldorf and Murphy consider the perceptions of risk and criminal justice pressures experienced by middle-class cocaine dealers. Their study examines a different segment of the drug dealing world from that of the previous chapter. Rather than being low-level street dealers with addictions of their own, these offenders were more rational, less likely to be users themselves, and less likely to be concerned with the sanction threat of the criminal justice system. ✦

Chapter 26
'E' Is for Ecstasy

A Participant Observation Study of Ecstasy Use

Wilson R. Palacios
Melissa E. Fenwick

In this selection, criminologists Wilson Palacios and Melissa Fenwick offer an insider's view of the Ecstasy culture in south Florida (Tampa). During a 15-month participant-observation study, they attended dozens of all-night (and sometimes several days in length) "clublike" parties, observing and asking questions of participants. Attending the nightclubs and parties where Ecstasy was freely available, the researchers were able to allay suspicion by presenting themselves as a couple interested in the music underground. In some cases they advised the others that they were researchers; in other cases, they did not, preferring to observe incognito. This chapter is a brief introduction to a continuing study—one of the first of its kind examining contemporary Ecstasy culture in America.

In *Writing on Drugs,* Sadie Plant argues that "every drug has its own character, its own unique claim to fame" (1999, 4). This is certainly true in the case of Ecstasy (MDMA). In 1986 Jerome Beck wrote:

> MDMA has been thrust upon the public awareness as a largely unknown drug which to some is a medical miracle and to others a social devil. . . . There have been the born-again protagonists who say that once you have tried it you will see the light and will defend it against any attack, and there have been the staunch antagonists who say this is nothing but LSD revisited and it will certainly destroy our youth. (305)

Beck's statements have proven to be timeless, as they accurately characterize the current media blitz surrounding the drug MDMA/Ecstasy. On July 1, 1985, at the behest of the U.S. Drug Enforcement Administration, MDMA/Ecstasy was temporarily placed in Schedule I of the Controlled Substance Act (CSA), with permanent placement achieved on November 13, 1986. While it may seem easy to understand the DEA's objectives in banning MDMA/Ecstasy, their actions inadvertently paved the way for a large international "underground" manufacturing and distribution network worth millions of dollars, and, to a greater extent, for a larger hidden population of users.

Law enforcement officials and politicians have led this new charge against MDMA/Ecstasy and its users. Newspaper headlines such as "Drug's Night Club Pull Seen Hard to Curb" (*The Boston Globe*), "Raving and Behaving: The Reputation of the High-Energy, All Night Dance Parties Outpaces the Reality" (*The Buffalo News*), and "Deputies: Ecstasy Overdose Killed Teen" (*St. Petersburg Times*) have been used to usher in a new "war on drugs" which, like our previous efforts with crack cocaine, stands to dramatically increase jail and prison populations with Ecstasy users and challenge our taken-for-granted notions concerning civil liberties.

Despite the attention from the criminal justice system, Ecstasy use and abuse has received minimal attention from the social scientific community, in particular criminology. Much of what we think we know about patterns of use and abuse concerning this drug stems largely from existing self-report surveys, such as Monitoring the Future (MTF); drug surveillance systems such as Drug Abuse Warning Network (DAWN); and the Arrestee Drug Abuse Monitoring (ADAM) program. Until now, there has been little in the way of active ethnographic fieldwork in this country concerning MDMA/Ecstasy use and its culture.

This chapter is derived from an ongoing, two-year ethnographic study concerning the use of "club drugs" (i.e., MDMA/Ecstasy, Ketamine/Special K, GHB, and nitrates) and club culture in Florida. The research focuses on the emotional state of individuals who ingest MDMA/Ecstasy, the local market for such drugs, and the vernacular of this drug culture.

The drug 3, 4-methylenedioxymethamphetamine (MDMA) is commonly referred to on the street as Ecstasy (Cohen 1998). While other names, such as Adam, the Love Drug, Mickey, X, Raven, and M&M's, are used to refer to MDMA, the term Ecstasy is the most recognizable. In the Hillsborough and Pinellas County area, the terms *bean(s)* and *rolls* are used interchangeably to refer to Ecstasy. When asked the origin of these terms, we were told that Ecstasy pills are called *beans* because they "look like little lima beans" and *rolls* because of the way they make you feel.

Ecstasy tablets are sold on the street according to distinctive designer logos pressed on one side of the pill. For example, in the field we came across Ecstasy pills sold under such names as Mitsubishi, Smurfs, Calvin Kleins, Nikes, Anchors, Rolls Royce (RR), Starburst, Pink Hearts, Double Stack Crowns, Navigator, KnockOuts, Blue Gene, and Red Gene. Many of the Ecstasy pills we encountered in the field were of various colors, although white was the most common. Moreover, we quickly learned that the popularity of these pills was solely dependent on word-of-mouth marketing from the individual consumer level. Ecstasy represents a marketing bonanza because of its ability to induce a physiologically and psychologically euphoric state so intense without the stigma associated with drugs like crack cocaine or heroin. In addition, it is a drug that many feel they can realistically walk away from or "schedule" into their lives on an as-needed basis. The following typify this attitude for some of our participants:

> It's not like doing crack or smack (heroin) . . . you don't hit a pipe or needle. . . . I wouldn't do that cause my friends would be like. . . . Hey, crack monster . . . or crack freak . . . and that's not cool . . . think about it . . . it's a little pill which takes you for a ride and then it's over . . . you don't fiend [crave] for it . . . you can do it every weekend or once a month or once or twice a year . . . just depends on what you've got going in your life and the people around you. (Jason, a single white male, 20 years of age)

> When I was in college I would roll [use Ecstasy] every weekend except for midterms and finals . . . but since I've been out I haven't rolled in the last two years. . . . I'm not saying that I won't . . . but I've just been busy with work and since I work for the system [referring to the criminal justice system] I know they drug test. . . . If I will do it again I'll just plan for it . . . it stays in your system from 2 to 5 days. . . . (Mark, a single white male, 29 years of age)

The intense physiological (amphetamine-like) rush from Ecstasy is referred to as *blowing up* or *rolling*. This experience varies across individuals. However, the overwhelming sensation of a heightened emotional and physical state was a commonly reported characteristic. The following comments typify this recurring theme:

> When you're blowing up it is like your fucking skin is going to come undone. Just imagine an orgasm but twenty or fifty times better and intense. That's the lure of X. (Jerry, a single white male, 25 years of age)

> I felt like I was coming undone from the inside. You can feel every inch of your skin, even the tiny little hairs on your arms and legs . . . feels that good. (Amy, single white female, 19 years of age)

Valter and Arrizabalaga (1998:13) argue that "the world-wide and still increasing use and abuse of MDMA (Ecstasy) is due to its euphoriant properties and capacity to enhance communication and contact with other people." Actually, because of this last property, Ecstasy is really a member of a small class of compounds called *entactogens* or *empathogens* (which means creating contact or empathy) and therefore should not be classified as a "hallucinogenic-amphetamine" drug (see Cohen 1998). This feeling of connecting with other people is what makes Ecstasy such a psychological draw for most people, including our participants:

> I know I could go to [local nightclub] and after I eat my pill I won't care what people think of me . . . I won't care if they think I'm fat, too skinny, or if I am wearing the wrong shoes . . . I just don't care because it becomes about meeting people and just meeting different kinds of people. (Betty, a single white female, 25 years of age, mother of two)

> It's about having a good time . . . I even don't have to worry about guys trying to hook up [reference to sex] with me. . . . If guys are rolling you know they are not looking at you that way . . . at least not when they are rolling . . . maybe later on the comedown [referring to the end of the night] but not during. (Carrie, a white Latina female, 21 years of age)

Blowing Up

Our participants gauged the strength and purity of a pill according to the intensity of their *blowing up* or *rolling* experience. Some acute reactions experienced by our participants during the blowing up or rolling stage were bruxism (teeth grinding), trismus (jaw clenching), uncontrollable fidgeting of extremities, rapid eye movements, and a heightened sensitivity to all external stimuli (touch, lights, sounds, etc.). In order for us to tap into these varied experiences, we asked the following; "How do you know you are/were blowing up?" These are some of the responses we received:

> It usually wouldn't come on until after thirty or forty minutes but when it did you would just feel this overwhelming sensation of all your emotions being flooded [released] throughout your body. I would say after forty-five minutes into it I would feel my eyes twitch and I would have this need to just massage everything and anything around me. One night I was massaging my arms so hard without realizing it or feeling any pain that the next day I woke up and had broken my skin. I was in pain the next morning but I did not remember feeling any pain when I was doing this . . . it just feel so good. (Tim, a white Latino male, 27 years of age, married)

> You can't help being or wanting to be touched. . . . I've seen men touching each other without all the worry about people thinking they were gay or anything . . . you know you're rolling when somebody comes up to you and begins massaging your neck, shoulders, or back . . . it feels just so good that one time I had my girlfriend massage my lower back so hard that she made me pee in my pants—now that was a good bean . . . you can't know what I'm talking about unless you've been there. (Stacie, a white single female 18 years of age)

> The first time I rolled I didn't feel a thing . . . I was pissed because I spent some money and everyone around me was rolling their asses off and I was the only one in the group sitting there like a dumb fuck . . . but the second time I rolled . . . that's when I can tell you that I honestly blew up. . . . I first noticed it because of the lights . . . everything was clearer and brighter. . . . I could see the bright colors from the corner of my eyes and then my feet started swaying to the music. . . . I looked at my feet and it was like they weren't even mine. . . . I kept wanting to get up and just walk around and talk to people. . . . I didn't care what people thought of . . . I just wanted to be around people. (Lady X, a single white female, 23 years of age)

> I really don't like anything speedy. . . . My father died of a heart attack at a young age. . . . I don't think I have a heart condition but I just don't want anything speeding my heart. . . . I usually like the ones that are not speedy. . . . I like for it [Ecstasy] to come on slow and gradually over the night. . . . I want it to last . . . I'm not one for dancing or stuff like that, I just want to sit there and take it all in. (Jane, a single white female, 27 years of age)

Side Effects

Of all of the possible acute reactions—papillary dilation, headache, hypertension, nausea, tachycardia, blurred vision, hypertonicity, and tremors—that Ecstasy induces, jaw clenching and teeth grinding (trismus and bruxism) were among the side effects most cited by our participants:

> You must always have something to chew on or you'll end up loosing your teeth. (Mary, a single white female, 21 years of age; has been using Ecstasy for 2 years)

> The only thing I hate about rolling is how your jaw feels the next morning. You just can't help chewing gum but you can chew the same piece of gum all night long and not realize it . . . you can keep chewing because you need something in your mouth but you don't realize how much pain your jaw is going to be the next day. There have been times when I couldn't even open my mouth for one or two days after rolling . . . it's a good thing I didn't want to eat. (Ms. S, a single Latina female, 18 years of age)

> The next day I noticed a lot of sores in my mouth . . . probably from my teeth grinding down on my gums . . . the inside of my mouth hurts for about 2 or 3 days after. (Joe, a single white female, 21 years of age)

A number of our participants used candy such as Gummy Bears, Starbursts, Jolly Ranchers, and BlowPops to help mitigate the unpleasantness of their jaw muscles clenching. Actually, any form of hard candy or chewing gum would do as long as it kept them from grinding their teeth and straining their jaw muscles:

> I've worn away all of my back teeth and I have four sores in my mouth from just grinding the inside of my teeth. I chipped my front teeth one night after dropping [ingesting] five beans. . . . I was blowing up hard . . . I felt my eyes roll towards the back of my head. I also bit my lip because I didn't realize I was biting down on it until I went to the bathroom at this club

and looked in the mirror and noticed a little bit of blood from my upper lip . . . no biggie but it scares the shit out of you looking in the mirror and seeing blood. (Ms. G, a single Latina female, 29 years of age)

A Blowpop or a piece of gum never tasted so fucking good as when you are rolling . . . but it helps not lose your teeth because with a good bean your teeth will chatter. (Greg, a single white male, 24 years of age)

Buying Ecstasy

Ecstasy's street price makes it attractive and affordable. Currently, in the Tampa area the price ranges from $10 to $20 per pill, with an average cost of $15. Factors that determine the price of a pill are market availability and whether or not one is known to the dealers. Market availability is just that . . . supply and demand. When a large number of pills are on the market, prices are lower. As might be expected, prices to strangers are usually higher than those to people known to the dealer. Prices at nightclubs are also more expensive than pills bought in other locations. We asked one dealer whom we had met during a rolling party whether he overcharged people at nightclubs. He offered the following view:

If I don't know the person I will and definitely if it's in a club . . . it's the price of doing business in a club. . . . I have to worry about the bouncers [security personnel], off-duty undercover cops and narcs [people working for the police] . . . just too much hassle. But I'm going to make my money . . . people just have to pay. . . . If I know you, I'll cut you a break but not by much . . . I really just don't like dealing in clubs. . . .

Our participants preferred to buy and take Ecstasy prior to arriving at their destinations as a way of minimizing the risk of detection from law enforcement. The following statements are typical:

I always buy a few days before I know I am going out. That way I don't get caught up with people saying that they can or can't get it [Ecstasy] and then having to go the club and buying something from I don't know who . . . a narc or undercover, and paying something crazy like $20. (Vanessa, a twenty-something Latina female)

We would always drop [take Ecstasy] at our apartment and then go to the clubs . . . we knew that we would be at the clubs like in twenty minutes so we knew that our rolls wouldn't kick in yet or they would start to kick in just as we were in line to get into the clubs . . . that's how we'd do it . . . we would never have anything on us . . . just in case they would search you at the door. (Jimmy, a white male, 19 years of age)

Onset of Effects

The average user begins to feel the effects from one Ecstasy pill in about 30 to 45 minutes. The time period is contingent on what and how recently people have eaten and on their unique physiology. The overall effects of Ecstasy, or an "E trip" as it is commonly known, can last from 4 to 6 hours, depending on the person's physiology, on his or her prior food intake, and most important on whether the pill has adulterants in it. In recent years the media and some ill-informed law enforcement officials have alleged that Ecstasy pills contain substances like rat poison and crushed glass, as well as other illegal drugs such as cocaine, heroin, and LSD. However, others have shown (see Cohen 1998; Saunders and Doblin 1996; Beck and Rosenbaum 1994) this to be more myth than reality.

According to DanceSafe, a harm-reduction organization, recent adulterant screening efforts have revealed the presence of such drugs as dextromethorphan, phenylpropanolamine, ephedrine, pseudoephedrine, glyceryl guaiacolate, other amphetamine-like substances (i.e., MDA, MDEA, DOM, 2-CB, and DOT), caffeine, Ketamine, and only trace amounts of such substances as heroin and LSD (DanceSafe 2001). It is believed that underground manufacturers in clandestine laboratories add many of these substances purely as a cost-saving method, although some of these ingredients do increase the risk for negative reactions, including overdose.

The fact that they could be ingesting a host of other substances in addition to MDMA did not appear to concern our subjects greatly. Our participants would take Ecstasy one of three ways: (1) orally, (2) snorting, or (3) "parachuting" or "packing." Some participants elected either one or a combination of all three methods during the evening depending on when they wanted to feel the effects of their pill. With oral ingestion, initial effects were usually felt within 30 to 40 minutes. Snorting produced effects within 10 to 15 minutes, while parachuting or packing would produce effects within 5 minutes.

"Parachuting" Ecstasy involves inserting the pill into the anus, like a suppository. Parachuters believe the pill will be absorbed faster and the effects will be felt in a shorter time. Just how parachuting is done is described in the following fieldnote excerpt:

> The time was 6:15 a.m. and we had just left an after-hours club where we had spent the last three hours with a group of people we met up with at another club earlier in the evening. In leaving this after-hours club we all got into our cars and headed for a gas station nearby. I asked David, a white male about 29 years of age, what we were looking to get at this gas station. He answered, "I need to refuel. I need to stop and get some Red Bull before we continue or I'm not going to make it." The gas station was less than ten city blocks from the after-hours club and we were there within ten minutes. All three cars pulled into the gas station, and most of the passengers got out of their cars.
>
> In total there were five cars and ten people all together. One of the drivers, Jake, a Latino male in his early twenties, pulled his red Honda Civic to a gas pump, got out, inserted a credit card, and began to pump gas. I waited outside the car I was riding in for the rest of the group. I noticed that most were in line inside the gas station with items in their hands. Since it was early in the morning on a Sunday and no one was around, I decide to go inside just to be with the folks. In walking into the gas station I noticed that most had either Red Bull, Gatorade, or PowerAde sport drinks in their hands. Two individuals had two bottles of water, Evian, in their hands. I noticed that Fred, a white male in his late twenties, was walking towards the back of the gas station.
>
> Soon there was Henry, a white male in his early thirties, following behind him. I think Mary, a Latina female about 20 years of age, noticed I was looking at them, and, in a very low whisper, said, "They going to the bathroom to shoot." I asked, "To shoot what?" She replied, "They still have some beans left," and that's all she said. Now, I knew that shooting beans did not mean using a needle, since I have not seen anyone use this method for taking Ecstasy. So I thought she was referring to "parachuting" but I was not sure. It is a term I had heard before but I had never seen anyone actually do it. I could not help it, but curiosity got the better of me and so I headed for the bathroom, and just as I got to the door Fred looked at me and said, "Hey, professor, do you want to see something?" I replied, "What?" Henry replied, "Come see."
>
> There we were . . . in the men's bathroom, three males and I could not help think that under other circumstance this scene would represent something altogether different. However, there we were. I stood directly in front of the door and Fred, while reaching for his right pants pocket, said, "I know you've heard about 'parachuting.' " I replied, "Yeah . . . but I think I know what it is." Fred's reply was, "Well, here you go. . . ." As he said this he pulled out three beans from a small baggie . . . they were white in color and I knew they were known as RR or Rolls Royce because that was what the group had been taking for most of the night. As he produced the beans and threw the baggie on the floor, Henry walked over to a bathroom stall and tore off a piece of toilet paper, probably about less than one inch in length. He walks over to the faucet and just wets the piece of paper with a small amount of water. Fred then walks over and places the three beans into the center of the paper. Henry begins to fold the paper over the pills and forms a nice little wad of paper with its end twisted. He licks the twisted ends and I asked, "Why are you doing that?" His response, "To make sure that it's all nice and tight and that it doesn't come undone when it goes in." As he says this, Fred walks over to a bathroom stall, unzips his pants and lets his pants come down to his thigh area. Henry walks over to him and says, "Are you ready?" Fred's response: "Go ahead." Fred bends only halfway and Henry takes that wad of paper with the twisted ends and begins to insert it anally into Fred. There I am watching this and all I could say, "Why can't you do it yourself, Fred?" Fred stands up and as he zips up his pants he turns around and says, "I just don't like putting anything into me." Henry adds, "I do myself all the time and I do my girl this way." In almost a comic relief tone, Fred adds, "Now that's 'parachuting,' professor." My only response: "No confusing that one . . . that's 'parachuting.' "

Coming Down

Toward the end of the blowing up stage of an E trip, people respond in many different ways. Some just want to engage in a freeflowing conversation about their lives and their own personal anxieties and fears. There are those that just want to sit outside to watch the sun rise and to feel the cool morning breeze brushing up against their skin. A few have some difficulty in accepting that their experience is about to end and therefore consume marijuana as a method for "kicking it back in."

> I always like to have some kind bud [high-quality marijuana] on me to smoke towards the end . . . takes the edge off and kicks my roll back in . . . it won't be as intense, but you do feel it somewhat . . . just relaxes me and give me a smoother roll at the end. . . . (Diego, a white male Latino in his early twenties)

Some also consume drugs like Valium and Xanax as a way of coping with the edginess they felt from Ecstasy:

> The morning after I take a Xane bar [referring to Xanax] then I'm OK . . . I can go to sleep . . . if I don't, my fucking mind is not going to stop talking to me . . . it's like you want to go to sleep because you know you're tired but your mind won't let you go . . . a Xane bar or some Valium would do the trick. (Keith, a white male in his early thirties)

For some of our participants, the day or days after their use of Ecstasy consisted of moderate to intense fatigue. In communicating the nature of this psychological and physical exhaustion, they used the term *ate-up*. For most, this ate-up feeling was characterized as a loss of appetite, mental exhaustion, some nausea, intense thirst, and body aches. While it sounds remarkably similar to a hangover, many of our participants did not see such similarities:

> The only thing I hate about E is how I feel the next day . . . I just can't do anything. . . . I mean, I sleep all day so I waste an entire day and then I get up and just want to lay in my bed. . . . I can't think and if I do, I can't get the music or people out of my head. I really don't want to eat anything but I force myself to eat something. . . . I'm not hungry but I just force myself. (Christine, a white female in her twenties)

> I just can't do anything the next day . . . all I want to is sleep. . . . I love to take a shower when I get home because it feels good, but then I just head for my bed. . . . I get no headaches or feel like throwing up, but I just don't want anything. (Mike, a white male in his early twenties)

> I really don't feel ate-up the next day. . . . I sleep for about six or eight hours and get up. . . . I eat a little something and then I just sit around, turn the TV on but I really don't watch it. . . . I just want to sit there and think . . . my legs hurt a bit but that's from the dancing. . . . If that's ate-up, then maybe yeah, but nothing like what my friends feel. (Judy, a white female in her late twenties)

> For me, the worst is about three days after I rolled. I just feel down . . . can't start or really finish anything . . . I just want to lay in my bed and do absolutely nothing. . . . I stop and think that I won't ever do that again [use Ecstasy] but then I remember I had a good time on it and well . . . you know. . . . (Sue, a white female in her late teens)

Such after-effects are mitigated by the person's physiology, health status prior to use, frequency of use, concurrent drug use (such as with LSD, cocaine, heroin, or alcohol), and the type and amount of Ecstasy pills consumed. Therefore, the ate-up experience is never the same for any one individual.

Conclusion

Philippe Bourgois (1999:2158) argues, "A major task of participant-observers is to put themselves in the shoes of the people they study in order to see local realities through local eyes." As participant-observers we have presented a local picture of Ecstasy use among a diverse network of individuals. There is no denying that for our participants, taking Ecstasy—despite all the known risks—is pleasurable. A "local reality" is that Ecstasy is relatively affordable, does not have the same stigma associated with other illegal drugs, and is very much a part of the local youth culture (individuals between the ages of 18 and 35). Since this is an ongoing ethnographic study, there are many areas that we have not yet studied. We wanted to present a "local portrait" of Ecstasy use. We only hope that we remained true to our participants in setting out to accomplish this goal.

Questions for Thought and Discussion

1. In this study, the authors observed Ecstasy use and related activity occasionally posing as participants in the Ecstasy culture and at other times being

open with participants as to their purpose. What is your opinion as to the ethics of this kind of research?

2. How do the authors approach the subject of the safety of using these drugs? The legality?
3. As an ongoing research project, what more should the authors attempt to learn about Ecstasy use and the culture in which it thrives?
4. What theory or theories of criminal behavior are illustrated in this research?

References

Beck, Jerome. (1986). "MDMA: The popularization and resultant implications of a recently controlled psychoactive substance." *Contemporary Drug Problems,* 13: 305–313.

Beck, Jerome and Marsha Rosenbaum. (1994). *Pursuit of Ecstasy: The MDMA Experience.* New York: State University of New York Press.

Bourgois, Philippe. (1999). "Theory, method, and power in drug and HIV-prevention research: A participant-observers critique." *Substance Use & Misuse,* 34: 2155–2172.

Cohen, Richard S. (1998). *The Love Drug: Marching to the Beat of Ecstasy.* New York: The Haworth Press.

DanceSafe. (2001). Retrieved August 2001 from http://www.dancesafe.org/labtesting/.

Plant, Sadie. (1999). *Writing on Drugs.* New York: Farrar, Straus and Giroux.

Saunders, Nicholas, and Rick Doblin. (1996). *Ecstasy: Dance, Trance and Transformation.* Oakland, CA: Quick American Achieves.

Valter, Karel and Philippe Arrizabalaga. (1998). *Designer Drugs Directory.* New York: Elsevier.

 This project is supported by funds from USF Research & Creative Scholarship Grant #12-21-926RO. ✦

Chapter 27 The Drugs-Crime Connection Among Stable Addicts

Charles E. Faupel

I*n this piece Charles E. Faupel examines in detail the lifestyles and career patterns of hard-core heroin addicts and the controversial issue of the relationship between drugs and crime. He also considers the question of whether addict criminals are skilled, rational "professional" criminals or opportunists. Faupel arrives at many of the same conclusions regarding opportunism versus rationality as have other researchers represented in this book (see Cromwell et al., Chapter 11; Shover and Honaker, Chapter 4). The lifestyle depicted by Faupel as representative of the addict criminal is also similar to that noted by Shover and Honaker in their study of persistent property criminals. Regarding the drugs-crime nexus, Faupel concludes that drug use does not cause crime, but may be caused by crime or at least facilitated by it. His treatment of these issues supports an understanding of the heroin addict as a much more rational being than previously believed.*

Faupel notes four phases in the heroin-using career: the occasional user, the stable addict, the free-wheeling junkie, and the street junkie. In this selection he focuses on the stable addict—the mature, seasoned heroin user. He characterizes this stage in the heroin addict's life as analogous to the productive, established period in conventional careers.

In terms of research methodology this article is drawn from a long-term study of the relationship of drugs to crime. It is based on life history interviews with hard-core heroin addicts in the Wilmington, Delaware, area. Thirty heroin addicts were extensively interviewed—10 to 25 hours each in sessions lasting from two to four hours. The subjects were paid a small stipend for their time.

The subjects all had extensive criminal histories and at the time of the interviews, 24 were under correctional supervision (incarcerated, probation, parole, or work release). Women were slightly overrepresented, constituting 12 of the 30 respondents.

The sample consisted of 22 blacks and eight whites. Latinos were not represented because there is not a sizeable Latino drug-using population in the area where the study was conducted.

The complexity of the drugs-crime connection is perhaps most fully apparent during the stable-addict phase. One clear feature is the role that criminal activities plays in facilitating drug use. The participants in this study strongly concurred that their level of heroin consumption was a function of their ability to afford it, which was usually enhanced by criminal activity. "The better I got at crime," remarked Stephanie, "the more money I made; the more money I made, the more drugs I used." She went on to explain, "I think that most people that get high, the reason it goes to the extent that it goes—that it becomes such a high degree of money—is because they make the money like that. I'm saying if the money wasn't available to them like that, they wouldn't be into drugs as deep as they were."

Contrary to the "drugs cause crime" hypothesis, which suggests that increases in the level of heroin consumption are necessarily followed by stepped-up criminal activity, the dynamics reported by the addicts in this study are quite the opposite: increased heroin consumption is preceded by increased criminal activity as measured by estimated criminal income. This does not necessarily imply a greater frequency of crime, for, as I shall highlight below, stable-addict status usually brings with it greater sophistication in skill and technique, often resulting in higher proceeds per criminal event.

These life history data also reveal, however, that the relationship between drug use and crime is much broader and more complex than simple causality. As I suggested earlier, increased criminal income not only enhances drug availability, but also provides the basis for an expanded life structure, an alternative daily routine. Because these criminal routines usually provide greater flexibility than do most forms of legitimate employment, they free the addict from prohibitive roles and social contacts that may be imposed by more rigid schedules. Drug-using activities are certainly facilitated under these more flexible routines. Nevertheless, criminal routines do impose certain constraints on the addict life-style. Moreover, they provide an important structure to one's drug-using activities. It is in this respect that Old Ray likened the routine of dealing drugs to legitimate employment: "When you're working, the world has its rhythm, its time clock. You have your eight-to-five time clock. Well, it's the same way with dealing drugs." The result is a curious paradox. Criminal activity not only enhances availability thereby providing for heavier drug consumption, but also places broad limits on the amount of heroin consumed by providing some semblance of structure and routine. There is yet another paradox in the drugs-crime relationship for the stable addict. While it is true that crime facilitates heroin use, many of the addicts I interviewed indicated that heroin and other drugs played a utilitarian role in their commission of crime as well. While it is commonly assumed that addicts are most likely to commit crimes when they are sick and desperate for a fix, the addicts in this study reported quite the opposite. The following comments from Joe and Belle highlight the importance of being straight (not experiencing withdrawal) when committing crimes:

> [Joe] It would be awful hard for me if I was sick to be able to hustle. A lot of times if you're sick you go in and grab stuff. And run without caution. But if I was high it was a different story. I could take my time and get what I wanted.

> [Belle] Most people say about drug addicts [that] when they're sick is when they do their most damage. But that's the lying-est thing in the world. When a dope addict is sick, he's sick. He can't raise his hand if he's a drug addict. . . . They say when a dope fiend's sick he'll do anything to get money, but how the hell is he going to do it if he can't even go on the street and do it?

The prostitutes I interviewed found heroin especially functional in their criminal activities. Never knowing if their next *trick* (client) might be a freak (one who enjoys violence or sadomasochistic acts), carry a disease, or simply have unpleasant body odor, prostitutes understandably approach many of their dates with a good deal of apprehension. They reported that heroin allows them to work under otherwise difficult conditions:

> [Belle] I think that a woman that tricks has to do something. If they wasn't an alcoholic, they had to be a dope fiend. 'Cause a woman in her right sense, you just can't sit up and do some of the things you do with a trick.

> [Penny] If I didn't have no heroin in me, I couldn't trick, because it turns my stomach. . . . I didn't feel nothin' then, I just went on and do it. . . . I always was noddin' before I even get to the date. And then when I get to the date, I go to the bathroom and get off again.

> [Helen] I could forget about what I was doing; I didn't give a damn about anything. I just felt good.

Heroin is not the only drug that addicts use for functional reasons in their commission of crimes. Amphetamines are also sometimes used to maintain necessary energy levels on particularly busy days. Boss, who was an armed robber among other things, reported that he would frequently use barbiturates before going out on a robbery. He found that they put him in the necessary belligerent mood to play the "tough guy" in order to pull off the robbery successfully. He also reported that he would frequently celebrate a successful robbery with heroin or cocaine or perhaps even a speedball (a heroin and cocaine combination):

> They'd be like a toast. Maybe nine-thirty or ten o'clock we'd done pulled a good score off and we're sitting there and say, "Hey man, let's go get us some good motherfucking dope." And it would carry you until two o'clock. Nodding in the apartment, everybody feeling all right because they got away with the crime, planning what you're gonna do with your half of the money. So it'd be like the cap for you. It'd be like a toast for a job well done.

Finally, the data from these life histories suggest that both drug use and criminal behavior are interrelated elements of a broader subcultural experience that cannot be fully understood in terms of a simple causal relationship. Particularly as stable addicts, these respondents regarded both drug use and crime as important parts of a challenging lifestyle. On the one hand, it is true that drugs provide an important perceptual framework from which addicts interpret their behavior. Boss commented on the importance of drugs in defining the meaning that he attached to his activities:

> The money is good, but I wouldn't want the money if I couldn't have what goes along with selling the money [for heroin]. . . . Like with the whores, I wouldn't want the whores if I couldn't spend the money on dope. . . . It's like a working man. A working man, he wants a home and nice family. Just like in the life of crime you got to have all those essential things that go with it or it's nothing. It would be nothing if I couldn't spend that money the way [I want to].

But while heroin is an important component of the subjective experience of addicts, it is only part of a more general lifestyle, the maintenance of which motivates the addict. Also part of that lifestyle for most addicts is a nice wardrobe, fancy cars (for men), a nice crib (home), and a reputation for generosity with friends. As Boss reflected:

> See, my concern wasn't catching the habit. . . . My thing was being able to make enough money to supply that habit and make enough money to keep my thing up to par—you know, my clothes, and my living standards . . . to stay up to par enough so if my mother or sister or brother needed some money I could loan them some money, plus keep my habit, plus buy some shoes or something, you know, rent a car for the weekend and just hang out like the guy that didn't have the habit. And in the course of that, that called for more crime.

As important as drugs and the fast lifestyle are in motivating addict behavior, one important fact remains: crime is a way of life with stable addicts. These people take pride in their ability to hustle successfully. Criminal success is a mark of stature in the subculture, and the more lucrative or difficult the hustle, the greater the recognition one receives. "The type of criminal activity he engages in, and his success at it determine, to a large extent, the addict's status among fellow addicts and in the community at large. The appellation of *real hustling dope fiend* (a successful burglar, robber, con man, etc.) is a mark of respect and status" (Preble and Casey 1969, 20; italics in original). Crime is a challenge that most stable addicts find tremendously appealing. It provides a source of excitement and a sense of accomplishment, similar to the challenge of climbing formidable mountain peaks or rafting turbulent white water. Mario compared the excitement of burglarizing a house with the anticipation experienced by a young child at Christmastime. Each package (house) has its own surprises, its own challenges. Some are located in wealthy sections of the city and have fabulous exteriors (pretty wrappings). Some of these promising houses resulted in a valuable *take* (loot), while others did not. What kept Mario going was the anticipation he experienced with each crime.

Mario's feelings reflect those of many of the addicts who took part in this study. Their perceptions defy any attempt to characterize criminal behavior as somehow being "driven" by an overwhelming need for drugs, even though heroin and other drugs constitute an important feature of a stable addict's motivational structure. For these addicts, drugs and crime are mutually reinforcing elements of a broader lifestyle, both of which play an important role in defining one's position in the criminal-addict subculture. Harry expressed it this way:

> It was never really the drug. It was the lifestyle I was trying to keep going. And the drug was a lot of that lifestyle. . . . Back then [before becoming a street junkie] . . . it was just that it was there and I had all this energy and no vent for it. And I had begun to vent it into getting drugs, knocking people in the head, taking their money, going into somebody's house, taking that stuff out, running into the fence, going to get the drugs—a full-time job. It was more than your basic forty hours a week. And that's what it was about, sustaining that lifestyle.

By way of summary, in contrast to the occasional-user period of addict careers where drug use and crime are independent, parallel activities, the stable-addict phase is marked by a close interdependence between these two sets of activities. This relationship is more complex than can be captured in the empiricist language of cause and effect, however. The transition to the status of stable addict is a function of increased drug availability and expanded life structure, which, in most instances, result from increased systematic criminal activities. In this respect, we might characterize the stable-addict period as one in which "crime causes drugs" or, at least, crime facilitates drug use. Having attained the status of stable addict, the user has succeeded in jockeying for position in the criminal-addict subculture. The stable addict is, at least by minimal definition, a successful participant in the subculture. Success in the subculture is defined by drug-using and criminal activity, both of which are motivating factors in the behavior of stable addicts. In this respect, the drugs-crime relationship is not so much causal as it is reciprocal, itself contributing to one's stature in the subculture.

Criminal Specialization Among Stable Addicts

The career transition to stable addict usually entails an increasing reliance on a small number of criminal hustles or, in some cases, on a single type of crime. I pointed out [earlier] that early occasional use is a time of experimentation, not only with various types of drugs, but also with a variety of criminal roles. As in other careers, this trial period usually gives way to more focused activity as developing addicts discover what criminal skills and penchants they may have by experimenting with different criminal routines. In short, assumption of the stable-addict role usually implies the development of one or more main hustles.

Developing a main hustle implies not only the achievement of increased specialization but also of increased skill and sophistication as a criminal. Stable addicts go beyond learning the nuts and bolts of their chosen trade(s) to master the subtleties of these criminal enterprises with a finesse more characteristic of a craftsman than of a stereotyped common criminal. Old Ray may have stated it most succinctly when he remarked, "You got to have a Ph.D. in streetology." There are three broad types of skills that the successful criminal addict acquires: technical, social, and intuitive skills (Faupel 1986).

Technical Skills

This category of criminal skills entails both the knowledge of how to perform the task as well as the physical adeptness for carrying it out successfully. Shoplifters stress the importance of being able to *roll* clothing items tightly with one hand with the clothes still on the hanger. Rolling loosely will not allow as many clothes to be packed in the bag, and keeping clothes on the hanger is important because empty hangers arouse suspicion. This must all be done with one hand because the other hand is used to finger through items on the rack, thereby creating the impression that the shoplifter is a legitimate customer. A slip in any one of the maneuvers involved in the complex process may mean failure to reach a quota for the day or, even more seriously, possible detection and arrest. Moreover, shoplifters must continually keep abreast of technological innovations designed to detect theft, including cameras, one-way mirrors, and alarm devices attached inside expensive clothing items.

Prostitutes also report the importance of developing technical skills, particularly streetwalkers who regularly *beat their johns* (rob their clients) out of credit cards and cash. Belle described her strategy for successfully stealing from her clients:

> The car was sweeter than anything else as far as getting money. Because once you get a dude's pants down, you got him where you want him. He just automatically forgets about he's got money in his pocket. . . . All she's thinking about is getting him in a position to get his mind off his pocket long enough for her to get in there. . . . She might take his pants with her and leave him stripped for nothing—'cause I've done it.

A prostitute must also be able to determine where her trick keeps his wallet, take the wallet from his pocket, and then return it—all in a matter of minutes and without the client's being aware that this activity is taking place. These are skills not readily acquired; developing them takes time and practice, as Penny described:

> When I started off I was scared. It took a little longer. . . . It might take four or five hours [on an all-night date] to get his wallet. . . . [Later] it didn't take me but a minute to get it and put it back in.

The acquisition of technical skills is critical to the success of other hustles as well. The technical skills required by burglars have been extensively discussed in the literature on professional crime (Letkeman 1973; Sutherland 1937). These same skills were also reported by the burglar-addicts who participated in this study. An intimate knowledge of alarm systems is part of the seasoned burglar's stock-in-trade. Moreover, because most burglars prefer to enter unoccupied homes, they commonly case a residential area for days or even weeks, meticulously noting the mobility patterns of the residents. Burglars working business districts also case their working areas to determine patterns of police surveillance. Paige recalled "staying up all night watching the pattern of the police officers and seeing how regularly he made his rounds of the establishment and charting all that stuff down and trying to get a fix on when's the best time for me to rip that store off."

Stable addicts are also involved in many other types of criminal offenses. The addicts in this study reported engaging in main hustles such as armed robbery, pickpocketing, forgery, fencing stolen goods, pimping, and drug dealing at one time or another during their careers. Each of these criminal enterprises involves its own modus operandi and requires the acquisition of specialized technical skills if one is to be a reasonably successful hustler.

Social Skills

Most criminal hustles require the addict to be verbally and socially skilled as well as technically adept. These social skills involve verbally and nonverbally manipulating the setting to the criminal's advantage such that the offense can be carried out smoothly and without risk of apprehension or arrest.

Social skills, like technical skills, are quite specialized. Shoplifters who work in pairs, for example, frequently find it necessary to engage in small talk with salespersons, thereby diverting attention from the actions of their partners. Moreover, when they are detected, good boosters are often successful in talking their way out of an arrest. Gloria found that she could intimidate lower-level sales personnel from referring her to management by taking on the persona of an indignant, falsely accused customer. Some shoplifters, such as Slick, used a modus operandi that relied primarily on verbal agility. In contrast to the surreptitious strategies employed by many shoplifters, such as hiding stolen goods in garbage bags and false-bottom boxes or underneath one's own clothing, Slick opted for the bold strategy of walking out of the store with his stolen merchandise in full view of store personnel, as if he had paid for it: "I would take McCullough chain saws. . . . I would just pick up the big box, set it up on my shoulders, and even get the store security guard at the door to open the door for me. I just got bold." Then, rather than sell the chain saw to a fence for about one-third the retail value, Slick would rely on his verbal skills once again by returning the item the next day to the very store he had stolen it from (or bring it to another store in the chain) for a full refund.

Needless to say, this sort of strategy requires a unique ability to play the role of a legitimate customer. A shoplifter with highly developed social skills tends to assume this role so completely that he or she takes on the attitudes, feelings, and perspective of the customer. To use Mead's (1934) term, the shoplifter quite literally "takes the role of the other." Socially skilled shoplifters do not take the role of just any customer, however; they assume the role of an assertive customer who takes complete command of the situation. Indeed, they must do so. A legitimate customer can perhaps afford not to be assertive, but a timorous shoplifter may well forfeit his or her career by failing to command credibility as a legitimate customer.

Check forgers make use of some of the same social skills employed by shoplifters. Indeed, social agility can probably be said to constitute the principal stock-in-trade of the check forger. The entire act revolves around successfully convincing a bank employee that the signature on the check is in fact that of the individual whose name it bears, and that the forger is that individual and therefore the rightful recipient of the amount of the check. All of this involves the ability to assume the role of an assertive individual with a legitimate claim, an ability Old Ray cultivated to his advantage:

> I found the hardest teller I could find and she sent me to the manager's office. . . . I went in there telling about this godsent check—a tragedy in my life. It was all acting. . . . You got to story-tell. But it was my check. It became my check the minute I walked into the bank. . . . Once I packed up that type attitude, I became the role. And it's easier to go to the top than the bottom. It's easier at the top to get to anybody. . . . The guy at the bottom, he's gonna give you hell . . . but the man at the top, he can afford to be benevolent.

Other criminal hustles require social skills of a slightly different nature. Prostitutes point out the importance of maintaining a position of dominance in the interaction between them and their tricks. Rose advised: "Always try to keep control of the conversation. Never let them see that you're soft. . . . They see one time that you stutter or aren't in control, they're gonna try to take advantage of you." By maintaining such control, the prostitute is also able to direct and focus her client's attention, which allows her to engage in acts of theft. Penny was so successful at this strategy that she was frequently able to rob her clients without even having to *turn the trick* (engage in sexual acts).

Drug dealing entails social skills with still another focus. Here the primary task is to maintain a relatively stable clientele. This involves advertising one's drugs and establishing a reputation as having "righteous" dope. Harry, who was heavily involved in burglary as well as selling drugs, understood successful dealing to be little more than hype and good salesmanship:

> Conning was part of everything. The whole thing is an image. Believe it or not, it's the American way! . . . So you learn how to hype. . . . One of my favorite lines was "You better do only half of one of these." And that just made them get all that much more motivation to do three or four of them. And they'd do three or four and they'd come back and say, "Hey, that shit was good!" Of course, if they did three or four of them, they did get fucked up.

Inevitably, however, drug dealers are confronted with dissatisfied customers who have reason to believe that they have been ripped off with poor-quality dope. There was no consensus among the dealers I interviewed regarding how they respond to discontented clients. Some would play it tough, on the theory that to give in to a client's demands sets a bad precedent and may serve as a signal to others that here is a dealer who can easily be taken. Others saw themselves as conscientious businesspeople and would quite readily supply a dissatisfied customer with more dope, urging them to spread the word that they were treated fairly. In either event, to borrow a phrase from the subculture of pick-pockets, dealers must "cool the mark out," employing all of the social skills they have at their disposal to maintain a stable clientele.

Intuitive Skills

This last category of hustling skills entails an acute sensitivity to one's environment. Sutherland (1937) describes this characteristic as *larceny sense,* a term that Dressler also employs to describe the professional criminal: "Larceny sense, it seems, is the ability to smell out good hauls, to sense the exact moment for the kill, and to know when it is wiser to desist" (1951, 255). Maurer (1955) applies the term *grift sense* to describe intuitive skills in his classic analysis of the professional pickpocket. But these skills are by no means limited to professional criminals. Gould et al. observe this ability among active heroin users: "Most successful dope fiends show an ability to size up people they meet in terms of trustworthiness and motivation, and have a good memory for people" (1974, 45–46).

The addicts I interviewed also emphasized the importance of intuitive skills. Like technical and social skills, intuitive skills are manifested differently in various criminal contexts, but their general purpose is to help facilitate the commission of a crime or to help the criminal avoid detection and arrest.

Intuitive skills can facilitate the commission of crime by providing the addict with the ability to sense a profitable and reasonably safe opportunity. "I could see money. I could smell money," claimed Old Ray. "I could walk by a store and see if it was vulnerable. . . . I could sense the whole setup." These are the skills that contribute to larceny (or grift) sense, and many of the participants in this study explicitly acknowledged their importance. Representative observations of a prostitute, a pickpocket, and a shoplifter illustrate how these skills are applied in various hustles:

> [Rose—a prostitute] Look for the nice dates. When you spot a man with the raggediest car and the oldest clothes, he's probably got the money. Because he's cheap, he don't wanna spend all of that money. It's usually the man that's got all this and that [who] ain't got a dime because he's paying out so many bills. [Rose went on to point out that she would probably have to steal his money because he is unlikely to be generous with her either.]

> [Boss—a pickpocket] As I got better, I could spot people with decent money, and you play them. Whereas in the beginning, on the amateur thing, I might play anywhere from ten to fifteen wallets. But when I got professional, I might just play one or two wallets.

> [Booter—a shoplifter] All days aren't the same for boosting. . . . If there's no situation where you can make some money you just don't go in and make a situation. You understand what I'm saying? The situation has to be laid out for you. And to be really good at it, you got to be the type of person that can recognize a laid-out situation. If you get in there and try to make a situation, then you're rearranging the whole thing and it could be detrimental.

Intuitive skills are also instrumental in avoiding detection and arrest. The addict criminals in this study repeatedly stressed the importance of being able to detect and avoid undercover police officers, floorwalkers, and potential informants. This ability was regarded as absolutely crucial to their success in criminal roles:

> [Harry—regarding drug dealing] I learned the ropes . . . how you spot cops. He [a friend] pointed out . . . those undercover detectives with the bee stingers on their cars, little teeny antennae on top; and how you could pick those cars out; and how two detectives in a car, how there were certain characteristics about them that were always the same. You could smell them a mile away. He really schooled me criminally, you know.

> [Stephanie—a check forger] When she [the bank teller] sees the check, if she has to look up [or] if she has to call another teller or something like that, it ain't no good. . . . If the teller has to pick up the phone, then you tell her, "That's all right, there's something I have to do."

> [Penny—on shoplifting] I can tell [who the floorwalkers are]. They constantly keep walking the floor looking at me. . . . They're still in that same department and ain't bought nothing.

> [Fred—a drug dealer] Never take a deal that sounds too good to be true. . . . This guy came by and wanted to buy fifteen bags for $10 apiece—no shorts. Now any kind of a hustler junkie coming off the street and he's got $150, he's not gonna come to you wanting fifteen bags. He's gonna come to you wanting twenty-five or thirty. You know what I'm saying? The deal was too good to be true.

These observations illustrate the diffuse qualities characteristic of intuitive skills. It was difficult even for the study respondents to articulate their precise nature. Pagie recalled: "I always had a knack for sensing the police. I don't know why. I don't know if it's an ESP thing or what, but I always could sense when the police was there." It is because of their rather imperceptible quality that I have used the term *intuitive skills* to refer to this important set of abilities. It is important to understand, however, that they are not hereditary talents. These are skills that are acquired through the same process of socialization as are technical and social skills. Together, these three sets of skills distinguish successful stable addicts from beginning occasional users.

I have attempted in this discussion to demonstrate that contrary to stereotyped depictions of addict criminality, stable addicts are skilled criminal entrepreneurs. The level of criminal sophistication required to sustain a livelihood of the magnitude reported by these hard-core addicts is acquired only after spending considerable time in the subculture. Such skills are simply not part of the beginning occasional user's stock-in-trade. In the process of becoming stable addicts, however, most users narrow the range of their criminal activities considerably. I certainly do not wish to represent the stable addict as a professional in the tradition of a Chic Conwell (Sutherland 1937) or Vincent Swaggi (Klockars 1974) nor necessarily as specialized as Preble and Casey (1969) imply in their watershed study of addict criminals. The addicts I interviewed, however, do favor a small number of crimes among the vast variety they could be committing. I am suggesting that as stable addicts, these hard-core users are sufficiently successful at their main hustles such that they seldom find it necessary to deviate from their preferred crimes. They attain a level of specialization not characteristic of amateurs nor even of their own criminal patterns during other periods of their careers. Indeed, I contend that it is only by such specialization that these addicts are able to develop the requisite skills for a successful career. There is thus a mutually reinforcing relationship between the development of a main hustle and the acquisition of technical, social, and intuitive skills that correspond to this specialization. The acquisition of these skills is, in the first place, dependent upon some level of specialization; at the same time, these skills provide the very foundation for stable addicts to maintain their main hustles.

These main hustles, which constitute more or less full-time criminal roles, also have other important consequences. As I suggested earlier, they provide an alternative basis for life structure that is capable of accommodating higher levels of drug use and consumer activity generally. At the same time, however, the routine nature of the main hustle prevents one's habit from getting out of hand. The stable addict's heroin use still takes place within a rather well defined, though modified, life structure. Moreover, full-time hustler roles provide addicts with increased dependable income. Unlike the marginal criminality of occasional users, the main hustle is both a primary means of income and a source of identity and prestige in the subculture. The study respondents were quick to distinguish between a main hustle typical of stable addicts and the more amateur or impulsive *flat-footed hustling* style characteristic of less criminally routine lifestyles. Gloria emphasized her distinctive status as a booster: "I'm not a thief—I'm a booster. There's a difference between a thief and a booster. A thief . . . takes anything and everything from anywhere." Booter understood his role as a pimp in entrepreneurial terms, viewing his *who's* (prostitutes) as an investment:

> You try not to spend too much money unless it's important. You're playing economics here. Like I got some stock. . . . In order for her to collect the capital, she has to be a product. You have to have something that you can sell. You don't try to give up too much, but say you are into a new girl. . . . You have to put some clothes on her, put some capital into that to make her look presentable. . . . You're expecting her to get that money back.

Thus, the stable-addict phase is characterized by a comparatively high degree of criminal specialization, complete with the technical, social, and intuitive skills that contribute to success in the criminal role. As shown by this research and in previous studies, stable addicts are successful and sophisticated criminal entrepreneurs.

Questions for Thought and Discussion

1. What types of skills must a stable addict maintain in order to survive?
2. How does crime facilitate drug use? Do you think that drug use may also facilitate crime?
3. What is meant by an addict's "main hustle"?
4. What theory or theories of criminal behavior are illustrated by this research?

References

Dressler, David (1951). *Probation and Parole.* New York: Columbia University Press.

Faupel, Charles E. (1986). "Heroin use, street crime and the main hustle: Implications for the validity of official crime data." *Deviant Behavior* 7: 31–45.

Gould, Leroy, Andrew L. Walker, Lansing E. Crane, and Charles W. Lidz (1974). *Connections: Notes From the Heroin World.* New Haven, CT: Yale University Press.

Klockars, Carl (1974). *The Professional Fence.* New York: The Free Press.

Letkeman, Peter (1973). *Crime as Work.* Englewood Cliffs, NJ: Prentice-Hall.

Maurer, David W. (1955). *Whiz Mob: A Correlation of the Technical Argot of Pickpockets with Their Behavior Patterns.* Gainesville, FL: American Dialect Society.

Mead, George Herbert (1934). *Mind, Self, and Society.* Edited by C.W. Morris. Chicago: University of Chicago Press.

Preble, Edward and John H. Casey (1969). "Taking care of business: The heroin user's life on the streets." *International Journal of the Addictions,* 4, 1 (March): 1–24.

Sutherland, Edwin H. (1937). *The Professional Thief.* Chicago: University of Chicago Press.

Chapter 28
Inside the Drug Trade

Trafficking From the Dealer's Perspective

Kenneth D. Tunnell

In the past decade most states and the federal government have enacted increasingly severe sentences for drug offenses. How effective are these policies? Is drug-related crime decreasing? Are the new policies capturing the intended individuals—high-level dealers? This study argues that we know little about trafficking networks, strategies for connecting with buyers, or the nexus between drug dealing and using. To answer these questions, the author selected a sample of 10 men incarcerated for drug dealing in a medium-security prison. Interviews were conducted focusing on their experiences dealing drugs, their personal use of drugs, and any prior incarcerations. He found that all of the men were low-level drug dealers who sold small amounts of drugs or were employed as "runners" for other drug dealers. Most of these men had long sentences more appropriate for the "higher-ups" in the drug-dealing profession. Eight of the 10 were addicted to the drugs they sold, and claimed that they dealt in order to support their addiction. The author concludes that the public policies regarding drug use and sales need to be rethought—that we need to cease to rely on a "war on drugs" and develop and encourage prevention and treatment programs.

Over the past decade, the social control of drugs has become a war-like campaign, as policy makers and law enforcement communities use increasingly innovative strategies to inhibit drug manufacturing and distribution (e.g., air interdiction, asset seizure and forfeiture, military operations) (e.g., Potter, Gaines, and Holbrook, 1990). Recent figures indicate that the monetary and social costs of this war are staggering. The Federal Government alone increased its drug war expenditures from $1.5 billion in 1981 to $5.9 billion in 1990; state and local governments spent $12 billion in 1990—a record high (and yet these are conservative figures) (Drug Trafficking, 1989). The vast majority of these monies has been earmarked for law enforcement, interdiction, and prison construction with little allocated for prevention and rehabilitation programs. As a result of policing and law enforcement expenditures, drug traffickers are now apprehended, convicted, and imprisoned at greater rates than at any time before. For example, in 1987, as compared to 1980, adult arrests for drug selling and manufacturing increased 113 percent (BJS, 1988a). Federal drug convictions increased 213 percent during the 1980s, and the numbers of convicted drug offenders sentenced to prison increased from 72 percent in 1980 to 86 percent in 1990 (BJS, 1992).

At the state level, drug traffickers constitute 26 percent of first-time incarcerees and the number is rapidly swelling (BJS, 1988b; Reuter and Haaga, 1989). Drug traffickers sentenced to state prison increased from 37 percent in 1986 to 41 percent in 1988 (BJS, 1991a). Not only are arrest, conviction, and incarceration rates increasing, but prison sentences are likewise. The average sentence for Federal drug offenders increased from 47 months in 1980 to 81 months in 1990—a 72 percent increase; similar trends are found at the state level (BJS, 1992; 1991b).

Even with such unprecedented numbers of detected drug offenders, researchers have given drug trafficking erratic attention. Early and recent research describes drug dealing as low-level, fragmented and unsophisticated (Redlinger, 1975; Leib and Olson, 1976; Mieczkowski, 1986). Research with heroin addicts/dealers describes their existence as a continuous search for drugs (Preble and Casey, 1969) while more recent research indicates that heroin and marijuana users and dealers make drug connections informally rather than within formally organized networks (Atkyns and Hanneman, 1974; Fields, 1984, 1986). Research consistently describes drug dealing as fragmented, disorganized, and composed of unprofessionals—markedly different from images propagated by the media and political pundits.

Although mid-level marijuana and hashish dealers (i.e., those who buy and sell in large quantities) have received only little attention, these studies refute commonly held images of dealing as a sophisticated criminal organization and dealers as seducers of young children into addiction (e.g., Preble and Casey, 1969; Langer, 1977). Studies of high-level dealers and their organizations inform us of the process of gaining entree into drug markets, the longevity of such organizations, and the nature of "middling" and wholesaling drugs (Adler, 1985; Reuter and Haaga, 1989). As earlier studies on garden-variety crimes inform us of "drifting" into crime (e.g., Matza, 1964), recent research describes the process of "drifting" into and desisting from "careers" in drug trafficking (e.g., Murphy, Waldorf, and Reinarman, 1990; Waldorf, Murphy, and Lauderback, 1989). One characteristic of most drug trafficking research, as opposed to research on other types of criminality (e.g., property crime), is samples have been composed of un-incarcerated active or once-active dealers rather than incarcerated offenders.

The objectives for this descriptive study were twofold. First, in the tradition of drug trafficking research, I sought the dealer's perspective to understand the relationships among dealing and drug use, the nature of making connections with both buyers and sellers, and the dealers' buying and selling networks. Second, I sought those dealers who have fallen victim to the criminal justice system, that is, those who have been netted in the escalating war on drugs. Thus, I learned of drug dealing from former traffickers who have been apprehended and sentenced to prison during the most recent and intensive war on drugs. . . .

Getting Started Dealing

Previous research informs us that those who sell drugs often are "stash" dealers, that is, they sell to maintain consistent access to drugs for their own consumption (e.g., Fields, 1986; Murphy, Waldorf, and Reinarman, 1990). Such findings are also indicative of this sample who began dealing very early in life and primarily to maintain a supply for their own use. Early in their dealing careers, they had already experimented with a variety of drugs and discovered that selling provided both "free drugs" and a regular, yet intimate, clientele. These dealers typically developed drug use patterns before selling (c.f., Atkyns and Hanneman, 1974).

One sample member, a 37 year old serving his first prison sentence for trafficking, although having been arrested several times for various drug offenses, recalled that he first began selling to have drugs for his own personal consumption. Later, selling provided him status as he developed informal connections with would-be buyers.

> When I first started selling, at age 16, we used to go down to the beach and find somebody selling acid. If you sold ten hits for them, they'd give you one.

And a second individual, at a very young age, began selling acid to acquaintances again, to have drugs for his own use.

> If I went to the swimming pool, it wouldn't take no time to sell 50 to 100 hits of acid, in one night. And hell, I'd get free acid and a little pocket change.

A third individual, serving a 20-year prison sentence, his second, related that he first sold marijuana at the age of 12. He was both able to earn income and to personally use marijuana at no monetary cost to himself. He represents Fields' (1984) "rider," that is, one who sells at the street level on consignment for a mid-level dealer.

> I had a friend of mine that was an older guy and he introduced me to selling marijuana to make a few dollars. I started selling a little and made a few dollars. For a young guy to be making a hundred dollars or so, it was a lot of money. So I got kind of tied up in that aspect of selling drugs.

According to him, he had nearly immediate success in moving his product because he had knowledge of who bought marijuana and where.

> Down the street there was a corner with a liquor store and little beer joint. Whole lot of guys hung down this corner and a few guys sold marijuana. I would go down there and say, "I've got good marijuana." And I would sell like 10 or 15 ten-dollar bags in a few hours. I would take my friend his money back and he would say, "You did good. Here's some more." I'd go and do it again. I did that for a long time.

Selling provided him a stash, money, and social rewards of developing informal networks with older buyers—benefits from dealing recognized by previous researchers (e.g., Adler, 1985; Weisheit, 1991). Beyond that, he aspired to and later became what Fields (1986) coined "a weedslinger," and hired younger boys to sell for him. His upward mobility in the drug trade is due, in part, to his social skills conducive to such advancement and the autonomy to sell on a regular basis, having quit school at that time. He had committed himself to dealing as a profession, and when describing that period in his life, showed that even then he easily developed the necessary entrepreneurial knowledge and skills for dealing at the street level and beyond. Interestingly, this individual was only one of two who progressed from street-level sales to a more lucrative mode. Such requisites for upward mobility in dealing are also described by Fields (1984; 1986).

These men typically started using and selling drugs at a very young age and sold them for both pecuniary and non-pecuniary benefits. . . . They desired access to a fairly consistent supply of drugs and money, although nominal, from their dealing. Beyond that, they enjoyed excitement associated with dealing and status from both their younger and older friends. This latter finding is similar to that of other researchers' descriptions of the social, non-pecuniary rewards obtained from drug dealing (e.g., Weisheit, 1991; Adler, 1985; Blum et al., 1972).

Making Connections With Buyers and Sellers

Previous research informs us that dealers, while not necessarily making conscious decisions to participate in long-term drug dealing, find over time that they develop long-term network connections for buying and selling their wares (e.g., Langer, 1977; Murphy, Waldorf, Reinarman, 1990). Likewise, these men reported that their initial connections for both buying and selling drugs were made very informally and sometimes nearly accidentally. They apparently "drifted" into dealing and learned, by "word of mouth," where and from whom to purchase. The words of a 29 year old dealer illustrate the loose structure which characterizes such low-level, informal drug trafficking.

> Q. How did you meet the person that you scored from?
>
> A. Through family. My older brother.
>
> Q. Is that the person you continued buying from?
>
> A. No. Here and there, I got introduced to other people through friends.

Making connections with mid-level or wholesale dealers for buying drugs to re-sell occurred through casual conversation, by having been in the right place at the right time, and by having been introduced to well-connected individuals. In other words, establishing such necessities of the business occurred very informally and did not require conscious decisions to become "drug dealers."

These informal methods also typify the way that connections were made for selling drugs, indicating they did not operate within a formal network. Making connections for selling, apparently, was loosely structured.

> Once you start selling drugs and you're in a tight-knit community, and if you got good drugs, don't take people long to say, "Well that guy's got the best drugs." You just meet people. I might meet you and you might bring your buddy. Next time, I meet him and sell him some. Next time he brings his buddy. So, it's a chain.

One 46 year old, serving his sixth prison sentence, offered a revealing analogy about the informality of buying and selling.

> A. It's like a circle, like a club, a bridge club. You've got certain people come to a certain place and play bridge. You've got certain people who come to a certain place to buy drugs. There's no problem with getting drugs. I might not know their full names, but I could go to about 100 people that use Dilaudid.[1]
>
> Q. So, does that informal system typify the way that you bought and sold until you caught this last charge?
>
> A. Yeah. If you don't have it, you know somebody that you can call, and if they don't, they know somebody that they can call that'll have it. It's just one big circle.

Thus, these men approached dealing, especially early in their careers, very casually and informally. They made connections with buyers and sellers through friends, family, by word of mouth, or by street knowledge of where buyers and sellers were likely found.

Low-Level Dealing

One fundamental characteristic of these men is that each was a low-level dealer[2] who neither sold large amounts of drugs nor employed others as "drug runners." One individual, and typical for this sample, dealt drugs for years but only to a small circle of friends who, like him, had addictions. After his second conviction for selling small quantities of drugs, he was sentenced as a Persistent Felon to 40 years in prison. We had the following conversation.

Q. It sounds like, from what you've told me here today, that it was basically just you on your own, that there was no "drug ring." Did you ever work with partners?

A. No. You had your own little connections, scratch my back and I'll scratch yours. Just a big circle was all it was, and we sold to each other. They got to realize that there's a difference in being big wheeler-dealers and what we did. It's hard to constitute what a trafficker is. I know it's somebody who sells drugs, but anybody who uses them, sometime in their life, they're going to sell to their brother, their friend, or somebody. If they can save a buck, they're going to do it. Plus, they feel they're doing a friend a favor.

Another man of 45 years, whose selling and Dilaudid addiction experienced periods of oscillation, claimed to have wholesaled drugs only within a small circle of friends and personal acquaintances (c.f., Adler and Adler, 1983; Adler, 1985; Waldorf, Murphy, and Lauderback, 1989) and claims his sales were low-level.

I would wholesale to get enough money to meet my needs, whatever they were. I didn't live high on the hog, drive a new Lincoln, and have Mr. T. starter kits around my neck. Some guys, that's a statement for them. That's the way they say, "I'm the dope dealer." As far as the big money operators, you either find them in the federal penitentiary or you'll find them still on the street in a big condo somewhere. Most of the drug traffickers here are guys that have sold to informants or sold to just people they chipped around, just used drugs occasionally and the police were watching them or had them set up.[3]

His comments on those imprisoned for trafficking, at least among this sample, were accurate—former traffickers imprisoned in Kentucky operated on a very small scale; they made very little money from their risky ventures and typically dealt to maintain a steady supply of drugs. Similarly, earlier research indicates that although low-level heroin dealers sell frequently, their incomes are surprisingly inconsequential, and they usually are paid with drugs which they consume rather than cash income (Johnson, Kaplan, and Schmeidler, 1990: 209).

The following comment of a 31 year old who dealt acid, cocaine, and marijuana across many years, is indicative of low-level dealers, their desire for drugs rather than income, and in the end, how they have little to show for their labor (c.f., Langer, 1977; Reuter and Haaga, 1989).

I never got that big in money. Whatever money I made was always spent up on drugs. I have nothing to show for it.

Only two of the participants had established connections to any semblance of a formalized drug trafficking network. Of the two, one operated for only a few months by hiring young men to deal "curb side" in an inner-city (similar to the descriptions of Fields, 1986; Mieczkowski, 1986). His words describe his business expansion as he advanced from being a low-level dealer to employer.

A. I'm selling cocaine through my beeper, me and three guys. There's a street in Louisville that's known as a drug corner. So, we got a plan together in our mind. We just set up shop on this street corner. We just come down here and sell our cocaine, won't have to keep running all over town. This is what we do. We get us three or four young teenage guys, give them the dope, they run, they sell the cocaine. We wanted to have an organization. We sort of tried to move up in the world, you know?

Q. Was that the first time you had tried that kind of organization with drug dealing?

A. Yeah. Every other time I've been on my own.

A second individual had dealt drugs as part of a formally structured criminal enterprise—a California organized crime family. He worked as a "middle-man" in their drug business by dealing "wholesale." Of the sample, he is the lone middle-man and the only one connected to a sophisticated drug dealing network.

A. I was working as a middle-man selling heroin for this Mexican family. I was dealing in quarter ounces.

Q. How many middlemen did this family employ?

A. It was numerous cause they had about six main people they supplied. Those six main people supplied the others. I dealt with about 10 people on a weekly basis. And they ran all the dope from California to Washington. They had a pretty good business going.

Q. How did you know the family and these 10 people?

> A. They were friends of mine. I grew up with them. They were sending me dope in the mail. They'd send me an ounce and I'd sell it, send them their money by Western Union. Then they'd get me another ounce Overnight Express. They'd mail it like 2:00 in the evening and I'd get it the next morning.

Although firmly entrenched in a formal organization, he had developed those connections very informally and casually through friends he had known most of his life. Interestingly, within the sample, only this man and the individual who employed young boys to sell curbside had large quantities of drugs in their possession when arrested; one had two ounces of cocaine and the other four. The other eight, at the time of their arrests, possessed only small quantities. They all were arrested after having sold small quantities to informants and undercover police officers, or after having been "squealed" on (doubtless, typical modes of arrest among low-level drug traffickers).

These individuals may typify the growing numbers of drug dealers who not only are being incarcerated in state prisons at increasing rates but who are being incarcerated for longer periods of time as fixed prison sentences for drug traffickers are now common. Such sentences undoubtedly are being imposed on low-level dealers and not solely on professional or organized dealers. These small-scale dealers, as those found in earlier studies, have little in common with the media's drug-dealing images which have become transformed, through high-tech media and political rhetoric, into symbols for nearly everything that is wrong with America (see also Tunnell, 1992; Humphries, 1993).

Drug Dealing as a Career

Doubtless, drug dealing is sometimes viewed as an exciting, autonomous, and financially rewarding occupation. Due to the pecuniary and non-pecuniary rewards, some individuals aspire to such a vocation. However, drug dealing was an occupational choice for only two of these men. The others began dealing after acquiring a fondness for drugs and desiring a readily available stash, or after having become addicted. Other studies show similar patterns among drug traffickers (e.g., Murphy, Waldorf, and Reinarman, 1990). Unlike individuals who are committed to dealing as a career and who aspire to upward mobility (e.g., Adler and Adler, 1983), these men, while experiencing some flux during their dealing careers, did not have an image of themselves as dealers or pursue dealing as a profession or occupational choice. Furthermore, they made no attempt to advance from their low-level operations to mid-level or beyond to upper-level sales and smuggling (c.f., Langer, 1977).

Three of the men made decisions that changed the nature of their dealing. Although arguably, each altered his dealing so that it became farther removed from small-scale, none particularly aspired to deal on a larger scale than before and incidentally, none advanced beyond low-level activities. The following comment is that of a 32 year old serving a 20-year prison sentence. Although gradually investing in larger amounts of marijuana, he did not pursue advancing to middle- or upper-level dealing.

> I sold marijuana for many years. I eventually worked my way up to a quarter pound. Then I worked up from there to a half pound and then from there to a pound. But I really didn't go much over that.

He continued selling to his small circle of friends and acquaintances and remained uncommitted to dealing as an occupation. His self-perception was something other than "dealer." A second individual described how the frequency of his selling decreased as he changed his dealing style from retail to wholesale.

> Well, when I first started there was times that I sold every day due to the fact that that was the way that I would get money for myself to fix. But then when I sold wholesale, it was less often. The dealing never became bigger other than wholesaling. And the reason why I wholesaled was so I wouldn't have to deal with a lot of people. I could deal with one person.

A third individual, a 37 year old who had been arrested several times on drug-related charges, but serving only his first prison sentence for trafficking, described how his dealing became more lucrative as he sold larger quantities of marijuana. Nonetheless, his trafficking methods remained those of a low-level dealer. He demonstrated none of the characteristics commonly associated with upper-level drug dealers. For example, he lived a very simple, back-to-nature lifestyle in a small, secluded house without electricity. He had a self-imposed curfew at night to prevent friends and buyers from disrupting his privacy and to minimize the chances of alerting the police. His persona and way of life were anything but that of an upper-level dealer described by Adler and Adler (1983:196) as "a fast lifestyle which emphasized intensive partying, casual sex, extensive travel, abundant drug consumption, and lavish spending on consumer goods." Dealing had never been a career choice for him and he had no aspirations for the upper echelons of the drug dealing profession.

> Q. You just said that you did the growing and selling yourself. So, did you or not have a middle-man who dealt it out in smaller quantities?
>
> A. I used to have a guy that came and picked it up and get it all at once. I always sold in pounds to somebody who would sell in ounces and half ounces. One guy would take it all. Usually I didn't grow that much on my own. The last year I grew as much as I could and then quit.

After making connections with a cocaine dealer, he soon began trafficking cocaine from Miami to Kentucky both to sell and to have a stash for himself, since by that time, he had developed an addiction. Although the volume of cocaine increased, his operation remained small scale, absent of partners, and with little sophistication, as his words indicate.

> A. First time I just brought back an ounce. About half a year after that I was getting keys, one every two months.
>
> Q. When you flew back with it, how did you get it back?
>
> A. I hid it in my pants.

These men were neither professional nor lucrative dealers. Their self-image was as something other than "real dealers" as they continue to believe that real dealers either remain unapprehended or incarcerated in Federal prisons. Since they neither considered themselves dealers nor dealt on a large scale, they enjoyed benefits other than large sums of money, status, and the fast lifestyle indicative of upper-level dealers (e.g., Adler, 1985). Blum et al. (1972) describe similar findings from their study and suggest that their sample enjoyed latent benefits from the occupation of dealing—benefits such as available drugs, socializing with other users, buyers and sellers, and the autonomy that a deviant lifestyle often affords—commonalities also of this sample.

Addiction and Drug Dealing

Although dealing and addiction are two concepts inextricably wedded in the literature, the issue of the reality of addiction is a tenuous one (e.g., Lyman and Potter, 1991; Preble and Casey, 1969; Redlinger, 1975). Debates continue on whether addiction is physiological or psychological (e.g., Peele, 1985). For this sample, and perhaps others like them, addiction and the role it plays in drug dealing is conceptually useful, for a critical point is that these men defined their addictions as important for explaining their continued dealing. Thus, their definitions of their situations, that is, their beliefs that they were addicted, and that their addictions were the impetus for drug dealing, are important for understanding their lives as drug users and low-level dealers (e.g., Becker, 1963).

While dealing, eight of the 10 were always addicted to one drug or another, and at various times during their careers, each had an addiction (Dilaudid and cocaine being the most common). They claimed that they dealt drugs for one reason—to support their addictions. A 31 year old who had been addicted to both alcohol and drugs offered the following words:

> A drug user loses his morals. He lets go of his values, his honor, he don't care. Dope is the most important thing to you, out of your family and everything. You just don't care what the outcome is going to be. You'll continue doing what you're doing, period.

Another described how his addiction, rather than a desire for profit maximization, drove his dealing.

> Well it wasn't long after I was addicted that I sold drugs. And when I say, "I sold drugs," it wasn't to John Q. Citizen or the little kids up the street. When you become addicted it becomes a way of life to you. It's part of your life. After a period of six months or a year of every day use of those type of drugs, you lose weight, you lose any real initiative as far as wanting to do anything and you get kind of laid back.

The following words are those of the man who at one time employed young boys to run cocaine for him. Although only one of two participants not addicted consistently across his drug dealing career, his words describe his severe addiction and its effects on his dealing—it dwindled to a smaller scale.

> In the meantime, I've got a hell of a habit myself. I started smoking cocaine and shooting cocaine in my arm. And I was getting this habit on. So, after about a year, I was shooting and I was using more drugs than I was selling. So, I blew my thing. I just laid in California and caught a habit. I seen a friend one day and he said, "Man, do you want to make some money?" I said, "Yeah, I want to make some money." He said that he could front me a couple of ounces of cocaine. So, I've got this habit and he fronted me the cocaine. I start selling $25, $50, $100 pieces of cocaine, whatever you want. Now I'm dealing with the street people. This is the level I've dropped to now. I'm selling to street people. Whoever wants some, that's who I'm selling to.

Table I illustrates the types of drugs these men dealt and were addicted to. Although they sold a wide array of drugs, to have an accessible stash they dealt the type that they were addicted to, as a 45 year old serving his first prison sentence explained.

> Q. You said that you tried to quit. Do you mean quit using or quit dealing cocaine?
>
> A. I could quit dealing it cause I had money. I didn't need to sell it. If I wasn't doing it, I wouldn't have needed to sell it. But, I couldn't quit using it.

Among this sample, Dilaudid was the most common drug of addiction. These men avoided potentially dangerous drugs, (i.e., those "stepped on") and opted for a synthetic, clean, and reliable drug (see also Murphy, Waldorf, and Reinarman, 1990). This fondness for Dilaudid may be a reflection of these men's ages; they are older than participants of previous studies and desire a "mellow" high rather than a stimulant. The following words of a 46 year old illustrate this point.

> Dilaudid, to a lot of your old timers, your old junkies, or old users, we don't go for this old cocaine, this crack, this ice, and stuff like that. Something that makes us hyper and run up and down the streets like a maniac. We want something that will mellow us out and that's why narcotics is our drug of choice. With coke, unless you really know the person you're getting it from, there's no telling what they cut it with. Plus, hell, I don't want to be high. Not in that sense that I'm talking about being high.

Table I

Drugs of Addiction and Drugs That Were Dealt: By Number of Participants

	Dilaudid	Cocaine	Heroin	Marijuana	Acid
Addicted	6	3	1	0	0
Dealt	6	3	1	4	2
N = 10					

Occasionally, when describing their dealing and how it changed across their lives, these men could not help but focus on their addictions as the single most important variable in accounting for its dynamics. They defined their situations as such that they had few alternatives available other than dealing to maintain their personal habits. The following words succinctly capture one's definition of addiction and the belief that dependency is an illness rather than deviance.

> You got to realize that it's a damn sickness. I can honestly say in my heart-of-hearts that I know that I was sick rather than bad. I got introduced to drugs early and that's all I knew.

These men do not represent greedy, calculative, violent drug lords. Rather, they constantly engaged in dealing for accessible drugs that, as a result of their illegality, have both limited availability and almost unlimited price (e.g., Reiman, 1990). They reiterated this point during the interviews and their prison files confirmed the point—they had not been arrested for any violent crime and possessed little material wealth when arrested. Their files indicate that they lived "hand-to-mouth," dealt drugs, were addicted to drugs, and did not engage in violent crime. These characteristics are likewise incongruous with media and political images of drug dealers which are typically violent, greedy, would-be drug lords jockeying over turf and willingly selling to anyone, including school children. Yet these men, poor, uneducated, non-violent, low-level addict/merchants of illegal wares, have received inordinately long prison sentences. This issue was important to them as they volunteered their views and opinions regarding current criminal justice drug policies.

Reactions to a Punitive Criminal Justice System

Nearly all of these men are serving long prison sentences and believe that in their cases, the punishment far exceeds the crime severity. . . . Their definitions of themselves are incongruous with those of criminals who cause grave social harm. They believe their crimes, especially compared to violent crimes, are of little danger. One individual described the severity of his sentence compared to that of violent offenders.

> Ironically, a guy that was charged with killing a baby was snitching on people to get out of his charge. So he had set up a deal with this guy that I got busted with. They put me in here for 30 years when I've seen guys come in with manslaughter charges for three and five years. I know I hurt some people but, people don't know how bad I was hurting since I was eight years old and on drugs.

His words further indicate that he believes the State should have treated his problem rather than criminalize it.

> Every time I've been to prison, in '79 and '80 and in '85, I was never given drug rehabilitation. Never. They just lock you up.

Another individual shared his thoughts on the war on drugs, how society could more effectively deal with the drug problem, and about the "threat" that he believes he was to society.

> They're going about this drug war all wrong. I feel that if people want to stop, they ought to have more rehabilitation centers, education early, get your professional help when you need it instead of just throwing you out of school like I was. They didn't offer me no professional help or nothing. I'm kind of pissed at society in that aspect. If only I would have got help a long time ago. I'm no threat to society whatsoever.

These men complained that formal punishments for drug offenses are overly severe, especially compared to violent crimes.

Unlike property offenders of earlier studies (e.g., Tunnell, 1990) these participants nearly always had critical words about "justice," how "justice" varies from case to case, and the sociolegal concept of "equal justice." Justice, for them became a commodity.

> I hate to say this but it's the truth, you got to buy justice by the pound. It's as simple as that. I didn't have no money.

Another man, serving his sixth prison sentence, likewise had some harsh words for justice, the drug war, and the media's depiction of drug dealers. He also revealed his motivation for participating in this study—to educate the public about the character of low-level drug dealing and dealers (c.f., Langer, 1977).

> Another reason I wanted to come and talk to you is to let folks really know that everybody that's out there dealing drugs, they're not out there selling to school kids, they're not out there to make a big pile of money where they can go to the Riviera. They're out there taking care of their drug habits. And when the police get a guy like us on a trafficking charge, then they go and portray him as a big drug trafficker and he's really nothing. He's nobody and he admits that he's nobody. And they're having society think they're really cleaning up the streets. "Boy we're getting the drug traffickers." And they're getting poor Joe Schmoe here.

Their comments on a system that defines their addictions as criminal which in turn makes it increasingly difficult to acquire the addictive drugs, and then severely punishes them for doing just that, are revealing insights about the offenders/victims of the war on drugs.

Conclusion

This research is but one more study in a growing line of studies that enlightens us about the disorganized nature of drug dealing, the individuals caught up in it, and the social response to them and their violations. From both official and self-report data, we learn that this sample was composed of almost entirely low-level drug traffickers; they neither made large sums of money nor sold large sums of drugs. Rather, they sold because of their own addictions. They specialized in dealing, but chose not to commit themselves to a career and upward mobility in the drug trade. In fact, they had very little opportunity for advancement since their connections with upper-level dealers were nearly non-existent. Of the sample, only two progressed beyond low-level sales while others dealt primarily for survival and on a very low scale. Judging solely from the amounts that they typically sold, only one could be considered even remotely a "mid-level" dealer. Each dealt powerful narcotics at some point in their drug dealing stints—typically cocaine or Dilaudid—and one sold marijuana that he had personally cultivated. Given the limits of their dealing, it is conceivable that they may not be those dealers that concern the general public. In other words, these men, engaged in a drug war with the government, may not well represent those dealers that apparently cause grave social and moral harm.

Presently, the dominant social solution for these and increasing numbers of other (although perhaps not necessarily similar) nonviolent drug offenders is severe punishment for their illegal actions. As much as these men are criminals, they also are victims of a particular historical time—a time like no other in recent history—where drug users and addicts are met with antagonistic intolerance and when states mandate increasingly severe penalties for drug dealers. As much recent attention as decriminalization proposals have received, there is little hope for any immediate relaxation in laws governing drug use and trafficking (see e.g., Lyman and Potter, 1991; Trebach, 1987). Such enlightened social policies are fundamental for re-thinking the drug problem, the drug war, and the growing numbers of individual traffickers who are being sentenced to increasingly longer prison terms. Likewise, a rethinking of spending priorities is essential for lessening the dysfunctional effects of drug abuse in our society. As a start, public monies must be invested at greater rates in educational, preventative and treatment programs and a lesser rate in law enforcement strategies and prison building programs. We must cease to rely on a "war" mentality where police are socialized into roles of soldiers in a moral crusade and where the innocent and guilty suffer irreparably. Not only are law violators being treated harshly in this war, but law-abiding citizens have witnessed their own individual rights diminish as new laws and court rulings place the State and its power over the rights of individuals (e.g., Jenkins, 1992).

Notes

1. Dilaudid is "a hydrogenated ketone of morphine, a narcotic analgesic. Small doses of Dilaudid produce effective and prompt relief of pain usually with minimal disturbance from nausea and vomiting" (*Physicians Desk Reference,* 1977: 871). It is also the drug of choice among older junkies since it is produced in safe, laboratory conditions and its effects are reliable.
2. Although the term "low-level" appears in an abundance of drug dealing literature, the term (as well as "mid-level" and "upper-level") is rather vague. Deducing from the literature, a low-level dealer is one who deals at the street level and who occasionally wholesales, but typically does not. Low-level dealers usually do not pursue trafficking as a full-time occupation but deal when they have access to drugs and customers. They are usually users or addicts themselves, unlike upper-level dealers. They make very little money for their efforts and because they are stash dealers, earn drugs rather than income. Furthermore, they do not engage in social activities characteristic of upper-level dealers and described by Adler and Adler (1983).
3. "Chipping, " a term used by junkies and dealers, means injecting drugs socially without forming an addiction. Although we know that some individuals use drugs intravenously during weekends and hence "chip, " there is, at this time, no estimate of the number of Americans who presently engage in such casual drug use.

Questions for Thought and Discussion

1. What policy issues does the author suggest for dealing with the drug/crime problem?
2. What is the process by which new drug dealers begin their careers?
3. Other than the financial aspects, what are the "rewards" of drug dealing?
4. What are the various positions on the issue of dealing and addiction?

References

Adler, P. A. (1985). *Wheeling and Dealing: An Ethnography of an Upper Level Drug Dealing and Smuggling Community.* New York: Columbia University Press.

Adler, P. A., and Adler, P. (1983). "Shifts and oscillations in deviant careers: The case of upper-level drug dealers and smugglers." *Social Problems* 31 (2): 195–207.

Atkyns, R. L., and Hanneman, G. J. (1974). "Illicit drug distribution and dealer communication behavior." *Journal of Health and Social Behavior* 15: 36–43.

Becker, H. S. (1963). *Outsiders.* New York: The Free Press.

Blum, R. H., and Associates. (1972). *The Dream Sellers.* San Francisco: Jossey-Bass, Inc.

Bureau of Justice Statistics. (1992). "National Update." Washington, DC: U.S. Department of Justice 1 (3).

———. (1991a). "National Update." Washington, DC: U.S. Department of Justice, 1 (1).

———. (1991b). "Drugs and Crime Facts, 1990." Washington, DC: U.S. Department of Justice, August.

———. (1988a). "Drug Law Violators, 1980–86." Washington, DC: U.S. Department of Justice, June.

———. (1988b). "Profile of state prison inmates, 1986." Washington, DC: U.S. Department of Justice, January.

Drug Trafficking: A Report to the President of the U.S. 1989. A Report Compiled by the U.S. Attorneys and the Attorney General (August 3). Washington, DC: U.S. Department of Justice.

Fields, A. (1986). "Weedslingers: Young black marijuana dealers." In George Beschner and Alfred S. Friedman (eds.), *Teen Drug Use*. Lexington, MA: Lexington Books, pp. 85–104.

———. (1984). "Slinging weed: The social organization of street corner marijuana sales." *Urban Life* 13: 247–270.

Humphries, D. (1993). "Crack mothers, drug wars, and the politics of resentment" in K. D. Tunnell (ed.), *Political Crime in Contemporary America: A Critical Approach*. New York: Garland.

Jenkins, P. (1992). "Fighting drugs, taking liberties: The effects of the drug war." *Chronicles* May: 14–18.

Johnson, B. D., Kaplan, M. A., and Schmeidler, J. (1990). "Days with drug distribution: Which drugs? How many transactions? With what returns?" In Ralph Weisheit (ed.), *Drugs, Crime and the Criminal Justice System*. Cincinnati: Anderson Publishing Company, pp. 193–214.

Langer, J. (1977). "Drug entrepreneurs and dealing culture." *Social Problems* 24: 377–386.

Leib, J., and Olson, S. (1976). "Prestige, paranoia, and profit: On becoming a dealer of illicit drugs in a university community." *Journal of Drug Issues* 6.

Lyman, M. D., and Potter, G. W. (1991). *Drugs in Society*. Cincinnati, Ohio: Anderson.

Matza, D. (1964). *Delinquency and Drift*. New York: John Wiley and Sons.

Mieczkowski, T. (1988). "Studying heroin retailers: A research note." *Criminal Justice Review* 13: 39–44.

———. (1986). "Geeking up and throwing down: Heroin street life in Detroit." *Criminology* 25: 645–666.

Murphy, S., Waldorf, D., and Reinarman, C. (1990). "Drifting into dealing: Becoming a cocaine seller." *Qualitative Sociology* 13(4).

Peele, S. (1985). *The Meaning of Addiction*. Lexington, MA: Lexington Books.

Physicians Desk Reference. (1977). "Product information." Oradell, NJ: Medical Economics Company.

Potter, G., Gaines, L., and Holbrook, B. (1990). "Blowing smoke: An evaluation of marijuana eradication in Kentucky." *American Journal of Police* 9 (1): 97–116.

Preble, E., and Casey, J. J. (1969). "Taking care of business: The heroin user's life on the street." *The International Journal of the Addictions* 4: 1–24.

Redlinger, L. (1975). "Marketing and distributing heroin." *Journal of Psychedelic Drugs* 7: 331–353.

Reiman, J. (1990). *The Rich Get Richer and the Poor Get Prison* (3rd edition). New York: Macmillan.

Reuter, P., and Haaga, J. (1989). *The Organization of High Level Drug Markets: An Exploratory Study*. Santa Monica, CA: Rand.

Trebach, A. S. (1987). *The Great Drug War*. New York: Macmillan.

Tunnell, K. D. (1992). "Film at eleven: Recent developments in the commodification of crime." *Sociological Spectrum* 12 (3): 293–314.

———. (1990). "Property criminals as the lumpen proletariat: A serendipitous finding." *Nature, Society, and Thought* 3 (1): 39–55.

Waldorf, D., Murphy, S., and Lauderback, D. (1989). "Cocaine sellers: Self-reported reasons for stopping cocaine sales." Paper presented to the American Society of Criminology, Reno, Nevada, November.

Weisheit, R. A. (1991). "Domestic marijuana as a growing concern." Paper presented to the Academy of Criminal Justice Sciences, Nashville, March.

Chapter 29
Perceived Risks and Criminal Justice Pressures on Middle-Class Cocaine Dealers

Dan Waldorf
Sheigla Murphy

In this chapter, the authors examine the perceptions of risk and the criminal justice pressures experienced by middle-class cocaine dealers. Waldorf and Murphy dispel the myth that drug dealers are all from lower socioeconomic areas of the community and are deeply involved in the criminal underworld culture. The sample consisted of interviews with 80 ex-cocaine sellers from eight different levels of sales. To be eligible for the study a respondent had to have sold cocaine steadily for at least a year and had to have stopped selling for at least six months. In-depth interviews indicated that these ex-suppliers of cocaine felt that by controlling the network of buyers they could avoid arrest and prosecution. Rather than being concerned about arrest and prosecution, they reported that their major concerns were angry buyers, police informants, and being "ripped off" by other criminals. They recognized that their own drug use and the associated paranoia was of greater concern to them than the sanction threat of the criminal justice system.

Introduction

Despite the pronouncements of successive "drug wars" and extensive efforts by law enforcement agencies, cocaine, in both powdered form and as crack, is readily available to large segments of users in most of the urban centers of the United States. Drug sales has become for many people not only a way to get drugs they might use but also a means to attain some of the All-American dream—house, car and all the attractive consumer goods that are part and parcel of our notions of the "good life." Periodically politicians and criminal justice representatives promise interdiction of supplies by increased funding for narcotics law enforcement, special task forces, and various changes in laws that allow police more latitude to arrest and incarcerate drug sellers. Most recently, changes in laws have taken the forms of new legislation that allows the police to arrest sellers as continuing criminal enterprises (RICO) and allowed prosecutors to confiscate money and property of sellers derived from drug sales prior to actual trials. With the implementation of these two laws it would appear on the surface that risks for drug sellers are becoming greater and greater. And it was [with] this new legislation in mind that we undertook an exploratory, descriptive study of the perceived risks associated with cocaine sales and criminal justice pressures to quit sales. . . .

Perceived Risks of Drug Sales

In general, the study envisioned that perceived risks associated with drug sales could be categorized into eight groupings:

- General Fears of Arrest,
- Fears About Informants,
- Fears About Police Investigations,
- Fears About Confiscations of Property by Police or Other Authorities,
- Fears About Internal Revenue Service Audits,
- Fears About Robbery and Violence,
- Fears Associated with Customers or Suppliers, and
- Unanticipated Risks.

Each category was explored in the in-depth focused interviews with questions that asked how individuals viewed such risks, what were their specific experiences of risks, and what actions were taken to minimize risks. We begin our description with general fears of arrest.

General Fears of Arrest

In general, most respondents realized that there was a general possibility that they might be detected and apprehended by the police for drug sales, but it was not an abiding concern of most of the sellers. In fact, most believed that they could minimize this possibility of arrest by restricting their sales to a small group of friends, people who they work with and associates—people who they have known for some time and were known *not* to be police or persons who would reveal their activities to the police. In short, they believed that they need not fear arrest if they restricted their sales activities to persons they knew and trusted. Here is a typical example of a seller who had little concern about the risks involved in drug sales:

> I didn't think I was at any risk. My biggest risk was when I had to go over and pick up from my dealer. But I didn't think I was at any risk at all when I was selling.

Other persons were more cognizant of how to minimize the risks involved as one kilogram and pound dealer explained:

> Yeah, well I think the major thing is just keep your network closed, you know. If you've got a network, you only expand it to the people that you know and the people that they know. And if they want to buy for them, and if you could afford to give them a deal so they can go sell to their friends, you know . . . and in that way they can start their own small network. I think that was the easiest way. Like I had ten interactive networks going [that he sold to], you know, expanded families type thing.

One way to manage possible risks or to minimize the general possibility of arrest was to establish personal rules about who one would sell cocaine to. For example, an ounce dealer expressed some concerns about traffic in and out of his house to buy cocaine and rules about who he sold to:

> . . . I worried about like traffic, so most of the time I would deliver the product, you know. I kept decent hours, you know, if somebody wanted to come over late at night I refused, you know, I kept control of it pretty much so I wasn't worried in that sense. It's like the police, the only thing that could happen is like somebody introducing you to somebody and just being a little sloppy or a little greedy. If you deal with the same people, or let someone roll over . . . otherwise I think it's really hard for them to legitimately bust you, you know.

Traffic seemed to be an important consideration when sellers dealt out of their homes, most particularly, how neighbors would respond to a large volume of persons coming to and from a house or apartment. The strategies to deal with traffic were various. Some persons delivered the drugs themselves rather than have customers come to their home. Some were sure to locate their homes in areas that had high densities and large natural traffic, rather than live on a suburban cul de sac where traffic would be obvious. Other sellers required that buyers act like friends and other visitors and stay for a period of time, rather than rush in and out. One very outgoing and social pound dealer made it a point of inviting policemen that he knew socially to come to his house to socialize, feeling that if neighbors saw him socializing with the police that they would never suspect that he was a drug seller.

The rule about restricting sales only to persons known by the seller generally works for wholesalers, but is rather difficult to maintain for street and bar dealers. Street and bar dealers contact customers in public places and are more likely to take on new customers that they do not know; therefore, they are anxious to develop new customers and expand their business. Selling cocaine in small units, parts of grams and grams requires a larger number of customers to realize a reasonable profit. If a street or bar seller is ambitious and/or is using his own product too much then he may be less prudent about screening the persons he will sell to. And the less careful you are and more willing you are to develop new customers the more likely you are to sell to an undercover narcotics officer.

Fears About Informants

Cocaine sellers usually know that most arrests for drug sales come as the result of information provided to the police by informants. The use of informants by narcotics police has a long and enduring history for perhaps several reasons: drug sales with the exception of street sales [are] usually clandestine; drug users do not, as a rule, complain to the police about drug sellers; investigations of sellers require a good deal of time and effort; and most undercover police are easily identified as such.

Fears about informants is a particular concern for heroin users who sell cocaine because of ways the police use heroin-addicted informants to gather information. This was illustrated very well by a heroin addict who sold ounces and parts of ounces of cocaine for six years and was arrested only after he went to treatment for his heroin addiction:

> **(R)** Like when I did get busted I had a feeling in the beginning [that something was wrong] and then these guys kept calling. . . .
>
> **(I)** How did you meet that guy, the fisherman?
>
> **(R)** [Through] the one guy that I was in treatment with in the hospital.
>
> **(I)** He introduced you?
>
> **(R)** When he came in the first time, he says I want to come and see you, right, I'm at the bar and they both [two DEA agents] come in and they both look scruffy as hell, they both looked like they just came in, you know, like they both had been fishing in Alaska. And he [the informant] introduces me to the guy and he [the undercover agent] says, "We're fishing in Alaska and I got a chance to make some big money in Alaska and we need some coke," and I said, "Well, I don't do it anymore," and he said, "Well can you get me a quarter gram or something so we can snort now?" So I go down to the end of the bar and get him a quarter gram and that in turn was one of the counts [charges] against me. There were three different counts, it was a pound sale that they got me the last time and then I got a quarter of an ounce the next time they came into the bar and I set it up to get him a quarter of an ounce but he brought this guy in and he leaves the scene. Marty, the guy that I knew, and the other guy came.
>
> **(I)** So the guy in treatment he is an informant?
>
> **(R)** He is a paid informant. Paid informant, that's all. He wasn't in trouble, it's just that he wanted money.
>
> **(I)** Right. And so he introduced the DEA to you?
>
> **(R)** Right. Sure. I mean it's hard when you like somebody and you open up to somebody, I mean you're not thinking of everything you're saying is going to be used against you. I mean this guy had his kids over to the house and I met his family, you know.

Another woman who was selling parts of grams in a Latino community in Oakland expressed similar concerns about an informant. In this case it was her sister-in-law, who became angry with her brother who was selling heroin and informed on him to the police. This police activity against her brother was also viewed as a possible threat to herself.

Again street and bar dealers are also subject to this risk more than larger, more clandestine dealers because of their high visibility and their lack of caution.

Fears About Police Investigation

Fears about a possible police investigation were perceived as a regular risk for most of this group of sellers. This usually took one of two forms. The first form had to do with individuals' cocaine consumption and was most apparent when individuals were abusing the drug. The second form had to do with actual or possible police observations of individual sellers and the people they were associating with.

In the case of the first, fears associated with a seller's own cocaine consumption, there is a general paranoia that accompanies regular and/or heavy use which causes many dealers to imagine possible police surveillance and instigates certain cautions. One female dealer who sold parts of pounds for her lover described this form in combination with concerns about traffic:

> We heard a lot of people say, "Well we know that the cops are watching this house for sure." But sometimes when somebody puts that in your mind that they [the police] can be upstairs . . . like I would walk through the halls and I would be tweaking out and feel like they were following me upstairs . . . stupid sick stuff. But it would make you wonder. You would look outside and you would see figures in other houses across the street. And I would think people were watching me through binoculars. I'm sitting there not moving because I'm tweaked out but that figure would just be there not moving too. Like I thought this lamp was a person that just never left and this person always watched us. It's sick. (Case #042).

Eventually this woman became so cautions about concerns with her neighbors and the fears of being observed by the police that she developed a rather elaborate scheme where she did not allow anyone to come to their house for the drug and she went to considerable trouble to deposit the drug in an airport locker and then sold the key to the locker to the buyers.

Actual police observation was reported by a Latino smuggler who made regular forays to Mexico to bring back kilograms of cocaine which was eventually distributed by persons which he called the "Mexican Mafia."

(I) Do you think that you ever had your phone tapped or they were investigating you at all?

(R) Yeah. For sure they were investigating me at one point. The last part of the year that I was dealing I'm positive of that. I was stopped more than a few times and they were drug agents that were stopping me.

(I) Oh really, in your car?

(R) I think basically because of the association. Like the people that I knew were heavily into it and of course there was always arrests of people like that. You know when they get one person. . . .

(I) When you got stopped what would they do to you?

(R) Just give me a bunch of shit, you know, search me and the vehicle I was in. Feed me a bunch of bullshit.

(I) And you never had any on you?

(R) No, they'd always tell me something like, "We're going to get you. We know what you're doing and you know so and so." And I said, "I don't know that person," And they say, "You know so and so." And I say, "No I don't." They'd say, "Well we seen you with him." I said, "Well, I don't know that person by that name so I don't know who you're talking about." I said, "I have a lot of friends." So they always, you know, the fact that they were watching other people.

Fears About Confiscations of Property by Police or Other Authorities

In general, sellers did not express much concern that police would confiscate their personal property derived from drug sales should they be arrested. Low level sellers did not believe that the police would use that tactic with them because they had so little property that it would not matter to the police. High level sellers knew about the powers of the police to confiscate property and were either careful not to buy property or large conspicuous material items if they could not prove that the purchases came from legal income or did not spend drug money on items that could be confiscated. Only one seller reported that she felt considerable concerns about possible appropriation of her property. She was a long time marijuana and cocaine seller who regularly received kilograms and sold pounds and half-pounds to a small network of eight customers. She became concerned about her property when an old marijuana supplier who she had not done business with for four years was arrested and had all his property confiscated as well as all the property of his parents. Eventually, the parents of the accused regained their property, but the seller never did. Her way of handling the risk was to always work at a legal job and speculate on the stock market so that she had some way of verifying any purchases that she and her husband might make.

Fears About IRS Audits

In general, most sellers who did not work, did not file income tax returns and always dealt in cash. None had any problems with the IRS when they returned to work and filed returns. For persons who worked regularly while they sold cocaine it was seldom an issue, they just reported their legal income and forgot their illegal income. Some of the large sellers had legitimate businesses in which they invested cash and had ways to launder illicit money to make it appear that they earned the money legally.

Fears About Robbery and Violence

When sellers felt comfortable with the persons they were buying or selling cocaine from [or to] they had no particular fears about robberies or violence, but if they felt uncomfortable then it was a very real possibility. There was also some concern about customers revealing their activities to thieves who in turn might rob them. This was a particular concern for some women who dealt on their own, without the assistance of a man.

There were only six mentions of robbery, violence or threats of violence and we will illustrate three. The first is a robbery. A forty-six year old woman, who had worked as a prostitute for twenty years and sold cocaine for four years, reported how she was robbed and both she and her lover were badly beaten by three men.

> I didn't have any drugs in the house. I had some money but I didn't have any drugs and it was about four in the morning and a bunch of people had just left my house and these people [the thieves] must have been waiting outside . . . and there was a knock on the door and I went downstairs and I was really high and the guy knocked on the door and I asked, "Who is it?" He goes, "It's me, open the door," and I thought it was my son. But that was not my son, my son was in his room asleep. And I opened the door and three of them came in with stocking masks on their face

and one of them said, "Let's blow them away now," and then the other one said, "no man, don't do that." And one beat me so bad that they had to shave my whole head. They knocked my old man out and took his jewelry and they got about $1,000 in the envelope that I had just laying around but the rest of my money they didn't get. But they got $1,000 and they pulled a gun on my son and they told him to freeze before they blew his brains out. And I played like I was passed out because I knew if the guy was to pull me outside he was gonna kill me. But when he did that to my son, I didn't care about me anymore. I go, "Please don't hurt my son" and he goes, "We know, we won't hurt your kid." So they left and after that I stopped dealing and I went back to prostitution. And then about a year later I started dealing again and I dealt for about six months and then I stopped.

The second illustration is of a woman who dealt multiple kilograms with her lover until he was murdered. She was not exactly sure if he was killed because of his sales activity, but we were advised by an associate of the woman that the police believed her husband's death was drug-related.

(I) But basically you do believe that his death was drug-connected?

(R) Yeah, it was either someone jealous because they knew he had a lot of money or maybe they . . . it could have been that he was robbed and they could have taken a package that he had that I just didn't know about. Or they could have taken the money because when he got killed I didn't have the money and it wasn't found in his place. So, you know, I don't really know what happened to the money. I don't know. He had been telling me that he wasn't transacting any more business and, you know, there was a time when I tested him because I didn't believe he was really out of the business. So I called him up and I said, "Hey, you know so and so, it will be simple cut and dry," and I'm talking like a $10,000 or $15,000 transaction and a lot of profit for us and he did not do it. I don't know whether he realized I was testing him and he said no or if he was really sincere and was out of the business. But it was either someone robbed him and he lost his life through that or, you know, he had couple little girl friends who didn't want to see him get married. And they could have really been angry and feeling like they had been used and they could have set him up for the robbery, you know, and didn't realize he was gonna get killed too. I really don't know. He was the kind of person who kept a lot of protection around those he love. . . .

Another good illustration of threats of violence was related by a thirty-eight year old black seller who sold pounds of powder and crack to several sellers in San Francisco housing projects. It also illustrates how a gang took over his crack business by use of violence against his network of customers.

(R) Well the thing that really caused me to get out of the business is the fact that . . . the whole process is being organized and organized crime is moving in. Okay they've got the L.A. Crypts [*sic*] that are up here now. . . . Well I started getting some heat and I started getting people beat up on the street and threatened not to come back out there.

(I) So someone knew it was your man.

(R) No, they didn't know it was my man but I mean people were coming back to me saying, "Hey man, somebody robbed me and took all of my shit," or "Somebody told me not to come back out there unless I've got a gun." And the clientele really started to really decline so that's why I got out of it. And you would have to deal with people that, you know, if you turned your back they would steal the white off of your teeth . . . that's when I decided to get out of it and, you know, the people getting killed and robbed and stabbed and I didn't want that around. And I made a couple of enemies too because people would sit up and start getting high and they would want me to give them credit or give them some or something and it's like I'm sorry. Then, you know, they're like, "Well this mother fucker is selling coke up in that house," and before you know it they tell another person and the other person says, "Yeah well he's selling coke and he's got a bunch of freaky women up there," and they keep the story on until it snowballs to where it's I'm selling coke and selling women and selling hot cars and apartments and everything else.

There was a second report of gang activity to take over drug sales by a kilogram/pound dealer who reported that he was approached by a friend of a customer (who vouched for him) about putting together a ten kilogram deal. After he arranged to get the ten kilograms and the transaction was made the customer returned with two others, who were heavily armed, and demanded that he buy back the cocaine, not for the $100,000 for which he sold it for but $150,000. Furthermore, they demanded that he deal with them exclusively in the future and made threats that he could not disregard. His response to this threat was to pay them $150,000, take his family on a long vacation and retire. He was in a position to do this because he had bought several income producing properties and did not need either the trouble or the money from cocaine sales.

Fears Associated With Customers or Suppliers

Customer Fears. Customers of sellers can be a problem for sellers. Very often customers will make unusual demands upon the seller that become irritating—calling at all hours of the day or night, talking about drugs on the telephone, being unable to pay for the drugs that they wish to buy and consume, and as we saw earlier by introducing narcotics police into the network who could pose some threat to the seller.

Freebasers, crack smokers and persons who cannot afford to buy the drugs they are using are considered to be particularly problematic. Sellers usually establish rules to deal with some of these issues, but there is a general rule that many dealers lived by, "Do not make your customers mad at you so they would not drop a dime on you." This usually translated into not turning troublesome customers down when they approached them for cocaine, but telling them that you did not have any cocaine for sale. As one man explained:

> No, not too many deals went bad because we would give more [when customers complained about quality or short weight] . . . we didn't want to have any complaints or hassles. We didn't want anybody to snitch on us, you know.

A white, male gram dealer expressed his problems with customers:

> Being woken up in the middle of the night by phone calls from customers who wanted to score. Having trouble collecting money from people who owed it to me. Having that lead to cutting people off and then having arguments with them about that and then being afraid of retaliation.

Freebasing customers could be particularly problematic as a twenty-nine year old female, black ounce dealer elucidated:

> **(R)** Well the people around me, the people who were buying from me, were getting a little bit weird . . . a lot of people started basing and I didn't want any part of that or feel like I was contributing to that.
>
> **(I)** How about the friends you were hanging with?
>
> **(R)** They started using a lot more too, you know. . . . They wanted more and asking for more and wanting to base and stuff and it just started getting out of control and when it's out of control it's bad and you run more of a risk of getting busted when it's out of control. . . .
>
> **(I)** So did you just suddenly say you were going to quit?
>
> **(R)** It started building up in me and then one day I just said this is it. I think I went and bought some more and paid off the last one and I said this is it. But I didn't tell my connection that or anybody else. . . . Made one more cop and cleaned it out, paid the man and I said that's it for me.

Some sellers have continuing problems with customers and found them to be extremely troublesome to deal with:

> **(R)** Well as I learned how difficult coke fiends are to deal with, when it come to money and their reliability and how they will transgress on your life in order to get their powder, and you see people in really bad shape coming to you with nothing, you know, with fantastic stories of how they can pay you later cause something has happened to them, they just sold a screenplay or, you know, all this weird stuff they're telling you so you can front them just a few lines of blow, cause they're jones'n [addicted]. And seeing that too often and then having people who were real nice to me when I had blow and when I didn't have any or wouldn't sell to them, have them scream at me and threaten me, and I think well Jeez, I don't want this guy to be picked up by the police. . . .
>
> **(I)** Yeah. Did you have a lot of bad customers?
>
> **(R)** . . . No, no, they aren't actually all bad customers, no. No, I sold many times without any problems at all.
>
> **(I)** But there were some bad customers. What did bad customers do?
>
> **(R)** They would call you at any hour of the night, okay, to see if you had something. They might show up at your door, any hour of the day or night, whether or not the lights were on then knock on the door to see if you just went to bed, maybe you

just went to bed, "I was seeing if you just went to bed," it's 3:30. . . . So they're extremely egotistical and uhhh, and oh just coke fiends. Often they had no money at all, and would have all these stories they could pay you later and sometimes they are friends of yours and you figure you can front them the stuff, then each one of your friends always owes you $25 for the latest quarter and you're out a few $100. . . . It strains relationships too. Cause you're letting their drug problem, their inability to pay for their drugs, put you out.

Most sellers try to develop rules in dealing with customers; rules that will provide structure to the transactions much the same way shop keepers have rules about when businesses will be conducted, who will be given credit, etc.:

> . . . I only sold to the people that I knew and they knew they weren't suppose to bring anybody to my house, not even parked outside or anything like that. . . . Yeah, and they knew that they shouldn't call me after ten and if they did my machine was usually on.

One gram dealer who had a number of troublesome customers had a particularly good tactic for dealing with them. He sold them very heavily diluted cocaine and they did not return. Upon getting his supply he would organize it into three baggies—his own personal stash which was not cut, a cut supply for good customers, and a very heavily cut supply for customers he wished to stop selling to. The tactic worked every time. Suppliers were plentiful and customers would not return to a seller that sold them low-quality drugs. His customers were persons who would not come back and demand their money back and the tactic seemed to work for nonviolent customers, but by no means are all customers nonviolent.

Supplier or Connection Fears. Some large sellers were potentially violent, but most sellers were not fearful of connections unless they had problems paying for drugs that were being fronted. Again, freebasers and persons who injected the drug were particularly vulnerable to threats from connections when they could not make payments for fronted drugs. One ounce dealer, who was also an injector of both heroin and cocaine, told of one incident he had with an old friend who was connected to "the mob" and supplied him with large supplies from Miami.

> **(I)** You didn't feel any risks with the mob?
>
> **(R)** No, well one time I owed them money. I think I was into them for about four or five grand and I get a phone call and, uh, they are at the Miami airport. . . . Perry who I would only see at his home in Fort Lauderdale, uh, my old roommate from years that past says me and Frank . . . are on our way out here. Now I owed him like, I don't know, four or five thousand and I don't have any money on me and I don't have any coke and they want me to rent them a car and they'll be here in five hours right so I get real nervous but at that time I was using a lot of drugs and strung out on heroin. . . . So I'm loaded, so I got the car with a credit card and I met them at the airport and we drive like two miles outside the airport and Perry tells me to pull over and I go "Oh shit," you know, and I am thinking, "Get in the fuckin' trunk," right and we get out and he slaps me, you know, not hard, you know, "Hey you fucked up and don't do it again, okay," and I say, "Okay." . . . And after that they proceeded to give me like three or four pounds of cocaine and I mean I don't know, I just beat them for like $4,000 and he slaps me in the face and you do it again I'm going to hurt you, that's what he said, "If you do it again I'm going to hurt you, now take care of business," you know.

A second case, a smuggler, told us that he regularly shaved off five or six ounces from kilograms that he smuggled across the Mexican border. He used these purloined supplies for his own rather outrageous freebasing sessions. Eventually the persons who financed his Mexican forays discovered the shortage and approached him about it. He denied the pilferage, but felt that he was in real danger of being shot or killed. He eventually convinced them that he did not do it, but felt that he only got away with it because he was related to one of the major financiers. Eventually when his own use began to get out of control the group simply cut him off from all money and supplies.

Unanticipated Risks

To our surprise we found only one person who did not use the product he sold. This man is an ex-convict (and was one of the models of John Irwin's "straight raised youth" in his book *The Felon*) who has seldom used drugs other than alcohol even though he always had access to them, even in prison. While in San Quentin prison he was the cellmate of an infamous addict (who has gone on to become a well-known novelist and movie script writer) who always had heroin and other drugs smuggled into prison, but the respondent never used heroin or cocaine himself. He was literally allergic to cocaine so he never had any problems with his own consumption of the drug. He remarked that he was in a perfect position to sell cocaine since he never used it.

Many persons found that their personal use got completely out of control so that it either cut down on their profits or they had trouble meeting their debts to suppliers who were fronting them supplies. For example: one woman who sold for ten years and did very well when she only snorted the drug became a compulsive user and an unreliable seller when she began to freebase it:

> **(R)** . . . let me tell you what happened. When I started freebasing, I started losing money, you know, but the people that I was involved with and I had been involved with the same people for so many years they could not believe that I wasn't capable of doing it anymore. So they kept giving me these amounts of drugs, you know, half-pounds, you know. And then they'd cut it down and I would end up with part of their money and not all of their money. Then they gave quarter pounds and would come back with hardly no money but, I mean, the average person would have been dead because they would have been killed probably. But by me knowing them since I was like nineteen or twenty years old and I had been dealing with them for so long and I'm sure I probably made them a lot of money too as well as for myself . . . they kept trying it but I kept slipping backwards. After awhile . . . after I started basing I tried to sell it for about a year after that and I couldn't. I just went so far in debt.
>
> **(I)** Okay now let's talk about the circumstances that caused you to make a decision to stop selling. What caused you to come to that decision to stop selling cocaine?
>
> **(R)** My own use. Freebasing. When I was using and selling, well, when I was snorting and selling cocaine, you know, I made money and I didn't have any pressure. Because like I said, over the years I had built my clientele to where they were all very close to me. Everything that I did worked out fine. . . . But in my head to quit selling cocaine completely was when I knew I couldn't handle it anymore and I couldn't make it pay . . . do you understand? It was costing me too much. Everything I had lost, just everything that I had. I tried to obtain more and the more I would try to climb the farther I would slip back. And it became a problem when I started freebasing cocaine because it gave such a craving that you can't stop. Whatever you have, whatever you're doing, whatever money you've got, you're gonna spend it. I haven't seen anyone do any different either.

Another twenty-four year old student ounce dealer, reported similar problems of being out of control, losing the confidence of his suppliers and physical problems:

> **(R)** My own use was getting way out of hand and I was real skinny and way undernourished and I couldn't even stay awake anymore because I was . . . physically fatigued and I couldn't even keep my eyes open . . . so exhausting. I've been more tired from a night of bingeing than I could have ever been from back packing for two weeks and hiking one hundred miles a day. That's when my grades dropped in school because I was too tired for school, too tired to do anything. I would spend a lot of time in the shower or trying to suck some food down just to be somewhat nourished.
>
> **(I)** So when you did decide to quit, what did you do? Did you leave the scene or did you get out for awhile?
>
> **(R)** Well it also kind of happened the same time when my dealers weren't trusting me anymore. I was getting out of hand and not paying the debts fast enough and finally I think they got nervous. They were getting bigger and they had other customers so they didn't need me really as much anymore. And so they were kind of giving me the cold shoulder and cutting me out. And they were tired of me scaring them because I was scaring them to death. . . . I was getting too out of hand.

With only a few exceptions most persons who sold cocaine tended to use it very heavily and with heavy use came various unanticipated physical and psychological problems. There were of course certain variations among users, in the ways that they used the drug, but it was a very common occurrence for sellers to have myriad problems with their own use.

One man who was a very heavy drinker as well as a prodigious user of cocaine reported that he nearly died of peritonitis while he was using and selling cocaine.

One young, female pound dealer became anorexic with her heavy use and had to go to the hospital with a urinary infection:

> **(R)** I was like anorexic. I probably ate ten times that year or maybe more like twelve times, like once a month. No really, I would not eat. I would maybe eat a bag of potato chips and that would keep me going for three days. Then I would sleep and I would wake up and I might have a piece of toast . . . would be sick all the time. I would be nauseous, faint. . . . I had a constant cough that year and I would always be able to cough up black stuff.
>
> **(I)** So no serious illness?
>
> **(R)** No, the urinary infection was serious. I got to the point where I couldn't walk and I bled. . . . I thought I was on my period for a full month and I knew something was going on. I put it off for another week and it was a urinary infection that went into my kidneys and it was in my back and I was bent over . . . and I was so thin and weak I just had to stay like that until they took me to the hospital. I was too weak to even pull myself up. I was just drained and I had no color. I had these big black things on my face and they would peel. Oh God. . . .

Criminal Justice Pressures

Our exploration of criminal justice pressures to stop selling cocaine were conceived as being of two types—direct and indirect criminal justice pressures. The first was pretty obvious—an arrest for some violation of the law, either drug related or not. Indirect pressures were a little more complicated—arrest of someone from a supplier's network, arrest of someone from a customer network, arrest of a drug selling partner, fears of being investigated by the police and fears of going to prison.

In general, the majority of ex-sellers we interviewed reported that they did not experience any criminal justice pressures to quit, neither direct nor indirect. Forty-eight persons or 60% of the eighty respondents reported that they did not experience any criminal [justice] pressures to quit. Of the remaining thirty-two who reported some pressures, sixteen (20%) said that they stopped selling because of some arrest, the majority of which was for sales and possession; and sixteen (20%) reported indirect pressures to quit.

Direct Pressures

The most direct criminal justice pressure, as might be expected, was arrest for sales and possession of cocaine and six persons were arrested for sales and possession. Another four were arrested for possession of cocaine with intent to sell, one for possession only and another two for possession of other illicit drugs.

One kilogram and pound dealer was arrested after being stopped for a traffic violation and the police officer discovered that there was an outstanding warrant for his arrest in Nevada on a conspiracy charge. The respondent hired a well-known criminal lawyer and was finally released from the charge when the prosecutor's file was lost. Both the respondent and the interviewer, who has known this man for six years, believed that the attorneys had arranged to have the file stolen by someone in the prosecutor's office. As a result of the arrest the respondent lost his customers, they stayed away from him while he was awaiting trial, and never did resume sales when the charges were dropped.

Three respondents were arrested for other crimes: one for driving under the influence, another for assault, and a third turned himself into the police for check forgery under the pressure of his live-in girl friend.

Indirect Criminal Justice Pressures

Indirect pressures to stop sales could take several forms, as we mentioned earlier. The most common form was arrest of someone from a supplier's network; ten people gave such responses. A good illustration of this was the case of a forty-year-old ounce dealer who sold cocaine on and off for six years. In general, she was very careful about restricting her sales to a small group of customers that she knew and trusted, but her major connection, who drank very heavily, was not as careful. Just prior to her voluntary retirement two incidents happened.

The first incident involved four thieves masquerading as police who broke into her connection's house, held him, his wife and two children at gun point and stole $30,000 and approximately a pound of cocaine. Three weeks later police contacted the wife of the connection and told her that they knew that her husband was selling cocaine and asked for their cooperation in identifying the gang. Both agreed to help the police, but could not identify anyone in a police line up. The connection continued to sell despite the protests of his wife.

The second incident occurred one month later. Whenever the connection went out of town she assumed delivery to several of his suppliers in the South Bay. On this occasion she was out of town herself, taking her children to a Girl Scout camping outing, and an associate took over the tasks of delivery. The associate was arrested with several ounces and the respondent believed that had she made the delivery the same thing would have happened to her. She decided that it was time to quit selling shortly thereafter.

A second illustration is the account of a forty-six year old pound dealer who regularly traded guns for pounds and kilograms of cocaine. The guns were not military weapons, but rifles and pistols that were eventually smuggled to Mexico by his connection who was said to be part of the "Mexican Mafia."

> **(I)** What were the circumstances of your decision to quit selling?
>
> **(R)** Well the circumstances is that this whole network seemed to have gotten busted and I haven't heard from any of them in about thirteen or fourteen months.
>
> **(I)** So your connection dried up.

One stock-broker seller told an unusual story about his growing concerns about being arrested, a portentous dream he had that his whole supplier's network was arrested and his subsequent decision to retire from drug sales:

> **(R)** I don't remember any significant changes until I started feeling that these people [his connections] are sloppy. And there is a lot of busts going down, and I suggested to them [his suppliers] several times that they cool the activities and let this storm [possible arrests] that is obviously coming blow over and we will see how the waters are at that point but everyone else was really into it and so I pretty much pulled the plug on it. And I also had these dreams. I had this dream three times it was like the movie, "Little Big Man" where I had certain morality play . . . but the bottom line was that I kept dreaming that everybody got caught. And, uh, and the vividness where it took place and what happened and how it went down it was like playing a video tape. It was the same dream three times. Well I had stopped dealing [regularly], . . . somebody had asked me to pick something up for them and this was a very important guy. . . .
>
> **(I)** You are saying that you stopped dealing already?
>
> **(R)** These were the one occasions where I would say, "Okay at my convenience I will do this for you." I think I did it once or twice. And one time there was this painting crew at the house next door [to the connection] and they were there painting. . . . I think I made three trips in four days or five days and this fuckin' crew of painters was there for five days and there were about nine guys. I mean you could have painted a Taj Mahal in five days. And I said, "I don't like this at all." I mean they had this van parked out there and nobody had paint on them and they were all standing around and doing their stuff and I don't know what was going on. I expected that they were filming everybody walking in and I don't know what the hell they were doing but it was weird and it scared me a little bit.
>
> And another time I went back, there was a cement truck there. I went back in the morning and my dealer was not there he blew an appointment on me. And I went back later that day and there was the same cement truck, the license plate was the same. The cement pump truck had been there for eight hours and he would have to be pumping it by the shovel full to be there that long. And nobody rents a cement truck that long, I mean it just didn't make any sense . . . anyway there was two circumstances there that I felt very uncomfortable about.
>
> I was able to cover my going in and out in front of these people because I had luckily met the nurse that lived upstairs and ran into her one day and ran into her roommate the other day and introduced myself and talked and stuff like that in front of these people. And I felt fortunate well there is a sly cover there and maybe they think I'm here to see the nurse on floor 2 instead of [the] dealer on floor 3. . . . So a couple of weeks later I'm coming back from Tahoe on the behalf of these people that I decided to make an exception for and I phoned [the connection] and phoned and nobody is there. And, uh, then I picked up the newspaper and there is everybody in a drawing. They picked up so many people they are all being arraigned in a jury box 'cause there are so many of them and I said, "The heat's gone done."
>
> **(I)** Your people?
>
> **(R)** My people and all of their North Bay connections and all of the lower people in

the Haight. Everything blew over and around, and somehow I ducked and I missed it all.

(I) So your dream came true, everybody got busted but you.

(R) And they didn't finger me. By that time I'd been out [of it] for a few months and they didn't see me on a weekly basis or any kind of regular basis. I was the drop-in.

Arrest of Customers

Indirect pressures stemming from the arrest of customers was not reported as a reason to stop selling cocaine. When customers were arrested sellers usually denied them all access, refused to take phone calls, refused to sell to them and generally avoided them.

Arrest of Business Partners

Arrest of drug selling partners was viewed as indirect pressure and was reported by two cases. One was a woman who sold ounces and parts of ounces for four years and who at one point financed two lesbian friends to go to South America to smuggle cocaine into the United States. The two eventually became regular and reliable connections for the respondent. This woman's partner (another woman) was arrested for possession of one gram of cocaine was judged to be guilty and served six months in a county jail. During her imprisonment she suffered considerable psychological distress and her hair turned gray. . . . The respondent thought that the sentence was severe and, noting the effect it had upon her partner, she decided to stop using and stop selling herself.

Another woman who sold kilograms and pounds and was closely associated with Colombian smugglers stopped her activities when the DEA arrested fifteen persons in her supplier and customer network, one of whom was her brother-in-law. When she was not arrested herself, other Colombians in the supply network threatened her and others with violence to make sure that they did not reveal information to the DEA.

Police Investigations

Only two cases reported that they stopped selling cocaine because of an imminent police investigation. One woman first sold marijuana for three years and when the price of marijuana was increasing she and her lover decided to move on to cocaine. Initially, they traded marijuana for cocaine, but eventually they found a good supply for high quality cocaine and began to buy three or four kilograms a month. They sold it to a small group of eight trusted customers who would buy pounds, half-pounds and ounces.

Early in their transition from marijuana to cocaine sales she was arrested by the police for possession of marijuana after a police informant directed narcotic officers to her home with the information that they sold cocaine. The police did not find the cocaine that was hidden there, but they did find several ounces of marijuana. She remained in jail over a weekend, plead guilty to the charge, and was sentenced to a diversion program which she described as a joke. "The counselor regularly asked me to score for him and tried to convince me to give up my marijuana use by utilizing meditation techniques."

Upon being released from jail she and her boyfriend (who she eventually married) moved to a new location and kept selling both drugs but at a reduced rate. Gradually they increased their business and began to make regular money, but she continued to work throughout the whole time that they sold cocaine. During the last year of their cocaine-selling career they learned that an old marijuana supplier who lived in Arizona had been arrested by the police and was being prosecuted. Police confiscated the supplier's property and began to arrest other customers of the supplier. Although they had not done business with the old supplier in a number of years, they began to feel that they might be investigated themselves. To avoid possible investigation they moved a second time to a town in another county and were careful not to give out their new address and telephone number to any of their old associates. At the time her husband was using the drug very heavily and experiencing paranoid ideation about the investigation. Both became fearful that the police were imminent and decided to cut back on their sales activity. Six months later after she took on a new more responsible job [and] separated from her husband, they both stopped selling completely.

Fears of Re-Arrest or Imprisonment

Two respondents reported that they stopped selling because of fears of re-arrest or imprisonment. Sellers who had previous convictions for drug sales and possession and/or were ex-convicts who had a good deal to lose if they were re-arrested had considerable fears about going to or returning to prison. This naturally acted as an indirect pressure on some to stop selling. One ex-convict illustrated this type of indirect pressure very well. He had a long and checkered arrest history from an early age and had spent ten years in San Quentin and Folsom prisons and had no desire to return. Prior to going to prison he had sold various types of drugs—opiates, cocaine, barbiturates, amphetamines. After serving his last prison term he built a small but profitable contracting business and managed to change his life considerably. He was a regular user of marijuana and on occasion he used cocaine. When cocaine became more plentiful he undertook selling ounces and parts of ounces to a very small network of friends to finance his own and his wife's use. He knew his connection very well, she was the best friend of his wife, so he had no fears on her part. He never allowed customers to bring any strangers into the house and on one instance when it happened he became livid with the culprit.

In general, he felt he had too much to lose if he were arrested and this acted as continuing indirect pressure on him to limit the scope of his sales activities. Eventually he decided to stop when his connection stopped selling and he did not seek any other sources, even though two others were available to him.

Other Reasons to Stop Selling Drugs

There are of course other pressures exerted on sellers to stop—pressures from family, spouses/lovers, friends and children that can be just as effective, though not as obvious, as criminal justice pressures. There are as well other reasons why drug sellers stop selling. Some are simply inept as sellers, some can not meet the financial responsibilities of fronted supplies, some have severe physical and psychological problems with their own drug abuse. Some do not view drug sales as an enduring career and go into other illegal occupations.

Summary

The general possibility of arrest for sales was perceived by middle-class ex-cocaine sellers as a risk that most could minimize by restricting their selling activities to small networks of persons that they knew and trusted. Such a possibility was not an abiding concern, but very clearly sellers put themselves at risk when they sold to strangers or people who were not personally known by the seller. Sellers were generally more concerned about disgruntled customers, informants and possible rip-offs and violence than they were of police investigations, possible confiscation of personal property by the police and IRS audits and investigations.

Heavy abuse of their product causes many persons to become generally paranoid about their drug sales and to maintain some caution about customer traffic and possible police surveillance. Abuse also causes many to experience unanticipated physical and psychological problems with the drug which are important factors in their reasons to stop sales.

Criminal justice pressures, either direct or indirect, were not a particularly recurrent factor in this sample's accounts of their decisions to stop selling cocaine. More than half reported that they felt no criminal justice pressures at all to stop sales. Of those who reported pressures there was near equal percentages of direct and indirect pressures. The most frequently mentioned indirect pressure to stop was an arrest of a member of a supply network.

Questions for Thought and Discussion

1. By what method(s) did the cocaine dealers in this study minimize their risk of arrest?
2. In what ways do the dealers in this study resemble those in the study by Patricia Adler (Chapter 21)?
3. What were the risks of dealing that most concerned the dealers in this study? Why?
4. What theory or theories of criminal behavior are illustrated by this research?

References

Becker, H. S. 1953. Becoming a marijuana user. *American Journal of Sociology* 59:235–42.

Biernacki, P. 1986. *Pathways From Heroin Addiction.* Philadelphia: Temple University Press.

Biernacki, P. and D. Waldorf. 1981. Snowball sampling: Problems and techniques of chain referral sampling. *Sociological Methods and Research* 10:141–63.

Feldman, H. W. 1968. Ideological supports to becoming . . . and remaining a heroin addict. *Journal of Health and Social Behavior* 9:131–9.

Irwin, J. 1970. *The Felon.* Englewood Cliffs, N.J.: Prentice Hall.

Lindesmith, A. 1968. *Addiction and Opiates.* Chicago: Aldine.

Preble, E. and J. H. Casey, Jr. 1969. Taking care of business—the heroin users' life on streets. *The International Journal of the Addictions* 4:1–24.

Waldorf, D., S. Murphy, C. Reinarman, and B. Joyce. 1977. Doing coke: An ethnography of cocaine users and sellers. Washington, D.C.: Drug Abuse Council, Inc.

Waldorf, D., C. Reinarman, and S. Murphy. 1991. *Cocaine Changes: The Experience of Using and Quitting.* Philadelphia: Temple Univ. Press.

Section IX

Quitting Crime

Do criminals continue their careers over a lifetime? Do they desist at some point or begin to engage in less serious offenses? What motivates causes these changes in criminal activity? Desistance has been a controversial topic in criminology. Research has generally shown a decline in criminal activity as offenders age.

This final section contains studies in which researchers have delved into the dynamics of desistance, attempting to learn from the offenders themselves the factors which lead to "quitting crime."

In the first selection, "Getting Out of the Life: Crime Desistance by Female Street Offenders," Sommers, Baskin, and Fagan study how women offenders attempt to leave their past criminal existence and live a more conventional life. Their research found that fear of punishment was the primary dynamic in this attempted transition.

In the next selection, "Aging Criminals: Changes in the Criminal Calculus," Shover's research reveals that as offenders get older two factors have significant impact on their lives: (1) development of conventional social bonds, and (2) strengthened resolve to abandon crime entirely or to restrict their criminal activities. Other factors related to desistance identified by Shover include a greater interest in the rewards of a noncriminal lifestyle and a more rational decision making process. The risk-gain calculus employed by criminals tends to shift as they age and mature, exhibiting a greater concern with the possibility of apprehension and punishment.

Finally, Shukla discusses desistance from marijuana use ("An Examination of Decision Making and Desistance From Marijuana Use." She found that four categories of factors influenced desistance from marijuana use: lifestyle activities, social considerations, health concerns, and availability. ✦

Chapter 30
Getting Out of the Life

Crime Desistance by Female Street Offenders

Ira Sommers
Deborah R. Baskin
Jeffrey Fagan

This selection considers the role of life events and the relationship of cognitions and life situations to the desistance process. The authors are concerned with whether the social and psychological processes and the events leading up to their desistance from crime vary by gender. In other words, do men and women differ in the processes and events which bring them to the decision to give up crime?

The authors constructed a sample of 30 women. Initially, 16 subjects were recruited through various drug and alcohol treatment programs in New York. An additional 14 women were obtained through a chain of referrals process. To be included in the sample, a woman had to have had at least one official arrest for a violent street crime and to have desisted from crime for at least two years prior to the study. Life history interviews were conducted by the first two authors. Each interview lasted approximately two hours.

The subjects had engaged in a wide range of criminal activities. Eighty-seven percent were addicted to crack, 63 percent had been involved in robberies, 60 percent had committed burglaries, 94 percent had sold drugs, and 47 percent had at some time been involved in prostitution. The mean number of prior incarcerations was three.

The authors found that the reasons for desistance from crime were remarkably similar to those found for men. Like the male subjects in Shover's (1985, Chapter 31 in this volume) desistance study, the women in this study had begun to take the threat of incarceration seriously and attempted to reestablish links with conventional society while severing relationships in the deviant subculture.

Studies over the past decade have provided a great deal of information about the criminal careers of male offenders. (See Blumstein et al. 1986 and Weiner and Wolfgang 1989 for reviews.) Unfortunately, much less is known about the initiation, escalation, and termination of criminal careers by female offenders. The general tendency to exclude female offenders from research on crime and delinquency may be due, at least in part, to the lower frequency and comparatively less serious nature of offending among women. Recent trends and studies, however, suggest that the omission of women may seriously bias both research and theory on crime.

Although a growing body of work on female crime has emerged within the last few years, much of this research continues to focus on what Daly and Chesney-Lind (1988) called generalizability and gender-ratio problems. The former concerns the degree to which traditional (i.e., male) theories of deviance and crime apply to women, and the latter focuses on what explains gender differences in rates and types of criminal activity. Although this article also examines women in crime, questions of inter- and intragender variability in crime are not specifically addressed. Instead, the aim of the paper is to describe the pathways out of deviance for a sample of women who have significantly invested themselves in criminal social worlds. To what extent are the social and psychological processes of stopping criminal behavior similar for men and women? Do the behavioral antecedents of such processes vary by gender? These questions remained unexplored.

Specifically, two main issues are addressed in this paper: (1) the role of life events in triggering the cessation process, and (2) the relationship between cognitive and life situation changes in the desistance process. First, the crime desistance literature is reviewed briefly. Second, the broader deviance literature is drawn upon to construct a social-psychological model of cessation. Then the model is evaluated using life history data from a sample of female offenders convicted of serious street crimes.

The Desistance Process

The common themes in the literature on exiting deviant careers offer useful perspectives for developing a theory of cessation. The decision to stop deviant behavior appears to be preceded by a variety of factors, most of which are negative social sanctions or consequences. Health problems, difficulties with the law or with maintaining a current lifestyle, threats of other social sanctions from family or close relations, and a general rejection of the social world in which the behaviors thrive are often antecedents of the decision to quit. For some, religious conversions or immersion into alternative sociocultural settings with powerful norms (e.g., treatment ideology) provide paths for cessation (Mulvey and LaRosa 1986; Stall and Biernacki 1986).

. . . A model for understanding desistance from crime is presented below. Three stages characterize the cessation process: building resolve or discovering motivation to stop (i.e., socially disjunctive experiences), making and publicly disclosing the decision to stop, and maintaining the new behaviors and integrating into new social networks (Stall and Biernacki 1986 . . .). These phases . . . describe three ideal-typical phases of desistance: "turning points" where offenders begin consciously to experience negative effects (socially disjunctive experiences); "active quitting" where they take steps to exit crime (public pronouncement); and "maintaining cessation" (identity transformation):

***Stage 1* Catalysts for change**

Socially disjunctive experiences

- Hitting rock bottom
- Fear of death
- Tiredness
- Illness

Delayed deterrence

- Increased probability of punishment
- Increased difficulty in doing time
- Increased severity of sanctions
- Increasing fear

Assessment

- Reappraisal of life and goals
- Psychic change

Decision

- Decision to quit and/or initial attempts at desistance
- Continuing possibility of criminal participation

***Stage 2* Discontinuance**

- Public pronouncement of decision to end criminal participation
- Claim to a new social identity

***Stage 3* Maintenance of the decision to stop**

- Ability to successfully renegotiate identity
- Support of significant others
- Integration into new social networks
- Ties to conventional roles
- Stabilization of new social identity

Stage 1: Catalysts for Change

When external conditions change and reduce the rewards of deviant behavior, motivation may build to end criminal involvement. That process, and the resulting decision, seem to be associated with two related conditions: a series of negative, aversive, unpleasant experiences with criminal behavior, or corollary situations where the positive rewards, status, or gratification from crime are reduced. Shover and Thompson's (1992) research suggests that the probability of desistance from criminal participation increases as expectations for achieving rewards (e.g., friends, money, autonomy) via crime decrease and that changes in expectations are age-related. Shover (1983) contended that the daily routines of managing criminal involvement become tiring and burdensome to aging offenders. Consequently, the allure of crime diminishes as offenders get older. Aging may also increase the perceived formal risk of criminal participation. Cusson and Pinsonneault (1986, 76) posited that "with age, criminals raise their estimates of the certainty of punishment." Fear of reimprisonment, fear of longer sentences, and the increasing difficulty of "doing time" have often been reported by investigators who have explored desistance.

Stage 2: Discontinuance

The second stage of the model begins with the public announcement that the offender has decided to end her criminal participation. Such an announcement forces the start of a process of renegotiation of the offender's social identity (Stall and Biernacki 1986). After this announcement, the offender must not only cope with the instrumental aspects (e.g., financial) of her life but must also begin to redefine important emotional and social relationships that are influenced by or predicated upon criminal behavior.

Leaving a deviant subculture is difficult. Biernacki (1986) noted the exclusiveness of the social involvements maintained by former addicts during initial stages of abstinence. With social embedment comes the gratification of social acceptance and identity. The decision to end a behavior that is socially determined and supported implies withdrawal of the social gratification it brings. Thus, the more deeply embedded in a criminal social context, the more dependent the offender is on that social world for her primary sources of approval and social definition.

The responses by social control agents, family members, and peer supporters to further criminal participation are critical to shaping the outcome of discontinuance. New social and emotional worlds to replace the old ones may strengthen the decision to stop. Adler (1992) found that outside associations and involvements provide a critical bridge back into society for dealers who have decided to leave the drug subculture. With discontinuance comes the difficult work of identity transformations (Biernacki 1986) and establishing new social definitions of behavior and relationships to reinforce them.

Stage 3: Maintenance

Following the initial stages of discontinuance, strategies to avoid a return to crime build on the strategies first used to break from a lengthy pattern of criminal participation: further integration into a noncriminal identity and social world and maintenance of this new identity. Maintenance depends in part on replacing deviant networks of peers and associates with supports that both censure criminal participation and approve of new nondeviant beliefs. Treatment interventions (e.g., drug treatment, social service programs) are important sources of alternative social supports to maintain a noncriminal lifestyle. In other words, maintenance depends on immersion into a social world where criminal behavior meets immediately with strong formal and informal sanctions.

Despite efforts to maintain noncriminal involvement, desistance is likely to be episodic, with occasional relapses interspersed with lengthening of lulls in criminal activity. Le Blanc and Frechette (1989) proposed the possibility that criminal activity slows down before coming to an end and that this slowing down process becomes apparent in three ways: deceleration, specialization, and reaching a ceiling. Thus, before stopping criminal activity, the offender gradually acts out less frequently, limits the variety of crimes more and more, and ceases increasing the seriousness of criminal involvement.

Age is a critical variable in desistance research, regardless of whether it is associated with maturation or similar developmental concepts. Cessation is part of a social-psychological transformation for the offender. A strategy to stabilize the transition to a noncriminal lifestyle requires active use of supports to maintain the norms that have been substituted for the forces that supported criminal behavior in the past.

Findings

Resolving to Stop

Despite its initial excitement and allure, the life of a street criminal is a hard one. A host of severe personal problems plague most street offenders and normally become progressively worse as their careers continue. In the present study, the women's lives were dominated by a powerful, often incapacitating, need for drugs. Consequently, economic problems were the most frequent complaint voiced by the respondents. Savings were quickly exhausted, and the culture of addiction justified virtually any means to get money to support their habits. For the majority of the women, the problem of maintaining an addiction took precedence over other interests and participation in other social worlds.

People the respondents associated with, their primary reference group, were involved in illicit behaviors. Over time, the women in the study became further enmeshed in deviance and further alienated, both socially and psychologically, from conventional life. The women's lives became bereft of conventional involvements, obligations, and responsibilities. The excitement at the lifestyle that may have characterized their early criminal career phase gave way to a much more grave daily existence.

Thus, the women in our study could not and did not simply cease their deviant acts by "drifting" (Matza 1964) back toward conventional norms, values, and lifestyles. Unlike many of Waldorf's (1983) heroin addicts who drifted away from heroin without conscious effort, all of the women in our study made a conscious decision to stop. In short, Matza's concept of drift did not provide a useful framework for understanding our respondents' exit from crime.

The following accounts illustrate the uncertainty and vulnerability of street life for the women in our sample. Denise, a 33-year-old black woman, has participated in a wide range of street crimes including burglary, robbery, assault, and drug dealing. She began dealing drugs when she was 14 and was herself using cocaine on a regular basis by age 19.

> I was in a lot of fights: So I had fights over, uh, drugs, or, you know, just manipulation. There's a lot of manipulation in that life. Everybody's tryin' to get over. Everybody will stab you in your back, you know. Nobody gives a fuck about the next person, you know. It's just when you want it, you want it. You know, when you want that drug, you know, you want that drug. There's a lot of lyin', a lot of manipulation. It's, it's, it's crazy!

Gazella, a 38-year-old Hispanic woman, had been involved in crime for 22 years when we interviewed her.

> I'm 38 years old. I ain't no young woman no more, man. Drugs have changed, lifestyles have changed. Kids are killing you now for turf. Yeah, turf, and I was destroyin' myself. I was miserable. I was . . . I was gettin' high all the time to stay up to keep the business going, and it was really nobody I could trust.

Additional illustrations of the exigencies of street life are provided by April and Stephanie. April is a 25-year-old black woman who had been involved in crime since she was 11.

> I wasn't eating. Sometimes I wouldn't eat for two or three days. And I would . . . a lot of times I wouldn't have the time, or I wouldn't want to spend the money to eat—I've got to use it to get high.

Stephanie, a 27-year-old black woman, had used and sold crack for 5 years when we interviewed her.

> I knew that, uh, I was gonna get killed out here. I wasn't havin' no respect for myself. No one else was respecting me. Every relationship I got into, as long as I did drugs, it was gonna be constant disrespect involved, and it come . . . to the point of me gettin' killed.

When the spiral down finally reached its lowest point, the women were overwhelmed by a sense of personal despair. In reporting the early stages of this period of despair, the respondents consistently voiced two themes: the futility of their lives and their isolation.

Barbara, a 31-year-old black woman, began using crack when she was 23. By age 25, Barbara had lost her job at the Board of Education and was involved in burglary and robbery. Her account is typical of the despair the women in our sample eventually experienced.

> . . . the fact that my family didn't trust me anymore, and the way that my daughter was looking at me, and, uh, my mother wouldn't let me in her house any more, and I was sleepin' on the trains. And I was sleepin' on the beaches in the summertime. And I was really frightened. I was real scared of the fact that I had to sleep on the train. And, uh, I had to wash up in the Port Authority.

The spiral down for Gazella also resulted in her living on the streets.

> I didn't have a place to live. My kids had been taken away from me. You know, constantly being harassed like 3 days out of the week by the Tactical Narcotics Team [police]. I didn't want to be bothered with people. I was gettin' tired of the lyin', schemin', you know, stayin' in abandoned buildings.

Alicia, a 29-year-old Hispanic woman, became involved in street violence at age 12. She commented on the personal isolation that was a consequence of her involvement in crime:

> When I started getting involved in crime, you know, and drugs, the friends that I had, even my family, I stayed away from them, you know. You know how you look bad and you feel bad, and you just don't want those people to see you like you are. So I avoided seeing them.

For some, the emotional depth of the rock bottom crisis was felt as a sense of mortification. The women felt as if they had nowhere to turn to salvage a sense of well-being or self-worth. Suicide was considered a better alternative than remaining in such an undesirable social and psychological state. Denise is one example:

> I ran into a girl who I went to school with that works on Wall Street. And I compared her life to mine and it was like miserable. And I just wanted out. I wanted a new life. I was tired, I was run down, looking bad. I got out by smashing myself through a sixth-floor window. Then I went to the psychiatric ward and I met this real nice doctor, and we talked every day. She fought to keep me in the hospital because she felt I wouldn't survive. She believed in me. And she talked me into going into a drug program.

Marginalization from family, friends, children, and work—in short, the loss of traditional life structures—left the women vulnerable to chaotic street conditions. After initially being overwhelmed by despair, the women began to question and reevaluate basic assumptions about their identities and their social construction of the world. Like Shover's (1983) male property offenders, the women also began to view the criminal justice system as "an imposing accumulation of aggravations and deprivations" (212). They grew tired of the street experiences and the problems and consequences of criminal involvement.

Many of the women acknowledged that, with age, it is more difficult to do time and that the fear of incurring a long prison sentence the next time influenced their decision to stop.

Cusson and Pinsonneault (1986) made the same observation with male robbers. Gazella, April, and Denise, quoted earlier, recall:

> **Gazella:** First of all, when I was in prison I was like, I was so humiliated. At my age [38] I was really kind of embarrassed, but I knew that was the lifestyle that I was leadin'. And people I used to talk to would tell me, well, you could do this, and you don't have to get busted. But then I started thinking why are all these people here. So it doesn't, you know, really work. So I came home, and I did go back to selling again, but you know I knew I was on probation. And I didn't want to do no more time.
>
> **April:** Jail, being in jail. The environment, having my freedom taken away. I saw myself keep repeating the same pattern, and I didn't want to do that. Uh, I had missed my daughter. See, being in jail that long period of time, I was able to detox. And when I detoxed, I kind of like had a clear sense of thinking, and that's when I came to the realization that, uh, this is not working for me.
>
> **Denise:** I saw the person that I was dealing with—my partner—I saw her go upstate to Bedford for 2 to 4 years. I didn't want to deal with it. I didn't want to go. Bedford is a prison, women's prison. And I couldn't see myself givin' up 2 years of my life for something that I knew I could change in another way.

As can be seen from the above, the influence of punishment on these women was due to their belief that if they continued to be involved in crime, they would be apprehended, convicted, and incarcerated.

For many of the women, it was the stresses of street life and the fear of dying on the streets that motivated their decision to quit the criminal life. Darlene, a 25-year-old black woman, recalled the stress associated with the latter stage of her career selling drugs:

> The simple fact is that I really, I thought that I would die out there. I thought that someone would kill me out there and I would be killed; I had a fear of being on the front page one day and being in the newspaper dying. I wanted to live, and I didn't just want to exist.

Sonya, a 27-year-old Hispanic woman, provided an account of what daily life was like on the streets:

> You get tired of bein' tired, you know. I got tired of hustlin', you know. I got tired of livin' the way I was livin', you know. Due to your body, your body, mentally, emotionally, you know. Everybody's tryin' to get over. Everybody will stab you in your back. Nobody gives a fuck about the next person. And I used to have people talkin' to me, "You know, you're not a bad lookin' girl. You know, why you don't get yourself together."

Perhaps even more important, the women felt that they had wasted time. They became acutely aware of time as a diminishing resource (Shover 1983). They reported that they saw themselves going nowhere. They had arrived at a point where crime seemed senseless, and their lives had reached a dead end. Implicit in this assessment was the belief that gaining a longer-range perspective on one's life was a first step in changing. Such deliberations develop as a result of "socially disjunctive experiences" that cause the offender to experience social stress, feelings of alienation, and dissatisfaction with her present identity (Ray 1961).

Breaking Away From the Life

Forming a commitment to change is only the first step toward the termination of a criminal career. The offender enters a period that has been characterized as a "running struggle" with problems of social identity (Ray 1961, 136). Successful desisters must work to clarify and strengthen their nondeviant identity and redefine their street experience in terms more compatible with a conventional lifestyle. The second stage of the desistance process begins with the public announcement or "certification" (Meisenhelder 1977, 329) that the offender has decided to end her deviant behavior. After this announcement, the offender must begin to redefine economic, social, and emotional relationships that were based on a deviant street subculture.

The time following the announcement was generally a period of ambivalence and crisis for the study participants, because so much of their lives revolved around street life and because they had, at best, weak associations with the conventional world. Many of the women remembered the uncertainty they felt and the social dilemmas they faced after they decided to stop their involvement in crime.

> **Denise:** I went and looked up my friends and to see what was doing, and my girlfriend Mia was like, she was gettin' paid. And I was livin' on a $60 stipend. And I wasn't with it. Mia was good to me, she always kept money in my pocket when I came home. I would walk into her closet and change into clothes that I'm more accustomed to. She started calling me Pen again. She stopped calling me Denise. And I would ride with her knowing that she had a gun or a package in the car. But I wouldn't touch nothin'. But that was my rationale. As long as I don't fuck with nothin'. Yeah, she was like I can give you a grand and get you started. I said I know you can, but I can't. She said I can give you a grand, and she kept telling me that over and over; and I wasn't that far from taking the grand and getting started again.

> **Barbara:** After I decided to change, I went to a party with my friend. And people was around me and they was drinkin' and stuff, and I didn't want to drink. I don't have the urge of drinking. If anything, it would be smokin' crack. And when I left the party, I felt like I was missing something—like something was missing. And it was the fact that I wasn't gettin' high. But I know the consequences of it. If I take a drink, I'm gonna smoke crack. If I, uh, sniff some blow, I'm gonna smoke crack. I might do some things like rob a store or something stupid and go to jail. So I don't want to put myself in that position.

At this stage of their transition, the women had to decide how to establish and maintain conventional relationships and what to do with themselves and their lives. Few of the women had maintained good relationships with people who were not involved in crime and drugs. Given this situation, the women had to seek alternatives to their present situation.

The large majority of study participants were aided in their social reintegration by outside help. These respondents sought formal treatment of some kind, typically residential drug treatment, to provide structure, social support, and a pathway to behavioral change. The women perceived clearly the need to remove themselves from the "scene" to meet new friends, and to begin the process of identity reformation. The following account by Alicia typifies the importance of a "geographic" cure:

> I love to get high, you know, and I love the way crack makes me feel. I knew that I needed long-term, I knew that I needed to go somewhere. All away from everything, and I just needed to away get from everything. And I couldn't deal with responsibility at all. And, uh, I was just so ashamed of the way that I had, you know, became and the person that I became that I just wanted to start over again.

Social avoidance strategies were common to all attempts at stopping. When the women removed themselves from their old world and old locations, involvement in crime and drugs was more difficult.

> **April:** Yeah, I go home, but I don't, I don't socialize with the people. I don't even speak to anybody really. I go and I come. I don't go to the areas that I used to be in. I don't go there anymore. I don't walk down the same blocks I used to walk down. I always take different locations.

> **Denise:** I miss the fast money; otherwise, I don't miss my old life. I get support from my positive friends, and in the program. I talk about how I felt being around my old associates, seeing them, you know, going back to my old neighborhood. It's hard to deal with, I have to push away.

Maintaining a Conventional Life

Desisters have little chance of staying out of the life for an extended period of time if they stay in the social world of crime and addiction. They must rebuild and maintain a network of primary relations who accept and support their nondeviant identity if they are to be successful (the third stage of this model). This is no easy task, since in most cases the desisters have alienated their old nondeviant primary relations.

To a great extent, the women in this study most resemble religious converts in their attempts to establish and maintain support networks that validate their new sense of self. Treatment programs not only provide a ready-made primary group for desisters, but also a well-established pervasive identity (Travisano 1970), that of ex-con and/or ex-addict, that informs the women's view of themselves in a variety of interactions. Reminders of "spoiled identities" (Goffman 1963) such as criminal, "con," and "junkie" serve as a constant reference point for new experiences and keep salient the ideology of conventional living (Faupel 1991). Perhaps most important, these programs provide the women with an alternative basis for life structure—one that is devoid of crime, drugs, and other subcultural elements.

The successful treatment program, however, is one that ultimately facilitates dissociation from the program and promotes independent living. Dissociation from programs to participate in conventional living requires association, or reintegration, with conventional society. Friends and educational and occupational roles helped study participants reaffirm their noncriminal identities and bond themselves to conventional lifestyles. Barbara described the assistance she receives from friends and treatment groups:

> . . . a bunch of friends that always confronts me on what I'm doin' and where I'm goin', and they just want the best for me. And none of them use drugs. I go to a lot like outside support groups, you know. They help me have more confidence in myself. I have new friends now. Some of them are in treatment. Some have always been straight. They know. You know, they glad, you know, when I see them.

In the course of experiencing relationships with conventional others and participating in conventional roles, the women developed a strong social-psychological commitment not to return to crime and drug use. These commitments most often revolved around renewed affiliations with their children, relationships with new friends, and the acquisition of educational and vocational skills. The social relationships, interests, and investments that develop in the course of desistance reflect the gradual emergence of new identities. Such stakes in conventional identity form the social-psychological context within which control and desistance are possible (Waldorf et al. 1991).

In short, the women in the study developed a stake in their new lives that was incompatible with street life. This new stake served as a wedge to help maintain the separation of the women from the world of the streets (Biernacki 1986). The desire to maintain one's sense of self was an important incentive for avoiding return to crime.

> **Alicia:** I like the fact that I have my respect back. I like the fact that, uh, my daughter trusts me again. And my mother don't mind leavin' me in the house, and she don't have to worry that when she come in her TV might be gone.

> **Barbara:** I have new friends. I have my children back in my life. I have my education. It keeps me straight. I can't forget where I came from because I get scared to go back. I don't want to hurt nobody. I just want to live a normal life.

Janelle, a 22-year-old black woman, started dealing drugs and carrying a .38-caliber gun when she was 15. She described the ongoing tension between staying straight and returning to her old social world:

> It's hard, it's hard stayin' on the right track. But letting myself know that I'm worth more. I don't have to go in a store today and steal anything. I don't deserve that. I don't deserve to make myself feel really bad. Then once again I would be steppin' back and feel that this is all I can do.

Overall, the success of identity transformations hinges on the women's abilities to establish and maintain commitments and involvements in conventional aspects of life. As the women began to feel accepted and trusted within some conventional social circles, their determination to exit from crime was strengthened, as were their social and personal identities as noncriminals.

Discussion

The primary purpose of this study was to describe—from the offenders' perspective—how women embedded in criminal street subcultures could end their deviance. Desistance appears to be a process as complex and lengthy as that of initial involvement. It was interesting to find that some of the key concepts in initiation of deviance—social bond, differential association, deterrence, age—were important in our analysis. We saw the aging offender take the threat of punishment seriously, reestablish links with conventional society, and sever association with subcultural street elements.

Our research supports Adler's (1992) finding that shame plays a limited role in the decision to return to conventional life for individuals who are entrenched in deviant subcultures. Rather, they exit deviance because they have evolved through the typical phases of their deviant careers.

In the present study, we found that the decision to give up crime was triggered by a shock of some sort (i.e., a socially disjunctive experience), by a delayed deterrence process, or both. The women then entered a period of crisis. Anxious and dissatisfied, they took stock of their lives and criminal activity. They arrived at a point where their way of life seemed senseless. Having made this assessment, the women then worked to clarify and strengthen their nondeviant identities. This phase began with the reevaluation of life goals and the public announcement of their decision to end involvement in crime. Once the decision to quit was made, the women turned to relationships that had not been ruined by their deviance, or they created new relationships. The final stage, maintaining cessation, involved integration into a nondeviant lifestyle. This meant restructuring the entire pattern of their lives (i.e., primary relationships, daily routines, social situations). For most women, treatment groups provided the continuing support needed to maintain a nondeviant status.

The change processes and turning points described by the women in the present research were quite similar to those reported by men in previous studies (Shover 1983, 1985; Cusson and Pinsonneault 1986). Collectively, these findings suggest that desistance is a pragmatically constructed project of action created by the individual within a given social context. Turning points occur as "part of a process over time and not as a dramatic lasting change that takes place at any one time" (Pickles and Rutter 1991, 134). Thus, the return to conventional life occurs more because of "push" than "pull" factors (Adler 1992), because the career of involvement in crime moves offenders beyond the point at which they find it enjoyable to the point at which it is debilitating and anxiety-provoking.

Considering the narrow confines of our empirical data, it is hardly necessary to point out the limits of generalizability. Our analysis refers to the woman deeply involved in crime and immersed in a street subculture who finds the strength and resources to change her way of life. The fact that all the women in this study experienced a long period of personal deterioration and a "rock bottom" experience before they were able to exit crime does not justify a conclusion that this process occurs with all offenders. Undoubtedly, there are other scenarios (e.g., the occasional offender who drifts in and out of crime, the offender who stops when criminal involvement conflicts with commitments to conventional life, the battered woman who kills) in which the question of desistance does not arise. Hence, there is a need to conceptualize and measure the objective and subjective elements of change among various male and female offender subgroups.

Furthermore, the evidence presented here does not warrant the conclusion that none of the women ever renewed their involvement in crime. Because the study materials consist of retrospective information, with all its attendant problems, we cannot state with certainty whether desistance from crime is permanent. Still, it is also clear that these women broke their pattern of involvement in crime for substantial lengths of time and have substantially changed their lives.

Questions for Thought and Discussion

1. What are the major variables that led the women in this study to consider "getting out of the life"?
2. Once the criminal has left the "life," what must he or she do to stay out?
3. Explain the three stages of desistance.
4. What theory or theories of criminal behavior are illustrated by this research?

References

Adler, Patricia. 1992. "The 'Post' Phase of Deviant Careers: Reintegrating Traffickers." *Deviant Behavior* 13: 103–126.

Biernacki, Patrick A. 1986. *Pathways from Heroin Addiction: Recovery Without Treatment.* Philadelphia: Temple University Press.

Blumstein, Alfred, Jacqueline Cohen, Jeffrey A. Roth, and Christy A. Visher. 1986. *Careers and Career Criminals.* Washington, DC: National Academy Press.

Cusson, Maurice, and Pierre Pinsonneault. 1986. "The Decision to Give Up Crime." In *The Reasoning Criminal: Rational Choice Perspectives on Offending,* edited by Derek Cornish and Ronald Clarke. New York: Springer-Verlag.

Daly, Kathy, and Meda Chesney-Lind. 1988. "Feminism and Criminology." *Justice Quarterly* 5: 101–143.

Faupel, Charles. 1991. *Shooting Dope: Career Patterns of Hard-Core Heroin Users*. Gainesville: University of Florida Press.

Goffman, Erving. 1963. *Stigma: Notes on the Management of Spoiled Identity*. Englewood Cliffs, NJ: Prentice-Hall.

Le Blanc, Marc, and M. Frechette. 1989. *Male Criminal Activity from Childhood Through Youth: Multilevel and Developmental Perspective*. New York: Springer-Verlag.

Matza, David. 1964. *Delinquency and Drift*. New York: Wiley.

Meisenhelder, Thomas. 1977. "An Exploratory Study of Exiting from Criminal Careers." *Criminology* 15: 319–334.

Mulvey, Edward P., and John F. LaRosa. 1986. "Delinquency Cessation and Adolescent Development: Preliminary Data." *American Journal of Orthopsychiatry* 56: 212–224.

Pickles, Andrew, and Michael Rutter. 1991. "Statistical and Conceptual Models of 'Turning Points' in Developmental Processes." In *Problems and Methods in Longitudinal Research: Stability and Change*, edited by D. Magnusson, L. Bergman, G. Rudinger, and B. Torestad (pp. 110–136). New York: Cambridge University Press.

Ray, Marsh. 1961. "The Cycle of Abstinence and Relapse Among Heroin Addicts." *Social Problems* 9: 132–140.

Shover, Neil. 1983. "The Latter Stages of Ordinary Property Offenders' Careers." *Social Problems* 31: 208–218.

———. 1985. *Aging Criminals*. Newbury Park, CA: Sage.

Shover, Neil, and Carol Thompson. 1992. "Age, Differential Expectations, and Crime Desistance." *Criminology* 30: 89–104.

Stall, Ron, and Patrick Biernacki. 1986. "Spontaneous Remission from the Problematic Use of Substances: An Inductive Model Derived from a Comparative Analysis of the Alcohol, Opiate, Tobacco, and Food/Obesity Literatures." *International Journal of the Addictions* 2: 1–23.

Travisano, R. 1970. "Alteration and Conversion as Qualitatively Different Transformations." In *Social Psychology Through Symbolic Interaction*, edited by G. Stone and H. Farberman (pp. 594–605). Boston: Ginn-Blaisdell.

Waldorf, Dan. 1983. "Natural Recovery from Opiate Addiction: Some Social Psychological Processes of Untreated Recovery." *Journal of Drug Issues* 13: 237–280.

Waldorf, Dan, Craig Reinerman, and Sheila Murphy. 1991. *Cocaine Changes*. Philadelphia: Temple University Press.

Weiner, Neil, and Marvin E. Wolfgang. 1989. *Violent Crime, Violent Criminals*. Newbury Park, CA: Sage.

Chapter 31 Aging Criminals

Changes in the Criminal Calculus

Neal Shover

In this selection, Neal Shover compares the decision-making processes of juvenile and young adult offenders to those of older criminals to discover the changes in the criminal calculus—the perception of risk and gain associated with a criminal opportunity—as offenders age. "Clearly," he argues, "something about advancing age produces reduced participation in ordinary crime, even by those with extensive criminal records." Shover concludes that aging offenders undergo a number of changes, including development of new commitments and increasing fear of incarceration. This causes them to alter their calculus—to evaluate the risks and benefits of crime differently.

Shover's research methodology involved identifying, locating, and interviewing a group of men aged 40 and over who were involved in ordinary property crime earlier in their careers. Shover and his assistants interviewed 50 subjects whose dominant criminal pattern consisted of ordinary property offenses such as grand larceny, burglary, robbery, and auto theft. All had been convicted of such offenses at least once. The research subjects were identified through the files of the U.S. Probation Offices in Baltimore and Washington, D.C. (22), and U.S. Probation Offices in other cities (5), through introduction by an ex-convict employed to work on the project (13), and by referral from an ex-convict who had been part of an earlier study (4). Six additional subjects were interviewed in federal prisons. Interviews, which were tape recorded and later transcribed, lasted from 30 minutes to three hours, averaging two hours.

Calculus and Offenses of Youth

For many juveniles, involvement in delinquency contains a rich variety of motives and subjective meanings. Juveniles "slide into" their initial delinquent acts for a variety of nonrational, often situationally based reasons (Matza 1964). Although there is little new in this, it is interesting that the interview subjects recalled their earliest crimes this way. A 45-year-old man said,

> I was, like years ago, I was a peeping Tom—when I was a kid, you know. . . . I enjoyed this, you know. . . . But, anyway, then I got married young, and I had two children. And I had bills, you know. I was a kid and I had a man's responsibility. . . . Now, what's the best way to make money? With something you know. I had been peeping in windows when I was a kid. So, I knew, you know, like where the windows would open, where the—you understand what I mean? And then [I] broadened my sense. After awhile I started mixing business with pleasure, you know. I would peep and then later come back and, you know, take this or that.

Another man told of his adolescent fascination with automobiles. As a youth, he often roamed through parking lots, admiring the steering wheels of cars. From there it was a short, tentative step to breaking into the cars and stealing their contents.

A great deal of delinquency begins simply as risk-taking behavior and it is only later, with the benefit of accumulated incidents, that it takes on the character and meaning of "crime" (Short and Strodtbeck 1965). Braley (1976, 11–12) writes,

> I began to steal seriously as a member of a small gang of boys. We backed into it, simply enough, by collecting milk and soda bottles to turn in for the deposits, but, after we had exhausted the vacant lots, empty fields, and town dumps, we began to sneak into garages . . . and, having dared garages and survived, we next began to loot back porches, and, finally, breathlessly, we entered someone's kitchen. . . . Clearly, this was an exercise of real power over the remote adult world and I found it exciting. I liked it. . . . [A]nd it is only now, some forty years later, that I begin to see how stealing cast me in my first successful role.

Many of the crimes committed by youth are impulsive and poorly planned:

> Q: Did you do a lot of stickups [when you were young]?
>
> A: Oh yeah, you know. . . . [We] stole and shit like that, you know. I didn't give it no thought, no plan, don't know how much money's in it. You know what I mean?

> Just go in there and say, "we're gonna do it, we're gonna do it." . . . That was it.

The spontaneous pursuit of fun and excitement provides the impetus for some delinquency:

> [When I was a kid] I wasn't a sports enthusiast. I played sports very rarely, but it just wasn't exciting enough. . . . None of [the "normal" adolescent activities] were exciting to me. . . . It's just that we, there was a feeling of participating in something that was daring and dangerous.

To some extent, these collective definitions of misconduct based on expressive vocabularies of motive explain why participants do not always see their activities as criminal. Instead of resulting from a rational decision-making process, they simply "happen," and participants do not appreciate sufficiently the seriousness. A former gang member writes,

> It's funny, but we didn't see ourselves as delinquents or young criminal types. Most of what we were into was fighting other gangs. . . . Sure, we got into other kinds of scrapes sometimes, like vandalism and petty larceny from a street vendor or a store. Most of the time we thought of that kind of stuff as "just playing around"—never as crime. (Rettig et al. 1977, 28)

For other youths, participation in delinquency results from the interactional dynamics of peer groups. Some boys experience a situational need to maintain personal status and face with their peers (Short and Strodtbeck 1965; Jansyn 1966). Theft or other acts of delinquency may function to buttress or solidify one's informal ranking within a small group. Youths may occasionally use them as a dramatic, incontrovertible demand for a higher as compared with a lower rank:

> Everybody would look up to me, you know, when I was young. . . . And seem like every time they wanted something, they'd come to me and say, "Jack, well, come on and do this," or "help me do this," you know. Fuck it, you know. I had an image I had to live up to, you know. I'd say, "fuck it, man, come on."

Precisely because many of the criminal incidents of youth are responses to group dynamics or moods, they occasionally "break out" in situationally propitious circumstances. An interview subject related an incident of armed robbery that occurred when he was young. His account illustrates some of the foregoing observations about the impetuous nature of juvenile crime:

> [One day] we were just walking up First Street and [one of my companions] said as we were approaching Rhode Island Avenue, "let's go in here and rob this drug store," because [another companion] had a gun. We said, "okay, let's go in here and rob the drug store." Went in there, the soda fountain was filled up . . . robbed everybody on the stools. Went back in the post office, stole money orders and stamps and stuff, took the cash box. And we turned our backs on everybody in the store, going out! We didn't know whether the proprietor had a gun or what, but it just so happened that he didn't. But, that's just the atmosphere in which, you know, that took place.

Overall, the interview subjects said that as juveniles and young adults they pursued crime with considerable intensity:

> [W]hen you're young, or when—the people that I've known who are young, it was nothing to go out and break into two or three places a week just *looking* for money.

Similarly, a retired English thief writes that "when you're young you tend to have a go at anything" (Quick 1967, 142).

While juvenile crime is impetuous and fun, it is also monetarily rewarding. Indeed, to juveniles from economically deprived backgrounds it may appear more rewarding than any legitimate employment available to them. The sums of money garnered from crime may seem princely indeed. Crime opens up for them new worlds of consumption and leisure activities. The 49 imprisoned armed robbers studied by Petersilia et al. reported that often their youthful crimes were motivated by a desire for and pursuit of "high times" (1978, 76).

It seems apparent that many youth become involved in property offenses without having developed an autonomous and rationalized set of criminal motives. Petersilia et al. discovered a similar pattern in their research on imprisoned armed robbers. Their subjects reported using little or no sophistication in planning the offenses they committed in their youth (1978, 60–65). At the same time, they found that the juvenile offenses committed by men in their sample included "expressive elements" far more than was true of the offenses they committed later (1978,

76). (Expressive reasons for committing offenses include such things as hostility, revenge, thrills, or peer influence.)

Juveniles and young adults often have little awareness or appreciation of the legal and personal repercussions of their criminality. This is true especially of their perceptions of time spent in institutions such as training schools and prisons:

> I've seen the time in my life, man, where it might seem foolish, 'cause it seems foolish to me now. When I was in the street, hustling, I'd say, "if I get knocked off and don't get but a nickel"—five years—I said, "hell with it," you know. The only thing would be in my mind, if I got busted could I hang around, try to have my lawyer try to get me some kind of plea or something so I wouldn't get but a nickel. 'Cause I knew I could knock five years out.

A 47-year-old man echoed these remarks, saying that when he was young,

> I don't know, man, I just didn't give a fuck, you know. I was young, simple, man. I didn't care, you know. Shit, doing time, you know, I didn't know what doing time was all about. Doing time to me was nothing, you know.

The net result of these youthful meanings and motives is that the potential repercussions of crime to some extent are blunted. Juveniles neither possess nor bring to bear a precise, consistent metric for assessing the potential consequences of delinquent episodes. They fail to "see" or to calculate seriously their potential losses if apprehended. For many youth, crime is a risk-taking activity in which the risks are only dimly appreciated or calculated.

Calculus and Offenses of Young Adults

This poorly developed youthful calculus is transformed both by the approach of adulthood and by the experience of arrest and adult felony confinement. Young adults develop the ability to see, to appreciate, and to calculate more precisely some of the potential penalties that flow from criminal involvement. Consequently, by late adolescence to their early 20s men begin to develop a keener awareness of the potential costs of criminal behavior. Gradually supplanting the nonrational motives and calculus of youthful offenders is a more clearly articulated understanding of the price they will pay if convicted of crime. In this sense, aging and its associated experiences are accompanied by an increasing rationalization of ordinary property crime.

Their growing rationalization of crime seems to be a turning point for many ordinary property offenders. As Zimring (1981, 880) has noted,

> At some point in adolescence or early adult development, most of those who have committed offenses in groups either cease to be offenders or continue to violate the law, but for different reasons and in different configurations. Either of these paths is a significant change from prior behavior.

A substantial majority of the uncommitted apparently drop out of crime at this point.

Paradoxically, others—this includes many unsuccessful and most successful offenders—respond to their developing rationalization of crime with a strengthened belief that they can continue committing crime and make it a lucrative enterprise. This is because they convert their developing rationalization of crime into an increased confidence that they can avoid arrest.

For those who continue at crime, theft increasingly springs from a more autonomous set of motives and meanings. The salience of "expressive elements" gradually declines in the process of criminal decision making. Offenders also develop an awareness of the importance of making crime a rational process. They learn the importance of assessing and committing crimes on the basis of an increasingly narrow and precise metric of potential benefits and costs. In this sense as well, their crimes became more calculating and rational. Money increasingly assumes more importance as a criminal objective. After serving a term in the National Training School, one subject and his friends began robbing gamblers and bootleggers. I asked him,

> Q: Did the desire for excitement play any part in those crimes?
>
> A: No, I think the desire for excitement had left. It was, we recognized that it was a dangerous mission then, because we knew that gamblers and bootleggers carried guns and things like that. And it was for, you know, just for the money.

Another man made the same point succinctly, saying that "whatever started me in crime is one thing. But at some point I know that I'm in crime for the money. There's no emotional reason for me being into crime." Finally, an ex-thief has written,

> When I first began stealing I had but a dim realization of its wrong. I accepted it as the thing to do because it was done by the people I was with; besides, it was adventurous and thrilling. Later it became an everyday, cold-blooded business, and while I went about it methodically . . . I was fully aware of the gravity of my offenses. (Black 1926, 254)

Interestingly, during their young adult years the 49 California armed robbers expressed a new confidence in their ability to avoid arrest for their crimes (Petersilia et al. 1978, 69–70). They reported a marked increase in the sophistication of their criminal planning (although the researchers indicate the men never achieved tactical brilliance) (1978, 60). Pursuit of "high times" declined in importance as a motive for crime (1978, 78) and the need to meet ordinary financial exigencies became more important (1978, 76). Concern about arrest declined substantially (1978, 70).

Young men, however, tend to exaggerate their ability to rationalize their crimes and to commit them successfully:

> Whenever I began to steal it was always with the rationale I wouldn't make the mistakes I had made before. . . . It didn't occur to me there were literally thousands of ways I could get caught. I was sustained by the confidence nothing truly awful could happen to me. (Braly 1976, 65)

Often they confidently assume there are a finite, manageable number of ways that any particular criminal act can fail (Shover 1971). Consequently, they analyze past offenses for information they believe will lead to ever more perfect criminal techniques and success. Parker's interview (Parker and Allerton 1962, 149) with an English thief reveals this reasoning process:

> Q: When you're arrested, what are your reactions at that moment?
>
> A: I think the first thing's annoyance—with myself. How could I be so stupid as to get nicked? What's gone wrong, what have I forgotten, where have I made the mistake?

In most cases, young adult offenders' newly acquired faith in their ability to rationalize theft and thereby make it safer proves to be self-defeating. Few of them are equipped by temperament, intelligence, or social connections to follow through on their plans and dreams. Consequently, subsequent offenses usually only repeat the pattern established in their youthful criminal forays.

Calculus and Offenses of Aging Adults

As men age, fail at crime, and experience . . . [other] contingencies, their rationalization of the criminal calculus changes apace. Now they enter a third and final stage of their criminal careers. Increasingly, they realize that the expected monetary returns from criminal involvement are paltry, both in relative and in absolute terms.

Simultaneously, their estimation of the likelihood of being arrested increases, as do the objective probabilities of arrest (Petersilia et al. 1978, 36–39).

Because of the nature and length of their previous criminal record, they generally assume that they will be sentenced to prison again if convicted of another felony. There is evidence to support this assumption (Petersilia et al. 1978, 39). Also, older men assume that any prison sentence they receive, given the length of their previous criminal record, will be long. Finally, those who experience an interpersonal contingency are increasingly reluctant to risk losing their new-found social ties. For all these reasons, aging men begin to include factors that previously were absent from their calculus of potential criminal acts. A 46-year-old former addict said,

> If I go out there and commit a crime now, I got to think about this: Hey, man, I ain't *got* to get away. See what I'm saying? I have—man, it would be just my luck that I would get busted. Now I done fucked up everything I done tried to work hard for, man, you know, to get my little family together.

Perhaps it is not surprising that they increasingly begin to see that their potential losses, if imprisoned again, will be immense.

In sum, as offenders age, their expectations of the potential outcome of criminal acts changes. Their perception of the odds narrows. Now the perceived risks of criminal behavior loom larger. Note that the Rand Corporation's research on 49 armed robbers found that fear of arrest increases during this age period (Petersilia et al. 1978, 70). Little wonder then that a 56-year-old man said,

> I realized that, even though in crime, even though you might get away, let's say 99 times, the one time eliminates your future. You don't have no future. Regardless of what you have gained, you lost all of that. A rabbit can escape 99 times and it only takes one shot to kill him. So, I was a rabbit. . . . I want to enjoy life. But I know I can't do it successfully by committing crimes.

This does not mean that men cease *thinking* about crime altogether. Rather, they develop a more complex set of reasons for avoiding it in most situations. However, in more advantageous circumstances, some believe they still are capable of resorting to crime:

> Now, I'm not going to tell you that if you put $100,000 on that table and I saw an opportunity, that I felt that I could get away with it, that I wouldn't try to move it. But there's no way, even now, there's no way that I would endanger my freedom for a measley four, five, ten thousand dollars. I make that much a year now, you know. And I see the time that I wasted—well, I figure I wasted four or five years when I was younger.
>
> Q: What do you mean, you "wasted" it?
>
> A: In and out of jail.

Those men who continue to pursue a criminal career change their approach to crime. Most decide to avoid some of the crimes more characteristic of their youth. They shift to offenses that are less confrontative and, therefore, less *visible.* Armed robbery is the prototypical highly visible and highly confrontative offense. Shoplifting or selling marijuana represent the other extreme. An imprisoned man said,

> When I go out, I'm goin' for the "soft" stuff. I'm going to book the numbers, you know . . . but *hard* crime . . . I gave that up a long while ago.

Thus, there is evidence that ordinary property offenders, once their fear of arrest and confinement increases, shift to other types of criminal activities. In doing so, they believe that they simultaneously reduce the chances of arrest and, even if arrested, increase the chances of receiving less severe penalties:

> You know, it's funny but there's only a few things that a man goes to the penitentiary for: burglary or robbery or something like that. But how many ways of making money are there that you don't have to revert to robbery or burglary? Thousands. I mean [where you're] between being legit and being crooked. You're skating on thin ice and if that ice breaks it's not going to break bad. You might get your foot wet, you might get a fine or something. What they're [police, prosecutors, courts] really concerned with are these violent cases, man, these people who are causing these headlines and stuff. . . . If I am going to be a thief I might as well be the one who is skating on that thin ice. And a person who is skating on thin ice is less likely to go to the penitentiary. . . . 'Cause if you get arrested boosting, shoplifting, it is generally a fine. If worse comes to worst, you're going to have to have to do a year in the county jail—in some places, nine months.
>
> I caught one number—that ten years, all them robberies—and then, you know, everything I did then was more like a finesse thing. . . . I'm not gonna stick no pistol in nobody's face, man, you know. I'm not gonna strong arm nobody, you know. I'm not gonna go in nobody's house. You understand what I'm sayin'? I'm not gonna do that.
>
> Q: You figure as long as you don't do those things you won't go to the penitentiary?
>
> A: Hey, you better believe it. You better believe it.

Along with this reduction in the visibility of their offenses, men try to reduce the *frequency* of their crimes. One subject, who still engages occasionally in nonviolent felonies, told me how he had changed:

> I done got a little *softer,* you know. I done got, hey man, to the point, you know, where, like I say, I don't steal, I don't hustle, you know. But I don't pass the opportunity if I can get some free money. I'm not gonna pass. . . . I don't hustle, you know. I don't make it a everyday thing. I don't go out *lookin'* for things, you know.
>
> Another man said,
>
> When you're younger, you can . . . steal to pay the rent, you know. Hell, you can go out and steal seven days a week. And sooner [or later] . . . you learn that—to me, it's exposure time, you know. You don't want to get "exposed" too much.

Petersilia et al. (1978, 27) found the same pattern. The average monthly offense rates reported by their subjects decreased from 3.28 when they were juveniles to 0.64 in their adult years. After changing their approach to crime, some men do continue to commit crime for several years, but eventually they desist from crime. Only a handful of ordinary property offenders continue their criminal behavior into old age. . . .

Negative Cases

Three aspects of the experiences of successful offenders distinguish them from the other types of offenders. First, the former usually develop an autonomous, rationalized calculus of crime at an earlier age, albeit in the same general fashion discussed here. By their late teens, some successful offenders are engaging in carefully planned crimes primarily for the expected monetary gains. Even some successful thieves, however, never entirely slough off all nonmonetary meanings of and motivations for crime:

> I know a guy who's relatively well connected, if you know what I mean, with the Outfit. [Nevertheless, he would] [g]o on any score! Now he needed money like I need a double hernia. But [he] just loved—don't care if there's any money there or not. "Let's go." [It was] [t]he thrill. I never got any thrills like that myself. . . . The only thrill I got [was] counting the money.

Second, the crimes of successful offenders generally are substantially more rewarding than the crimes committed by other types of offenders. Third, they are more successful than other types of offenders in avoiding incarceration; they spend fewer years in prison. For these reasons, failure at crime does not produce in successful offenders the same impetus to modify their criminal calculus as it does in their unsuccessful peers.

Despite these differences, however, some successful offenders also experience one or more of the contingencies described [earlier]. . . . In such circumstances, they respond in ways similar to unsuccessful offenders (Hohimer 1975).

Unlike unsuccessful offenders, however, they sometimes make adjustments in their criminal activities without discontinuing them entirely. They can do so, in part, because their theft activities provide them late career opportunities not available to unsuccessful offenders. For example, because some of them establish extensive social contacts through their work, they can change the nature of their criminal involvement. They are able to shift to other roles in the social organization of theft. Now they eschew the role of *front-line participant* in favor of the role of *background operator* (Mack and Kerner 1975 . . .). Still others manage to save enough money from their working years to retire with a degree of material comfort. One man suggested these two strategies account for most late-life patterns of successful offenders like himself. As he put it, "[T]hey're either sitting in the rocking chair or out finding something soft for somebody else to pick up."

Nevertheless, a substantial percentage of successful offenders apparently continues "going to the well" despite advancing age. An English thief, who already had served several prison sentences, has written,

> I content myself with the dream—the one that all criminals have—that one day I'll get the really big tickle. . . . That's all I can do now, take my time and wait for the chance to come. I've no intention of going straight, I'm just being more careful, that's all—and I'm getting cagey, I won't take unnecessary risks. It used to be I wanted a fifty-fifty chance, now I want it better than that, somewhere like seventy-five to twenty-five. But sooner or later it'll come, the job will be there, I'll do it, get the big tickle, and then I'll retire. . . . This is it, this is the dream, the great rock candy mountain that beckons us all. (Parker and Allerton 1962, 189)

This man subsequently was reimprisoned several times (Parker 1981).

Among the unsuccessful offenders, there are two distinctly different categories of negative cases. Some men simply do not experience the orientational and interpersonal changes described [earlier], and so they fail to modify significantly their calculus of ordinary property crime. In assessing their past criminal behavior these men use almost identical verbalizations: "They [police and the courts] could never get even." They use this description to support their contention that they have avoided arrest and prosecution for so many crimes that, even if they were caught in the future, the ledger books still would show an advantage for them. A man who shoplifts almost daily as a means of support had this to say:

> Q: Have you ever thought that you were a good thief, or a good hustler?
>
> A: Yeah, I am. . . .
>
> Q: What makes you think you're a good hustler?

A: 'Cause I *produce*.

Q: Yeah, but you've done a lot of time, too, haven't you?

A: Yeah, but considering, you know, in comparison, I ain't did that much. I think, if they gave me 199 years they couldn't get even. . . . They couldn't get even.

Questions for Thought and Discussion

1. What is it about aging that causes offenders to question their involvement in crime?
2. How does the criminal calculus of youth differ from that of older offenders?
3. Explain the three stages of a criminal career.
4. What theory or theories of criminal behavior are illustrated in this research?

References

Black, Jack (1926). *You Can't Win*. New York: A.L. Burt.

Braly, Malcolm (1976). *False Starts*. New York: Penguin.

Hohimer, Frank (1975). *The Home Invaders*. Chicago: Chicago Review Books.

Jansyn, Leon R., Jr. (1966). Solidarity and Delinquency in a Street Corner Group. *American Sociological Review* 31 (October): 600–614.

Mack, John and Hans-Jurgen Kerner (1975). *The Crime Industry*. Lexington, MA: D.C. Heath.

Matza, David (1964). *Delinquency and Drift*. New York: John Wiley.

Parker, Tony (1981). Letter to the Author (July 10).

Parker, Tony and Robert Allerton (1962). *The Courage of His Conviction*. London: Hutchinson.

Petersilia, Joan, P. W. Greenwood and M. Lavin (1978). *Criminal Careers of Habitual Felons*. Washington, DC: National Institute of Justice.

Quick, Harry (1967). *Villain*. London: Jonathon Cape.

Rettig, R. P., M. J. Torres and G. R. Grant (1977). *Manny: A Criminal Addict's Story*. Boston: Houghton Mifflin.

Short, James F. and Fred L. Strodtbeck (1965). *Group Processes and Gang Delinquency*. Chicago: University of Chicago Press.

Shover, Neal (1971). *Burglary as an Occupation*. Ph.D. dissertation, University of Illinois, Urbana.

Zimring, Franklin (1981). Kids, Groups, and Crime: Some Implications of a Well-Known Secret. *Journal of Criminal Law and Criminology* 72 (Fall): 867–885.

Chapter 32
An Examination of Decision Making and Desistance From Marijuana Use

Rashi K. Shukla

This article presents findings from an exploratory, qualitative study of desistance from marijuana use. Retrospective, semistructured interviews were conducted between 2000 and 2002 with a sample of 51 adult current and former users of marijuana in Oklahoma City, Oklahoma. Subjects were recruited using a snowball, chain-referral sampling strategy aimed at finding individuals with a range of perspectives and levels of involvement with marijuana use (i.e., past and present). Subjects queried about patterns of drug use and decision-making processes related to initiation, continuation, and desistance from marijuana use. The specific focus on desistance evolved during the course of the study when it was discovered that regardless of current marijuana use status, all of the individuals interviewed were able to discuss desistance from marijuana use. The definition of desistance, defined as a voluntary stop or quit of marijuana use as perceived and experienced by the individual, was grounded in the data and defined according to how individuals experienced desistance. To gain a better understanding of the desistance experience, an event-level analysis of periods of desistance from marijuana (N = 87) was conducted. Periods of desistance varied in terms of duration, outcome and influence of decision-making. Four categories of factors influenced desistance from marijuana use: lifestyle activities, social considerations, health concerns, and availability. By taking the perspective of the individual into account, it is evident that individuals purposely stop using marijuana at different periods of time and that not all periods of desistance are attempts to stop marijuana use permanently.

Researchers who study desistance are interested in examining the cessation of criminal activity, or why people stop offending. Within criminology, desistance is described as the "least studied process" (Laub and Sampson 2001; Loeber and LeBlanc 1990; Farrington 1986; Fagan 1989; Shover 1983). At the most simplistic level, desistance can be defined as "ceasing to do something" (Laub and Sampson 2001, p. 5). There is no consensus, however, on the precise definition of desistance. Research on desistance is plagued with conceptual, methodological, and measurement issues (Laub and Sampson 2001). To a great extent the conceptualization and measurement difficulties inherent in the study of desistance have contributed to the paucity of research on the topic (Piquero and Mazerolle 2001). Desistance, conceptualized as the end of the criminal career, is difficult to measure because permanent desistance can only be assessed retrospectively (Frazier 1976) and cannot be measured while individuals are still alive and thus capable of reoffending. Researchers have conceptualized desistance to refer to the end of the criminal career (Laub and Sampson 2001), to the end of a specific form of criminal behavior (Shover 1983, 1985, 1996; Cusson and Pinsonneault 1986; Biernacki 1986; Waldorf, Reinarman, and Murphy 1991), and to the maintenance of a crime-free lifestyle (Maruna 2001). Two primary approaches have been used to study desistance from criminal behavior. In the first approach, the focus is on explaining desistance from multiple forms of criminal or delinquent behavior. These studies seek to explain the more general movement to nonoffending by individuals involved in multiple types of criminal or deviant behaviors. The second approach focuses on explaining desistance from specific forms of criminal behavior, such as property offending, and illicit drug use, including opiates and marijuana. Both types of studies have contributed to our understanding of desistance, and the types of factors associated with desistance from criminal offending. In summing up the literature on desistance, Laub and Sampson (2001) note:

> On the basis of our review of the literature, desistance stems from a variety of

> complex processes—developmental, psychological and social—and thus there are several factors associated with it. The key elements seem to be aging; a good marriage; secure legal, stable work; and deciding to "go straight," including a reorientation of the costs and benefits of crime. Processes of desistance from crime in general, specific types of crime, and multiple problem behavior seem to be quite similar. (3)

However, few exploratory studies of desistance have been conducted. While studies have provided information on the motives related to desistance from different types of behaviors, in-depth analyses of differences in desistance experiences have not been conducted. The findings from this study complement other studies that have sought to understand desistance from the perspective of the individual (see Biernacki 1986; Maruna 2001; Shover 1985, 1996; Sommers et al. 1994). One of the most important contributions on the role decision making plays in desistance has been provided by the work of Shover (1985, 1996). In his research on persistent thieves, Shover found that desistance could be explained by changes in the criminal calculus that occurred as individuals aged. He concluded that the decision-making processes of youth offenders (i.e., youth calculus) were different from the decision-making processes of adult offenders (i.e., adult calculus). As offenders got older, they were more likely to consider the risks of their involvement with crime. Further, he found that while those who desist may continue to think about crime, they "develop a more complex set of reasons for avoiding it in most situations" (1996, 140). His research provided a great deal of insight on how and why changes in decision-making processes influence changes in behavior (i.e., desistance).

There is growing evidence that drug users make decisions and choices about their drug use (see Bennett 1986; Parker, Aldridge, and Measham 1998). The rational choice perspective (Clarke and Cornish 1985, 2001; Cornish and Clarke 1986) allows for the study of desistance from marijuana use to be approached from a decision-making perspective. Given that most individuals eventually stop using illicit drugs in adulthood there is a need to better understand desistance from illicit drug use. Few studies have specifically examined desistance from illicit drug use through a decision-making perspective. The present research focuses on involvement with marijuana because marijuana is the most commonly used illicit drug (Office of National Drug Control Policy 2001; Substance Abuse and Mental Health Services Administration 2002). Many people use marijuana. Many people stop using marijuana. A number of factors have been found to be associated with desistance from marijuana use, including lack of interest or negative experiences (Cohen and Kaal 2001), reductions in time spent with peers after getting married (Warr 1998), frequency of marijuana use and age (Chen and Kandel 1998), and degree of prior involvement with marijuana use (Kandel and Raveis 1989). Although marijuana use is more normative and less serious than other forms of criminal behaviors, it remains worthy of study because of its prevalence and significance within the criminal justice system. Marijuana-related offenses account for a disproportionate number of drug arrests,[1] and individuals who use marijuana are engaged in an illegal activity that inherently carries a certain degree of risk with it.

Purpose of the Study

The purpose of this study is to present an inductive examination of desistance from marijuana use. Specifically, this study describes patterns of desistance, examines variations in decision-making processes related to desistance, and outlines the main types of considerations that influence desistance from marijuana use.

Patterns of Desistance

The specific focus on examining desistance evolved when it was discovered that all of the individuals in the study, regardless of current marijuana use status, were able to discuss desistance from marijuana use. Patterns of desistance were identified using an event-level analysis of periods of desistance from marijuana use (N = 87). Used most recently in the study of violent events (see Wilkinson and Fagan 2001; Wilkinson 2002), event-level analyses allow for the examination of specific situations or events, in this case periods of desistance from marijuana use. Periods of desistance were included in the analysis if they met the following criteria: made reference to a specific situation when marijuana use was stopped, were perceived as a quit or stop by the individual, occurred within a period of more stable marijuana use, and contained identifiable data on the dimensions of interest (e.g., duration). Periods of desistance varied on the following dimensions: duration (i.e., length of time), outcome, and the influence and nature of decision making on desistance. The number of periods of desistance discussed by each individual ranged from one to four (see Table 32.1). The majority of individuals discussed two distinct periods of time they had desisted from using marijuana.

Duration

Individuals stopped using marijuana for different lengths of time. Individuals talked about stopping their marijuana for weeks (n = 5), months (n = 37) and years (n = 45) at a time (see Table 32.2). In most of the periods of desistance, individuals stopped using marijuana for one or more years. These periods of desistance are important to consider because they provide evidence that involvement with marijuana use is dynamic and is subject to change over time. Case #007, a 35-year-old male, talks here about his multiple, long periods of desistance:

> 007: I've quit a bunch of times. For a year at a time, for a couple years one time. It just wasn't around, so I didn't use it. I just didn't think about it. I mean, really, I didn't, that's the funny thing.

In his case, his preference for using alcohol over marijuana helped to explain the periods during which he desisted from using marijuana. However, periods of desistance from marijuana use were common experiences among the individuals in this sample.

Outcome

Not all individuals permanently stopped using marijuana after a period of desistance from marijuana use. Individuals resumed using marijuana after 68 of the periods of desistance. In the majority of instances, individuals resumed using marijuana at the same level of use that preceded a period of desistance. What is interesting about these periods of desistance is that while there was often a clear intention by an individual to stop the use of marijuana for a specific reason, there was little evidence to indicate that these individuals had experienced a failed attempt to permanently stop their marijuana involvement. Instead, the periods of desistance were viewed as being temporary or short-term stops influenced by other considerations (e.g., work, health, etc.). One can see from the way this 33-year-old regular marijuana user (Case #021) talks about the different times in his life that he's stopped using marijuana that his periods of desistance were purposeful, but not ever intended to be permanent. Rather, his periods of desistance were influenced by changes in his life situation.

> 021: . . . actually, the times I quit had to do with either logistics of where I was staying, cause I did have to move back with my folks for a little while after I left college, and, and so, it, it really had nothing to do with, "Oh my God, I'm becoming a marijuana junkie," as much as it had to do with just the logistics of my situation, or you know, maybe I had a drug test, if I was to have a new job and I was concerned about a drug test . . . and if I really, really wanted to, I always knew enough people where I could just go get it, I mean it was never truly unavailable to me.

Individuals also talked about short-term periods of desistance as meaningful from their perspective. Individuals sometimes talked about stopping their marijuana use for shorter periods of time (e.g., weeks) as a way to maintain or regain control over their level of marijuana use. Here, Case #001 dis-

Table 32.1
Number of Periods of Desistance Discussed Per Individual

Number of Periods of Desistance	Discussed by Individuals N = 45[2] n	%	Periods of Desistance N = 87 n	%
1	12	26.7	12	13.8
2	26	57.8	52	59.8
3	5	11.1	15	17.2
4	2	4.4	8	9.2

Table 32.2
Duration and Outcome of Periods of Desistance[3]

Periods of Desistance N = 87	Weeks n	%	Months n	%	Years n	%
Use Resumed	5	100.0	35	94.5	28	62.2
Not Resumed	0	–	2	5.4	17	37.7
Total	5	100.0	37	100.0	45	100.0

cusses stopping her marijuana use on a short-term basis during a period of time when her use was heavy:

> Q: Why did you quit the first time?
>
> 001: Just because things in my life are real crazy and I wanted to stop smoking to think clearly, to kinda take the fog off, because when things are just real intense . . . you don't really notice but when you're high all of the time you're under a cloud, and it's harder to concentrate on the important issues when you're like that all of the time. And I wanted to stop because I wanted to, I was trying to get to the most inner parts of myself and I wanted to make sure there was nothing standing in my way.

Other subjects also discussed stopping their marijuana use to deal with other issues in their life (Case #006):

> 006: I had to deal with things, and anytime you're intoxicated, no matter what, you're not going to be able to deal emotionally with things.

These desistance experiences were evidence that users sometimes purposefully stopped using marijuana as a way to maintain a certain level of control over their use, or when they felt like their marijuana use might be interfering with other things in their lives. Most viewed their marijuana use as a primarily recreational activity, of secondary importance to other life considerations.

For a few of the individuals in the study, a significant change in level of marijuana use followed a period of desistance. Case #049, a 31-year-old marijuana user, described how the frequency of his marijuana use declined after he graduated from law school. On his level of use during college, he stated:

> Q: How often would you use it at that time?
>
> 049: On the weekend, uh-huh [yeah]. Every day in college, yeah, it progressed to every day in college. Yeah, in New Orleans, you have to understand going to college in New Orleans, college is college everywhere, but if you're in a city where, the city itself is a, I mean people go to New Orleans to party. So imagine going to college there, when it's just, it's nonstop, so in my opinion, I probably wouldn't have done as many drugs, or partied as much, had I gone to a different school, cause the city just offered so many different environments conducive to partying, Mardi Gras, and Jazz Fest, and 16 different food festivals a year and all that stuff.

Having used marijuana daily during most of his college years, he purposefully stopped using marijuana after graduating from law school. He viewed this period of desistance as a time to "clean up," a time that was directly related to his transition between law school and the job market.

> Q: Have you ever quit using marijuana?
>
> 049: Yeah, I quit smoking pot for over a year.
>
> Q: When was that, and why did you quit?
>
> 049: Uh, it was when I graduated from law school, 'cause I'm done smokin' it.

When he began using marijuana again, he resumed using marijuana with less frequency.

> Q: How often do you use marijuana now?
>
> 049: Eh, couple times a week, if I had to average it.
>
> Q: Sometimes more, sometimes less?
>
> 049: Uh-huh.
>
> Q: And what does that depend on?
>
> 049: What kind of day I had, what's going on in the weekend.
>
> Q: Like what, free time, or if things are hectic or. . . .
>
> 049: Well, if I've had a long day, sometimes I want a little to relax, usually on the weekend I would say we always smoke it, if we go play golf, smoke a little, or if we're out drinking with the friends, we'll smoke a little, not always.
>
> Q: So you don't use marijuana every day, or all day long?
>
> 049: Oh no. Oh no.

Such changes in level of marijuana use were evident for others as well. Case #015 is a 50-year-old marijuana user who used marijuana on a daily basis for many years when he was younger. He stopped using marijuana after reaching a crisis point in his life, when his health began to deteriorate due to stress-related health problems associated with his overly demanding job at the time. On his current level of use with the marijuana, he said:

> Q: Do you currently use marijuana?
>
> 015: Very occasionally. . . . Maybe, maybe once every two months, and I'm not

> really, I'm not really a social user either. I prefer to do it alone, when I do it.

Although Case #015 still refers to himself as a marijuana user, his use patterns have changed significantly from when he was younger. On the rare occasions he uses marijuana now, he prefers to use it alone, and uses it because it enhances the music he listens to. While these individuals resumed using marijuana after a period of desistance, the types of changes in the level of use that followed the periods of desistance suggest that for some individuals, periods of desistance may serve as a transition point in an individual's use career. These changes, while representing real changes in the marijuana use experience for those who use marijuana, would likely be missed by most measures of use and desistance.

Decision Making

Is making a decision to desist an important component of the desistance experience? The literature on desistance is mixed with regard to the importance of decision-making for desistance (see Laub and Sampson 2001). For example, in his study of ex-opiate addicts Biernacki (1986) found that three different types of decisions led to the resolution to stop using opiates among the individuals in his study: 1) quitting without making a firm decision; 2) an explicit, rational decision to stop; and 3) hitting rock bottom and existential crisis. While not all of those who stopped using heroin made a formal decision to do so, decision making was relevant for a number of individuals. However, in their study of desistance among a sample of 30 female street offenders, Sommers et al. (1994) found that although the process of desistance was lengthy and complex, all of the women who desisted made a decision to stop their criminal involvement. The data in the present study contribute to what is known about decision making and desistance by illustrating the complex nature of decisions to desist and changes in behavior that follow. While the findings suggest that decision making is clearly associated with the desistance experience, not all who desist necessarily make a decision to stop using marijuana.

In a majority of periods of desistance, a decision to stop using marijuana preceded the period of desistance from marijuana use. Evidence of a decision to stop using marijuana was apparent in 74 of the 87 desistance periods. For some, the decision to desist is intended to be permanent. Case #026 is a 40-year-old ex-user of marijuana who talked about making a decision to stop using marijuana completely. Having used marijuana regularly for a number of years, he stopped using it after a series of life changing experiences led to a reevaluation of his marijuana involvement. His reevaluation of marijuana use was influenced by the suicide of a close friend and an ongoing divorce:

> 026: I mean it was just one of those things, just like now, you know with all the stuff I had been going through, you know, going through a divorce, losing my family, me and my wife were together 20 years, and the first thing I thought about was, "Man, I could sure use a joint," you know, you go through them days, like oh. . . . I got to thinking about how I used to feel, and then I was like, nah, nah, you got to do something else, and then, the fact that, at work, they drug tested you, you know, that's another thing 'cause I know a lot of guys got these jobs and they were always worrying about doing things, "You know I got to pass this drug test, got to do this and this. . . ." That's too much stress, if you don't do it you ain't got to worry about it, so that was another reason, I'm like, well I'm not going to worry about that anymore.

In his case, the first time he desisted from using marijuana he made a decision to stop using marijuana permanently:

> Q: Was that the first time you had stopped using marijuana?
>
> 026: That was um, from the time I had started, um, that was the first time I, I just stopped, and the first and last time, made a decision, prayed about it, and like I, I say, that's how it came to me, you know, stopped. Stopped.

An interesting variation in the data on making a decision to desist is demonstrated by cases where individuals made decisions to stop using marijuana without making any decisions about their future use. This is illustrated by Case #048, a 21-year-old marijuana user who describes how her decision about future marijuana use was primarily noncommittal the last time she stopped using marijuana.

> Q: Did you make a decision to quit?
>
> 048: Well, I don't, it's more of a, like I'll be sitting there, and, God you know I'm just doin' it way too much, you know I just, you know I need to stop for awhile, it's

just a decision that I make, and then I won't do it for awhile, and it's not a forever thing, um, and it, it might be a forever thing, it's not definite, I'm stopping, I may go back, I may not go back, depending on how I feel.

The few individuals who fit this pattern were infrequent social marijuana users who differ from those who have made a decision to desist from using marijuana completely. Those who desist without making a decision to desist permanently make decisions about marijuana use on an ongoing basis, as opportunities to use present themselves. Case #023, a 31-year-old marijuana user, is a singer who has decreased the frequency of her marijuana use to less than five times a year. Concerned about the health implications of smoking on her vocal cords, she purposely reduced the level of her marijuana use without making a decision to stop using it permanently. When asked whether or not she has considered stopping her marijuana use completely, she stated:

023: I don't think I can answer that question. I have no clue. I'm just one of those people that "lives for the moment." I may never use it again, but I may use it tomorrow.

Through examining the decision-making processes of these individuals, it is evident that individuals do not always predetermine whether or not they will resume using marijuana in the future. Such cases demonstrate the potential difficulties of measuring desistance, particularly among those individuals who may desist for long periods of time, yet remain noncommittal about their future involvement with the behavior of interest, in this case marijuana use.

While making a decision to desist is a step that preceded the majority of periods of desistance, making a decision to desist is not the same thing as being successful in one's attempts to desist. This point is raised by Maruna (2001), who uses the example of cigarette smokers who make multiple attempts to quit smoking to support his argument that making the decision to stop is not the same thing as the process of actually maintaining a state of desistance. This distinction is clearly relevant for the two individuals in this study who experienced difficulties trying to stop using marijuana after deciding they wanted to stop. In essence, they experienced difficulties "making the decision stick." Case #013 is a 22-year-old ex-user of marijuana who discussed making a decision to desist several times before he was able to completely go through with it. He described his overall pattern of marijuana use as one that was characterized by cycles of using and stopping:

Q: How often did you use it?

013: The way that marijuana worked for me, is that I would smoke it, occasionally, and then I would smoke it more and more and more and more, and be, end up smoking it like once a day. And then I would stop, for like five or six months, and just not smoke at all.

Q: And then would you start again?

013: Yeah, and then I would start again, and do the same thing, and then pretty much, after I realized just like, that occupied so much of my time, then I would just quit, but, you know, and then it would just seem like the thing to do. . . .

Q: So you would go through cycles of using and progressing?

013: Yeah, but I think it's pretty easy to quit, as well, and um, I mean, I think it's easy, like easy to like downsize it, but um, it's just the way that it kinda happened, plus, I had a lot of free time, as well.

His periods of desistance were attempts to regain control over his marijuana use during periods of heavy use. On the difficulty he experienced maintaining his decision to desist, he said:

Q: Did you make a decision to quit?

013: Yeah, I made a decision to quit. I think probably for like a day or two I might have smoked like a *little* bit, but pretty much it was just cold turkey, you know.

Q: Did anything specific trigger that [quitting]?

013: Um, I just came to the conclusion that I shouldn't be doing it, like, and I mean I did that probably like three times, came to this sort of coalesce [*sic*] of, you know, smoking pot fairly regularly, and then would realize, well, [I was going to stop], and then after it happened the first time, like the second time and third time I was like, well I can't, I decided already that I wasn't going to do this and now I'm like going to the same conclusion, and why didn't I do it in the first place, you know, so. . . .

By engaging in an ongoing reevaluation of his marijuana use, he finally came to a point where he was able to stop using marijuana completely. Such cases where individuals discussed experiencing difficulties desisting from marijuana use were rare, and no one in this study had to attend treatment to stop using marijuana.

Not everyone made a decision to stop prior to desisting. No decision to desist was made in 13 of the periods of desistance. Decision making is important but not necessary for desistance to occur. Case #040, a 27-year-old ex-user of marijuana, explains how she phased out of using marijuana without making a specific decision to desist. What is interesting about her situation is that although she didn't make a decision to stop using marijuana at the time she initially stopped, she talked about making a decision to desist as something that became important later:

> Q: Did you think about quitting or make a decision to quit before you did?
>
> 040: I think I just phased out if it, and then, when it starts getting, like in the past year, it's been offered to me a lot, and I think I just made a decision, not to.
>
> Q: It's been offered to you a lot in the past year?
>
> 040: Yeah, and I just don't. I'm not interested.

The interrelationship between making a decision to desist and desistance is complex. While making a decision to desist was a common theme associated with periods of desistance from marijuana use, a decision to desist is not always necessary.

Factors Influencing Periods of Desistance From Marijuana Use

Individuals weigh a number of diverse types of considerations when making decisions to desist from marijuana use. A preliminary, inductive typology of the types of considerations that influenced periods of desistance is presented here. Four primary categories of factors influenced periods of desistance from marijuana use: lifestyle activities, social considerations, health concerns, and availability (see Table 32.3). Although the categories are presented as distinct, in reality there is a great deal of overlap between the different categories of considerations; the types of considerations discussed here were often interrelated with one another.

Table 32.3
Factors Influencing Periods of Desistance (N = 87) From Marijuana Use

Category	Number of Mentions n	%
Lifestyle Activities	72	82.8
Health Concerns	34	39.1
Social Considerations	35	40.2
Availability	15	17.2

Lifestyle Activities

Lifestyle activities were most commonly mentioned in relation to periods of desistance from marijuana use. They were identified as important in 72 of the 87 periods of desistance. Lifestyle activities were discussed in terms of alternative activities individuals were invested in and spent time being involved with. Such activities were related to different areas in an individual's life, including work, family, and leisure activities. Most commonly, lifestyle activities were other conventional behaviors individuals were involved with. Inasmuch as these considerations are influenced by the particular lifestyle of an individual at a given time period, their influence on desistance is subject to change over time. Within this category the following factors influenced desistance from marijuana use: life events, occupation, other drug use, situational factors, and passage through a phase of drug use. In all of these subcategories, with the exception of passage through a phase of drug use, alternative activities individuals participated in or that were related to a transition in their lives influenced periods of desistance. Some examples of the types of statements subjects made follow:

> Q: Did you make a decision to quit?
>
> 028: Yeah, and then also, honestly, I was . . . I was trying to get a pharmaceutical job, and I knew they were going to drug test me, and there was no way I was going to have anything in, so it's not been a problem, and actually, I like that excuse, so when people offer it to me I'm like, "Oh, I get drug tested." I don't get drug tested anymore, but you know.
>
> 003: I've quit for long, long periods of time. Long periods of time being, oh I don't know, years sometimes, you know. It's been quite a while since I quit. Let's

see, since I moved back to ______ in '95, the longest period of time that I've quit for has been a few months. I mean deliberately quit. And, you know, again, that was just because I was busy, you know, with the job and the demands of that didn't really allow for it. I was pretty into triathlons for awhile, so I was exercising a lot. . . . And I've thought about quitting, but you know, just sort of as a means of assessing where I'm at in my life, and what I am doing.

024: I quit for six months, when I joined the army.

Q: Did you make a decision to quit?

024: Had to, yeah, I had to, to join. You couldn't do nothing, couldn't drink, couldn't smoke, nothing. Had to have clean urine.

002: Well, when I started doing the cocaine, I literally did away with the smoking dope [marijuana], almost. Every once in awhile I'd smoke. But I did away with it, because the high wasn't good enough compared to the coke.

Social Considerations

Desistance from marijuana use was also influenced by social relationships individuals maintained. Relationships with parents, peers, spouses or intimate partners, and children were discussed in relation to desistance from marijuana use. Social considerations were mentioned as an influence on desistance from marijuana use in 35 of the 87 periods of desistance. The influence of social relationships on periods of desistance changed over time. While considerations related to parents and peers were most likely to be related to periods of desistance while individuals were younger, considerations related to significant others or spouses and children became more important as individuals moved into adulthood. Examples of statements about the influence of social relationships on desistance are provided here:

Q: Do you think you would ever use marijuana again?

050: Yeah, I'm not, well, in a way, I'm not opposed to it, I mean, I don't think it's that big a deal, but I also kinda think, that, you know, I'm an adult now, I'm married and I have a child, and I have responsibilities, and that's just not a good idea. . . . I'm not opposed to using again, I think if I were to use it, it would probably be recreational, I mean, I could, foresee a circumstance where I go home for Christmas break for example, and meet up with the old crew of kids, and the situation is right, and I smoke some pot, I can see that happening, it's not going to happen though, I mean, I'm an adult, I'm a parent, I got, you know, I can't do that anymore, you know.

023: Well I was married for four years, and I was a military wife, so obviously I didn't use it then.

003: It is interesting, I think, to think about how it affects your relationships, because that definitely plays a part in my decision to, or not to use it.

009: I didn't really like the feeling of it. In a way, I kinda wanted to be different from everybody too, 'cause everybody smoked and I kinda wanted to be different, you know, I didn't want to do it because everybody else was doing it. I wanted to do it because I wanted to, and I didn't really want to, so I didn't.

048: The friend that I was living with didn't smoke, no one, no one I was around smoked. . . . But I don't like being high around a bunch of sober people. 'Cause I feel like, everyone knows, it, it makes me, I don't like the way you get paranoid, and you're just like, it's not worth it to me.

Health Concerns

As individuals get older they begin to think about the health concerns associated with smoking marijuana. Health concerns were related to desistance in 34 of the 87 periods of desistance. The category of health concerns included the following: concerns that related to the method of use (i.e., smoking it), concerns associated with the physical or mental effects of marijuana, and other health issues. Health considerations were discussed in relation to actual periods of desistance, as well as a type of consideration that might lead to desistance at a later period of time. Here are examples of the types of statements subjects made:

Q: When did you quit using marijuana?

052: [When I g]ot pregnant.

Q: Why did you quit using marijuana at that time?

052: I went to the Health Department and they told me I was pregnant, and I said, "Well," and asked them, you know, what the side effects were with the baby, if you, if you were a pot user, she told me somethin', might come out brain damaged, doin' things like that, and I was determined with me bein' 16 years, I already had that problem. My baby comin' out with some kind of deformity, being as young as I was. So I wasn't going to add to his, his or her suffering.

015: [On the last time he used] I was just like really high for like several hours, which is a lot of the reason I don't do it, 'cause I have a life, you know, and it really, it really interferes with, you know, I felt miserable the next day at work because I'd been up 'til two in the morning.

031: Oh, I would quit, in younger life, teens or early twenties, I would quit it, when I very first started using, I would notice the effects of it, for days, yeah, and I could feel, the, I could feel that it was, I felt like it was not good for me physically, and would quit, because of the, basically, my concern over good health.

Q: What do you dislike about marijuana?

017: Yeah, I think the physical effects, sometimes coughing, that kind of thing, are worrisome, I worry about that as I get older, you know I've been doing this for 30 years, and I should quit, that kind of thing.

Availability

Individuals also talked about stopping marijuana use at different times due to considerations associated with the availability of marijuana. Individuals discussed not having access to marijuana at a specific period of time, the cost of marijuana, and concerns about being involved with the illegal market. Some examples of the types of statements subjects made follow:

Q: Have you ever quit using marijuana?

011: I have, um, when I got laid off from my job at ______ back in 1992 and moved back to ______, I couldn't afford it, and I really didn't buy any because I knew that I didn't want to spend my money on it, and for a year and a half, I didn't smoke any marijuana, then I got a better job, got another job, so when I could afford it, then I started buying again and started smoking.

008: [Last time I quit I d]idn't have enough contacts, probably the longest stretch of time would have been two months maybe, in fact, probably five, six years ago.

034: Yeah, like right now, I got two bicycles in the back, my kid's birthday, well I got three, he already got his bike cause his is in September. I got a son, his birthday was the seventh of this month, my daughter's the twenty-second. If I was a bad user, my kids, all three of 'em wouldn't have bicycles this year. I got two bikes right now, in my bedroom waiting for my kids next weekend, so they can have they bicycles. I had a choice, the bike or the marijuana, and I say well, I want that bike.

029: I've quit for awhile, but only because I couldn't afford to be a daily user. . . . That's why I don't really smoke anymore, 'cause [my money] goes to the boy [my son] instead.

The analyses of data on decision-making processes related to desistance from marijuana use demonstrate that decisions to desist are multidimensional. Individuals discussed a number of different types of factors as influential on periods of desistance from marijuana use. To the extent that decisions to desist from using marijuana are influenced by factors that are subject to change, decisions about desistance are likely to change over time.

Conclusions

The purpose of this study was to examine patterns of desistance and decisions to desist from using marijuana. The majority of individuals discussed multiple times when they stopped or quit using marijuana. The findings support those reached by Cohen and Kaal (2001), who also found that cannabis users often go through lengthy periods of abstinence during their marijuana use careers. Given that the focus on desistance evolved during the course of the study, it is likely that more periods of desistance would likely have been identified if this study had originally been designed specifically to study desistance from marijuana use. The distinction between purposeful periods of desistance that are never intended to be permanent, and relapses, where individuals attempt to stop using marijuana completely and fail, is an important one to consider. Individuals were not always intending to stop using marijuana permanently during periods of desistance. Some resume involvement with marijuana use after a period of desistance. These findings challenge the notion that desistance is always permanent and suggests that different types of desistance experiences may exist. Future studies should continue to examine differences between transitory periods of desistance and desistance experiences that are intended to be final or permanent.

The findings demonstrate the utility of approaching the study of desistance from a decision-making approach. Decisions to desist from using marijuana are multidimensional and subject to change over time. Individuals were able to discuss the specific reasons they stopped using marijuana, suggesting that periods of desistance were often purposeful. The findings lend support to the notion that desistance can be viewed as a process that occurs over time. As individuals experience changes in their lives, they are likely to reevaluate their marijuana use behavior and desist whenever they deem it necessary or appropriate. The findings that individuals are not always intending to stop using marijuana permanently and do not always make decisions about their future use of marijuana demonstrate some of the potential difficulties inherent in measuring permanent desistance. These findings contribute to our understanding of why individuals sometimes resume their criminal behavior even after desisting and fit into a developing body of literature on the process of desistance. For example, in his study of persistent thieves Shover (1996) also found that desistance is a process that is not always "accomplished abruptly and cleanly" (122). In particular, he suggested that even offenders who have desisted "may not stop committing crime entirely" and "may reduce the frequency of their offenses but continue committing crime for months or even years" (122). In their study of cocaine users, Waldorf et al. (1991) also found that many of the individuals who stopped using cocaine also occasionally used cocaine after desisting. Cumulatively, these findings provide evidence to support the notion that it is difficult if not impossible to measure while individuals are still alive.

The findings from this study apply primarily to the individuals in the sample. The specific findings on decision making and desistance only apply to their marijuana use and desistance experiences in adulthood. These research findings are limited to the degree that they focus on a small sample of adults in Oklahoma City. The sample represents a restricted population with regard to lifestyle, location, and geographic influence. The sample is predominantly white and middle-class. They live in a conservative, Midwestern state that aggressively enforces illicit drug violations. They do not have lifestyles that are immersed in criminal and drug-using behaviors. This population is very different from populations of individuals heavily enmeshed in drug-using lifestyles and criminal behavior. For these individuals, marijuana is not addictive in the sense that they can and do stop, most often without difficulty. This has been found in other studies of marijuana users as well (National Commission on Marihuana and Drug Abuse 1972; Zinberg 1984). The adults in this study stopped using marijuana on their own. They stopped when they wanted to. They stopped when they needed to. Stopping was not difficult for them; withdrawal symptoms were minimal or nonexistent. This is supported by the data on desistance. This study demonstrates the utility of examining desistance from a grounded approach that takes the perspectives and experiences of individuals into account.

Notes

1. Of the 1,586,902 arrests for drug abuse violations in 2001, 40.4 percent were for marijuana possession, and 5.2 percent were for "sale/manufacturing" violations (FBI 2002, 232–233).
2. Data from six subjects were eliminated from this analysis because the data on desistance collected from these individuals did not fit the inclusion criteria for the periods of desistance analysis.
3. Percentages may not equal 100 percent due to rounding.

Questions for Thought and Discussion

1. In what ways do the findings in this study agree or disagree with those in the studies in the previous chapters by Sommers et al. and Shover?
2. What role did aging play in the desistance of marijuana users? Potential legal consequences?
3. What other variables appear to be involved in the decision to desist?
4. What theory or theories of criminal behavior are illustrated in this research?

References

Bennett, Trevor. 1986. "A Decision-Making Approach to Opioid Addiction." In *The Reasoning Criminal: Rational Choice Perspectives on Offending,* eds. Derek Cornish and Ronald Clarke, 83–102. New York: Springer-Verlag.

Biernacki, Patrick. 1986. *Pathways From Heroin Addiction: Recovery Without Treatment.* Philadelphia: Temple University Press.

Chen, Kevin, and Denise B. Kandel. 1998. "Predictors of Cessation of Marijuana Use: An Event History Analysis." *Drug and Alcohol Dependence* 50(2):109–121.

Clarke, Ronald V., and Derek B. Cornish. 1985. "Modeling Offenders' Decisions: A Framework for Research and Policy." In *Crime and Justice: An Annual Review of Research,* Vol. 6., eds. M. Tonry and N. Morris, 147–185. Chicago: The University of Chicago Press.

———. 2001. "Rational Choice." In *Explaining Criminals and Crime,* eds. Raymond Paternoster and Ronet Bachman, 23–46. Los Angeles: Roxbury.

Cohen, Peter D.A., and Hendrien L. Kaal. 2001. *The Irrelevance of Drug Policy: Patterns and Careers of Experienced Cannabis Use in the Populations of Amsterdam, San Francisco and Bremen.* Amsterdam: CEDRO/UvA. Funded by the Dutch Ministry of Health, Welfare and Sport.

Cornish, Derek B., and Ronald V. Clarke, eds. 1986. *The Reasoning Criminal.* New York: Springer-Verlag.

Cusson, Maurice, and Pierre Pinsonneault. 1986. "The Decision to Give Up Crime." In *The Reasoning Criminal,* eds. D.B. Cornish and R.V. Clarke, 72–87. New York: Springer-Verlag.

Fagan, Jeffrey. 1989. "Cessation of Family Violence: Deterrence and Dissuasion." In *Crime and Justice: A Review of Research* Vol. 11, eds. Lloyd Ohlin and Michael Tonry, 377–425. Chicago: University of Chicago Press.

Farrington, David P. 1986. "Age and Crime." In *Crime and Justice; An Annual Review of Research* Vol. 7, eds. M. Tonry and N. Morris, 189–250. Chicago: University of Chicago Press.

Federal Bureau of Investigation. 2002. *Crime in the United States 2001: Uniform Crime Reports.* U.S. Department of Justice. Washington, DC: U.S. Government Printing Office.

Frazier, Charles E. 1976. *Theoretical Approaches to Deviance: An Evaluation.* Columbus, Ohio: Charles E. Merrill Publishing Company.

Kandel, D.B., and V.H. Raveis. 1989. "Cessation of Illicit Drug Use in Young Adulthood." *Archives of General Psychiatry* 46:109–116.

Laub, John H., and Robert J. Sampson. 2001. "Understanding Desistance From Crime." In *Crime and Justice: A Review of Research* Volume 28, ed. Michael Tonry, 1–69. Chicago: University of Chicago Press.

Loeber, Rolf and Marc LeBlanc. 1990. "Toward a Developmental Criminology." In *Crime and Justice: A Review of Research* Vol. 12, eds. M. Tonry and N. Morris, 375–473. Chicago: University of Chicago Press.

Maruna, Shadd. 2001. *Making Good.* Washington, DC: American Psychological Association.

National Commission on Marihuana and Drug Abuse. 1972. *Marihuana: A Signal of Misunderstanding.* March. Washington, DC: U.S. Government Printing Office.

Office of National Drug Control Policy. 2001. *What America's Users Spend on Illegal Drugs,* NCJ 192334, http://www.whitehousedrugpolicy.gov (in publications database).

Parker, Howard, Judith Aldridge, and Fiona Measham. 1998. *Illegal Leisure: The Normalization of Adolescent Recreational Drug Use.* Adolescence and Society Series. New York: Routledge.

Piquero, Alex, and Paul Mazerolle. 2001. "Introduction." In *Life-Course Criminology,* eds. A. Piquero, and P. Mazerolle, viii–xx. Belmont, CA: Wadsworth.

Shover, Neal. 1983. "The Later Stages of Ordinary Property Offender Careers." *Social Problems* 31(2):208–218.

———. 1985. *Aging Criminals.* Beverly Hills: Sage.

———. 1996. *Great Pretenders: Pursuits and Careers of Persistent Thieves.* Boulder, CO: Westview Press.

Sommers, Ira, Deborah R. Baskin, and Jeffrey Fagan. 1994. "Getting Out of the Life: Crime Desistance By Female Street Offenders." *Deviant Behavior* 15:125–149.

Substance Abuse and Mental Health Service Administration. 2002. *Results From the 2001 National Household Survey on Drug Abuse: Volume 1. Summary of National Findings.* Office of Applied Studies. NHSDA Series H-17, DHHS Publication No. SMA 02-3758, http://www.samhsa.gov/oas.nhsda/2k1nhsda/PDF/O1SOFchp2_W.pdf.

Waldorf, Dan, Craig Reinarman, and Sheigla Murphy. 1991. *Cocaine Changes: The Experiences of Using and Quitting.* Philadelphia: Temple University Press.

Warr, Mark. 1998. "Life-Course Transitions and Desistance From Crime." *Criminology,* 36(2):183–215.

Wilkinson, Deanna L. 2002. "Decision-Making in Violent Events Among Adolescent Males: An Examination of Sparks and Other Motivational Factors." In *Rational Choice and Criminal Behavior,* eds. Alex R. Piquero and Stephen G. Tibbetts, 163–196. New York: Routledge.

Wilkinson, Deanna, and Jeffrey Fagan. 2001. "What We Know About Gun Use Among Adolescents." *Clinical Child and Family Psychology Review* 4(2):109–131.

Zinberg, Norman E. 1984. *Drug, Set and Setting.* New Haven: Yale University Press.